NOVELL'S

Guide to Troubleshooting
NetWare® 5

NOVELL'S

Guide to Troubleshooting
NetWare® 5

R I C K S A N T ' A N G E L O

Novell Press, San Jose

Novell's Guide to Troubleshooting NetWare® 5

Published by
Novell Press
2211 North First Street
San Jose, CA 95131

Copyright ©1999 Novell, Inc. All rights reserved. No part of this book, including interior design, cover design, and icons, may be reproduced or transmitted in any form, by any means (electronic, photocopying, recording, or otherwise) without the prior written permission of the publisher.

ISBN: 0-7645-4558-2

Printed in the United States of America

10 9 8 7 6 5 4 3 2

1B/QX/QV/ZZ/FC

Distributed in the United States by IDG Books Worldwide, Inc.

Distributed by CDG Books Canada Inc. for Canada; by Transworld Publishers Limited in the United Kingdom; by IDG Norge Books for Norway; by IDG Sweden Books for Sweden; by IDG Books Australia Publishing Corporation Pty. Ltd. for Australia and New Zealand; by TransQuest Publishers Pte Ltd. for Singapore, Malaysia, Thailand, Indonesia, and Hong Kong; by Gotop Information Inc. for Taiwan; by ICG Muse, Inc. for Japan; by Norma Comunicaciones S.A. for Colombia; by Intersoft for South Africa; by Le Monde en Tique for France; by International Thomson Publishing for Germany, Austria and Switzerland; by Distribuidora Cuspide for Argentina; by Livraria Cultura for Brazil; by Ediciones ZETA S.C.R. Ltda. for Peru; by WS Computer Publishing Corporation, Inc., for the Philippines; by Contemporanea de Ediciones for Venezuela; by Express Computer Distributors for the Caribbean and West Indies; by Micronesia Media Distributor, Inc. for Micronesia; by Grupo Editorial Norma S.A. for Guatemala; by Chips Computadoras S.A. de C.V. for Mexico; by Editorial Norma de Panama S.A. for Panama; by American Bookshops for Finland. Authorized Sales Agent: Anthony Rudkin Associates for the Middle East and North Africa.

For general information on IDG Books Worldwide's books in the U.S., please call our Consumer Customer Service department at 800-762-2974. For reseller information, including discounts and premium sales, please call our Reseller Customer Service department at 800-434-3422.

For information on where to purchase IDG Books Worldwide's books outside the U.S., please contact our International Sales department at 317-596-5530 or fax 317-596-5692.

For consumer information on foreign language translations, please contact our Customer Service department at 800-434-3422, fax 317-596-5692, or e-mail rights@idgbooks.com.

For information on licensing foreign or domestic rights, please phone +1-650-655-3109.

For sales inquiries and special prices for bulk quantities, please contact our Sales department at 650-655-3200 or write to IDG Books Worldwide, 919 E. Hillsdale Blvd., Suite 400, Foster City, CA 94404.

For information on using IDG Books Worldwide's books in the classroom or for ordering examination copies, please contact our Educational Sales department at 800-434-2086 or fax 317-596-5499.

For press review copies, author interviews, or other publicity information, please contact our Public Relations department at 650-655-3000 or fax 650-655-3299.

For authorization to photocopy items for corporate, personal, or educational use, please contact Novell, Inc., Copyright Permission, 1555 North Technology Way, Mail Stop ORM-C-311, Orem, UT 84097-2395; or fax 801-228-7077.

For general information on Novell Press books in the U.S., including information on discounts and premiums, contact IDG Books Worldwide at 800-434-3422 or 650-655-3200. For information on where to purchase Novell Press books outside the U.S., contact IDG Books International at 650-655-3021 or fax 650-655-3295.

Library of Congress Cataloging-in-Publication Data

Sant'Angelo, Rick, 1947-

   Novell's guide to troubleshooting Netware 5 / Rick Sant'Angelo.

      p.   cm.

   ISBN 0-7645-4558-2 (alk. paper)
   1. NetWare (Computer file) 2. Local area networks (Computer networks)--Maintenance and repair.   I. Title.
TK5105.8.N65S26   1999
005.7'1369--DC21   98-52718
                                                              CIP

Trademarks: Novell, NetWare, GroupWise, ManageWise, Novell Directory Services, and NDPS are registered trademarks; Novell Press, the Novell Press logo, NDS, Novell BorderManager, Z.E.N.works, and Novell Distributed Print Services are trademarks; CNE is a registered service mark; and CNI and CNA are service marks of Novell, Inc. in the United States and other countries. All brand names and product names used in this book are trade names, service marks, trademarks, or registered trademarks of their respective owners. IDG Books Worldwide is not associated with any product or vendor mentioned in this book.

John Kilcullen, *CEO, IDG Books Worldwide, Inc.*
Steven Berkowitz, *President, IDG Books Worldwide, Inc.*
Richard Swadley, *Senior Vice President & Publisher, Technology*
is a registered trademark or trademark under exclusive license to IDG Books Worldwide, Inc. from International Data Group, Inc. in the United States and/or other countries

Marcy Shanti, *Publisher, Novell Press, Novell, Inc.*
Novell Press and the Novell Press logo are trademarks of Novell, Inc.

Welcome to Novell Press

Novell Press, the world's leading provider of networking books, is the premier source for the most timely and useful information in the networking industry. Novell Press books cover fundamental networking issues as they emerge — from today's Novell and third-party products to the concepts and strategies that will guide the industry's future. The result is a broad spectrum of titles for the benefit of those involved in networking at any level: end user, department administrator, developer, systems manager, or network architect.

Novell Press books are written by experts with the full participation of Novell's technical, managerial, and marketing staff. The books are exhaustively reviewed by Novell's own technicians and are published only on the basis of final released software, never on prereleased versions.

Novell Press at IDG Books Worldwide is an exciting partnership between two companies at the forefront of the knowledge and communications revolution. The Press is implementing an ambitious publishing program to develop new networking titles centered on the current version of NetWare, GroupWise, BorderManager, ManageWise, and networking integration products.

Novell Press books are translated into several languages and sold throughout the world.

Marcy Shanti
Publisher
Novell Press, Novell, Inc.

Novell Press

Publisher
Marcy Shanti

IDG Books Worldwide

Acquisitions Editor
Jim Sumser

Development Editors
Kevin Shafer
Stefan Grünwedel
Kurt Stephan

Technical Editor
Kevin Moore

Copy Editors
Brian MacDonald
Robert Campbell

Production
IDG Books Worldwide Production

Proofreading and Indexing
York Graphic Services

Illustrator
Donna Reynolds

About the Author

Rick Sant'Angelo, CNE and Microsoft Certified Product Specialist, is the author of several books on NetWare, including *NetWare Unleashed*, *Optimizing NetWare*, and *Putting NetWare Lite OS to Work*. He frequently contributes articles to *LAN Times*, *PC Week*, *NetWare Technical Journal*, and other publications. He is also an active speaker at Networld/Interop, Networks Expo, and NetCom.

Preface

Novell's *Guide to Troubleshooting NetWare 5* was designed as an essential support tool — a survival guide — for installing, configuring, maintaining, optimizing, and troubleshooting your NetWare 5-based network. I sincerely trust you will appreciate its direct approach to these topics.

▶ • ◀

Read This Book If You Manage NetWare Networks

This book is for professionals who support NetWare networks. Support personnel fall into two categories: user/software administrators and computer/network implementers. This book is for the computer/network implementers, most of whom support network services and network operating systems. You will therefore find little about NDS, user management, or security in this book.

▶ • ◀

Written for Intermediate to Advanced Networking Professionals

Novell's Guide to Troubleshooting NetWare 5 is aimed at intermediate to advanced technicians. I therefore assume that you are familiar with Windows, DOS, basic personal computer configuration, and only the most elementary networking issues. This book is for support professionals who may or may not be CNEs. NetWare 5 and its pure IP implementation introduce topics that may be new to many CNEs.

▶ . . . . ◀

About NetWare 5

NetWare 5 marks a new era in technology for NetWare professionals. Novell has grafted TCP/IP into NetWare as a native protocol, which can completely replace IPX/SPX transport services or work in conjunction with them. TCP/IP networking requires a set of skills and knowledge that many Novell professionals, certified or not, may need to improve upon. Novell technicians are used to IPX networking, where addressing, subnetworking, masking, name resolution, and a host of other issues were not required. This book pays special attention to TCP/IP configuration with NetWare 5, addressing this topic in a way that does not assume that you have any existing knowledge of TCP/IP.

NetWare 5 has many features that make it the most advanced network operating system on the market by a long shot. NetWare 5 installs with all required services set up and activated so you can get the product running with very little effort. However, the complexity of this product mandates that every NetWare 5 administrator must learn about several new subsystems—many of which you may never have dealt with before.

This book is forthright and profound in its approach to supporting this product. It is designed to provide both experienced and inexperienced network professionals with all the essential background, procedural instructions, and troubleshooting assistance required to properly install and administer NetWare 5's basic set of services. The material is presented in the most succinct and compact manner, wasting very few words on trivial details or non-essential services.

As a well-seasoned NetWare support specialist, I have used my insights, gleaned from 15 years of supporting NetWare to isolate the key knowledge factors and support issues that you will deal with. As a professional instructor, consultant, and writer, I have written this book to be easy to read, understand, and implement.

▶ . . . . ◀

Terminology Used in This Book

You may find that terms in this book vary slightly from the way they have been used elsewhere. Since 1983, Novell has attempted to align its terminology with other networking industry vendors, resulting in many synonyms and much confusion. Terms commonly used in TCP/IP networking and terms commonly used in NetWare networking are sometimes at odds. It is common for terms to become more confusing, especially where internetworking is concerned. As an author I have found that the more words I use, the harder it is for the reader to understand.

It does not help much when you are laboring to understand how to assign a network address to a logical network. If you are confused, how can you properly configure your internetwork, network interfaces, and routers? Network addressing is at the heart of configuring an internetwork, and foundation terminology is key in discussing how to assign network numbers. Any discussion of internetworking mechanics should be explicit and succinct. This often is not possible when two, three, or even four different terms are used with overlapping and inconsistent meanings. For example, the terms *LAN, network, topology,* and *segment* are often used interchangeably. The terms *LAN* and *network* both are used as vague, general terms referring to a network "cloud." Sometimes you see the terms *topology* and *segment* used to refer to the type of LAN or to a specific addressable network. *Segment* is a term that is also used to refer to a data stream segment and a cabling segment. Using these terms without definite distinctions is much like referring to "that" or a "thing." The key to understanding network addressing is predicated on your understanding of what a *logical network* is, which is in turn complicated by the confusion over the terms I just mentioned. In this book, once you understand the definitions of the terms *network segment, LAN,* and *bridge domain,* the discussion of a logical network is clear. Of course, all this is predicated on being able to point to each component with clear, consistent vernacular.

In this book, the term *LAN* is used more explicitly than elsewhere—the term *LAN* refers to an Ethernet, Token Ring, or other type of local area network. *Topology* is a specific term discussed in IEEE specifications, and it has no such meaning in that context. When *topology* is used to identify a local area network, people trained in local area networking but not trained with NetWare are often confused. It was found that using the terms *LAN, topology, network,* and *segment* interchangeably makes the internetworking discussion needlessly complex. In this book, pay close attention to the terms *LAN, network segment, logical network, bridge domain,* and *collision domain.*

What's in This Book

Novell's Guide to Troubleshooting NetWare 5 focuses on NetWare 5, but takes into consideration all current versions of NetWare. Most network implementers who work with NetWare 5 also work with NetWare 4 and 3.

You will find this book divided into four parts:

▶ Part I, *Networking with NetWare* — This section contains four chapters, each explaining the foundation knowledge upon which the rest of the book is based. Pay close attention to terminology in this section — words are used with explicit meanings in this book.

▶ Part II, *Installing and Configuring* — This section includes eight chapters, each one containing instructions on installing and configuring the network, NetWare servers, clients, TCP/IP services, and remote access options. Read this section when installing and configuring components of your network. Many network problems relate back to incorrect configuration or missing components.

▶ Part III, *Troubleshooting and Maintenance* — Each chapter in this section addresses the most important configuration issues that are known to cause problems, the most common problems support personnel experience, and diagnostic/troubleshooting procedures.

▶ *Appendixes* — This section, which appears as PDF files on the accompanying CD-ROM, contains support documentation that serves as reference for the rest of the book. The appendixes constitute a powerful library to be used for troubleshooting and optimizing your network. Reference materials too detailed and specialized for inclusion in the text of the book are included, along with URLs for dozens of support resources. You will find everything you need from utility syntax to detailed protocol analysis codes.

What's on the CD-ROM

This book includes a CD-ROM with the appendixes mentioned previously in electronic form (PDF files), Adobe's Acrobat reader to view the PDF files, URLs for valuable Web resources, useful hardware configuration guides, and helpful shareware/freeware utilities. Use this disk as a support tool when reading the book and when troubleshooting. See Appendix A for more information.

Contents at a Glance

Contents

PART I

Networking with NetWare

CHAPTER 1

NetWare Basics

As Enslo's third law of communications states, *"Terminology is 85 percent of data communications — technology accounts for 15 percent."*

Understanding basic terminology when discussing networking is essential to effectively troubleshooting your NetWare network. This chapter discusses many of NetWare's terms and capabilities. Terms used in this chapter establish common definitions used consistently throughout this book. Capabilities, specifications, and features of each current NetWare version are also discussed to provide you with a valuable foundation knowledge of the NetWare product line.

▶ · ◀

Terminology

Terminology is used quite loosely in the computing industry. Various standards organizations, Novell, Microsoft, other vendors, and independent software developers may use words with slightly different meanings. Even within a single organization such as Novell, it is quite difficult to maintain consistent terminology throughout all documentation. Therefore it is essential to establish a common language at the outset and be quite consistent with use of terminology throughout this book.

TIP

Please pay close attention to definitions in this chapter and at the beginning of each chapter. I have made every effort to define terms when they are first used — early in the book and early in each chapter. Later discussions throughout this book are succinct and assume that you have adopted the uses of terms previously established in this book.

The alternative to this recommendation is to extract the meaning of various terms from context. This is too common in our industry, and technical material is complex enough without this handicap.

Whenever you feel a little uncomfortable with the way a term is used, please first consult the Glossary. Every advanced term defined in this book appears in there. Next you should refer to the Concepts book in your NetWare documentation. If all else fails, refer to *Novell's Encyclopedia of Networking* (Kevin Shafer, Novell Press). These are the reference works I have relied on to establish consistent and meaningful use of terminology.

Several terms are pivotal in your understanding of NetWare and networking mechanics. Though you may have a good knowledge of these concepts, it is in your best interest to review the definitions used in this book. Later chapters will use this same terminology and will be succinct. Your understanding of more advanced concepts depends upon synchronizing your understanding with the definitions used in this chapter. Defining terms is also a good way to explain foundation information. Please study how the following terms are used in this book before proceeding.

Network versus Local Area Network

Though most of us assume we understand the term LAN, we are often confused over its use until we derive the author's meaning from context. In fact, the terms *LAN* and *network* are both vague and general terms that are used interchangeably. This is not the case in this book.

The terms LAN and network are clearly defined in this book, and each is given a distinct meaning. As you will see, network addressing relies on using terms with more precise understanding.

CHECKLIST

Network is a general (and vague) term used in this book to refer to any type of data communication medium.

CHECKLIST

Local area network, or LAN, is a specific type of network. In this book, the term LAN only refers to an Ethernet, Token Ring, FDDI, or other type of LAN that connects computers together over a limited distance.

Many writers and speakers use the term LAN interchangeably with the term network, causing difficulty in references to network addressing and protocols. The definition in this book is not intended to invalidate how others use this term; it is only to clarify functional network layers for the purpose of communicating within the context of this book.

Most dictionaries will define a LAN as "a system of computers connected over a limited distance." Xerox coined this term in the early 1970s when the company first invented Ethernet. This definition is not explicit enough for our purposes anymore. Early LANs were not separate from the rest of the computer system; today, however, all LANs are separate subsystems within a network. The LAN, servers, workstations, networking software, and protocols all work together, though each component is a separate subsystem of the network.

In this book, a LAN is a communications medium consisting of network interface cards (NICs), cabling (or an unbounded medium such as infrared), and all physical layer devices, such as repeaters, hubs, or wiring concentrators. Figure 1.1 illustrates the LAN portion of a network. This distinction is important, as you will see because many networks contain multiple LANs, and we must have appropriate labels to discuss this likelihood.

CHECKLIST

A *network interface card* (NIC) connects a computer to a LAN. You will sometimes see the terms NIC, network card, network board, network adapter, or LAN adapter used to refer to this piece of LAN hardware.

CHECKLIST

A *node* is an intelligent device connected to a network. Generally, this term is used to mean any computer connected to a LAN. When discussing LANs, the term node more specifically means a NIC or chip set that has a physical address and appears as a sender/receiver for LAN traffic.

F I G U R E 1.1

A LAN is the data communications portion of a network.

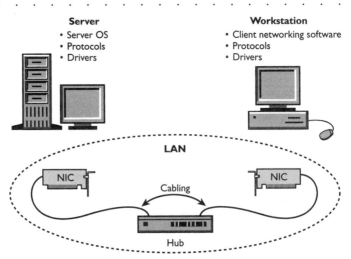

Server
• Server OS
• Protocols
• Drivers

Workstation
• Client networking software
• Protocols
• Drivers

LAN

NIC

NIC

Cabling

Hub

CHECKLIST

A _frame_ is a protocol data unit generated by a LAN node. Frames are exchanged between nodes in order to move data over the LAN. Many things you read will use the terms frame and packet interchangeably, but this books draws a definite distinction between these two categories of protocol data units.

LAN frame formatting is defined in LAN or WAN standards, such as those developed by the Institute of Electrical and Electronic Engineers' (IEEE) 802.3 workgroup. Figure 1.2 shows an Ethernet frame. Frame formatting is discussed in Chapter 2.

F I G U R E 1.2		Destination address	Source address	Length		CRC
An Ethernet frame						
		6	6	2	|←— 48 – 1500 —→|	4

As you can tell from the frame format, the header contains just a few pieces of information: the physical addresses of source and destination (also known as MAC address or node address), the length of the data field (which contains the packet), and a cyclical redundancy check. This is all that is needed to deliver the frame, and therefore its payload, to a destination node. At this layer, addressing is physical — the address is physically assigned to a NIC (or WAN communications card). In an Ethernet LAN, frames are broadcast to all nodes connected to a common medium (cables, perhaps connected together with a wiring concentrator or hub). If the destination address matches the physical address of the NIC, the frame is accepted; otherwise, the frame is simply ignored, with one exception: a broadcast frame (destination address FFFFFFFFFFFF) is accepted by all NICs.

Two basic mechanisms allow a LAN to deliver data: the access protocol and the frame format. Because several nodes share a common medium (for example, cable), the access protocol controls access to the medium. Some types of WANs work in a very similar manner, but most WANs do not require an access protocol because they are point-to-point connections where only two nodes are in play at any time: a sender and a receiver. In almost every case LANs and WANs use a frame to transport data. The X.25 protocol is an exception; it uses a routable packet. Another exception is Asynchronous Transfer Mode (ATM), in which packets are broken into smaller units called _cells_.

CHECKLIST

A *packet* **is a protocol data unit generated by the networking software. The packet may (or may not) contain a segment of data and does not contain a trailer. The packet header contains protocol information to be communicated between nodes at higher levels, such as function calls that indicate what is to be done with the data segment. Each packet relies on a delivery mechanism such as a frame to get it to its ultimate destination node.**

CHECKLIST

Protocols **are rules of communications. Protocols are** *stacked,* **or layered upon one another. Protocols work together (like a team) to provide network functionality while each protocol does its part of the job. Protocol information is stored in the frame and packet headers (and frame trailers) to be communicated to the receiving node.**

The LAN (or WAN) has a very simple function — it transports data from one LAN node to another. The data to be delivered is formatted into packets. Each packet is encapsulated into a frame for delivery as shown in Figure 1.3. Once the packet is delivered, the packet is delivered to a packet driver (software). The receiving node's packet driver reads the packet header to determine what should be done with the packet.

▶ · ◀

FIGURE 1.3

Network packets are encapsulated into frames for delivery over a LAN.

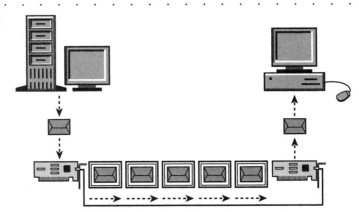

Network Operating System

The NOS is the software package that provides network services. Protocols and drivers as discussed in this chapter are integrated into the NOS, along with other functions. Most NOSes provide shared file access, shared printing, and login security. The most popular NOSes on the market today include Novell's NetWare, Microsoft's Windows networking, IBM's Warp Server, and Banyan's Vines. All NetWare versions that are currently supported will be discussed later in this chapter.

A *network operating system* (NOS) is networking software that provides a set of connectivity services. More than just a protocol stack, the NOS provides access to shared resources, such as file systems, printers, and security.

NOSes connect servers and client workstations, LANs, and other peripherals into an integrated network. Most NOSes enable connectivity between computers even though they may be running different operating systems. A NOS generally consists of a server operating system and client workstation connectivity software. In some cases, however, the NOS is added to an existing operating system to provide network services (for example, Artisoft's LANtastic). In other cases, NOS functionality is built into the operating system (for example, Windows 95 and Windows NT).

Open Data Link Interface

A driver provides an access point between two layers of protocol. Novell and Apple Computer codeveloped the Open Data Link Interface (ODI) driver architecture in the mid 1980s. The ODI architecture includes drivers for NICs as well as higher-level packet drivers. Apple's interest in codeveloping ODI was to assist Novell in supporting both DOS and Macintosh clients at the server end. Novell later leveraged this standard to support NetWare, TCP/IP, and Microsoft networking protocol stacks.

Multiple Link Interface Drivers

ODI architecture is a design specification that encompasses entire protocol stacks, but the Multiple Link Interface Driver (MLID) driver is the driver that interfaces a NIC to the network protocol (for example, IPX or IP). MLID drivers are part of ODI architecture. These drivers effectively interface various types of LANs/WANs with NetWare and other protocol stacks. In the ODI map, everything below the MLID is network hardware, whereas everything above the MLID is pure hardware-independent software.

Each type of LAN and NOS requires a NIC driver that enables the network protocol (for example, IPX) and the access protocol (for example, Ethernet) to work together as a team. Because of this design, different types of LANs and WANs can be used with a NOS, such as NetWare. By the same token, Ethernet and other types of LANs and WANs can work with different NOSes and applications.

The most basic type of driver most system integrators are familiar with is the NIC driver. The system integrator installs a NIC driver to complete the interface between the NIC to the NOS. Novell and other NOS developers write the drivers for the protocols that reside above this level (for example, IPX or IP packet drivers), and the integrator never needs to modify them. As a result, most mere mortals are not familiar with anything except NIC drivers.

MLID drivers are mainly written and maintained by third-party NIC developers. Though Novell distributes many MLID drivers with NetWare, primary responsibility for developing, updating, and supporting MLID drivers lies with the NIC developer. However, Novell takes responsibility for supporting many drivers, because this is such an essential part of supporting their product.

ODI allows a single MLID driver to handle more than one protocol stack. If you used both NetWare and TCP/IP prior to this, you would need to load NetWare drivers, then reboot and load TCP/IP drivers. You could not use both protocol stacks at once.

Network Device Interface Specification

Microsoft developed a similar specification to Novell's MLID. Network Device Interface Specification (NDIS) drivers are used in Microsoft networking for NIC (and other network adapter) drivers. Most vendors develop MLID and NDIS drivers so that their products can be used in both environments.

When DOS and Windows 3.x dominated the desktop, 16-bit DOS MLID drivers were loaded to terminate and stay resident in memory before loading Windows. However, Windows 95 and Windows NT Workstation required new 32-bit drivers. Microsoft developed their own NDIS drivers to be used with Microsoft networking, and Novell developed their 32-bit MLID/ODI drivers to be used with Windows 95/Windows NT. When you installed the Novell MLID driver, it ran side by side with the Microsoft NDIS driver.

Novell has incorporated the ability to use Microsoft's NDIS drivers in lieu of Novell MLID drivers with Windows 95, 98, and NT workstations. When you configure Windows 95, 98, or NT workstations with Microsoft networking and then add Novell's client software, ODI packet drivers are installed that work with the existing NDIS drivers. Novell's support for NDIS drivers reduces the number of drivers and protocols required to support these clients, which translates into less complexity and less memory usage.

Client/Server versus Peer-to-Peer Networking

Clients are workstations that attach to a server. Servers share resources, such as shared file systems, printers, and communications resources. In a NetWare environment, clients are never servers, and servers are never clients. In a NetWare network, a clear distinction is maintained between clients and servers.

In a peer-to-peer network, a computer can be both a server and a client. Until recently, peer-to-peer NOSes like Artisoft's LANtastic were popular. Because Windows 95 and Windows NT include peer-to-peer networking, such products have all but disappeared. In a Microsoft network even a Windows NT server can be both a server and a client. This often confuses technicians because the terms server and client are often replaced with the term "computer." A Microsoft network is a blend of client/server and peer-to-peer elements.

CHECKLIST

A *workstation* is a personal computer. A workstation can be a fully equipped stand-alone computer, or it can be network-attached. The term *terminal* is used for a dumb device that is a slave of a host computer, such as a minicomputer or mainframe computer. NetWare is built to provide services to network-attached workstations but does not support user terminals like a UNIX system does.

Novell Directory Services

Prior to NetWare 4, each server was the center of a network, providing login, file sharing, print sharing, and other services. When clients needed to connect to multiple servers, separate user accounts and administration were required for each server. Taking the International Standards Organization's X.500 specifications as a basis, Novell developed a service that allows a single login to the network, regardless of how many servers the user needs to access.

Novell Directory Services (NDS) does far more than consolidate logins. NDS is a hierarchical object-oriented structure for containing and managing users and resources of an entire enterprise. In NDS, users and resources can be grouped into logical containers instead of servers. This allows the organization of logical objects to differ from the network's physical infrastructure. Administrators and their responsibilities can be established over logical containers instead of being handcuffed to servers and the resources they contain.

CHECKLIST

Larger networks are often very complex with more than one server, more than one LAN, and often more than one administrator. The term *enterprise* is used to describe any type of organization (business, government agency, nonprofit organization, and so on) where a complex network exists.

NDS allows both centralized control as well as distributed administration that can be individually tailored to meet the needs of any organization. For example, NDS allows the network administrators to put servers in a locked building, while departmental administrators can still manage their own user accounts, rights to files and directories, and network printers.

NDS's hierarchical design permits differing degrees of administrative rights. For example, a departmental administrator may have NDS rights to add users and manage user rights within his/her container but not have NDS rights to alter server configuration, add/delete disk storage/volumes, and so on. NDS rights can pertain to a specific container or extend down the branches of the tree to allow various levels of administration while establishing precise control over users and resources under the administrator's control.

NDS is a perfect fit for virtually any organization, especially for enterprise networks. However, NDS benefits can be quite attractive even for smaller organizations. An NDS tree can be simple, with just one container — or complex, designed like a corporate organizational chart. NDS has numerous features, too detailed to discuss in this chapter. See Chapter 11 for more details on NDS.

Internetwork

Enterprise networks most often consist of complex internetworks that include multiple LANs, WANs, routers, gateways, and other network resources. Even smaller networks often include this type of complexity. Many organizations have outlying branches that are served by a central facility.

An *internetwork* is a complex network consisting of multiple LANs and perhaps WANs.

CHECKLIST

Generally, we consider an internetwork to consist of LANs linked together with routers, but bridges can also connect LANs together into internetworks. Since 1985, Novell has incorporated a router into its server operating systems, making internetworking with routers a built-in feature. Network integrators generally prefer routers over bridges where routable protocols, such as IPX/SPX or TCP/IP, are used. For these reasons, internetworking and routing are generally part of the same discussion. Internetworking, bridges, and routers will be discussed in Chapter 2.

Intranet

Networking with PCs has grown in sophistication and complexity. Many enterprises started with separate LANs—islands of computing—where each department had their own server, LAN, and system administrator. It was only logical that they should link these "islands" together with the built-in routers found in NetWare and most UNIX servers. When these systems are linked together with one or more routable protocols (such as the Novell and TCP/IP protocols), that internetwork is called an *intranet*.

An *intranet* is an internetwork owned by and confined to a single enterprise. An intranet provides the network infrastructure for delivering client/server services.

CHECKLIST

The key feature of an intranet is providing server-based services to users all over the intranet. When discussing client/server applications, most people think of TCP/IP "daemons" (UNIX server-based applications) such as Web service, FTP (file transfer protocol) and LPR (line printer redirector), or Internet e-mail.

Though these services are indeed reason enough to link users together all over an enterprise, some non-TCP/IP server-based applications are of equal importance. Novell's GroupWise for E-mail is a very popular intranet e-mail server, NDS is an intranet server, and many other server-based services exist that are not based on TCP/IP. More appropriately, intranets are vehicles for delivering server-based services to all network users.

Intranets are mainly TCP/IP-based, probably due to the original TCP/IP services as well as the UNIX system developers who made this type of architecture popular. TCP/IP simply enables network connectivity; it does not have any built-in features of a NOS such as security or real-time file sharing.

NetWare Versions

NetWare has evolved through at least twenty-one unique versions, plus a few supplemental versions (such as ELS NetWare). From the original NetWare86, which ran on a PC XT, to NetWare68, which ran on a Novell server with a Motorola 68000 processor, to NetWare 5, NetWare has retained its status as the most advanced NOS in the market, and to this date it is still the best performer.

In this book, however, we are only concerned with NetWare versions that are in wide use — NetWare 3, 4, and 5. It has been a Novell policy to continue to sell and support an existing version when a new version is introduced. An older version is discontinued only when demand falls to the point that it is not feasible to support it any longer. NetWare 3 is still a strong seller, and Novell has not indicated that the company is prepared to discontinue it at this time. This section discusses the primary design features that will help you select the current NetWare version that is right for you.

NetWare 3

NetWare/386, introduced in 1987, was the first 32-bit server operating system. Arriving very shortly after the 80386 processor, this product took advantage of the 80386's memory architecture, which made it possible to address vast amounts of memory and is still used in current 486 and Pentium processors. NetWare/386, as it was originally known, could address up to 4GB of RAM and 32TB of disk storage.

The industry was not so quick to adopt NetWare/386. NetWare 2.15 was very stable, and most network engineers were pretty jaded by previous ".0 releases" from Microsoft and IBM. Later, when the 486 processor shipped, Novell referred to this product as NetWare 3 instead of NetWare/386, since it was also quite suitable for the 486 and future processors. When version 3.1 was introduced, the product was well endorsed and overwhelmingly accepted by the industry.

It is hard to say that any one factor led to NetWare 3's unprecedented success. Here are a few of the many developments that occurred between 1987 and 1992 that fueled the networking market: Novell experienced tremendous growth during these years. TCP/IP networking also skyrocketed during the same time period, but no one company experienced the benefits to the extent that Novell did at the time.

Novell had previously divested themselves of its NIC and disk adapter divisions, opting to focus on the NOS market. NetWare 3's open architecture allowed third-party hardware developers to produce devices that integrated well with NetWare. These vendors joined Novell in driving the networking industry to a new level. In the early 1990s, Novell's Yes program was very prominent in identifying nonproprietary network devices that were certified to work with NetWare. This strategy coupled Novell's and hardware developers' marketing efforts.

NetWare 3 also generated a new wave of server-based applications. This environment was a better development platform than NetWare 2. Software developers who developed NetWare 3 server apps (NetWare Loadable Modules), became development partners, assisting in making NetWare 3 more popular.

NetWare 3.11's introduction was very timely. The U.S. Congress had mandated TCP/IP capability in all government computer systems as a temporary stepping-stone to GOSIP. NetWare 3.11 included TCP/IP capabilities. When no other NOSes qualified for government contracts, Novell inherited large contracts that had been granted to other NOS vendors.

Another factor that rocketed NetWare 3's acceptance was the Certified NetWare Engineer program. (I was one of the first, receiving my CNE in June 1990.) The gap between networking promises, networking hardware, and qualified technicians closed in the early 1990s, and NetWare 3 was at the heart of it all.

At about the same time, 3Com's codevelopment efforts with Microsoft ended, and NetWare was about the only game in town. Microsoft made a half-hearted attempt to convert 3Com 3+ Open customers to LAN Manager, but the lion's share of the market upgraded to Novell. 3Com had over seven percent of the NOS market, and Microsoft turned it into less than one percent almost overnight. It seems as though these developments forced customers to use NetWare.

All these factors conspired to grow the networking industry, and NetWare 3 garnered a substantial majority of the NOS market. At present, probably more NetWare 3 servers are in use than any other server operating system. It is impossible to tell how many users log into NetWare 3 servers every day, but suffice it to say, many do.

Current Release

Novell's policy has been to freeze development on an older version once a newer version is released. Novell will continue to issue fixes, patches, and drivers as long as the product is officially supported. NetWare 3.12 was officially the end of the NetWare 3 product line; however, Novell issued several fixes and enhancements and then incorporated them into a new release, renamed 3.2.

Version 3.2 contains the following revisions over 3.12:

- A Windows-based SYSCON utility

- Stable server support for most popular CD-ROM disk storage formats

- Improved network performance

- Year 2000 readiness

- Improved network reliability

- Netscape Navigator versions 3.01 and 4.04

- An evaluation copy of intraNetWare

- Availability in English, French, German, Italian, Portuguese, and Spanish

NOTE You can order the NetWare 3.2 Enhancement Pack to upgrade NetWare 3.12 for a nominal fee from any Novell Authorized, Gold, or Platinum Partner. For more information, contact your local Novell office or call the Novell Customer Response Center at 801-228-4CRC (801-228-4272). Or in the United States and Canada, call toll free 888-321-4CRC (888-321-4272). You may also visit Novell's World Wide

Web site at `http://www.novell.com` or use **Novell's Product Information FaxBack system at 801-861-3030. Or in the United States and Canada, call 800-209-3500.**

Recommendations

NetWare 3.2 is a great product that is extremely stable, simple, powerful, easy to use, and widely supported. Many NetWare 3 servers are currently in use because there is no compelling reason to upgrade. The following conditions may persuade you to choose NetWare 3.2:

- ▶ Small networks where administrators and support personnel are already familiar with NetWare 3

- ▶ Support for older disk storage or LAN hardware that is not supported with NetWare 4 drivers

- ▶ Support for server-based NLMs that run only under NetWare 3

TIP

You might consider NetWare for small business use, because it is the most affordable 4.11 version for networks of 25 users or less. It features simple installation, easy administration, Internet access, GroupWise for E-mail, calendaring, scheduling, task management, and document management.

NetWare 4

In 1994, Novell introduced NetWare 4.0. NetWare 4 had many operating system enhancements, but the big news was NetWare Directory Services (the name was later changed to Novell Directory Services). NDS was, and still is, the definitive answer to enterprise networking issues. NDS, based on the International Standards Organization's X.500 standards, was developed to manage larger networks and internetworks on a more modular, departmentalized basis without sacrificing central control. NDS, among other features, allows a single login to all required servers and services and includes bulk user management features that significantly reduce administration efforts in larger networks.

For many installations, another compelling reason to use NetWare 4 is System Fault Tolerance III (mirrored fault tolerant servers). This feature makes NetWare a true 24 × 7 (24 hours/day, 7 days/week) server architecture. Combined with high-availability server hardware, a NetWare SFT III system can provide top protection from server failure for mission-critical applications.

Current Release

Version 4.11 is the current product release; no future release is planned at this time. Though Novell has not made a formal announcement, Novell has a proven track record of continuing to support its products until demand for support is no longer required. For example, Novell still supports NetWare 3.12 and has only recently discontinued support for NetWare 3.11 (as of January 31, 1999), several years after replacing the product. Novell will continue to provide fixes and updates to support this product far into the foreseeable future.

Recommendations

You have no reasons to purchase NetWare 4.11 instead of NetWare 5. You will find that NetWare 5 is stable, is robust, and contains additional features not included in NetWare 4. However, if you prefer to purchase NetWare 4.11, this product will remain on the market. Novell has established a policy of keeping previous versions available until demand no longer warrants it.

Some organizations have taken the position that they will not purchase any ".0" software products until the first "service pack" is released or until the product reaches its first revision. Improvements in NetWare 5 do not warrant typical ".0" release concerns — this product has been developed from a base of highly mature and proven code.

NetWare 5 was put to the most severe challenges and is used in production by thousands of users — at Novell, Inc., where NetWare 5 has been used internally, and in customer beta sites. In all cases, NetWare 5 has proven to meet Novell's strict standards for final release. Novell has an excellent track record of responding to consumer reports and posting fixes quickly. Reviews and news reports on NetWare 5 have verified that this product is sound and stable. In short, Novell fully supports moving to NetWare 5 without reservation.

Upgrading

Some organizations have a policy of retaining an existing software version until a compelling reason forces them to upgrade. No bug fixes or design flaws would compel you to upgrade from NetWare 4. Other organizations make it a policy to always upgrade to latest version of a software product. Even such a policy does not automatically oblige you to upgrade NetWare. However, all networks based on NetWare 4's advanced features will benefit from improvements in NetWare 5.

See the following section on NetWare 5 to see if a powerful incentive exists for you to upgrade your NetWare 4 servers. At the very least, all new installations should take advantage of NetWare 5's advanced features.

NetWare 5 integrates seamlessly into existing NetWare 4 networks. However, be sure to apply the NetWare 4.11 updates contained on your NetWare 5 operating system CD before installing NetWare 5 servers.

NOTE

NetWare 5

NetWare 5 incorporates a host of new features. If a single theme characterizes NetWare 5, it is a move to more open systems and Internet/intranet compatibility with other systems. Among other features, NetWare 5 can be configured with pure, native TCP/IP. For the TCP/IP purist, this is a long-awaited development. For network administrators who prefer to manage only one protocol stack, NetWare 5 is the ultimate solution.

New TCP/IP Developments

Several new TCP/IP features are integrated into NetWare 5. The following features provide a native TCP/IP environment without compromising NetWare functionality:

- *Pure (native) IP* — In previous NetWare versions Novell supported the use of IP between NetWare servers and clients, but NetWare services were tunneled inside of IPX packets (an IPX packet was encapsulated within a TCP/IP packet). This meant that IPX traffic was still present on the network, and superfluous layers of protocol were required for NetWare services (see Chapter 2 for a brief description of NetWare protocols). In NetWare 5 all NetWare higher-layer protocols have been re-engineered or replaced to eliminate the need for IPX. Though NetWare still relies on NetWare Core Protocols for basic NetWare services, they are now natively handled by TCP/IP. Like UNIX, NetWare is now a true, native TCP/IP environment — but unlike UNIX, NetWare makes Novell services (such as

NDS security and real-time file sharing) available to NetWare clients. Novell has upstaged Microsoft on this one. Though all current Windows versions run on TCP/IP, the NetBIOS protocol is required for all Windows networking services. Not only does NetBIOS waste valuable resources, it is also not routable. Windows Internet Name Service (WINS) and NetBIOS broadcasts over UDP are required to enable host name resolution.

▶ *Service Location Protocol (SLP)* — Novell developers also implemented a new Internet standard protocol called Service Location Protocol (SLP) (RFC 2165). SLP replaces Novell's Service Advertising Protocol (SAP), which was required to locate servers and their services. SLP handles server identification without a need for periodic broadcasting as is the case in SAP. SLP reduces periodic broadcast traffic for the optimal use of bandwidth.

▶ *IPX Core Support* — NetWare 5 can still support IPX services. For each NIC in your server, you can bind IPX, IP, or both protocols. This feature allows pure IP for IP clients and pure IPX for IPX clients simultaneously. Administrators will like this because they will not have to choose between the two or reconfigure all nodes during migration. If an administrator wants to migrate nodes over to IP, this can be done one workstation at a time.

▶ *IP-IPX Compatibility Mode* — IPX-related services are available to pure IP clients through the Compatibility Mode. This mode is a gateway service that provides three functions:

  • Backward compatibility with IPX applications

  • Migration Agent compatibility services for IPX and IP (discussed previously)

  • Bindery Agent for NetWare 3 bindery compatibility

The IP-IPX Compatibility Mode protects your investment for existing NetWare networks and NLMs and third-party services. For example, GroupWise for E-mail services will handle both IPX and IP clients' e-mail without an upgrade. Another example is that you can use an existing IPX backbone LAN or WAN to link two NetWare 5 IP-only systems, or you can use an IP backbone to link two IPX-only servers. The Migration Agent allows tunneling of either protocol to make migration to an all-IP solution seamless. Compatibility Mode capabilities are discussed in detail in Chapter 11.

▸ *DNS, DHCP, and NDS integration* — Dynamic Host Configuration Protocol (automatically assigns IP addresses), and Domain Name Services (looks up IP addresses when only the host name is known) are incorporated into the replicated NDS database. This aligns information necessary to access IP nodes all over the network with NDS and uses NDS's replication service instead of using traditional DNS replication methods. Incorporating these services into NDS increases valid name resolution responses, virtually eliminating failure to resolve DNS names. Integrating DHCP and DNS into NDS also provides automated client information for discovering client NDS configuration data. This feature eliminates the need to manually enter NDS configuration data at the client workstation. This may seem like a small factor, but in large networks it can save many man-hours. There is nothing proprietary about this solution; it is fully supported in the latest RFCs for DHCP.

▸ *Dynamic DNS* — NetWare 5 incorporates the new Internet standard for Dynamic DNS. Instead of manually updating DNS tables, the DDNS service accumulates IP address and name resolution information by listening to the network and updating its tables automatically. This virtually eliminates DNS system administration while improving successful DNS name resolution. Many benefits are now available due to this service. For example, notebook users can now plug into any subnet, and their location is accessible because their address and name information is updated immediately without manual intervention.

Web- and Internet-Related Features

NetWare 5 is fully Java-compliant and includes components that make NetWare the premier platform for Web services. NetWare 5 includes the following components to base your Web services on NetWare and make your system 100 percent compatible with industry standards.

▶ *Netscape FastTrack Server (Web server)* — Netscape's popular FastTrack Server Web service is bundled with NetWare 5. Web clients can access this server over an intranet or the Internet. FastTrack's cross-platform environment enables you to deploy Web service and database access on a NetWare server. Web users will not be able to tell the difference between Web sites loaded on a UNIX, NetWare, or Windows NT server. FastTrack Server includes the highest degree of secure Web access, with Lightweight Directory Access Protocol (LDAP) support for centralized user and group management. FastTrack Server is extremely simple to set up and is tuned for best performance.

▶ *Lightweight Directory Access Protocol (LDAP) Services for NDS* — LDAP is an industry standard for integrating various directory services. NetWare 5 features a server-based LDAP version 3 interface. This allows LDAP-compliant services such as FastTrack Server to access information contained within NDS. Administration is reduced significantly because user accounts and security restrictions can be drawn from your existing NDS database. Even custom applications can use the LDAP interface for security data because it runs under Secure Sockets Layer version 3 (SSL). In the past, each user list required separate setup and administration. With LDAP support built into NetWare 5, you should never have to set up users and security again.

▶ *Active Directory Services Interfaces (ADSI) NDS Provider* — This service provides LDAP integration with other directory services, including Microsoft Active Directory.

New System Administration Features

NetWare 5 is easier to manage than previous versions. Novell developers have engineered ways to manage client desktops centrally and more efficiently. The following features reduce or eliminate the need to visit clients or have clients spend time configuring their systems:

▶ *Java-based install* — A new GUI-based install program ushers you through the server setup, or you can choose the older-style character-based program. All Novell products will eventually be installed with a common look and feel. Novell's autodetection of existing hardware further simplifies installation.

▶ *Zero Administration Network Works (Z.E.N.works)* — Z.E.N.works enables administrators to install desktop software centrally, eliminating the need to install software locally on each workstation. NetWare Application Launcher (NAL) and NetWare Application Manager (NAM) enable you to install an application for an NDS application object using NAM. NAL is installed on each desktop and in turn uses NAM to load the software. The result is a desktop object that requires no local maintenance. Z.E.N.works eliminates the need for local Registry entries in Windows 95 and Windows NT workstations. By installing and managing applications centrally, you reduce the need for support significantly. Z.E.N.works has other powerful features. For example, when you add a user in NDS, a user account is automatically created in a Windows NT Workstation. This reduces the need to perform this task in both NetWare Administrator and Microsoft User Manager.

▶ *NDS for NT (available at additional cost)* — This product provides full support for a single-user login and centralized administration for integrated NetWare and Windows NT domain environments. NDS for NT enables you to manage NT domains and Microsoft BackOffice services through NDS. Windows NT Server domains can be placed into NDS containers and controlled through NDS security. You can add users in NetWare Administrator, and the user accounts will simultaneously be added in the Windows NT Server domains.

▶ *NetWare Management Agents (NMAs)* — Three NMAs enable you to manage NetWare server operating systems from a desktop using HP OpenView, Novell ManageWise, CA UniCenter, IBM Tivoli, SunNet Manager, and other SNMP-based software.

▶ *Migration Wizard* — A new Windows 95 migration utility helps move NetWare 3 servers and objects into your NDS tree. The utility enables you to view bindery objects and NDS trees offline, move them to the appropriate containers, and then execute your migration. This is a simple tool that makes the prospect of migrating older servers into NDS less imposing.

▶ *New backup utility* — A new Windows 95 client-based backup utility provides many scheduling options and autoloader support. This new utility can be used by IPX or IP clients and is subject to NDS control and security.

Application Server Support

The NetWare 5 operating system has been redesigned with new components added to be a more stable and effective platform for server-based applications.

▶ *New multiprocessing kernel* — Novell's multiprocessing design offers NetWare's traditional nonpreemptive processing for core services, plus preemptive processing with several new enhancements for server-based applications. The multiprocessing kernel includes fault-tolerant memory protection, virtual memory, increased performance, and an integrated debugger.

▶ *Java Server framework* — NetWare 5 delivers on the Java promise to "write once, run anywhere" with a Java Virtual Machine running on the server. This makes NetWare 5 the perfect platform for developing and implementing industry-standard applications that use Java and Java scripting. Java developers can write object-oriented, multithreaded, and dynamically linked applications using the Java language and a fully exposed set of APIs. NetWare 5 contains a Java Software Development Kit (JSDK) with Common Object Request Broker Architecture (CORBA) ORB, a VBScript-compatible NetBasic interpreter, JavaBeans for NetWare, JavaScript, and Perl 5. A server-based Java graphical user interface (GUI) is used for server utilities. Everything from installing your NetWare 5 server to monitoring its functions is now GUI-based.

▶ *Cryptographic services* — Standards-based international cryptographic services are built into NetWare 5 core services provides fundamental security features. This new service includes confidentiality, integrity authentication, and nonrepudiation. It has a secure loader and an interface manager so that only signed modules can be used.

▸ *Secure Authentication Services (SAS)* — NetWare 4.11 is the first and only operating system to receive C-2 security certification when network-attached. NetWare 5 extends that security to the next level with SAS authentication. SAS is an industry-standard mechanism that includes a framework for distinguishing between authentication mechanisms of various qualities, as well as supporting third-party authentication services. SAS provides server-based user applications with controlled access to files and NDS objects based on the user's SAS authentication. SAS supports Secure Sockets Layer (SSL) version 3, and SAS APIs can establish encrypted SSL connections.

▸ *Public Key Infrastructure Services (PKIS)* — Now NetWare 5 administrators can support public key cryptography and digital certificates using PKIS. You can establish a Certificate Authority (CA) container with NDS to perform certificate key management within the umbrella of NDS. PKIS supports certificate-based security services such as Secure Sockets Layer (SSL) security for LDAP servers. PKIS allows use of NetWare 5's CA as well as third-party CA services.

Other Improvements

The advanced technologies in NetWare 5 set it apart as the most advanced NOS in the industry. Novell has always lead the industry in NOS features, and NetWare 5 again pioneers new capabilities.

▸ *Novell Storage Services (NSS)* — NSS is a powerful new 64-bit indexed file system that increases storage capacity and cuts volume mounting time to a minimum (just a few seconds even for the largest volumes). NSS's 64-bit addressing provides for billions of volumes and directories and increases the maximum file size to 8TB, yet it reduces memory usage during volume mount. At Comdex '98, Novell demonstrated a crash-repair operation for a 3TB volume. The procedure took less than 10 seconds. NSS is the fastest, most durable file system in the industry.

▸ *Novell Distributed Print Services (NDPS) version 2* — NDPS eliminates the complexity of traditional queue-based printing services and provides improved printer communication and feedback. This service provides automated setup and bidirectional communications for printers. It features plug-and-print, automated driver download, and single-point administration. NDPS enables users to easily locate available printers, and it provides the end user with printer features, status, and a list of pending jobs. NDPS offers advanced printer management/configuration, reduces job polling traffic, and eliminates SAP broadcasts. By reducing print and protocol traffic, NDPS benefits your entire network.

▶ *Hot Plug PCI* — NetWare 5 support the new Hot Plug PCI standard for replacing server PCI interface cards without a shutdown. NetWare 5 installed on a Hot Plug PCI server platform makes 24 × 7 a realistic goal.

▶ *I_2O Support* — NetWare 5 supports intelligent I/O technology commonly known as I_2O. I_2O is an industry standard in computer design that offloads I/O traffic to an additional I/O processor. I_2O alleviates bottlenecks in servers, improving performance especially for server-based applications.

▶ *Oracle 8* — You will find an Oracle 8 server with a five-user license included with NetWare 5. The Oracle 8 server is tuned for optimal performance with NetWare. Oracle 8 features integration with NDS, providing access to a wealth of objects already defined in your network.

▶ *Catalog Services* — NetWare 5's Catalog Services provides a flat-file customizable catalog of NDS allowing users/developers to search and extract NDS information. Catalog Services provides the capability to enable logins without specifying a login context.

▶ *WAN Traffic Manager* — The WAN Traffic Manager enables you to create policies to control NDS replication over WAN links.

▶ *Auditing Services* — A new audit log file object has been added to the NDS schema to allow auditors to be assigned as trustees as required. Audit logs can thus be protected so that system administrators are denied access to auditing information.

Recommendations

NetWare 5 has proven stable — the final release is ready for prime time. Though the server operating system has major revisions, much of the core development code is retained and is quite mature. Many of the services (for example, NDS) have experienced minor revisions, while most of the new features have been added, not revised. The product in its current form is ready for production use in the largest environments.

Of course any new product should be experienced like a fine wine, with patience and awareness. Reason mandates that you try NetWare 5 in less than mission-critical roles until you gain confidence in it. Once you do, you will probably be amazed at the technology and power that has been integrated into this product.

NetWare 5 servers can integrate into NetWare 4 NDS environments with little or no difficulty. Migration does not have to be a major operation. With the new migration utility, you may decide that the time is right to move your NetWare 3 servers into NetWare 5.

When integrating NetWare 5 into a NetWare 4 tree, you must update your NetWare 4 servers. NetWare 5 includes updates to extend the NDS schema for full interoperability with NetWare 4.11. See Chapter 8 for details.

NOTE

Check for news about NetWare 5 at `http://www.novell.com/netware5` on the World Wide Web. You can locate the latest patches, drivers, updates, and service packs for NetWare 5 and all Novell products at Novell's Product home page, `http://support.novell.com/misc/patlst.htm`.

Product Features

You can find this and the other tables shown in this chapter in Appendix B, and on the CD that accompanies this book.

NOTE

Table 1.1 compares the product features of NetWare 3, NetWare 4, and NetWare 5.

TABLE I.I

Product Features

	NETWARE 3	NETWARE 4	NETWARE 5
General	32-bit server operating system	Multithreaded, multiprocessing (requires Pentium processor)	New multiprocessing kernel
	Support for large storage and large amounts of server RAM		Java Server framework
	Support for virtually any popular client desktop		
	Connectivity to virtually any popular minicomputer or mainframe computer		
	Compatibility with thousands of third-party applications and services		
	Stable server support for most popular CD-ROM disk storage formats (version 3.2)		
Administration	Powerful network management capabilities, including remote management	A single, integrated view of your multiserver network through Novell Directory Services (NDS)	Java-based install
	Resource management and accounting features	NDS database distribution and fault tolerance through partitioning and replication	Z.E.N.works workstation management
	Support for an interface for IBM's NetView network management system	NetWare Administrator Windows-based comprehensive administration utility	NDS for NT

Product Features (continued)

	NETWARE 3	NETWARE 4	NETWARE 5
Administration *(continued)*	DOS Menuing system	More flexible resource accounting and licensing management	NetWare Management Agents (NMAs)
	Easy installation from CD-ROM	More automated CD-ROM-based installation and migration tools	Migration Wizard
	Simple upgrade from previous NetWare versions	Built-in support for most CD-ROM and optical disk formats	Hot-Plug PCI
	Online documentation in English, French, German, Italian, Portuguese, and Spanish	Data migration to/from secondary storage	
	Interoperates with other NetWare versions	Significantly improved performance, especially over wide area links	
	Windows-based SYSCON utility (version 3.2)	Symmetric multiprocessing (SMP) for scalability	
	Improved network performance (version 3.2)	Modular client and server architectures so you can add services easily	
	Year 2000 ready (version 3.2)	Improved memory management	
		Multiple simultaneous language support at server and client	
		More flexible NetWare licensing (additive server licensing)	

Continued

T A B L E   1.1

Product Features (continued)

	NETWARE 3	NETWARE 4	NETWARE 5
File System	Exceptional data protection and system reliability	Enhanced file services	Novell Storage Services (NSS)
	Long name space support for Macintosh, OS/2, and UNIX filenames		Active Directory Services Interfaces (ADSI) NDS Provider
Intranetworking	Internal routing for IPX and IP	Multiprotocol routing for IPX/SPX, AppleTalk, and TCP/IP	Pure (native) IP
	IP forwarding, IPX tunneling over IP	NetWare/IP for better integration for IP and IPX networks	IPX core support
	Support for SNMP and other IP services		IP-IPX Compatibility Mode
			DNS, DHCP, and NDS integration
			Dynamic DNS
			Lightweight Directory Access Protocol (LDAP) Services for NDS
Security	Advanced network security	Unsurpassed network security and C-2 compliance	Cryptographic services
			Secure Authentication Services (SAS)
			Public Key Infrastructure (PKI) Services
Backup	Complete backup services	System Fault Tolerance Level III (two-server clustering — additional cost for upgrade)	New Backup utility

TABLE 1.1

Product Features (continued)

	NETWARE 3	NETWARE 4	NETWARE 5
Backup *(continued)*		Enhanced backup capabilities	
Printing	Advanced print services		Novell Distributed Print Services (NDPS)
Internet	Netscape Navigator Web browser; versions 3.01 and 4.04 (version 3.2)	NetWare server-based Web server for access to intranets and the Internet	Netscape FastTrack Server

Product Specifications

Table 1.2 compares product specifications for NetWare 3, NetWare 4, and NetWare 5. These specifications are limited by current computer hardware design.

TABLE 1.2

Product Specifications

	NETWARE 3	NETWARE 4	NETWARE 5
Logical users supported	5, 10, 25, 50, 100, or 250	5, 10, 25, 50, 100, 250, 500, or 1,000 (Provides additional licenses in 10-, 25-, 50-, 100-, and 250-user increments)	5, 10, 25, 50, 100, 250, 500, or 1,000 (Provides additional licenses in 10-, 25-, 50-, 100-, and 250-user increments)
Concurrent open files per server	100,000	100,000	10 quintillion (10^{19})
Directory entries per volume	2,097,152	16 million	10 quintillion (10^{19})
Volumes per server	64	64	No limit
Logical Drives Per Volume	32	1,024	No limit

Continued

TABLE 1.2

Product Specifications
(continued)

	NETWARE 3	NETWARE 4	NETWARE 5
Maximum disk storage capacity	32TB	32TB	8TB
Maximum RAM	4GB		
Maximum file size	4GB	4GB	8TB

Product System Requirements

Table 1.3 compares product system requirements for NetWare 3, NetWare 4, and NetWare 5.

TABLE 1.3

System Requirements

	NETWARE 3	NETWARE 4	NETWARE 5
Server	Intel 386, 486, Pentium, Pentium Pro, or Pentium II processor	Intel 386-based PC or higher	Pentium-based PC or above
	6MB (up to 4GB) RAM (More RAM may be required, depending on the number of users, NLMs, and server disk storage)	16MB of RAM (more RAM may be required to support NLMs and larger disk drives)	64MB of RAM (128MB recommended)
	15MB DOS-formatted boot volume (more space is recommended to support NLMs and future upgrades)	Unpartitioned disk space sufficient to support your applications and data	
	20MB (up to 32TB) unformatted disk space	55MB or more of free disk space in a DOS boot volume.	1GB hard disk space
	A NIC connected to a LAN	One or more NICs connected to a functional LAN	One or more NICs connected to a functional LAN

TABLE 1.3

System Requirements
(continued)

	NETWARE 3	NETWARE 4	NETWARE 5
Server	CD-ROM (can be on workstation)	SO 9660-compliant ICD-ROM drive, DOS device drivers, and Microsoft CD extensions or equivalent	CD-ROM reader for installation
DOS client workstation	Intel 386 or higher processor; MS-DOS, PC-DOS or Novell DOS 3.1 or higher; MS-DOS 2.x. 3.x. 4.x. 5.x, or 6.x; DR DOS 6.0; or Novell DOS 7	MS-DOS 3.x, 4.x, 5.x, or 6.x, DR DOS 6.0, or Novell DOS 7; NetWare Client for DOS/Windows (included with NetWare 4.11)	DOS 3.3 or higher (DOS 7 included with NetWare 5 License disk); NetWare Client for DOS/Windows 3.1x
Windows workstations	Windows 3.0, 3.1 or 3.11 with MS-DOS 3.1 or higher; Windows 95; Windows 98; Windows NT 3.51 or 4.0	Windows NT, Windows 95, or Windows 3.x; NetWare Client for DOS/Windows (included with NetWare 4.11)	Windows NT (4.0), Windows 95/98, or Windows 3.x; NetWare Client for DOS/Windows 3.1x
UNIX NFS workstations	UNIX NFS clients (with NetWare NFS installed at server)	UNIX workstation (see your UNIX vendor for workstation requirements); NetWare NFS Services 2.1 or higher—NetWare 4 Edition on server (available from Novell at additional cost)	
OS/2 workstations	OS/2 v 1.1, 1.2, 1.3, 2.0, or 2.1, Standard or Extended editions (see OS/2 hardware requirements)	Any version of OS/2; NetWare Client for OS/2 (included with NetWare 4)	

Continued

TABLE 1.3

System Requirements
(continued)

	NETWARE 3	NETWARE 4	NETWARE 5
Mac OS workstations	Macintosh System 6 or higher (with NetWare for Macintosh installed at server)	Mac OS System 6 or above; NetWare for Macintosh 4.x (included with NetWare 4.x at no additional cost)	

CHAPTER 2

Internetworking Basics

Networked computers are physically linked with LANs and WANs, but protocols enable communications over these connections. A network engineer must understand physical infrastructure and logical communications, or suffer myopia in troubleshooting. Conversely, a good understanding of internetworking and protocols will equip you with a keen ability to diagnose.

This chapter discusses the underlying mechanics used in all current NetWare networks. The information in this chapter is the foundation for much of what follows in this book. You will configure protocols when you build your internetwork, you will accommodate protocols when you optimize your network, and you will resolve problems based on your knowledge of how communications flow. Therefore this chapter is very important to you if you want to master your network. Some of the material in this chapter will serve as a reference for future troubleshooting efforts.

This chapter deals with configuration aspects of network infrastructure — you must understand physical infrastructure before you can properly configure protocols. If you are about to install a system, this is a good place to start. This chapter contains information that is indispensable for the system analyst or designer.

You need not remember all the details contained in this chapter, but you might need to refer back to some of them when you suspect that your network is configured improperly. This chapter is intended to serve as an introduction and overview. Later chapters build on the concepts and terminology discussed in this chapter.

In reading this chapter, expect to learn foundation concepts that will help you understand:

- ▸ NetWare protocol mechanisms

- ▸ Internetworking design

- ▸ Sources of network errors

- ▸ Network optimization

Internetworking Hardware

Actually, the workings of a network are quite simple to understand. This section discusses the basic hardware used in internetworks.

LANs and WANs

LANs and WANs transport packets of data (IPX or IP in a NetWare network) from one node to another over a common medium. A LAN is a data communications medium with high bandwidth over a limited distance. A LAN has many users sharing a common medium (normally cabling). LANs are privately owned and contained within buildings and/or campuses (series of buildings occupied by one company).

WANs are generally owned by data communications providers, such as telephone companies or long distance carriers (for instance, AT&T, Sprint, MCI). WANs generally move data at lower bandwidths over longer distances. Most WANs are based on point-to-point connections over leased digital lines. In these WANs, data communications flow between just one sender and one receiver at any given moment.

Bridging and Routing

Bridges and routers connect LANs and WANs into larger systems called internetworks. Several years ago, it was enough to build a LAN, and many departments in larger organizations did so, creating separate islands of computing. More recently, larger organizations began linking these LANs together. For a while the networking industry was at odds whether to employ bridges or routers. Industry leaders like IBM and Microsoft originally stood firm on using bridges for internetworking. UNIX, NetWare, Digital, and Apple integrators preferred routers. The vendors' preferences were based on the protocols they used. In some cases, the terminology got pretty confusing. In recent years routing has clearly emerged as the preferred strategy in larger organizations. The preference is based on a larger strategy involving the widespread employment of IPX/SPX and TCP/IP (routable) networking protocols.

Network Segments

The term *network segment* is central to many internetworking discussions in this book. To be perfectly clear when discussing internetworking, consistent use of terminology must be established. It is quintessential to define elements of an internetwork distinctly as they are used in this book, or you will get lost in the more complex discussions that follow. A *network segment* is an individual LAN (as the term is used in this book) or WAN. It is a physical network to which data communications are directed.

CHECKLIST

A *network segment* is a separate data network to which nodes are connected, and to which data communications are directed. In this book, this term will be consistently used to describe an addressable portion of an internetwork. All of the following terms are used in the networking industry to describe a network segment: *LAN* (as used in this book), *collision domain* (used in Ethernet LANs), *ring* (used in Token Ring LANs), *subnetwork, segment* (as opposed to cable segment), *subnet* (used in IP networking). Please be aware that these terms are often used interchangeably elsewhere, but not in this book.

You will always be confused about internetworking to some degree until you get one concept very clear: Any type of node (server, client, router, and so on) is connected to one or more network segments, not the other way around. Bridges and routers form connections, and therefore boundaries, between network segments. There is no discussion of servers in this subject — it is an issue of network hardware and infrastructure. This distinction is a very powerful one, yet it is one most network professionals seem to overlook.

The confusion over such terms and concepts is deep-rooted in networking history. IBM and Microsoft networking has traditionally been very host-centric, seeing the host computer (be it server, minicomputer, or mainframe) as the center of the network. In a routed network this model is problematic. When discussing system administration, likewise the server (or directory service) is the center of the network. Let me suggest that as we discuss internetworking, you focus on network segments and think of servers only in terms of their being connected to these network segments. Better yet, forget servers and user administration for the balance of this chapter, and just consider the internetwork itself.

Bridges and routers connect network segments. Each network segment is a separate data network to which nodes are connected. Each network segment uses a separate frame for delivery—the source and destination addresses are physical addresses identifying nodes located on that network segment.

The term *LAN* as used in this book corresponds closely to a network segment until a bridge is introduced. The term *collision domain* also comes close but is not a perfect fit because it only applies to Ethernet. A *bridge domain* is a very good fit: It is addressed as a single network segment, but many folks are not familiar with this term. The term *ring* is close, but the term only applies to Token Ring and FDDI, and two bridged rings constitute one addressable network segment. In IP networking, the term *subnet* has its own meaning, which is not necessarily the same as a network segment. The term *subnetwork* is a good synonym but is too close to the term *subnet* to be used distinctly. The term *segment* can describe a cabling segment and is therefore not appropriate. All these terms leave gray areas undefined. Only the term *network segment* fits the definition used in this book and will therefore be used consistently.

Think of a network segment as a street. Houses and businesses are located on the street, not the other way around. Likewise, a server is located on a network segment, not the other way around. In many cases multiple servers reside on a single network segment, and servers are often connected to multiple network segments. Just as each street is identified with a unique name, network segments must be identified with a unique network number. In the following two chapters, where addressing is discussed, this simile of a street will help you. Your IPX network number must map to a network segment.

Bridges

A bridge is one of two types of devices that can connect multiple LANs and WANs into an internetwork. Bridging is a strategy that has been favored in IBM and Microsoft networking where nonroutable protocols are employed.

Bridges are basically network hardware devices, linking the two LANs together at the LAN protocol (frame) layer. As far as NetWare and other routable protocols (for example, TCP/IP or AppleTalk) are concerned, a bridged network appears to be a single network (or subnetwork as the term is used in TCP/IP networking).

CHECKLIST

A *bridge* is a network device that links two LANs together. As far as networking protocols are concerned, a bridge makes the two LANs appear as one, though frame traffic may be separated. Bridges work at the LAN protocol level, filtering and forwarding frames as required to get them to their destination nodes.

A bridge connects two or more LANs together. A bridge works at the LAN/WAN protocol layer. The bridge filters frames that are addressed for delivery on the same LAN, and it forwards frames that need to be delivered to another LAN to which the bridge is connected. Bridges come in different types, the simplest being a MAC bridge. The process is very simple: If both the source and destination nodes reside on the same LAN, the frame does not need to be forwarded, so it is filtered. If the source node resides on one LAN, and the destination node resides on the other side of the bridge, the bridge will forward the frame.

NOTE

In case you missed the definition in Chapter 1, in this book the term *frame* **describes the LAN protocol data unit, as opposed to the** *packet,* **which is an IP or IPX protocol data unit.**

A bridge never processes the packet header protocol information. Instead, it only looks at the very first few fields of the frame header information (the physical address) to make its filter versus forward decision. The bridge knows where the physical node addresses are because it monitors frames circulating on each LAN (which correlates to a port). The bridge maintains tables relating the node addresses to ports. If the source and destination are the same, no action is taken, but if the source and destination ports are different, the frame is forwarded to the appropriate port. A typical bridge is shown in Figure 2.1.

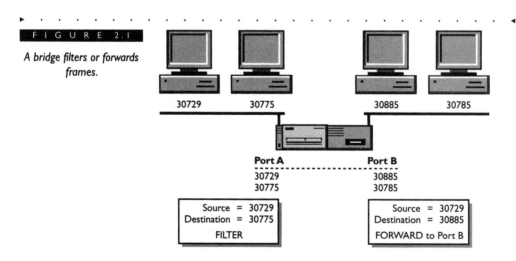

FIGURE 2.1

A bridge filters or forwards frames.

This process makes the bridge "protocol independent." In other words, the bridge will work with IP, IPX, NetBIOS, SNA, and other packet protocols, regardless of whether it is routable or not. Because IBM mainframe systems rely on the SNA protocols, which are not routable, bridges are generally used. However, when routable protocols are used (IP and IPX), network integrators generally rely on routers to connect LANs together.

Bridges are used to segment larger LANs into smaller LANs. If the network design is good, this should result in less traffic on each LAN but still allow traffic to flow from one LAN to the other when necessary. Bridges are also used to connect remote LANs with a LAN link between them. When LANs are bridged together, the resulting network is called a *bridge domain* and each LAN is called a *collision domain*.

MAC bridges are easy to install, and they normally plug-and-play; however, they suffer from some major deficiencies. MAC bridges are not equipped to handle multiple routes or complex networks. Figure 2.2 shows a situation that a MAC bridge cannot handle, where two paths are available. Normally bridges forward frames on all collision domains when the destination node address is not known. The scenario depicted in Figure 2.2 would result in a loop, where the frame would be forwarded, circulated, then forwarded back, circulated, forwarded, and so on.

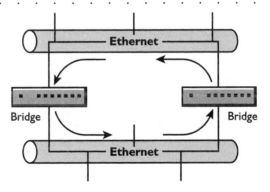

FIGURE 2.2

MAC bridges forming multiple paths may result in a loop.

In situations like this, the bridges might be equipped with Spanning Tree Protocol. This protocol eliminates loops by first establishing a root (main) bridge, identifying redundant paths, comparing the paths, and blocking alternate paths.

IBM Token Ring LANs generally use source-routing bridges. These bridges use the 802.2 Logical Link Control Protocol to determine path selection when multiple paths are present. When a workstation first boots, a discovery frame is broadcast, searching each path. One reply is returned for each path; the first one to make it back contains LLC data identifying the selected path.

A typical bridge is very simple to install; generally little or no configuration is necessary. Routers are far more intelligent and robust. Generally bridges are employed internally within a campus or building, whereas routers are preferred for more complex internetworks and WAN links between campuses.

Network integrators must be careful never to use bridges in parallel paths with routers. This type of configuration will cause router configuration errors that can corrupt the integrity of routing data.

NOTE

Routers

A router connects LANs and WANs together at the packet level. The router provides LAN-to-LAN (or LAN-to-WAN) connectivity at a higher protocol layer. Routers receive frames, extract the packets, and read the protocol headers in the packets. Bridges never view the packet headers; they function by reading the frame headers. (See why I make a big deal out of using terms distinctly?) Bridges and routers operate at two completely different layers of protocol.

Routers are basically software modules, though most router vendors call the computer that runs the routing software a router. Some routers, such as Novell's MultiProtocol Router, can be implemented on any computer. Other routers, including most Cisco routers, are special-duty computers that contain a proprietary operating system, routing software, and massive bus capacity. Cisco also markets software-only routers.

A *router* switches packets from one LAN or WAN to another. The router receives a packet, examines the packet header and its internal routing tables to see where the destination node is, and then forwards the packet to the appropriate LAN or WAN.

CHECKLIST

Routers are preferred over bridges for several reasons. Though they are more difficult to install, configure, and manage, they are more robust in many ways. Like many system administrators, they are dynamic, intelligent, and flexible!

Routers dynamically determine which path a packet will take, whereas bridges are generally static (think of a bridge as like a concrete street bridge, where the path always is the same). Routers communicate with one another to keep up to date on the latest path information. If a new path appears that is better, the routers automatically start using the new path. If a path goes down (for example, a WAN link goes down), the routers send the packets over an alternate path (if one exists).

Routers are far more intelligent than bridges. Because routers must read protocol headers to determine the routing path to take, they often have protocol filtering capabilities. For example, most routers can be configured to filter out print traffic over a WAN, or to prevent specific workstations from accessing a WAN. Some routers are used as firewalls to keep out uninvited guests. Many protocol fields can be used to enable filtering of many functions.

Routers exchange routing information with one another using protocols. Each router builds a routing table; when a packet is processed, the destination address is checked against the routing tables, and the least-cost path is selected. Routers can dynamically change paths if a more efficient path is established. The following (simplified) process occurs when a router receives a frame from a LAN:

1. The router's NIC receives the frame, and the driver extracts the IP packet.

2. Routing information in the IP packet header is read.

3. IP packets are forwarded to the router's NIC to which the destination IP subnet is attached (directly or indirectly).

In this illustration, the frame is not used for routing decisions. The router is the destination on the first leg, and another router is the source on the last leg. The frame has done its job in delivering the packet to the router.

Internetworking Infrastructure

A brief mapping of network architecture helps to understand the complexity of a network. NetWare protocols and network mechanisms rely on the underlying network as a platform. This section discusses the infrastructure of an internetwork.

To begin with, you should understand how various protocols are used to move data over a network. All NOSes work pretty much the same way, using the same functions and procedures, but different combinations of protocols. This is a very brief general discussion of how data is moved over a network using a stack of protocols.

Frames and Packets

The unit of data that moves data from one node to another on a LAN or WAN is called a *frame* (as discussed in Chapter 1, some WANs do not use frames). A frame contains protocol information that precedes the data segment, and a trailer that follows the data segment. The data segment a frame carries is in virtually all cases a packet. Figure 2.3 shows a frame carrying a packet.

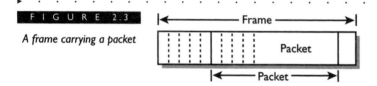

F I G U R E 2.3

A frame carrying a packet

NOTE

Many descriptions you read use the terms *frame* and *packet* interchangeably. In this book the frame defines the unit of data that is used by the LAN or WAN (the data-link layer of the OSI model).

Virtually all data networks, NetWare included, are packet-switching networks. Packets are encapsulated into frames for delivery on the local network segment. When necessary, packets can be extracted from one frame and then inserted into another frame—a process called *routing,* which is discussed in the following section. Networks are designed to packetize data and then transport it through any one of several types of LAN or WAN on the way to its ultimate destination. A router is used to connect network segments—its responsibility is to switch packets from one network segment to the other, even when the networks are dissimilar.

CHECKLIST

Encapsulation is the process of inserting packets into frames for delivery on a local network segment. Frames are specific to the type of network (LANs and WANs), but routable packets such as IP and

IPX can be switched between many types of frames, a capability that provides protocol-independent networking over a variety of networks.

An Example: Delivering Containerized Freight

Packet switching through a series of networks is analogous to transporting containerized freight. The payloads to be transported may be quite different, but the mechanics are quite similar. The following illustration compares moving containerized freight to moving a packetized data segment.

Assume that you have a shipment of widgets that are to be packed into a sealed freight container and shipped from a manufacturer in Los Angeles to a warehouse in Chicago. Along the way trucks and railways will be used to ship the sealed container to its final destination. Here are the steps that will be taken to deliver the container:

1. The container is loaded at the factory in Los Angeles, and a routing slip is attached to it.

2. The sealed container is put on a truck bed and then driven to the Los Angeles train yard.

3. A crane is used to take the sealed container off the truck bed and place it onto a railroad car.

4. The railroad car is taken to Chicago.

5. At the Chicago rail yard, a crane is used to take the container off the railroad car and place it on a truck bed.

6. A truck transports the container to the final destination, a warehouse in Chicago.

Table 2.1 shows how this example correlates to packet switching.

T A B L E 2.1	EXAMPLE	EQUIVALENT TO
A Packet Switching Example	Freight container	Packet
	Routing slip	Packet header
	Manufacturer in Los Angeles	Node on source LAN
	Truck bed in Los Angeles	Frame
	Road in Los Angeles	Source LAN
	Crane in Los Angeles	Router at sender node
	Moving the sealed freight container	Routing a packet
	Railway	WAN
	Crane in Chicago	Router at destination node
	Truck in Chicago	Frame
	Road in Chicago	Destination LAN
	Warehouse in Chicago	Node on destination LAN

The trucking company in Los Angeles has the job of picking up the container somewhere in Los Angeles and delivering it to the railroad yard, also in Los Angeles. In a very similar manner, the first LAN's only job is to transport the packet from the source node to the router, which are both on the same LAN. The router is connected to the first LAN and to the WAN. The LAN uses a frame that is addressed from the source to the router.

The railroad has the responsibility to transport the container from its Los Angeles train yard to its Chicago train yard. The railway is like a WAN, and the cranes at each end are like routers. The WAN's job is to move the packet from the Los Angeles router to the Chicago router, and it uses a WAN frame to move the packet.

In Chicago, another trucking company has the job of moving the container from the train yard to the warehouse. In a similar manner, the second LAN moves the packet from one node (the router) to the destination node, the warehouse.

Routable Protocols

The protocols used in NetWare networks are routable, meaning that they can be transported over LANs and WANs that are linked by routers. Not all networking protocols are routable, but only a couple are not: IBM SNA (mainframe and midrange) and Microsoft NetBIOS/NetBEUI. NetWare, TCP/IP, and Apple Computer networks use routable protocols.

Routing Protocols

Routers communicate with one another to maintain routing information independent of servers and network nodes. Routers are driven by just a few routing protocols — some are proprietary, whereas others are standardized by the Internet Engineering Task Force (IETF). Routers exchange routing information using these protocols, dynamically updating one another as path changes occur. Control over routing issues is exercised by adjusting routing protocols and their parameters. Some routing protocols do not allow much adjustment, whereas others have a plethora of adjustments. Routing configurations are adjusted by logging onto a router and accessing its management console.

Large internetworks are often divided into routing domains. One routing protocol can be used internally within a routing domain, whereas a different routing protocol handles the link between routing domains. When two protocols are used in this manner, the local facilities using the interior protocols are called *autonomous systems* but the protocol used between facilities is called a *gateway protocol* as shown in Figure 2.4.

More commonly used protocols include:

▸ Novell's Routing Information Protocol (RIP)

▸ Routing Information Protocol (RIP) as used with TCP/IP

▸ Open Shortest Path First (OSPF)

▸ Novell's NetWare Link Services Protocol (NLSP)

▸ Interior Gateway Routing Protocol (IGRP, Cisco)

▸ Exterior Gateway Protocol (EGP) and Border Gateway Protocol (BGP)

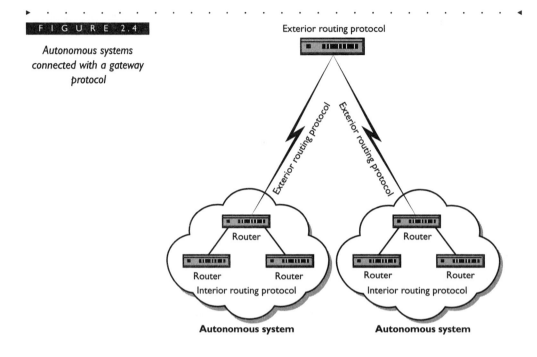

F I G U R E 2.4

Autonomous systems connected with a gateway protocol

Exterior routing protocol

Exterior routing protocol

Exterior routing protocol

Router

Router

Router

Router

Interior routing protocol

Router

Router

Router

Router

Interior routing protocol

Autonomous system

Autonomous system

Routing Information Protocol

RIP is a very simple protocol. Novell's RIP, based on Xerox Network Systems' RIP, only works with IPX. Another version of RIP developed for the original Berkeley sockets UNIX version is used with IP and is an Internet standard. Both versions are very similar and employ the same mechanics. Both determine the best route according to the number of hops over routers (or time). In a RIP internetwork, every router is a peer of every other router. RIP is simple, usually requiring little or no configuration. It is therefore used frequently in smaller autonomous systems.

The following are characteristics of this protocol:

▶ Propagation involves periodic broadcasts.

▶ All routers are peers of one another (flat space intradomain algorithm).

▶ Path decisions are based on hops or time (distance vector based).

▶ Each router only exchanges information with its nearest neighbors.

RIP supports very limited routing decisions. The hop count alone is used to determine the "least-cost" path. Though time can be substituted for hop information, this protocol's use should be limited to smaller internetworks. When there are no more than 30–40 servers in a zone, you might consider upgrading to a more efficient routing protocol.

Each NetWare server contains an internal router. Novell's RIP is the default routing protocol used in all NetWare 3 servers up to NetWare 4.01. This protocol is perfectly adequate for most NetWare networks.

Whenever many NetWare servers are present in your intranet, you might encounter two problems: First, RIP broadcasts can consume a substantial portion of a WAN link's capacity. Servicing RIP broadcasts can dominate servers' processing power once every broadcast cycle (every 60 seconds).

Some router vendors have developed routing protocols and techniques that mitigate bandwidth consumption issues. Some suppress WAN traffic by storing repeated broadcasts at one end of a WAN, broadcasting the same information locally from a cache at the other end. Cisco's IGRP (used between Cisco routers) reduces the need for WAN broadcasting. These solutions can reduce WAN congestion, but they do not reduce the processing power required for a NetWare server to support many other NetWare servers.

Novell's RIP and RIP for IP protocols are discussed in greater detail in the next two chapters of this book.

Open Shortest Path First
This protocol is used in most UNIX systems, is an Internet standard, and is supported in most routers. It is highly flexible and programmable. The following are characteristics of this protocol. OSPF:

▸ Is not broadcast-based (it is link state-based).

▸ Can be organized hierarchically and divided into zones.

▸ Uses a wide variety of programmable metrics.

▸ Can provide quality of service priority according to Type of Service (TOS) (highest-layer protocol).

OSPF can be configured to use time delay and/or other metrics (routing statistics) to determine the least-cost path. In RIP, only hops are used, and sometimes time is substituted for hops, but with OSPF you can establish a higher cost for a high-capacity link to discourage its use. This will allow traffic to flow over a lower capacity WAN until the link becomes saturated, when traffic will automatically be redirected to the high-capacity link. For example, you might have dedicated a 64Kbps WAN for the internetwork backbone but have a T1 (1.544Mbps) line that is shared. RIP would either direct traffic over the T1 or not have a preference. With OSPF you can program your routers to use the 64Kbps link until it becomes congested and then take the more expensive route (the T1). This is only one example of OSPF flexibility.

OSPF is discussed in greater detail in Chapter 4, "TCP/IP Protocols, IP Addressing, and Name Resolution."

Novell's NetWare Link Services Protocol

Novell developed NLSP to resolve both RIP and service advertising limitations. It can be used both in autonomous systems and as a gateway protocol. NLSP is a proprietary link service protocol that reduces broadcasts and is available at no cost for all current NetWare versions (NetWare 3, 4, and 5). NLSP is the default protocol used when installing NetWare 4.10 and higher versions. NLSP is supported by most router vendors.

Each NLSP router contains route information for all routes, by contrast with RIP routers, which only contain information about the next hop. NLSP routing tables grow exponentially as the number of routes increase. NLSP routers can be separated into routing domains as shown in Figure 2.5 to reduce the amount of data in the routing tables. Each router in a routing domain contains routing information for all routes in its own routing domain. Requests for destinations outside of the default routing domain are directed to a root server that handles interaction between routing domains. This allows NLSP to scale up to the largest of internetworks.

NLSP is discussed in greater detail in Chapter 3.

X-REF

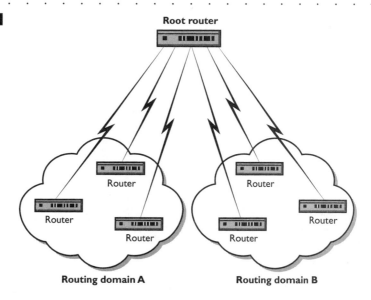

FIGURE 2.5

NLSP routers can be configured into routing domains.

Interior Gateway Routing Protocol

IGRP, developed by Cisco Systems, was designed for larger internetworks where network segments may have different bandwidth and delay characteristics. This protocol is used between Cisco routers to optimize network performance and supports autonomous systems running other routing protocols as shown in Figure 2.6. IGRP replaces less efficient protocols in a backbone, reducing bandwidth required to support periodic broadcasts, and can be configured hierarchically.

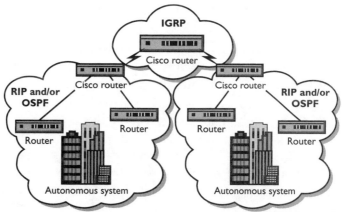

FIGURE 2.6

IGRP used between Cisco routers

This protocol has the following characteristics:

▶ Is hierarchical, intradomain

▶ Uses distance vectors

▶ Uses a wide variety of programmable metrics

▶ Offers multiline load balancing with failover

Cisco routers can be configured as gateways to support RIP, OSPF, and other popular protocols within a campus. IGRP also provides gateway service to larger internetworks, including the Internet, where the Border Gateway Protocol (BGP) is used between privately owned internetworks and higher-level Internet service providers (ISPs).

Exterior Gateway Protocol and Border Gateway Protocol

These protocols are standardized gateway protocols used to link smaller autonomous systems together. Exterior Gateway Protocol (EGP) and Border Gateway Protocol (BGP) routers communicate with interior protocols and even use interior protocols to pass routed traffic through autonomous systems. BGP was developed as a replacement for EGP and has replaced EGP in practical use. These protocols are also used to connect privately owned systems to the Internet.

The Open Systems Interconnection Model

The most common model used to define and compare network architecture is the Open Systems Interconnection (OSI) model, developed by International Standards Organization (ISO). OSI defines typical networking protocols and functions. In this model, each layer is responsible for rules of communications to allow computers to communicate seamlessly over a network without specific user interaction. Because all networks use similar functions, OSI is generally used as a model to distinguish functions between protocol layers.

 How various protocols compare or map to the OSI model is a matter of opinion. If you compare charts from Novell, Sun Microsystems, Digital, Hewlett-Packard, and other companies, you will find

NOTE

**differences in where various protocols map to OSI layers. The
discussion in this book clarifies the basic functionality of protocol
layers and may disagree with Novell and with other discussions of OSI
found in other books.**

**When studying for Novell certification (for *Networking Technologies* or
Service and Support exams), please refer to Novell official course
material, not this book.**

Table 2.2 defines the seven layers and a very brief description of functionality
in the OSI model:

TABLE 2.2	OSI LAYER	FUNCTION
OSI Layers and Basic Functionality	Application	Client/server application communications
	Presentation	Function calls (how to handle the data) in a common format segmentation and reassembly of data for transport
	Session	Virtual connection establishment
	Transport	Transport of the data segment and error control, generally through an acknowledgment mechanism
	Network	Delivery and routing from ultimate source to ultimate destination
	Data-link	Intra-LAN/WAN communications between nodes on a given network
	Physical	Encoding of signals, electrical and physical circuitry/design

In this model, data is segmented and encapsulated into protocol units called
packets (layers 3–5), which in turn are handed off to the LAN or WAN for delivery
(layer 1 and 2). At the receiving end, the LAN/WAN frame is received, the packet
headers are read and processed, and the data is reassembled.

Another way to look at the OSI model is to correlate it to the data units to be
handled, as shown in Table 2.3.

	LAYER	DATA UNIT	EXAMPLE
TABLE 2.3	7	Messages	FTP client–FTP server file transfer request
OSI Model Data Units	6	Segments	NCP, NFS, SMB
	3–5	Packets	IPX, IP, NetBIOS, NetBEUI
	2	Frames	LAN access protocol, frame driver
	1	Bits	NIC firmware, cabling, hub

No matter how you characterize OSI layers, the bottom line is that protocol functions are divided into linear layers — one layer interfaces with the next, which in turn interfaces with the next, and so on. In one computer a layer logically communicates with the same layer on another computer, even though the protocol is handled by other protocols. The protocols work together as a team to accomplish the task of handling a request from a remote computer.

NOTE

Don't get too caught up in the specifics of OSI; it is only used as a model to compare other protocols with. The only practical implementation of this model is Digital's Phase V protocol stack option, which is not very popular — most Digital customers opt for TCP/IP instead.

Physical Addressing

LAN or WAN frames are addressed, much like an envelope is addressed, from one node to another. Each node is assigned a physical address, which is used in the LAN or WAN frame header to indicate which node is sending the frame and which node is to receive the frame.

The addresses used in most LANs are programmed into firmware on the NIC, and therefore each NIC has a preassigned physical address. This address is often called a "MAC address" because the addresses are assigned in accordance with IEEE 802 committee Media Access Control (MAC) specifications. Due to this specification, each NIC that meets IEEE 802 specifications has a unique MAC address. Sometimes the term "node address" is used because this address identifies a node that is attached to a LAN or WAN.

In this book, we will consistently use the term *physical address*; however, be advised that the terms "MAC address" and "node address" are also used interchangeably in other material.

When we view the frame header of any type of LAN or WAN, we will find physical addressing. The mechanics of delivery assume that both the source and the destination node reside on the same network.

Logical Addressing

Addressing is also used at the packet level in routable protocols. At this level the addressing is not physical; it is assigned by a system administrator and must be tracked by the routers. This level of addressing identifies the ultimate source and ultimate destination regardless of whether that node exists on the same LAN or a different one.

Figure 2.7 illustrates packet-level addressing as end-to-end, with three frames required to deliver the packet to the ultimate destination. In this figure the first frame carries the packet from the client to the first router (frame #1 addressing) on one Ethernet LAN, a second frame carries the packet over a WAN from router A to router B, and a third frame carries the packet from router B to the server on another Ethernet LAN. The dotted line indicates the end-to-end addressing at the packet level, while the solid lines indicate physical frame addressing.

In the example of the containerized freight, the routing slip would be addressed from the manufacturer to the warehouse. The Los Angeles trucking company is only concerned with the physical trip segment from the manufacturer to the Los Angeles train yard. In much the same manner, a routable protocol header identifies the ultimate source and destination addresses. The routers are left to decide which paths to take to get the packets to their ultimate destinations.

Nonroutable protocols have no such logical addressing, and routers cannot identify paths without this information. For example, NetBIOS uses a computer name to identify each network computer.

FIGURE 2.7

Packet-level addressing is end-to-end, whereas frame addressing is from physical node to physical node.

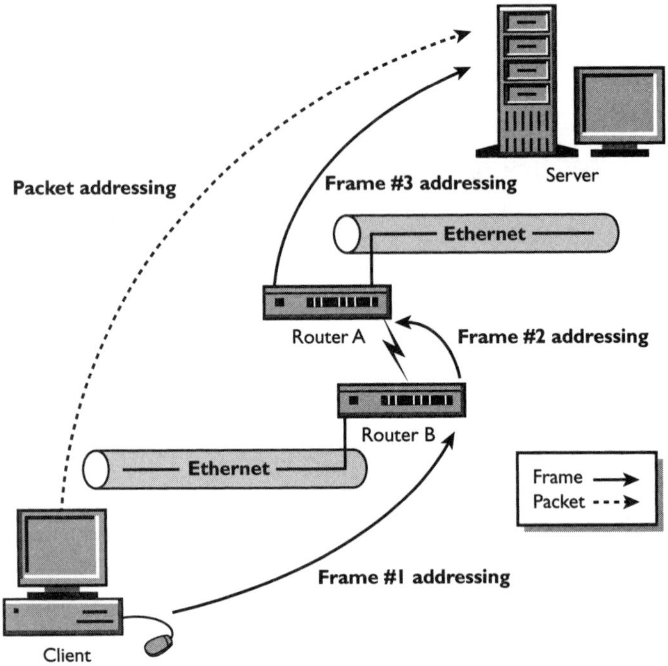

The system administrator groups these addresses into network segments (which are also called "logical networks"). Network segments are correlated to router ports, and a path can be calculated by relating the address with network segment information that the routers share with one another. The addresses are called logical because address and path information must be processed to calculate each path.

Connection-Oriented versus Datagram Service

Some protocols are connection-oriented, and some are not. When protocols are stacked, only one needs to do the job of guaranteeing delivery. A packet that delivers data without connection service is called a *datagram*. The datagram delivers data efficiently, whereas a connection-oriented protocol uses additional overhead to ensure that every packet makes it to its destination. The two protocols work together to reliably deliver each and every packet.

A datagram is a packet that works just like a mail envelope: It encapsulates the data (normally a connection-oriented packet), addresses it, and sends it.

Communications are established in one direction only, and delivery is assumed, just as when you mail a letter. The transaction is complete when the datagram is shipped.

Connection-oriented protocols guarantee delivery but normally do not incorporate the ability to address and send the data; that is left to the datagram in which it is encapsulated. This type of protocol typically uses an acknowledgment (reply) to verify that data has been received. Much as in the case of certified mail, the sender receives verification that the packet was received. This process establishes two-way communications between the sender and the receiver: A packet is sent, and the receiver acknowledges that the packet has been received. This process is much like sending a letter by certified mail: You fill out a little card that is attached to the envelope, the recipient signs the card upon receiving the letter, and then the card is returned to you.

In order to track delivery, each transaction is traced back to a connection. A connection is established through a handshake procedure, much like this: The query is sent, "Are you there, IP address 204,10,210,34?" and the reply comes back, "I am listening and ready to receive a request." Each connection-oriented protocol establishes two-way communications, labels the connection, and then refers to the connection in the process of communicating. This process is much like giving verbal instructions and then having the instructions repeated back to ensure that a common language is being used and the listener understands the instructions.

Most higher-level protocols relay function calls in the packet header, transfer data, and are connection-oriented to guard against the likelihood that some packets may be lost or damaged. Most higher-level protocols depend upon datagrams for delivery. The higher-level packet is encapsulated in the datagram for delivery.

NetWare establishes such a connection before login and does not take it down until after logout. The server delivers data to the connection, which is correlated to a logical address for datagram addressing. Other protocols work similarly. For example, TCP establishes a temporary connection between two ports, data sent to the destination port is encapsulated into IP datagrams for delivery, and when the transfer is finished, the connection is terminated.

In most cases, connections are established by the same protocol that sends the data. First, a connection request is sent; the receiver acknowledges the request and grants a connection. Next, the data is transferred. Last, the receipt of each packet, and therefore the entire message, is acknowledged. These three steps are accomplished and coordinated by varying methods, but every connection-oriented protocol uses these three steps.

The packet that is originally sent is called a *request*, and the acknowledgment is called a *reply*. As with most terms in networking, you will observe variations of these terms. A request is sometimes called a *send packet*. A reply is often called an acknowledgment or in rare cases a *receive packet*.

CHAPTER 3

Novell Protocols and IPX Addressing

This chapter is about Novell's NetWare protocol stack. A *protocol stack* is a combination of protocols that work together as a team, one protocol stacked above the other, and used in linear sequence. All NetWare networking is driven by a single protocol — NetWare Core Protocol (NCP) — at the top of the stack. NCP is then transported by one of two transport options: IPX/SPX or TCP/IP. This chapter discusses NCP, the IPX/SPX transport mechanisms, and related topics. Just as in Chapter 2, the material discussed in this chapter is required foundation knowledge for the rest of this book.

CHECKLIST

A *protocol stack* is a combination of protocols designed to work together. Each protocol in the stack performs specific functionality; working together the protocols in the stack operate much like a team.

By comparison with Chapter 2, this material is a bit more technical, but if you have read the previous chapters it should not be hard to absorb. If you are already familiar with NetWare protocols, skim this chapter, paying attention to general mechanics. If this material is new to you, you do not need to understand everything here in detail. In either case, you will probably refer back to this chapter if you ever use a protocol analyzer. This chapter not only helps you understand and configure NetWare protocols, it can also help when you are troubleshooting network communications.

If you are a Novell certified professional, one of the more important aspects of this chapter is terminology. You will have learned to use several terms interchangeably. This chapter establishes distinct usages for terms related to internetworking that will be used throughout this book. If you take the time to skim this chapter and pay close attention to how just a few terms are used, you will find the rest of the book quite explicit.

In any case, pay close attention to the following terms:

- ▸ Network segment

- ▸ Logical network

- ▸ Network address/network number

▶ Bridge domain

▶ Packet versus frame

These terms define specific internetworking elements. In this book terms are used with consistency, but you must remember the definitions as presented in this book.

The following sections discuss each of the protocols used in the native NetWare protocol stack. This chapter discusses protocol characteristics, protocol header description, and protocol dialog to assist you in understanding the mechanics used in network communications.

Read this chapter for a general understanding of how these protocols work. As with any technology, understanding how it works makes all the difference in understanding how to optimize and troubleshoot. When troubleshooting with a protocol analyzer, you can use this chapter to recognize defective communications and understand error messages better. You will find more specific details of each protocol contained in Appendix C, "Protocol Reference Guide," and in the Protocol Reference Guide on the CD that accompanies this book.

▶ · ◀

The NetWare Protocol Stack

The original Novell protocol stack is made up of the following protocols:

▶ Internetwork Packet Exchange (IPX)

▶ Sequenced Packet Exchange (SPX)

▶ Sequenced Packet Exchange II (SPX II)

▶ Service Advertising Protocol (SAP)

▶ Router Information Protocol (RIP)

▶ NetWare Core Protocol (NCP)

▸ Packet Burst (previously called Burst Mode)

▸ NetWare Link Services Protocol (NLSP)

IPX, SPX, RIP, and SAP were adapted from Xerox Network System (XNS) protocols. Really, the only differences between XNS and the basic Novell protocols are the function codes and names. However, Novell developers developed NCP, Packet Burst, NetWare Link Services Protocol (NLSP), and Service Location Protocol (SLP). Very few network developers have ever engineered a new network protocol from scratch or defined new functionality as Novell has (though many of us wish they would).

Table 3.1 shows Novell's protocols organized by function, related to OSI layers, and includes a brief description of which function each protocol serves. OSI layers are discussed in Chapter 2.

	PROTOCOL	OSI LAYER	FUNCTION
TABLE 3.1	IPX	Network	Accomplishes end-to-end delivery through routers if necessary.
Novell Protocols	SPX	Network	Accomplishes end-to-end delivery through routers if necessary.
		Transport	Guarantees delivery via acknowledgment mechanism.
	NCP	Presentation	Segments and reassembles data to be transferred, establishes common communications formats, sequences packets, and exchanges function codes for data handling.
		Session	Establishes virtual connection (at server end).
		Transport	Guarantees delivery via acknowledgment mechanism.
	SAP	Session	Broadcast service establishes server-to-server connections, propagates server IPX address, type of service.
	RIP	Network	Exchanges routing information between servers and clients and between routers.

T A B L E 3.1	PROTOCOL	OSI LAYER	FUNCTION
Novell Protocols (*continued*)	NLSP	Network	Exchanges routing information, handshakes, sets communications parameters, propagates server addresses.
	Session		Establishes server-to-server connections, server-to-client connection.

Each protocol is discussed in greater detail in the following sections of this chapter.

. . . .

NetWare Core Protocol

Novell continually updates and refines the NetWare Core Protocol (NCP). Before NetWare 5, NCP relied exclusively on IPX as its transport mechanism. Novell developers reengineered NCP to run over TCP/IP and in the process developed their iteration of the Service Location Protocol to replace the IPX-based Service Advertising Protocol (SAP). Whether you use IPX/SPX or TCP/IP, NCP still sits at the top of the stack.

Novell developers have done more protocol engineering than any other group of developers in history. Novell protocol development is the most sophisticated and optimized in the industry.

Protocol Description

NCP is the main workhorse of NetWare networking; the vast bulk of NetWare traffic contains NCP communications. NCP handles file access, file system rights and attributes, virtual connections, login and security authentication, NDS context and rights, print spooling, synchronization, and statistics. Plus, NCP guarantees delivery of every packet. You might conclude that NDS is the drive train that NetWare runs on.

Two of NCP's primary functions are to read and write data from and to NetWare volumes. Many other activities that NCP handles are related to file access, such as checking/enforcing rights to files and directories, checking/enforcing file attributes, and adding/changing rights to directory listings. Though NCP includes many functions, shared file system access comprises the bulk of NCP requests.

Protocol Characteristics

NCP does not have any mechanism for delivery or addressing. Instead, NCP packets are encapsulated into IPX packets for delivery. In NetWare 5 networks, NCP can be encapsulated directly into TCP/IP packets for delivery. In NetWare/IP, NCP packets must be encapsulated into IPX packets, which in turn are encapsulated into TCP/IP packets.

NOTE

In NetWare 3 and 4 networks using NetWare/IP, NCP packets are encapsulated into IPX packets, which in turn are encapsulated into TCP/IP packets. This is a process called *tunneling*. However, in NetWare 5 networks tunneling is not necessary; NCP can be encapsulated directly into TCP/IP packets for delivery without an IPX layer.

NCP is *connection-oriented*, which means that communications are two-way — each NCP request is answered with an NCP reply. Every NCP packet must be acknowledged by a return NCP packet indicating that the original request was received. Before the next NCP packet is sent, the previous request must be acknowledged as shown in Figure 3.1. Connection-oriented protocol communication is discussed in Chapter 2.

In NetWare 3.12, 4.x, and 5.x versions Packet Burst enhancement to NCP is used, which allows multiple packets to have one acknowledgment. You must have a recent client software version to enable this feature. If you have any recent version of NetWare and the most recent client software, this feature is automatic and does not require any configuration or adjustments. Look for a discussion of Packet Burst enhancements immediately following this section of this chapter.

NOTE

You should always verify that your client software is a newer version and is properly set up to support Packet Burst. This enhancement boosts network performance, especially where any delays are introduced, such as a congested LAN, a busy router, or a low-bandwidth WAN. It is best to stay current with the latest client software updates for your desktop operating systems (the latest client updates are always available on Novell's Web site at no cost).

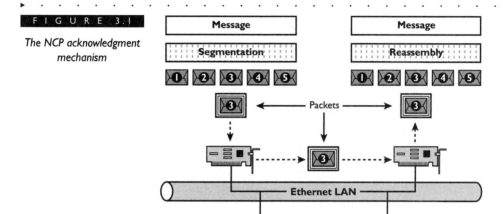

FIGURE 3.1

The NCP acknowledgment
mechanism

If an NCP reply (acknowledgment packet) is not received within a given amount of time, a duplicate NCP request is sent (this process is called a *retry*). If repeated requests are not acknowledged, the connection is assumed to be lost, the connection is removed, and a network error is sent to the workstation console.

Like all connection-oriented protocols, NCP must have a virtual connection in which to operate. Virtual connections are established by other protocols (RIP and NLSP discussed later in this chapter) when the workstation first attaches to a server during boot. The NCP connection is left open all the time the client is attached (unlike TCP, which establishes and destroys connections for each transfer). Fifteen minutes after logout, the server should normally drop the NCP connection.

NCP also segments and reassembles larger messages. Because LAN and WAN frames can carry a limited amount of data in each frame, NCP breaks messages into smaller segments. Each segment is preceded by an NCP header, encapsulated into an IPX (or TCP) packet, which is in turn encapsulated into a frame for delivery. When the NCP packet reaches its destination, the segments are reassembled back into a complete message, as shown in Figure 3.2. The mechanism that allows segmentation and reassembly is the sequence number in the NCP header.

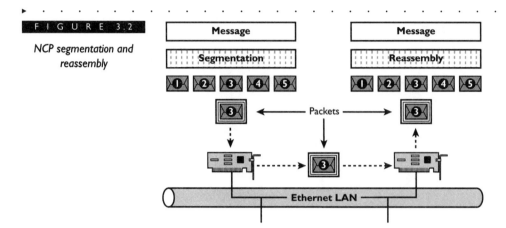

FIGURE 3.2

NCP segmentation and reassembly

During the connection request NCP negotiates a maximum packet size. A single NCP packet is always encapsulated into a single IPX packet, which is encapsulated into a single LAN/WAN frame. Therefore the maximum frame size for any part of the path between a client and the server to which it is connected must be set to the lowest common denominator. The maximum packet size is therefore calculated according to the largest packet size available over the connection (this was not the case in earlier NetWare implementations). For example, if the connection were to be established from an Ethernet workstation, through a router or switch, to a server that is connected to an FDDI backbone, the maximum size would be the lowest common denominator. In this case, Ethernet permits a maximum packet size of 1,518 bytes. Even though FDDI permits a larger packet size (4,500 bytes), the connection will be configured for the lowest common denominator, which in this case cannot exceed 1,518 bytes.

NOTE

Each NetWare NCP/IPX packet is encapsulated into a single LAN or WAN frame. The only exceptions to this rule are ARCnet and ATM. In these cases, IPX packets are segmented into smaller data units, transmitted, and reassembled. However, this process is done at lower protocol levels (the NIC driver in ARCnet, and in LAN Emulation in ATM).

NCP's primary mechanism is the function code and subcode. This information is contained in the NCP header indicating the purpose of the request and controls protocol processing. Though you will find many packets that contain data transfers, a substantial proportion of NCP traffic is simply protocol function codes being exchanged with little or no data. Request codes are categorized into request types (see the protocol header section that follows), and further broken down into function subcodes.

Protocol Header Description

Protocol functions are implemented in header fields and codes or values inserted into those fields. Understanding a protocol requires that you know what information is stored in the packet headers. Table 3.2 shows the NCP header fields and their functions.

NOTE

Each protocol discussed in this chapter will include a header description and a brief discussion of how the protocol works. You will also find supporting codes and descriptions in Appendix C, "Protocol Reference Guide."

T A B L E 3.2	FIELD NAME	# BYTES	DESCRIPTION
Standard NCP Packet Header Fields	Request Type	2	Identifies request (4 types) or reply (3 types).
	Sequence Number	1	Unique number identifies each request.
	Connection Number Low	1	Indicates server connection number (shown on server MONITOR screen).
	Task Number	1	Tracks multiple client requests pending.
	Connection Number High	1	Is used only in 1,000-user versions.
	Completion Code	1	Indicates successful completion of transaction (this field is only present in a reply).

Continued

TABLE 3.2	FIELD NAME	# BYTES	DESCRIPTION
Standard NCP Packet Header Fields (continued)	Connection Status	1	Used to indicate that a server has been downed (this field is only present in a reply).
	Data	variable	Contains any data or data segment, such as a file transfer.

NOTE

The completion code and connection status fields are only found in a reply and are omitted in a request (type 3333, 7777, or 9999 — refer to the Request Type field).

Protocol Dialog

The NCP packet's data field will often contain a function code, which is related to the request or reply type. The data field will often also contain other protocol information, such as a function subcode, security verification, or file attribute information. If the request is to use a file, the file will be segmented and transferred to the client after the file handle has been located, related security is checked, and other housekeeping activities are performed. These tasks generate an exchange of NCP function codes between the client and the server. Once all the preliminary activities have been set up, the file transfer proceeds, one segment (offset) at a time. Each segment will be transferred and acknowledged, then a successful completion will be acknowledged, and the task will be terminated.

NCP connections are established at boot-up and left open as long as the user remains connected (see "Watchdog" under the section entitled "Miscellaneous NetWare Protocols" later in this chapter). Within each connection, multiple tasks can be pending at any given time. The Task field tracks which specific task this particular packet is addressing.

A connection request differs depending upon whether the server to service your connection is running RIP/SAP or NLSP. NetWare 4.10, 4.11, and 5 servers use NLSP by default. All earlier versions have NLSP as an option but do not implement it by default. Request type 1111 is a request to establish a connection.

The following request types are currently used:

▶ (Request) Create a service connection

- ▸ (Request) Service request

- ▸ (Request) Destroy connection

- ▸ (Request) Packet Burst transfer

- ▸ (Reply) Service reply

- ▸ (Reply) Packet Burst connection

- ▸ (Reply) Request being processed (server busy)

Troubleshooting Gems

A Request type 9999 should send up a red flag that the server is backlogged. During periods of high activity a few 9999s are normal, but witness more than just a few of these, and you clearly have a server that cannot keep up with pending requests.

Any value other than 0 in the Completion Code field indicates that a transaction was not completed successfully.

If you have a protocol analyzer or packet viewer, look carefully for these two circumstances. If more than just a few of these two problems are discovered, you should trace the transactions to which they apply and find out what the cause is.

See Appendix C, "Protocol Reference Guide," for a full listing of NCP request types, function codes, and function subcodes. Most protocol analyzers will explain these codes (decode), but decodes often are not very descriptive.

NOTE Protocol analyzers decode protocol fields with short descriptions, which often differ from the official Novell descriptions offered in Appendix C. When using a Network General Sniffer, consult the decodes in Appendix C. Network General uses XNS decodes, which often do not describe NetWare functions as precisely as this list does. You will also find the Protocol Reference Guide on the CD that accompanies this book.

A typical server connection request proceeds as follows:

1. A SAP broadcast queries for the "nearest server" (see the section entitled "Service Advertising and Routing Protocols" later in this chapter).

2. All servers that can receive the request send a SAP reply with IPX addressing and routing data.

3. The client then selects the SAP reply with the lowest hop count.

4. A RIP routing request is sent to the selected server.

5. The server issues a RIP reply with its internal network address and all next-hop network addresses along with their hop counts.

6. The client then issues an NCP Create Service Connection request (type 1111) with information in the data field detailing the client software version, node address, and other related information.

7. The exchange then negotiates the largest possible packet size.

8. A logout is issued to clear any previous connections that are open for this workstation (which normally fails, leaving the other connection open anyway).

9. Other connection-related information is exchanged.

10. The server opens a connection and provides the connection number to the client.

11. A Get File Server Date and Time request is issued.

12. The attaching server responds with the server's date and time.

13. The client's local clock is updated.

The connection is now available for a login.
A typical client file open and read request will proceed as follows:

1. An NCP service request (type 2222) is issued; the data field will contain a function code, filename, and other related information.

2. The server searches for the file (searching the working directory first, and then drives). Each step taken is relayed to the client, where it is acknowledged and the next step is issued (such as searching the next directory in the path).

3. Once the file is located, the server reads file and security information and returns a service reply (type 3333) including various related information in the data field, including the NetWare path name, file attributes, and so on.

4. A Packet Burst transaction is initiated (in most later NetWare versions), and a burst transfer (type 7777) is initiated. NCP packet fragments (each packet in a burst is called a fragment) will contain a file segment (called an offset).

5. An acknowledgment is returned from the client for each burst (the burst is regulated often with protocol exchanges within this transaction).

6. When the entire file has been transferred, successful completion is acknowledged (Completion code = 0).

These protocol dialogs can take just a few or thousands of requests (packets) to complete. Fortunately, each packet only consumes a negligible amount of network bandwidth, but the delay between requests and replies is a very significant factor in performance. If the network is saturated or excessive delays exist between the two communicating stations, the delay will be multiplied. Each step must be completed successfully and acknowledged before the next step can proceed.

This problem will be further discussed in the next section of this chapter, as well as in Chapter 14, "Client Connectivity," and Chapter 17, "NetWare Servers."

When network problems occur, you might consider using a protocol analyzer to trace these dialogs. The information provided in this book can help most technicians trace dialogs and locate problems that are not evidenced elsewhere. Protocol analyzers start at under $1,000 and can cost $25,000 or more. Novell's LANalyzer for Windows (3.1 and 95/98) retails for about $1,500 and has most of the features that a network manager will find useful. LANalyzer functions as a server-based agent and is included in Novell ManageWise, along with many other support features. Some protocol analyzers include special hardware, whereas others like LANalyzer for Windows do not. Software-only analyzers like LANalyzer for Windows utilize "promiscuous mode" NIC drivers and will only work with NICs that are designed with this special feature.

NCP Packet Burst

In earlier NetWare versions (v3.11 and earlier, and 4.01 and earlier), each NCP packet required an NCP acknowledgment packet. In v3.12, 4.10, and later versions, *Packet Burst* was employed. Packet Burst allows one acknowledgment for a series of packets (typically seven or eight requests to one reply).

Packet Burst can impact performance significantly, especially when congested WANs or routers cause excessive delay. In older NCP communications, an acknowledgement must be returned for each outstanding request before the next request can be sent, as shown in Figure 3.3. If any delays exist, such as a congested router or WAN, the delay will be multiplied many times for each data transfer. With Packet Burst, several requests can be sent before NCP must wait, as shown in Figure 3.4. This cuts the effect of delay to a minimum.

NOTE

Packet Burst was originally called Burst Mode, and then Novell changed the name. You will still find many references to Burst Mode in Novell documentation and related material. Both refer to the same protocol enhancement to NCP.

You can upgrade earlier NetWare 3 and 4 networks to add this functionality by adding a patch to your servers and upgrading the client software.

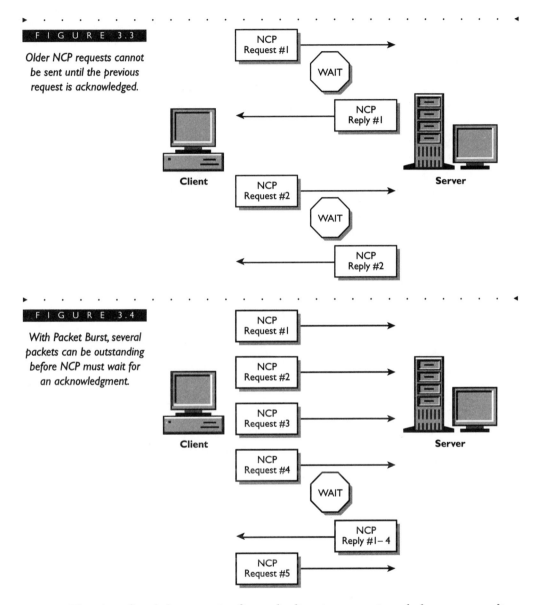

FIGURE 3.3

Older NCP requests cannot be sent until the previous request is acknowledged.

FIGURE 3.4

With Packet Burst, several packets can be outstanding before NCP must wait for an acknowledgment.

The size of each burst varies for each client/server pair and changes according to changing network conditions. This automatic adjustment feature has changed since Packet Burst's original implementation.

Packet Burst is self-adjusting to yield the best performance under changing network conditions. Do not attempt to adjust client protocol settings unless there is a specific reason to do so.

NOTE

Be sure you are using the latest client software available. Packet Burst may not work as efficiently as it does in later software revisions.

Each packet in a packet burst is called a *packet fragment*. Each burst of packet fragments is treated as a single packet, and the packet fragments are preceded by an enhanced NCP packet header that contains special handling functions. The packet burst acknowledgment reports the last packet received in the burst. If any fragments are missing, the sending node retransmits the missing packet fragment and all remaining packet fragments in the burst.

IPX/SPX Transport Mechanism

This section discusses the transport mechanism found in the IPX, SPX, and SPX II protocols.

IPX

IPX is Novell's basic mechanism for delivering packets of data from end to end. All other protocols in this stack rely on IPX for delivery (see the note later in this chapter in the section entitled "SPX"). Think of IPX as like the mailing envelope shown in Figure 3.5 — all other NetWare packets are encapsulated into IPX for delivery, much as you would put correspondence into an envelope, address it, and send it.

Protocol Characteristics

IPX is a *connectionless* or *datagram* protocol, which means that it uses one-way communications, no replies being required. Packets are simply addressed and sent — much as one mails a letter.

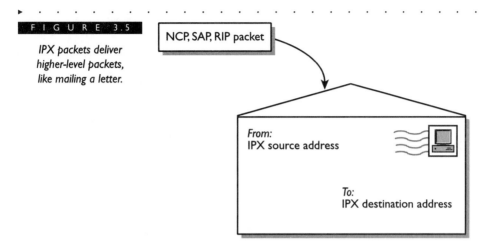

F I G U R E 3.5

IPX packets deliver higher-level packets, like mailing a letter.

IPX's main function is delivery, which depends upon addressing. An IPX address identifies the physical address of the recipient, and the network segment on which it resides. Routers read the network address portion of the IPX packet header and forward the packet as required. Once the packet has been delivered to the destination network segment, the node address is read by the router and used to physically address the frame.

The IPX socket address categorizes the request. Packets are cached when received by the server and are not always processed in the same order as received. Processes in the server's operating system correspond to a socket number. When a process becomes available, the next packet with the appropriate socket number is processed. If you are familiar with TCP port numbers, IPX sockets serve much the same purpose.

In IPX packet indicates how many routers it has traversed. The Transport Control field of the IPX packet header is incremented by one each time the packet crosses, or "hops," a router. The maximum number of hops is 16, which eliminates the possibility of looping. A loop occurs when a packet is forwarded to a destination that forwards it back, causing the packet to be forwarded once again, and so on. This field is also useful to diagnose the efficiency of the path chosen by the routers.

The packet includes a Checksum field, which is not used by default. Because all NetWare higher-level communications are connection-oriented, all data is guaranteed or the faulty connection is terminated. The chances of any acknowledged data containing errors is extremely low. However, you can activate this feature to ensure data integrity by manipulating workstation and server protocol configurations.

Packet Header Description

The IPX packet header handles little more than addressing. The Table 3.3 lists IPX header fields and their functions.

TABLE 3.3

IPX Packet Header Fields

FIELD NAME	# BYTES	DESCRIPTION	COMMENT
Checksum	2	Header checksum	Normally not used (value FF FF).
Length	2	Length of packet	Includes IPX header and data field.
Transport Control	1	Hop count	Counts the number of hops over routers.
Packet Type	1	Type of service	Indicates type of packet contained in the data field (5 = SPX, 17 = NCP, 0,4 = all others).
Destination Network	4	Destination network address	Network number of destination
Destination Node	6	Destination node address	Physical address of destination node
Destination Socket	2	Socket number	Identifies type of request.
Source Network	4	Source network address	Network number of source
Source Node	6	Source node address	Physical address of source node
Source Socket	2	Socket number	Identifies type of request.
Data	variable		This field always contains a higher-layer packet header plus a data segment (if any).

More details of protocol field values are contained in Appendix D, "Protocol Reference Guide."

Protocol Function

This sequence of steps describes an IPX request:

1. When a higher-level protocol sends data, it is encapsulated into an IPX header for delivery.

2. Each IPX header is addressed with the source and destination network, node, and socket addresses and sent.

3. If the destination network address is the same as the source, the packet is sent to the local network. If the destination is on a remote network, the frame is sent to the router, identified in the client's server connection.

Name resolution is performed even before the request is sent and is internal. No name resolution server is required, as is the case in a TCP/IP and/or Microsoft network. Servers and clients know the IPX addresses because each connection is marked with the corresponding IPX address. Requests are handled by name; the NCP protocol directs the request to a connection, and then the connection configuration addresses the IPX packet header. Furthermore, no logical-to-physical address lookup is required (as is the case in TCP/IP and/or Microsoft networks), because the physical address is part of the IPX address.

SPX

All NetWare client/server traffic is connection-oriented at the highest layer. When another higher-layer protocol is not connection-oriented, SPX is substituted for (or appended to) IPX. SPX's function is to carry data — most commonly a print job, although it is used in some communications applications.

Novell developers expected that software developers would use SPX where NCP is not required, but it is rarely employed outside of NetWare print services. SPX can severely impact network performance because it is not very efficient. Novell has released a more recent version (see the later section in this chapter entitled "SPX II") that is better, but it is also rarely used.

Protocol Characteristics

SPX is *connection-oriented*, which means that communications are two-way — each SPX request (packet) must be acknowledged with an SPX reply before another SPX packet is sent. SPX is normally described as a connection-oriented substitute for IPX — a statement that is debatable. The initial fields in the SPX header are the same as the IPX headers, or you can say that the SPX header follows the IPX header. NetWare client/server communications are always connection-oriented, a function that NCP typically fulfills. Therefore SPX is used when the higher-level protocol is not connection-oriented. For example, print jobs do not use NCP, so SPX is substituted for IPX to provide connection-oriented delivery.

SPX's maximum packet size is 594 bytes, including headers. This restriction was placed on the protocol to accommodate the smallest potential frame size, which was ARCnet. Because ARCnet is rarely used today, this artificial size restriction causes unnecessary network traffic.

NOTE

You can say that the SPX packet is the same as the IPX packet with a few more header fields, or you can say that the SPX header follows the IPX header. An SPX header is identified with the value 5 in the IPX header's Type field.

Packet Header Description

Table 3.4 shows the SPX header fields (excluding the IPX header) and their functions.

TABLE 3.4

SPX Packet Header Fields

FIELD NAME	# BYTES	DESCRIPTION	COMMENT
Connection Control	1	Request/reply	Identifies packet as a request or a reply to a request.
Datastream Type	1	End of communications marker	Marks the body of the request, last request, or reply to last request.
Source Connection ID	2	Unique SPX connection number	Each SPX connection is identified with a unique number; all SPX packets in that connection are identified with this number.

TABLE 3.4

SPX Packet Header Fields
(continued)

FIELD NAME	# BYTES	DESCRIPTION	COMMENT
Destination Connection ID	2	Unique SPX connection number	(See the preceding field.)
Sequence Number	2	Request number in datastream datastream	Each request or reply in a is sequentially numbered.
Acknowledgment Number	2	Number to be used by reply, expected sequence number for the acknowledgment, or next request.	
Allocation Number	2	Number of receive buffers	The number of receive cache buffers allocated (first is numbered 0, so a value of 5 indicates 6 cache buffers allocated) regulates sender when processing is slower at receiving end.
Data	variable, 0 to 576		This field contains data segments, such as print job segments (if any).

Protocol Dialog

SPX connections are established for the duration of a specific datastream and then removed. For example, when a print job is sent, the following dialog is established:

1. An SPX request is sent to a server (such as a print server).

2. A connection is initialized by the server, and an acknowledgment is returned with a unique connection ID.

3. The sender initiates a datastream (a stream of several request packets, each containing a segment of the print job).

4. Each packet is acknowledged (a reply is returned).

5. The reply (acknowledgment) must be received before the next request packet in the datastream is sent. If an acknowledgment is not received within a given timeout period, a copy of the lost request is resent.

6. The last packet in the datastream is marked accordingly (value = FE in the Datastream Type field).

7. An SPX reply is sent acknowledging that the last packet has been received and the connection has been removed (value = FF in the Datastream Type field).

If an SPX reply (acknowledgment packet) is not received within a given amount of time, a duplicate SPX request is sent (this process is called a *retry*). If repeated requests are not acknowledged, the connection is assumed to be lost, and a network error is sent to the workstation (or server) console.

SPX II

SPX II is different from its predecessor in the following ways:

- ► 1,518 byte packet size (big enough for the largest Ethernet frame)

- ► Windowed acknowledgment, one reply for a burst of requests

- ► An additional header field (the Extended Acknowledgment) to accommodate windowed bursts

- ► Some additional values added for the Connection Control field

During an SPX II connection request, the packet size is negotiated. Normally the packet size will equal the LAN packet driver's size up to the Ethernet maximum packet size of 1,518 bytes (the packet size is the size of packet that fits into the data portion of the Ethernet frame).

SPX II is backward compatible with SPX. If the recipient is not SPX II–enabled, the negotiation yields SPX parameters.

Service Advertising and Routing Protocols

How do clients find servers? The answer is quite complex in some network architectures but pretty simple in NetWare. Three service advertising protocols are used with NetWare, one for older versions, one for newer versions with IPX, and another for NetWare 5 with TCP/IP. IPX-related protocols are discussed later in this chapter.

Service Advertising Protocol

In order to provide shared services over a network, a NOS must use some type of service advertising or locating service. A Service Advertising Protocol (SAP) broadcast announces to all listening that a specific service is available and provides the service's IPX address.

SAP is broadcast-based and must use IPX for delivery. There are three types of SAP packets: service queries, service responses, and periodic service information broadcasts.

Service Queries

When a NetWare client software is executed, it broadcasts a SAP service query looking for the "nearest server." The broadcast elicits a response from each server, and then the client selects a server based on the number of hops counted in the reply packet header.

Service query broadcast packets include just two fields, shown in Table 3.5.

TABLE 3.5	FIELD NAME	# BYTES	DESCRIPTION
SAP Service Query Packet Header Fields	Packet Type	2	Value of 3 indicates a service query.
	Server Type	2	Indicates what type of server is requested.

Service Responses

When a service query is broadcast, each server of the type requested responds with the information shown in Table 3.6.

Server Name, Network Address, Node Address, Socket, and Intermediate Networks fields make up a set of data. Up to seven sets can be returned in one packet.

NOTE

FIELD NAME	# BYTES	DESCRIPTION
Packet Type	2	Value of 4 indicates response to service query.
Server Type	2	Indicates what type of server is requested.
Data Set 0–6		
Server Name	48	Server name is padded with null characters to 48-byte fixed length.
Network Address	4	IPX network address of server
Node Address	6	IPX node address of server
Socket	2	Indicates which socket will be used in requests to this server.
Intermediate Networks	2	Number of hops over routers between this server and the client.

SAP Service Response Packet Header Fields

TABLE 3.6

Periodic SAP Information Broadcasts

SAP broadcasts proceed as follows:

1. *Initial broadcast* — Each server advertises its services with a Service Advertising Protocol (SAP) broadcast when it is booted. SAP includes the IPX network and node address of the server.

2. *Discovery* — All servers and routers receive SAP broadcasts. Each server stores the server information in its bindery or directory service (NDS) as an active logical object. Each router forwards the SAPs to other network segments and broadcasts them.

3. *Availability* — The server shares the server or resource as a logical object (by name) in its bindery or directory service subject to its security, making it available (by name) to users.

4. *Name resolution* — The server provides the server's destination IPX address to users when requested.

SAP is effective but can hog network resources. In order to maintain up-to-date listings of available server services, the service must be "kept alive." Each server broadcasts SAP packets once every 60 seconds. If a server stops broadcasting, the other servers will drop the name from its bindery/directory service. If a broadcast is not heard for three minutes, it is assumed that the server is down, and the object's service is made unavailable.

SAP broadcasts are issued every 60 seconds from each server (including application servers, such as print servers, communications servers, and database servers). SAP information must be "kept alive," meaning that regular broadcasts are required or access to the service will be discontinued.

Under NetWare/IP, SAP is encapsulated into UDP packets for broadcast. In NetWare 5 with TCP/IP, SAP is replaced with the Service Location Protocol, which does not require IPX.

Table 3.7 describes SAP information broadcast packet header fields.

TABLE 3.7	FIELD NAME	# BYTES	DESCRIPTION
SAP Information Broadcast Packet Header Fields	Packet Type	2	Value of 4 indicates response to service query.
	Server Type	2	Indicates what type of server is requested.
	Data Sets 0–6		
	Server Name	48	Server name is padded with null characters to 48-byte fixed length.
	Network Address	4	IPX network address of server
	Node Address	6	IPX node address of server
	Socket	2	Indicates which socket will be used in requests to this server.
	Intermediate Networks	2	Number of hops over routers between this server and the client
	Data set 1–6		(Up to six sets of data in each packet)

NOTE

Data sets consist of Server Name, Network Address, Node Address, Socket, and Intermediate Networks fields. Up to seven sets can be returned in one packet. Each server issues one SAP for itself and up to six other servers that is available through its bindery or NDS database.

Protocol Dialog

SAP has been used in older NetWare networks and can be used today, but it is no longer the default when installing NetWare 4.10 or 5. Here's how SAP works.

Each server contains a router, which forwards SAP broadcasts from each LAN to every other LAN. When forwarding SAP data, servers consolidate up to seven data sets in each packet, reducing the number of SAP broadcasts. This process has a tendency to multiply broadcasts when servers have multiple NICs. Router developers and network managers do not like broadcasts. More users and more servers translate to more broadcasts — the number of broadcasts grows exponentially as the network gets larger. Broadcast traffic can overwhelm networks and routers by flooding them with requests once every 60 seconds. The amount of bandwidth used on a LAN is negligible, but traffic can be significant on limited-bandwidth WANs.

Another problem with SAP broadcasting is the load that results from servicing many servers and many network routes. In a network with hundreds of servers, each server will need to relay hundreds of SAPs along with its own. Every 60-second cycle can flood the server's processor, causing performance degradation for user requests.

NOTE

Many routers have a *spoofing* feature that can be turned on to reduce broadcast traffic on your WANs. Spoofing suppresses SAP broadcasts on WANs by capturing them from LAN ports in the router and then forwarding them only once each time they change. A copy of the SAP is stored at the other end. The "keep-alive" broadcast is serviced from the stored copy, thus reducing the need to broadcast on the WAN.

SAP is inefficient and was replaced with NLSP, which is discussed in further detail later in this chapter. NLSP replaces two protocols and reduces broadcast traffic to an absolute minimum. Service Location Protocol (SLP) is used with TCP/IP and is also discussed in the Chapter 4, "TCP/IP Protocols, IP Addressing, and Name Resolution."

Routing Information Protocol

A mentioned earlier in this chapter, routers are intelligent. Their intelligence is based on maintaining routing tables, which get their information from router-to-router communications. Novell adapted Routing Information Protocol (RIP) from the XNS stack to handle propagation of routing information.

Protocol Characteristics

RIP is broadcast-based. Every 60 seconds, each NetWare server's router receives routing information from each network segment, updates its routing tables, and then relays updated information to all other network segments to which the router is attached. On each network segment, each router/server receives RIP packets from every other router/server. The information is incorporated into its routing table and then relayed to every other network segment during the next broadcast cycle.

RIP routers only receive RIP packets from other routers directly connected to the same network segments. Routing information for remote network addresses are contained within these RIP packets and are available by forwarding.

Like SAP, this process must be kept alive. RIP information omitted for three minutes is purged from the routing tables. This mechanism automatically removes routing information for paths that may have gone down. For example, if a server were to crash, within three minutes servers and routers on adjacent network segments would drop the route from their routing tables because they would not receive regular keep-alive broadcasts. However, because each router forwards RIP routes on the next broadcast cycle, an additional minute would be added for each hop before the routing information would be purged. In very large internetworks this propagation delay is problematic.

RIP is not as bandwidth-intensive as you might assume. Each server sends a separate RIP broadcast for each network segment, but each RIP packet can contain up to 50 RIP data sets, one for each available network segment. When an internetwork has more than 100 servers and many of those servers have multiple NICs, the amount of RIP broadcasting and processing can cause a server to freeze for a few seconds every broadcast cycle.

Protocol Header

Table 3.8 describes RIP packet header fields.

TABLE 3.8	FIELD NAME	# BYTES	DESCRIPTION
RIP Packet Header Fields	Packet Type	2	1 = request, 2 = reply
	Data Sets 0–49		
	Network Address 0:	4	
	Hops away	2	
	Time	2	

Each Data Set contains Network Address, Hops Away, and Time fields for another available route. Up to 50 Data Sets in total can be contained in a single RIP packet.

NOTE

Protocol Dialog

RIP is used in NetWare for two purposes: client connection setup, and router-to-router communications.

When a client first boots, it issues a SAP query broadcast requesting the "nearest server." When servers reply, the workstation selects a server and then issues a RIP request for routing information. The server responds with a RIP reply listing the server's internal network address and all network addresses that are available through its router. An NCP connection request is then issued.

Generally, only one RIP packet is required to service a connection request, because one packet can contain up to 50 data sets of network addresses and hop counts.

Routers use RIP for five functions:

▶ *Router initialization* — When an IPX router comes up, it broadcasts its availability. Other routers respond, providing all available routes.

▶ *Router synchronization requests* — Routers will occasionally need to request information of other routers and provide routing information to other routers. This synchronizes their routing tables. One case that initiates a synchronization request is when a router detects conflicting information.

▶ *Periodic keep-alive broadcasts* — Every 60 seconds each IPX router broadcasts a listing of all current routes available. These are called "keep-alive" packets because a router will remove any routing information that has not been kept alive for three minutes. If a router were to crash, this allows other routers to notice the missing routes within a few minutes and remove them from their tables.

▸ *Change notification* — When a change occurs in routing information, the router advertises the changed information immediately. This allows routers to update their tables before their next periodic keep-alive broadcast.

▸ *Router going down* — When a router is shut down, it broadcasts a notification to remove its routes from all routers' tables.

RIP's bandwidth utilization is not so inefficient as the amount of server processing time that is required to service the keep-alive broadcasts. RIP has been replaced by NLSP in later NetWare versions as discussed in the next section.

NetWare Link Services Protocol

To overcome the limitations inherent in SAP and RIP protocols, Novell engineers developed NetWare Link Services Protocol (NLSP). NLSP is a link-state routing protocol, much like Open Shortest Path First used in TCP/IP environments. NLSP is not broadcast-based — it uses multicasts (request packets addressed to multiple nodes) instead. When the server first comes up, it broadcasts its availability, but from that point on, multicasts are sent only when changes occur. The "keep-alive" broadcasts are eliminated, and the load of updating tables and relaying the routing information every minute is also eliminated.

NLSP is very quiet. It reduces overhead on network segments as well as processing load on servers. It also is more efficient. RIP-based routers are only aware of traffic on immediate networks, but NLSP routers maintain routing information for their entire routing domain. No keep-alive broadcasts are required. When routing information changes, changed information is multicast (one request addressed to multiple routers) to all affected routers. This reduces propagation delay to a minimum as well as reducing processing and bandwidth requirements.

NLSP is also scalable to the largest internetworks. RIP-based routers are organized in a single level that extends over the entire network (internetwork). NLSP routers can partition large internetworks into routing domains, a capability that reduces each router's table to manageable portions. Routing domains can be organized in a hierarchical manner.

NLSP was released with NetWare 4.01, but SAP was retained as the default. Beginning with NetWare 4.10, NLSP is the default, and you can configure the server to use SAP instead. An upgrade is available at no cost for NetWare 3.11. NetWare 3.2 includes the enhancement, but SAP is the default. NetWare 3.12 owners can upgrade to NLSP by downloading the latest service pack over the Internet.

NLSP is also quite flexible; it is backward compatible and will work with SAP and RIP in other servers. You can reconfigure NLSP and SAP from the server's console.

NOTE

Protocol definitions for NLSP are not contained in this book for a few reasons. First, NLSP is quite complex. Second, NLSP routing is automatic and requires little or no analysis. Finally, NLSP is not used with TCP/IP.

Should you wish a more detailed discussion on NLSP, you will find that *Novell's Guide to LAN/WAN Analysis: IPX/SPX* by Laura Chappell (IDG Books Worldwide) has a very detailed description of NLSP.

Miscellaneous NetWare Protocols

The vast bulk of traffic on a NetWare network uses the previously described protocols, but there are a few minor protocols that might be found on your network. The following protocols perform specific functions not handled by other protocols discussed previously.

Watchdog

Logins and logouts occur over an established connection. Once a client workstation attaches to the network by executing the network drivers, the connection stays open. Before a client logs in, and after he/she logs out, the connection is shown as "Not logged in" (these conditions are sometimes called NLIs). These connections can tie up connections that are allocated for logged users. Each NetWare server provides enough connections to service the licensed number of users plus a few extra connections for miscellaneous use, such as a print server or third-party NLMs. At times a user will log out, and then a new connection will be created when the user logs in again. Because the server will allow only the licensed number of logins, and only the allowed number of connections, NLIs can sometimes cause the server to refuse connections.

Watchdog monitors connections and attempts to terminate NLIs. By default, a *watchdog packet* is sent about every five minutes on each inactive connection. If a user is logged in, the client will automatically reply and the cycle will start again. If the user is not logged in, more queries will be sent, once each minute. If after 10 retries there is still no response, the NLI connection will be cleared.

 NOTE **The watchdog parameters just described can be adjusted using server SET parameters. Some routers filter watchdog packets by filtering IPX type 4 packets (used by watchdog). You can configure NetWare 5 to use type 0 instead with a SET parameter so that connections over routers will clear.**

Watchdog packets contain only two fields and are carried by IPX packets:

▸ Connection number (one byte)

▸ Signature character (one byte)

Watchdog requests have a null character in the Signature field and expect a Y in the acknowledgment if the user is logged in. No reply indicates that the user is not logged in, in which case watchdog initiates the retry process before terminating the connection.

Serialization Packets

A *serialization packet,* also called a *copyright protection packet,* searches the network for other servers using the same serial number. Each server broadcasts a serialization packet once every 66 seconds. When a server receives a serialization packet that contains the same serial number as its own, it beeps and displays a copyright violation message to the server console and to all connected users.

The serialization packet contains only one six-byte field and is carried by an IPX packet.

Message Packets

Messages can be sent to other users and connections by using the SEND command line utility or the SEND console command. These messages are sent directly and are not stored for later forwarding. Many software packages also use an API to convey messages through this service. Message packets carry these messages.

Message packets contains three fields and are carried by IPX packets:

▶ Connection number (one byte)

▶ Signature character (one byte)

▶ Data (the message in plain ASCII)

The sending client directs the message to the server (or NDS) using an NCP request. The bindery or NDS is searched for the user or connection. The reply provides the connection number to which the message will be directed. The sending client then sends the message packet.

IPX Addressing

An IPX address has two parts: the network number (network address) and the node address. Each network node must have an IPX address. IPX delivery mechanisms depend upon proper IPX addressing. Because IPX is a routable protocol, an IPX network number must be assigned to each network segment to which a NetWare server or router is connected.

IPX and IP addressing are pretty similar, but IPX is simpler. If you already familiar with IP administration, you will find IPX administration simpler in three ways:

▶ IPX addresses are preassigned. Each node discovers the IPX network address from the server servicing its connection as it connects. The IPX node address is copied from the physical address.

▶ Because the IPX address includes the physical address as part of its logical address, the need for other protocols to solve for physical addressing (such as ARP, used with IP, and NetBIOS, used with Microsoft) is eliminated.

▶ NetWare servers perform name resolution for their clients, so name resolution protocols (such as DNS and WINS) are not required.

The network address is also called the network number in the server INSTALL application and in server utilities. This address is generally expressed in hexadecimal format, so a total of eight hex characters are used (leading 0's are added if omitted), which fit into four bytes of address space.

This address is assigned during server installation when the IPX protocol is bound to the NIC driver. The address is recorded in the AUTOEXEC.NCF file as a suffix to the BIND command. In servers where more complex protocol configurations are used, you will find the network address assignment in the INETCFG server utility.

The node address is a six-byte number that is copied from the NIC's assigned physical (MAC) address. This number is generally shown in hex format, which translates to 12 hex characters. Because each NIC is assigned a unique number by the manufacturer, duplicate address assignments are virtually impossible. The assigned address can be overridden, but overriding it can result in duplicate IPX addresses.

Network Numbers

An IPX *network number*, also called the *network address,* must be assigned to each IPX network. This number is assigned when a server is installed. Normally, an IPX network maps to a network segment (see the discussion of the term "network segment" in Chapter 2, "Internetworking Basics"). An IPX network is a logical network where IPX communications have been established.

A unique IPX network number is typically assigned to each network segment. A network segment is typically a LAN or a WAN; however, there are some exceptions: when bridges are used, and when multiple frame types are used with a single NIC. The following sections discuss all the situations you might encounter when assigning IPX network numbers.

When you install your server, the IPX address is assigned when the IPX protocol is bound to the NIC driver. This section conceptually addresses IPX network address assignment. In this book you will find separate chapters for installing each current version of NetWare. There you will find more explicit instructions on how to assign those numbers.

To change an IPX network number assignment, use the server INSTALL utility (NWCONFIG in NetWare 5) or EDIT.NLM to edit the AUTOEXEC.NCF file. In some cases, the INETCFG server utility is used to edit protocol configurations.

Once you change a network number, you will need to either down and restart the server, or unbind and bind the protocol manually so that the network number will be bound to the NIC driver. If you use the manual method, you should unload the NIC driver and reload it to prevent bind errors. You should down and restart the server to make sure that the startup file edits you made will work properly.

Typical IPX Network Number Assignment

IPX network numbers are assigned during server installation. When assigning the number, consider that your server is connected to a network segment, not the other way around. Think of a network segment as a street and the server's NIC as one address located on that street. That's the way IPX sees it.

Figure 3.6 illustrates a simple one-server and one-LAN configuration. Notice that the Ethernet LAN depicted in this illustration is labeled with the network number.

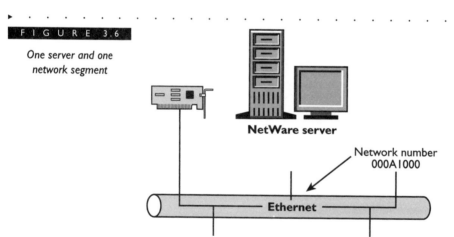

FIGURE 3.6

One server and one
network segment

NetWare server

Network number
000A1000

Ethernet

Though you will associate the network number with the NIC, remember that you are actually indicating that the IPX logical network is connected to the network segment identified by this network number.

If two servers are connected to the same network segment, the same network address will be assigned to both servers. Figure 3.7 illustrates the same network number assigned to a NIC in each of two servers. When binding the NICs in each server in Figure 3.7, the installer will assign the same network number.

More Than One NIC in a Server

You can have up to 16 NICs in a NetWare server. More precisely, the server's router can handle no more than 16 logical networks. If more than one frame type is used, or more than one protocol is bound, you will not be able to use as many as 16 NICs. This should not trouble you because it is quite difficult to find a server that has enough expansion slots for this many NICs.

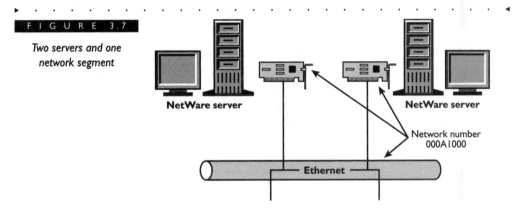

FIGURE 3.7

Two servers and one network segment

Assign an IPX network number to each network segment. Figure 3.8 illustrates one server with two NICs, each connected to a separate network segment.

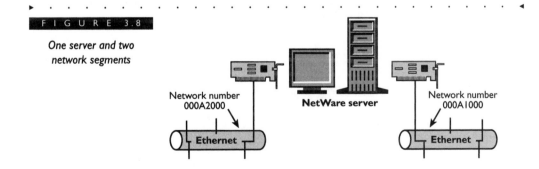

FIGURE 3.8

One server and two network segments

By default, you will not be allowed to assign the same network number to more than one NIC in a server. It is assumed that each NIC will connect the server to a different network segment. The internal router makes this assumption to reduce complexity.

Assigning One Network Number to Two Server NICs

NetWare will not allow you to assign the same network number to two NICs in a NetWare server by default. However, you may want to assign the same number to two NICs if they are to be attached to the same network hub. This option is good for load balancing and NIC fault tolerance.

You can bypass this restriction using Novell and third-party utilities. For information on how to assign the same network address to two or more NICs, look for:

▸ *Resource* — Novell Technical Information Documents, available in the Novell Support Connection CD or on Novell's Support Web site.

▸ *Document* — #2909238, "How to Enable Load Balancing" (June 17, 1998)

Using More Than One Frame Type

NetWare drivers and the IPX protocol support virtually all known LAN frame types. Some types of LANs have multiple frame types — Ethernet, for example, has four possible frame types, all of which are supported with IPX protocol. When you bind more than one frame type to a server NIC, the LAN is partitioned into multiple logical LANs. Each logical LAN is assigned a different network address.

In Figure 3.9, two frame types are bound to the same NIC driver. In this case, two different network numbers are assigned, one for each frame type.

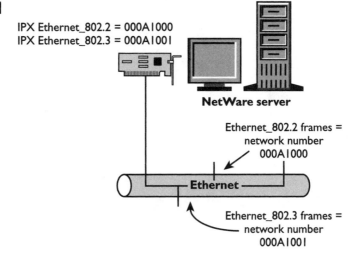

F I G U R E   3.9

*Two frames types bound
to one NIC driver*

IPX Ethernet_802.2 = 000A1000
IPX Ethernet_802.3 = 000A1001

NetWare server

Ethernet_802.2 frames =
network number
000A1000

Ethernet

Ethernet_802.3 frames =
network number
000A1001

When two different frame types are used, nodes can only communicate with other nodes using the same frame type even though they share the same network segment. Therefore two separate sets of network communications are established. Each is a logical network, and therefore two separate network addresses must be assigned, one for each logical network.

Bridge Domains

When two or more LANs or WANs are bridged together, they form a single logical network, which is often called a *bridge domain*. IPX routers cannot detect bridges, at least not for the purpose of segmenting LANs or WANs. As far as IPX and IPX routers are concerned a bridge domain is a single logical network segment and is to be addressed accordingly. For a discussion on what constitutes a bridge domain, look for the section entitled "Bridging and Routing" in Chapter 2.

Internal Network Number

Each NetWare server is assigned an internal network number. This number identifies the location for services contained in each NetWare server. Clients address requests to the internal network number to access resources available through the attached server. Servers service each client connection, even in an

NDS environment. Though the internal network number is an IPX address, it is required even in a pure TCP/IP NetWare 5 environment.

Figure 3.10 shows that the internal network number is assigned to the server, in addition to network numbers being assigned to network segments.

FIGURE 3.10

An internal network number is assigned to each server's internal processes.

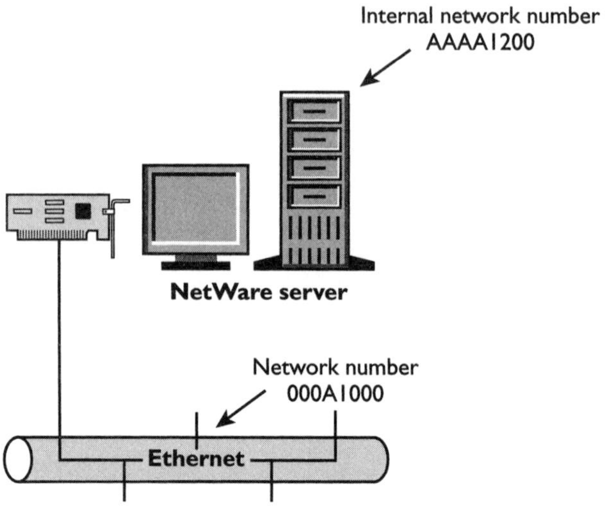

Internal network number
AAAA1200

NetWare server

Network number
000A1000

Ethernet

The internal network that this number represents is a logical network, not a physical one. Access to the internal network shows up as a hop in your router information and in routing tables. For example, when a client directly accesses a server, the server will show up with one hop. The router has to handle routing packets directed to the internal network, but no physical handling or LAN frame encapsulation is required.

All client requests will be routed through your attached server's router to an internal network. Once a client attaches to a server, all accesses to network services are routed through this internal network or passed off to another server's internal network.

Purpose of an Internal Network

The reason for this internal network goes way back to a problem that was evident in NetWare 2 systems. When a server has more than one NIC, NetWare 2 used to point network services to the first network number. This caused irregularities in routing information; there appeared to be fewer hops when accessing a server over one NIC than a second. The problem is solved by putting all services on the internal network and associating one hop with access from any NIC in the server.

Unique Network Number

Each internal network number must be unique, distinguished from every other network number, internal or external. During installation a random number will be assigned in an attempt to prevent duplicate numbers. You can edit this default number, and you probably should.

When installing NetWare servers, you can use the internal network number to identify each server. You are restricted to using up to eight hex characters (0–9, A–F). Identify each server by building number, department number, or some other identifying characteristic. Later on you will be able to identify servers when viewing your Router Tracking screens, when using protocol analyzers, or at other times when routing information is available. This is helpful for troubleshooting and maintenance procedures too numerous to mention.

CHAPTER 4

TCP/IP Protocols, IP Addressing, and Name Resolution

This chapter discusses foundation knowledge for implementing and configuring a TCP/IP intranet. Any experienced NetWare system administrator should be able to use this chapter to assist in setting up NetWare with TCP/IP.

This chapter can also be used as a basis for more advanced troubleshooting and protocol analysis. Protocol analyzers assist you to see details of protocol activity, but knowledge of the protocol functions and mechanics are necessary to make use of your captured packets. This chapter is not intended to be a tutorial on protocol analysis or TCP/IP protocols, but a basic guide on how the protocols work.

You will find additional detailed protocol information in Appendix C, "Protocol Reference Guide." This guide is also to be found on the CD that accompanies this book.

TCP/IP Development

The U.S. Department of Defense (DoD) Advanced Research Project Agency (ARPA) originally developed TCP/IP. The original intention was to establish a wide area data network enabling data communications between various DoD agencies, research facilities (such as universities), and defense contractors. TCP/IP was released to the public domain when source code was furnished to universities and computer developers. It was left up to these organizations to take on the task of furthering developing and managing TCP/IP. In the early 1970s UNIX source code and rights were conveyed to University of California at Berkeley, where TCP/IP was integrated into UNIX and a set of UNIX-like network service utilities were developed that functioned over a network. Berkeley also provided a new operating system abstraction called *Berkeley sockets* and resold developed, networked source code under Berkeley Software Distribution (BSD). Many computer vendors built on this foundation, using TCP/IP as their native protocol stack along with their customized versions of UNIX.

In the late 1970s the Request for Comment (RFC) system was developed to democratically manage TCP/IP development. Today, the Internet Engineering Task Force (IETF) manages TCP/IP development and the Internet. As part of the Internet Architecture Board (IAB), IETF is a consortium of industry engineers pledged to support open standards.

TCP/IP is nonproprietary, is used in many networked computer systems, and is the only protocol allowed on the Internet today. Integrating TCP/IP into local internetworks allows communications to be handled in a uniform manner. One client TCP/IP stack can be loaded in each client workstation to access all TCP/IP resources regardless of the platform that hosts them.

TCP/IP is the platform that spawned client/server development. Many TCP/IP server-based applications have been developed that can reside on any platform and can be accessed from any platform using TCP/IP. It is only logical that Novell would eventually engineer the ability to replace IPX/SPX with TCP/IP in a NetWare network.

Novell and the TCP/IP Protocol

TCP/IP is supported at two entry points to the network: at the clients and at the servers. In the mid-1980s Novell showed avid interest in TCP/IP and UNIX through acquisitions and internal development. In 1986 Novell purchased Excellan, which included some of the best TCP/IP developers in the industry and their products. This combined with the ODI/MLID driver architecture (discussed in Chapter 1, "NetWare Basics") provides client support for all TCP/IP services at the client end. The new development team built TCP/IP support into NetWare 3.11, which was introduced in 1987, and also developed protocol monitoring tools and products. Congress mandated TCP/IP capability in government systems in 1988, and Novell inherited many existing contract dollars. Later introductions of NetWare NFS and Flex/IP added another important dimension to the Novell promise of interoperability.

Today, Novell leads the industry with native TCP/IP support in NetWare 5. This product marks the first truly native TCP/IP implementation in a network operating system (NOS). Though UNIX was there first, NetWare provides file service and security far beyond what is offered in the combination of UNIX and Network File System (NFS). Microsoft's Windows operating systems may have TCP/IP, but the need to support NetBIOS over TCP/IP in NT and all Microsoft operating systems is problematic. In NetWare 5, RIP and SAP protocols are eliminated in favor of Service Location Protocol (SLP) when using TCP/IP, and NCP runs on IP without any need for IPX or any use of proprietary protocols. You will find that Novell protocols and Novell's TCP/IP implementations are the most stable, refined, and optimized in the industry.

Novell's ODI/MLID driver architecture provides support for multiple protocol stacks. In 1987 NetWare 2 and 3 products included MLID drivers (NetWare 2.15 still used monolithic IPX drivers — they supported only the IPX/SPX protocols — as the default, whereas NetWare 3 required the MLID and IPX ODI drivers for full functionality). Novell did not include any IP packet drivers or TCP/IP client software in NetWare. By adding LAN Workplace for DOS, Windows, OS/2, or Macintosh (or a third-party TCP/IP client product), the client could concurrently access both NetWare and TCP/IP resources. These products ran on top of MLID drivers.

NetWare server support for TCP/IP varies from one NetWare version to another. NetWare 2 had no server support for TCP/IP. Each successive NetWare version was introduced with progressively increasing levels of TCP/IP support.

NetWare 3's TCP/IP Support

NetWare 3 (starting with 3.11) includes limited server support for TCP/IP. NetWare 3.11 and later versions support loading dual protocol stacks for each server NIC.

Each server NIC can be configured as an IP node, an IPX node, or both. NetWare versions 3.11 through 3.2 support the following features:

▸ The server can forward IPX-based packets over an IP network (a process called *tunneling*).

▸ The server can route IP packets.

▸ The server can accept and store SNMP traps.

▸ A server console application can monitor TCP/IP traffic statistics (TCPCON.NLM).

▸ Server-based applications can be added to provide additional TCP/IP-based services (for example, NetWare NFS, Flex/IP, LANWorkGroup for the server).

In addition to this support, Novell and third parties developed NetWare server-based software modules for traditional TCP/IP-based services. NetWare 3 was designed to provide an operating system platform for server-based applications called NetWare Loadable Modules (NLMs).

NetWare 4's TCP/IP Support

Novell developed NetWare/IP to run with NetWare 4.01. This product became a free add-on and was included in distribution shipments with NetWare 4.10. NetWare/IP added support for NetWare client services over IP. However, NCP, RIP, and SAP protocols still required IPX for transport. NetWare/IP encapsulates IPX inside of IP packets, only partially fulfilling the promise to support IP clients. NetWare protocols were still present on the network, even though they may have been masked by IP headers.

Until recently, NetWare 4 clients had to use Novell MLID/ODI drivers—they could not use other vendor's TCP/IP protocol drivers. Configuring client ODI drivers was cumbersome—a DOS workstation's NET.CFG file contained dozens of protocol adjustments. More recently, NetWare clients for Windows 95 and Windows NT could choose between the Microsoft NDIS or Novell MLID NIC drivers with the Novell packet drivers and client modules. Using existing NDIS drivers reduces configuration requirements and the need to support dual NIC drivers.

NetWare/IP provides client access to both NetWare and TCP/IP hosts using a common protocol. However, many network engineers and IS managers perceive NetWare/IP as limited because it still requires IPX to deliver higher-layer Novell protocols (NCP, SAP, RIP, NLSP, and so on). NetWare/IP was often disregarded for this reason. Given that NetWare/IP requires servicing two protocol stacks, why employ it? NetWare/IP did not gain much acceptance, probably because many system administrators did not see much benefit except to eliminate the need to purchase LAN Workplace or another TCP/IP protocol stack.

NetWare 5's Native TCP/IP

In NetWare 5, TCP/IP can totally replace IPX/SPX service. All NetWare services can be transported with TCP/IP without the additional IPX layer that was required in previous NetWare versions. NetWare 5 still supports both TCP/IP and IPX/SPX clients and even provides a gateway for IPX clients to access IP services, as well as a gateway for IPX clients to access IP services.

NetWare 5 with TCP/IP offers all the TCP/IP services that UNIX and Windows NT Server can offer, plus a rich set of NetWare services. The protocol reengineering that was required to make NetWare 5 a native TCP/IP implementation is a great accomplishment. NetWare is as native as UNIX but can still run NetWare services over TCP/IP without adding unnecessary broadcasts or redundant layers of protocol, as is the case with Windows NT and previous NetWare versions.

You do not need to replace your existing client TCP/IP stacks; simply add the latest Client for Windows 95 or Windows NT (also called Client 32). You will have an option to select IPX, IP, or both. The client modules shipped with NetWare 5 enables you to add NetWare client services to an existing Windows workstation, using the built-in Microsoft NDIS drivers and TCP/IP protocol stack.

NetWare 5's protocol support is significant for at least one reason: TCP/IP can now be the only protocol stack used to transport all network traffic. In addition Microsoft, NetWare, UNIX, and other operating systems can share a common protocol stack. No protocol reconfiguration or adjustments are required to adapt a Windows or UNIX TCP/IP workstation as a NetWare client — just install the NetWare client (NCP) module and bind it to TCP/IP. Services such as DNS and DHCP will interoperate across all operating systems. Even without the NetWare client module, TCP/IP workstations can access TCP/IP services on any one of these three platforms. For example, a Windows workstation with TCP/IP networking installed can access FTP servers on Windows NT, NetWare, and UNIX hosts. By adding the Client for Windows 95 or NT, you can give the same workstation full access to NetWare 5 systems, including a Novell Directory Services (NDS) login.

NOTE

NetWare 5's native TCP/IP implementation provides a powerful incentive to upgrade your networks from previous NetWare versions and Windows NT. Protocol usage has been optimized to conserve bandwidth and handle name resolution/routing communications more efficiently than any other NOS on the market today.

Windows networking, including Windows NT, Windows 95, and Windows for Workgroups, requires NetBIOS to handle Microsoft service advertising and network services. You will find Novell's implementation to be more reliable and efficient than Microsoft's TCP/IP implementation.

Network Connectivity versus NOS Features

TCP/IP provides connectivity, delivery, and transport services but does not provide higher-layer services found in NetWare and other NOSes. In a NOS environment, TCP/IP is used as it is elsewhere, plus it becomes the transport mechanism for the highest-level NOS protocol. Figure 4.1 illustrates a common NIC, driver, and protocol stack that support two separate high-level services.

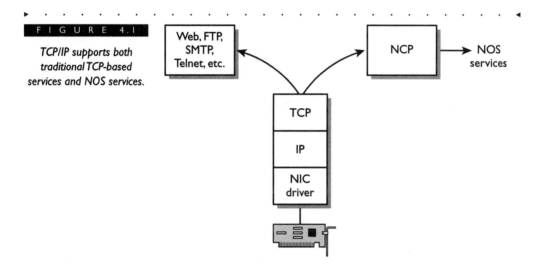

FIGURE 4.1

TCP/IP supports both traditional TCP-based services and NOS services.

TCP/IP is used in all UNIX systems, but the combination of TCP/IP and UNIX is not a NOS. The TCP/IP protocol stack does not provide many network features, such as file sharing and login security authentication. In most TCP/IP networks, services are exposed without any network security. In most UNIX shops, you will find that security, database sharing, and print services are delivered via server-based applications, which is like reinventing the wheel again and again. This means that each application has separate mechanisms and procedures in order to provide these services. For example, a user may need to log into an Oracle application and then log in again to a Web server. Netscape and other companies provide a directory services server to provide centralized security, but this solution is years away from where NDS is today, and each application must develop its own security mechanisms. NDS provides a unified login for all network services and provides C-2 level security.

In a UNIX shop, data sharing is enabled within a server-based database server, such as Oracle. Or Network File System (NFS-Sun Microsystems) is used to work with TCP/IP to provide shared file access to NFS volumes. NFS also has no security provisions and does not perform as well as NetWare. NetWare's NDS provides far more performance, security, and control than any competing NOS. NDS can be extended to include UNIX and NT servers. UNIX and NT applications are available to incorporate UNIX and NT servers into NDS and manage them from the NetWare Administrator utility.

NetWare uses NCP and other higher-layer protocols to deliver NOS services. When you are using NetWare with TCP/IP, all TCP/IP services are supported, and all NetWare features are available. There is no downside in NetWare 5's TCP/IP implementation; even setup and configuration are simplified and a graphical server user interface (GSUI) is provided to simplify server installation and management.

IP Addressing, Subnetworking, and Masking

IP addresses are logical addresses — they are used to enable end-to-end addressing over routed internetworks. IP addressing is designed with a very large address space, which allows each host connected to an internetwork to have a unique IP address. IP is the only protocol allowed on the Internet, and current addressing is sufficient to accommodate anticipated address demand for the next few years.

Each organization that would like to connect to the Internet can apply for and receive a block of IP addresses for its own use. The largest organizations may apply directly to ARIN (http://www.arin.net), a contractor working under IETF's jurisdiction. Smaller organizations should simply apply to their local Internet access provider (ISP or telco). The IETF manages the Internet, defining the IP protocol and all related protocols and mechanisms. IP addresses are often issued in blocks as discussed in the text that follows. Once an organization receives a block of addresses, the organization's role in administration is to assign these addresses in a manner that will prevent duplication of assignments. Any organization that uses TCP/IP but does not intend to access the Internet can assign addresses without looking to ARIN or their local provider for address assignment.

Exposing an organization's internal internetwork to the Internet is risky business. It is somewhat dangerous to do so, as hackers can access any computer that has sharing enabled. Many organizations have opted to use private IP addressing within their internal internetwork and provide Internet access via a proxy server or Network Address Translation (NAT) gateway. Proxies and NATs support private IP addressing on the inside interface and registered IP addresses on the outside interface. Proxies multiplex requests from multiple users on the inside through a single registered IP address on the outside. NAT gateways work in a similar manner but typically require a pool of Registered IP addresses that are dynamically allocated to each requesting user on the inside. These products are considered a form of *firewall*, but the term firewall has many definitions. Novell's BorderManager provides proxy, NAT, firewall, and many other services that secure your network and provide enhanced performance and manageability.

IP Address Dotted Decimal Notation

The current version of IP, version 4 uses a 32-bit address. The address is divided into four octets, which are delimited with periods. These addresses are normally expressed in decimal format. Each octet represents 256 numbers (decimal 0–255), which is the maximum number of decimal values possible for an eight-bit binary number.

For example, IP addresses expressed in decimal format look like this:

XXX.XXX.XXX.XXX

The following is a valid class C IP address:

204.010.210.022

Leading 0's are typically dropped, such that the format used for the preceding address looks like this:

204.10.210.22

Except for masking, the numbers 0 and 255 are reserved and may not be assigned in any octet for a host address. The value 0 is reserved for a network number, and the value 255 is reserved for broadcasts to all hosts on a subnet — only the numbers 1-254 are to be assigned to hosts. For example, the number 204.10.210.0 is the subnet number on which the node 204.10.210.22 resides.

Network Addressing and Masking

A network number, often called a network address, identifies a logical IP network. The concept of a logical network was discussed in the previous chapter with regard to the IPX protocol and its network number. Like an IPX logical network, each IP subnet can exchange information locally without calling on a router for processing. To move an IP packet from one subnet (or network) to another requires the services of an IP router.

NOTE

Elsewhere you may find the terms *network address, network number, netid, network, logical network, subnetwork,* and *network* used interchangeably. In this book, each of these terms has an explicit meaning and is used with consistency. In most IP documentation, you will find that terms are often not well defined, and meaning must be extracted from context. If you study the following definitions before reading on, you will find this book to be much clearer and easier to understand.

The terms *logical network, network segment,* and *bridge domain* all have slightly different meanings. For clarification, refer to Chapter 2 or the Glossary. The important factor to consider when discussing these systems is the fact that logical communications, such as broadcasts, are propagated on this segment of the network. If you understand the definitions of each of these terms, you can pick the one that applies to the IP subnets in your internetwork. Terms will differ because network devices will differ from internetwork to internetwork.

CHECKLIST

A *network address* is a number assigned to an organization for internal use. The *network number* is the numeric value itself of that network address. The *address space* in IP version 4 is 32 bits, generally divided into four octets. The *network address space* is the portion of the IP address assigned to the organization. For example, the network number 204.10.210.0 identifies a network address assigned to an organization — the network address space is the first three octets (204.10.210) of the network address. The zero identifies this number as a network address.

A network address in IP is similar to a network number in IPX networking. IP routers are boundaries between logical networks and use the network address to identify and direct communications to the appropriate router port. All hosts that share the same network address must be connected to the same network segment. More than one IP subnet can be connected to the same router port, but the opposite is not permissible. In order for IP packets to be delivered to the appropriate router port, all addresses within each subnet must be related to just one router port.

Masking

IP addresses are divided into two parts: the *network address* and the *host address*. IP addressing is flexible; the division between these two parts can be drawn at the first, second, or third octet. A *default mask* is used to identify the network address.

▸ The network address, often called a network number, identifies the organization to which the network address has been issued.

▸ The host address identifies the host (node) to which the IP address is issued.

CHECKLIST

The *mask* identifies the network and host address spaces within the 32-bit IP address space. For example, in the IP address 204.10.210.1, the mask 255.255.255.0 identifies the first three octets as the network address space and the 0 identifies the fourth octet as the host address space.

Just like an IPX network number the IP network address identifies the network number, while the host address identifies the node (which in IP nomenclature is called a *host*). In IPX, the network and node address space is fixed. In IP addressing, the 32-bit address space is defined by the system administrator by assigning a mask. The mask is entered in several places where IP addresses are configured. Without a mask, the IP protocol and IP routers cannot identify which part of the IP address space identifies the network address space.

Network addresses are normally masked to include the first octet, the first two octets, or the first three octets of an IP address.

The mask is based on the binary value that the decimal number represents. The decimal number 255 (all 1's in binary) is used to indicate that the entire octet is masked to be part of the network address. The decimal number 0 is used to indicate the address space allocated to the host address. The following mask identifies the first three octets as the network address space and the last octet as the host address space:

```
255.255.255.0
```

In binary, this address is:

```
11111111.11111111.11111111.00000000
```

The router reads the binary 1's to determine which portion of the address applies to the network address space, and it reads the binary 0's to determine which portion of the address space applies to the host address space. In the preceding example, the decimal number 255 in the first three octets indicates that all bits in the first three octets are allocated to network address space.

The following mask identifies the first two octets as the network address space and the last two octets as the host address space:

```
255.255.0.0
```

In binary, this address is:

```
11111111.11111111.00000000.00000000
```

IP addresses can be broken down further or *subnetted*. The process of breaking network addresses into smaller units is discussed in the section "Subnetting" later in this chapter.

Network Address Classes

IP network addresses are categorized into class A, B, C, D, and E addresses. Class A, B, and C addresses are issued as needed, but IETF reserves class D and E addresses for uses other than network addressing. A class of address is established by dedicating one or more of the four octets in the IP address space to the network address space, and the remaining octets to the host address space, as shown in Figure 4.2.

F I G U R E   4.2

IP network address classes
and their masks

Class A NNN. HHH.HHH.HHH

Class B NNN. NNN. HHH.HHH

Class C NNN. NNN. NNN. HHH

NNN = netid
HHH = hostid

IP network address classes are identified by the value in the first few bits of the first octet. In decimal format, all numbers from 1 through 126 represent class A addresses, all numbers from 128 through 191 represent class B addresses, and all numbers from 192 through 223 represent class C addresses. If you refer to the binary numbers that these decimal numbers represent, you will see that class designation maps to the first few bits of the first octet. Addresses are assigned as shown in Table 4.1.

T A B L E   4.1

IP Address Classes and Their
Designations

CLASS	DEFAULT MASK	DECIMAL VALUE IN FIRST OCTET	BINARY VALUE IN FIRST OCTET
A	255.0.0.0	1-126	00000001-01111110
B	255.255.0.0	128-191	10000000-10111111
C	255.255.255.0	192-223	11000000-11011111
D	255.255.255.0	224-239	11100000-11101111
E	255.255.255.0	240-254	11110000-11110111

The address range starting with 127 in the first octet is reserved for loopback testing and diagnostic functions.

The key to locating the class is the binary value found in the first few bits of the address. Routers look at the first few bits of each IP packet and determine which class the packet belongs in. Next the router looks at the mask to identify the network address space. The router then compares the network number against its routing table to determine the destination logical network to which the IP datagram is to be delivered.

Only 126 potential class A network addresses are available, each of which can issue up to 16,777,214 host addresses. These addresses were issued to the largest organizations and are no longer issued. Class A addresses were assigned to DoD, IBM, AT&T, @Home, Xerox, the U.S. Postal Service, and other very large organizations.

Of the 16,384 potential class B network addresses, each one can issue up to 65,534 host addresses. These addresses are generally issued to larger organizations that may have tens of thousands of clients. Class B addresses are rarely issued today.

Class C addresses are used for the bulk of commercial applications. For each of the potential 2,097,152 class C network addresses, the local system administrator can issue up to 254 host addresses. When more than 254 host addresses are needed, more than one class C address is required. Addresses in this range are currently available.

Class D network addresses are reserved for multicast group usage. There are no network or host addresses in this range. Instead a given class D number identifies an IP packet that is to be sent to more than one destination IP host. For example, a class D address was provided to Cisco Systems for multicasts to be used in the Enhanced Interior Gateway Routing Protocol. For more discussion of multicasting, see the section "Enhanced Interior Gateway Routing Protocol (EIGRP)," later in this chapter.

Class E addresses are experimental. Currently some addresses in this range are used for Internet testing, but others are reserved for future use.

In the United States you can apply for a range of Internet addresses by contacting your local Internet service provider (ISP) or the American Registry for Internet Numbers (ARIN) at the following addresses:

> ARIN
> 4506 Daly Drive, Suite 200
> Chantilly, VA 20151
> hostmaster@arin.net
> http://www.arin.net/intro.html
> Telephone: 703-227-0660
> Fax: 703-227-0676

To apply for domain names, contact InterNIC Registration Service by mail or e-mail at the following addresses:

Network Solutions
InterNIC Registration Services
505 Huntmar Park Drive
Herndon, VA 22070
hostmaster@internic.net
http://rs.internic.net or http://www.internic.net

Outside of the United States, check with InterNIC for the agency that administers the assignment of network numbers.

Internet network numbers are running in short supply. Many experts disagree on exactly when the remaining supply of addresses will be exhausted, but all agree that within a few years there will be no new network addresses left to issue. Classless addressing (discussed later in this chapter in the section entitled "Classless and Classful Addressing") extends the current number of network addresses that can be assigned. In the long run, IP version 6 (IPv6), which uses a 128-bit address, will resolve this problem. In addition to providing a much larger address space, IPv6 provides security and encryption, and the last 48 bits can be used for the physical address to eliminate the need for local address resolution.

IPv6 was designed so that the industry can migrate smoothly from IPv4. IPv6 is backward compatible with IPv4. To make the different address configurations work together, the IPv4 32-bit address is preceded with 80 zero bits followed by 16 bits of all ones or all zeros. This allows devices that support both protocol versions to handle the IPv4 address within an IPv6 header.

Subnetting

Class A, B, or C network address space can be divided into smaller units, known as *subnets*. Subnetting allows network addresses to be divided into smaller portions to be assigned to network segments, or to designate departments, divisions, regions, and other categories found in larger organizations. Organizations with class A and B addresses must use this option to manage large numbers of host addresses. Even class C addresses are often subnetted because routers must identify each logical network with a different network or subnet number.

CHECKLIST

Class A, B, or C network address space can be broken into smaller divisions known as *subnets*. Subnets are created by masking bits in the host address space to identify part of this space as the subnet address space.

Up to this point, you have read about dividing IP addresses at the network address level. However, you can mask almost any number of bits within the host address space to create a subnet. When you receive a class A, B, or C network address, you must always use it; however, what you do with the remainder of the address space is up to you. The remaining bits can be further subdivided at your discretion (with a couple of exceptions).

For example, a class A network address can be divided into 254 subnet addresses by designating the second octet as the subnet address space. The mask would then be 255.255.0.0. In this case, each of the 254 subnets could accommodate the same number of hosts as a class B address, 65,534. Likewise, a class B network address can be divided into 254 subnets by masking the third octet (with the number 255). This would produce 254 subnet numbers (256 minus the numerals 0 and 255 as discussed previously). In this case, each of the 254 subnets could accommodate the same number of hosts as a class C address, 254.

NOTE

The mask 255.255.255.0 does not necessarily identify a class C network address, nor does the mask 255.255.0.0 necessarily identify a class B network address. Though these are the default masks for class A and class B network addresses respectively, these masks may be used to divide class A or B network addresses into subnets. In a class B network, the subnet mask 255.255.255.0 can accomplish the same objective as a class C network address assignment—the address space is divided into smaller networks.

Subnet addresses are identified with a subnet mask, which in turn identifies which bits are allocated to subnet address space. For example, the decimal value 192 identifies the first two bits of an octet. The decimal number 192 in binary is 11000000. By masking a network address with the number 192, you direct the router to consider the first two bits of the designated octet as subnet address space.

CHECKLIST

In this book the term *network address* is used to identify the address assigned to an organization, whereas the term *subnet address* refers to the subnet address assignment within the organization.

As an example, consider a class C address subnetted with the decimal mask 192:

```
decimal mask: 255.255.255.192

binary mask: 11111111.11111111.11111111.11000000

potential subnets: 00, 01, 10, 11
```

As you can see, the 192 subnet mask divides the class C network address into four potential subnets.

The decimal number 224 directs the router to consider the first three bits of the fourth octet as the subnet mask. Consider a class C address with the decimal mask 224:

```
decimal mask: 255.255.255.224

binary mask: 11111111.11111111.11111111.11100000

potential subnets: 000, 001, 010, 011, 100, 101, 110, 111
```

As you can see in this example, the 224 subnet mask divides the class C network address into eight potential subnets.

In the preceding examples, however, two subnet numbers are invalid in each mask. Subnet numbers consisting of all 0's or all 1's are invalid when used with class C network addresses. The number of valid subnets for the 192 subnet mask is reduced to two; the number of valid subnet masks for the 224 subnet mask is reduced to six.

You must follow three basic rules in subnetting:

1. Subnet masks consisting of all binary 0's or 1's are invalid. All 0's in the subnet address space is used to identify the subnet number itself. All 1's in the subnet address space are used for broadcasts.

2. Each logical network (separated by a router) must be assigned a unique network or subnet number.

3. All 0's or all 1's in the host address space are invalid and cannot be used.

NOTE The rule invalidating subnet masks consisting of all 0's and all 1's has been relaxed and can be safely ignored under the proper circumstances, as discussed later in this chapter in the section entitled "Classless and Classful Addressing."

In the 192 subnet example, although there are four potential subnets, only two of them are usable — 01 and 10. The subnets 11 and 00 cannot be used because of rule number one. Within the subnet address space, those numbers are reserved for subnet numbers and broadcasts respectively.

In the 224 subnet mask, although there are eight potential subnet masks, only six of them are usable — 000 and 111 are invalid per rule number one.

For the same reason, the subnet mask 128 is invalid and cannot be used in any octet. Because the binary equivalent of this decimal number is 10000000, the first bit is designated as the subnet mask. The only potential values for this mask are 1 or 0, both of which are invalid.

Because some subnet masks are invalid, host address space that is contained within the invalid subnets is also not usable. As you can see, calculating how many valid subnets and host addresses are available for each subnet mask can become quite complex. Rather than attempt to calculate subnet masks, use Table 4.2 to subnet your networks. This will eliminate the possibility of using an invalid subnet mask. Because you may need to refer to these tables periodically, they are repeated in Appendix C, "Protocol Reference Guide."

NOTE The following tables are for subnetting classful network addresses. Under the proper conditions, classless addressing allows the subnet addresses shown as invalid to be used. To determine whether you can use subnet numbers shown as invalid in these tables, see the section entitled "Classless and Classful Addressing" later in this chapter.

TABLE 4.2

Subnetting in Class A, B, and C Networks

CLASS A NETWORKS SUBNET MASK	BINARY MASK IN SECOND OCTET	NUMBER OF SUBNETS AVAILABLE	NUMBER OF HOST ADDRESSES AVAILABLE
255.0.0.0 (default mask)	00000000	0	16,777,214
255.128.0.0	10000000	0	Not valid (see the preceding note)
255.192.0.0	11000000	2	4,194,302
255.224.0.0	11100000	6	2,097,150
255.240.0.0	11110000	14	1,048,574
255.248.0.0	11111000	30	524,286
255.252.0.0	11111100	62	262,142
255.254.0.0	11111110	126	131,070
255.255.0.0	11111111	254	65,534
CLASS B NETWORKS SUBNET MASK	BINARY MASK IN SECOND OCTET	NUMBER OF SUBNETS AVAILABLE	NUMBER OF HOST ADDRESSES AVAILABLE
255.255.0.0	00000000 (default mask)	0	65,534
255.255.128.0	10000000	0	Not valid, see the preceding note
255.255.192.0	11000000	2	16,382
255.255.224.0	11100000	6	8,190
255.255.240.0	11110000	14	4,094
255.255.248.0	11111000	30	2,046
255.255.252.0	11111100	62	1,022
255.255.254.0	11111110	126	510
255.255.255.0	11111111	254	254

Continued

T A B L E   4 . 2

*Subnetting in Class A, B, and
C Networks (continued)*

CLASS C NETWORKS SUBNET MASK	BINARY MASK IN SECOND OCTET	NUMBER OF SUBNETS AVAILABLE	NUMBER OF HOST ADDRESSES AVAILABLE
255.255.255.0 (default mask)	00000000	0	254
255.255.255.128	10000000	0	Not valid, see the preceding note
255.255.255.192	11000000	2	62
255.255.255.224	11100000	6	30
255.255.255.240	11110000	14	14
255.255.255.248	11111000	30	6
255.255.255.252	11111100	62	2
255.255.255.254	11111110	(Not valid, host address can never be 0 or 1.)	
255.255.255.255	11111111	Host addresses 0 and 1 are not valid.	

In Table 4.2 for the Class C networks, you can see that the mask 255.255.255.252 is valid, but it should rarely be used because it is very inefficient — it only contains two hosts in each of 62 subnets. Likewise, the masks 255.255.255.252 and 255.255.255.240 would rarely be used. In a class C network address, the masks 255.255.255.192 and 255.255.255.224 are most common but result in the loss of many host addresses.

Subnetting enables you to design your internetwork to suit organizational requirements as well as segment network traffic. The subnetting scheme appropriate for each organization depends on the size of the organization; the number of campus locations; the number of buildings, floors, departments, and workgroups; and the total number of hosts, users, router interfaces, and shared resources. It is very important to give careful attention to this decision, for once deployment has begun, changing course can be costly and time-consuming.

You may also need to subnet your network address to accommodate the rule about assigning hosts to separate subnets when they are separated by routers. This subject is discussed later in this chapter, in the section entitled "Designing an IP Internetwork."

Classless and Classful Addressing

Class A, B, and C network addresses are considered *classful* addresses. The Internet's increasing popularity in the past few years has caused a logistical problem in assigning classful network addresses. When the classes were developed, today's conditions were not anticipated. Classful addressing is accompanied by two problems: inefficient network address assignment and wasted host addresses lost due to subnetting rules. IETF developed *classless* addressing for better efficiency in assigning Internet network addresses and to eliminate addresses lost to inefficient subnetting rules.

CHECKLIST

The term *classful* refers to class A, B, and C network numbers. The Internet now issues *classless* numbers that are not class A, B, or C— they fall somewhere in between classes.

A large gap exists between the number of host addresses supported in each class — a class C address has 254 potential host addresses, a class B address has 65,534 potential host addresses, and a class A address has 16,777,214 potential host addresses. Many organizations that apply for Internet addresses require support for a number of host addresses that falls between classes.

Classless network addresses are assigned in a manner that provides an intermediate number of host addresses. If your organization requires less than 254 host addresses, you will receive a single class C address. If you require more than a few class C addresses, you will probably receive a classless network address that you can then subnet and distribute throughout your organization. These network addresses are equivalent to blocks of eight class C addresses, each block supporting up to 2,032 host addresses. Classless network addresses do not just handle one block of eight class C addresses but can be assigned for blocks of any multiple of eight class C or class B addresses. Each block is treated as one network address.

Classless addressing not only supports greater flexibility in Internet address assignment but also features relaxed rules for subnet addressing. Because certain subnet masks are invalid in classful addressing, organizations require additional network addresses to compensate for host addresses that are lost to subnetting. Classless addressing significantly reduces this problem, making subnetting and host assignment more efficient. This mitigates the address depletion problem and extends address assignments for another few years.

Classless addressing eliminates wasted subnet and host addresses lost because of subnetting rules. When routing protocols and routers are used that support classless addressing, valid subnet addresses can consist of all 1's and/or all 0's. As discussed earlier in this chapter, classful addressing prohibits using the mask 128 in any octet. When using the mask 192, two of four potential subnets and associated host addresses are invalid. Classless addressing eliminates this inefficiency by restoring these masks as valid.

The following are just two examples of subnet and host addresses that are invalid in classful addressing but can be used in classless addressing:

▸ *Subnetting a class B network address with the mask 255.255.128.0* — In classful addressing, this subnet mask is not valid. In this mask, the first bit in the third octet is marked as subnet address space. Only the numbers 0 and 1 are available, and both are invalid because a subnet mask that consists of all binary 1's or 0's cannot be used in classful addressing. That this mask is valid in classless addressing makes two more subnets available — each containing 124 host addresses.

▸ *Subnetting a class B network address with the mask 255.255.192.0* — This subnet mask divides a class B network address into four subnets. In this mask, the first two bits of the third octet are marked as part of the subnet mask. The third octet's first two bits can be 00, 01, 10, or 11. In classful addressing, 00 and 11 are invalid, so two subnets are lost along with 62 host addresses in each of those subnets. In classful addressing these two subnets and their host addresses are valid.

These are only a couple of examples of relaxed subnetting rules. Table 4.3 lists subnet masks and the number of subnets available in classful versus classless addressing.

	CLASS	MASK	SUBNETS AVAILABLE IN CLASSFUL	SUBNETS AVAILABLE IN CLASSLESS
T A B L E 4.3 *Subnets Available for Classful versus Classless Networks*	A	255.128.0.0	2	invalid
	A	255.192.0.0	4	2
	B	255.255.128.0	2	invalid
	B	255.255.192.0	4	2
	C	255.255.255.128	2	invalid

In very large organizations, these changes can restore thousands of subnet and host addresses that were previously invalid. The impact that classless addressing has on the Internet's total available addressing potential is quite significant.

NOTE

Using all 1's or all 0's in the host address space is never supported under any conditions. A host address of 0 identifies the subnet, and an IP datagram sent to host address 255 (decimal) is a broadcast. Classless addressing cannot change this basic mechanism, but it can make subnet mask values of 0 and 255 available, thereby increasing the number of subnet addresses available when subnetting a class A or B network address.

Your ability to implement classless addressing in your network depends upon three factors:

▸ Assignment of a classless network address block (if connecting to the Internet)

▸ Using a routing protocol that supports classless addressing

▸ Using routers that support classless addressing

When implementing an independent TCP/IP network (not connected to the Internet), you can consider your network to be classful or classless, and you can subnet almost any number of bits you choose. However, it is recommended that organizations adhere to the private network addressing guidelines defined in RFC 1918. When connecting your network to the Internet, you must apply for network address assignments so that your intranet will not conflict with addresses used in other organizations.

Supernetting

Establishing classless network addresses in routers is known as *supernetting*. Because loads on the Internet's backbone have increased dramatically in the past few years, supernetting is very important in order to maintain optimal performance. Classless Inter-Domain Routing (CIDR) records are used in Internet gateway routers to recognize classless network addresses. CIDR reduces the number of route entries in these routers, consolidating eight entries (or multiples of eight) into one routing table listing. CIDR reduces the size of routing tables in Internet backbone routers, reducing latency and improving efficiency. For example, an organization that had eight class C network addresses would require eight routing table listings. CIDR allows those eight class C network addresses to be reduced to one network address listing.

Fragmented network addresses have caused considerable routing inefficiency in the Internet. IETF has asked organizations that have been assigned nonsequential class C addresses to turn them in return for a supernetted block of classless network addresses. This is an especially big problem in the 192 range — the first class C address value to be handed out. Many organizations have received additional network address assignments at different times. In this range we find addresses that are spread all over the world, and in many cases organizations in a geographical location will have several class C addresses that are noncontiguous, which is exceptionally inefficient. Assigning contiguous blocks of addresses to a single organization can reduce route complexity and restore better efficiency.

Supernetting affords significant benefits to private TCP/IP internetworks as well as the Internet. Supernetting can be applied in private internetworks where backbones connect autonomous systems.

NOTE

Refer to your router documentation for supernetting support. This feature requires a routing protocol that supports CIDR and classless addressing. You typically have to configure your router to support classless addressing, and enter CIDR configuration data. RIP, which is the most common routing protocol in use, does not support these features.

Designing an IP Internetwork

Each IP subnet must be correlated to a single router port—no exceptions can be allowed. In other words, each router port must be assigned a unique IP subnet address. An optional configuration referred to as *secondary IP addressing* permits assigning multiple IP subnet addresses to a single router port. To make a routing decision, IP routers only read the network and subnet portion of the IP address in an IP packet (as designated by the mask). Figure 4.3 shows six network segments connected by two routers. Notice in this illustration that different subnet addresses have been assigned to each network segment including a network address for the WAN.

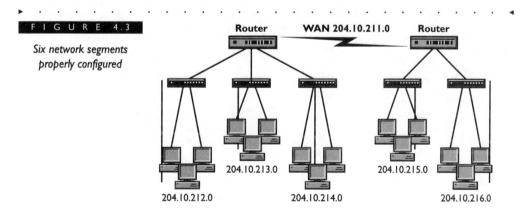

FIGURE 4.3

*Six network segments
properly configured*

More than one subnet can be attached to a single router port as shown in Figure 4.4 (secondary IP addressing). This type of configuration is not recommended because it is inefficient, but it is allowable. In the intranet depicted in Figure 4.4, the router must handle traffic between the subnets, even though they are both physically located on the same network segment. This increases the router's load and doubles network traffic on that network segment.

▶ . . . . ◀

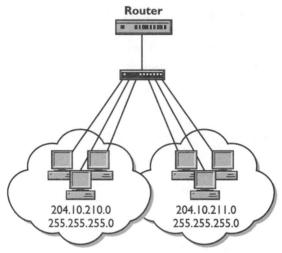

F I G U R E   4.4

Two subnets connected to a single router port will work, but such a configuration is not recommended.

204.10.210.0
255.255.255.0

204.10.211.0
255.255.255.0

A subnet may not span more than one router port. Figure 4.5 shows an invalid configuration: The router cannot determine which port should be the destination for a node in subnet 204.10.210.0. This configuration will cause router protocol errors.

▶ . . . . ◀

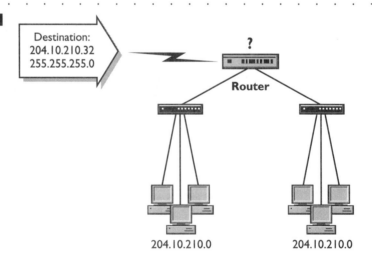

F I G U R E   4.5

The router cannot determine which port contains the destination host.

Destination:
204.10.210.32
255.255.255.0

204.10.210.0

204.10.210.0

TCP/IP Protocols

This section discusses the TCP/IP protocol stack and individual protocols used by Novell. Detail in this section is sufficient to provide the basics of integrating and troubleshooting TCP/IP. For a far more detailed discussion of this topic, see *Novell's Guide to NetWare 5 and TCP/IP*, by Drew Haywood (IDG Books Worldwide). You will find much more by way of detail, background, and descriptions than can be devoted to this topic in this book.

You can reference the official Internet RFCs at InterNIC's site at `http://www.internic.net`.

A couple of very good indexes for searching RFCs and related material are:

▶ `http://www.cis.ohio-state.edu/hypertext/information/rfc.html` (Ohio State University)

▶ `http://www.nexor.com/public/rfc/index/rfc.html` (Nexor Corporation)

The protocols described in this section are part of the TCP/IP protocol stack and are used with NetWare.

This section discusses protocols employed in the TCP/IP protocol stack, IP-related routing protocols, and IP-related services. Use this section to understand the mechanics at work in a NetWare pure IP network. You may need to refer to this chapter when using later chapters for configuration and troubleshooting. As you learn about these protocols, you will become better prepared to understand how to manage and maintain your IP-based network.

Internet Protocol

Internet Protocol (IP) is a basic mechanism for delivering packets of data from end to end, in a very similar manner to IPX. All higher-layer protocols in this stack rely on IP for delivery. Think of IP as like a mailing envelope — all other higher-layer packets are encapsulated into IP for delivery, much as you would put correspondence into an envelope, address it, and send it.

Protocol Characteristics

This protocol is a *connectionless* or *datagram* protocol, which means that it uses one-way communications — no replies are required. Packets are simply addressed and sent — much like mailing a letter.

IP datagrams are fragmented when forwarded over networks that cannot accommodate the packet size as configured. For example, Ethernet can accommodate a 1,518-byte packet size, but ARCnet uses a 512-byte packet size. Each packet originating on an Ethernet LAN would have to be fragmented into three packets for delivery over an ARCnet LAN. Fortunately, Token Ring, FDDI, and other common LAN and WAN technologies can accommodate larger packet sizes, so fragmentation is rarely required.

The current version of IP (IP v.4) supports a hierarchical 32-bit addressing scheme that is used to identify the network, subnet, and host address. By comparison, IPX supports a 32-bit + 48-bit addressing scheme in which the 32-bit portion identifies the IPX network and the 48-bit portion identifies the node (host). The 48-bit host address is based on each station's MAC address, which is interoperable between many vendors' products. An IP address identifies the network layer address of the recipient, as well as the network and subnet (logical network) on which it resides. Routers process the IP address and its mask to discover the subnet where the destination host resides and the paths available to deliver it. Address Resolution Protocol (ARP) is used to obtain the MAC or physical address for the MAC layer frame.

IP addressing is more complex than IPX addressing. The address is entirely logical, so another protocol (ARP) is required to locate the physical node address. By contrast, the IPX address contains the physical node (also called *host* or *station*) address and is therefore more efficient. This also implies that IPX supports a much larger address space than does IP version 4.

The Time to Live (TTL) field specifies how long, in seconds, a datagram is allowed to remain in the internetwork. Routers and hosts that process a datagram must decrement the TTL field value and remove the datagram from the network when the TTL has expired. This field can also be set through an API, allowing software, routers, and other network handlers to limit the distance the packet can travel.

With Routing Information Protocol (RIP), IP and IPX datagrams are limited to traversing no more than 15 hops. The sixteenth router hop is considered infinity or unreachable. This field can also be set through an API, allowing software, routers, and other network handlers to limit the distance the packet can travel.

The Type of Service field provides a mechanism for establishing a quality of service. Precedence can be established. This field allows this protocol to tolerate long delays where needed.

IP headers are designed for 32-bit computing. The header, some fields, and smaller groups of fields must end on 32-bit boundaries. Padding must be added to accommodate this need where required.

Packet Header Description

The IP packet header is uncomplicated. See Appendix C, "Protocol Reference Guide." You will find IP packet header details and descriptions in the table entitled "IP Packet Header Fields."

You will also find the "Protocol Reference Guide" on the CD that accompanies this book. You will find this comprehensive guide indispensable if you analyze protocols on a NetWare network.

NOTE

Protocol Function

IP has many functions that are not available in IPX. Higher-level protocols such as TCP, UDP, and ICMP are encapsulated in an IP packet for delivery. The IP protocol performs the following functions:

1. A checksum is calculated and compared against the value in the Checksum field.

2. Each IP header is addressed with the source and destination addresses, which identify the subnet and node of the ultimate source and destination.

3. If the destination subnet is the same as the source, the packet is sent to the local subnet for delivery.

4. If the destination is on a remote subnet, the frame is sent to the physical address of an internetwork router (also called a *default gateway* — or *default router*). The IP address of at least one default router must be provided to the IP protocol stack installed on each host. This information may be entered statically on each host or provided dynamically via DHCP. The router then forwards the IP packet to the appropriate intermediate subnet for delivery to the router that is connected to the destination subnet (as determined by routing information exchanged between routers).

5. Each time the packet traverses a router, the Time to Live field is decremented by one. If the value in this field equals 0, the packet is removed from the network ("killed," eliminating loops).

Other field headers are provided for specialized purposes and are used by some routers, the next-higher layer of protocol, and applications. Some of the fields are optional and may not contain any data.

Transport Control Protocol

Transport Control Protocol (TCP) is relatively complex in comparison to the protocols previously discussed. This protocol has many functions and options. TCP establishes communications between hosts, handles data transfers, and acknowledges delivery.

Source and destination *ports* identify the type of request or reply within a host. The port acts as a "trap door" to funnel traffic to the appropriate destination. The destination port number forwards the request to a specific process or application. Port numbers are standardized for FTP, Telnet, SNMP, HTTP, and so on, whereas custom numbers (above 1000) can be assigned to applications. The source port identifies the sending process, which in turn is used to direct the reply appropriately. For a listing of TCP port numbers, see the "Common TCP Port Numbers" table in the TCP "Protocol Reference Guide" on the CD that accompanies this book.

Protocol Characteristics

As a connection-oriented protocol, TCP establishes reliable two-way communications. Reliable delivery is required for at least one level in network communications, or network errors will cause serious problems. Each request must receive an acknowledgment. However, several requests are grouped into "windows," which are acknowledged with a single request. The size and marker for the window moves as acknowledgments are received, making the window flexible as network conditions change.

TCP packets are sized by the operating system regardless of packet size accommodated by the physical network. TCP packets are segmented to fit in IP packets, which are sized according to the maximum frame size supported by the physical network and reassembled at the receiving end. This differs from IPX networking, in which NCP negotiates a packet size that fits the IPX packet, which in turn fits the maximum packet size for the physical network. This is also in addition to the fragmentation and reassembly of the data to be transferred. This protocol is well suited for large internetworks with significant delays and multiple routes. In larger networks (for example, the Internet) it is possible that IP packets will travel over different routes, arriving out of order. The sequence number in the TCP header allows the packets to be reassembled into the correct order.

The Flag field in the header enables limited quality of service, permitting packets marked as urgent to be processed ahead of less urgent packets. The Options field can be used to designate a specific route or other information available to developers via APIs. To be useful, all internetworking devices end to end across the network must support this feature.

Packet Header Description

TCP headers are designed for 32-bit computing. The header, some fields, and smaller groups of fields must end on 32-bit boundaries. Padding must be added to accommodate this need where required. For details refer to the "TCP Packet Header Fields" table in the "Protocol Reference Guide" on the CD that accompanies this book. You will also find the "TCP Flag Values" table in that same document.

Pseudo-Header

A TCP pseudo-header precedes each TCP packet that has been segmented for delivery in multiple IP datagrams. The pseudo-header contains five fields (12 octets) that provide IP addressing in case the TCP segments arrive out of sequence.

Refer to the "Pseudo-Header Fields" table in the "Protocol Reference Guide" for a listing of the fields and their functions.

Protocol Dialog

TCP establishes a miniconnection for each data transfer with an OPEN request, a socket is opened, a port number is assigned for the connection, and the connection information is returned. Once this process has occurred, a data stream can be sent to the port.

Each TCP protocol data unit transferred between two machines is called a *segment*. Each data stream to be transferred, such as a data file, is segmented for delivery. TCP segments may contain connection establishment information, data, acknowledgments, and window size advertisements. Hosts at both ends of a connection establish a maximum segment size during connection establishment. TCP uses the Options field to negotiate a maximum segment size between two hosts — each TCP host advertises its maximum acceptable segment size. Protocol stack parameter settings involve the Maximum Segment Size (MSS) & Maximum Transmission Unit (MTU), respectively.

Each segment is preceded by a TCP header containing the port number for the source and destination, and much overhead information for maintaining segmentation, sequencing, windowing, and acknowledgment.

When a TCP packet is to be fragmented for delivery in multiple IP packets, a pseudo-header is added which controls the fragmentation — reassembly at the IP — TCP level and prevents lost TCP segments.

TCP's *sliding window* allows multiple segments to be outstanding at any given time, making this a full-duplex protocol — data can flow in both directions at the same time. The acknowledgments cause the window to "slide" as the segments are returned, changing the number of segments in a window and moving the window accordingly. The sliding window automatically adjusts to network conditions and delay characteristics, which are constantly changing on a large internetwork.

As shown in Figure 4.6, for example, the first position for the window include segments 1–8, and an acknowledgment is returned for 1–5; then the window slides to 6–10, and an acknowledgment comes back for 6–9; then the window slides again, to 10–14.

The TCP connection is used only for the duration of data stream transmission. When a data stream has been received and acknowledged in its entirety, the connection is taken down. This makes TCP an ideal protocol for the Internet, where connections can be intermittent. By reducing the connection time to very short cycles, TCP makes windowing and acknowledgment simpler than it would be with the overhead required to maintain a virtual connection over such a complex network with long and variable delays.

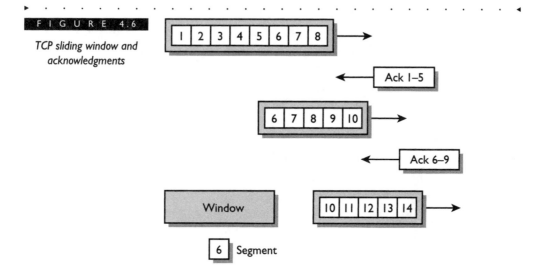

FIGURE 4.6

TCP sliding window and acknowledgments

User Datagram Protocol

User Datagram Protocol (UDP) substitutes for TCP when acknowledgments are not required. Broadcasts, SNMP traps, and NFS packets, among other forms of protocol traffic, are transported by UDP. For these protocols, setting up and destroying connections constitutes excessive processing with little or no benefit.

In most cases UDP uses the same port numbers as TCP, and therefore it has the same basic functionality—to deliver a higher-layer packet without TCP's associated overhead. The UDP header has only has four header fields, just enough to transport data over IP.

UDP uses a checksum to ensure accurate delivery in lieu of an acknowledgment. When the packet arrives, the checksum is recalculated and checked against the value in the header. If the two checksums do not agree, a negative acknowledgment is sent back, which elicits a retransmission.

Protocol Characteristics

UDP is connectionless; no acknowledgments are used. Packet integrity is guaranteed by a checksum. If the checksum at the receiving end is incorrect, a negative acknowledgment (NACK) is returned requesting retransmission of data.

UDP cuts down network traffic. Because it is not acknowledged, it is used to transport broadcast traffic, such as NetBIOS and ARP.

Packet Header Description

The UDP packet header has just four fields: source port, destination port, packet length, and checksum. The ports have the same (or similar) port numbers and functions as for TCP. Refer to the "UDP Packet Header Fields" table in the "Protocol Reference Guide" for descriptions. You will find this guide on the CD that accompanies this book.

Pseudo-Header

A UDP pseudo-header precedes each UDP packet that has been segmented for delivery in multiple IP datagrams. The pseudo-header contains five fields that provide IP addressing in case the UDP segments arrive out of sequence.

The UPD pseudo-header has the same fields and functions as the TCP pseudo-header. See the previous section on TCP for details of this header.

Address Resolution Protocol

IP addresses ultimately map to physical addresses of NICs and WAN network cards. However, nothing in IP version 4 provides addressing information for the frame, which will carry the IP packet. In an IP network, Address Resolution Protocol (ARP) is used to locate the physical node to address the LAN frame. When an IP datagram is sent, ARP is used to find the next delivery point. When an IP datagram arrives at its destination network, an ARP request will query for the physical address so that IP can finalize delivery.

Protocol Characteristics

ARP is an acknowledged broadcast. The broadcasts elicits a response from the target host. ARP is used by hosts and routers. Because most hosts and routers cache ARP information, this protocol does not burden the network with excessive broadcast traffic.

Packet Header Description

The ARP packet header identifies the type of LAN (Ethernet, Token Ring, and so on), the protocols (IP), an operation code, the source and destination hardware addresses (physical or MAC address), the source and destination IP addresses, and a function code. The primary operation and function codes are used to request and respond and to identify the hardware type and addressing. Refer to the "ARP Packet Header Fields" and related tables found within the "Protocol Reference Guide" on the CD that accompanies this book.

Protocol Dialog

ARP provides mapping between logical IP addresses and physical addresses through ARP broadcasts. ARP is a simple protocol that broadcasts on a network requesting the physical address for a given destination IP address. If a host's IP address matches the broadcast request, a response is sent providing the physical address of the destination host.

Local ARP Requests and the ARP Cache   If the destination host is on the same subnet, a normal ARP request is broadcast on the local subnet. Before the ARP request is broadcast, however, the local workstation checks its ARP cache. Every time an address is resolved, the IP and physical addresses are stored locally for a limited period of time — which varies according to TCP/IP software used in the workstation. If an entry is found in local cache, the address is resolved and an ARP broadcast is not required.

The ARP cache timeout period for Windows 95 and Windows NT hosts is set at 10 minutes. Each time an entry is used, it is time-stamped. When the local ARP cache table is full, the entries are purged on a first-in-first-out basis according to their time stamps. You can modify the ARPCacheLife parameter in a Windows 95 or NT Registry. You can also manually enter permanent ARP entries in a workstation's local ARP cache table to reduce the need for ARP broadcasts.

Locating Physical Addresses on Remote Subnets   ARP is only used to resolve addresses on local subnets — routers do not forward ARP broadcasts. When an IP datagram is addressed to a host on the same subnet (netid), an ARP query is broadcast on the local network segment.

When the IP datagram must be routed, the IP address of the default gateway (router) becomes the intermediate path that the packet will take to arrive at its destination. In this case, ARP queries the gateway's physical address on the local network segment and uses it to physically address the frame to the gateway. Routers are configured with the netids, masks, and physical addresses for router ports. Different routing protocols handle the process of forwarding the IP packet according to different rules and procedures. However, routers are normally configured with other routers' physical port addresses for delivery on the next link along the preferred path. Once the destination network is reached, the router uses ARP to query the destination network for the destination host's physical address. As discussed in Chapter 2, "Internetworking Basics," routers communicate with one another to maintain routing tables that contain path information for all subnets.

Internet Control Message Protocol

IP datagram service is connectionless and therefore does not provide reliable delivery. If an IP datagram does not reach its destination, IP has no mechanism to recover. Internet Control Message Protocol (ICMP) notifies the sender with an error code when an IP datagram is not deliverable. Normally, reliable delivery is handled by TCP; however, if another higher-layer protocol is used, there is no reliable delivery. Even when TCP is used, it is helpful to receive ICMP notifications. ICMP messages provide an indication of why the datagram never reached its destination.

ICMP messages are quite important to monitor — they generally provide clues to the reason why network communications fail. Monitoring ICMP is a simple task; only a few function codes are used. ICMP packet header format is defined in the "Protocol Reference Guide" on the CD that accompanies this book. Look for the "ICMP Packet Header Fields" table and related information.

TIP   **If you have access to a protocol analyzer, watching for ICMP traffic is your best bet in quickly locating problems. For the most part, you will not see ICMP traffic unless a problem exists, and decoding ICMP will point you to the problem and explain the type of problem.**

Routing Protocols

Several routing protocols are used in TCP/IP networks. Because each protocol works differently, it is almost impossible to say how a router is going to work, or how it is to be configured. Much of that information depends upon the routing protocol the router uses. In some cases, you have a choice of several routing protocols.

Interior and External Routing Protocols

Routing protocols that are used internally within an organization are called *internal* routing protocols. The internal network is sometimes referred to as an *autonomous system* or *domain*. When autonomous systems are linked together, an *exterior* routing protocol is used. Figure 4.7 illustrates the relationship between an interior routing protocol, an exterior routing protocol, gateways, and autonomous systems.

CHECKLIST

An *internal* routing protocol is used within a private network or campus. The private network is called an *autonomous system*. An *external* routing protocol connects autonomous systems, usually over a WAN. The external protocol limits the amount of routing information that must be propagated over WANs and forwarded to other autonomous systems.

FIGURE 4.7

Interior routing protocols, exterior routing protocols, gateways, and autonomous systems

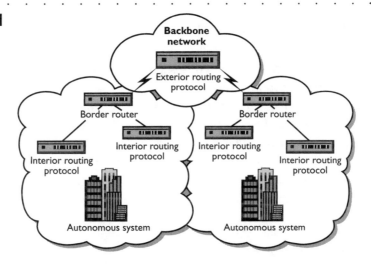

The router that connects one autonomous system to another autonomous system must use both routing protocols; it is called a *gateway*, or sometimes it is called a *border router*. Normally the term *gateway* refers to a device that uses one protocol on one side and another protocol on the other. In this case, indeed the gateway uses two different routing protocols. From another perspective, the gateway is a router that only supports one network protocol—IP.

A *gateway* is a device that converts protocols. In one respect, the gateway router filters and forwards the same protocol on both sides: IP. However, the router is called a gateway because it translates between internal and external routing protocols.

Several interior routing protocols have been developed to work with TCP/IP: Router Information Protocol (RIP), Open Shortest Path First (OSPF), and Cisco's Interior Gateway Routing Protocol (IGRP) or Enhanced IGRP (EIGRP). Several exterior routing protocols are also available: Exterior Gateway Protocol (EGP) and Border Gateway Protocol (BGP version 4). An exterior gateway protocol is not required when only one connection exists between autonomous systems. In such cases the border routers may be configured to use static route/default route. The most common configurations use static route/default route or BGP-4.

Router Information Protocol and RIP II

Router Information Protocol (RIP) for IP is similar to Novell's RIP, which was discussed in Chapter 3, but this is a different RIP protocol, used for routing IP. RIP is the simplest routing protocol of all, and by far the most common. RIP's favorable aspects are that it is simple and easy to configure. RIP suffers from the same deficiencies as Novell's RIP: It is broadcast-based, which in a large intranet may require excessive router processing power. Several other limitations restrict the size of the network, the ability to influence path selection, slow convergence, and the formation of looped paths. With all those deficiencies, it is still the most popular routing protocol because it is the simplest to set up and maintain.

Protocol Characteristics

RIP is a *distance vector* routing protocol, meaning that paths are chosen on a simple hop-count metric, which is considered to be the total cost for each path. In RIP, cost is simply the total number of router hops the path contains. The router administrator can substitute a value for each link within a path to influence path selection. RIP's metric can range from 1 to 15. A path with a lower metric is considered the lower-cost or best path.

RIP comes in two flavors: RIP I and RIP II. RIP I is an earlier implementation that does not support variable-length subnetting, classless addressing, supernetting (CIDR), or the use of subnet addresses 0 or 1. RIP II supports these options, plus password protection in router configuration and multicasting. Multicasting allows a single datagram to be transmitted to a group of hosts. The IP class D address of 224.0.0.9 is assigned for multicasts to RIP II routers.

The procedure used to discover routes is known as *route convergence*. This process involves propagation and processing the information into routing tables. RIP routers use the following method to discover path and metric information:

1. Every 30 seconds, each router broadcasts its entire routing table.

2. Each time a RIP broadcast is received, the router updates its routing table.

3. At the next 30-second broadcast cycle, the updated routing table is broadcast to all network segments, and incoming routes are incremented by one for all network segments. The source network segment is labeled as one hop.

RIP's route convergence process causes path information to ripple over the internetwork, propagating from router to router. Path information received from one network segment is relayed to routers on other network segments, then relayed again by the next router, and so on. Approximately 30 seconds separates every relay cycle. When an update is received, the router must incorporate the change into its routing table and then include the change in its next broadcast. In a large network with several hops, changes in path information may take several minutes to reach the furthest ends of the network.

The router administrator has three options to reduces loops from occurring:

- Split horizons

- Triggered updates

- Poison reverse

Split horizons prevent a router from broadcasting information received from a network back to the same network from which it came. Due to the periodic broadcast cycle, however, invalid path information continues to be disseminated even after the path has gone down. The propagation delay causes confusion in routing tables, and broadcast of erroneous path information at times. Eventually the path information will be resolved, but in the meantime, loops can occur that can cripple network performance.

Triggered updates are sent immediately when a change occurs instead of waiting for the next broadcast cycle. Triggered updates reduce but do not eliminate the time it takes for changes to ripple over the internetwork, because RIP requires routers to retain a route entry for 180 seconds after that route was last advertised. The possibility that loops will occur is also reduced but not eliminated. However, the cure can exceed the illness. Triggered updates can cause excessive broadcast traffic, which is also a concern in busy networks.

Poison reverse is a technique used to reduce convergence delay. When a router advertises a lost route or connection, that router retains the bad entry for several update periods and changes the metric to 16—which is infinity and labels the path as unreachable. Poison reverse is effective at accelerating the time required to converge and eliminates the possibility of looping, but it increases the number of entries in the routing tables. This normally is not a significant problem in smaller internetworks, but poison reverse limits internetwork scalability, takes substantial bandwidth, and can increase convergence delay in larger internetworks.

Path Selection Limitations

Another problem for RIP is how to handle redundant paths. Redundant paths may have the same hop count but may differ significantly in performance; RIP, however, does not take this fact into consideration. For example, one path may be over a T-1 line (1.544Mbps) while another is over a fractional T-1 (64Kbps). RIP would identify both paths with the same number of hops—nothing in this protocol differentiates between the two by default. However, the system administrator can assign higher costs to a link in an attempt to compensate for this shortcoming. When assigning higher costs, you limit the diameter of the autonomous system by reducing the potential number of hops available. The maximum number of router hops is reduced each time the hop metric is artificially increased on a router port.

Each time RIP broadcasts are received, each router must update its tables; it must then broadcast its routing table on the next broadcast cycle. In networks with a lot of routers and network segments, this places a heavy load on the router. RIP routers are often noticeably burdened by this load, causing delays in routing traffic.

Another problem is the limited nature of the metrics. Because the metric value is limited to 15, any routes that contain more than 15 hops are out of reach. This limitation limits internetwork scalability. The maximum number of hops over routers is 15. When a packet has reached a metric of 16, the packet is removed from the network.

Path Information Stored in Routing Tables

RIP routing tables include one entry for each potential path containing the following information:

- ▸ IP address

- ▸ The metric for the path

- ▸ The host name or IP address of the next router to reach the destination

- ▸ A flag indicating the last update to this record

- ▸ Timers

Gateway Address

Each workstation must be configured with the *default gateway address,* which is the IP address of the router NIC connected to its network segment. RIP routers have no provision for discovering this address automatically. Workstations that are not configured with the default gateway address on their local network segment will not be able to send data over the router. Some vendors refer to the default gateway as the *default router,* or merely the *gateway.* DHCP can be configured to automatically provide this information.

Open Shortest Path First

Open Shortest Path First (OSPF) was developed to address RIP's numerous shortcomings — it is designed to reduce broadcasts and to reduce the bandwidth required for servicing the network. In many ways it is far superior and more robust than RIP. It is also more complex and makes router configuration more difficult.

This design reduces both broadcast traffic and router processing time. Additionally, OSPF propagates path changes immediately, preventing loops. Is there more? You bet! OSPF is also more programmable. The system administrator has quite a bit of flexibility in assigning values for links that are used to calculate routing metrics, valid link values ranging from 1 to 65,535. This provides more logic and control over path selection and can reduce situations in which two paths end up with the same total cost.

OSPF supports variable-length subnet masks — you can subnet network addresses to smaller units as discussed earlier in this chapter. OSPF supports CIDR and can also use the first bit in the second or third octet of an IPv4 address. This capability provides capacity for more subnets and hosts when subnetting a class A or B address.

OSPF routers can also balance loads over multiple paths. If two paths have the same total cost, traffic is spread equally over them. This feature is automatic and enables automatic fail-over should a path go down.

In large networks, OSPF routers can be grouped into areas, restricting the amount of routing information required in each area. OSPF routers can also be configured into border routers, where they can hand off to another routing protocol. This allows OSPF to interface with RIP, IGRP, BGP, and just about any other routing protocol.

For many reasons, OSPF is an outstanding routing protocol that is efficient, scales up to very large internetworks, and is flexible in many ways. OSPF is newer than RIP and a bit more difficult to set up and manage, but it has become the top protocol used in the majority of routers — except between Cisco routers, where their own protocol — IGRP — is still frequently used. Cisco routers also support OSPF.

OSPF is more complex than RIP, with more configuration options and metric adjustments. This section provides a general overview. If you need to troubleshoot an OSPF internetwork, most routers have their own monitoring and diagnostic software that will help you locate problems. Most newer routers send RMON alerts — discussed later in this chapter in the "Simple Network Management Protocol" section — which notifies system administrators when problems occur.

Protocol Characteristics

OSPF is a *link-state* routing protocol — as opposed to distance vector routing protocol such as RIP. Link-state routing protocols allow each router to maintain a comprehensive view of all paths in the internetwork. In comparison, RIP routers only describe routes in relation to adjacent network segments and routers to which they are connected.

Link-state protocols do not broadcast their routing tables on a periodic basis. Updates are triggered any time a change to a path occurs. Because updates are immediate instead of based on periodic broadcasts, no need arises to protect against loops, and route convergence occurs throughout the network with little or no delay. Broadcasts are used upon initialization, but from then on OSPF uses multicasts to send updates. This reduces broadcast traffic, and all routers forward multicasts, which is not true of broadcasts.

How OSPF Works

During router setup, each link — or network — is assigned a cost value from 1 to 65,535. When routing metrics are calculated, they are based on the sum of costs for links in the path. When assigning link cost values, the router administrator can take into consideration any factors that should affect path selection. This provides extensive flexibility in path selection. During router setup each port is assigned an IP address, and then network addresses and masks are entered for each port.

When the routers are booted, the hello process identifies neighboring computers connected to the same network segment. Routers are then grouped into *adjacencies*. In each adjacency, a *designated router* (DR) is elected that is responsible for sending and receiving updates and then distributing them to the other routers in the adjacency.

During the hello process, each router considers itself to be the root of an internetwork and maps all paths in the internetwork. Each potential path is assigned a total cost based on the combined cost of links in the path. When redundant paths are present, the lower-cost path is selected and higher-cost paths are discarded. Loads are balanced equally over redundant paths that have equal costs.

OSPF updates are very efficient and contain only routing information that is pertinent to the receiver. When a router detects a path change, applicable updates are sent to adjacent DRs. Only changes are sent, not full routing tables as is the case in RIP. Changes that do not affect other adjacencies are not sent — changes are multicasts, which are directed only to routers. In RIP, erroneous routing information is propagated throughout the internetwork, but not so for OSPF — each router only has routing information obtained from routers that were involved in the change first hand. Once a DR updates its routing table, it synchronizes other routers in the adjacency. When changes occur, updates are sent out immediately, and directly to affected routers. This leaves no time gaps for erroneous information to exist, alleviating the problem of loops appearing.

Consider Figure 4.8. Path A may have one router and two networks (links) between the source router and the destination router, whereas path B has no router and just one network. Each network is assigned a cost value: Path A includes two links and two link costs, which are added to produce one total cost metric. Path B has only one link and one link cost, which adds up to one total cost.

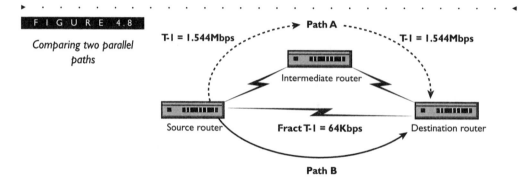

FIGURE 4.8

Comparing two parallel paths

Path A

T-1 = 1.544Mbps   T-1 = 1.544Mbps

Intermediate router

Source router   Fract T-1 = 64Kbps   Destination router

Path B

The metrics for each path are compared to determine the least-cost path. Each link can be assigned a value from 1 to 65,535 for a wide range of costs.

Now consider that path A might consist of two T-1s with a 1.544Mbps bandwidth, whereas path B contains a single fractional T-1 with a 64Kbps bandwidth. OSPF enables us to assign different values to the links. In this example a value of 1 might be assigned to each T-1, and a value of 6 might be assigned to the fractional T-1. The metrics would compute as follows:

Path	OSPF	RIP
A	1 + 1 = 2	2
B	6	1

In this example, RIP would choose path B because it has a lower metric, with a hop count of 1. However, OSPF would choose path A because the metric is lower for that path. The link costs for both links in path A are added and compared against the value assigned to the single link in path B. Though there is a hop in path A, it is the better choice. OSPF's programmability enables administrators to factor in many considerations and to fine-tune path selection. RIP's limited programmability limits the administrator's ability to accomplish the same level of path control.

On the other hand, the system administrator may wish to discourage traffic on the T-1s because they are burdened with traffic from competing departments or because their actual costs per month are higher. Assigning different values to each link can compensate for differing bandwidths, causing path selection to vary according to administrative strategies. Router administrators often build formulas or spreadsheets to take many factors into consideration when calculating cost values for links.

This example also points out that OSPF has not taken into consideration the latency factor that may be introduced by the intermediate router. If the intermediate router becomes congested, excessive delay may cause path A to become slower. Other routing protocols, including IGRP, discussed in the text that follows, take additional factors such as delay into consideration.

Areas

An OSPF internetwork can be partitioned into areas. Each area works like an autonomous system, with connection points between the areas. This reduces the size of the routing tables required in each router and provides less complexity for local routing, with slightly more complexity for interarea routes. This configuration is recommended for networks with many routers and links where most of the traffic stays in the local area.

Area Border Routers (ABRs) are connection points between areas. ABRs form a backbone internetwork of higher-level routers to exchange data between areas. Each router has a complete view of all paths in the area, but when traffic is to go out of the area, it is handed off to an ABR.

Border Gateways

OSPF can also interface with other routing protocols such as RIP and BGP. A router that connects two autonomous systems is called an *autonomous system border router* (ASBR). The ASBR becomes a gateway between the two routing protocols. This makes OSPF even more flexible and compatible with existing systems and with the higher-level protocols discussed in the text that follows.

Interior Gateway Routing Protocol

Interior Gateway Routing Protocol (IGRP) is a distance vector routing protocol used within autonomous systems in Cisco routers. Cisco developed IGRP to replace RIP in autonomous systems before link-state protocols were developed. IGRP has many improvements over RIP and is generally used in Cisco routers rather than RIP or OSPF. Because Cisco has most of the routing market, IGRP is used quite extensively.

Several improvements over RIP make IGRP far more desirable and even make IGRP preferred over OSPF — according to Cisco. This routing protocol features programmable routing metrics that enable the system administrator far more control over routing decisions. The factors about to be discussed are IGRP features.

Programmable Routing Metrics

IGRP takes five factors into consideration when calculating routing metrics. A router administrator can manipulate the following factors:

▶ *Bandwidth* — A value between 1 and 255 is assigned to each link. Values are assigned according to bandwidth. In comparison, RIP is based on hops, and links can be assigned a value of 1–16, where 16 is out of range.

▶ *Delay* — Values of 1–2^{24} power can be assigned for each link, generally based on the amount of time over a link when PINGed. Delay is a significant factor that is overlooked in RIP and OSPF.

▶ *Reliability* — A variable can be assigned to compensate for lack of stability.

▶ *Load* — A variable can be assigned to compensate for expected loads generated by routing and other systems sharing bandwidth.

▶ *User Definable Algorithm* — A "wildcard" algorithm can be defined by the system administrator to account for other factors, such as the actual cost (in dollars) of using a link.

Multipath Routing, Load Balancing, and Automatic Fail-Over

IGRP permits multiple paths and balances loads over them. When metrics for two paths are equal, traffic is balanced over them. When a metric for one path is lower, that path will be used more often, but the alternate path is available and is also used — if a metric for one path is twice as low, the path is used twice as often. When a link fails, traffic is automatically switched over to a less favorable path.

Preventing Loops

IGRP uses a periodic broadcast to update routers, and each router relays updates. This opens a possibility that routers will advertise invalid path information during the time that updated information is disseminated. Hold-downs, split horizons, and poison reverse features can be used to compensate for this possibility. Some or all of these features are also used in various routers that use RIP.

Hold-downs are used to suppress potentially conflicting routing information. When a router receives an update triggered by a downed link, it retains conflicting information received about the affected path until the maximum amount of time necessary for convergence to occur throughout the internetwork. In RIP, both the new information and old information are broadcast, which extends the amount of time the internetwork can contain erroneous information.

Split horizons are used to prevent routing information received from a network from being sent back to the same network. Split horizons are discussed earlier in this chapter in reference to RIP. In IGRP the combination of split horizons and hold-downs further reduces occurrences of loops.

Poison reverse is used when routing loops are suspected. An increase in routing metrics often indicates that a large loop has slipped past the hold-downs and split horizons. In this case, poison reverse route information (as discussed previously in this chapter) is sent to the affected router to force the suspected loop into a hold-down condition.

Timers

IGRP employs a variety of timers and variables containing time intervals:

▸ *Update timers* control the frequency of broadcast updates instead of using a fixed period. The default broadcast period is 90 seconds.

▸ An *invalid timer* is used to declare a route invalid when updates are not received for that route. The default invalid timer is three times the update timer interval.

▸ A *hold-time* timer regulates the period that suspected loop path information is suppressed by the hold-down feature. The default is three times the update timer plus ten seconds.

▸ A *flush timer* regulates the amount of time before a route should be flushed from the routing table if no regular update is received. The default value is seven times the routing update period.

These timers make the internetwork more stable and enable updates to propagate as quickly as possible according to the internetwork's size and complexity.

Enhanced Interior Gateway Routing Protocol

Enhanced Interior Gateway Routing Protocol (EIGRP) uses *Diffusing Update Algorithm* (DUAL), which was developed by SRI International to combine the advantages of distance vector and link-state routing protocols. EIGRP is the standard routing protocol used in all newer Cisco routers; it reduces broadcast traffic and router processing. EIGRP features the following enhancements:

▸ *Fast convergence* — When a failed path is detected, routers check with their neighbors for updated path information.

▸ *Variable-length subnet masks* — You can subnet network addresses to smaller units as discussed earlier in this chapter. EIGRP supports CIDR and can also use the first bit in the second or third octet of an IPv4 address. This provides capacity for more subnets and hosts when you are subnetting a class A or B address.

▸ *Partial bounded updates* — Instead of periodic broadcasts, only changed path information is sent. Updates are bounded to restrict them to affected routers only.

▸ *Multiprotocol network layer support* — EIGRP acts as a border router to support several interior and exterior routing protocols including:

- Novell RIP and SAP

- IP RIP

- OSPF

- BGP and EGP

- Apple RTMP

- IS-IS

EIGRP has many new features and improvements that make it one of the most effective and efficient routing protocols. IGRP and EIGRP are partially responsible for the overwhelming market share that Cisco has accumulated. It is estimated that well over half of all routers in use are Cisco routers.

Exterior Routing Protocols

Exterior routing protocols are used to connect autonomous systems together. Generally an interior routing protocol such as RIP or OSPF is used in the autonomous systems, while one of the exterior routing protocols is used to connect the autonomous systems together.

The classic model of a large intranet consists of two or more campuses and a WAN backbone. Figure 4.9 demonstrates the most common configuration, in which a star backbone is used, hosted by a root router, border routers, and autonomous systems in each campus. Exterior routing protocols are used between the border routers and their root router, whereas an interior routing protocol is used in each campus.

FIGURE 4.9

A classic intranet with three campuses and a star backbone WAN

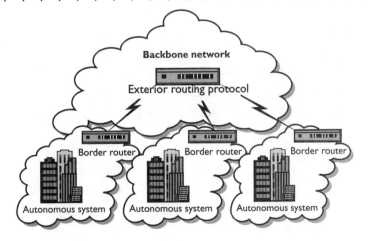

The most common exterior routing protocols are:

▸ Exterior Gateway Protocol

▸ Border Gateway Protocol

Exterior Gateway Protocol

Exterior Gateway Protocol (EGP) was the first common exterior gateway protocol to be used to connect systems to the Internet. EGP connects autonomous systems to one another or to the Internet. EGP is still used in many Internet border routers but has been replaced for backbone internetworks connecting autonomous systems. EGP is a bit outdated and is not used in newer installations. Most Internet border routers have been upgraded to BGP, which was built on EGP but has many improvements.

EGP is considered more of a reachability protocol than a true routing protocol. This fact makes it suitable for an Internet border router but limits its effectiveness for intranets. EGP's major flaw is its tendency to develop loops in a backbone. Several other flaws limit EGP's use as a backbone technology.

Border Gateway Protocol

Border Gateway Protocol (BGP) is a more popular exterior routing protocol that is used to connect autonomous systems to one another and to the Internet. Though BGP was developed from EGP, it is not backward compatible with EGP. Because of its improvements BGP has replaced EGP in most intranets and is used in place of EGP in newer installations. BGP is slowly replacing EGP border routers for connection to the Internet.

You might use BGP to link autonomous systems based on RIP and/or OSPF together over a backbone WAN. Most router vendors and larger organizations prefer to use OSPF in autonomous systems and BGP in the WAN backbone connecting them.

TCP/IP Services

TCP/IP services are applications that use open standards that allow interaction between client and server host computers and their software over TCP (and UDP) protocols. The TCP/IP services discussed in this section are responsible for the birth of open systems networking. To this day industry developers compete on the front of open systems versus proprietary applications and protocols. TCP/IP applications provide open system support for all major operating systems.

Remember that NOS services are separate from TCP/IP-based applications, though they share the same transport services. TCP/IP-based applications interface with TCP port numbers — no login to a host is required. Any security must therefore be provided by the server application. TCP is designed such that access to multiple server modules and perhaps login to a host NOS can be accomplished through a single protocol stack.

The following services are used extensively in TCP/IP networks.

Dynamic Host Configuration Protocol

In a typical TCP/IP network, the system administrator assigns addresses manually. This process is called a *static* address assignment. Dynamic Host Configuration Protocol (DHCP) was designed and standardized to eliminate this labor-intensive task. DHCP addresses are assigned and managed centrally instead of requiring a visit to each client workstation.

NOTE **Some hosts should not use DHCP address assignments. For example, a DHCP server must use a static IP assignment. A DNS server must also have a static address assignment, or DNS queries will be lost. You should consider using static address assignments for all servers and DHCP for clients.**

DHCP Elements

DHCP servers assign IP addresses when workstations boot. DHCP assigns IP addresses from a *pool*, which is a range of addresses configured for the DHCP server. To define or change a pool of addresses, the administrator need only edit the DHCP pool. DHCP pools have *inclusions* and *exclusions*. IP addresses, usually in blocks, are included in the pool, and statically assigned addresses can be excluded, either individually and/or in blocks. NetWare 5's DHCP has a *ping ahead* feature. When this feature is enabled, it pings an IP address before assigning it. This eliminates the possibility of assigning an address that is already in use.

DHCP *leases* addresses. IP address assignments are assigned for a period of time, as defined in the pool. When a lease expires, the old address is reserved for a period of time and then the address is released so that it can be assigned to another client. Under certain circumstances this enables the administrator to extend the number of addresses to more clients than the number of addresses actually available. For example, remote users can dial into the network and receive a DHCP address lease, which will expire when the client disconnects. Internet service providers (ISPs) use this feature to parlay a few IP addresses to cover hundreds of users. The ISP need only have enough IP addresses to service the modems or network connections in use at any given time.

DHCP Service Dialogs

The DHCP client service uses BootP (the Bootstrap Protocol) to request an address assignment when a system boots. The address assignment process is illustrated in Figure 4.10. When the IP packet driver is loaded, a BootP broadcast goes out on the local network segment (request A). One or more DHCP server responds, offering to provide an IP address (reply A). The client then selects an offer and sends a new request addressed to the selected DHCP server (request B). The DHCP server responds, issuing the IP address lease from its pool (reply B).

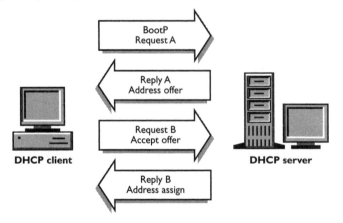

FIGURE 4.10

The DHCP client/server dialog and resulting IP address assignment

BootP
Request A

Reply A
Address offer

Request B
Accept offer

Reply B
Address assign

DHCP client

DHCP server

Recommended Configuration

You can have several DHCP servers on your network, but when employing multiple DHCP servers, you should follow just a few basic guidelines:

1. Have one DHCP server on each network segment. Because BootP requests are broadcasts, routers are often configured to filter broadcasts and will therefore confine them to the local network segment. You can overcome this limitation by enabling BootP and UDP broadcast forwarding in your router, but that may flood your WANs with unwanted broadcasts.

2. When more than one DHCP server is present, be sure that the addresses contained in their pools are mutually exclusive.

3. Be sure to exclude all static IP address assignments. Check all servers, printers, intelligent network devices, and so on before defining a pool. All servers that provide name resolution and address assignment, such as DHCP, DNS, and gateways, must have static IP assignments.

NOTE

NetWare 5's DHCP records are stored within the NDS database. NDS's replication makes a single DHCP server as fault-tolerant as your NDS replication configuration. Some of the factors you would normally consider for DHCP servers can therefore be eliminated when using NetWare 5's DHCP.

Domain Name Service

Host names are often used to access remote hosts. Every time you access a host over TCP/IP, the IP address must be discovered in order to address IP packets. Domain Name Service (DNS) handles name-to-IP address mappings through DNS servers that maintain tables of host names and IP addresses.

DNS is not software requiring user intervention outside of setup and configuration. A DNS server is a software service, and DNS client software is integrated into your TCP/IP client workstation software. Name-to-address resolution can be a simple process that is done on your own network, or it can be conducted over the Internet to access hundreds of thousands of hosts. Once name resolution is accomplished, communications can flow over the TCP/IP protocol stack. Without name resolution, IP addresses would need to be somehow discovered. If IP addresses were to change (as is the case in DHCP), each client would somehow have to renew its link to the new IP addresses. You can address this issue by implementing a Dynamic DNS server to import DHCP address assignments into the DNS database.

Host Names

Host names are assigned to every host in a TCP/IP network. In many cases data is directed to the host name. DNS must look up the name and find the IP address. This is where the IP destination address comes from that is placed in the IP packet header. Without name resolution, we would have to access every host with an IP address.

NetWare Host Names In NetWare networking, computer names are only assigned to servers; the workstation does not require a name. As discussed in Chapter 3, "Novell Protocols and IPX Addressing," no client name resolution is necessary in IPX networks. The server stores the IPX address in its connection table — a name never enters into the formula. In NetWare 5 with TCP/IP each host must have a valid DNS name, which can be resolved by a DNS server. When using NetWare with TCP/IP, you must assign NetWare servers names that conform to the lowest common denominator between NetWare and DNS naming conventions.

Microsoft Host Names In Microsoft networking, the NetBIOS name is the way the host is known to the network. Each computer is assigned a NetBIOS host name; this includes both servers and peer workstations on which the server service — or file and print sharing — is enabled. In NetBIOS over TCP/IP — also known as NBT — the NetBIOS name needs to be resolved to an IP address. This consideration applies to all Windows NT, Windows 95/98, and Windows for Workgroups clients. Windows 3.1 and other DOS clients do not have the server service and therefore do not require host names.

Additional considerations arise in a Windows environment because NetBIOS names and DNS names do not have the same name space requirements. A NetBIOS name is limited to 15 user-defined characters, whereas a DNS name can have as many as 256 characters. Several characters are valid in NetBIOS name space that are not permitted in DNS name space — such as space ( ) and underscore (_) for example.

One of a few methods can be used to resolve NetBIOS names to IP addresses:

▸ NetBIOS broadcasting

▸ Windows Internet Name Service (WINS)

▸ Use of DNS for WINS resolution

▸ Use of DHCP for WINS resolution

▸ The LMHOSTS file

Each one of these methods has some qualifications.

NOTE

Name resolution must be configured properly for Windows 95/98, NT, and Windows for Workgroup clients to work properly in a TCP/IP environment. The following discussion of DNS name resolution can be somewhat different for Windows clients depending upon how they are configured. See Chapter 18, "Network Communications and Protocols," for details on troubleshooting and correcting name resolution problems in Windows clients.

UNIX Host Names   UNIX hosts must be assigned names. UNIX host names conform to DNS naming conventions and should present no problem in DNS.

Printer Host Names   Printers that are used with TCP/IP or Appletalk are assigned host names. The printer name is only significant when access is required using TCP/IP or Appletalk. Printers that are configured as NetWare printers do not use the name; instead, they use the print queue name as the destination for print traffic. Access to NetWare queues is controlled by NetWare bindery or NDS security. NetWare 5 uses Service Location Protocol and/or printer setup to locate the appropriate IP address.

Local DNS Name Resolution

Local name resolution is normally very simple when all hosts are in a single DNS domain. Each host is configured with at least one DNS server address, which directs name resolution requests to that server. Whenever access to a host is required, your client software checks with the DNS server in the domain to find the corresponding IP address.

The system administrator must manually enter host names and corresponding IP address records into the DNS server's tables. A DNS server can run on any platform. If you have intraNetWare or NetWare 5, you can use a NetWare DNS server. A UNIX DNS daemon or Windows NT Server DNS service will provide the same function.

NOTE

Though the previous statement is true in theory, if you are implementing a firewall, check the firewall developer's release notes concerning cross-platform DNS servers. Windows NT Server's built-in DNS server may not respond properly to some firewalls when a reverse lookup is required.

NetWare 5's DNS is preferred for many good reasons. Integrating DNS into NDS provides fault tolerance and reduces the need for primary and secondary name servers for each domain. Novell DNS's logical zones also remove many restrictions implicit in a typical DNS domain configuration.

Name Resolution on the Internet and Larger Intranets

When a large number of hosts are in a single domain, the tables in the DNS servers can become cumbersome, especially within very large internetworks like the Internet. In a large internetwork, a hierarchical DNS system may be employed. In the Internet, for example, DNS servers are arranged hierarchically from local or ISP DNS servers to root DNS servers hosted by first-tier ISPs.

DNS Name Space Hierarchy and Naming DNS names have hierarchical structure that maps to DNS domains within a root. The host is called a *leaf*, which maps to a *domain*, which can be a child of another domain and so on until we reach a *root*. Names are delimited with periods (.). The structure is as follows:

- The first name on the left starts with the leaf, followed by a period.

- The next name is a domain that contains the leaf, followed by a period.

- The next name is a parent domain that contains the child domain preceding it, followed by a period.

▸ Each child domain is contained within a parent, followed by a period.

▸ The last name is a root name — also called the *top level domain* — with no period following it.

The format would look like this:

`leaf.childB.parentA.root`

For example:

`myhost.mainofc.corp.com`

In this example, *myhost* is a host name registered in the *mainofc* DNS server, which is in turn registered in the *corp* domain, which is in the *com* root.

Next to locate a user name established in the host, we would precede the DNS name with the user name followed by an "@" character. For example, my name might be:

`rick@myhost.mainofc.corp.com`

For example, let's assume we want to send an e-mail message to Bill Smith, whose mailbox is located in the e-mail server within the ftbliss child domain. The name to be used is:

`bsmith@email.ftbliss.army.mil`

In this example, *bsmith* is the user name, *email* is a leaf host, and *ftbliss* is the child of the army domain, which is in turn a child of the *mil* root.

The host name comes first, followed by the @ character, followed in turn by the domain name arranged with the root at the end. The name described in this example is:

`bsmith@email.ftbliss.army.mil`

▸ *bsmith* is a user account (or mailbox) in the *email* host, which is an e-mail server located in the *ftbliss* domain.

▸ *ftbliss* is a child domain of the *army* domain.

▸ *army* is a domain in the *mil* root.

Each domain (*ftbliss* for example) must be registered with its parent domain (the *army* domain in this example). In turn the *army* domain is registered in the *mil* root. An entry in a DNS server is called a *registration*.

Example of Internet Name Resolution   The name used in the preceding example will be used in the following example. Assume that we would like to send e-mail to Bill Smith at the address just given. Assuming our ISP's DNS server is a registered host anywhere on the Internet, the following procedure would occur:

1. Mail is sent, addressed to `bsmith@email.ftbliss.army.mil`.

2. A DNS name resolution query is sent to the sending ISP's DNS server.

3. The ISP's local DNS server refers the request to the mil root server.

4. The mil root DNS server looks up the registered IP address for the army domain's DNS server.

5. The query is referred to the army DNS server.

6. The army DNS server looks up the IP address for the registered DNS server in the ftbliss domain.

7. The query is referred to the ftbliss DNS server.

8. The ftbliss DNS server looks up the IP address for the registered host e-mail.

9. The IP address of the host e-mail is returned to the sender.

10. The mail message is sent to the IP address for the host e-mail.

11. The message is delivered to the bsmith mailbox, located within the host e-mail.

To expedite DNS requests on the Internet, all ISPs and most commercial domains are registered in the root of their top-level domain. These organizations can then create child domains, which are managed internally, not by the Internet.

For example, my ISP is Transport Logic, and their domain name is transport.com. This allows DNS queries for most of the Internet to be handled with just two referrals: The first is from the sender ISP's DNS server; the second is from the root-level's DNS server back to the recipient ISP's DNS server.

Root-Level Domains   Several top-level domain names are used as roots. The following top-level domains are currently in use on the Internet:

- *net* — ISPs and Internet administration authorities, such as `www.internic.net`

- *com* — Commercial (business) entities, such as `www.novell.com`

- *gov* — Nonmilitary government agencies, such as `www.irs.gov`

- *mil* — Military and Department of Defense agencies, such as `www.army.mil`

- *edu* — Educational organizations, such as `www.uiowa.edu`

- *org* — Nonprofit organizations, such as `www.libertynet.org`

- *int* — Includes domains established by international treaties, such as `www.nato.int`

- *xx* — Two-letter country code, such as `www.tomtom.co.uk` (a very fine cigar store in England)

- *num* — Phone numbers

Several new root-level domains have been established. For the most up-to-date listings see `http://www.alternic.net/TLDS.html` or check the InterNIC Web site at `http://www.internic.net`.

Domain Name Registration   You can register your own domain name directly with InterNIC, an ISP, or one of many other domain registration providers. It is simple enough to register a domain name yourself. Simply access InterNIC's Web site or registration server, search to see if the domain name you wish to use is already in use, pay the fee, and then register. Once you determine that your chosen domain name is available, you need to get the name hosted on both primary and secondary DNS servers (with an Internet connection) and then register the domain name with InterNIC (you will need the IP addresses of the primary and secondary DNS server hosting your domain name). You may pay by check or credit card. The current fee is $70 for the first two years and $35 per year thereafter. Pricing is subject to change.

You can reach the InterNIC registration services at `http://www.internic.net`.

If you use a third party to register your domain name, they tack on a small fee (usually $50.00). Their job is simply to handle the search, registration, and payment for you. See your local ISP or use an Internet search engine (such as Yahoo or AltaVista) to locate a domain registration provider.

There is really no requirement to use the root-level domain under which an organization is categorized. Several new root-level domains have been established, and more are under consideration. A movement is under way to transfer management of the Internet and domain registrations to an international organization.

To check a list of the latest root-level domains and their definitions, see `http://www.alternic.net/TLDS.html`.

Configuring DNS

Setting up a DNS server is not a difficult task in the NetWare environment. NetWare 5 and intraNetWare come with DNS servers that can be used within your organization. If you wish to connect to the Internet, your DNS server must be registered with an ISP. Registration consists of entering your domain name and IP address in the parent DNS server's tables. You must provide both primary and secondary DNS servers. You may provide one and your ISP, the other, or you or your ISP may provide both.

DNS *zones of authority* are used in NetWare 5's DNS. This allows one or more than one domain to be placed into a zone, and it enables local administrators to manage part of a domain or more than one domain. Zones of authority disassociate the physical and logical configurations of domains. Typically each domain has a primary and secondary DNS server—each domain is managed locally at the server console. Domains can be fractured into several zones, or more than one domain can be in one zone. In NetWare 5 DNS, each zone needs only a primary DNS server; a secondary server is not needed, because NDS replication takes care of fault tolerance. Zones allow administration to be configured by location, while the domain names can be logically divided without the overhead of two DNS servers. For example, if three domains were in one location, a single zone could collapse six DNS servers into one. Normally three domains would be managed by three administrators, three primary DNS servers, and three secondary DNS servers. Zones enable you to fit existing domain structures into existing NDS structures.

Primary DNS servers are used to establish the root of a private domain or zone. Primary DNS servers must be registered with an ISP's DNS server for access to the Internet. *Secondary DNS servers* obtain domain or zone data from a primary DNS server that controls a parent domain or zone. *Caching-only servers* are used to improve performance in large networks. *Resolvers* are used to pass DNS requests between applications and DNS servers.

To configure DNS or register a DNS server in a parent domain, you must enter the host name and IP address pointer records manually into the parent DNS server. Then the DNS local server's IP address must be added to the client configuration. If the local DNS server is to be a child of a parent domain or zone, the child's DNS server is configured as secondary to the parent. Once this is done, the secondary server will request updates from the primary on a regular basis. The procedure for configuring your NetWare 5 DNS service is discussed in Chapter 11, "Configuring TCP/IP with NetWare."

Common TCP/IP Applications

The underlying purpose for developing TCP/IP was to enable software applications to interoperate between multiple hosts, even when they run different operating systems. A few client/server applications have been used since the early 1970s to enable software interaction over TCP/IP. Several client/server applications were developed along with the original TCP/IP protocol stack to enable services over TCP/IP. These applications are platform-independent, meaning that they can operate between servers running one operating system and clients running the same or a different operating system.

TCP/IP applications consist of client/server modules that do not communicate through the hosts' operating systems. Instead they direct communications to a TCP port number, which is then redirected to the target host computer. Server and client modules can be developed and run on virtually any operating system, as long as they both use TCP/IP.

Of the many TCP/IP applications, only the most common are discussed in this book. In addition to the original TCP/IP-based applications many client/server applications are available from independent software developers. Such applications as Web servers–Web client browsers, database systems (among them Oracle, SQL server, and Informix), and electronic mail systems extend TCP/IP's capabilities and popularity. Many of these applications are UNIX-based, but the NetWare server has also become a favored platform for client/server applications.

File Transfer Protocol

File Transfer Protocol (FTP) is used to copy files stored on one host to another host (or client workstation). FTP client software communicates with FTP server software to enable file transfers between them. FTP was originally developed as a character-based command line utility for terminals and workstations. Today's applications, such as browsers and Web servers, use FTP to provide file transfers without requiring the user to know or execute FTP commands.

FTP software development is guided by RFCs that ensure platform independence. You can use any brand of FTP software on a server, and a different brand of FTP software on your client. FTP software for NetWare servers is available from Novell and many third-party software developers.

FTP provides:

1. Reliable and efficient file transfers between hosts

2. File transfers of both plain ASCII text and binary executables (applications, images, and other complex data)

3. Indirect and/or implicit file access to remote hosts via client/server applications

4. Shielding from variations in different operating systems and file systems

FTP is simply a client/server file transfer program and does not provide file sharing as do NetWare and other NOSes. FTP allows an entire file to be copied but does not enable read/write access or real-time file sharing to the files. FTP provides a basic mechanism for simply transferring ASCII and binary files stored on a host — it is up to the senders or receivers to be sure that binary files are usable on their systems. In fact, the majority of FTP servers on the Internet are UNIX servers that host files to be used in other operating systems. For example, various NIC, disk, and other peripheral drivers for Windows 95, Windows NT, and NetWare servers are posted on UNIX-based FTP servers that enable you to list and download the required files via your own FTP client.

An FTP client can list or browse the FTP server's directories, select files, and then request a download. The server receives the FTP client request and initiates a file transfer to the client over TCP. Many FTP servers are accessible from Web browsers or applications. FTP transfers data formatted into pages. FTP page headers provide information about how a page of data is formatted.

Telnet

Telnet is a terminal emulation program that allows remote users to log into a terminal session on a UNIX multiuser host over a network or dial-up connection. UNIX systems are multiuser, meaning that multiple users load and execute applications on a shared host CPU and host operating system using dumb terminals. Telnet software has the capability of emulating many different terminal models to enable a user to log into the UNIX host's secure and often unique environment and to use the host's UNIX operating system to execute software applications.

Simple Mail Transfer Protocol

Simple Mail Transfer Protocol is a basic e-mail protocol that was designed to provide reliable and efficient transfer of e-mail messages. Originally SMTP's character-based client application was used to send/receive e-mail, but today client e-mail software and e-mail servers use SMTP to forward e-mail messages and attachments to destination hosts over the Internet. E-mail client software sends e-mail messages to an SMTP relay (usually the same host as the ISP's mail server). The SMTP relay is responsible for transmitting the messages to the appropriate destination mail server. The destination mail server then holds these messages in the appropriate user's *e-mail box*, folder, or directory until that user next logs into the mail server.

Many modern e-mail servers use SMTP for Internet mail but use another protocol for local e-mail delivery. E-mail servers use *message transfer agents* (MTAs) to exchange e-mail in one format to connectors and gateways that convert each message to the appropriate format. E-mail servers that use other protocols must contain an SMTP gateway to exchange e-mail over the Internet.

Post Office Protocol

An e-mail server stores all e-mail messages received for all users with a valid account on that system. E-mail client software connects to the e-mail server; the user logs into his or her account and is authenticated via a password. The e-mail client then uses Post Office Protocol (POP3) to request all e-mail messages for that account, and the messages are then transferred to the client system. When the user replies to a message, SMTP is once again used to transmit the message to the SMTP relay, which in turn transmits the message to the destination mail server.

Internet Message Access Protocol

Internet Message Access Protocol (IMAP) is an Internet standard that is a more advanced alternative to POP3. IMAP mail servers permit a client e-mail program to access messages stored in the e-mail server as if they were on the local client system. For example, e-mail stored on an IMAP server can be manipulated from a computer at home, at the office, or from a notebook computer in a hotel room, without the need to transfer all of the e-mail messages between these computers. IMAP provides the client a summarized list of all messages including sender, date/time, size, and if any attachments are present. The client user may then opt to download some messages, store others on the IMAP server for later use, and delete some messages without ever reading them. IMAP was conceived in 1986 at Stanford University. However, it did not command the attention of many e-mail vendors until a decade later, and it is still not as widely deployed as earlier and less-capable alternatives such as POP3. The current standard is IMAP4.

Simple Network Management Protocol

Simple Network Management Protocol was developed to gain access to errors and statistics detected in network devices and printers. SNMP agents are embedded in devices such as LAN hubs, routers, switches, bridges, printers, and servers. Workstation-based management station software is used to interact with SNMP agents to monitor networks and devices. Though SNMP is mainly used for detecting network errors, Hewlett-Packard uses SNMP for communications between HP printers and their hosts. SNMP v.1 & SNMP v.2 are currently in use.

SNMP is the most universal mechanism used to monitor and manage network devices. Many software develops use SNMP to centrally manage a network from an administrator's workstation. Popular network monitoring packages include

Novell's ManageWise, Hewlett-Packard's OpenView, Sun's NetManager, Tivoli TME, and Computer Associates' TNG Workstation just to mention a few.

Communities   Many intelligent network devices include embedded SNMP agents, including everything from Ethernet wiring concentrators to Cisco routers. Larger networks often have many SNMP agents and management workstations. SNMP *communities* group agents and workstations. Some internetworks have several communities, each one with several agents and one or more management stations. When configuring SNMP agents and management workstations, the administrator specifies which community the SNMP device is to be part of. SNMP messages are then confined to the specified community. Some communities allow public read access, while others are restricted to managers with read and write access.

Traps and Management Information Infobases   SNMP *traps* (error notifications) are sent to management stations. When setting up a management station, a Management Information Base (MIB) is configured to receive and store SNMP traps for a given community.

The MIB format becomes the data exchange standard. Two basic MIB formats have been accepted, MIB and MIB II. Several MIB formats are currently in draft form. When vendors use draft standards, they run the risk that some of their SNMP messages cannot be used by other vendors' software and vice versa. You will find more detail on MIBs in Chapter 11, "Configuring TCP/IP with NetWare."

Request Functions   SNMP has five basic functional requests implemented as packet types, each of which contains management information data. The data contained in the data field of the SNMP protocol data unit contains specific information about the nature of the request; it is formatted in one of several MIB formats.

The following packet types are used:

► *GetRequest* — Queries the agent for information such as current level of network utilization.

► *GetNextRequest* — Reads the next data record in the agent.

► *GetResponse* — Bears the agent's response to a GetRequest or GetNextRequest.

▸ *SetRequest* — Sets a value for the agent's setting (that is, the value for a threshold setting such as network utilization percent).

▸ *Trap* — Sends information to management stations.

NOTE

For more on SNMP, look for SNMP FAQ on the CD that accompanies this book. You will also find a helpful 32-bit Windows SNMP utility by Thomas R. Cikoski, who is also the author of the FAQ files.

Remote Network Monitoring   Remote Network Monitoring (RMON) is an extension to SNMP that was developed to monitor and manage network devices more closely. While SNMP is used to query devices after errors have occurred, RMON is used to monitor RMON agents in real time using the SNMP protocol. Using standard SNMP requests, the RMON MIB format is extended to include network management. RMON-compliant software and devices can report network conditions as they occur. RMON agents monitor and alert management workstations when network conditions exceed normal operating ranges (thresholds).

RMON 2 extends RMON to include reporting on protocol traffic. For example, Novell's ManageWise uses RMON 2 agents installed on NetWare servers to make packet captures and protocol analysis available to a central management console.

Network File System

Network File System is a presentation layer protocol developed by Sun Microsystems for remote file access. NFS is the networking software used in UNIX systems when sharing a remote file system is necessary. Though NFS was developed for UNIX, NFS client support is available for virtually every operating system. NFS server software is available for most operating systems. Several companies — including Novell — market NFS software.

When NFS server software is installed, any TCP/IP workstation running NFS client software can attach the remote file system to the local file system, extending it to include shared NFS storage systems. NFS has no features, such as security, found in a NOS. UNIX systems generally develop their own security to layer on top of NFS sessions.

Novell makes NetWare NFS to allow NFS clients to access the NetWare server where it is loaded. NetWare 3, 4, and 5 servers load NFS name space support to allow support for NFS/UNIX filenames. Novell's LAN Workplace provides NFS client support and is available for DOS, Windows, OS/2, and Macintosh. UNIX workstations can purchase NFS support from their UNIX vendor or one of many third parties.

Miscellaneous Applications

Several miscellaneous applications have been developed and are standardized under RFCs. The following list includes applications that are not used as frequently as the applications discussed previously. These services were used from Telnet sessions, but most now have been upgraded to graphical utilities. To use these services, use Telnet to contact a host and then log in with the application name.

- ▸ *Archie* — Catalogs files on FTP servers.

- ▸ *Gopher* — Provides access to files and Internet services; easier to use than FTP.

- ▸ *Veronica* — Indexes gopher sites.

- ▸ *WAIS* (Wide Area Information Servers) — Maintains indexes of catalogued resources on the Internet.

Many TCP/IP command line utilities are used for a variety of purposes. Check out Appendix D, "TCP/IP Utilities," for a listing of utilities and their syntax. You will also find this document on the CD that accompanies this book.

PART II

Installing and Configuring NetWare

CHAPTER 5

Preparing the Server and LAN

This chapter addresses several aspects of system design that you should consider, including:

- ► Selecting or building a server

- ► Selecting or building disk subsystems

- ► Selecting LANs and NICs

- ► Cabling requirements

- ► Power conditioning and monitoring

- ► Setting up the server and LAN

These issues are discussed in sufficient depth to assist you in planning your own network in a way that will serve you well into the future. You will find a checklist at the end of the chapter so that you will not forget any of the recommended preparation steps.

Planning a departmental network is a much bigger job than it used to be. Along with open system design comes the responsibility of selecting the very best components from several vendors' offerings. You may decide to have one brand of server; another brand of SCSI disk drive; a different brand of SCSI host adapter; several brands of workstations; and one or more brands of NICs, hubs, and so on. Getting all these items to work together is no simple task.

Designing a campus-wide or an enterprise-wide internetwork involves even greater complexity. The use of NetWare's internal and external routers, third-party external routers, plus the complexity of WANs add more layers of integration and planning to your task. Data communications services add further complexity and additional vendors; both a long-distance company and a local telephone company are involved in bringing a leased line to you.

Generally, though, the biggest problems are political, and internetworks cross more organizational lines than departmental networks. They therefore require far more planning, and centralized or committee-oriented decision making is necessary unless mandates are received from a central authority.

This chapter outlines the decisions that need to be made when you integrate or upgrade any current NetWare version. If you are an experienced networking expert, skip this introductory chapter and go on to the more detailed component-specific parts of this section. However, if you are not a networking expert, you will find this chapter will help you to avoid mistakes that consume valuable resources and perhaps dozens of hours of your time.

One last warning: Do not buy from marketing materials; they are often misleading. Check out technical specifications, talk with support personnel, and discuss your considerations with peers in other organizations. The toughest part of your job has to do with errors of omission — it is difficult at best to anticipate some of the costly aspects of system integration.

WARNING

Research your hardware selections thoroughly. **On many occasions, I have seen thousands of dollars' worth of hardware components on my clients' shelves because of unresolved integration issues. Always ask yourself "What might I have overlooked?" Do your best to find the hidden "gotchas" that the marketing folks don't talk about. For example, check Novell's and other vendors' support Web sites for documents revealing problems with a vendor's product. Check to see if a product evaluation is possible before buying.**

Building or Selecting a Server

You have two basic choices for selecting a server and its subsystems: You can purchase a computer that was designed to be a server, or you can purchase a computer and then select and install your own components. Computer design and input/output (I/O) subsystems have been standardized so that almost any computer you purchase can be built with the same level of performance.

You can purchase a PCI-based motherboard, powerful SCSI disk subsystems, and lots of RAM to build your own server. However, you may run into some very time-consuming challenges if you do. Sometimes components do not work together very well, and drivers may be hard to find or prove "buggy." In short, building your own server can be a nightmare, especially when you integrate the latest technology.

It used to be that you paid a premium for a powerful server. Due to the competitive nature of the computer hardware business, computers that are factory-built as servers are normally very cost-effective. Purchasing a factory-configured server can often save you dozens of hours in preparing your server for installation. Additionally, the server you build may be fraught with incompatibilities or mismatches that reduce performance. Major original equipment manufacturers (OEMs) provide a valuable service and are forced to price their servers at bargain prices. It is hardly worth your time to integrate components on your own. They also have to support the server and all its components comprehensively. They often even have a money-back guarantee in case you are dissatisfied.

Today, many computer vendors bundle factory-configured servers below the cost you would pay for individual components, plus the hardware is all installed and factory tested. Some vendors will even install the NetWare version of your choice at no additional cost. In these systems, subsystems are matched to provide the best performance. You will often find that minor details you might have overlooked were included in a factory-built server. The vendor's reputation depends on the product it puts out. Computer vendors often build systems that are far better than you might build on your own because they have matched components and worked out all the integration glitches.

Stay away from proprietary hardware. The integration of proprietary hardware currently affords no significant performance advantages and can actually penalize you with excessive replacement costs and limited availability of parts. For these reasons, the entire industry has turned toward equipment that is standards-based and nonproprietary. Table 5.1 lists theoretical throughput characteristics of major server components. Add them up for yourself and be sure you have sufficient bus capacity to handle peak loads.

TABLE 5.1 Usable Throughput Characteristics of Server Components	COMPONENT	THEORETICAL CAPACITY (MB/SEC)	USABLE THROUGH-PUT (MB/SEC)
	Ethernet NIC	1.25	0.875
	Fast Ethernet NIC	12.5	8.75
	FDDI NIC	12.5	11.25
	Token Ring-16	2	1.8
	SCSI-1	5	5
	Fast SCSI-2	10	10

TABLE 5.1	COMPONENT	THEORETICAL CAPACITY (MB/SEC)	USABLE THROUGH-PUT (MB/SEC)
Usable Throughput Characteristics of Server Components (continued)	Fast-Wide SCSI-2	20	20
	Ultra-Wide SCSI	40	40
	EIDE disk	1.5	0.8
	SCSI UW disk	3–5	3–5
	EISA bus	33	33
	PCI bus	132	132

Most important, your server should be designed to handle the specific job, and you should consider your future demands. Project your network's growth over the lifetime of the server, and build the server to meet your highest projections.

TIP

For better reliability and latest technology, replace your server every two or three years. Most servers have a useful lifetime of several years; however, you should replace them more frequently. If you are in an environment where new user workstations are acquired on a regular basis, consider giving the old server to a user and replacing it with a new server.

By updating, your maintenance will be lower and you can feel more secure knowing the new server is probably more dependable than an aging one. This also will enable you to project future demands more accurately because the foreseeable server lifetime will be defined more accurately.

Internal Components

Having given this advice, let's take a look at components you should choose when building or selecting a server. You should focus on four areas:

- Processor(s)

- Memory

▶ Bus design

▶ Disk adapters and disk storage subsystems

Processors

NetWare only runs on Intel *x*86 family of processors: the 386, 486, Pentium, Pentium Pro, Pentium II, or Pentium Xeon. NetWare 4 and 5 take advantage of the Pentium's multithreading capabilities, which increases performance significantly. When selecting a server, be sure to get the most powerful processor you can afford. Research the latest technology by visiting Intel's Web site (http://www.intel.com). Higher-speed processors are more beneficial for sure. NetWare does not burden your processor as much as UNIX or Windows NT, but more is better.

Select a processor with as much internal (L1) and external (L2) cache as possible. Server performance tests show that most server tasks are repetitive and benefit from a larger processor cache.

Motherboards   If you purchase your own components down to the board level, select a major-brand motherboard. Intel makes motherboards that are available in the aftermarket and are a good value — several OEMs use Intel motherboards, and so can you. You will find that very inexpensive imported motherboards are poorly made. Manufacturing defects often show up just after the warranty period is over. The difference in cost between an Intel motherboard and a cheap clone normally is less than $100. A server is too important to scrimp on this component — purchase a quality motherboard from a reliable vendor.

The memory bus is a very important aspect of server design. Many of the newer computer designs have a dedicated bus between the processor and memory. Intel's Slot 1 design and other similar designs expedite data movement between the processor and memory, which can make a lot of difference in heavy processing environments. New developments are appearing daily in this area, such as the "look through or look aside" cache architecture.

Multiprocessors   If the server you select is to serve multiple duty as a Web server or other type of application server, consider a multiprocessor system. Multiple processors benefit NetWare application servers — there is limited benefit to be gained by adding multiple processors for file and print services.

Don't be swayed by claims that servers are upgradable. Upgrading a server sounds good but is often not a practical idea. Competition and new technology yields increasingly more powerful computers for less money each year. More often than not, a new server is less expensive and more powerful than upgrading an old one.

WARNING Adding a second or additional processors at a later date is not practical — you are generally better off purchasing a dual- or quad-processor system from the outset. Multiprocessor requirements generally require that processors are identical — typically from the same manufacturing lot. As your server ages, you may not be able to locate matching processors without replacing the original processor. You might have to pay a premium to find four matched processors.

Memory

Memory is one of the most important parts of your system. Though RAM is cheap and normally carries a lifetime warranty, there are differences in memory types and memory module design. If you ever do experience a parity error, your system will crash unless you have error correcting code (ECC) memory. ECC memory is more expensive than other types of RAM but very important for servers. You cannot just substitute ECC memory; your motherboard must support this option.

Bus Design

The type of bus in your computer is the single most important aspect of high-performance I/O. Fortunately, PCI is normally included in every new computer and is quite standardized and stable. You can use the ISA slots in a motherboard, but read on to find out why this is not a good idea.

PCI versus ISA and EISA The most important aspect you can control in building a server consists of the bus and adapters you install in the server. NetWare operating systems and drivers are optimized for 32-bit operation. You should never hamper the system design by using any 16-bit ISA adapters or bus.

The standard bus used in the original AT computer is currently called an industry standard architecture (ISA) bus. This 16-bit bus is poorly suited for multitasking and lacks capacity to move data as fast as the rest of your system. Plus, ISA depends upon the central processor for moving I/O.

Extended Industry Standard Architecture   IBM developed the Microchannel Architecture (MCA) bus to alleviate bus traffic jams and then attempted to charge OEMs a license fee to use it. The industry answered back with Extended Industry Standard Architecture (EISA), which matched MCA but was designed to accommodate ISA adapters in the same slot if desired. EISA was an open system design, governed by industry standards, so it became far more popular than MCA, which has been discontinued.

EISA was a good design, but high-performance I/O devices such as SCSI adapters soon outgrew its limitations. It was also expensive to develop adapters for this architecture — much design work was left up to the adapter developer, giving larger hardware developers a competitive edge. EISA adapters were expensive, typically over $500 and often over $1,000.

PCI   The Peripheral Component Interface (PCI) bus has the greatest capacity of any standardized bus on the market today, and it is the least expensive. Intel developed this design and made it an industry standard. They were smart enough to release the specifications but to make PCI bus controller firmware for such low prices that no one was willing to compete with them. PCI buses are built into every x86 computer built today. It has replaced all other buses except the ISA bus, which for some reason remains incorporated into workstation motherboards, but not for long. Intel and Microsoft have now issued policy statements indicating that all new computers should cease to include ISA buses by the year 2000.

Building PCI components into the motherboard and card design is very simple. PCI specifications and designs are provided at no cost, and most of the logic is embedded into the PCI controller on the motherboard anyway. Building a PCI adapter is a matter of building a board from design specifications and purchasing firmware. Most PCI adapter cards sell for under $200 at retail, and many very fine cards are priced under $100.

The only server bus you should plug an adapter into should be a PCI bus. Generally, ISA bus slots are provided for backward compatibility with older devices. PCI cards are just as inexpensive as ISA, and the only reason you would pick an ISA card for your server is if you did not know any better. Table 5.2 shows burst rates for recent bus designs. You can see from this table why newer computers always have PCI slots.

TABLE 5.2	BUS	MAXIMUM BURST RATE (MB/SEC)	WIDTH
Bus Throughput Rates and Specifications	ISA	5	16 bit
	EISA	33	32 bit
	MCA	40	16 and 32 bit
	PCI	132	32, 64, and 128 bit

In addition to its wide bandwidth (132MB/sec), PCI has many features that make data flow more efficient. Because the bus is designed for multitasking and has its own processor, the load you put on your server's processor is reduced. Typically, a PCI card will generate 90 percent less CPU utilization than a comparable ISA card.

NOTE

Note that throughput statistics are stated in megabytes per second (MB/sec). You will read many articles where bus and card throughput statistics are stated in megabits per second (Mb/sec or Mbps). Most LAN standards are managed by the Institute of Electrical and Electronic Engineers (IEEE), where statistics are stated in Mbps to be consistent with other data communications standards. Computer I/O statistics are handled by American National Standards Institute (ANSI) and member organizations, who state specifications in MB/sec. The latter is eight times the former. You will often read articles in computer magazines where the two are confused.

I make note of this detail because I have seen PCI bus capacity stated erroneously in many articles and books for this very reason.

Multiple Buses   Many high-end servers include two PCI buses. This feature provides two 132MB/sec bus channels for NICs, SCSI adapters, and other I/O devices. If you add more than two Ultra-Wide SCSI adapters and a few 100Mbps NICs, you might consider this option. The "Disk Subsystems" section of this chapter discusses SCSI technology in greater detail.

Hot Plug PCI   Hot Plug PCI was developed by Compaq and shared with the rest of the industry. You can add and remove interface cards from PCI computers equipped with this feature while they are running. Without a doubt, this is an important feature if you require 24 × 7 service (24 hours/day, 7 days/week uptime).

NOTE

NetWare is truly designed for 24 × 7 service, but Windows NT is not. Hot Plug PCI will enable you to physically change or add NICs and SCSI adapters without downing your system only if your operating system does not require reboot after loading new drivers. All current NetWare versions enable you to load drivers, bind protocols, partition drives, create volumes, and mount new volumes without downing your server. When you change a driver in Windows NT, you must reboot for the driver to be loaded.

High Availability

Servers that are designed for *high availability* are your best bet for 24 × 7 service. No industry standard definition exists for the term "high availability," but vendors reserve this label for their most durable hardware. Many high-end servers include:

▸ Top engineering and manufacturing quality control beyond the level considered adequate for most computers

▸ Dual fault-tolerant internal power supplies

▸ Dual fault-tolerant cooling fans

▸ ECC memory

▸ Hot Plug PCI bus

▸ 24 × 7 expert technical support

▸ Cross-shipping and standby server loan during warranty repairs

When you add up the alternative costs, you will find that factory-built servers are tremendous cost-savers. Any server that faces downtime costs you money. Alternative costs are reflected in other budget items, such as worker productivity and lost revenues.

Disk Subsystems

The disk storage systems on your server are the heart of your network. If drive performance is poor, all users will experience impaired production. Should a disk drive fail, data will be lost, and you may have to reinstall your operating system before restoring backups. Without a doubt, a server's disk subsystem is one of the most critical components in your network, if not the most critical. Other systems may fail, but when your disk drives fail, you have a more severe and time-consuming problem on your hands.

PCI's expanded capacity has pushed the boundaries of disk adapter performance. Before the PCI bus was developed, it was not feasible to produce high-capacity disk drives, so disk adapter and drive technology for PCs was at a standstill. Normal ISA design did not enable sufficient data throughput for existing designs to be fully exploited. Development of powerful 32-bit PCI disk adapters has expanded the performance envelope. Therefore, developers have now extended the capabilities of disk subsystems. More important, bus-mastering small computer system interface (SCSI) adapters enable NetWare's built-in split seek features to be activated without taxing CPU utilization or interfering with concurrent NIC transfers (as long as all devices are well-designed bus masters).

Integrated Drive Electronics and Small Computer Systems Interface

Older disk designs, including MFM, RLL, and ESDI, have become virtually obsolete. Integrated Drive Electronics (IDE) and Extended IDE have become the standard for desktop storage. IDE's low cost, small form-factor, capacity, speed, and durability are well suited for desktop computers. An IDE drive is fine for a light-duty server with just a few users. When serious server power is required, however, you should use Small Computer Systems Interface (SCSI) drive systems or RAID subsystems in your server.

IDE and SCSI are actually bus designs — they combine a host adapter in the computer bus with intelligent embedded controllers on each disk drive. In SCSI, each drive is intelligent and has the capability to read and write independently and concurrently from the other SCSI devices – this is not the case for IDE. New IDE and SCSI standards have come along in the past few years, providing a plethora of options.

IDE Operating System Drive and SCSI Data Drives   Consider building your server with a good IDE drive for the operating system and a more powerful SCSI disk system to house applications and data. The operating system itself does not benefit greatly from the enhanced performance characteristics of a SCSI system and can be located on an IDE drive. Your user applications and data should reside on SCSI drives. This is where performance is critical.

You also might want to use an IDE CD-ROM drive and other IDE-based peripherals. If you do, you might find that booting from SCSI drive is sometimes a challenge. The SCSI adapter's BIOS (basic input/output system) chip controls booting. Sometimes the BIOS does not allow you to boot from a SCSI device when an IDE adapter is present. Using an IDE boot drive may be a good solution to BIOS problems you might encounter.

Another good reason to use an IDE boot drive is the fact that your operating system and data are located on separate physical disk drives. If a drive were to fail, you would lose either your operating system or data, but not both. The system disk can be IDE or SCSI.

WARNING

Should you decide to mirror IDE drives, be sure to use a dual-channel adapter with each drive configured as the master on each channel. If you connect two IDE drives to the same channel, when one drive fails, the other often also stops working. Mirroring is discussed in a later section of this chapter entitled "NetWare Disk Mirroring."

SCSI Terminology, Designs, Standards, and Terms   SCSI comes in many flavors, called *levels*, such as Fast SCSI and Ultra SCSI. These levels define products that have many levels of performance, use different connectors and cables, and have various levels of throughput. SCSI includes many standardized designs, some of which have been officially sanctioned by American National Standards Institutes (ANSI) and some that have not.

In leading-edge technologies such as SCSI, standards are implemented while they are still in the draft stage. When a new design is developed, it is given a common name agreed upon by general consensus among SCSI developers, and then the ANSI standard is proposed. During the approval process, the proposal becomes a de facto standard, logic chips are put into production, and products appear almost immediately. Drive and adapter manufacturers develop and ship product based on the draft proposal. If the official standard differs, the vendor usually provides a BIOS update without cost to the purchaser if desired. In many cases, BIOS chips are flash-upgradable — so they can be updated by executing a file.

NOTE

You will find that some de facto standards are synonymous with official ANSI standards, while others may not have been officially approved in the form of an ANSI standard. For this reason, SCSI levels often have two names: the common name and the ANSI standard name. For example, before ANSI approved the *SCSI-2* standard, it was commonly called *Fast-Wide SCSI* by disk adapter developers. Some of the features included in a de facto standard may not make the final standard. For this reason, industry names and ANSI standards are mostly the same, but some differ slightly. Manufacturers like Adaptec use the common names most often in their marketing literature and use the ANSI name in their technical documentation. Could this be why many people get confused about SCSI standards?

SCSI supports either 8 or 16 devices per channel, depending upon the SCSI level and type of cable. The adapter counts as a device, so you are able to connect either 7 or 15 devices to a SCSI adapter. Table 5.3 defines popular SCSI terms referenced to their standards, along with throughput statistics.

For more extensive tables and information on SCSI features and configurations, refer to DELEC's Web site at http://www.delec.com. You will find a copy of DELEC's SCSI guide on the CD that accompanies this book.

Multichannel SCSI Adapters   Some adapters have multiple cables; and some have multiple channels, which act as two or more adapters. Multiple cables do not necessarily mean that the card has multiple channels. For example, the Adaptec AHA-2940UW is a PCI card that has two SCSI connectors: one wide and one narrow; however, they are both in one channel. With this adapter, you can connect no more than 7 devices to the narrow connector, and no more than 15 devices to the wide connector, but you can connect only 15 devices in total. The Adaptec AHA-3940UW has two Ultra-Wide SCSI channels and two 68-pin (wide) connectors. You can connect up to 15 drives on each cable, for a total of 30 drives. More important, each channel can accommodate up to 40MB/sec of traffic from its disk drives — using both channels doubles the adapter's capacity.

TABLE 5.3

*SCSI Terms/Names
and Maximum Data
Transfer Rates*

TERMS	NAME	MHZ	BUS WIDTH (BITS)	THROUGHPUT IN MBYTE/SEC
SCSI-1	SCSI-1	5	8	5
Fast SCSI	SCSI-2	10	8	10
Fast-Wide SCSI	SCSI-2 /			
SCSI-3	10	16	20	
Ultra SCSI	SCSI-3	20	8	20
Ultra-Wide SCSI	SCSI-3	20	16	40
Ultra2 SCSI	(SCSI-4)	40	8	40
Ultra2-Wide SCSI	(SCSI-4)	40	16	80

Footnotes:

[1] Notice that the term MHz is used to specify speed, since MByte/sec changes with the bus width.

[2] Fast-Wide SCSI is actually SCSI-2; however, many cable manufacturers refer to the 68-pin plugs as SCSI-3.

[3] The SCSI-4 definition is not yet final.

[4] Most SCSI 1–4 devices can be mixed on the same bus; however, the slowest device/controller may determine the bus speed. Check with the adapter vendor for specifics.

[5] You cannot mix single-ended and differential or LVD devices/controllers on the same SCSI bus.

[6] Please note that Fast-Wide SCSI-2 is also sometimes called SCSI-3 (in particular when referring to the 68 HP connector).

[7] Table 5.3 and footnotes courtesy of DELEC, 23376 Caminito Basilio, Laguna Hills, CA 92653, U.S.A. Telephone (714) 859-8592, Fax (714) 859-8593.

Multichannel adapters allow you to leverage the number of drives you can connect to a single bus slot. For example, you could connect up to 120 disk drives to four dual-channel adapters. A multichannel adapter increases the total bandwidth available for a single bus slot.

Use multichannel adapters for:

▸ Servers with a mix of SCSI level devices (such as SCSI-1 and SCSI-2)

▸ Multiprocessor servers

▸ Multimedia servers

▸ Servers with many storage devices, such as CD-ROM servers or optical juke boxes

▸ Large transaction-processing and database servers (such as SQL or Oracle servers)

Configuring SCSI Devices and Buses   SCSI connections are subject to several rules, which depend upon the SCSI level used. In general, you can connect lower SCSI-level devices to higher SCSI-level adapters. In many cases this will reduce total throughput over the channel to the speed of the lowest SCSI-level device. Here are some general rules about connecting SCSI devices:

▸ The adapter counts as one device and electrically terminates its end of the cable. You can theoretically connect 8 devices on an 8-bit SCSI connection, but the adapter counts as one. Though you can theoretically connect 16 devices on a 16-bit SCSI connection, the adapter counts as one.

▸ Each device must be configured with a SCSI device number. No two devices can be assigned the same device number. Device numbers are typically configured with jumper settings on the drive (or device) itself.

▸ The last drive on cable must be terminated — other drives must not be terminated. Most drives have an electrical termination option. In this case the terminator is physically installed, and a jumper or switch bypasses the terminator according to a signal from the adapter. This feature is an option on most later-model SCSI adapters and disk drives.

▸ SCSI-1 cannot mix device types.

▸ SCSI-2 and up can mix different types of devices (for instance, disk drive and CD-ROM).

▸ You can connect up to 7 devices (8 minus the adapter) on an 8-bit (50 pin) SCSI connection.

▸ You can connect up to 15 devices (16 minus the adapter) on a 16-bit (68-pin) SCSI connection.

NOTE **Look for DELEC's SCSI Guide on the CD that accompanies this book. You will find this to be a comprehensive guide for SCSI standards, including standardized rules for configurations. The DELEC SCSI Guide was provided by *DELEC Online* of Laguna Hills, California.**

SCSI technology moves quickly. Any published facts on leading-edge technology will become outdated very quickly. This book and references on the CD can be updated by checking the DELEC Online Web site as discussed previously.

You can find the latest facts concerning SCSI technology in the comp.periphs.scsi document found on a few Web sites. This document is updated from public comment and then compared to industry standards and products. The updated document is posted monthly on the following Web sites:

```
http://www.cis.ohio-state.edu/hypertext/faq/usenet/scsi-faq
http://www.ultranet.com/~gfield/gary/scsi.html
```

You will find a wealth of information on SCSI standards, features, products, and configurations from the following Web sites:

```
http://www.delec.com/guide/scsi
http://www.quantum.com/src/
```

SCSI Adapter and Drive Recommendation   Here are some recommendations that will go a long way toward providing the utmost disk performance and best value for server disk subsystems:

1. To derive the best value for your expenditure, select Ultra-Wide SCSI or later level adapters and disk drives. This technology provides 40MB/sec through a single disk channel to which you can attach up to 15 devices. Price differential between older designs and Ultra-Wide SCSI-2 adapters and drives is very small. Here's why you should use Ultra-Wide SCSI:

   a. On SCSI-1, you cannot mix devices. SCSI-2 and higher adapters enable you to connect several types of drives to a single adapter, including disk drives, CD-ROM drives, tape drives, optical drives, and so on.

b. SCSI-1 does not support command-tag queuing, which allows up to 256 disk requests to be queued at the adapter. This feature dramatically increases server performance for concurrent disk I/O requests. Without this feature, each physical disk write request must be completed and acknowledged before the next request can be sent to a disk drive.

c. Ultra-Wide SCSI allows up to 40MB/sec over a single disk channel. This is normally sufficient to allow up to 15 high-performance disk drives to operate simultaneously without traffic jams in the disk channel.

2. Check your adapter and driver documentation to be sure that command-tag queuing is enabled. In some cases, the adapter firmware and driver have this feature disabled even though the adapter is capable of it.

3. Separate slower and faster SCSI devices on different adapters or channels — always use the highest-performance devices available that are matched to the channel's capabilities. For example, never connect a SCSI-1 drive to a Fast SCSI adapter. If you do, the channel and all drives on it will operate at 5 MHz instead of 10 or 20 MHz, which will cut your potential throughput in half or less. When integrating tape drives, CD-ROMs, and other devices that do not take advantage of Fast-Wide technology, use a separate adapter or channel on a multichannel adapter.

4. Use only PCI bus-mastering adapters. PCI is the only standardized bus that provides sufficient bandwidth for high-powered SCSI adapters and 100Mbps NICs. Bus mastering lowers CPU utilization and is more efficient in transferring large amounts of data between a host adapter and the destination. For example, disk I/O requests can be serviced directly from the adapter to cache without going through the processor. Bus mastering allows up to eight bytes in a stream to be preceded by a single address byte. Without bus mastering, each byte requires a separate address byte.

5. Use cables that are rated and certified for the SCSI level of your adapter. For example, Fast SCSI uses the same type of cable as SCSI-1, but SCSI-1 cables may not support higher signaling rate without causing many errors.

6. If you have more than one Ultra SCSI channel in a computer, consider a dual-bus computer design. Calculate total potential throughput of all adapters and their devices. If the total approaches 100MB/sec, a dual-bus computer is recommended.

NetWare Disk Mirroring

You can mirror disk drives on any current NetWare version. Mirroring makes your drive system fault tolerant by writing the same data to both drives. If one drive fails, the other continues to provide uninterrupted access to data without a moment of downtime. When the failed drive is replaced, all the data from the primary drive is copied to the secondary drive in a lower-priority background mode without interrupting user access.

Duplexing   Duplexing is when mirrored drives are connected to separate adapters (or a multichannel adapter) as shown in Figure 5.1. Duplexing provides additional fault tolerance, since the adapters are duplicated. Duplexing can also provide additional performance under the right conditions. When duplexing, you will need to load two disk drivers — or if your adapters are identical, you will need to load the same disk driver *reentrantly* (a second time).

When duplexing, you realize a performance bonus when your server handles concurrent physical read and write requests. Because NetWare has two disk drivers, unverified write requests can delay read requests. While the disk subsystem is busy with write requests and a read request is issued, one adapter services the read request while the other services the write request. If data is written to one drive, the write operation can be verified. At the first opportunity, the other drive will be synchronized to the first.

Requirements for Mirroring   When mirroring drives, you must have two logical partitions that are identical in size. A logical partition is the available disk space that a NetWare volume can be placed on after Hot Fix has been allocated. Hot Fix space is allocated for bad sectors that are found while in use. If one drive is physically larger than the other, some space will remain after you have mirrored the two drives. In this case, you may place another NetWare volume on the remaining space in the logical partition as long as it exceeds 10MB.

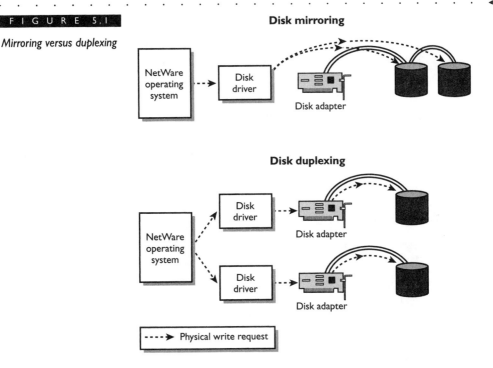

FIGURE 5.1

Mirroring versus duplexing

Disk mirroring

Disk duplexing

You can mirror drives during installation or anytime afterward. When a drive contains data and you add a new drive, you can select the new drive, pair it to the existing drive, and establish mirroring. Mirroring will occur in a background mode as discussed previously. See later chapters discussing installing your NetWare version for specific details on how to mirror drives.

WARNING

When mirroring an existing drive with the NetWare INSTALL utility, be sure to select the existing drive as Primary, and the new drive as Secondary. When mirroring occurs, the Primary drive is copied to the Secondary. If you selected the drive with existing data as Secondary, the blank drive will be copied to the drive with data, destroying all existing files and directories.

RAID Disk Storage Options

Redundant Array of Inexpensive Drives (RAID) systems provide fault-tolerant disk storage — when a drive fails, operation continues without interruption. RAID also provides better performance by striping data over multiple disk drives.

You can implement RAID systems in three ways:

▸ In your NetWare operating system using standard hardware

▸ Using a special RAID SCSI adapter and standard disk drives

▸ Using special external RAID subsystems and a proprietary adapter

All three of these options are discussed in the following sections.

RAID Levels   Compaq was the first to develop RAID products in servers, but this technology is widely available today. There is no true RAID standard, but the first widely circulated document on RAID was a white paper published by University of California at Berkeley. This document defines six RAID levels and guides standard use of the term.

You have several RAID configuration options available, but only four levels are commonly used. Table 5.4 describes the benefits of the four basic RAID levels in use today.

T A B L E 5.4	RAID LEVEL	CONFIGURATION	BENEFIT
RAID Levels	0	Striping	Improved performance
	I	Mirroring	Fully redundant fault tolerance
	3	Striping w/parity on a separate drive	Better performance and fault tolerance with lower redundancy, is not hot-pluggable
	5	Striping w/parity striped over all drives	Same as RAID 3, but is hot-pluggable

CHECKLIST

Mirroring **writes data to two drives simultaneously, resulting in fault tolerance.**

Striping **is where a volume is created over multiple disk drives and data is written to multiple drives simultaneously, resulting in improved performance.**

Mirroring Drives

1. Use only SCSI adapters and drives. SCSI drives can read and write independently of one another — a feature that IDE drives are not able to perform. Without multitasking read/write operations, mirroring imposes severe penalties on disk read/write performance.

2. Use two SCSI adapters or a dual-channel adapter. Install a drive on each adapter or channel. This option, called *duplexing*, improves performance because disk read/write requests are split. One drive can perform a read operation while the other writes.

All current NetWare OSes enable you to implement RAID 0 and RAID 1 in your server without any special hardware. You can stripe a volume over multiple drives (RAID 1), and you can mirror drives (RAID 0).

RAID 5 is the most popular configuration for four basic reasons:

▶ *Fault tolerance and economy* — RAID 5 provides fault tolerance, but a small percentage — typically only 10–15 percent — of available disk storage is allocated to the RAID parity data. In a mirrored pair, fully 50 percent of total disk storage is used up to make the system fault tolerant.

▶ *Hot plug capability* — You can replace a downed disk drive without bringing the system down or interrupting I/O operations. RAID 3 is not hot-pluggable. When a drive is lost, the drive must be replaced with the server down.

▶ *Online reconstruction* — When a new drive replaces a failed drive, reconstruction can be accomplished without interrupting user disk access. Most RAID 3 systems require offline reconstruction.

▶ *Smaller block size performance* — RAID 5 handles smaller block allocation unit sizes better than RAID 3.

RAID 1 + 0   You can stripe and mirror in your server — which is unofficially called RAID 10 or RAID 1 + 0. You can stripe two pairs of drives and then mirror the pairs as shown in Figure 5.2. This configuration provides the highest level of performance in a NetWare server.

FIGURE 5.2

RAID 1 + 0

Disk duplexing

Disk driver

Disk adapter

Vol:

NetWare operating system

Mirrored

Disk driver

Disk adapter

Vol:

- - - ▶ Physical write request

TIP

Striped and mirrored drives (RAID 1 + 0) as discussed previously provide the highest level of disk performance possible in a NetWare server.

Aftermarket RAID SCSI Adapters   In the past, RAID logic was proprietary — you had to purchase a complete RAID subsystem at a premium price. The adapters and even the drives were often proprietary. In 1996, a couple of SCSI adapter developers began offering RAID adapters to computer OEMs. For example, when you purchased a Hewlett-Packard server with an internal H-P RAID system, the adapter was built by Mylex and resold by H-P.

In 1997, only two manufacturers sold SCSI RAID adapters to the aftermarket through OEMs. These adapters were mainly used by OEMs due to the technical difficulties encountered with compatibility and driver issues. The OEM was responsible for driver development, which kept the adapters off the aftermarket. Today you can build your own internal RAID subsystem with common adapters and drives for very little money. For example, Adaptec's AAA series RAID adapters use ordinary SCSI drives and cables. Prices start at $499 manufacturer's suggested retail.

It wasn't until early 1998 that nonproprietary RAID adapters became commercially viable when Adaptec introduced its first standard SCSI RAID adapter. The Adaptec RAID adapters were the first to integrate well in various brands and models of computers, and they had driver support for NetWare and other server OSes. When industry periodicals tested and compared available RAID SCSI adapters, the results were very favorable to Adaptec — their adapter was the easiest to set up and run and provided the best performance. When testing competing adapters, the testers were repeatedly frustrated with technical problems, poor documentation, poor support, poor performance, and high CPU utilization. Poor support is typical of companies that primarily cater to OEMs — they rely on the OEM to provide support when reselling their products. The Adaptec adapter was priced well below the few competing products that were available, and their technical support was well-suited for the aftermarket.

When building your own RAID subsystem, always purchase drives from different lot numbers, perhaps even different models or different manufacturers' drives. Defects in one drive are typically present in all drives from the same manufacturing run. When purchasing drives for a RAID system, be sure that all are Ultra-Wide SCSI or higher.

TIP

You can check Adaptec's Web site at http://www.adaptec.com **for complete product, technical, and pricing information on RAID adapters.**

Hardware-Based RAID Subsystems   In the past, proprietary RAID hardware subsystems were the only RAID options available, and they came at a premium price. Today many hardware-based RAID subsystems are available at prices that rival the cost of implementing your own RAID adapter and internal drives. Many use nonproprietary adapters and drives, but others still include proprietary components.

Here are a few features that might persuade you to consider a hardware-based RAID subsystem:

- External, expandable heavy-duty drive cabinet

- Dual, hot-pluggable fault-tolerant power supplies

- Drive cases that snap out for quick and easy on-the-fly replacement

- Multichannel Fast-Wide SCSI-2 or UltraSCSI PCI adapters

- RAID management and monitoring software

- 24 × 7 technical support with guaranteed immediate response

- Emergency replacement-part shipping via air carriers or priority overnight air

You can purchase any of these hardware items separately from various vendors, but consider the support options and software items just listed — where do you find that level of support? For example, your RAID adapter may fail on a Friday afternoon. When you call your hardware vendor, can they assure you that you will have a replacement by 10:30 the next morning? If a hardware-based RAID vendor cannot offer this level of support, they will not be successful in marketing their product.

WARNING   **Watch out for proprietary parts, especially adapters and drives. If your hardware-based RAID vendor discontinues a product, you might need to junk the entire system and your investment when a replacement part is needed.**

LANs

Which LAN to choose is not really a serious decision today. The majority of all LAN connections are Ethernet and Fast Ethernet. The only other LAN technologies that are commonly found are Fiber Distributed Data Interface (FDDI) and Token Ring. Most Token Ring networks are installed in IBM shops — organizations where large IBM mainframe-based systems dominate the network. Other technologies are almost rare, while Ethernet and Fast Ethernet are the de facto standards almost wherever you go. Ethernet/Fast Ethernet has extensive support in vendor offerings and is most cost-effective.

For workgroup LANs, choose Fast Ethernet (100Base-X) whenever possible. This technology is the default in the absence of any better new technologies. Token Ring is a good product but is generally more expensive than Fast Ethernet and does not come close in throughput. Fast Ethernet is a 100Mbps technology, while Token Ring is 16Mbps. Be sure to refer to cabling specifications discussed later in this chapter to be sure that Fast Ethernet products will work in your cabling system. Also, consult with your hub or switch vendor. Cabling rules are quite limited, and you need to be sure that your network design will handle the Fast Ethernet's low latency requirements.

For backbone LANs and high-capacity users, Gigabit Ethernet, FDDI, and ATM are the technologies of choice. You will find that these technologies are too expensive for typical desktops, and demand for this much bandwidth is rare for desktop users.

Campus Backbone LANs

FDDI at 100Mbps is far more expensive than Fast Ethernet but is valuable as a backbone technology. In a backbone, cost is not as important as it is in workstation LANs. The cost of a backbone LAN is distributed over the entire campus. In a typical campus, you can afford the better backbone technology but save money on the local network segments. FDDI is an excellent choice in backbones where local LANs are linked together into a campus-wide network as shown in Figure 5.3.

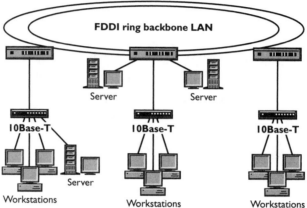

FIGURE 5.3

A backbone FDDI ring
connecting Ethernet
network segments

FDDI has much greater distance capabilities than Ethernet or Fast Ethernet. An FDDI LAN on fiber can stretch up to 60 miles in circumference in a ring and 1.2 miles between switches. Comparatively, the distance for a Fast Ethernet fiber optic cable segment is far more limited. Another reason FDDI makes sense as a backbone is usable bandwidth. Ethernet/Fast Ethernet can only use about 60–80 percent of its theoretical bandwidth. FDDI can operate at up to 95 percent utilization. Also, FDDI has several performance enhancements, error control features, and fault-tolerant design characteristics that are not available in Fast Ethernet.

When one is building an FDDI backbone, generally FDDI switches are used that bridge the FDDI backbone to the local Ethernet/Fast Ethernet network segments. In the network represented in Figure 5.3, the entire network is a bridge domain that acts as one logical network. This allows you quite a bit of flexibility in IP subnetting, since no routers are present in the local internetwork.

Asynchronous Transfer Mode (ATM) is the ultimate in backbones. However, ATM NICs are difficult to install and configure because LAN Emulation (LANE) is required. LANE also reduces usable bandwidth to 60 percent or less. ATM between switches is simple and effective and does not require LANE. ATM switches are an excellent solution if you use the same vendor switches throughout your backbone. Most ATM products employ 155Mbps bandwidth between switches and provide equivalent features to FDDI. ATM is the most expensive backbone technology you can employ but may be worth the expenditure. ATM is just about the only technology for the future; it has potential to reach 622Mbps and 1Gbps over extended distances.

Fast Ethernet is also often employed as a backbone technology. Cabling distances are quite restrictive, and usable bandwidth is limited, as discussed previously. However, price and simplicity are powerful factors that often tip the scales in favor of Fast Ethernet. When switches are used, cabling limitations are less significant—a switch bridges to a separate physical LAN, and the cabling budget starts over again.

Any backbone technology requires constant monitoring. Be sure that normal traffic patterns stay well below warning thresholds. The most important statistic to monitor is bandwidth utilization. Table 5.5 shows common thresholds used to determine when a network is too busy. Note that previous Table 5.2 lists the lowest to highest usable bandwidths in ascending order.

TABLE 5.5

LAN Thresholds and Usable
Bandwidth Utilization Levels

TYPE OF LAN	THRESHOLD (PERCENT)	THEORETICAL THROUGHPUT (MBPS)	MAXIMUM THROUGPUT (PERCENT)	MAXIMUM THROUGHPUT (MBPS)
Ethernet	30	10	70–90	7–9
Token Ring	80	16	95	15.2
Fast Ethernet	30	100	60–80	60–80
FDDI	80	100	90	90
ATM	50	155	90	139.5

Switching Hubs

A traditional Ethernet wiring concentrator is simply a multiport repeater. Every bit that is received on any cable segment is repeated on all other cabling segments. When normal wiring concentrators are used, bandwidth is shared among all connected users. Switched hubs can provide better throughput over the same cables, and with the same NICs.

Switches divide a network into separate segments. The ports switch between connected and nonconnected states. Using a little caching, LAN frames are cached at the switch and then sent to another cabling segment. This process eliminates the need to share bandwidth, as each cabling segment is dedicated to the attached user while transmitting the frame. Switch designs and features vary. Most often a switch connects two ports during a transmission and then switches the connection between two other ports as needed. Even if the destination port is busy, the switch's buffers can allow more than one node to send frames simultaneously.

Network Interface Cards

Though LANs are standardized, you will see a lot of design difference between NICs. Fast Ethernet NICs specially designed for servers are a good choice. In some cases, intelligent wiring concentrators (often called *hubs*) or switches must be used that are designed to take advantage of advanced features, such as duplex Ethernet. Though duplex Ethernet is not a standard, most vendors' products are interoperable.

Use PCI NICs

Always select PCI bus-mastering cards in a server. As discussed previously, PCI has much greater bandwidth than other bus designs and is an inexpensive technology. Select a card that is designed for a server. It often features a bus-mastering design that reduces CPU utilization by reducing processing required to service interrupts.

Using Multiple Adapters in a Server

One of the most important applications for bus-mastering products is where multiple NICs are installed in a server. Normal traffic generated by one NIC and one disk adapter is usually not a problem. However, when multiple NICs and/or multiple disk adapters are used in a server, bus traffic can become bottlenecked and CPU utilization can run very high, causing an additional bottleneck at the CPU. PCI, MCA, and EISA were designed specifically to alleviate this problem, but the computer and bus design only provide the *capability* for new performance levels. Your file server's performance relies heavily on the use of well-designed bus-mastering 32-bit adapters in that bus.

Full-Duplex Adapters

Full-duplex NICs almost double throughput, even above the stated theoretical bandwidth. Full duplex provides two channels: one for sending and one for receiving. A recent test in a major industry periodical tested the Intel PRO/100+ Management Adapter at 172 percent of its 100Mbps capacity when used in a full-duplex switched environment. Full duplex means that the NIC can communicate in both directions simultaneously. Full-duplex switches or wiring concentrators are required to take advantage of this feature.

Fault-Tolerant Server NICs

Intel's PRO/100+ Management Adapter was designed specifically for servers where fault tolerance is required. These NICs can be duplexed — two identical cards are configured to act as one adapter. This feature does not accommodate more traffic than a single full-duplex NIC, but it provides a fault-tolerant LAN connection. If one adapter were to fail, the other adapter maintains the connection with clients without interruption. Duplexed NICs constitute a breakthrough in fortifying critical failure points that can cripple your network.

LAN Cabling

This chapter discusses building a good media platform for your LAN. When designing your network, you will find that it pays to invest in a good cabling plant. Cabling problems affect the majority of LANs. Though LAN cabling accounts for only 10 percent of the overall cost of installing a network, support costs related to cabling cost organizations $250,000 per year per 100 users (according to a study commissioned by LeCroy, manufacturers of testing equipment). Other recent studies indicate that cabling accounts for well over half of LAN connectivity problems.

Cabling becomes a performance issue when poor cabling is installed. Ethernet/Fast Ethernet is especially sensitive to cabling faults. For example, cabling that cannot certify as category 5 can cause performance degradation for Fast Ethernet when bandwidth utilization is high. In many cases, no problems are evident until bandwidth utilization approaches recommended thresholds. A kink in a cable can cause strong reflections that appear to be collisions. Problems such as these can cause considerable intermittent problems with Ethernet networks.

Cabling rules used to be a major issue. Not so long ago, each type of LAN had different cabling rules. Within the past couple of years, the Telecommunications Industry Association (TIA) in conjunction with the Electronics Industry Alliance (EIA) developed and approved the EIA/TIA Structured Cabling System Design specifications. EIA/TIA specifications are used in wiring new buildings so that cabling throughout the building will be suitable for voice and data applications. These specifications also provide good cabling documentation for all common types of LANs and telecommunications equipment.

Structured Cabling System Design

The EIA/TIA Structured Cabling System Design specifies:

▸ Minimum requirements for telecommunications cabling within an office environment

▸ Recommended topology and distances

▸ Media parameters that determine performance

▸ Connector and pin assignments to ensure interconnectability

▸ The useful life of telecommunications cabling systems as being in excess of ten years

EIA/TIA's Structured Cabling System Design is an overall design specification for wiring an entire building from end to end.

Look for Anixter's condensed guide on structured cabling system design at http://www.anixter.com/techlib/standard/cabling/.

NOTE

Horizontal and Work Area Cabling Specifications — EIA/TIA 568A

These cabling specifications support all common LANs. If category 5 unshielded twisted-pair (UTP) is used with all category 5 connectors, and distance limitations are observed, you can install Ethernet, Token Ring, Fast Ethernet, FDDI, and ATM networks on the same cabling.

Be sure your cabling is up to EIA/TIA standards. Most network technicians simply test a cable segment for continuity and perhaps the correct pin-out. In order to test the adequacy of a cabling segment, you need to use a cable tester. Each cabling segment, from the hub or switch port to the NIC, should be tested to meet the category 3, 4, or 5 level. Many electronic characteristics for wiring vary according to length and must fall within allowable variances. Measurements and calculations are so complex that a cabling tester is the only practical way to certify installed cabling.

Figure 5.4 illustrates the aspects of horizontal cabling described in the text that follows.

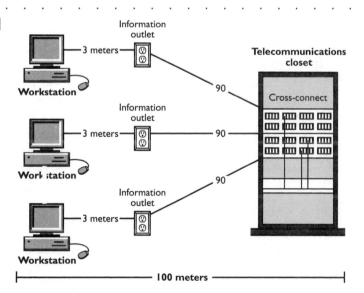

FIGURE 5.4

Maximum distances for horizontal cabling

Maximum Distances for Horizontal Cabling

Cable runs are limited to 100 meters (327 feet), no more than 90 meters between the wiring closet and the data outlet, a total of 10 meters is allowed for work area and telecommunications closet patch and jumper cables.

Telecommunications Outlet (Wall plate)

Each work area shall have a minimum of *two* information outlet ports, one for voice and one for data.

Media Types

Three media types are recognized as options for horizontal cabling, each extending a maximum distance of 90 meters:

1. 4-pair 100 ohm UTP cable (24 AWG solid conductors)

2. 2-pair 150 ohm shielded twisted-pair (STP) cables

3. 2 fiber 62.5/125 μm optical fiber cable

NOTE

UTP comes in voice-grade and data-grade levels. Most organizations use UTP category 5–rated cabling, which is data grade. The category rating was implemented to provide ratings that would make it simple to find cable that fit EIA specifications for various purposes. Category 3 is voice-grade UTP that supports telecommunications and Ethernet 10Base-T standards. Category 5 is a data-grade UTP that is required for 16Mbps Token Ring, Fast Ethernet (100Base-TX), FDDI on copper wire, ATM, and all other LANs that support 100Mbps transmission rates (up to 100 MHz).

Use category 5 solid or stranded wire to support all types of 100Mbps LAN technologies. The same type of cable should be used throughout your cabling system.

Eight-Position Modular Jack Pair Assignments for UTP (RJ-45)

Cable ends are to be pinned out as shown in Figure 5.5.

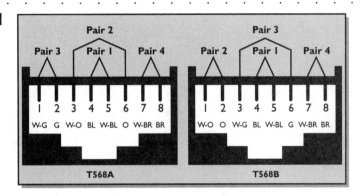

FIGURE 5.5

Eight-position modular jack pin-outs for local data networking

The outer cabling jacket should be trimmed to 3mm ($^1/_2$ inch). Be sure to use the correct type of modular jack — some are made for solid core wire; others, for stranded.

NOTE

Wires in your UTP cable must be paired properly. Split pairs result in excessive crosstalk, attenuation, noise, and so on. Cable that is improperly paired will show good link status, but any cable tester will reveal improperly paired wires.

General Comments

Cable alone is not enough to ensure that your wiring is up to specifications. Connectors, wiring blocks, and other connection/termination hardware must be up to category 5 specifications and must be installed in a manner that produces category 5 requirements when tested.

Care must be taken during installation to ensure good contacts at points where cabling is connected. Category 5 parts are designed to provide a positive connection, but when improperly installed they will not support high-performance LANs. Sloppy workmanship and faulty connectors are usually to blame for cabling that does not perform to expected levels.

TIP

When outsourcing cable installation, use a qualified electrical contractor who specializes in LAN cabling. Always specify in your contract to retain final payment until the cabling installation is certified in-house or by an independent contractor.

If cabling problems are suspected, either purchase a cable tester or outsource with a cabling engineer to scan your cabling system for category 5 compliance. Many cable testers are available that provide one-touch testing for UTP.

 For more complete information about the EIA/TIA 568A and 569 cabling specifications, see Anixter's Web site at `http://www.anixter.com/techlib/standard/cabling.`

Power Conditioning, Power Monitoring

A very important factor to consider is the power you put through your file server. All NetWare versions are sensitive to power inconsistencies, especially poorly conditioned power. Poorly conditioned power is very common in office buildings, and many pieces of office equipment introduce power surges, spikes, and noise. Power fluctuations can be radical enough to reboot computers. Over an extended period, power fluctuations can damage power supplies and electronic equipment on servers and peripherals.

You have three basic considerations with regard to servers and power:

- ▸ Source interruption

- ▸ Conditioning

- ▸ Supply monitoring

Uninterruptible Power Sources

Your file server cannot handle an interruption of power from your AC source. A momentary loss of power or drop in voltage can cause your servers to go down, which in turn can cause file damage. Because active files are cached in RAM on the server, loss of power causes loss of data updates and failure to update file system directory entry tables and file allocation tables. NetWare's Transaction Tracking System (TTS) will recover file damage, but some updates may be lost.

Two types of power supplies are sold for file server protection: uninterruptible power supplies (UPSs) and switching power supplies. Both types are commonly called UPSs, but a true UPS provides battery power to your server while AC power regenerates the battery. A switching power supply provides AC from your power receptacle and switches to battery power if the source is interrupted, as shown in Figure 5.6. A true UPS provides better protection and eliminates many types of power defects. A switching power supply is adequate if it can switch within four microseconds and provides adequate power conditioning. A good UPS provides superior protection, and although it is more expensive, it can be more cost-effective in filtering out power defects, as discussed next.

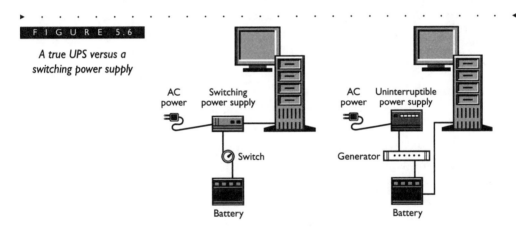

F I G U R E 5.6

A true UPS versus a switching power supply

Power Conditioning

Many types of power defects can shorten the life of your file server's internal power supply and integrated circuits. Some power defects can actually cause your server to crash, depending upon what thread is in process on the file server. Novell's Systems Research Department issued a research report in December 1991 ("Power and Grounding for Distributed Computing") that explicitly details power problems and solutions for NetWare servers.

WARNING

UPS protection is not enough for your server. Many power defects can cause your server to crash. Power in office complexes is often very poorly conditioned. Be sure you get a UPS designed for computer use that includes power conditioning. Study specifications; you will find that a good power conditioning UPS is not very expensive.

Special electrical specifications for electrical installations do not always work as planned, as electrical implementation is not governed by specifications alone. Very often, installations do not accomplish what electrical specifications say they should because electricians have ignored instructions that exceed code requirements. Every detail of an electrical installation must be accomplished according to engineering specifications to be effective. Quite often electricians take shortcuts that do not jeopardize safety but can adversely affect power conditioning. Inspectors only spot check, and for the most part they are only concerned with hazards to personal safety.

Surge protectors and suppressors do not do much (if anything at all) to protect your server. They are mainly designed for personal protection against large voltage or amperage surges and spikes, such as lightning strikes. Your computer power supply transforms all voltages to the lower voltages at which your computer's components operate anyway.

The problem with voltage or amperage surges or spikes is the edge speed of the transition — how quickly the voltage or amperage change occurs. A power fluctuation may be small enough to slip past a surge protector but fast enough in edge speed to cause damage or crash your server.

WARNING

If a circuit is not properly grounded, a voltage spike can charge through the common grounding wire and enter your computer's power supply through the ground on the motherboard, bypassing all protection. A good surge protector must have a capacitor to slow the speed edge of the voltage transition.

Surge protectors monitor voltage changes but do not monitor frequency modulation. Fluctuations in amperage can also damage computer equipment. More commonly, amperage fluctuations take their toll over an extended period.

Other grounding problems can cause excessive line noise and amperage fluctuation. If electrical installations were performed in strict compliance with codes, these problems would not be so common. Even well-constructed buildings suffer from various types of grounding deficiencies. The problem with electrical specifications is that they do not control how the installation is to be done, and often the method of installation cancels the expected benefits of the specifications.

TIP

You would not be able to detect some of these problems without a sophisticated power analyzer. If you have questions about your power protection, you should have your power line monitored with a Dranitz analyzer or similar piece of electrical test equipment that provides a trend chart record, like a heart monitor or seismograph. These devices can be rented to test your power source.

Many types of power transformers, power filters, and other devices are available, but the most comprehensive device to use is a good power conditioner that is grounded to a properly grounded circuit. This device should be employed with your UPS, not in place of it.

UPS Monitoring

NetWare includes the capability to automatically shut down the server OS when power is interrupted. The UPS.NLM file is provided for this service. A simple connection (via RS-232C or interface card and cable) between your power supply and server can notify the UPS monitoring application that power has been shut off at the supply side of your UPS. This feature requires no special vendor server software but does require a UPS equipped for UPS monitoring. Most UPSes designed for use with NetWare come with a cable that is pinned out for use with NetWare servers. Be sure your cable is pinned properly, or it will not work when you need it to.

Many UPS vendors also provide their own UPS monitoring software to run on your server as a NLM. NetWare's simple UPS.NLM will do the basic job of shutting down your server when the UPS detects that power has been interrupted, as long as the monitoring cable is properly constructed. Vendor applications often add such features as notification via pager and a graphical monitoring utility.

▶ . . . . ◀

Setting Up the Server and LAN

Before you begin your NetWare installation, use this checklist to make sure you are properly prepared:

I. Install all hardware devices in your server.

2. Partition your first drive, and prepare a bootable DOS volume, leaving all other drives unpartitioned.

3. Run testing and diagnostic software provided with your equipment.

4. Cable your server and one workstation.

5. Test your NIC and LAN connection.

6. Locate the latest certified drivers for your hardware devices.

7. Test and record all device settings for reference during installation.

Perform each of these steps, and any other preinstallation steps, methodically with careful attention to results. You will find that installation will be much smoother and less chaotic when you are absolutely certain about each aspect of your hardware. When problems occur during installation and you have not tested all devices thoroughly, you will find yourself retracing your steps and spending far more time recovering from problems than it would have taken to test in advance.

Be sure to have a pencil and paper handy to jot down additional steps you may discover during setup, or missing items you need to handle. Review all reference materials prior to installing hardware. Look for release notes that may be missing from the documentation.

Install All Hardware Devices

Before you attempt installation, you need to make certain that your hardware is properly installed and working. When hardware does not work, installation can become quite problematic. Most problems during installation are a result of improperly functioning hardware. The following list will help you to remember all the most important steps to take before attempting an installation.

Install Disk Adapters

Your system may come with an internal IDE adapter and hard drive. As discussed previously in this chapter, IDE drives do not provide adequate performance for high-powered server duty; however, you can put the operating system on the IDE drive and all applications and data on a SCSI system.

If an IDE adapter is integrated into your motherboard, you may need to enable or disable the disk adapter's primary channel. This is done by entering the computer's hardware setup program, stored in the computer BIOS. The hardware setup program is typically accessed by striking Delete or F1 during boot.

You also need to have the latest drivers for your server components. Without the proper drivers you can experience a wide variety of problems. You need to test and record your hardware device settings so that they can be input during installation. Use NetWare tested and certified drivers whenever possible.

Set Up SCSI Devices

SCSI devices need to be cabled, terminated, and addressed correctly or they will not work. Check the following items:

▸ Obtain the correct type of cable for your adapter or channel. Do not use standard 50-pin ribbon cables for Fast SCSI channels — you might encounter excessive error rates. More often you might not receive any errors, because the SCSI protocol will recover the errors. However, performance can be compromised.

▸ The last drive must be terminated. A terminator must be installed on the last drive, or on the last cable segment when external drives are used.

▸ Each drive must be configured with a SCSI address, which is normally done with jumper settings on the drive.

▸ To enable boot from a SCSI drive, you must enable the adapter's BIOS. Be sure that the interrupt, port, and memory addresses your adapter is using are available, or the BIOS will fail to load into memory during boot.

▶ Run the SCSI setup and testing program and select software configuration options. You access this program either during boot (watch for SCSI BIOS message) or from a disk after adapter installation.

Partition Your First Drive

Prepare a bootable DOS volume, format it, and put MS-DOS boot files on it. Make a partition large enough to accommodate future use. Give yourself plenty of extra space in your DOS boot volume. Allocate disk space of two and one-half times the amount of RAM in your server or at least 100MB, whichever is greater. You may need to save a "memory dump" to disk for diagnostic purposes. This requirement will be discussed in Chapters 6, 7, and 8, which pertain to installing NetWare 3, 4, and 5, respectively.

Do not include HIMEM.SYS or any memory management software in your startup files. NetWare needs unmodified linear memory to start up.

Leave all other drives unpartitioned — you will partition them later in the NetWare INSTALL utility. If you have put a partition on the drive, INSTALL may not be able to remove the partition.

Run Testing and Diagnostic Software Provided with Your Equipment

Run all testing and diagnostic software that is available to you. Most newer computers come with testing and diagnostic software. You need to be sure every device is installed and configured properly so that the NetWare drivers will load automatically.

NetWare is not a plug-and-play operating system. Set up all plug-and-play devices using the software provided with your adapter for DOS. Install the plug-and-play software on the DOS volume in case you need to reconfigure your plug-and-play devices at a later date.

Cable Your Server and One Workstation

It is best to get one workstation on line first and then add more workstations in succession. It seems as though problems come in groups. It is overwhelming at times to encounter several problems at once. For example, one workstation may have a bad cable, another, a bad NIC, and another may have the wrong settings for the NIC, or one computer can have all three of these problems. A one-step-at-a-time policy helps preserve your sanity. Once you have gotten your first workstation connected, you know everything is working properly and then you can handle additional problems one at a time.

To eliminate possible cabling or hub problems, you can use a crossover cable to attach a workstation directly to the server (without a hub between them). Normal LAN cabling is pinned straight through (pins 1-1, 2-2, 3-3, and 6-6). The hub crosses transmit to receive and positive to negative in each pair. When you directly connect, you need to establish the crossover in the cable. (A crossover cable is pinned 1-3, 2-6, 3-1, and 6-2.) A proven crossover cable works as a troubleshooting tool later on to help you make sure you have a good connection.

Test Your NIC and LAN Connection

Most NICs come with testing and diagnostic software — use it! Once you have physically installed your NICs, you may need to run a setup utility to select port addresses, interrupts, and perhaps memory addressing. Next, load the testing software and run all the tests that are available.

Many NIC testing software packages come with a server-client test. Boot your server and all connected workstations from DOS. Run the server test software on one computer (it does not matter which one), and then run the client test software on another computer. The client should send a series of frames to the server, and the server should respond without errors. If there is a serious cable fault, the test will tell you that the cable is not installed properly. Be sure to get an error-free reading before continuing.

WARNING

Be careful when handling adapters, or any time you open the case of your computer. Use a grounding strap if you work on computers frequently. At the very least, make sure you ground yourself before handling any electronic equipment. A static electrical spark is the most common cause for defective NICs and other adapters.

Locate the Latest Certified Drivers for Your Hardware Devices

Be sure you have the latest drivers for the version of NetWare that you will be installing. Carefully check to see that the drivers you have are for the proper make and model adapters and NICs you have physically installed.

NOTE   **Hardware often takes several months to make it from the manufacturer to you. During that period the driver software may have been updated, but the disks in the package will not have been updated. Check the manufacturers' Web sites for driver updates and release notes immediately before attempting NetWare installation.**

Always check release notes and all pertinent information you find on the manufacturer's Web site. It is common for a manufacturer to find irregularities from end consumers after their development and quality-control departments have released the device. You will often save a lot of time addressing these issues in advance instead of trying to correct them during installation.

Be sure that the drivers are Novell certified. This assures you that the product has passed extensive tests to be sure that it will work properly with the NetWare version you will install. Look for the "Yes" label with the Novell logo indicating that the product has been officially tested and approved.

Check the manufacturer's support policies before proceeding. Make sure that support personnel will be on hand when you are performing your installation. Whenever possible, make sure that the manufacturer provides support rather than relying on the vendor from which you purchase the item. Manufacturers are better equipped than vendors to handle problems with their products.

Test and Record All Device Settings for Reference During Installation

Verify all device settings before starting installation. Write them down or print them out if an option is provided. If something does not work during installation, you will find that your memory may not be as sound as you would like.

CHAPTER 6

NetWare 3 Server Setup

The purpose of this chapter is to guide you through installing NetWare 3.12's server OS and then upgrading it to 3.2. NetWare 3.2 does not have a new install — you must install 3.12 and then upgrade it with the 3.2 Enhancement Pack. If you are installing for the first time or upgrading from a previous version, you will find very few — if any — differences. This chapter is a simple step-by-step installation guide that addresses configuration issues that may arise. You may find tips and warnings in this chapter helpful in making your installation go easily with the greatest benefit of foresight.

This chapter assumes the following things:

▶ You have selected and assembled a computer to be the file server.

▶ Your LAN and cabling have been properly installed.

▶ Your NICs are installed and tested and do not conflict with other hardware or software devices.

▶ Your server has a CD-ROM drive that can be installed as a DOS device.

▶ You are installing a single server and just a few workstations.

Installing the NetWare 3.12 server operating system (OS) is as simple as executing the standard unconfigured OS file from DOS and loading drivers. If a driver fails to load, the configuration is obviously not correct, or the device is simply not functioning. The INSTALL program's simplicity is in striking contrast with other OS installations, but a little guidance prevents stumbling over some of the details.

Installation Options

NetWare can be installed from:

▶ Floppies

▶ CD-ROM

▸ Network drive

▸ Networked or shared CD-ROM drive

All NetWare server operating systems (OSes) are shipped on CD, but NetWare 3 can still be purchased on floppies. Installing from floppies is not only more expensive but also more labor-intensive. CD-ROM installation is the quickest and easiest way to install NetWare 3.

Every current version of NetWare requires a bootable DOS volume. All NetWare server OSes are executed from a DOS (or Windows 95) volume after the server has been booted. Though NetWare 3.12 can boot from a floppy, NetWare 3.2 and higher versions must be booted from a hard drive. All versions require DOS disk space to contain the server boot files. This chapter discusses preparing servers to receive NetWare 3 and then goes on to instructions for installing it.

Preparing the Server

Before you begin your installation, you need to:

1. Prepare a bootable DOS volume.

2. Install your CD-ROM DOS driver(s) and CD-ROM extensions (MSCDEX.EXE or equivalent).

3. Obtain the latest disk and NIC drivers for your server's internal adapters.

NOTE

Your drivers must be updated when upgrading from NetWare 3.11. Before updating an existing NetWare 3.11 server, compare and update the files in the NetWare server directory of your DOS volume from the DRIVERS directory on the Enhancement Pack CD.

4. Be prepared with your adapters' hardware configuration settings, your NetWare installation CD or floppy disks, and your NetWare SYSTEM_1 (or INSTALL) disk.

Check release notes and preinstallation instructions before proceeding. You will be able to view these files from within INSTALL, or you can look for README files on your NetWare CD. You will find README files in the \NW312\NETWARE.312\<_language_>\README directory on your NetWare installation CDs.

Creating a Bootable DOS Volume

Though NetWare 3.12 only requires 5MB of DOS disk space, NetWare 3.2 requires a minimum of 20MB. You should allocate at least 50MB for several reasons. You may decide to install NetWare Loadable Modules (NLMs), drivers, DOS external executables, DOS utilities, hardware diagnostic utilities, and virus scanning software on the DOS volume. If you decide to upgrade the server, more disk space may be required. In case of server crashes, you may wish to dump memory to a file for debugging, which requires enough disk space to accommodate the total amount of memory installed in your server. For the foregoing reasons, allocating disk space equal to two and one-half times the amount of installed RAM would ensure that you could safely save one, or possibly two, memory dumps. At least 100MB in your server's DOS volume is a practical suggestion.

Though NetWare 3.12 supports booting from a floppy disk, NetWare 3.2 does not.

If you boot from a SCSI drive, you will need to set up your SCSI system properly as discussed in Chapter 5. To make a SCSI drive bootable, you may need to enable your SCSI BIOS and configure the first SCSI drive as bootable in your SCSI utilities. If the SCSI BIOS is not used, DOS device drivers are required in your CONFIG.SYS.

To create a bootable DOS drive: Create a DOS primary partition, make it active, and format it with a system. This is typically done at the factory for most computers, but most computers are shipped with an entire drive allocated to DOS, Windows 95, or Windows NT. NetWare only needs a small DOS partition, and this often means repartitioning and reinstalling DOS.

In many cases, computer manufacturers provide their own setup utilities. You should review your computer owner's manual for any special considerations before attempting to partition your drive.
NOTE

You can use Novell DOS, located on the 3.x SYSTEM_1 disk, or any later version of DOS to create a bootable DOS volume. NetWare comes with a bootable floppy disk that contains the FORMAT and FDISK utilities in the DOSTOOLS directory. If you are not familiar with the procedure of creating a partition and formatting it, see your DOS manual. Here is a generalized set of instructions for this procedure used with all recent DOS versions:

1. Boot from a bootable DOS floppy.

2. Run the DOS FDISK utility. Check the existing partition information. Delete all partitions before continuing.

   a. Create a primary DOS partition.

   b. Do not allocate all free disk space to the partition, but instead enter the amount of space to be allocated to your DOS boot volume.

   c. Make the primary DOS partition active.

   d. Reboot to your DOS floppy disk.

3. Run the DOS FORMAT utility.

   a. Execute the command FORMAT C: /s (place a system on drive C:).

   b. Create a DOS directory and copy the external executable DOS utilities into this directory (optional).

4. Create or edit your CONFIG.SYS and AUTOEXEC.BAT files.

   a. Include the path to your DOS directory in the AUTOEXEC.BAT

   b. Do not load any memory management software (such as HIMEM.SYS) in your CONFIG.SYS.

5. Run your CD-ROM drive's DOS setup utility. A device driver is required in CONFIG.SYS, and a CD extensions utility is required in AUTOEXEC.BAT.

To create a branching DOS boot menu, see the section "Creating a Branching DOS Boot Menu," later in this chapter.

NOTE

6. Remove your DOS floppy disk from drive A: and reboot. Verify that everything works correctly, and that you can access files on a CD.

Do not load any memory management software (such as HIMEM.SYS) in your CONFIG.SYS. The NetWare server OS requires unconfigured memory. Any memory allocated as XMS memory is not available.

NOTE

Installing from Floppies

If you are installing from floppy disks, your installation procedure will be very much the same as the CD installation. You will be prompted to insert disks wherever appropriate. The disk label will be shown when you are prompted to insert the next disk.

A floppy installation starts with the INSTALL disk.

Installing from CD-ROM

Novell designed NetWare's server INSTALL program to be run from CD. For most computers, running a CD-ROM drive as a DOS device is the most practical way of using the drive for installation. When purchasing your CD-ROM drive, be sure that the device comes with everything that is needed to install it as a DOS device.

The CD-ROM drive may be an IDE or SCSI device — either is acceptable. However, NetWare drivers may not support older CD-ROMs as NetWare devices. You will need a DOS device driver (such as CR_ATAPI.SYS) and Microsoft CD Extensions (MSCDEX.EXE) or equivalent. If your CD-ROM drive is a SCSI device, you may need a CD driver (such as ASPICD.SYS) in addition to a DOS SCSI device driver and MSCDEX.EXE. The device drivers (files that normally have .SYS extensions) are installed into CONFIG.SYS, whereas MSCDEX.EXE (or equivalent) is installed in your AUTOEXEC.BAT file. CD-ROM drives that use MSCDEX.EXE are not shipped with it — you must use MSCDEX.EXE from your

DOS system software. CD extensions are not provided with Novell DOS that is included with NetWare.

Many computers have bootable CD-ROM drives, and many SCSI adapters can be configured to boot from CD. NetWare's installation program does not take advantage of this feature. If your computer has a bootable CD, you will need to create a bootable DOS volume and allocate enough space on which to install your server boot files. In most cases, you will find that installing DOS support files is the most efficient way — and perhaps the only way — to install from CD.

NOTE

Some computer manufacturers provide a bootable CD with partitioning and formatting programs on a system CD. See your computer's installation manual for details. Be sure to check read your setup documentation carefully so that you do not end up destroying this partition.

If you are installing NetWare from CD, a CD-ROM drive must physically installed, and DOS drivers must be loaded in the server. Once your NetWare server OS is installed, your system files contain NetWare drivers for all later model IDE and SCSI CD-ROM drives and a CD reader NLM to recognize CD file systems as NetWare volumes.

TIP

Do not mix different SCSI version devices on the same channel — all devices on the same channel will be configured to perform to the lowest performance level of any device. Each SCSI device should be configured properly to take advantage of its capabilities. For best performance, see Chapter 5 to be sure your SCSI devices are set up and configured properly. You will also find SCSI FAQ on the CD that accompanies this book.

Installing from a Network

A NetWare server can be installed over a network from a shared CD or from a network drive to which the NetWare server installation files have been copied. The process is simple and is recommended any time more than one server (of the same version) must be installed.

Installing from a Networked CD-ROM

To install from a networked CD-ROM drive, map a drive letter to the shared CD-ROM volume and enter the source path as any other network drive mapping. Wherever you are prompted to verify source and destination path names during INSTALL, substitute the network drive/directory path for the default.

Installing from a Network Drive

You can also install your NetWare server from a network drive or CD-ROM drive that is shared on the network. This option is perfectly acceptable and is used wherever integrators need to install several servers.

1. Use XCOPY to copy the \NW312\NETWARE.312\ENGLISH directory and all subdirectories on your CD to a network drive. When using XCOPY, be sure to include the /c and /e switches. You may use Windows Explorer to do the same by right-clicking the \NW312\NETWARE.312\ENGLISH directory on the CD and then selecting Copy from the menu. You will then right-click the destination drive or directory and select Paste.

2. Map root to the drive/directory you created in step 1.

3. Change directories to the mapped drive.

4. Execute INSTALL.BAT.

5. Use XCOPY to copy the \NW32 directory and all subdirectories on your CD to a network drive.

6. Load INSTALL.NLM at your server console.

7. Select Product Options.

8. Select the \NW32 directory. The PINSTALL.NLM application will automatically load the NetWare 3.2 Enhancement Pack.

Wherever you are prompted to verify source and destination path names during INSTALL, substitute the network drive/directory path for the default.

This procedure requires you to set up your new server as a client to another server before starting INSTALL, which requires almost as much effort as installing the server OS. However, when installing multiple servers, you will find that your setup time will have been spent judiciously.

▶ • ◀

Server Operating System Installation

The following sections discuss installing your server step by step in a quick start overview, and in detail.

Server Installation Quick Start

This section discusses a quick overview. If you are experienced with installing operating systems, you may be able to install from the steps that follow. If you have questions about anything you encounter during the installation, refer to the next section, where each step is covered in detail. If the following process does not seem to be very familiar, follow the same steps through this section for step-by-step instructions.

Once you have booted to DOS and your CD-ROM drive is available, installing the server OS comprises the following steps:

1. Change directories to the \NW312\NETWARE.312\<language> directory, and execute INSTALL.BAT from the CD-ROM.

   a. Assign a server name and an internal IPX network number.

   b. Configure the Country Code, Code Page, and Keyboard for your server.

   c. Select a filename format.

   d. Specify any special SET commands in STARTUP.NCF and instruct INSTALL to modify your AUTOEXEC.BAT to autoload SERVER.EXE.

   e. The server operating system will load.

2. Load SERVER.NLM.

3. Switch to your console (Alt+Esc) and load and configure your disk driver.

4. Create your NetWare disk partition(s).

5. Create your NetWare volume(s) and then mount the volume(s).

6. Copy the System and Public files.

7. Load and configure your server NIC driver(s).

8. Bind the IPX protocol to your NIC driver(s).

9. Bind additional protocols to your NIC driver(s).

10. Create and save the system startup files.

In the sections that follow, each step is discussed in depth.

NetWare 3.12 Installation Procedure

The following instructions will step you through the process of installing NetWare 3.12. You must first install 3.12 and then update the server to 3.2. At the end of this section you will find a section devoted to updating your 3.12 server to 3.2.

Step 1: Execute the INSTALL.BAT File from the CD-ROM

You will find this file in the \NW312\NETWARE.312\I<*language*> directory. The screen shown in Figure 6.1 will appear.

1. Select Display Information (README) File. This option will provide a wealth of installation instructions. You can review these files on any DOS computer without initiating the INSTALL utility.

2. Select the option you wish to use, either Upgrade from 3.1x or Install a New NetWare 3.12. This chapter shows the Install a New NetWare 3.12 option. The upgrade option is very similar but will not destroy your existing system configuration or security (bindery) files.

▶ . . . . ◀

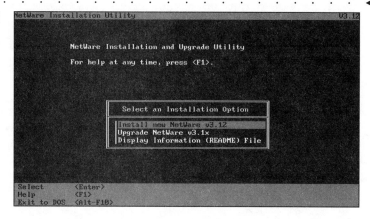

FIGURE 6.1

Select an Installation Option screen.

3. Accept the DOS partition, or create a DOS partition. When you proceed with the Install a New NetWare 3.12 option, you will be given the choice to retain your current partitioning or create a new DOS partition. If you have already made a DOS partition, go on by selecting Retain Current Disk Partitions. Follow the directions, which will create a bootable DOS volume and reboot your computer to DOS. You will then restart the install process from the beginning. If you elect to create your bootable DOS partition at this time, you will need to start INSTALL over again and proceed to this point again.

4. Enter the server name. The server name is not case sensitive; can contain between 2 and 298 alphanumeric characters (0–9, A–Z); and can contain underscores, hyphens, or periods, but not spaces. Only alphanumeric characters are to be used as the first character. INSTALL will not permit you to use an invalid name.

5. Accept or edit the IPX internal network address. Each server must be assigned a unique internal IPX network number as discussed in Chapter 3. An IPX network number is a four-byte number expressed in hexadecimal format (eight hex characters — 0–9, A–F). You will not be permitted to include illegal characters. INSTALL prompts you with a random number, but you should consider using a numbering convention for this address — it will help you identify your servers when viewing routing information. For more discussion on IPX network addressing, see Chapter 3.

6. Copy the startup files to your server's DOS volume. You will be prompted to insert the SYSTEM_1 disk into drive A. If you already have your SYSTEM_1 disk in drive A:, you will not see this prompt. The INSTALL.BAT utility will copy the appropriate files onto your DOS volume.

Your SYSTEM_1 disk contains a serialized NetWare OS executable file (SERVER.EXE). Be sure that you use the appropriate disk when installing your server or you will receive copyright violation errors when your server is running. You should make a duplicate of (diskcopy) this disk and protect the original; you may need the serial number on this disk to upgrade at a later date.

If you have copied vendor-provided disks or NIC drivers into your DOS boot directory, INSTALL will prompt you to decide whether they should be overwritten.

NetWare 3.2 includes updated LAN and disk drivers for an extensive selection of devices. However, your NICs and/or disk drivers may not be included or may be out of date. Always check with your device manufacturer before installation for the latest NetWare 3.x drivers.

Disk adapter vendors may require you to purchase a disk driver for NetWare separately. Drivers for SCSI disk subsystems come from the SCSI host adapter manufacturer or OEM.

7. Select the locale configuration for the server. Select the country code, code page, and keyboard mapping. Use the default values for English. For other languages see the README file pertaining to language on your NetWare 3.2 CD. Options other than the default support the use of various languages and associated keyboard characters on the server's keyboard and console.

Press F10 to continue.

8. Select the filename format. Unless you need to support a foreign character set on your server's file system(s), select the DOS filename format. The DOS file name format is not case-sensitive and does not contain foreign characters. The NetWare file name format is case-sensitive and is not recommended.

9. Specify any special startup set commands. Refer to documentation for your disk adapters and NICs for commands that are required in this file. This file is stored in your DOS boot directory, and it can be edited later if necessary.

10. Configure AUTOEXEC.BAT to load or not to load SERVER.EXE automatically. At this point, you can allow INSTALL to execute SERVER.EXE in your DOS AUTOEXEC.BAT file.

TIP

In the "Post-Installation Procedures" section of this chapter you will find a discussion on how to create a branching boot menu with version 6 of DOS or higher. You will find this option helpful any time you need to boot your server to DOS for maintenance.

Another helpful option is to strike the F5 key during boot (if your DOS version provides this feature) to prevent the startup files from executing.

INSTALL.BAT will now start the server OS, leaving you at a console prompt, which consists of the server name followed by a colon.

You may elect to abort the installation at this time and copy your latest 3.12 drivers onto your DOS volume. To do so, type **DOWN** at the colon (NetWare server console) prompt. Type **EXIT** to return to DOS, and copy new drivers into the NetWare boot directory. To restart the operating system, type **SERVER** from the NetWare boot directory (by default this is the C:\SERVER.312 directory). You will have to manually re-enter your server name and internal network address.

Your server operating system will automatically load at this point.

Step 2: Load and Configure the Disk Driver

1. Manually load your disk driver(s) from the DOS server boot directory. Many disk drivers were copied to this directory when your boot files were copied. This is your default directory until a valid NetWare volume has been created and mounted. If you have an updated driver or a driver provided by your disk adapter manufacturer or OEM, copy that driver into your DOS server boot directory (see the previous step). Load the driver using the command:

```
LOAD DRIVER_NAME
```

See your disk adapter's NetWare installation instructions for the driver name and any switches to be entered after the driver name. The default driver for an IDE drive is IDE.DSK.

2. Configure the driver. When the driver loads, it will present queries for hardware settings and configuration options that are required. You will be asked for the I/O port (base I/O address) and interrupt number (IRQ). The interrupt is expressed in hexadecimal. The default for a primary disk adapter is E, which is the hexadecimal equivalent of the decimal number 14.

TIP

If your driver fails to load, check to see that you have the correct driver and settings, and to see that the hardware is working properly. If you need to correct the problem, type DOWN at the server console prompt, fix the problem, restart the operating system, and then load INSTALL.NLM and try again.

Step 3: Load INSTALL.NLM

Load the server-based install program, INSTALL.NLM. At the colon prompt, enter the command:

```
LOAD INSTALL
```

The NetWare INSTALL NLM will load, and you will see the Installation Options screen shown in Figure 6.2.

▶ • ◀

FIGURE 6.2

INSTALL.NLM's Installation
Options screen

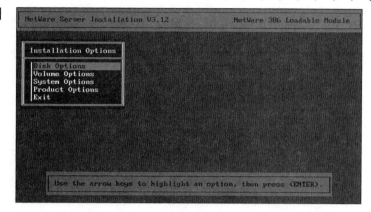

NetWare Server Installation V3.12   NetWare 386 Loadable Module

Installation Options
Disk Options
Volume Options
System Options
Product Options
Exit

Use the arrow keys to highlight an option, then press <ENTER>.

**You can switch between the console screen and the INSTALL
program by pressing Alt+Esc. Any time you hear a beep, switch to the
console screen to view a console message.**

NOTE

Step 4: Create NetWare Partition(s)

1. Select Disk Options, Partitions, Create NetWare Partition. If there are
multiple disk drives, select the drive that is to contain the operating system
and its directories and files. Each physical disk drive should be listed in a
menu if its driver has been loaded and it is working properly.

**If a drive is not listed, check to see if the driver was properly loaded.
Most drives are low-level formatted at the factory, but some must be
low-level formatted with the SCSI adapter utilities. Some SCSI
adapters require a setup program to be run before disk drives can be
recognized. See your adapter installation manual for instructions.**

NOTE

Once you have selected a drive, you will see the Partition Information screen
with partitioning and hot fix configuration options shown in Figure 6.3.

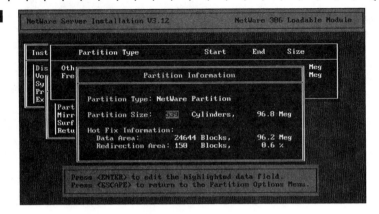

F I G U R E 6.3

The Partition Information screen

Do not change the existing DOS partition. This action will delete all data including your server boot files, requiring you to start your installation again from the beginning.

WARNING

2. Edit the partition information at your discretion. You should allocate as much disk space to the Data area as possible.

Table 6.1 explains configuration options on this screen.

T A B L E 6.1

Partition Information Options

PARAMETER	MEANING	EXPRESSED IN
Partition size	Size of NetWare partition	Cylinders (MB)
Data area	Area allocated to NetWare disk storage	Blocks (MB)
Redirection area	Hot Fix volume	Blocks (%)

You might consider reducing the Redirection area (Hot Fix space). The default value of 2.0 percent of disk space for the redirection area is far too much for most disk drives these days. You may reduce the size of the redirection area or increase the size of the data area. Either choice will adjust the value of the other accordingly. Use your judgment — the Redirection area does not need to be more than 10–20MB or so.

IDE drives use sector sparing, which serves the same purpose as Hot Fix. RAID subsystems also do not require Hot Fix. However, NetWare requires a Hot Fix area for each partition. In this case, make the Hot Fix area as small as possible.

NOTE

When installing an IDE or fault-tolerant disk subsystem (such as hardware-based RAID), enter the number "0" in the Redirection area option box. When you exit, an error box will tell you the minimum and maximum areas that may be allocated to Hot Fix. NetWare requires at least one track to be dedicated for this purpose even if the hardware does not use it. Enter the minimum value in the Redirection Area option box to satisfy this requirement.

3. Press Esc to save and exit. A query will verify that you wish to save the partitioning options. If you answer Yes, the disk partition table will be altered in real-time and you will be returned to the Disk Partition menu.

4. Select Return to Previous Menu or press Esc key to return to the list of available disk drives. You may then continue by partitioning other disk drives or exit by pressing Esc.

5. Surface-test your drives at your discretion. If you wish, you may perform a surface test of your disk for media defects by selecting the Surface Test option from the Disk Options menu. The test can be "destructive" or "nondestructive." A destructive test will destroy all existing data on the subject partition. A destructive test is more comprehensive and is preferred at this point, since no data resides on your logical partition just yet. This process will not damage your disk; it uses your disk driver to write/read data to each track and sector. You can use this test to be certain that the drive is working properly and no media defects are present.

6. Mirror drives. You may establish mirrored pairs at this time or after installation.

You can mirror any two physical disk drives if the logical partition size is exactly the same on two disk drives. The disk drives may differ physically and even may be slightly different sizes, but after partitioning and allocating the redirection area, the remaining data areas must be identical on the two physical disks. You may mirror drives following this procedure:

a. From the Available Disk Options menu, select Mirroring. You will see a Partitioning Mirror Status menu listing each logical partition you have created. The term *logical partition* refers to the data area that remains after the partitioning and allocation of the redirection area as shown in Figure 6.4.

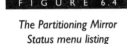

F I G U R E 6.4

The Partitioning Mirror Status menu listing

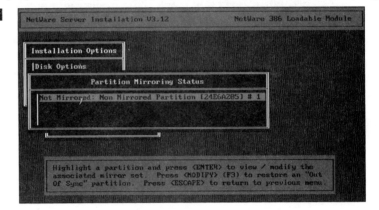

NOTE

Each logical partition is numbered in sequence, starting at "1." Physical device numbers identify physical disk drives and are numbered starting from "0."

b. From the Partitioning Mirror Status screen, select the logical partition to be designated as the primary disk in a mirrored pair. You will then see the Mirrored NetWare Partitions screen also shown in Figure 6.4. You may press Ins to bring up a list of eligible logical partitions. An eligible partition would be any other logical partition where the data area size is identical. To mirror the two logical partitions, simply select the logical partition to be designated as the secondary disk in the mirrored pair. From this point on, the two logical partitions will appear to be one.

If the logical partitions to be mirrored differ in size, INSTALL will change the secondary drive's logical partition size to meet mirroring requirements and then query for your approval before saving partitioning changes.

Your disk drive should have been low-level formatted prior to this point at the factory or by the vendor or by a vendor-supplied utility and should be perfectly okay. Running the surface test is therefore not necessary. If you elect to run the test anyway, expect it to take a while. You can interrupt it at any time without damage to the disk.

You may abort the test at any time by selecting Stop Surface Test. This option will not damage your disk or its formatting. When the surface test has finished one pass with no errors, select Return to Previous Menu or strike Esc to return to the list of drives and then press Esc again to return to the Available Disk Options menu.

Do not run the Format utility shown on this menu unless the disk drive instructions explicitly say to do so. This option will perform a low-level disk format (initialization) that can destroy the format of your disk drive(s), and render it unusable. Most disk drives are low-level formatted at the factory; others may require you to run a format utility from provided software under DOS, or from a BIOS chip on the adapter.

A high-level format, such as a DOS format, is not required for NetWare.

Step 5: Create NetWare Volume(s)

1. Escape to the Installation Options menu and select Volume Options. You will see a list of NetWare volumes, but it will have no volumes listed. Press Ins to create a new volume. The New Volume Information screen will appear as shown in Figure 6.5.

▶ . . . . ◀

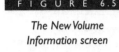

F I G U R E 6.5

The New Volume
Information screen

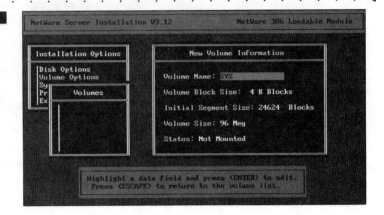

Your first volume must be named SYS:. You can select the block size. For the SYS: volume, you should select 4K, which is most efficient for smaller files.

If you would like to have larger block sizes, you should create a
separate volume (or volumes) to contain large files only.

TIP

2. Configure the size of the volume. You may skip the Initial Segment Size field if you would like the volume to fill the entire logical partition. If you wish to create more than one volume on a logical partition, edit Initial Segment Size and then reduce the number of blocks allocated to the volume. When you press Esc, the volume will be created.

You can span a volume across two or more logical partitions and therefore across two or more physical disk drives. If you have more than one physical disk drive, when you select a volume you will see another list of volume segments of which the current volume is composed. If you press Ins, a menu will appear listing free space available for volume segments (if any are available). You can span the selected volume onto an additional logical partition by selecting an available logical partition from the list, selecting the block size, and confirming that you wish to add the segment to the volume. If you have mirrored two disks, the volume(s) will be created on the mirrored pair.

NOTE

A single volume can span up to 32 physical drives for a total of no more than 32TB of disk storage for one (or for all) volumes.

If you span volumes, when new data is added and free space on both logical partitions exists, file sectors will automatically be striped across the physical disk drives. When SCSI drives are used in this manner, striping results in improved disk I/O.

3. Mount the volume(s) that has just been created. To mount the volume(s), select the volume from the list of volumes, select the Status field, and press Enter. Select Mount Volume and the volume will be mounted. Alternatively, you may press Alt+Esc to change to the console screen and then type **mount all**. If you would prefer to mount only a specific volume, enter the following command: **MOUNT** *volume_name*. You will now have access to the mounted volume(s). SYS: must be mounted to proceed with the installation.

Step 6: Copy SYSTEM and PUBLIC files

1. Escape to the Installation Options screen and select System Options, and then select Copy System and Public Files. The default path name is drive A:\. When installing from a CD, edit the path name.

2. Accept or edit the path names and press Enter to continue. The operating system and its files will be copied to the SYS volume. If your CD is drive D:, enter the path name D:\NW312\NETWARE.312\<language>. If you are installing from a network path, enter the drive letter and directory that contains the NetWare installation files.

Step 7: Load and Configure NIC Driver(s)

1. Load NIC (LAN) drivers from the console prompt. Return to the console screen by pressing Alt+Esc. Then type the command

```
LOAD NIC_driver_name
```

Substitute the name of the driver for your NIC. If you want to load an updated driver from your DOS volume, simply use the DOS path in the load command. For example,

```
LOAD C:\NW3\SMC8000
```

If you plan to load the driver more than one time to support multiple frame types and protocols, assign a name each time you load the driver. Assigning a name allows you to select each binding as if it were a separate NIC. The following command assigns a name:

```
LOAD SMC8000 NAME=A
```

If you have already loaded the driver and want to reload it with a name, unload the driver first using the UNLOAD command. Then you can reload the driver. For example:

```
UNLOAD SMC8000
```

```
LOAD SMC8000 NAME=A
```

Your driver will query for hardware settings and configuration options. Read your NIC driver installation instructions in the manual that came with your server NIC. Some NICs may require a few more steps to properly load the driver per instructions from your NIC driver installation guide. Some drivers require loading a support module or two before loading the driver. Most drivers load support modules automatically.

Novell provides drivers for several NIC brands and models. Each vendor has a different way of structuring its driver disks, but normally somewhere on the vendor's disk will be a driver for NetWare 3 servers.

TIP

It is rare that a NetWare driver would load if the NIC is not working, if the settings you have entered are incorrect, or if you have attempted to load the wrong driver. If the driver loads, and after binding the protocol you can receive data but cannot send data, you have entered the wrong interrupt number. When the incorrect interrupt has been entered, the driver may load, and you may be able to receive data, but your NIC will not be able to send data.

2. If your server has multiple NICs, load the next driver, or load the same driver again. When you load the driver, configuration information will be queried again, and you should respond by inputting the physical settings on your second NIC.

When you load the same driver a second time, the driver will ask:

```
Do you want to load another frame type for a previously
loaded board?
```

NOTE

When you load a driver more than one time, each incident of loading the board represents a *logical board*. INSTALL indicates that the driver is loaded *reentrantly*. When loading drivers reentrantly, you should assign an alias name to each logical board.

If you want to load the driver for another NIC, answer N for no. If you successfully load the same driver twice, you will see a message indicating that the driver has been loaded reentrantly . When loading the same driver twice, INSTALL will automatically assign an alias name for the second driver.

Repeat this process for each NIC installed in your server.

NOTE

Though most NIC drivers will load on your command, some NICs will not initialize until they are connected to a properly configured cabling system. For example, Token Ring NICs need to be connected to an active ring. Connect your Token Ring NIC to a MSAU, and configure the inactive ports per your installation instructions.

Step 8: Bind IPX to NIC Driver(s)

1. At the console prompt, type the command

```
BIND IPX to driver_name or alias_name
```

This command creates a binding between the NIC driver and the IPX packet driver. When you enter this command, you will be asked to enter a network number.

If you have loaded the same driver more than once and have not assigned name to each one, you will be prompted to select the driver to which to bind the protocol. If you have assigned a name to the board, bind the protocol to the alias name you assigned when you loaded the driver reentrantly.

2. Enter the IPX network number. This number is the IPX number assigned to the logical network to which the NIC is to be connected. At this point, you should input the network address assigned to the LAN. If no other servers are connected to this same LAN, this will become the network address for this LAN. The address you enter must be the same as the address entered for other server NICs that are connected to the same network segment that is using the same frame type.

If you are uncertain about what address to enter at this point, review the section on IPX addressing in Chapter 3, "Novell Protocols and IPX Addressing."

3. Bind additional frame types as required. Ethernet NICs can be configured with any one of four frame types. NetWare 3.12 drivers automatically select and load an Ethernet_802.2 frame type by default. Your server must use the same frame type as other NetWare servers and clients, or they will not be able to communicate. When loading your workstation drivers, you may need to select the appropriate frame type to match your server's frame type. You can load a second frame type for your server NIC to support nodes using the alternate frame type.

To bind a second frame type to a driver, load the driver for the NIC again. You will be asked:

```
Do you want to load another frame type for a previously
loaded board?
```

If you intend to support multiple frame types for the same NIC and driver, answer Y for Yes. The driver will then query which frame type to load and ask for the IPX network address for that logical network. In this manner, you can support all four frame types at the same time through one driver loaded into memory.

Though all frame types may share the same network segment, communications over each frame type constitute a separate logical network. Each logical network must be assigned a separate IPX network number.

NOTE

Step 9: Bind IP to your NIC Driver(s) (Optional)
1. Load the TCP/IP protocol. At the console prompt type:

```
LOAD TCPIP
```

See Chapter 11, "Configuring TCP/IP with NetWare," for switches to be used with TCPIP.NLM.

X-REF

2. Load your LAN driver again for the NIC that will support IP. When asked if want to add another frame type for a previously loaded board, answer Yes.

3. Select the Ethernet_II frame type. NetWare 3 only supports the Ethernet_II frame type for use with the IP protocol. You will be prompted to select from a list of reentrantly loaded drivers. Select the driver configured with the Ethernet_II frame type.

4. Bind the IP protocol to the logical board with your IP address and mask. If you do not enter the IP address and mask, you will be prompted to enter an IP address. When entering the IP address, enter the mask. If you do not enter the mask, the default mask for your IP network address class will be used. The following command should be used:

```
BIND IP TO driver_name ADDR=xx.xx.xx.xx MASK=xx.xx.xx.xx
```

TIP

If the numbers you enter are not valid, they will be rejected. If a valid IP address or mask is not accepted, enter the mask in hexadecimal. To find the hex equivalent to your decimal numbers, use your Windows Calculator. Execute the Calculator in the Accessories program group, check Scientific, enter each decimal number and then check Hex.

Step 10: Create and Save the System Startup Files

Next, all the commands that were typed to load and configure drivers and to bind protocols must be automated so that the server will boot without the user entering commands. Two files handle this: STARTUP.NCF and the AUTOEXEC.NCF. STARTUP runs when SERVER.EXE is executed; it therefore must be stored on the DOS partition (or disk) where SERVER.EXE is stored. AUTOEXEC.NCF is stored on the SYS: volume and is executed when the SYS: volume is mounted.

1. Create the STARTUP.NCF file. From your Available System Options menu, select Create STARTUP.NCF. Your disk driver will be loaded in this file. For example, you should find the command LOAD IDE.DSK for an IDE drive. You will be prompted to edit the path where STARTUP.NCF should be stored. Enter the server boot directory on the DOS boot volume.

2. Create the AUTOEXEC.NCF file. Next, from your Available System Options menu, select Create AUTOEXEC.NCF. You will see all the commands pertaining to bringing the server up, loading and configuring the NIC drivers, and binding the IPX protocol to the NIC drivers (including assigning network addresses). The appropriate syntax is used, so if you edit the file, be certain to retain the proper syntax.

NOTE

NetWare assumes it will find the NIC drivers in the SYS:SYSTEM directory. If you have used a vendor-supplied or updated NIC driver, copy your third-party NIC drivers into the SYS:SYSTEM directory. You will need to connect a workstation, log in as Supervisor, and then flag the driver file as read-only.

If you load the NIC drivers from the local hard drive, copy the file to the local DOS hard drive and then edit AUTOEXEC.NCF to include the local pathname (for example, load C:\NE2000.LAN). The working directory is SYS:SYSTEM when AUTOEXEC.NCF runs, so driver names that are not preceded by a path will be loaded from the SYS:SYSTEM directory.

3. Allow edit of your AUTOEXEC.BAT file. You will be asked if you want to allow INSTALL to edit your DOS AUTOEXEC.BAT file so that your server will load automatically when DOS boots.

NOTE

See "Post-Installation Procedures" for instructions on editing your DOS boot files to provide a menu selection for booting the server.

Once these options have been completed, your system is installed. You should then down your server and cold boot it to verify that all startup files will work properly. You may edit your server boot files by entering INSTALL again. Load INSTALL by executing SERVER.EXE from the DOS server boot directory and then load INSTALL from the console prompt with the command LOAD INSTALL.

NOTE

You may find that some of your BIND commands will not have been saved properly in AUTOEXEC.NCF. See the section later in this chapter on configuring protocols for details on entering BIND statements manually.

Post-Installation Procedures

Your server installation is now complete. You should exit the INSTALL module by pressing Esc from all menus and confirming your exit. As with all NLMs, you should exit from a menu selection rather than by typing an unload statement from the console.

Once you have installed your server OS, you will need to perform a few more operations. You should:

1. Verify that everything is working properly.

2. Install the 3.2 Enhancement Pack.

3. Install any additional server-based modules.

4. Install your online documentation.

5. Install any server-based applications that are required.

Once you have installed your NetWare server, you should shut down your server and reboot to verify proper boot execution. To shut down your server, enter the command **DOWN** at the server console (colon) prompt. Type **EXIT** to return to a DOS prompt. Next, cold boot your server to see if it will come up automatically. If it does not come up automatically, attempt to load your NetWare server OS manually by changing to the DOS server directory and executing SERVER.EXE.

If the server comes up but the disk and LAN drivers do not load, reload the disk driver manually, mount the volume (type **MOUNT ALL** at the colon prompt), load INSTALL.NLM, and check out the STARTUP.NCF and AUTOEXEC.NCF files. If the disk driver was not loaded, make sure your STARTUP.NCF is in the same directory with SERVER.EXE and has the appropriate disk driver load statement(s).

TIP

If the LAN drivers do not load, and your LAN driver(s) are not located in the SYS:SYSTEM directory, check the AUTOEXEC.NCF file to be sure that the drive letter is specified for where your drivers

are located. By default it is assumed during creation of this file that you will copy the **LAN** and disk drivers into the **SYSTEM** directory.

If the server loads, the volumes are mounted, and drivers load, but you cannot connect to the server, check cabling.

Installing the 3.2 Enhancement Pack

The 3.2 Enhancement Pack has several modifications you will find attractive. You will find a listing of new features in 3.2 in Chapter 1. If you run into any problems, check the 3.2 release notes in the file NW32\ENGLISH\README.TXT, which can be found on your NetWare 3.2 CD. You can also find this file and the latest information on 3.2 at Novell's support Web site.

For updated information, release notes, drivers, patches, and other useful information, see Novell's Support Connection site for NetWare **3.2** at http://www.support.novell.com/products/nw32top.

To install the enhancement pack, you will need a 20MB DOS volume, with at least 4MB of free space.

Loading the 3.2 Enhancement Pack

Follow these steps to load your 3.2 enhancements:

1. At your server console, LOAD INSTALL.

2. Select Product Options. Enter the path for your 3.2 Enhancement Pack files. On the NetWare 3.2 CD, you will find these files in D:\NW32\32ENH.

NOTE

NetWare 3 does not have a NetWare CD driver for IDE CD-ROM drives. You will need to access the 3.2 Enhancement Pack CD as a DOS device. Substitute the DOS drive letter assigned to your CD-ROM drive in step 2.

3. When the server installation NLM is found (PINSTALL.NLM), a file copy will begin.

4. Down your server and reboot.

Changes That You Should Make After Updating Your System

Make the following changes to your system:

▸ If you have enough RAM in your server, add the following SET command to your STARTUP.NCF file (found in the NetWare server directory of the DOS volume):

```
SET MINIMUM PACKET RECEIVE BUFFERS=500
```

▸ If you have 8MB of RAM and a small NetWare volume, this should work properly. However, if you have a large amount of disk storage, you may not have enough memory to load this many packet receive buffers. If this is the case, remove the SET command from your STARTUP.NCF file. You should add at least another 8MB of RAM to your server to provide more packet receive buffers if needed.

▸ If you have enough remaining memory, add the following line to AUTOEXEC.NCF:

```
SET MAXIMUM ALLOC SHORT TERM MEMORY=8000000
```

▸ When your server has over 16MB of memory, you may need to add lines to your STARTUP.NCF file and/or add switches to your driver load statements. See NW32\ENGLISH\README.TXT for more information. Newer computers and drivers should not require this modification.

Check for release notes and installation instructions in your hardware installation manuals and on your NetWare CD at NW32\ENGLISH\README.TXT.

Configuring Protocols

In NetWare 3, BIND statements are often not automatically added to your AUTOEXEC.NCF when drivers are loaded reentrantly. You must therefore edit your AUTOEXEC.NCF file manually when more complex protocol bindings are needed. A good example is when you add IP support. In this case, you must enter the commands necessary to load the TCPIP.NLM and bind the IP protocol to the driver.

The following example demonstrates how the entries should be added to AUTOEXEC.NCF to bind both the IPX and IP protocols to a single NIC and driver. Case is not sensitive.

 If you select Create AUTOEXEC.NCF File instead of Edit AUTOEXEC.NCF, your previous entries may be deleted.

NOTE

Your STARTUP.NCF file should contain the disk driver load statement and other SET parameters if required. A typical STARTUP.NCF will be found in the DOS boot directory and should look like this:

```
load IDE.DSK
```

Your AUTOEXEC.NCF file should look like this:

```
file server name NW32

ipx internal net AAAA1229


REM the following line was added by the 3.2 Enhancemnt Pack
installation
LOAD AFTER311
REM end of 3.2 enhancement modifications


REM the following lines support the IPX protocol over 802.2
load SMC8000 port=300 name=A frame=ETHERNET_802.2
```

```
bind IPX to A net=E100


REM the following lines support the IP protocol over E_II

load TCPIP

load SMC8000 port=300 name=B frame=ETHERNET_II

bind IP to B addr=204.10.210.16 mask=255.255.255.0


load monitor
```

Notice in AUTOEXEC.NCF that the logical boards are identified as A and B respectively. The aliased name identifies the reentrant driver from the original.

INETCFG can be used as an alternate method of editing startup files. INETCFG for NetWare 3 comes with server add-ons, such as NetWare IP and Multiprotocol Router. INETCFG transfers binding and related statements to a separate file and uses a more detailed menu interface for editing protocol configurations.

Creating a Branching DOS Boot Menu

At the outset of running the INSTALL batch file from CD-ROM, you were asked if you would like the server to boot automatically. If you answered Yes, AUTOEXEC.BAT will include the statement SERVER, which will load the NetWare file server OS when the computer is booted. If you did not answer Yes, you can manually type the command **SERVER** from a DOS prompt to load the server.

If you have opted to boot the server in your AUTOEXEC.BAT, you can interrupt the boot process to exit to DOS. MS-DOS 6 and above allows you to exit to DOS without executing your CONFIG.SYS or AUTOEXEC.BAT by pressing F5 when the message Starting MS-DOS appears. You can execute these files one line at a time by pressing F8 during boot.

Either way, it is a bit problematic when an inexperienced user is required to boot the server in an emergency. You can make a boot menu. MS-DOS 6 and above has the capability of creating a boot menu that will allow you to boot your server or exit to DOS. It can be configured to boot the server after a default time period.

You can create your own menu selections and include any commands that can be
included in your CONFIG.SYS and AUTOEXEC.BAT files.

Here is an example of a boot menu to be used with a later version of DOS:

```
CONFIG.SYS

[menu]                          | heading for boot menu

menuitem=DOS, Boot to DOS       | establishes branch variable

menuitem=NETWARE                | establishes branch variable

menudefault=NETWARE, 15         | default branch, and wait
                                  time


[DOS]                           | heading for branch
device=C:\DOS\HIMEM.SYS         | executed for this branch


[NETWARE]                       | heading for branch


[common]                        | heading for commands in
                                  common
files=12                        | all commands that are common
                                  to all branches

buffers=15                      |
device=C:\CDROM\MTMCDAI.SYS /d:MSCD0001 | CD driver


AUTOEXEC.BAT
@echo off                           | stops print to screen
```

```
path C:\DOS                        | sets path
C:\DOS\MSCDEX.EXE /d:MSCD0001 /m:10 | loads CD extensions
goto %CONFIG%                      | continues branch from
                                     CONFIG.SYS


:DOS                               | label: continues DOS
                                     branch
C:\DOS\SMARTDRV.EXE                | continues DOS branch
goto END                           | skips to END label


:NETWARE                           | label: continues
                                     NETWARE branch
CD \SERVER                         | continues NETWARE
                                      branch
SERVER                             | executes SERVER
goto END                           | skips to END label


     :END                          | label: exits both
                                     branches
```

The DOS boot file just listed can be found on the CD that accompanies this book. Look for 3AUTOEXC.TXT and 3CONFIG.TXT. Copy these files to drive C:, renaming them to CONFIG.SYS and AUTOEXEC.BAT as you do. Be sure to save backups of your existing CONFIG.SYS and AUTOEXEC.BAT files.

Installing Online Documentation

NetWare 3.2's documentation is Windows-based and is electronic. To make the documentation available to network clients, install the online documents through Product options in the INSTALL.NLM program.

To install the documentation, follow these instructions:

1. Load INSTALL at the server console.

2. Select Product Options.

3. Install the documents. Strike Ins and then enter the path **\NW312\INSTALL\IBM_PC\NETWARE\312\ENGLISH\312DOC** on your NetWare 3.2 CD. When the file upload is completed, you will be returned to the Currently Installed Products screen.

4. Install the document viewer. Strike Ins and then enter the path **\NW312\INSTALL\IBM_PC\NETWARE\312\ENGLISH\VIEWER**. When the file upload is competed, you will be returned to the Currently Installed Products screen.

You may also uninstall server-based software. To uninstall a module listed in the Currently Installed Products screen in Product Options, select the module and press Del.

Installing Other Server Products

Other products can be installed through the Product Options menu selection in the NetWare 3 INSTALL.NLM. This option is used to install server-based products, online documentation, client setup programs, and more. Look for PINSTALL.NLM files—these are installation programs written by the software developer, which automatically load server-based products on your server.

You will find the following products on your NetWare 3.2 CD:

- ▶ *NetWare 3.2 Enhancement Pack* — \NW312\32ENH

- ▶ *NetWare for Macintosh* — \NW312\NETWARE.312\ENGLISH\NW_MAC

- ▶ *Electronic documentation* — \NW312\INSTALL\IBM_PC\NETWARE\312\ENGLISH\312DOC

> *Electronic document viewer —*
  \NW312\INSTALL\IBM_PC\NETWARE\312\ENGLISH\VIEWER

> *BasicMHS electronic mail server —*
  \NW312\NETWARE.312\ENGLISH\BASICMHS

Several other server add-on products for NetWare 3 are available from Novell, including:

> Multiprotocol Router

> NetWare IP

> NetWare NFS

> SAA Services for NetWare

In addition to these products, many third-party vendors make server applications that can be installed on your NetWare server operating systems. In some cases third-party applications are installed with a server-based PINSTALL.NLM, their own server-based installation program, or a workstation-based installation program.

Adding Volume Name Space

NetWare 3 supports long file/directory names in Macintosh, OS/2, Windows 95, and Windows NT. However, support for longer names requires loading name space for the client file system. This is accomplished with two steps:

1. Load the name space module for the client operating system in the STARTUP.NCF file.

2. Upgrade NetWare volumes to support the name space.

The following name space modules are provided:

> MAC.NAM — Apple Macintosh

- ► OS2.NAM — IBM OS/2; Microsoft Windows 95, 98, and NT

- ► NFS.NAM — any UNIX version with NFS support

To provide name space support, load the appropriate name space support module as listed and then upgrade the volumes that will support those clients. For example, if you wish to support long file/folder names in Windows 95, 98, and NT, first add the following line to your STARTUP.NCF:

```
load OS2
```

To upgrade the SYS: volume for long filenames, execute the following command at the server console:

```
add name space OS2 to SYS
```

When performing this procedure, you should take the server offline or work when the system is not busy. It will take a few minutes to update the volume, and the process will impede user activity significantly.

Shadow listings will be created for each directory entry. DOS (default) name space directory listings use 256 bytes per listing. Other name spaces are enabled by adding an additional 256-byte "shadow" directory listing for extended attributes and the long file/directory names.

Loading name space will reduce available disk space and require more RAM in your server to mount volumes. Other than this consideration, you will find that loading name space does not affect performance.

WARNING

Once you add name space to a volume, running the VREPAIR utility will remove the name space from the volume, resulting in loss of data unless you follow the proper procedure. See Chapter 15, "Storage Devices and File Systems," for details on how to handle VREPAIR for NetWare 3 when name space has been added.

CHAPTER 7

NetWare 4 Server Setup

The purpose of this chapter is to guide you through NetWare 4.11, 4.2, and intraNetWare's server OS installation, and to help you troubleshoot configuration issues and common problems that occur during installation. If you are reinstalling, you will find very few — if any — differences from a first-time install.

If an installation has failed, this chapter will help you resolve your difficulties. If you are reinstalling NetWare 4 to work around previous problems, pay close attention to the configuration options that are presented to you — your installation may have been improperly configured. You may find tips, notes, and warnings in this chapter especially helpful in making your installation go easily with the benefit of the greatest degree of foresight. This chapter assumes these things:

1. You have selected and assembled a computer to be the file server.

2. Your LAN and cabling has been properly installed.

3. Your NICs are installed and tested and do not conflict with other hardware or software devices.

4. Your server has a CD-ROM drive that can be installed as a DOS device.

5. You are installing a single server and just a few workstations.

As with all NetWare versions, NetWare 4's server boot files are installed on a bootable DOS volume — it is not possible to boot and execute the server OS from a floppy. Therefore you must partition your drive and allocate a small portion for a bootable DOS volume. NetWare 4 requires only 15MB of disk space on your DOS volume; however, it is wise to allocate at least 50 or 100MB to contain DOS external executables, server and device diagnostic software, and other utilities. You will find a helpful document on the CD that accompanies this book that gives explicit instructions on creating a bootable DOS volume. You will also find instructions on using Windows 95 or Windows 98 as a boot operating system for a NetWare server.

NOTE

NetWare 4 does not support starting the NetWare server operating system from a floppy disk.

The installation process for NetWare 4.11 and 4.2 is similar to that for 3.12 with two exceptions: the installation process is automated, and you must enter NDS-related information. NetWare 4.11 and 4.2 also automatically scan for devices, making it easier to select the right driver and settings. From the time you start the installation program until you are finished, you are guided from step to step.

Because NetWare 4 features NDS, you must either create an NDS tree or install your NetWare 4 server into an existing tree. Installing a stand-alone server requires very little NDS knowledge. Installing a server into an existing tree requires some forethought and planning. This book focuses only on the establishment of the platform for your network. For help with designing an NDS tree, see your NetWare 4 documentation, or refer to *Novell's Guide to NetWare 5 Networks,* by Hughes and Thomas.

NetWare can be installed from:

▸ Floppies (available at extra cost)

▸ A local CD-ROM drive

▸ A network drive

▸ A networked or shared CD-ROM drive

Like other NetWare versions, NetWare 4 can be installed from CD, a network drive, or a networked CD-ROM drive. NetWare 4 is not shipped on floppies — if you really want floppies, you can purchase a set from Novell's fulfillment house after purchasing NetWare 4. Installing directly from the CD is the best option. NetWare 4.11 and 4.2 include software to use IDE and SCSI CD-ROM drives as NetWare volumes. Even the least expensive CD-ROM drive will be an asset to your server.

► · ◄

Preparing the Server

Before you begin your installation, you need to:

1. Prepare a bootable DOS volume.

NOTE **NetWare requires raw unconfigured memory. Any memory configured with HIMEM.SYS or other XMS memory managers will not be usable for NetWare.**

2. Install your CD-ROM DOS driver(s) and CD-ROM extensions (MSCDEX.EXE or equivalent).

3. Obtain the latest disk and NIC drivers for your server's internal adapters.

4. Be prepared with your adapters' hardware configuration settings, your NetWare installation CD or floppy disks, and your NetWare SYSTEM_1 (or INSTALL) disk.

NOTE **Check release notes and preinstallation instructions before proceeding. You will be able to view these files from within INSTALL, or you can look for README files on your NetWare CD. You will find README files in the \PRODUCTS\README\<language> directory on your NetWare installation CDs.**

Creating a Bootable DOS Volume

You should allocate 50MB plus the amount of RAM installed in your server to your DOS boot volume. Though NetWare 4.11 and 4.2 only require 15MB of DOS disk space, you should allocate more. You may decide to install NetWare Loadable Modules (NLMs), drivers, DOS external executables, DOS utilities, hardware diagnostic utilities, and virus scanning software on the DOS volume. If you decide to upgrade your server to NetWare 5, at least 50MB is required. In case of server crashes, you may wish to dump memory to a file for debugging, which requires enough disk space to accommodate the total amount of memory installed in your server. For these reasons, allocating even more than the recommended amount to your server's DOS volume is a practical suggestion.

TIP

You should allocate enough space to your **DOS** volume for future upgrades and a core dump. If you decide to upgrade to NetWare 5, at least 50MB of disk space is required. NetWare 5 requires more memory than does version 4 — 64MB at a minimum — you may want to add more. If you do not allocate enough space, an upgrade may require you to enlarge your **DOS** boot volume, which requires repartitioning. To avoid the need to destroy **DOS** and NetWare partitions and all existing server files when upgrading, make your **DOS** volume large enough to accommodate later NetWare requirements.

If you boot from a SCSI drive, you will need to set up your SCSI system properly as discussed in Chapter 5. To make a SCSI drive bootable, you will need to enable your SCSI adapter's on-board BIOS and configure the first SCSI drive as bootable in your SCSI utilities. In some cases, you may install DOS device drivers to substitute for the SCSI adapter's on-board BIOS.

NOTE

To make a **SCSI** drive bootable, you must configure the **SCSI** adapter **BIOS** and make the boot partition active. **SCSI BIOS** firmware sometimes has other requirements. For example, some **SCSI BIOS**es require that only **SCSI ID** 0 can be bootable.

Be sure your **SCSI** drives are set up properly. You must configure each drive with a unique **SCSI ID**, and only the last drive on the cable must be terminated. Sometimes improperly terminated drives may work, but they can cause I/O errors later on. All questions concerning SCSI specifications, cabling, and setup are discussed in the *DELEC Online SCSI Guide* on the CD that accompanies this book.

Create a primary DOS partition, make it active, and format it with a system. This is typically done at the factory for most computers, but most computers are shipped with an entire drive allocated to DOS, Windows 95/98, or Windows NT. NetWare only needs a small DOS partition, and this often means repartitioning and reinstalling DOS.

NOTE

In many cases, computer manufacturers provide their own setup utilities. You should review your computer owner's manual for any special considerations before attempting to partition your drive.

You can use Novell DOS (located on the license disk), any later version of DOS, or the OEM version of Windows 95 to create a bootable DOS volume. NetWare comes with a bootable floppy disk that contains the Novell DOS FORMAT and FDISK utilities in the DOSTOOLS directory. If you are not familiar with the procedure of creating a partition and formatting it, see your DOS manual.

To create a branching DOS boot menu, see the section of this chapter entitled "Creating a Branching DOS Boot Menu."

NOTE

Installing a NetWare Server on a Windows 95/98 Computer

Installing a NetWare server on a computer that is already running Windows 95 or Windows 98 requires some careful considerations. NetWare servers can be installed with Windows 95/98 in three ways:

1. You can create a bootable volume using the Windows 95/98 version of DOS (command prompt), the same way you would use a previous DOS version.

2. You can boot from a bootable floppy disk and then switch to drive C:.

3. You can interrupt the Windows 95/98 boot process to boot to the Windows 95/98 command prompt without executing the graphical portion of Windows.

All of these options require you to install your CD-ROM drive as a DOS device. Each option requires a few modifications to the original Windows 95/98 boot process.

The last option, interrupting the Windows 95/98 boot process and booting to the command prompt is a bit challenging. Once you have edited your computer boot files, you must remove most of the Windows 95/98 operating system files so that your computer will not boot to Windows 95/98 anymore. Every time your computer boots, you must intercept the boot by pressing F8. If you computer were to boot to Windows 95/98, your startup files would be edited and you would have to reconfigure your boot environment.

NOTE

You cannot access a FAT32 file system when booting from a DOS version that predates MS-DOS 6.22. Earlier Windows 95 versions used a FAT16 file system that is accessible from MS-DOS versions 6.0 and later. The FAT32 file system is not backward compatible with previous DOS or Windows 95 versions where the FAT16 file system was installed. However, this problem is easily overcome if you prepare your boot disk using the FAT32 utilities or the Windows Startup disk that was created during Windows installation.

You can verify your file system's configuration in FDISK. Windows 95 OSR2, Windows 98, and MS-DOS 6.22's FDISK will identify a FAT32 file system. FDISK from previous DOS versions will simply identify the volume as a non-DOS system.

TIP

The option to interrupt a Windows 95/98 boot by pressing F5 or F8 during boot is not a good idea. Should an untrained user need to reboot the server, this option may cause needless downtime.

Installing from CD

Novell designed NetWare's server INSTALL program to be run from a CD. For most computers, running a CD-ROM drive as a DOS device is the most practical way of using the drive for installation. When purchasing your CD-ROM drive, be sure that the device comes with everything that is needed to install it as a DOS device.

The CD-ROM drive may be an IDE or SCSI device—either is acceptable. However, NetWare drivers may not support older CD-ROM drives as NetWare devices. You will need a DOS device driver (such as CR_ATAPI.SYS) and Microsoft CD Extensions (MSCDEX.EXE) or equivalent. If your CD-ROM drive is a SCSI device, you may need a CD driver (such as ASPICD.SYS) in addition to a DOS SCSI device driver and MSCDEX.EXE. The device drivers (files that normally have .SYS extensions) are installed through CONFIG.SYS, while MSCDEX.EXE (or equivalent) is installed through your AUTOEXEC.BAT. CD-ROM drives that use MSCDEX.EXE are not shipped with it—you must use MSCDEX.EXE from your DOS system software. CD extensions are not provided with Novell DOS that is included with NetWare.

Many computers and many SCSI adapters can be configured to boot from CD. NetWare's installation program does not take advantage of this feature. Even if your computer has a bootable CD, you will need to create a bootable DOS volume and allocate enough space on which to install your server boot files. In most cases, you will find that installing DOS support files is the most efficient way — and perhaps the only way — to install from CD.

NOTE **Some computer manufacturers provide a bootable system CD with partitioning and formatting programs. See your computer's installation manual for details. Be sure to read your setup documentation carefully so that you do not end up destroying this partition.**

If you are installing NetWare from CD, a CD-ROM drive must physically installed, and DOS drivers must be loaded in the server. Once your NetWare server OS is installed, your system files contain NetWare drivers for all later model IDE and SCSI CD-ROM drives and a CD reader NLM to recognize CD file systems as NetWare volumes.

Installing from a Network

A NetWare server can be installed over a network from a shared CD or from a network drive where the NetWare server installation files have been copied. The process is simple and is recommended any time more than one server (of the same version) must be installed.

Installing from a Networked CD

To install from a networked CD-ROM drive, map a drive letter to the shared CD-ROM volume and enter the source path as any other network drive mapping. To install from a networked CD-ROM drive, map a drive letter to the shared CD-ROM volume and enter the source path as any other network drive mapping.

Installing from a Network Drive

You can install your NetWare server from a network drive or CD-ROM drive that is shared on the network. This option is perfectly acceptable and is used wherever integrators need to install several servers. Follow these steps to make NetWare server installation files and directories available over the network:

When installing from a network, be sure your source server has not been configured to filter RIP and SAP protocols. Check existing servers' MONITORs for protocol configuration options.

NOTE

1. From a client workstation use XCOPY to copy \PRODUCTS\NW411 and all subdirectories on your CD to a network drive. You may use Windows Explorer to do the same using a right-click when your arrow is on the \PRODUCTS\NW411 directory on the CD and then selecting Copy from the menu. You will then right-click on the destination drive or directory and select Paste. Copying these files requires 170MB.

2. Map root to the directory containing the new directory.

3. Start INSTALL from the mapped drive.

Wherever you are prompted to verify source and destination path names during INSTALL, substitute the network drive/directory path for the default.

This procedure requires you to set up your server as a client to another server before starting the INSTALL, which requires almost as much effort as installing the server OS. However, when installing multiple servers, you will find that your setup time will have been spent judiciously.

You can access the README files from any workstation by executing INSTALL.BAT, found in the root of your NetWare 4.11 or 4.2 operating system CD. Or you can use a text editor. Look for the README text files in the \PRODUCTS\README\<language> directory.

NOTE

Server Operating System Installation

The following section discusses installing your server step by step in a quick start overview, and in detail.

Server Installation Overview

This section discusses a quick overview. If you are experienced with installing operating systems, you may be able to install from this overview without having to follow the detailed steps that follow. If you have questions about anything you encounter during the installation, refer to the next section, where each step is covered in detail.

Installing the server OS comprises the following steps:

1. Configure INSTALL options.

    a. Execute INSTALL.BAT from the root of your CD (or mapped drive).

    b. Install in English or select the language you wish to install.

    c. Approve the license agreement.

    d. Select NetWare Server Installation.

    e. Select NetWare 4.11 or 4.2 or NetWare 4.11 or 4.2 SFT II, or else see the README files.

    f. Select Custom Installation of NetWare 4.11 or 4.2.

    g. Enter Server Name and Internal IPX address. A random IPX address will be generated by default. You will also be prompted to select the language to be used on the server.

    h. Select the filename format.

    i. Specify any special startup set commands.

    j. Configure AUTOEXEC.BAT to load or not to load SERVER.EXE automatically.

2. Select and configure disk and LAN drivers (automatic with new hardware).

3. View/modify protocol settings (will be configured by default).

4. Create NetWare disk partitions (will be created by default).

5. Mirror drives (optional).

6. Create NetWare volumes (will be created by default).

7. Install NDS establishing a new tree or into an existing tree.

8. Install server license from the license disk.

9. Create/edit server startup files, selecting Create to save the default configuration.

10. Install optional programs and files as needed.

In the following section, the installation procedure is discussed in detail.

NetWare 4.11 and 4.2 Installation Procedures

The following procedure discusses the NetWare 4.11 and 4.2 installation procedure in detail, step-by-step. Once a bootable DOS volume has been configured on your server and your CD-ROM drivers are installed, you can follow these instructions.

Step 1: Configure INSTALL Options
Start INSTALL.BAT.

1. Execute INSTALL.BAT from the root of your CD (or mapped drive).

2. Select this line to install in English or select the language you wish to install.

3. Approve the license agreement.

4. Select NetWare Server Installation.

5. Select NetWare 4.11 or 4.2 or NetWare 4.11 or 4.2 SFT II, or else see the README files.

6. Select Custom Installation of NetWare 4.11 or 4.2. You can select Simple Installation of NetWare 4.11 or 4.2, but you should avoid the Simple Installation so that you can have control over several server configuration options. You will be prompted to enter the following information.

For best results, select Custom Installation. Simple Installation enters some default configuration values automatically without your consent or knowledge. Custom Installation will prompt you with default values for many configuration options, which allows you to make changes and to be aware of the configuration options that have been selected.

a. Enter the server name. You can use between 2 and 47 alphanumeric characters, hyphens, and underscores in a server name.

b. Enter an IPX internal network number for this server. Each server must have a unique internal network number which can have up to eight hexadecimal characters (0–9, A–F). INSTALL will prompt you with a random number as a default. You should edit a network number that uniquely identifies this server when viewing routing tables or protocol decodes. See Chapter 3 for detail on IPX addressing.

Unless you have a system for assigning IPX internal network numbers, select the default number which was generated randomly. Assigning a number that is in use for any other internal or external IPX logical network will result in a conflict.

c. Verify or edit the source and destination directories for the server boot files on the DOS volume. The server boot files will be copied to the DOS volume in the directory you have chosen.

d. Select Country Code, Code Page, and Keyboard Mapping as shown in Figure 7.1. Do not edit the defaults unless you plan to support a language other than English on your server. These parameters are provided to enable support for characters and text unique to each language.

Select alternate settings only if you wish to support other than the U.S. format on your server's keyboard and console. The default setting is for U.S. keyboard and the default screen-generated character sets.

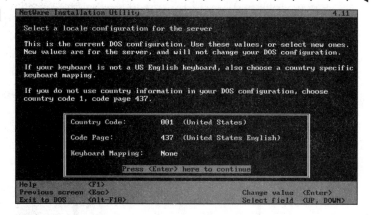

F I G U R E   7.1

*The Country Code, Code
Page, and Keyboard
Mapping screen*

e. Select the filename format. Unless you need to support a non-U.S. character set on your server's file system(s), select the DOS File Name Format. The DOS File Name Format is not case-sensitive and does not contain foreign characters. The NetWare File Name Format is case-sensitive and is not recommended except where non-U.S. character sets and case sensitivity in file names is preferred.

NOTE

This option does not affect long filenames for Windows 95, 98, NT, OS/2, UNIX, or Macintosh clients. Long filenames are supported by adding a name space, which is discussed later in this chapter under "Post Installation Procedures."

f. *Specify any special startup set commands.* You have an option to add commands to your STARTUP.NCF file. Refer to documentation for your disk adapters and NICs for commands that are required in this file. This file is stored in your DOS boot directory and can be edited later if necessary.

TIP

NetWare 4's default SET parameters have been adjusted to handle most common hardware. However, Token Ring and FDDI NICs may require additional SET statements in your STARTUP.NCF. Be sure to review your NIC installation guide for adjustments to receive buffer parameters.

g. Configure AUTOEXEC.BAT to load or not to load SERVER.EXE automatically. At this point, you can allow INSTALL to execute SERVER.EXE in your DOS AUTOEXEC.BAT file.

TIP

See the section "Post-Installation Procedures" for a discussion on how to create a branching boot menu with version 6 of DOS or higher. You will find this option helpful any time you need to boot your server to DOS for maintenance.

Another helpful option is to strike the F5 key during boot (if your DOS version provides this feature) to prevent the startup files from executing.

h. Add SMP support. If your server has multiple processors and NetWare 4's autoscan detects multiprocessor capability, you will be asked "Do you want to install Symmetrical Multiprocessing NetWare (SMP)?" If you want to load SMP support, answer Yes. INSTALL will scan for the Platform Specific Module (PSM) for your computer. Select the appropriate PSM driver to proceed. If a PSM is not automatically located or if the PSM was provided on a separate disk, press Ins to read the driver from your disk. You will be asked for the file location from which to read the PSM driver.

SMP and NetWare 4.10

Novell fully supports SMP in NetWare 4.11 and NetWare 4.2. In NetWare 4.10, however, SMP NetWare was only available from OEM server vendors and is only supported by the OEM vendor.

If you elect to add SMP at this time, the PSM will be copied and the following statements will be added to your AUTOEXEC.NCF file: LOAD *PSM_driver*.PSM (PSMs are vendor-specific and have a .PSM extension).

```
LOAD SMP.NLM

LOAD MPDRIVER.NLM ALL
```

TIP

Because SMP NetWare is more difficult to troubleshoot than normal NetWare, it is best to add SMP support after successfully installing and configuring your server. After your installation has been completed and you are satisfied that your server is running without problems, you can add SMP by loading INSTALL.NLM and then selecting the Multi-CPU Options menu selection. If have installed SMP and you experience server problems, first remove SMP using the Multi-CPU Options menu selection, resolve your problems, and then reinstall SMP support.

For detailed information and tips about troubleshooting SMP NetWare, see Technical Information Document #2924364. You can find this document on Novell's support Web site or on the Novell Support Connection CD.

Step 2: Select Drivers

In this step, INSTALL will scan your hardware for a disk adapter and for NICs. In most cases, the disk adapter will be recognized, settings will be discovered, and INSTALL will continue without displaying driver information. INSTALL often cannot detect SCSI adapters, especially when using legacy hardware. In this case, you will need to select disk drivers manually.

1. Manually select disk drivers. If INSTALL is unable to detect any disk adapters, the program will stop and present a list of drivers as shown in Figure 7.2. Select your driver, and use the Tab key to move your cursor to the top portion of the screen to edit the hardware settings.

To install a driver provided by a disk adapter manufacturer, move your cursor to the Select Additional or Modify Selected Disk/LAN Drivers menu selection, press Enter, move your cursor to the disk driver box, press Enter, and then either select a new driver or press Ins to select a driver from disk. Place the driver disk in drive A: and press F3 to edit the path name for the driver disk.

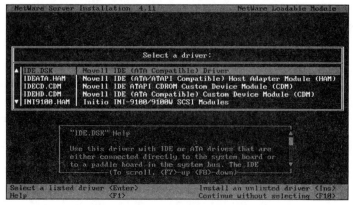

FIGURE 7.2

The disk driver list

2. Select LAN drivers. In this same screen, INSTALL will have scanned for your server network drivers (LAN drivers) and displayed them in the same screen as you disk drivers. If INSTALL cannot detect a NIC, it will stop and present a list of drivers as shown in Figure 7.3. Select your driver, and use the Tab key to move your cursor to the top portion of the screen to edit the hardware settings.

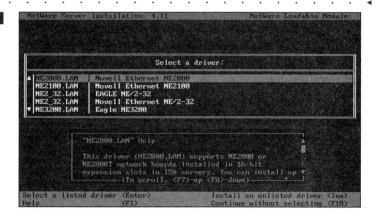

FIGURE 7.3

Selecting LAN drivers

Review the LAN driver list and save selections. Select another network driver if your server has multiple NICs.

3. Review the list of drivers and add more drivers if necessary. When you are finished selecting drivers, a screen showing the selected drivers will be displayed. If all the disk adapters and NICs installed in your server are not listed, move your cursor to Select Additional or Modify Selected Disk/LAN Drivers. Select Load an Additional Driver from the submenu and then press Enter to view the list of disk drivers. You can press Ins to read a third-party driver from a floppy disk.

Install will now copy the selected drivers to your DOS server boot directory.

Step 3: View/Modify Protocol Settings

Each NIC driver must be configured with LAN protocol options and IPX network addressing. The next screen you see will prompt you to install the IPX protocol. If you wish to install TCP/IP support, strike Ins to add and configure TCP/IP protocol and load statements.

NOTE

If you are installing NetWare/IP, or if your protocol options are somewhat complex, just configure the basic IPX options for now. After installation is completed, use INETCFG to configure LAN interfaces with multiple protocols as discussed in Chapter 12, "Novell Internet Access Server."

1. Select the protocol and frame type. To view or edit frame types or add protocols, cursor up to the Protocols Selected box and press Enter. IPX can use any one of four Ethernet and either of two Token Ring frame types. You must select the frame type that is used by other servers and clients with which you would like to communicate. You can select multiple frame types. If IP is selected, you will need to enter the IP address of this host. Each NIC must have a unique IP address assignment.

2. Enter IPX network numbers. Each frame type for each driver represents a separate logical network for communications. Therefore, each frame type will also have an IPX network address associated with it.

The terms *network address* and *network number* are used interchangeably. Each logical network must be assigned a unique network number. IPX network numbers are assigned to each logical network. When two servers are connected to the same logical network, the same network number must be assigned to all server NICs connected to it.

If IPX network addresses are not properly assigned, servers cannot communicate with one another. If you are unfamiliar with IPX network addressing, see Chapter 3, "Novell Protocols and IPX Addressing," for a brief discussion.

At this point, your disk and NIC drivers should load, and the IPX protocol should be properly bound to the driver. If a driver fails to load, you will hear a beep and see a dialog box indicating that the driver failed to load. Press Alt+Esc to view the console screen for a message indicating why the driver failed to load. Generally the problem is that you may have selected the wrong hardware settings, or that the NIC settings conflict with another adapter.

If a disk driver for the first NetWare volume does not load, you will need to exit, fix the problem, and then restart INSTALL from the beginning. If a NIC driver has not loaded properly, you can exit INSTALL, fix the problem, and restart your installation from the beginning. If the server is to be configured as the first server in an NDS tree, you can continue and address the driver problem after completing installation.

Step 4: Create NetWare Disk Partitions

Next, you need to place a physical NetWare partition on each drive. The NetWare OS recognizes NetWare partitions only while the server is running. You will have the option to create partitions automatically or manually.

1. Select Manually as the method for setting up NetWare disk partitions so that you can have more control over the partition configuration process. Automatically is okay, but you may not agree with some of the default choices, which will be automatically accepted.

2. Select Create, Delete, and Modify Disk Partitions.

. . . . .
NETWARE 4 SERVER SETUP

3. Review the list of available disk drives. When you select the first drive, notice that the DOS partition is shown, and free (unpartitioned) space is shown. If another partition has been created but is not in use, you can delete the existing partition and create a new one. Be careful when doing this, as deleting an existing partition causes all data on the partition to be lost.

WARNING

Do not change the existing DOS partition. This action will delete your server boot files, requiring you to start your installation again from the beginning.

4. Select Create NetWare Disk Partition. Select the free disk space on which to create the partition. Select a partition to contain your SYS (system) volume.

TIP

Your SYS volume must have a minimum of 100MB of available disk space to accommodate the operating system files. By no means is this amount of disk space adequate, however. You will need additional space for server modules, client installation software, online documentation, and of course, data.

It is a good idea to install the operating system and related files on the SYS volume and install a separate disk drive and volume for all software and data. Separating the server operating system and user-related files in this manner can often make backup and system recovery easier.

5. Edit the partition information at your discretion (see Figure 7.4). You should allocate as much disk space to the "Data Area" of each partition as possible. Refer to Table 7.1 for explanations of the configuration options on this screen.

You might consider reducing the Redirection area (Hot Fix space). NetWare 4.11 and 4.2 are somewhat intelligent about selecting a size for Hot Fix. You may reduce the size of the Redirection area or increase the size of the Data area. Either one will adjust the value of the other accordingly. Use your judgment — the Redirection area does not need to be more than 10–20MB or so.

. . . . .
267

FIGURE 7.4

Disk partitioning options

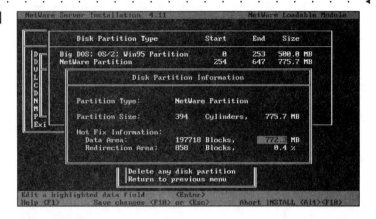

TABLE 7.1

Partition Information
Options

PARAMETER	MEANING	EXPRESSED IN	EXPRESSED AS
Partition size	Size of NetWare partition	Cylinders	MB
Data area	Area allocated to NetWare disk storage	Blocks	MB
Redirection area	Hot Fix volume	Blocks	Percentage

IDE drives use sector sparing, which serves the same purpose as Hot Fix. RAID subsystems also do not require Hot Fix. However, NetWare requires a Hot Fix area for each partition. In this case, make the Hot Fix area as small as possible.

NOTE

When installing an IDE drive or fault-tolerant disk subsystem (such as hardware-based RAID), enter the number "0" in the Redirection Area option box. When you exit, an error box will tell you the minimum and maximum areas that can be allocated to Hot Fix. NetWare requires that at least one track be dedicated for this purpose even if the hardware does not use it. Enter the minimum value in the Redirection Area option box to satisfy this requirement.

6. Save partition changes. Press Esc to save and exit. A query will verify that you wish to save the partitioning options. If you answer Yes, the disk

partition table will be altered in real time and you will be returned to the Disk Partition menu.

7. Partition remaining drives. Select Return to Previous Menu or press Esc to return to the list of available disk drives. You may then continue by partitioning other disk drives.

8. Surface test your drives at your discretion. If you wish, you may perform a surface test of your disk for media defects by selecting the Surface Test option from the Disk Options menu. The test can be "destructive" or "nondestructive." A destructive test is preferred at this point, since no data resides on your logical partition just yet. A destructive test is more comprehensive. This process will not damage your disk; it uses your disk driver to write/read data to each track and sector. You can use this test to be certain that the drive is working properly and no media defects are present.

TIP

Your disk drive should have been low-level formatted prior to this point at the factory or by the vendor or by a vendor-supplied utility and should be perfectly okay. Running this surface test is therefore not necessary. If you elect to run the test anyway, expect it to take a while. You can interrupt it at any time without damage to the disk.

You may abort the test at any time by selecting Stop Surface Test. This option will not damage your disk or its formatting. When the surface test has finished one pass with no errors, select Return to Previous Menu or strike Esc to return to the list of drives and then press Esc again to return to the Available Disk Options menu.

WARNING

Do not run the Format utility shown on this menu unless the disk drive instructions explicitly say to do so. This option will perform a low-level disk format (initialization), which can destroy the format of your disk drive(s), and render it unusable. Most disk drives are low-level formatted at the factory; others may require you to run a format utility from provided software under DOS, or from a BIOS chip on the adapter.

A high-level format, like a DOS format, is not required for NetWare volumes.

Step 5: Mirror Drives (Optional)

You may establish mirrored pairs at this time or after installation. To establish a mirrored pair, you must have two *logical partitions* that are precisely equal in size. The logical partition is the "Data area" as shown on your partitioning screens—it is the space remaining on the physical partition after the Hot Fix redirection area has been allocated. The disk drives may differ physically and even may be different sizes, but after partitioning and allocating the redirection area, the remaining data areas must be identical on the two physical disks. If you do not size your logical partitions equally, you will still be able to mirror disks. INSTALL will automatically lower the size of the larger logical partition to a size equal to the smaller logical partition to make mirroring possible. You may mirror drives following this procedure.

1. Select the physical device to be the primary drive in a mirrored pair. Return to the Disk Partition and Mirroring Options menu. Select Mirror and Unmirror Disk Partition Sets. You will see a list of accessible disk drives where NetWare logical partitions have been created as discussed in the previous step. Select the device (drive) that is to contain the logical partition you want mirrored. When you select a device, you will see a list of logical partitions contained on that device.

NOTE

Physical device numbers identify physical disk drives and are numbered starting from "0." Your CD-ROM drive is numbered also but will not appear on the device list. Each device should contain only one logical partition, with the exception of the first drive, which will contain a DOS partition and a NetWare partition.

2. Select the logical partition to be the secondary in the mirrored pair. Press Ins—you will see a list of logical partitions. If no logical partitions qualify because of unequal logical partition space, INSTALL will give you the option to adjust one of the partitions to make it fit. Review your selection carefully before accepting the changes—when you change the size of a partition, all data residing on the existing logical partition will be lost during the modification. Once you have mirrored two logical partitions, you will be returned to the Disk Partition Mirror Status screen, where mirrored pairs are listed. From this point on, each mirrored pair is treated as a single logical partition.

Step 6: Create NetWare Volume(s)

When you complete the partitioning options, INSTALL will move you to the volume creation options. The first logical partition will be automatically selected with default volume configuration as displayed on your screen. A summary of all volumes will be displayed on the next screen. You may edit the volume segmenting or configuration options for any volume(s).

I. Modify volume segmenting. Press F3 to modify volume disk segments, and the Volume Disk Segment List will appear as shown in Figure 7.5. By default, volumes have been suggested where one volume segment is placed on each logical partition. A volume segment is a whole volume that resides on a single logical partition, or a portion of a volume that resides on a single logical partition. Using this option you can place as many as eight volumes on each logical partition, or you can span a single volume over multiple drives. Volumes can consist of one or up to 32 volume segments.

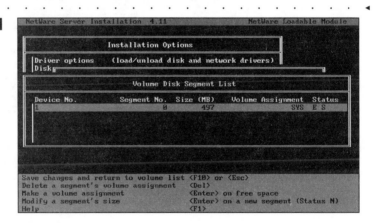

FIGURE 7.5

The Volume Disk Segment List screen

To change volume segmentation, you must first remove the proposed volume's volume assignment. Select each volume to be changed, and press Del to remove the current segmentation option. You can then create a new volume segment map by selecting the logical partition(s) on which the new volume will be created.

If you have mirrored two disks, the volume(s) will be created on the mirrored pair.

NOTE

A single volume can span up to 32 physical drives for a total of no more than 1 terabyte of disk storage for each volume. If you span volumes, when new data is added and free space on both logical partitions exists, file sectors will automatically be striped across the physical disk drives. When SCSI drives are used in this manner, striping results in improved disk I/O.

2. Modify volume information. You can modify volume configuration options, such as volume name and file compression. Select a volume and press Enter to view volume configuration options shown in Figure 7.6.

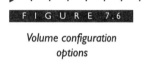

F I G U R E 7.6

Volume configuration options

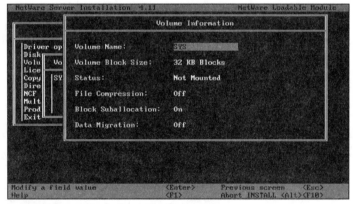

NOTE

You should edit your volume configurations. In most cases, you will want to turn file compression off. Problems associated with file compression are discussed in Chapter 15, "Storage Devices and File Systems."

Consider each of the options shown in Figure 7.6:

- *Volume Name* — The operating system volume must be named SYS, but you can rename other volumes at this time. Valid volume names consist of 2–15 alphanumeric characters and !@#$%&() and are case sensitive when NetWare Filename Format was chosen over DOS Filename Format at the beginning of your installation. Use simple volume names to make administration easier.

- *Volume Block Size* — The default of 64K for almost all drives should be left alone. NetWare 4's block suballocation takes advantage of large block read/write requests but stores data efficiently when Block suballocation is turned on.

- *File Compression* — The default is On, but it should be turned off in most cases. Files are compressed when they are not used for a period that can be specified at this point (the default is seven days). Files are uncompressed when accessed, which often causes serious performance degradation. Other problems, such as programs that will not recognize compressed files, may make this option unattractive.

WARNING

File compression should be turned off because it often causes problems. You can turn this option on at a later date, but you cannot turn it off. If you wish to have file compression for files that are seldom used, create a separate volume where file compression is turned on.

- *Block Suballocation* — The default is On, and *you should leave this on*. Block suballocation stores data in 512-byte suballocation units even though a larger (64K default) block size is configured for the volume. This improves storage efficiency without sacrificing economies of large block size read/write requests.

- *Data Migration* — The default is Off; you should leave this setting off unless you have a storage device that requires it.

3. Verify the source and destination paths for the preliminary file copy. When you proceed, the new volumes and the CD-ROM will be mounted as NetWare volumes if possible. The NetWare preliminary file copy will copy the basic OS files to the SYS volume that was just created.

NOTE

If you are installing from CD-ROM, you will see a menu allowing you to Continue Accessing the CD-ROM via DOS or select Try to Mount the CD-ROM as a NetWare Volume. If your CD-ROM drive will not mount as a NetWare volume, it is usually due to a conflict between the DOS and NetWare device drivers. To complete your installation, continue to access the device as a DOS volume. After installation, be sure to remove the DOS device driver statements from your

CONFIG.SYS and AUTOEXEC.BAT files. This should allow you to use the CD-ROM drive as a shared NetWare device from that point on.

Unlike NetWare 3.12, NetWare 4.11 and 4.2 have drivers to use IDE CD-ROMs as a NetWare device. However, it is fairly common that a driver conflict will occur when the CD-ROM is connected to the same disk adapter as the drive on which the SYS volume is located. To resolve this problem, see Technical Information Document #13590 on the Novell support Web site or the NetWare Connection CD.

If your server beeps during this process, an error message will be displayed on your screen. Switch to the console (Alt+Esc) to also read console error messages that may contain more detail. You must resolve most problems with disk drives and volumes in order to continue. If your CD-ROM drive cannot be mounted, you can continue the installation accessing the CD-ROM as a DOS device without incident.

TIP

If you have been successful in partitioning and volume configuration but some volumes will not mount, you should first suspect your disk drivers. Check your adapter installation guide to see if settings should have been placed in the STARTUP.NCF file. Visit your disk adapter's Web support site and search for problems with NetWare drivers. When using SCSI devices, you might also look at the hardware configuration options normally found in the BIOS setup program that is stored on ROM in your adapter. If you are using SCSI drives, check drive termination. When drives are not properly terminated, the drives may show up, but you may not be able to create a usable volume. For more discussion of SCSI drive termination, see Chapter 15, "Storage Devices and File Systems," or the DELEC SCSI Reference Guide on the CD that accompanies this book.

Step 7: Install NetWare (Novell) Directory Services

In this step, your NDS tree and basic objects will be created, or you will install your server into an existing NDS tree. Depending on which option is applicable for your installation, proceed to step 1(a) or step 1(b). After creating the tree name or adding the server to an existing tree, proceed to step 2.

NOTE

NetWare Directory Services was renamed to Novell Directory Services recently because NDS now supports several types of servers in addition to NetWare. Modules for several UNIX versions and Windows NT can be installed to incorporate them into NDS.

1(a). Install the first server in a tree.

You will install your server as the first server in an NDS tree if no NDS tree currently exists, or if you wish to initialize a new NDS tree. If you have no intention of merging your NetWare 4–based network with other servers or departments, create a new tree. If you may integrate your server with an existing NDS tree at some time in the future, consider installing your server in a new tree and merging it with an existing tree at some future date.

TIP

For recommendations on designing your NDS tree, see *Novell's Guide to NetWare 5 Networks* by Jeffrey F. Hughes and Blair W. Thomas (IDG Books Worldwide) or refer to your online documentation.

When you enter this step, you will see a menu that is titled Is This the First NetWare 4 Server?. If you wish to create a new NDS tree, you should select Yes, This Is the First NetWare Server.

   a. Enter the tree name. You can name your tree with up to 32 alphanumeric characters plus the underscore and hyphen. NDS names are not case sensitive, though they appear in upper/lowercase in various utilities. You should use short names, as names must be entered in many places.

   b. Configure the time server properties. Proceed to the section titled "Select time zone, then edit time configuration values."

1(b). Install a server into an existing NDS tree.

NOTE

Tree structure and configuration can vary significantly. You should check with your tree administrator for instructions, assistance, and/or permission before installing your server into an existing tree. For this reason, it is not possible to give precise instructions on how to proceed in this section. However, the instructions in this section should guide you, possibly with a little support from your tree administrator.

If other NDS trees exist in your organization, you should evaluate the possibility of joining an existing tree. You can merge your tree into an existing tree at some point in the future, though you should integrate into an existing tree during installation if possible.

NOTE

If any communications problem prevents you from detecting other NDS trees, you will not be able to complete this operation successfully. Before attempting to install a server into an existing tree, be sure to solve any potential communications problems.

a. Select No, Connect to Existing NetWare 4 Network. This option will check the network for existing trees and display a listing of existing trees.

b. Select the tree from the list. If any other trees can be detected on your network/internetwork, you will see a menu that prompts you to Install into Tree *TREE_NAME*.

From this menu, you have the option to select a tree from the list or to configure the tree information despite not being able to detect the tree. You can select the option to Specify NetWare 4 Network Name and Number without having verified the connection, you may have difficulty synchronizing NDS data with the NDS master replica server of the tree.

NOTE

If you have other trees on your network/internetwork and they are not displayed at this time, your server is unable to receive NDS communications. If you see Recheck for NetWare 4 Networks, this would indicate that your server is unable to communicate with the existing network. If you encounter this message, first check for obvious problems such as a disconnected network cable. If no obvious problems are found, you should exit INSTALL, fix whatever problems are present, and restart your installation at this time.

When you have checked and fixed communications problems, select the Recheck for NetWare 4 Networks menu selection. This option will cause the server to again search the network for NDS trees on all server NICs and network interfaces. If you still do not see a listing of tree names, this indicates that your NICs and network interfaces could not detect any other NDS servers.

Problems Detecting Trees

If no trees can be detected, you should check and correct network problems so that the tree information can be detected before continuing. Check the following items first:

1. First check the console screen (press Alt+Esc) to see that the NIC drivers have loaded properly.

2. Check frame types to be sure that this server and the first server in the tree are using the same frame type, or see that a usable router link is enabled between the two logical networks.

3. Check the IPX network number assignments for proper configuration. If you are unfamiliar with IPX addressing, see Chapter 3, "Novell Protocols and IPX Addressing."

4. Check cabling and hubs for link status and run NIC diagnostics tests to be sure that this server and other servers can communicate over the LAN.

5. Check the first server in the existing tree's MONITOR utility's Protocol Configuration selection to be sure that SAP and RIP filtering has not been enabled.

If you are still unable to detect other NDS servers on your network, proceed by selecting the option to Specify NetWare 4 Server Network Name and Number. Enter the tree and first server in the tree information as prompted, and then continue.

Depending upon your NDS configuration, the order and content of the following steps may vary slightly.

NOTE

▶ · ◀

Troubleshooting Directory Information

If you are not able to see existing trees during INSTALL and you proceed by manually entering tree information, your Directory information may not synchronize properly even after you have effectively fixed your communications problems. If you elect to proceed under these conditions you can recover by following these steps:

1. Complete the installation.

2. Troubleshoot and fix communications problems between this server and other servers.

3. At the server console type **track on** to display protocol communications between this and other servers. Look for tree advertising data to verify that tree information is being received before proceeding.

4. Use the INSTALL utility to remove Directory Services from this server.

5. Reinstall Directory Services on this server.

Once you have created a new tree or joined an existing tree, proceed with time configuration.

2. Select time zone and then edit time configuration values.

   a. Select your server's time zone. From the menu, select the local time zone for this server.

   b. Verify/Enter time configuration parameters (see Figure 7.7). The first server in a tree defaults to the value of Single Reference server. This means that the server will look to its own clock to provide time to this and all other servers in the tree.

   When your server has joined an existing tree, the time configuration screen will look like Figure 7.8. The default value of Secondary Server will be suggested.

FIGURE 7.7

The time configuration
screen

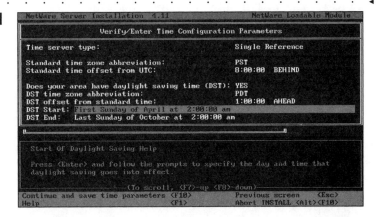

FIGURE 7.8

The time configuration
screen (server joined in
an existing tree)

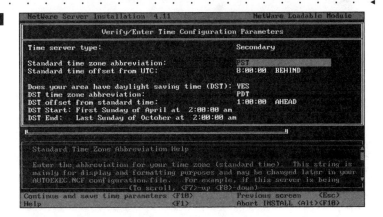

A Secondary time server is preferred in a local environment — that is,
where the senior time server is connected via LAN links within a
building or campus. A Secondary relies on one of the senior time
servers to provide time updates on a periodic basis and then provides
time to the clients it services.

You should configure your server as a Primary when the senior time
server is remote (on the other side of a WAN). A Primary time server
receives time from a Single Reference or Reference time server. If there
is no Single Reference or Reference time server, Primary time servers
vote to determine a time value, update their own time, and then
provide the determined time value to Secondary time servers and

clients. It is only necessary to configure one Primary in each location, with the exception of the location where the Single Reference or Reference time server is located.

Edit time configuration values for the other fields on this screen. The defaults will be correct in most cases, as they were selected according to the time zone you selected. In some cases, you will need to edit fields if your local government does not utilize daylight saving time (DST) the same way as general convention dictates. For example, in Arizona, daylight saving time is not observed at all. In other cases, the exact time that daylight saving time goes into effect or expires may differ from general conventions.

The DST offset from standard time is the number of hours your time zone differs from Greenwich Mean Time, which is now known as Universal Coordinated Time (UTC) per international treaty.

NOTE

Time server configuration can be edited if necessary after installation is complete. For detailed information on time service, see Chapter 18, "NDS Physical Infrastructure and Repair."

3. Specify a context for the server and its objects (see Figure 7.9).

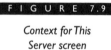

FIGURE 7.9

Context for This Server screen

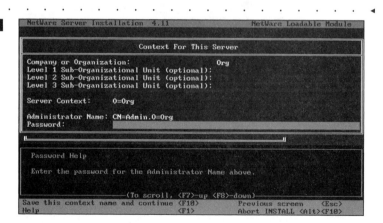

Fill in the following fields as discussed.

TIP

When configuring a small network or single-server tree that contains only one or two servers and does not contain WAN links, put all resources into the Organization container. This configuration makes your tree very easy to manage because all objects will be placed in a single container. This configuration is similar to a bindery-based single-server network and eliminates NDS rights and trustee assignment issues.

a. Fill in the Company or Organization field — which is the Organization container at this time. Do not define Sub-Organizational Units (OUs or containers) at this time except when using a container designated for the specific duty of containing resources. The lowest level you define is where your server and administrator user account will be created by default. The first server in a tree should be placed in the Organization container. For this reason, leave all Sub-Organizational Units fields blank at this time. You can add those containers in the Windows-based NetWare Administrator utility after your installation has been completed.

NOTE

Notice the server context field. Be sure the server will be placed in the appropriate container.

You should create only one Sub-Organization container at this time. One strategy for a Directory tree is to define a Sub-Organization container for servers and other resources and place your server into this container. Placing a server that will host an NDS replica into the Organization container will possibly cause NDS synchronization issues, especially if the tree will include WAN links.

NOTE

If this is a new tree, enter the organization name in the Company or Organization input field. Do not enter Sub-Organizational Units at this time except for the resource container; it is better to configure your tree in NetWare Administrator after your system is installed. By default the server will be installed into the lowest level you define at this time.

It is recommended that you do not install servers into the Organization container where your internetwork will contains one or more WAN links. Placing servers at this level has been known to cause NDS synchronization problems.

b. Enter the Administrator account name and password. Accept the default Administrator user account name, or enter the name you prefer to use. You will be required to enter a password and verify it.

If you have elected to install into an existing tree, you will be asked for the administrator's name and password for the existing tree. You will not be allowed to manage the changes to an NDS tree if you do not have sufficient NDS rights to do so. You will need to have Supervisory NDS rights to the container in which your server will be added. Normally, only the Administrator of the entire organization is permitted to modify the tree's physical infrastructure. In most cases, therefore, it is necessary to log in as the tree Administrator to install new servers in to the tree.

NOTE

Be sure the Administrator account (Admin by default) is created in the Organization level. Placing the Administrator account in a lower level can prevent the Administrator from managing higher containers and objects in them. For example, if the user name is Admin, and the Organization is Org, the Administrator name should read CN=Admin.O=Org. The administrator account will have NDS rights to administer the level in which the account is created and all levels below.

c. Select a context in which to place the server (see Figure 7.10). It is often best to install all servers into a Sub-Organization container designated for this server and related resources. Define the administrator account for this server in the same container. The administrator account defined in this step will have Supervisory NDS rights for the server and all volumes in this server. Container administrators can be defined at lower levels in the tree. Container administrators defined below this level will be able to manage their containers, but not containers above their level — therefore they will not be able to manage server and NDS configuration.

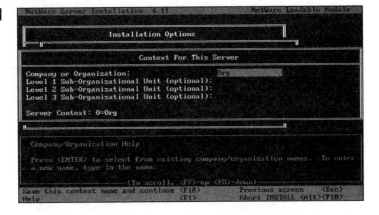

FIGURE 7.10

Placing the server into an existing context

Be careful where you place your server into an existing tree. Any user that has Supervisory NDS rights to the server's context has unlimited NDS rights to the server and its configuration. This includes Supervisory rights to files and directories for all volumes contained in the server.

WARNING

At this point, NDS information on this server and other NDS servers throughout the tree will be updated. The NDS schema will be updated on your local volumes, directories, and files.

If this step has been successful, do not remove this server from service unless you logically remove the server from the tree in NetWare Administrator and you remove any replicas in NDS Manager. Physically removing an NDS object without updating NDS through these utilities *will* cause repercussions throughout the tree.

WARNING

d. To accept the context information, press F10. After the verification menu is answered with a Yes, the NDS schema will be applied to the volumes, directories, and files in the server. When this step is complete, INSTALL will present the NDS information for the context in which the server was created, and the Administrator account and context (if installing into a new tree).

NOTE

Throughout this book examples will use the names **TREE** for the NDS tree and **O=ORG** for the Organization.

WARNING

Be sure to write down the **NDS** information as well as the administrator account name and password. Without this information, you will not be able to administer your **NDS** tree after exiting INSTALL. Forgetting your password or administrator context information would be like losing your key after locking the door.

Step 8: Install Your Server License

Insert your license disk into drive A: and press Enter. The license information will be read from the disk.

If you have purchased an upgrade from a previous version, the disk cannot be read until you have entered a valid key number. You will have to call Novell — they will verify the serial number of your original NetWare version and issue a key to unencrypt the server license. Read the instruction sheet that came with your upgrade for more details.

WARNING

Be sure to use the correct license disk, and do not reinstall it a second time. Server licenses are additive in NetWare 4 and 5 versions. Once you have installed a license, performing this step again will add the license to the existing license already installed. If the same license has been installed on another server on your network/internetwork, this will cause copyright protection error messages.

NetWare 4 licenses are additive — meaning that you can add a license to an existing license. For example, if you wanted to upgrade a 50-user license to support 70 users, instead of purchasing an upgrade to a 100-user license, you can purchase a new 25-user copy of NetWare. When you add the 25-user license to your existing 50-user license, you can support up to 75 users.

Step 9: Create/Edit Your Startup Files

The next step in your setup is to configure the servers' startup files. This includes STARTUP.NCF, AUTOEXEC.BAT, and AUTOEXEC.NCF. STARTUP.NCF contains the disk driver load commands and is executed when the server is started.

AUTOEXEC.NCF, shown later in Figure 7.11, is executed when the SYS volume is mounted. These files can be updated later if SET commands must be adjusted.

1. Create the STARTUP.NCF file. Check your installation manuals for your disk adapters and ask your NIC manufacturers for settings that may need to be included in this file.

   The STARTUP.NCF file is loaded when the OS loads. Certain OS configuration settings must be loaded at this time, such as reserved buffers. NetWare 4 includes a couple of settings that are required in many cases but may not be necessary in all cases. If you are certain that settings included in this file will not be necessary, just delete them. For example, unless you will have Macintosh clients, the line LOAD MAC is not necessary and can be safely eliminated.

NOTE

   To support long filenames for Windows 95, 98, NT, and OS/2 add the line LOAD LONG to your STARTUP.NCF file at this time. Once your system is up, you also need to enter the following command at the console (colon) prompt:

   ADD NAME SPACE LONG to SYS

   Enter the same command for each volume name. This procedure updates the volume's directory listings, adding shadow directory listings on the named volume. This step only needs to be entered one time for each volume. See the section at the end of this chapter that discusses adding name support for workstation operating systems for Macintosh, OS/2, and UNIX clients.

2. Create the AUTOEXEC.NCF file. This screen displays the AUTOEXEC.NCF file as it will be written if you agree. This file runs automatically when the SYS volume is mounted.

   You can add SET or LOAD commands at this time if required. You may add various LOAD commands to automatically load modules upon boot. For example, you might wish to load the MONITOR application when the server is booted. To do so, add the line LOAD MONITOR to the last line of the AUTOEXEC.NCF file.

3. Load Server from your AUTOEXEC.BAT. You may allow your DOS AUTOEXEC.BAT to load SERVER.EXE which boots the NetWare server.

Once you have agreed to these steps, your Main file copy runs, installing all remaining OS files and utilities to your SYS volume.

Step 10: Other Installation Items/Products

Finally, you can install server-based modules, services, and files. In the sections that follow, we shall discuss these options in depth. Before you end the INSTALL utility, the following steps will customize your server installation.

Post-Installation Procedures

After your basic installation has been completed, you may need to spend a little more time to put the finishing touches on your server installation, provide client support, and add services. The following sections discuss procedures that may be required before exiting INSTALL.

Mounting CD Volumes

Your CD-ROM drive should have been set up as a NetWare device during installation. When you copied your system and public files, they were copied from the CD mounted as a NetWare volume. After installation, however, CDs are not mounted as NetWare volumes unless you set them up for this process.

To mount a CD as a NetWare volume:

1. Insert your CD in the server's CD-ROM drive.

2. From the server console (colon prompt), enter **LOAD CDROM**.

3. Enter **CD DEVICE LIST**, noticing the No. (CD device number) listed for the CD.

4. Enter **CD MOUNT 1** (or substitute the No. listed for the CD you wish to mount). This command will mount whichever volume is shown in position number 1, which is, normally, any CD in the drive.

If the CD DEVICE LIST command does not list any devices, check to see that the appropriate drivers are loaded in your STARTUP.NCF file. See Chapter 15, "Storage Devices and File Systems," for more information about troubleshooting CD-ROM problems.

Your CD will be mounted, and the volume name on the CD (shown in the CD DEVICE LIST screen) will become the volume name. Provided you have the appropriate NDS rights and rights to files and directories to access the volume, you can locate the volume in Windows Explorer under Network Neighborhood.

You can then add these commands to your AUTOEXEC.NCF so that the volume will be mounted each time the server is started. To automatically mount the volume in your CD-ROM drive:

1. At your server console (colon prompt), enter **LOAD INSTALL**.

2. Select NCF files option → Edit AUTOEXEC.NCF.

3. Scroll down toward the end of the file and enter these lines (see Figure 7.11):

```
load CDROM

CD VOLUME LIST

CD MOUNT 1
```

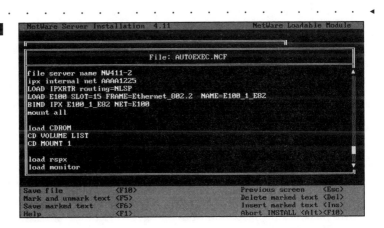

FIGURE 7.11

AUTOEXEC.NCF
file additions

4. Press Esc and then confirm the file save. Escape to exit INSTALL.

In most cases, this will mount any CD that is in your server's CD-ROM drive. In some situations, your CD DEVICE number will not be the number 1. If this is so, your CD volume will not be mounted. To load the volume, read the No. parameter in the CD DEVICE LIST or use the command CD MOUNT *<volume_label>*. Enter the CD's volume label that would be found if you viewed the CD in Windows Explorer or entered the VOLUME command in DOS with the CD in your drive.

Mounting CD Volumes

When you mount a CD volume, an NDS object appears in the NDS container with the server. Appropriate NDS rights and rights to files and directories must be granted to give the users access to the volume. The simplest way to grant these rights is to:

1. Create a group object in the same container as the volume.

2. Grant the group object the appropriate rights to files and directories.

3. Make all users members of the group who are to have access to the CD volume.

Configuring Protocols with INETCFG

When supporting multiple protocol configurations, it is often advisable to use the INETCFG utility. This utility moves protocol-related commands from your AUTOEXEC.NCF into separate files that are then managed with the INETCFG.NLM menu-driven utility. INETCFG makes managing protocol configurations much easier than entering character-based commands at the console. You will find explicit on-screen queries, and help is available. This is especially helpful when supporting the TCP/IP protocol and related services.

You will find that managing drivers, bindings, protocols, and settings from this system is much simpler than manually editing configuration files and settings. You will find context-sensitive help for each menu selection by pressing F1.

To move your protocol binding and configuration statements and manage them using INETCFG, follow these instructions:

1. Put the NetWare 4.11 or 4.2 operating system CD in your server CD-ROM drive.

2. From the server console (colon prompt), enter **LOAD INETCFG**.

Confirm that you want to transfer LAN driver, protocol, and remote access commands to other configuration files. You will see the Internetworking Configuration menu option shown in Figure 7.12.

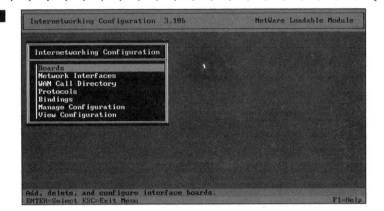

This utility supports the following configuration options:

▸ *Boards* — Used to add and configure NICs

▸ *Network Interfaces* — For assigning names to a logical board, and to view a status to see if a driver has been loaded

▸ *WAN Call Directory* — Used to add and configure WAN call destinations

▸ *Protocols* — Used to configure protocols and their configurations

▸ *Bindings* — Used to select and configure frame types, protocols, and network numbers

▸ *Manage Configuration* — Used for managing other protocol options not described here, including SNMP and remote access (RCONSOLE) support

▸ *View Configuration* — Used to view configuration statements and settings in read-only mode

Once you have migrated your internetworking configuration statements to INETCFG, you can no longer manage them in the AUTOEXEC.NCF — instead type **LOAD INETCFG** at your server console prompt to bring up the previous menu.

See Chapter 11, "Configuring TCP/IP with NetWare," for more detail on configuring TCP/IP protocols and services. In that chapter, INETCFG options are discussed in far more detail.

Adding Volume Name Space Support

NetWare 4 supports long file/directory names in Macintosh, OS/2, Windows 95, Windows NT, and UNIX/NFS. Support for longer names requires loading name space for the client file system and then configuring each volume to support the name space. This is accomplished with two steps:

1. Load the name space module for the client operating system in the STARTUP.NCF file.

2. Upgrade NetWare volumes to support the name space.

The following name space modules are provided:

▸ MAC.NAM (Apple Macintosh)

▸ LONG.NAM (Microsoft Windows 95, 98, NT, and OS/2)

▸ NFS.NAM (any UNIX version with NFS support)

To provide name space support, load the appropriate name space support module as listed and then upgrade the volumes that will support those clients. For example, if you wish to support long file/folder names in Windows 95, 98, and NT, first add the following line to your STARTUP.NCF:

```
load LONG
```

To upgrade the SYS: volume for long filenames, execute the following command at the server console:

```
add name space LONG to SYS
```

When performing this procedure, you should take the server offline or work when the system is not busy. It will take a few minutes to update the volume, and the process will impede user activity significantly.

Shadow listings will be created for each directory entry. DOS (default) name space directory listings use 256 bytes per listing. Other name spaces are enabled by adding an additional 256-byte "shadow" directory listing for extended attributes and the long file/directory names. Loading name space will reduce available disk space and require more RAM in your server to mount volumes.

Creating a Branching DOS Boot Menu

Once you have installed your NetWare server, you should take the following steps to stabilize your server and make it easy to manage:

I. Shut down your server and reboot to verify proper boot execution. To shut down your server, enter the command **DOWN** at the server console (colon) prompt. Type **EXIT** to return to a DOS prompt. Next, cold-boot your server to see if it will come up automatically. If it does not come up automatically, reload the disk driver manually, mount the volume (type **MOUNT ALL** at the colon prompt), load INSTALL.NLM, and check out the STARTUP.NCF and AUTOEXEC.NCF files. If the disk driver was not loaded, make sure your STARTUP.NCF is in the same directory with SERVER.EXE and has the appropriate disk driver load statement(s).

TIP

If the LAN drivers do not load and your LAN driver(s) are not located in the SYS:SYSTEM directory, check the AUTOEXEC.NCF file to be sure that the drive letter is specified of where your drivers are located. By default it is assumed during creation of this file that you will copy the LAN and disk drivers into the SYSTEM directory.

2. Edit the DOS AUTOEXEC.BAT. At the outset of running the INSTALL batch file from CD-ROM, you were asked if you would like the server to boot automatically. If you answered Yes, AUTOEXEC.BAT will include the statement SERVER, which will load the NetWare file server OS when the computer is booted. If you did not answer Yes, you can manually type the command **SERVER** from a DOS prompt to load the server. This is a bit problematic when an inexperienced user is required to boot the server in an emergency.

You should either add the SERVER command to your AUTOEXEC.BAT or make a boot menu. The following is an example of a boot menu to be used with a later version of DOS:

```
CONFIG.SYS:

[menu]                          | heading for boot menu

menuitem=DOS, Boot to DOS       | establishes branch variable

menuitem=NETWARE                | establishes branch variable

menudefault=NETWARE, 15         | default branch, and wait time


[DOS]                           | heading for branch

device=C:\DOS\HIMEM.SYS         | executed for this branch


[NETWARE]                       | heading for branch


[common]                        | heading for commands in
                                  common

files=12                        | all commands that are common
                                  to all branches

buffers=15                      |

device=C:\CDROM\MTMCDAI.SYS /d:MSCD0001 | CD driver


AUTOEXEC.BAT:
```

```
@echo off                           | stops print to screen
path C:\DOS                         | sets path
C:\DOS\MSCDEX.EXE /d:MSCD0001 /m:10  | loads CD extensions
goto %CONFIG%                       | continues branch from
                                      CONFIG.SYS


:DOS                                | label: continues DOS branch
C:\DOS\SMARTDRV.EXE                 | continues DOS branch
goto END                            | skips to END label


:NETWARE                            | label: continues NETWARE
                                      branch

CD \SERVER                          | substitute server directory
                                      name

SERVER                              | executes SERVER
goto END                            | skips to END label


 :END                               | label: exits both branches
```

3. Exit to DOS during boot. If the server comes up automatically and you
wish to exit to DOS, press F5 during boot when you see the "Starting MS-
DOS or Loading . . ." screen message (if your version of DOS supports this
feature).

NOTE

**The DOS boot file just listed can be found on the CD that
accompanies this book. Look for 4AUTOEXC.TXT. and
4CONFIG.TXT. Copy these files to drive C:, renaming them to
CONFIG.SYS and AUTOEXEC.BAT as you do. Be sure to save
backups of your existing CONFIG.SYS and AUTOEXEC.BAT files.**

Installing Online Documentation

Novell Online Documentation provides a full set of manuals for use with NetWare 4.11/4.2/intraNetWare. To install:

1. Insert your Novell Online Documentation CD into any Windows workstation.

2. Choose Run from the Windows File menu.

3. Enter the path/filename *D:\SETUPDOC.EXE* (substitute your drive letter for the CD-ROM drive) and then choose OK.

The setup program will walk you through installation. You can install your documentation on a local drive, install it on a network drive, or run it directly from the CD.

Installing Server Add-Ons

Other server-based modules can be installed by loading INSTALL.NLM and accessing Product Options with your product installation disk in any floppy drive. Several NLM products, including NetWare for Macintosh and NetWare NFS, are loaded this way.

Look for PINSTALL.NLM files. These are installation programs written by software developers that automatically load server-based products on your server. You can also unload server-based applications through this utility.

When loading other NLMs, be certain to watch your CPU utilization and some of your MONITOR statistics, such as Service Processes and Packet Receive Buffers. If they hit their default ceilings, you may need to adjust them upward.

NetWare IP

NetWare IP allows you to use the TCP/IP protocol between NetWare servers and clients. When you install NetWare IP, both IPX/SPX and TCP/IP transports are supported.

To load NetWare IP:

1. Insert your NetWare 4.11 or 4.2 operating system CD in your CD-ROM drive.

2. At the console prompt type **LOAD INSTALL**.

3. Select Product options.

4. Scroll up to Install NetWare IP. Press Enter to select this option.

5. Press Enter or F3 and edit the source path. You will find the NetWare IP PINSTALL.NLM in the \PRODUCTS\NW411\INSTALL\IBM\DOS\ XXX\<*language*> directory.

6. Follow the on-screen instructions for installing and configuring NetWare IP.

NetWare DHCP

NetWare DHCP assigns IP addresses to clients automatically. A DHCP server is configured with a *pool* of addresses from which assignments are made. Of course, before loading NetWare DHCP, you must add TCP/IP protocol support to your server's LAN interfaces.

To load NetWare DHCP:

1. Insert your NetWare 4.11 or 4.2 operating system CD in your CD-ROM drive.

2. At the console prompt type **LOAD INSTALL**.

3. Select Product Options.

4. Scroll up to Install NetWare DHCP. Press Enter to select this option.

5. Press Enter or F3 and edit the source path. You will find the NetWare IP PINSTALL.NLM in the \PRODUCTS\NW411\INSTALL\IBM\DOS\XXX\ <*language*> directory.

6. Follow the on-screen instructions for installing and configuring NetWare DHCP.

For more information on installing, configuring, and using NetWare DHCP, see Chapter 11, "Configuring TCP/IP with NetWare."

Install NetWare Web Server

The NetWare Web Server is a Web server in NetWare 4.11 and 4.2 that provides access to Web pages/sites for an intranet or for the Internet.

 NetWare 4.2 ships with Netscape FastTrack Server for NetWare. You can obtain an update to Netscape FastTrack Server for NetWare from Novell's Web site.

NOTE

To load NetWare Web Server:

1. Insert your NetWare 4.11 or 4.2 operating system CD in your CD-ROM drive.

2. At the console prompt type **LOAD INSTALL**.

3. Select Product Options.

4. Scroll up to Install NetWare Web Server. Press Enter to select this option.

5. Press Enter or F3 and edit the source path. You will find the NetWare Web Server PINSTALL.NLM in the \PRODUCTS\NW411\INSTALL\IBM\DOS\ XXX\<language> directory.

6. Follow the on-screen instructions for installing and configuring NetWare IP.

Installing Netscape FastTrack Server for NetWare 4

FastTrack Server is installed from a Windows 95, 98, or NT client. You must use client version 3.01 for Windows 95/98 or version 4.11a or later for Windows NT. The client must be configured to run IPX, and the server must be version 4.11 or higher. NetWare 4.11 server must have at least 32MB of RAM and should preferably have 16MB more than the server otherwise requires. If you are to integrate users and groups with a database server, you will also need to install Novel's NLDAP server, which is available from Novell's Web site. FastTrack Server requires 100MB of available space on the SYS volume on which FastTrack will be installed, and a DNS server must be available with a pointer record to the FastTrack Server host.

1. Log in with Supervisory rights to the SYS volume and server on which the FastTrack server will be installed.

2. Start SETUP.EXE, which is located in the root of your Netscape FastTrack Server for NetWare CD. Execute this program from the Run menu or Windows Explorer.

3. Specify a root directory for the Web server. This directory will contain your Web page data.

TIP **Be sure you put the Web root directory in a location that can be managed by the Web administrator. You may create a Directory Map object and then assign Supervisory NDS object rights to the Administrator.**

NetWare for Macintosh

NetWare for Macintosh provides support through AppleTalk's built-in networking for Macintosh computers. When NetWare for Macintosh is loaded and configured properly, networked Macintosh computers can access the server as they would access any other AppleTalk server — no protocol support needs to be added at the client end.

To load NetWare for Macintosh:

1. Insert your NetWare 4.11 or 4.2 operating system CD in your CD-ROM drive.

2. At the console prompt type **LOAD INSTALL**.

3. Select Product options.

4. Scroll up to Install NetWare for Macintosh. Press Enter to select this option.

5. Press Enter or F3 and edit the source path. You will find the NetWare for Macintosh PINSTALL.NLM in the \PRODUCTS\NW411\INSTALL\IBM\ DOS\XXX\<language> directory.

6. Follow the on-screen instructions for installing and configuring NetWare for Macintosh.

NOTE

Once your Macintosh clients have been set up and configured properly, you must load Macintosh name space support for volumes that will contain Macintosh file listings. See the section titled "Adding Volume Name Space Support" earlier in this chapter.

Administrative Tools

The following options are available to be installed from the Product options selection in INSTALL:

▶ *Create Client Installation Directories on Server* — This option will put the NetWare client setup files on a network drive so that you can upgrade clients remotely without using a CD or floppy disks.

▶ *Make Diskettes* — This option will make a set of setup disks for clients.

▶ *Install Legacy NWAdmin Utility* — This option will install a 16-bit Windows version of NetWare Administrator.

▶ *Upgrade 3.1x Print Services* — This option will update a NetWare 3.11 or 3.12 print server, queues, and printers to NetWare 4 and NDS.

▶ *Install an Additional Server Language* — Use this option to install additional language support for your server and network.

▶ *Change Server Language* — This option switches the language that is used on the server.

▶ *Install NetWare Client for Mac OS* — This option provides support for Macintosh workstations to access NetWare servers and trees using the IPX protocol. When this product is used, NetWare for Macintosh is not required.

NOTE

Once your Macintosh clients have been set up and configured properly, you must load Macintosh name space support for volumes that will contain Macintosh file listings. See the section titled "Adding Volume Name Space Support" earlier in this chapter.

▶ *Configure NetWare Licensing Service (NLS)* — Use this option to install or update your client licenses. As discussed previously, licenses can be added together to add support for additional clients.

▶ *Create Registration Diskette* — You can create a disk that will contain your software registration data.

Additional intraNetWare Services

If you have purchased intraNetWare, the following services are also included.

FTP Services for intraNetWare and NetWare UNIX Print Services

FTP Services for intraNetWare provides file transfer services to TCP/IP workstations. NetWare UNIX Print Services software supports print gateways between NetWare and UNIX hosts.

To install:

1. Put your FTP Services for intraNetWare CD in your CD-ROM drive.

2. From your server console (colon prompt), type **LOAD INSTALL**.

3. Select Install a Product Not Listed.

4. Edit the path. Press F3, and enter the path **NWUXPS:\NWUXPS** or **D:\NWUXPS** if the drive is located as local drive *D:*.

Novell Internet Access Server 4

This disk contains software that will connect an intranet to the Internet and extend those services to both IP and IPX clients. Internet Access Server contains the following product components:

▸ *NetWare 4.11 and 4.2 updates* — Includes all OS updates, patches, and additional utilities to support the products on this disk.

▸ *NetWare MultiProtocol Router 3.1* — This router supports routing IP, IPX, and AppleTalk protocols with RIP, RIP II, and OSPF routing protocols.

▸ *IPX/IP Gateway* — Supports IPX client access to IP services, such as Web and FTP services.

▸ *WAN Extensions 3.1* — Adds more robust support for WANs.

▸ *Netscape Navigator* — Adds browser support for 16-bit and 32-bit Windows clients.

To install Novell Internet Access Server 4:

1. Put your Novell Internet Access Server 4 in your CD-ROM drive.

2. From your server console (colon prompt), type **LOAD INSTALL**.

3. Select Install a Product Not Listed.

4. Edit the path. Press F3, and enter the path **NIAS4:\INSTALL** or **D:\INSTALL** if the drive is located as a local drive *D*:.

To install Internet Access Server 4's online documentation from a workstation:

1. Put the Internet Access Server 4 CD in your workstation's CD-ROM drive.

2. Select Run from the Windows File menu.

3. Enter or select SETUP.EXE.

For more information on managing these modules, refer to Chapter 12, "Novell Internet Access Server."

CHAPTER 8

NetWare 5 Setup

The purpose of this chapter is to guide you through the installation of NetWare 5's server OS, and to help you troubleshoot configuration issues and common problems that occur during installation. If you are reinstalling or upgrading, you will find very few — if any — differences from a first-time install.

If an installation has failed, this chapter will help you work around your difficulties. If you are reinstalling NetWare 5 to work around previous problems, pay close attention to the configuration options that are presented to you — your installation may have been improperly configured. You may find tips, notes, and warnings in this chapter especially helpful in making your installation go easily with the greatest benefit of foresight.

This chapter assumes the following:

▸ You have selected and assembled a computer to be the file server.

▸ Your LAN and cabling have been properly installed.

▸ Your NICs are installed and tested and do not conflict with other hardware or software devices.

▸ Your server has a CD-ROM drive that can be installed as a DOS device.

▸ You are installing a single server and just a few workstations.

As in all NetWare versions, NetWare 5's server boot files are installed on a bootable DOS volume — it is not possible to boot and execute the NetWare 5 server OS from a floppy. Therefore you must partition your drive and allocate a small portion for a bootable DOS volume. NetWare 5 requires 50MB of disk space on your DOS volume; however, it is wise to allocate at least 100MB plus the amount of memory installed in the server. This amount of disk space allows room for DOS executables, server boot files, and an operating system core dump if necessary. Free space of 50MB should allow for server add-ons or future upgrades. It is a good idea to allocate an entire physical drive to the operating system, separate from all data and applications.

The NetWare 5 installation process is similar to that of previous versions with a couple of exceptions: the NetWare Graphical Server Interface guides you through part of the installation, and automatic hardware detection makes driver selection and configuration easier. As in NetWare 4, INSTALL guides you through the installation process step by step.

WARNING

Upgrade all NetWare 4 servers before attempting to install NetWare 5 into an existing NetWare 4 tree. Failure to do so may damage your NetWare 4 replicas during NetWare 5 installation. NDS updates are provided on your NetWare 5 operating system CD.

Because NetWare 5 features NDS, you must either create an NDS tree or install your NetWare 5 server into an existing tree. Installing a stand-alone server requires very little NDS knowledge or experience. Installing a server into an existing tree requires some forethought and planning. For basic information on NDS, see your NetWare 5 online documentation or *Four Principles of NDS Design* by Jeffrey F. Hughes and Blair W. Thomas (IDG Books Worldwide).

Installation Options

NetWare 5 can be installed from a:

▸ Bootable local CD-ROM drive

▸ Local CD-ROM drive

▸ Network drive

▸ Networked or shared CD-ROM drive

What's new with NetWare 5? Installation from a bootable CD is, for one thing. You will find this option a time-saver. If your computer or SCSI adapter supports booting from a CD, you won't need to set up your CD-ROM drive as a DOS device. When you boot from a CD, you are given an option to create a bootable partition. After you choose whether you want to change the partitioning and you select the size of the boot partition, you will reboot. If you boot again from the CD, you can elect not to change the partitioning and proceed with the install process the same way you would if you booted from a bootable hard drive.

NOTE **Booting from the CD requires less effort than other installation methods. You will not need to create a boot volume and install your DOS CD-ROM drivers before starting your installation. This step is handled within INSTALL from menu selections.**

Like other NetWare versions, NetWare 5 can be installed from a CD, a network drive, or a networked CD-ROM drive. The NetWare 5 setup program is not configured to support floppy disk installation. Installing directly from the CD is the best option. Even the least expensive CD-ROM drive will be an asset to your server — NetWare 5 includes software to use IDE and SCSI CD-ROM drives as NetWare volumes.

Preparing the Server

Before you begin your installation, you need to:

1. Verify that your server has sufficient resources to support NetWare 5. See the section on NetWare 5 resource requirements in this chapter.

2. Prepare a bootable DOS volume. This can be done through the setup program, but doing so requires restarting the installation after this step is finished.

3. Install your CD-ROM DOS driver(s) and CD-ROM extensions (MSCDEX.EXE or equivalent). This step is not necessary if you have a bootable CD-ROM drive.

4. Obtain the latest disk and NIC drivers for your server's internal adapters.

5. Be prepared with your adapters' hardware configuration settings, your NetWare operating system CD, and your NetWare 5 LICENSE floppy disk.

NOTE

Check release notes and preinstallation instructions before proceeding. You will be able to view these files from within INSTALL, or you can look for README files on your NetWare CD. You will find README files in the \PRODUCTS\README\<language> directory on your NetWare installation CDs.

NetWare 5 Resource Requirements

NetWare 5 requires far more RAM and disk storage than previous NetWare versions. The resources listed in Table 8.1 are required.

TABLE 8.1	RESOURCE	MINIMUM	RECOMMENDED
NetWare 5 Resource Requirements	Processor	Pentium (100 MHz)	Pentium II or Xeon
	RAM	64MB	128MB
	Video	VGA	SVGA
	DOS disk space	50MB	100MB + amount of server RAM
	SYS volume disk space	350MB	500MB or more
	Mouse	0	1
	3 ½" floppy disk drive	1	1
	CD-ROM drive	1	1

Your CD-ROM drive must be capable of reading ISO 9660–formatted CDs. Bootable CD-ROM drives must fully support the El Torito specifications.

Compatibility with NetWare 3 and 4

NetWare 5 and NetWare 3 coexist on the same network with no modifications. NetWare 3 servers use the bindery mode and are not fully integrated into NDS. NetWare 4 and 5 servers will integrate together within NDS trees, and NetWare 4.2 requires no modifications. However, NetWare 4.11 servers require the following upgrades:

- ▶ DS.NLM 5.99 or higher

- ▶ DSRepair.NLM 4.58 or higher

- ▶ Novell Licensing Services

NetWare 4.10 servers require the following upgrades:

- ▶ DS.NLM 5.13 or higher

- ▶ DSRepair.NLM 4.58 or higher

WARNING

When integrating a NetWare 5 server into a NetWare 4 tree, you must upgrade NDS on your version 4 servers. During NetWare 5 INSTALL, you will be given an opportunity to update the NetWare 4 servers over the network. Be sure to update *all* NetWare 4 servers before restarting your NetWare 5 server.

You will find these updates on your NetWare 5 operating system CD in the \PRODUCTS\411_UPG directory. See the file 411_UPG.TXT for more details. To update NetWare 4.10 servers, see Novell's Web site.

WARNING

Failure to upgrade NetWare 4.11 servers to NDS version 5.99 or higher can result in damage to existing NDS replicas. Be sure you update your NetWare 4.11 servers prior to attempting to install a NetWare 5 server into an existing tree. NetWare 4.2 is updated and requires no modifications to be fully compatible with NetWare 5.

Upgrading a Previous Version to NetWare 5

NetWare 3.1*x*, 3.2, and 4.1*x* servers can be upgraded to NetWare 5. To upgrade a server from a pervious version, 35MB of free disk space in the DOS boot volume is required. The SYS volume must have at least 100MB of free space.

Upgrading NetWare 4 servers running the Novell Web Server is not supported.

When upgrading NetWare 4.11 servers where Novell Licensing Services is installed, check and record the LSP object's attributes, and delete the LSP object before upgrading. After upgrading the server, create a new LSP object and modify its properties to restore the previous configuration.

Creating a Bootable DOS Volume

NetWare 5 requires 50MB of DOS disk space, but you should allocate at least 100MB for several reasons. You may decide to install NetWare Loadable Modules (NLMs), drivers, DOS external executables, DOS utilities, hardware diagnostic utilities, and virus scanning software on the DOS volume. In case of server crashes, you may wish to dump memory to a file for debugging, which requires enough disk space to accommodate the total amount of memory installed in your server in addition to the 50MB minimum. For these reasons, allocating 100MB or more to your server's DOS volume is a practical suggestion.

TIP

You should make your DOS volume at least 100MB plus the amount of installed RAM. A future upgrade may require you to enlarge your DOS boot volume, which would then require repartitioning.

If you boot from a SCSI drive, you will need to set up your SCSI system properly, as discussed in Chapter 5. To make a SCSI drive bootable, you will need to enable your SCSI adapter's on-board BIOS and configure the first SCSI drive as bootable in your SCSI utilities. In some cases, you may install DOS device drivers to substitute for the SCSI adapter's on-board BIOS. See your owner's manual for details.

NOTE

To make a SCSI drive bootable, you must either configure the SCSI adapter BIOS or make the boot partition active. SCSI BIOS firmware sometimes has other requirements. For example, some SCSI BIOSes require that only SCSI ID 0 can be bootable.

Be sure your SCSI drives are set up properly. You must configure each drive with a unique SCSI ID, and only the last drive on the cable must be terminated. Sometimes improperly terminated drives may work, but they can cause I/O errors later on. All questions concerning SCSI specifications, cabling, and setup are discussed in the DELEC Online SCSI Guide on the CD that accompanies this book.

IDE CD-ROM drives have become faster and cheaper. NetWare 5 includes IDE CD support modules that make it possible to use IDE drives as NetWare volumes. Later computer BIOS programs also make booting from CD possible. Usually, you have to configure your computer's BIOS setup program for this feature.

Creating a primary DOS partition, making it active, and formatting it with a system is typically done at the factory for most computers. Most computers are shipped with an entire drive allocated to DOS, Windows 95, Windows 98, or Windows NT. NetWare only needs a small DOS partition — clients can only access valid NetWare volumes over the network. This often means repartitioning and reinstalling DOS.

In many cases, computer manufacturers provide their own setup utilities. You should review your computer owner's manual for any special considerations before attempting to partition your drive and accepting the resulting loss of data.

NOTE

You can use Novell DOS, located on the LICENSE disk, any later version of DOS, Windows 95, or Windows 98 to create a bootable DOS volume. NetWare comes with a bootable floppy disk that contains the Novell DOS FORMAT and FDISK utilities in the DOSTOOLS directory. If you are not familiar with the procedure for creating a partition and formatting it, see your DOS manual or refer to the CD that accompanies this book.

You will find detailed instructions on creating a bootable DOS volume on the CD that accompanies this book.

NOTE

Installing a NetWare Server on a Windows 95/98 Computer

Installing a NetWare server on a computer that is already running Windows 95 or Windows 98 requires some careful considerations. NetWare servers can be installed with Windows 95/98 in three ways:

▶ You can create a bootable volume using the Windows 95/98 version of DOS (command prompt), the same way you would use a previous DOS version.

▶ You can boot from a bootable floppy disk and then switch to drive C:.

▶ You can interrupt the Windows 95/98 boot process to boot to the Windows 95/98 command prompt without executing the graphical portion of Windows.

All of these options require you to install your CD-ROM drive as a DOS device. Each option requires a few modifications to the original Windows 95/98 boot process.

NOTE

You cannot access a FAT32 file system when booting from a DOS version that predates MS-DOS 6.22. Earlier Windows 95 versions used a FAT16 file system that is accessible from MS-DOS versions 6.0 and later. The FAT32 file system is not backward compatible with previous DOS or Windows 95 versions where the FAT16 file system was installed. However, this problem is easily overcome if you prepare your boot disk using the FAT32 utilities or the Windows Startup disk that was created during Windows installation. You can verify your file system's configuration in FDISK. Windows 95 OSR2, Windows 98, and MS-DOS 6.22's FDISK will identify a FAT32 file system. FDISK from previous DOS versions will simply identify the volume as a non-DOS system.

The last option, interrupting the Windows 95/98 boot process and booting to the command prompt is a bit challenging. Once you have edited your computer boot files, you must remove most of the Windows 95/98 operating system files so that your computer will not boot to Windows 95/98 anymore. Every time your computer boots, you must intercept the boot by pressing F8. If you computer were to boot to Windows 95/98, your startup files would be edited and you would have to reconfigure your boot environment.

Installing from CD

Novell designed NetWare's server INSTALL program to be run from CD. For most computers, running a CD-ROM drive as a DOS device is the most practical way of using the drive for installation. When purchasing your CD-ROM drive, be sure that the device comes with everything that is needed to install it as a DOS device, or be sure that the CD-ROM drive is bootable and uses the El Torito specifications. You generally need to activate CD-ROM boot options in your computer BIOS or your SCSI adapter BIOS setup programs.

NOTE

If your CD-ROM drive is bootable, you can ignore all instructions concerning setting up your CD-ROM drive as a DOS device. If you do not have a bootable CD-ROM drive, DOS drivers must be loaded in the server so that you can execute INSTALL from the CD.

The CD-ROM drive may be an IDE or SCSI device—either is acceptable. However, NetWare drivers may not support older CD-ROM drives as NetWare devices. You will need a DOS device driver (such as CR_ATAPI.SYS), and Microsoft CD Extensions (MSCDEX.EXE) or equivalent. If your CD-ROM drive is a SCSI device, you may need a CD driver (such as ASPICD.SYS) in addition to a DOS SCSI device driver and MSCDEX.EXE. The device drivers (files that normally have .SYS extensions) are installed into CONFIG.SYS, whereas MSCDEX.EXE (or equivalent) is installed in your AUTOEXEC.BAT. CD-ROM drives that use MSCDEX.EXE are not shipped with it — you must use MSCDEX.EXE from your DOS system software. CD extensions are not provided with the Novell DOS that is included with NetWare.

Many computers have bootable CD-ROM drives, and many SCSI adapters can be configured to boot from CD. NetWare's installation program does not take advantage of this feature. Even if your computer has a bootable CD, you will need to create a bootable DOS volume and allocate enough space on which to install your server boot files. In most cases, you will find that installing DOS support files is the most efficient way — and perhaps the only way — to install from CD.

 If your system hangs right after starting DOS, your CD probably does not use El Torito specifications.

NOTE

If you have a bootable CD-ROM drive, you can boot from the NetWare 5 operating system CD and create your bootable DOS partition from NetWare INSTALL. Before proceeding with your installation, remove your CD and boot from your hard drive to verify that the drive is bootable. Once you resume the installation, you will skip the partitioning step and continue as normal regardless of whether you booted from CD or from your hard drive.

Once your NetWare server OS is installed, your system files contain NetWare drivers for all later-model IDE and SCSI CD-ROM drives and a CD reader NLM to recognize CD file systems as NetWare volumes.

Installing from a Network

A NetWare server can be installed over a network from a shared CD or from a network drive where the NetWare server installation files have been copied. The process is simple and is recommended any time more than one server (of the same version) must be installed.

Installing from a Networked CD

To install from a networked CD-ROM drive, map a drive letter to the shared CD-ROM volume and enter the source path as any other network drive mapping. To install from a networked CD-ROM drive, map a drive letter to the shared CD-ROM volume and enter the source path as any other network drive mapping.

When installing over the network from a CD-ROM on a NetWare 5 server, you must unload CDROM.NLM and load CDINST.NLM. CDROM.NLM mounts a CD as a NSS volume, which does not support the server-to-server install.

NOTE

When installing over the network from a CD-ROM on a NetWare 4 server, you must update your CD-ROM's storage adapter driver to the latest version. Older drivers have been known to cause abends during network installations. You can obtain the updated file from Novell's Web site or from the Support Connection CD.

WARNING

Installing from a Network Drive

You can install your NetWare server from a network drive or CD-ROM drive that is shared on the network. This option is perfectly acceptable and is used wherever integrators need to install several servers. Follow these steps to make NetWare server installation files and directories available over the network:

I. From a workstation, use XCOPY to copy the entire operating system CD and all subdirectories on your CD to a network drive. You may use Windows Explorer to do the same by right-clicking when your arrow is on the root directory of the CD and then selecting Copy from the menu. You will then right-click the destination drive or directory and select Paste.

For example, assume that your CD-ROM drive is drive D:, you want to install from SYS:\NW50, and SYS: is mapped as drive F:. To XCOPY the CD to this directory, type the command:

```
XCOPY D:\*.* F:\NW50 /s /e
```

This will copy the root of D: and all subdirectories (/s) even if they are empty (/e).

2. Create a bootable DOS partition on the new server.

3. Install the Client for DOS from your Z.E.N.works Starter Pack.

4. Edit the client NET.CFG file to include the following command under the DOS REQUESTER section:

```
FILE CACHE LEVEL = 0
```

5. Log in using an NDS account with access to the installation files.

6. Map root to the directory containing the preceding directory.

7. Start INSTALL from the mapped drive.

Wherever you are prompted to verify source and destination path names during INSTALL, substitute the network drive/directory path for the default.

This procedure requires that you set up your server as a client to another server before starting INSTALL, which requires almost as much effort as installing the server OS. However, when installing multiple servers, you will find that your setup time will have been spent judiciously.

NOTE

You can access online documentation immediately by clicking the RUNME.EXE file on your Z.E.N.works CD in the \NOVDOCS directory.

Server Operating System Installation

The following section discusses installing your server step by step in a quick start overview, and in detail.

Server Installation Quick Start

This section discusses a quick overview. If you are experienced with installing operating systems, you may be able to install from this overview without having to follow the detailed steps that follow. If you have questions about anything you encounter during the installation, refer to the section later in this chapter where each step is covered in detail.

When installing NetWare 5, you will find that the first three screens are character-based, and the fourth will load the Graphical Server User Interface. If you are upgrading, the first through fourth screens are character-based, and the fifth screen starts the Graphical Server User Interface. If your server is unable to display the graphical screens, character-based screens will be used throughout the installation.

Installing the server OS comprises the following steps:

1. Execute INSTALL.BAT from the root of your NetWare 5 operating system CD.

2. Select the type of installation and regional settings.

3. Select and configure device drivers.

4. Create a NetWare partition and SYS volume.

5. Assign the server name.

6. Install the NetWare 5 server file system on additional drives.

7. Install networking protocols.

8. Set the server time zone.

9. Set up Novell Directory Services.

10. Install your NetWare 5 server license.

11. Select other networking products to install.

12. Customize your installation.

Once you have completed installing your server, you can further customize your NetWare 5 server installation by loading NWCONFIG.NLM. This new application replaces INSTALL.NLM.

Server Installation Procedure

The following procedure discusses the NetWare 5 installation procedure in detail, step by step. Once a bootable DOS volume has been configured on your server and your CD-ROM drivers are installed, you can follow these instructions.

Step 1: Starting INSTALL

1. Execute INSTALL.BAT in the root of your operating system CD. You will be prompted to accept the license agreement and then to continue.

2. If you have created a bootable DOS volume, continue without changing partitioning. If you are booting from CD, you can create a bootable DOS volume at this time. You will then be prompted to enter the size of the partition. Once accepting the boot volume options, you will be prompted to reboot and start again. Once you have created your boot partition and rebooted, you should then choose the option to continue without changing the partitioning.

3. The splash screen (a graphical NetWare 5 logo screen) will appear.

NOTE

If the splash screen does not display properly, just wait. INSTALL will proceed to a character-based screen, and you will have an opportunity to change video driver configuration. This problem indicates that your video card and/or monitor will not work properly with the default NetWare server video driver to produce Super VGA output. You may be able to continue if you select the Standard VGA video driver in the next step.

4. Accept or edit your mouse and video modes. Cursor up to select the correct port for your mouse. The NetWare server video driver is a universal driver that only supports two video modes: VGA 640 × 480, 16-color or Super VGA 640 × 480, 256-color. If your video adapter and monitor will not support one of these two options, you will need to proceed with the character-based installation.

Step 2: Select the Type of Installation and Regional Settings

1. Answer which type of installation: upgrade or new server, as shown in Figure 8.1.

▶ . . . . ◀

F I G U R E   8.1

Select New Server or Upgrade and the directory for server boot files.

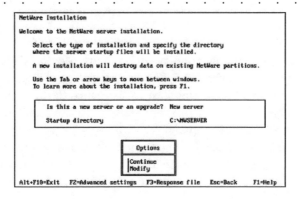

```
NetWare Installation

Welcome to the NetWare server installation.

    Select the type of installation and specify the directory
    where the server startup files will be installed.

    A new installation will destroy data on existing NetWare partitions.

    Use the Tab or arrow keys to move between windows.
    To learn more about the installation, press F1.


      Is this a new server or an upgrade?    New server

      Startup directory                      C:\NWSERVER


                          Options
                          Continue
                          Modify

    Alt+F10=Exit   F2=Advanced settings   F3=Response file   Esc=Back   F1=Help
```

WARNING

If you select New Server, all existing NetWare data partitions will be deleted automatically later during disk partitioning. If you are upgrading a server from a previous version, be sure to scroll up to the New Server field, press Enter, and then select Upgrade from 3.x or 4.x.

2. Accept or edit the directory name for server boot files. The server boot files will be placed on your local DOS drive.

3. Enter your locale settings: country code, page, and keyboard. For the United States, leave the defaults intact. For other countries, select the appropriate configuration to support your native language on your server.

TIP

Select alternative settings only if you wish to support other than the U.S. format on your server's keyboard and console. The default setting is for U.S. keyboard and default screen-generated character sets.

When you continue, the NetWare boot files will be copied to the DOS boot volume. Be patient; this file copy will take a while.

Step 3: Select Device Drivers

Next, your server's internal hardware devices are scanned and disk adapters are identified.

TIP

If a plug-and-play device is not automatically found, the device settings probably conflict with another device. If this is the case, you must run the DOS PnP configuration utility, configure the device, and record the settings. This will ensure that the device is properly configured and the proper settings are used. ISA PnP devices often do not autodetect properly and are not recommended for server usage. Always use PCI NICs and disk adapters in servers. Not only does PnP work better in a PCI environment, but you will find that PCI adapters use less server processing power and perform better.

a. Add the Platform Support Module and the HotPlug Support Module if required. It may be necessary for you to select Modify and manually add the appropriate drivers.

NOTE

Platform Support Modules are required for multiprocessor and other specially designed servers to be used with NetWare 5. HotPlug Support Modules are required for servers that support the HotPlug feature, which enables you to add interface cards without shutting your server down. Both of these types of drivers are provided by the server OEM.

Check to see that all disk drivers are listed. To add a driver, scroll up to the driver field, press Enter, and then press Ins to view a list of drivers located on your operating system CD. If you have an updated driver on a floppy disk, press Ins again. You can then read the driver from a floppy disk or edit the path from which the driver will be read.

NOTE

Be sure to add a storage adapter driver for each disk adapter or channel (for example, SCSI or IDE). When you are partitioning your storage devices, disk drives will not appear if the adapter driver was not loaded.

When you continue, the Platform Specific Module, HotPlug Module, and storage adapter drivers will be loaded.

NOTE

If a driver fails to load, you will hear a beep and see a message indicating that a driver failed to load. Press Alt+Esc to switch to the server console screen to view messages displayed by the disk driver during load. You can then press Alt+Esc to switch back to the INSTALL program. If your driver failed to load, it is the wrong driver, the hardware settings are not properly configured, or else the device conflicts with another device.

▶ • ◀

Troubleshooting Storage Adapter Drivers

If a storage adapter driver fails to load:

1. Check to see that the correct driver was selected. If the driver is correct, check to see that the driver is the latest driver provided by the adapter vendor and that it is certified for use with NetWare 5.

2. Check the adapter configuration settings in INSTALL. Be sure that the correct slot, I/O address, interrupt, memory address, and other settings are entered as the device is configured.

3. Exit INSTALL and test the hardware device. Fix configuration problems, test the device using installation and configuration utilities provided by the device manufacturer, and then restart your installation from the beginning.

When you continue, the driver summary listing will be displayed as shown in Figure 8.2.

NOTE

Device drivers (.HAM, .CDM, and .PSM files) may fail to load automatically upon reboot if autodetect was not successful. If this occurs, you must manually copy the device drivers from the \Startup\Drivers directory on the NetWare 5 operating system CD to the DOS server boot directory (NWSERVER by default).

F I G U R E   8.2

*The storage device and
network board driver
summary screen*

b. Accept or add disk drivers and network board (NIC) drivers. If a NIC is installed in your computer but does not appear on this screen, you will have to select the driver for it manually. A missing driver is not a problem; it simply indicates that hardware detection could not communicate with the unlisted adapter.

c. Add NLMs to load during boot. Driver support files, (that is, .ndi files) are sometimes required with a driver. Read your device documentation for specifics on required support files.

Selecting Additional Drivers

To select an additional driver:

1. Move your cursor up to Storage Devices or Network Boards.

2. Press Enter and then Ins to view a list of drivers on the NetWare 5 OS CD.

3. Locate the appropriate driver, or press Ins to load a driver from a floppy disk. A driver on a floppy disk must have the driver, a driver data file, and in some cases support modules.

▶ · ◀

Editing a Driver's Configuration

To edit a driver's configuration:

1. Select the driver from the list, using the up arrow to cursor up to driver line.

2. Press Enter, select Modify, and then press Ins.

3. Select the driver. If your device is not listed, press Ins to read a driver from a floppy disk or other storage location. Drivers can be stored on any type of DOS device in your server but must include at least two files: the driver file and the driver data file. In addition, some devices require support files.

4. After adding a driver, you will see the driver properties list. Enter the device settings and then press F10 to save the settings and return to the previous menu. When you are finished selecting drivers, select Return to Driver List and then Return to Driver Summary.

5. Repeat this procedure for each NIC installed in your server.

NOTE

Check your NIC and storage adapter installation guide for special instructions requiring NLMs to be loaded. Normally this is not required, since most drivers autoload required support modules. Do not add server applications at this point—you will have an opportunity to do so later during INSTALL or after installation is completed.

When you continue, the storage device and NIC drivers will be loaded. If you hear a beep and see a message indicating that the driver failed to load, press Alt+Esc to switch to the server console to view driver messages.

NOTE

If you are unable to successfully load storage adapter drivers, you will not be able to partition drives connected to the adapter and update those drives with NDS data. If you are unable to load NIC driver(s), you will not be able to join an existing NDS tree during installation. Though you can proceed without successfully loading NIC drivers, you should exit INSTALL and correct any device and driver problems before proceeding.

▶ . . . . ◀

Troubleshooting Drivers

If the driver has failed to load:

1. See that you have selected the correct NIC driver.

2. Check to see that the proper NIC settings have been entered. You may press Esc to return to the previous INSTALL instructions and reenter your configuration settings.

3. Exit INSTALL and check hardware settings and check for hardware conflicts. When you correct the problem, you will need to restart INSTALL from the beginning.

Step 4: Create a NetWare Partition and SYS Volume

In this portion of INSTALL, you will create a NetWare partition and the SYS volume that will contain the operating system. If this is a new installation, you will see a screen similar to the one shown in Figure 8.3. In a new installation, this screen may be part of the graphical installation. If this is an upgrade, this step will be character-based.

To create the SYS volume, accept the SYS volume summary as shown in Figure 8.3 or modify the partition and volume properties.

▶ . . . . ◀

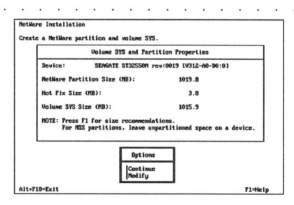

FIGURE 8.3

The Volume SYS and Partition Properties screen

If the selected device is not the drive on which you wish to create the SYS volume, you can select an alternative storage device by selecting in the Device field shown in Figure 8-3. You will have an opportunity to add partitions and configure volumes on additional disk drives later during INSTALL or in the NWCONFIG utility after installation is completed.

You can create just the SYS volume, or you can configure all disk drives at this time or during the Customize step at the end of the installation. If you attempt to configure all disk drives at this time, be sure you do not inadvertently place the SYS volume on the wrong drive.

NOTE

To edit the SYS volume's properties, press F3. You will see the Volume Information screen shown in Figure 8.4.

► · ◄

F I G U R E   8.4

*The SYS Volume
Information screen*

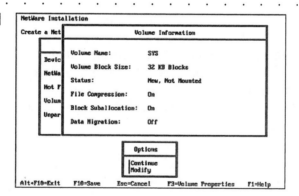

In the Create a NetWare Volume screen, NetWare 5 enables you to eliminate Hot Fix entirely. You should set Hot Fix to 0 for fault-tolerant RAID subsystems, since Hot Fix is not needed.

NOTE

To accept changed data and return to the menu, press F10.

Turn off compression on the SYS volume unless there is a compelling need to use it. It can be turned on at a later date, but it can never be turned off without deleting the volume. Use compression only on volumes that will contain archived data. Refer to Chapter 15, "Storage Devices and File Systems," before you invoke compression.

TIP

Never turn off block suballocation — it has never been known to cause problems. This feature enables you to use the default large block size with the economy of a small block size. Data is read and written to large blocks, typically 64K per block. However, blocks are actually stored in smaller block suballocation units of 512 bytes. Block suballocation is totally transparent to your software applications and requires no administration. The traditional NetWare volume with block suballocation is as dependable as any file system.

Use data migration only when storage devices will be installed that will use it. Data migration is used for two types of devices: backup devices and disk jukeboxes. Backup devices use data migration to automatically migrate unused data off primary storage units onto optical and tape storage magazines. Optical and CD jukeboxes use data migration to move data from disks onto a hard drive swap disk. Either way, the data appears to be located on a NetWare volume but is actually located on a storage device.

NOTE

The first server volume must be named SYS, and minimum partition size for the SYS volume to accommodate a minimum installation is 350MB with 500MB or more recommended. The SYS volume will contain the operating system, a swap file, server add-on modules, and print queues. Be sure to provide ample disk space for future upgrades and additions in this volume. This volume cannot be configured as an NSS volume.

When you are in the Modify mode, you can press F1 to see a listing of volume space requirements. NetWare 5 requires the following amounts of space on the SYS volume:

▸ NetWare 5 OS only — 350MB

▸ NetWare 5 OS with all modules, but without Online Documentation — 375MB

▸ NetWare 5 with all modules and online documentation — 550MB

Once you have finished viewing the partition, Hot Fix, and volume configuration, press F10 to save, and cursor to Continue.

The SYS volume and your CD volume will be mounted, and then the basic OS files will be copied to the SYS volume. If the installation is being performed from a network drive, you will be prompted to reconnect to the network at this time.

When you continue, the SYS volume will be mounted, and the CD-ROM will be mounted as a NetWare device. System files will then be copied to the SYS volume. A status screen will show progress as the file copy proceeds.

NOTE

This step may take a while, depending upon the speed of your storage peripherals and processor. Files are expanded and checked aggressively during this stage to ensure that OS files have been copied without error, so be patient. A File Copy Status bar indicates progress and may remain at a given level for an extended period. Wait several minutes watching to see if the status bar is updated before assuming your system has hung.

TIP

If file copy progress stalls at this point, check the termination on your SCSI drives. Failure to properly copy files indicates an intermittent disk drive failure or indicates that your SYS volume is full.

Step 5: Assign the Server Name

In a new installation, the NetWare Graphical Server Interface starts showing the Server Properties screen.

NOTE

If your mouse does not work, the wrong mouse port may have been selected, the mouse port or hardware may not be working, or your mouse may not be not supported.

If you do not have a mouse, or your mouse will not work, the keystrokes shown in Table 8.2 will get you through the installation. You can edit the mouse port configuration after installation from the server's graphical Start menu.

TABLE 8.2	KEYSTROKE	ACTION
Keystrokes	Tab	Move cursor to next element
	Shift+Tab	Move cursor to previous element
	Enter	Select
	Up-arrow (keypad 8)	Move cursor up
	Down-arrow (keypad 2)	Move cursor down
	Right-arrow (keypad 6)	Move cursor right
	Left-arrow (keypad 4)	Move cursor left
	Hold Shift while pressing keypad	Accelerate cursor movement
	Keypad 5	Select or click an object
	Keypad 0	Lock a selected object (for dragging)
	Keypad . (period)	Unlock a selected object (to drop)
	Keypad + (plus)	Double-click an object
	Alt+F7	Move to next window
	Alt+F8	Move to previous window

You will see the Server Properties screen. Enter the name to be assigned to this server into the server identification screen shown in Figure 8.5. You can use between 2 and 47 alphanumeric characters, hyphens, and underscores in a server name. You can use a period (.) in the server name, but a period cannot be the first character in the name.

F I G U R E   8.5

The server name screen

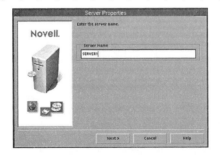

You should not use underscores in the server name when using TCP/IP to prevent name resolution problems. Underscores are invalid in DNS and are typically converted to hyphens.

TIP

If you are upgrading a previous version server to NetWare 5, this portion of INSTALL will be character-based. The existing server name will be used by default. To edit the server name, press F2.

Step 6: Configure File Systems on Additional Storage Devices

The Configure File System screen, shown in Figure 8.6, will display all storage devices. You may configure NetWare volumes on any free space listed on this screen. If all free space has been allocated to the SYS volume, you may select the Continue button.

▶ · ◀

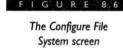

FIGURE 8.6

The Configure File System screen

If one or more of your drives do not show up on this list, your Storage adapter driver may not have loaded properly, or your disk storage system is not working properly.

NOTE

Follow these instructions to create NetWare volumes:

1. Create a partition on the free space on each drive. In the Configure File System screen select the free space on a drive and click the Create button. You will then see the New Volume screen.

2. Name and select free space to be allocated to the volume. In the New Volume screen, select free space from the list and enter the volume name

and type of volume. Volume names can be 2–15 characters, consisting of alphanumeric characters and the characters _ ! - # @ $ % & ( ). Volume names cannot begin with an underscore (_) or contain two or more consecutive underscores (_).

Two types of volumes are available in NetWare 5:

- *Traditional NetWare volume* — NetWare 5's volume format is improved over previous NetWare file systems to provide even better performance. Like NetWare 4 volumes, the traditional NetWare volume supports block suballocation, compression, and Transaction Tracking System (TTS).

- *NSS volume* — NSS is a new feature in NetWare 5 that provides advanced file system technology for management of large files, large volumes, name spaces, and storage devices. You will find that the amount of time it takes to mount an NSS volume is significantly reduced from the traditional NetWare volume. However, NSS does not support mirroring, striping, data migration, file compression, Transaction Tracking System, File Transfer Protocol (FTP), VREPAIR, Network File System (NFS), or file name locking.

See Chapter 1, "Networking with NetWare," and Chapter 15, "Storage Devices and File Systems," for detailed discussions on the choice between Traditional and Novell Storage Services volume types.

3. Add additional free space to the volume (optional). To span a volume over multiple disk drives, in the New Volume screen, select free space on a second drive, and then select the Apply to Volume button. For more discussion of spanning volumes, see Chapter 15, "Storage Devices and File Systems."

4. Save the partition and volume configuration. Select OK to create the partition and return to the Configure File System screen.

You may repeat this procedure to create partitions and volumes on remaining storage devices.

It is not necessary to configure additional storage devices at this
time; you can partition, Hot Fix, and create volumes with the
NWCONFIG.NLM utility after installation has been completed.

NOTE

The Mount Volumes screen will appear. You may mount the additional volumes
at this time, or leave them unmounted until the next time you boot your server.
Upon reboot, all volumes will be mounted automatically.

Step 7: Select and Configure Networking Protocols
The Protocols screen will appear (see Figure 8.7). You will see a listing of NICs
listed under your server.

FIGURE 8.7

*The Protocols
configuration screen*

I. Select a protocol. In the Protocols screen, select a NIC, and then select
   which protocols are to be supported on this interface. You have the choice
   to select one of four protocol configurations:

   • *IP (IP with IPX Compatibility Mode)* — If you check the IP box only, IP
     is installed with Compatibility Mode support for IPX. Because IPX is
     required to receive communications from existing NetWare servers,
     Novell chose to retain support for receiving IPX communications under
     all circumstances. Compatibility Mode receives IPX communications
     over the IP protocol stack and functions as sort of a gateway.

When you configure a network board with IP, IPX compatibility is
automatically configured and the Compatibility Mode Driver will
be installed.

NOTE

- *IP and IPX* — If you select both the IP and the IPX boxes, both protocol stacks will be installed, but IPX support is direct without the benefit of the Compatibility Mode.

- *IPX Only (with no IP)* — If you check only the IPX box, only the IPX protocol will be installed and supported. This option does not differ from previous NetWare versions.

- *IP Only* — If you have chosen to check only the IP box, and you later find that IPX support is no longer required, you can remove the Compatibility Mode Driver load statement (load SCMD.NLM) from your AUTOEXEC.NCF file. SCMD receives IPX packets, encapsulates them into IP packets, and forwards them to the IP address of the server. You can read more about Compatibility Mode in Chapter 11, "Configuring TCP/IP with NetWare."

2. Configure the protocols. Select IP and/or IPX protocols to configure.

   a. If you have selected the IP protocol box, move your cursor to the IP Address field and enter the IP address, subnet mask, and router (gateway) address for this NIC. IPv4 and IPv6 addresses are supported. The mask identifies the subnet to which this NIC is connected, and the gateway is the IP address of the router port connected to the local subnet. For more detail on IP addressing, subnet masking, and gateways, see Chapter 4, "TCP/IP Protocols, IP Addressing, and Name Resolution," and Chapter 11, "Configuring TCP/IP with NetWare."

NetWare 5 will discover the router address automatically, but if you enter an address for the router, the designated router port must be connected to the same local network segment as this NIC.

NOTE

   b. If you have selected the IPX protocol, the IPX protocol will be bound to the NIC. You will not enter an IPX network number at this time, but later during INSTALL you will need to enter the IPX network number to which the NIC is connected.

Step 8: Set the Server Time Zone

Select the time zone for this server. If your area uses Daylight Saving Time, check the box accordingly.

Step 9: Set Up Novell Directory Services

The next screen will prompt you to install this server into an existing NDS tree, or create a new NDS tree. When a new tree is created, the server you are installing will become the master replica server for the NDS tree you are creating. If you are installing into an existing tree, please take special note of the following warning:

WARNING

If you are integrating NetWare 5 into an existing NetWare 4.11 NDS tree, you must first update NetWare 4.11 servers with NDS version 5.99 or higher. *Failure to do so may disable NDS on the entire existing tree, resulting in immediate denial of login and access to all resources.* If this is the first NetWare 5 server you are installing into an existing NetWare 4.11 tree, you will be prompted to update the NetWare 4.11 servers. If you agree, the updates will be automatically applied over the network. If you are unable to communicate with any 4.11 servers at this time, they will not be updated. You must manually update them before you introduce the NetWare 5 server to avoid damage to the replicas contained on those servers. You will find this update on your NetWare 5 operating system CD in the \PRODUCTS\411_UPG directory.

Configuring an NDS tree requires strategic planning and understanding of NDS. This section discusses only the basic default configuration. Consult your online documentation for help on how to organize and manage your NDS tree.

TIP

For recommendations on designing your NDS tree, see *Novell's Four Principles of NDS Design* by Jeffrey F. Hughes and Blair W. Thomas (IDG Books Worldwide) or refer to your online documentation.

Creating a New Tree   If you have chosen to create a new tree, follow these steps:

1. Enter the Tree name. In this step you are defining a new NDS tree and this server will become the master replica server for the new tree.

2. Create the container in which the server will be created. By default, the server will be placed in the lowest container you define in the tree at this time.

TIP

In a small network with no WAN links, you should install your first server into the Organization container of your tree. In a larger tree, a good strategy is to create a separate resource container for servers and other devices such as printers. If you use this technique, be sure to give administrators the appropriate NDS rights to manage the server container. Whenever WANs link portions of the tree, do not place the server into the Organization container. This configuration is known to cause NDS corruption problems.

a. Select the tree applet to the right of the Context for server applet to bring up the NDS Context Browser screen.

b. Select the Add button to bring up the New Container screen. By default, this server will be installed into the last container you define.

c. Define the Organization container. With the Organization radio button checked, enter a name. For a small organization without WAN links, this is a good container for your server object. In a very simple tree, this is the only container you will need to configure. Select the OK button to continue.

NOTE

Avoid using the Country container if at all possible. The Country container causes additional naming restrictions and adds complexity that may not be necessary. In many cases you can use the Organization container for the same purposes.

d. Define Organizational Unit containers. You need only define the container in which the server will be placed. Select the OK button to continue.

e. Define additional Organizational Unit containers if desired. You can define additional Organizational Units later in the server Console One utility or in NetWare Administrator. In the NDS Context Browser screen, select OK to return to the main NDS screen.

f. Verify the context for the server and for the Administrator account. Enter the Administrator password and enter it a second time to verify. You can place the Administrator account in any container. Select the Next button to continue. The network will be checked for duplicate tree information, and then NDS will be installed on your server.

When defining the first server in the tree, the Administrator account is given NDS Supervisory Object rights and Supervisory Object Property rights in the [root] of the tree. This will give this Administrator account full rights to the entire tree, including full rights to files and directories to all volumes in the tree. By default, this account is the only account to have global supervisory rights to the entire tree. Be sure to protect the password for this account, and do not lose it.

3. INSTALL will present an NDS Summary screen. Be sure to write down the tree information and administrator's password for future reference. Verify the NDS summary information and continue.

Installing into an Existing Tree If you have chosen to install into an existing tree, follow these steps:

Tree structure and configuration can vary significantly. You should check with your tree administrator for instructions, assistance, and/or permission before installing your server into an existing tree. For this reason, it is not possible to give precise instructions on how to proceed in this section. However, the instructions in this section should guide you, possibly with a little support from your tree administrator. When adding servers to an existing tree, INSTALL automatically analyzes your tree's NDS physical infrastructure and creates replicas where required. After installation you can optimize the NDS topology for best performance and fault tolerance. See Chapter 18, "NDS Physical Infrastructure and Repair," for detail on replication and partitioning, and how to optimize your NDS infrastructure.

1. Enter the Tree name to which this server will belong. You will have the option to locate the tree by IP or IPX address.

If any communications problem prevents you from detecting other NDS trees, you may not be able to complete this operation successfully. Before attempting to install a server into an existing tree, be sure to resolve communications problems.

2. Log in as a tree administrator. In the Administrator Login box enter the tree administrator user account name and password. You may use the NDS search applet to search the tree for the Administrator account. Enter the complete administrator name with full context (for example, Cn=Admin.O=Org). The administrator account was defined when the tree was created. By default, the administrator name is Admin. Also by default, only this account has global Supervisory rights to create server objects throughout the tree.

If you are not able to log into the tree, you will receive a dialog box indicating that you are not able to connect to the target server. If this occurs, proceed with the next step, and attempt to use the Not Listed button to establish communications.

3. Enter or select the context in which the server is to be created. You may click the tree applet to access the NDS Context Browser to search for existing trees and Directories. In the NDS Context Browser you can add or edit containers in an existing tree. Select OK to continue and return to the main NDS screen. When you select Next, tree information will be checked and NDS will be installed on your server.

NOTE

You can only view trees and directories where your login account has NDS Browse object rights. In order to add a server to an existing tree, you must have Create rights in the target container. In most cases, the account to be used at this time should be the global Administrator of the tree, which by default would have been the Admin account.

If the NDS Context Browser cannot locate the tree to be joined, you can select the Not Listed button and enter the tree name, IP address, and server ID (IPX internal network address) of the master replica server. This option is provided in case the server is separated by a router and the routing information has not been established. If this method is successful in locating the tree, you will be allowed to log in with the Administrator account.

Synchronizing the Tree

Trees may fail to show up due to incomplete routing configuration at this time. Follow these steps to ensure proper synchronization with the rest of the NDS tree:

1. Using the Not Listed button, attempt to discover the existing tree you wish to join. If communications can be established, you will be logged into the tree and the NDS Context Browser should show the tree and directories.

2. If the Not Listed button fails to establish communications with the tree, you should attempt to resolve communications problems before proceeding. Check cabling, connectors, routers, and other network communications as discussed in Chapter 13, "LAN and Cabling."

3. If you still cannot find the tree, you can configure the server to be in the tree without establishing communications. However, keep in mind that this action may allow you to finish the server installation without a successful NDS installation.

4. After finishing your installation, attempt to establish communications between your server and the master replica server (first server) in the tree you wish to join. Troubleshoot internetwork communications problems as discussed in Chapter 17, "Network Communications and Protocols." You may need to resolve LAN/WAN communications, NIC hardware, NIC driver, IP or IPX protocol configuration, or router configuration problems.

5. Once you have established communications between your server and the master replica server, check NDS synchronization in the DSRepair utility as discussed in Chapter 18, "NDS Physical Infrastructure and Repair." If synchronization with the rest of the tree has not been established, remove and reinstall NDS on this server using the NWCONFIG.NLM utility.

4. Record NDS information displayed on your screen. NDS will now install on the server. The INSTALL program will progress as it would regardless of whether this is a new tree or whether you are adding a server to an existing tree. The NDS Summary screen will indicate the tree name, server context, and any other objects that can be ignored.

If you create new volumes after this point, you will need to update the new volume(s) with NDS using the NWCONFIG.NLM utility.

NOTE

Step 10: Install Your NetWare 5 Server License

You must install the server licensing data into your server. Put your LICENSE disk into drive A: and be sure that the path A:\ is entered in the License Location field. If more than one license exists in the selected location, you will be prompted to select a license from a list. You may check the Install without License box and install your license in NetWare Administrator after finishing installation.

Each server must have a valid and unique server license. Users will not be able to connect to this server until a valid license is installed. After installation is completed, you can install licenses in NetWare 5's NetWare Administrator utility.

NOTE

Step 11: Install Additional Products and Services

You will view a list of products and services. You can install them at this time, or you can install them after server installation is completed. You have the option to install any one or all of the following products/services at this time. Notice that the amount of required disk space for each of these options is listed on the right of the screen.

▸ *Novell Distributed Print Services (NDPS)* — Provides updated print services without the need for queues and print servers.

When you install NDPS, INSTALL will check for existing NDPS print brokers. If none are available, a print broker will be installed on this server. Note that NetWare 5's NDPS is version 2.0 and does not work with NetWare 4.11's NDPS version 1.0. You can update your 4.11 servers to NDPS version 2.0 from your NetWare 5 operating system CD.

NOTE

▸ *LDAP Services* — Installs an LDAP server, which allows access to directory listings via the LDAP protocol.

▸ *NDS Catalog Services* — Provides a catalog database for definable lists of directory objects.

▸ *WAN Traffic Manager Service* — Enables you to control NDS access to WAN links by applying usage policies.

▸ *Secure Authentication Services* — Provides Secure Sockets Layer version 3 support.

▸ *Novell PKI Services* — Provides public key cryptography and digital certificate services for Public Key Infrastructure (PKI).

▸ *Novell Internet Access Server* — Installs Multiprotocol Router, and enables you to support remote users over analog, digital, and Internet connections.

▸ *Storage Management Services* — Provides backup software for NetWare volumes and client workstations.

▸ *Novell DNS/DHCP Services* — Provides DNS and DHCP servers modules to be installed on this server. See Chapter 11, "Configuring TCP/IP with NetWare" for additional steps required to configure DNS and DHCP.

From this point on, setup screens for each additional product and service will be presented. Each additional product and service screen provides help for configuration information. You will see a summary screen like the one shown in Figure 8.8. Select the Customize button, and you will see a list of products queued to be installed and their disk space requirements. You can review, add, and change configuration options for additional products and services at this time.

▸ · ◂

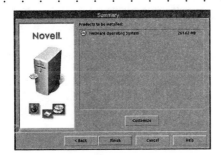

FIGURE 8.8

The Summary screen

Step 12: Customizing Your Installation

Before exiting, select the Customize button on the Summary screen (see Figure 8.8). A customized hierarchical view similar to Figure 8.9 will be created showing configuration aspects of your server that have been chosen during installation. You can select an object and then click the Properties button to edit configuration or add more configuration options. You will find a Help button on most screens with detailed information on how to perform steps in each screen.

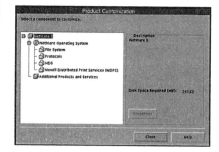

FIGURE 8.9

The Product Customization screen

TIP

Select each configuration object and explore its Properties. You will find that you can configure options that you were not able to configure in previous sections of INSTALL.

Here are some of the more important options that you can select and customize:

1. *NetWare Operating System* — You can select this object and then Properties to edit the following server properties:

   • *Server Properties* — You may edit the server ID (previously known as the IPX internal address). This is an four-byte hexadecimal number.

   • *Languages* — Select the languages to be used for the server utilities and console.

   • *Licenses* — View server license information.

   • *Components* — View the components (file system, protocols, NDS) to be installed on the server.

2. *File System* — You can select and edit volume configuration options by selecting a volume and then selecting a button on the right of the screen. Notice that the onscreen help prompts for help on performing volume operations.

3. *Protocols* — Select the Protocols object and then Properties. You will see four tabs:

• *Protocols* — You can edit IP and IPX addressing configurations.

• *Compatibility Mode* — If you have elected to install IP, the Load IPX Compatibility option will be on. The IPX Compatibility Mode box allows this NetWare 5 server to function as a Migration Agent, tunneling IPX communications over IP networks, and tunneling IP communications over IPX networks. For more explicit instructions on supporting the Compatibility Mode Migration Agent, see Chapter 11, "Configuring TCP/IP with NetWare."

 NOTE

The Compatibility Mode Migration Agent service depends upon the services of an SLP Directory Agent. To support this service, you must load the SLPDA.NLM in your AUTOEXEC.NCF.

• *Domain Name Service* — If you have elected to install IP, this tab will be available to enter. Enter the domain names to be serviced in this tree.

• *SNMP* — Configure SNMP data for this server in this screen.

4. *NDS* — Select the NDS object and then Properties. You can view and reconfigure the following items:

• *NDS Summary* — This screen shows the NDS summary information that was previously shown when NDS was configured.

• *Time Zone* — This screen shows the time zone and daylight saving time configuration options.

• *Time Synchronization* — This screen shows the time server type. Click a radio button to change the time server configuration.

5. *Additional Products and Services* — Select the Properties button to add or delete Additional Products and Services to be installed. Each product or service that was selected in this screen will have a configuration object under this heading. The following options are most important to configure at this time.

- *Novell DNS-DHCP Services* — In this screen the container for the Locator, DNS/DHCP Group, and Rootsrv Zone objects are shown. These objects should be placed in the Organization container and will be created as INSTALL completes.

NOTE

When Novell DNS/DHCP Services is installed, the Locator, DNS-DHCP Group, and the Rootsrv Zone objects are created. This will not need to be done later when setting up DNS/DHCP services. Configure DNS/DHCP separately using the DNS/DHCP Console Manager. This utility requires a Windows 95, 98, or NT workstation with the Z.E.N.works Starter Pack client provided with NetWare 5 configured with IP. See Chapter 11, "Configuring TCP/IP with NetWare," for complete instructions on installing NetWare 5's DNS/DHCP.

Click Finish to accept and start file copy. You may need to insert additional NetWare CDs to support additional products and services that you have selected.

When the file copy completes, you will see the Installation complete screen shown in Figure 8.10. This screen indicates that your installation has been successful and gives you the option to view the README file or restart your server.

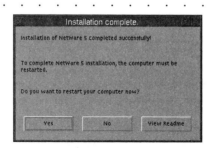

FIGURE 8.10

The Installation Complete screen

NOTE

View the README file. This file contains the latest release notes available at the time your NetWare 5 operating system CD was created. This file may contain important notes that are not reflected elsewhere.

▶ · ◀

Post-Installation Procedures

Once you have finished installing your server, a few steps may be necessary to make it ready for service.

Mounting CD Volumes

Unlike previous NetWare versions, NetWare 5 servers automatically load CD-ROM drivers and mount any CD that is in the CD-ROM during boot.

Configuring Protocols with INETCFG

When supporting multiple protocol configurations, it is often advisable to use the INETCFG utility. This utility moves protocol-related commands from your AUTOEXEC.NCF into a database that is then managed with the INETCFG.NLM menu-driven utility. INETCFG makes managing protocol configurations much easier than entering character-based commands at the console. You will find that explicit on-screen queries and help are available. INETCFG is accessed from Novell Internet Access Server or separately.

You will find that managing drivers, bindings, protocols, and settings from this system is much simpler than manually editing configuration files and settings. You will find context-sensitive help for each menu selection by pressing F1.

To move your protocol binding and configuration statements and manage them using INETCFG, follow these steps:

1. From the server console (colon prompt), enter LOAD INETCFG. To access the console, press Alt+Esc until you see the console screen.

2. Confirm that you want to transfer LAN driver, protocol, and remote access commands to other configuration files. You will see the Internetworking Configuration menu option shown in Figure 8.11.

FIGURE 8.11

The Internetworking
Configuration menu

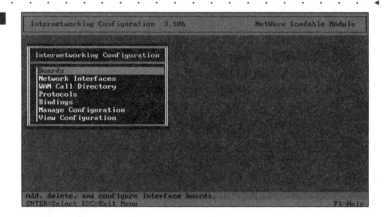

This utility supports the following configuration options:

▶ *Boards* — Used to add and configure NICs

▶ *Network Interfaces* — For assigning names to logical boards, and to view status to see if a driver has been loaded

▶ *WAN Call Directory* — Used to add and configure WAN call destinations

▶ *Protocols* — Used to configure protocols and their configurations

▶ *Bindings* — Used to select and configure frame types, protocols, and network numbers

▶ *Manage Configuration* — Used for managing other protocol options not included here, including SNMP and remote access (RCONSOLE) support

▶ *View Configuration* — Used to view configuration statements and settings in read-only mode

Once you have migrated your internetworking configuration statements to INETCFG, you can no longer manage them in the AUTOEXEC.NCF — instead type **LOAD INETCFG** at your server console prompt to bring up the previous menu.

See Chapter 11, "Configuring TCP/IP with NetWare," and Chapter 12, "Novell Internet Access Server," for more detail on configuring TCP/IP protocols and services.

IP-IPX Gateway

It is not necessary to install an IP-IPX Gateway in your server; the Compatibility Mode Driver is installed automatically when IP is installed.

NOTE

The IP-IPX Gateway is called the IPX Compatibility Mode in some of your Novell documentation.

Creating a Branching DOS Boot Menu

Once you have installed your NetWare server, the following steps should be taken to stabilize your server and make it easy to manage:

1. Shut down your server and reboot to verify proper boot execution. To shut down your server, enter the command **DOWN** at the server console (colon) prompt. Cold-boot your server to see if it will come up automatically. If it does not come up automatically, reload the disk driver manually, mount the volume (type **MOUNT ALL** at the colon prompt), load NWCONFIG.NLM, and check out the STARTUP.NCF and AUTOEXEC.NCF files. If the disk driver was not loaded, make sure your STARTUP.NCF is in the same directory with SERVER.EXE and has the appropriate disk driver load statement(s).

2. Edit the DOS AUTOEXEC.BAT. At the outset of running the INSTALL batch file from CD-ROM, you were asked if you would like the server to boot automatically. If you answered Yes, AUTOEXEC.BAT will include the statement SERVER, which will load the NetWare file server OS when the computer is booted. If you did not answer Yes, you can manually type the command **SERVER** from a DOS prompt to load the server. This is a bit problematic when an inexperienced user is required to boot the server in an emergency.

You should either add the command to your AUTOEXEC.BAT or make a boot menu. Here is an example of a boot menu to be used with a later version of DOS:

```
CONFIG.SYS:

[menu]                         | heading for boot menu
menuitem=DOS, Boot to DOS      | establishes branch variable
menuitem=NETWARE               | establishes branch variable
menudefault=NETWARE, 15        | default branch, and wait time


[DOS]                          | heading for branch
device=C:\DOS\HIMEM.SYS        | executed for this branch


[NETWARE]                      | heading for branch


[common]                       | heading for commands in
common
files=30                       | all commands that are common
to all branches
buffers=30                     |
device=C:\CDROM\MTMCDAI.SYS /d:MSCD0001 | load CD driver


AUTOEXEC.BAT:
```

```
@echo off                                 | stops print to screen

path C:\DOS                               | sets path

C:\DOS\MSCDEX.EXE /d:MSCD0001 /m:10  | loads CD extensions

goto %CONFIG%                             | continues branch from
CONFIG.SYS


:DOS                                      | label: continues DOS branch

C:\DOS\SMARTDRV.EXE                       | continues DOS branch

goto END                                  | skips to END label


:NETWARE                                  | label: continues NETWARE
branch

CD \NWSERVER                              | substitute server directory
name

SERVER                                    | executes SERVER

goto END                                  | skips to END label


:END                      | label: exits both branches
```

3. Exit to DOS during boot. If the server comes up automatically and you
wish to exit to DOS, press F5 during boot when you see the "Starting
MS-DOS or Loading . . ." screen message (if your version of DOS supports
this feature).

NOTE   **The DOS boot files just listed can be found on the CD that
accompanies this book. Look for AUTOEXC.TXT. and CONFIG.TXT.
Copy these files to drive C:, renaming them to CONFIG.SYS and
AUTOEXEC.BAT as you do. Be sure to save backups of your existing
CONFIG.SYS and AUTOEXEC.BAT files.**

Installing Netscape FastTrack Server

FastTrack Server is installed from a Windows 95, 98, or NT client. You must use client version 3.01 for Windows 95/98 or version 4.11a or later for Windows NT. The client must be configured to run IPX, and the server must be version 4.11 or higher. NetWare 5 servers must have at least 16MB more RAM than the server otherwise requires. If you are to integrate users and groups with a database server, you will also need to install Novell's NLDAP server, which is available from Novell's Web site. FastTrack Server requires 100MB of available space on the SYS volume on which FastTrack will be installed, and a DNS server must be available with a pointer record to the FastTrack Server host.

I. Log in with Supervisory rights to the SYS volume and server on which the FastTrack server will be installed.

2. Map a drive letter to the root of the SYS volume on the server where FastTrack Server will be installed.

3. Start SETUP.EXE, which is located in the \Products\Webserv directory of your NetWare 5 operating system CD. Execute this program from the Run menu or Windows Explorer.

4. Specify a root directory for the Web server. This directory will contain your Web page data.

TIP

Be sure you put the Web root directory in a location that can be managed by the Web administrator. You may create a Directory Map object and then assign Supervisory NDS object rights to the Administrator.

Installing Online Documentation

Online documentation is added from your Z.E.N.works Starter Pack. Select RUNME.EXE in the \DOCUMENTS directory, or follow instructions when the CD's autorun starts.

Supporting Compatibility Mode

To fully support Compatibility Mode, you will need to load the Service Locator Protocol Directory Agent (SLPDA.NLM) and the Compatibility Mode Migration Agent (SCMD.NLM) on a replica server. The first time you load the SLPDA and SCMD, a brief setup utility will run, creating objects and granting NDS rights as needed. See Chapter 11, "Configuring TCP/IP with NetWare," for details on loading these modules.

CHAPTER 9

DOS/Windows 3.x Clients

Novell Client for DOS and Windows 3.*x* is 32-bit software that provides access to NetWare servers, NDS trees, and all NetWare resources. The Novell client includes several new features, including Remote Access Services, which provides dial-out access to external bulletin boards, NetWare servers, and Internet service providers (ISPs).

NetWare 5's client software will support legacy DOS and DOS/Windows 3.*x* versions (Windows 3.1 and Windows for Workgroups 3.11) client workstations. You should upgrade all your clients with the NetWare 5 client software — the latest client software is always backward-compatible to support all NetWare versions.

In any Windows system, you should always use the Novell client software to access NetWare servers and NDS trees. The client software that is provided with Windows 3.*x* will not support access to NetWare 5 systems and lacks many of the support options for legacy NetWare systems that is provided in Novell's client software.

NetWare 5 comes with the Z.E.N.works (Zero Effort Networks) Starter Pack. Z.E.N.works was designed with the busy system administrator of a large system in mind. It provides client setup and many other utilities to make your job easier. This chapter discusses using the Z.E.N.works CD for installing clients.

NOTE

NetWare 5 comes with the Z.E.N.works Starter Pack. This CD has client setup software for DOS and all Windows clients, and many utilities that make administering your network easier. You can use this CD to update all clients to support access to NetWare 3, 4, and 5 servers. NetWare client stacks are always backward-compatible, and it is recommended that you upgrade all clients to the latest Novell client software.

Client Setup Options

To install a DOS or Windows 3.*x* client, run the NetWare 5 client setup utility for your workstation operating system:

- ▶ INSTALL.EXE text-based utility for DOS or Windows 3.*x*

- ▶ WINSETUP.EXE graphical utility for Windows 3.*x*, 95, 98, or NT

DOS clients use INSTALL.EXE. Windows 3.*x* clients can use either WINSETUP.EXE or INSTALL.EXE.

Novell has made using these programs as bulletproof as possible, but beware — there are several configuration files to be updated. Be sure that all NetWare support files are installed, all Windows and NetWare configuration files are updated, and your DOS boot files (CONFIG.SYS and AUTOEXEC.BAT) have been updated. Because your DOS and Windows configurations can vary significantly, one or more files may not get updated. For this reason, installing client support files manually is no longer a viable option.

NOTE

Before starting your installation, make copies of your CONFIG.SYS and AUTOEXEC.BAT files. For Windows 3.*x*, make copies of the WIN.INI, SYSTEM.INI, and PROTOCOL.INI files. If you need to troubleshoot your installation, or reinstall, you may wish to start from the beginning again, as if you had never installed the client in the first place.

You can set up your clients:

▶ Directly from the Z.E.N.works CD

▶ From a network directory

▶ From a shared CD volume

▶ From a set of client setup floppy disks

Regardless of which method you use, your setup program is the same. The only difference is the path from which you will execute the setup utility, and disk swapping as required.

NOTE

To automate client installation and updates, see your Z.E.N.works Starter Pack. It has many options to make centralized system administration much easier. For a complete reference on Z.E.N.works, open your online documentation in the Z.E.N.works Starter Pack and then select Contents → Desktop Management Services → Z.E.N.works Overview.

Copying Client Setup Files to the Network

You can set up clients from the network if they are already attached to an existing tree or server from the Z.E.N.works Starter Pack or from files downloaded from Novell's Web site. The following text provides instructions for both procedures.

Installing Client Setup Files from the Z.E.N.works Starter Pack

You can install setup files for all your clients on a network server from your Z.E.N.works Starter Pack. The process is automated with the help of the Z.E.N.works Setup Wizard. To load client software for DOS/Windows 3.*x*, Windows 95, 98, and NT clients:

1. Log in to a tree or server with sufficient rights to create, install, and access a directory to be created to house the client files, from a workstation running the Novell Client for Windows 95/98, or NT software.

2. Insert your Z.E.N.works CD into your CD-ROM drive.

3. Run the Z.E.N.works Setup application (SETUP.EXE) from the \Products\Zenworks directory.

4. Follow the instructions provided by the Z.E.N.works Setup Wizard shown in Figure 9.1.

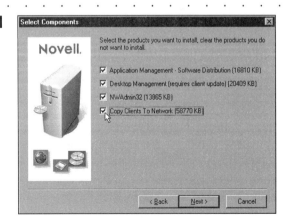

FIGURE 9.1

The Z.E.N.works Setup Wizard

Manual Network Directory Preparation

To prepare a network directory for installation, follow these steps:

1. From a client workstation, copy the DOS/Windows client setup directory and all subdirectories from your Z.E.N.works CD (\PRODUCTS\ DOSWIN32) to a directory located on a shared volume. For example, if the CD is in drive D: and you wish to copy to the SYS:PUBLIC\CLIENTS directory, type:

```
XCOPY D:\PRODUCTS\DOSWIN32\*.* F:\PUBLIC\CLIENTS\DOSWIN /s
/e
```

Using the NetWare NCOPY command, type:

```
NCOPY D:\PRODUCTS\DOSWIN32\*.* SYS:PUBLIC\CLIENTS\DOSWIN
/s /e /c
```

2. Map root a drive letter to the directory you have just created. To map drive letter I: to the same directory as discussed in the preceding step, type:

```
MAP ROOT I:=SYS:PUBLIC\CLIENTS\DOSWIN
```

3. Assign Read and File Scan Rights to Files and Directories to the setup network directory. For example, to assign Read and File Scan rights to the Admins group, type the following command:

```
RIGHTS SYS:PUBLIC\CLIENTS\DOSWIN RF /GROUP=ADMINS
```

To set up a client, log in as a member of the Admins group (assuming that group has been created and has sufficient NDS rights to use the network install directory) and then execute INSTALL.EXE from the mapped drive.

Networked CD Preparation

You can update a client that is already connected to a server by installing from a networked CD. Installing from a networked CD also requires mounting the CD as a NetWare volume. This step was done during server installation, but the process may not have been automated.

To mount a CD as a NetWare volume on a NetWare 5 server:

1. Insert the CD into the CD-ROM drive.

2. Switch to the console screen (colon prompt).

3. Type the command **LOAD CDROM**.

4. Add the LOAD CDROM statement to your AUTOEXEC.NCF file to load
support full-time for CD-ROM drives.

NOTE

**On a NetWare 5 server it is not necessary to issue any commands to
mount a CD volume once the CDROM.NLM module is loaded. When
you remove a CD, the volume will be dismounted. When you insert a
CD, the volume will be mounted automatically.**

CDROM.NLM supports ISO 9660 format CDs. To load support for Apple HFS-
format CDs, at your server console type the command **CDHFS.NSS**. To mount a
CD as a NetWare volume on a NetWare 3 or 4 server:

1. Insert your CD in the server's CD-ROM drive.

2. From the server console (colon prompt), enter **LOAD CDROM**.

3. Enter **CD DEVICE LIST**, noticing the No. listed for the CD.

4. Enter **CD MOUNT 1** (or substitute the No. listed for the CD you wish to
mount). This command will mount whichever volume is shown in position
number 1, which is, normally, any CD in the drive.

You can map to the volume using the CD volume label as the NetWare volume
label. For example, if the Z.E.N.works CD is in your server's CD-ROM drive, map
drive I: with the following command:

```
MAP ROOT I:=NW5_CLNT:PRODUCTS\DOSWIN32
```

You may then execute INSTALL.BAT from drive I:.

Upgrading Existing Clients with Automatic Client Upgrade

You can install clients using Automatic Client Upgrade (ACU) when running the INSTALL.EXE or WINSETUP.EXE utility with the /ACU switch. ACU enables system administrators to add a section in the login script that will upgrade the client if the client's files are older than the server-based setup utilities. WINSETUP.EXE in the Z.E.N.works Starter Pack has several switches to assist in setting up clients.

To use ACU, see your Z.E.N.works Starter Pack documentation. Refer to the Novell Client for DOS and Windows 3.1*x*, Setting Up, Installing with ACU section.

Requirements and Limitations

DOS and Windows 3.*x* clients have new requirements. More space is needed to install support files than in previous client software products. For both DOS and Windows 3.*x* clients, the same memory-resident driver and support files are loaded. NetWare 5 client files have changed significantly — you will have to upgrade your DOS and Windows 3.*x* clients to connect them to a NetWare 5 system. You should upgrade all your clients with the latest client modules, which are backward compatible with previous NetWare versions.

Client Hardware and Software Requirements

To install and use the Novell client software with DOS and Windows 3.*x* clients, make sure that your client workstations have at least the following resources available:

▶ 386 processor

▶ 15MB of free disk space

▶ 8MB of RAM

▶ XMS memory manager (HIMEM.SYS or equivalent)

> ▸ NIC and latest MLID driver

> ▸ Connection to a NetWare-based network

To install your Windows 3.*x* client software, you must have Windows 3.1 or Windows for Workgroups 3.11 installed and working properly. In addition to your Windows requirements, your workstation must have disk space available for optional product modules, which are discussed in a later section of this chapter. Additional disk space is required for optional Windows 3.1*x* software components.

The Windows client setup utility will check your system for available disk space and display how much disk space is available and how much is needed.

NetWare 5 Servers

If your NetWare 5 server is configured with the TCP/IP protocol only, you can still support IPX clients through the Compatibility Mode. However, you must load the Compatibility Mode driver on the NetWare 5 server that will service client attachments. Compatibility Mode allows support for IPX-only clients and services over IP communications.

DOS clients cannot take advantage of this interface. Windows 3.*x* clients must load the IP-IPX gateway (Compatibility Mode client drivers), in addition to the Compatibility Mode at the NetWare 5 server end.

To support NetWare IP clients, you must have the NetWare IP server and the TCP/IP protocol loaded and configured on a NetWare server that will service client attachments. See Chapter 11, "Configuring TCP/IP with NetWare," for details on installing the Compatibility Mode on your NetWare 5 servers.

Client Protocols

IPX support is required for all DOS and Windows 3.*x* clients to communicate with NetWare 5 system. Though this has always been a requirement for NetWare 3 and 4, Novell does not support pure TCP/IP for DOS-based clients. Even when using NetWare IP, IPX support is also required.

To support DOS and Windows 3.*x* clients on a NetWare 5 system, you must install one of the following three options on your client side:

▸ IPX protocol

▸ IP-IPX gateway (Windows is required for this option)

▸ NetWare/IP

NetWare 3 and 4 servers should be updated with the latest patches and fixes. You can obtain these files from Novell on CD or on their Web server at http://www.novell.com.

Though you have three options, the simplest way to support your legacy clients is to use the IPX protocol stack. The IP-IPX gateway requires Windows at the client side and will connect you to a NetWare 5 system that is configured to use IP only and CMD. NetWare IP requires additional resources at the client and server end and is less efficient than the other two options.

NOTE

DOS and Windows 3.x clients are limited to IPX only — you cannot use native TCP/IP to communicate with NetWare 5 servers and trees. However, you can support Windows 3.x clients through the IP-IPX gateway.

NIC Drivers

You have two Multiple Link Interface Driver (MLID) options that can be installed for your client workstations: You can use older 16-bit DOS memory-resident drivers, or you can use the very same 32-bit drivers used on a NetWare server. Novell engineers developed the NetWare I/O Subsystem (NIOS) module to load server MLID drivers on a DOS workstation. Now only one driver — the server driver — needs to be created to support NetWare servers and clients. This assures you that driver developers will not abandon support for older DOS-based clients.

The chapter is divided into two sections: one for DOS text-based setup, and one for Windows 3.x graphical setup. Using 16-bit memory-resident and 32-bit server drivers is covered.

Online Documentation

Online documentation is provided in HTML format; however, print and search functions are not supported for DOS or Windows 3.*x* operating systems. Search and print options requires Netscape Navigator 4 or Internet Explorer 4 (or later versions) for Windows 95, Windows 98, or Windows NT.

To view your online documentation, execute RUNME.EXE or VIEWDOC.EXE, which you will find on your Z.E.N.works Starter Pack CD in the \NOVDOCS directory. RUNME.EXE enables you to view or install online documentation, while VIEWDOC.EXE executes Navigator and accesses the index to the online documentation.

If you wish to have printed documentation, it is available from Novell's fulfillment house at additional cost. Online documentation and ordering information for printed documentation is in the NOVDOCS directory of the Z.E.N.works Starter Pack. Read the README text files for more information.

Running INSTALL for DOS Clients

To install a DOS client, you can use the text-based INSTALL.EXE application. You will find this utility in the PRODUCTS\DOSWIN32 directory of your Z.E.N.works CD. Though this utility provides support for DOS and Windows 3.*x* clients, you should use the WINSETUP.EXE utility discussed later in this chapter for Windows 3.*x* clients.

When you execute INSTALL.EXE, you will see the screen shown in Figure 9.2.

FIGURE 9.2

The Novell Client INSTALL.EXE text-based application

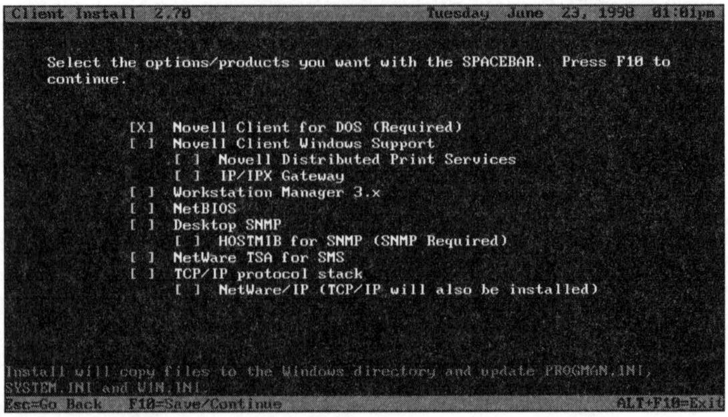

You are prompted to configure the opening screen before any files are installed or modifications are made to your system. Prior to completion, you can exit this utility at any time without any repercussions. The following options are available:

▸ *Novell Client for DOS (Required)* — This option installs the DOS client for NetWare, creates directories, edits your CONFIG.SYS and AUTOEXEC.BAT files, creates a STARTNET.BAT file that loads your drivers, and otherwise builds a client for NetWare 5 and earlier versions.

▸ *Novell Client Windows Support* — Use this option when installing with Windows 3.*x*. When this item is selected, you will be prompted to enter the path where Windows 3.*x* is installed. This utility supports installations where shared Windows files are stored on a network volume.

▸ *Novell Distributed Print Services* — Use this option when NDPS is used in your network. See Chapter 19, "Printing and NPDS," for details.

▸ *IP-IPX Gateway* — Use this option when your NetWare 5 server supports only TCP/IP clients. This option is only available for Windows clients.

▸ *Workstation Manager 3.x* — This option provides control over the client desktop and applications. Workstation Manager is discussed in your Z.E.N.works online documentation.

▸ *NetBIOS* — Installs NetBIOS support when the workstation will use Novell drivers for access to both NetWare and Microsoft servers. This version of NetBIOS is the Novell version designed to run on IPX.

▸ *Desktop SNMP* — This option installs SNMP monitoring on this workstation. SNMP workstation monitoring is discussed in your Z.E.N.works online documentation.

▸ *HOSTMIB for SNMP* (SNMP required) — This option installs an MIB database on this computer in conjunction with Desktop SNMP.

▸ *NetWare TSA for SMS* — This option installs a memory-resident module that enables sharing so that the workstation's storage devices can be backed up from a server. You can only use this option if SMS and an SMS-compatible backup device and driver are installed on your server.

▸ *TCP/IP protocol stack* — Install this option to provide support if the client is to use Internet dial-up and/or NetWare IP.

This utility should update all Windows configuration files and options; however, Windows 3.x updates are often problematic. If you encounter problems after running this application, try running WINSETUP.EXE from within Windows. If you still have difficulties accessing Microsoft servers, install NetBIOS support in this utility, and add IPX support in your Microsoft servers.

TIP

Procedure

The following procedure will install your DOS client software:

1. Select the options you want to install. Move your cursor to the options shown in Figure 9.2 — use the spacebar to toggle the X on or off.

You will be asked to agree to the Novell license agreement, and then you will be asked two questions: The first question asks if you plan to support multiple country codes on your workstation. Answer Yes only if you want keyboard support for languages other than English. The second question asks about a shared Windows path. Answering Yes will enable you to support workstations that have some of their Windows 3.x files stored on a server.

Supporting Windows 3.x shared files is problematic and should be avoided. You will experience fewer support problems if all operating system and Windows files are stored locally. This does not necessarily apply to Windows applications, just the operating system and Windows itself.

NOTE

2. If you have selected to install TCP/IP, you will be prompted to configure the workstation IP addressing parameters. As shown in Figure 9.3, you can check whether your workstation is to have a static address assignment (manually configured at the workstation) or to receive an IP address assignment using one of the methods shown in Figure 9.3.

FIGURE 9.3

IP addressing options

```
Client Install 2.70                              Tuesday  June  23, 1998  02:33pm

    Does a TCP/IP server provide IP addresses automatically for you?  Use the
    SPACEBAR to select and F10 to continue.

                        [X]  No: User Specified

                        [ ]  Yes: DHCP

                        [ ]  Yes: BOOTP

                        [ ]  Yes: RARP



    You want to specify your own TCP/IP address.
    Esc=Go Back    F10=Save/Continue                              ALT+F10=Exit
```

To use DHCP, you must have a DHCP server attached to the same logical network as your workstation. The DHCP server can be a NetWare, NT, UNIX, or any type of DHCP server. Some routers have DHCP server services built in. Be sure that you have the correct IP address of the DHCP server, and that the subnet number and mask match those of your workstation. If you have selected one of the address assignment mechanisms, you may be asked for additional configuration information, such as DHCP servers' addresses.

3. If you have chosen to install TCP/IP and you have selected No: User Specified in the screen shown in Figure 9.3, you will be prompted to input static IP addressing information for your network as shown in Figure 9.4.

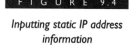

F I G U R E 9.4

Inputting static IP address information

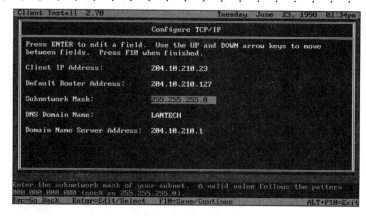

a. Enter the IP address to be assigned to the client workstation.

b. Enter the Default Router Address (the address of the router NIC connected to the same subnet that the workstation is connected to).

c. Enter the subnet mask.

d. Enter the name of the DNS domain to which the workstation belongs (optional).

e. Enter the address of a local DNS server (optional) used to resolve DNS names.

Without the static address assignment, default router address, and proper subnet mask, you will not be able to access resources that are separated from your logical network by a router.

NOTE

4. If you have selected SNMP options, you will be prompted to enter SNMP Parameters. See your Z.E.N.works Online Documentation for more information on configuring SNMP with NetWare.

5. If you have selected the TSA option, enter the name of the server that has the backup device and SMS installed, the name assigned to your workstation, and an (optional) password to protect your system from remote access. You can also make a list of local drives you want to back up.

6. Select the appropriate driver type — 16-bit ODI or 32-bit server drivers. To read a driver from a floppy disk, select User Specified 16-bit or 32-bit Driver. If your floppy disk contains the proper files, you will be prompted to select the appropriate driver from a list (see Figure 9.5).

FIGURE 9.5

Select a driver

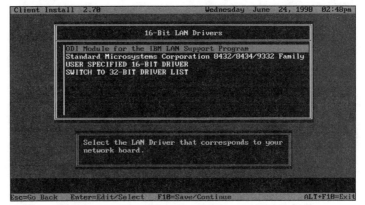

7. Configure the driver with your current NIC hardware settings.

NOTE

Be sure that you select the correct driver for your NIC and that the settings you enter are the correct current NIC settings. Before running the client setup utility, you should configure and test your NIC. Write your settings down so that you will be certain that the settings you enter are correct.

If your NIC is designed for plug-and-play, run the DOS plug-and-play utility that came with it.

TIP

To prevent wasted time and effort, check the NIC vendor's Web site for the latest information about your drivers. Always use the latest drivers and scan all release notes for references to your NIC driver.

8. Verify the Installation Configuration Summary screen options. Be sure that the appropriate Windows and client software directories, and the correct driver(s) are listed. Your CONFIG.SYS and AUTOEXEC.BAT files will be updated accordingly.

INSTALL will now update your system. All directories will be created, all files will be installed, and all configuration files will be created or edited. You should check the following files and make note of the changes that were made.

▸ *CONFIG.SYS* — The line "Device=LOCATION.EXE" may have been added to this file if you have configured more than one location. Your previous CONFIG.SYS will be saved as CONFIG.OLD.

▸ *AUTOEXEC.BAT* — The Novell client software directory should have been added to the path. CALL STARTNET.BAT should also have been added. This command will shell to the STARTNET.BAT file in the Novell client software directory and then return to AUTOEXEC.BAT. Your previous AUTOEXEC.BAT will be saved as AUTOEXEC.OLD.

▸ *STARTNET.BAT* — This file is located in the Novell client software directory and contains the list of drivers and modules to be loaded. Check the switches on the LAN driver line(s) to see that the correct hardware settings and frame types have been configured. Your previous STARTNET.BAT will be saved as STARTNET.OLD.

▸ *WIN.INI* — The command "load=nwpopup.exe C:\windows\system\ dpmw16.exe" (substitute the correct directory path) should have been added to the [windows] section. Your previous WIN.INI will be saved as WIN.000.

▸ *SYSTEM.INI* — The "netcard" entries in the [386Enh] section should have been commented out (with a semicolon). The ODI drivers will be used instead. Several changes should have been made to the [Network] section, the [NetWare] section should have been added, and the vnetware.386 driver should have been included. Your previous SYSTEM.INI will be saved as SYSTEM.000.

Login

After your Novell DOS client files have been configured and loaded, they should execute when your computer is booted. When the CLIENT32.NLM module is executed in the STARTNET.BAT file, you should see a message indicating that you have attached to a server. If you cannot verify this step, press F8 during boot to execute startup files one line at a time.

Once you have attached to a server, you can log in. Switch to your first NetWare drive (typically drive F:), and type **login**. You will be prompted to enter your user name and password. You can log in either before running Windows or when Windows executes and you see the Novell Login screen.

TIP

To verify that each command executes successfully, press F8 during boot (for DOS 6 and above). This will enable you to execute your boot files, including STARTNET.BAT, one line at a time. Read each screen message carefully, looking for error messages.

Troubleshooting a DOS Client Installation

The following lines represent files for a typical DOS IPX client installation. Check to be sure the following items have been updated on your DOS client installation:

```
CONFIG.SYS
FILES=40
BUFFERS=30
LASTDRIVE=M (or higher)


AUTOEXEC.BAT
PATH = <existing path>;%PATH%
@CALL <Novell client directory path>\STARTNET.BAT
```

```
STARTNET.BAT
```

SET NWLANGUAGE=ENGLISH (or supported client language)

C:\NOVELL\CLIENT32\NIOS.EXE

LOAD C:\NOVELL\CLIENT32\NBIC32.NLM

LOAD C:\NOVELL\CLIENT32\LSLC32.NLM

LOAD C:\NOVELL\CLIENT32\CMSM.NLM

LOAD C:\NOVELL\CLIENT32\ETHERTSM.NLM (or other TSM support module)

LOAD C:\NOVELL\CLIENT32\<NIC_driver.LAN> <hardware settings and frame type parameters>

LOAD C:\NOVELL\CLIENT32\TRANNTA.NLM

LOAD C:\NOVELL\CLIENT32\IPX.NLM

LOAD C:\NOVELL\CLIENT32\SPX_SKTS.NLM

LOAD C:\NOVELL\CLIENT32\CLIENT32.NLM

Running Winsetup for Windows 3.x Clients

Using WINSETUP.EXE — the graphical Novell client setup utility — is recommended for installing your NetWare client software with Windows. This same file is executed to set up NetWare client support for all Windows versions. When WINSETUP.EXE initializes, you will have an opportunity to select which Windows operating system you will install, as shown in Figure 9.6.

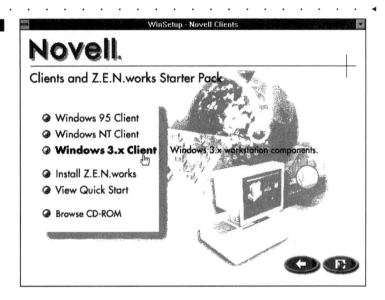

*The Novell Clients and
Z.E.N.works Starter Pack
client selection screen*

Procedure

You will find the WINSETUP.EXE file in the root of the Novell Z.E.N.works Starter Pack CD. Windows does not have to be set up for networking at the time you run Winsetup. You should have your Windows setup disks available — in many cases files will be required from those disks.

Follow this procedure to install your NetWare client for either Windows 3.1 or Windows for Workgroups 3.11:

1. Start WINSETUP.EXE. Select Program Manager → File → Run, and then select WINSETUP.EXE in the root directory of your Z.E.N.works Starter Pack CD. The screen shown in Figure 9.6 will appear. Select Windows 3.x Client. WINSETUP.EXE will autostart if this feature is enabled in Windows.

2. Select the language to be supported at this workstation, and then select Install Novell Client. Select the Yes button to agree to the license statement, and view release notes if you have not already done so.

3. Choose optional modules from the list as shown in Figure 9.7. You can click the Help button for detail on the optional modules.

▶ • ◀

FIGURE 9.7

Choose optional modules

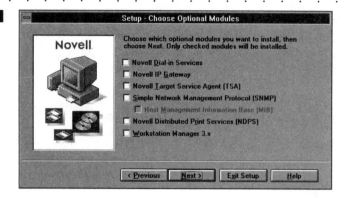

4. Accept or edit the path name where the Novell client files are to be installed. A disk space check will let you know if you have sufficient space. A complete installation should take no more than 4.5MB. The directory will be created, and client files will be installed into that directory.

5. Select the first network drive. This will be the drive letter where you will find the NetWare login prompt. If there is no LASTDRIVE= statement in your CONFIG.SYS, no drive letter will be available.

6. If you selected the Novell Target Service Agent option shown in Figure 9.7, you will see the Configure Novell Target Service Agent screen. The TSA server name is the server that contains the backup device and the SMS utilities. Enter a computer name to be assigned to your workstation for sharing, enter a password if desired, and list which local drive letters should be backed up. The next screen will ask for locations and additional name information.

7. If you checked the Simple Network Management Protocol (SNMP) box in Figure 9.7, you will be prompted to enter SNMP configuration information.

8. Accept or edit the name to be assigned to the program manager group for your NetWare client utilities. The default name is Novell Client.

9. Create a Location Profile. If you do not elect to create a location profile, a single default location profile will be created. A desktop computer only

requires one location, but if you use a notebook computer, it may serve you to create multiple locations — one for each way you connect with your network. For example, you may have one location for using your notebook at your desk in a docking bay, and another for use on the road when you dial in. You will be prompted to give the location a name.

10. Configure NIC settings. You will proceed to the LAN adapter (NIC) configuration screen as shown in Figure 9.8.

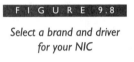

FIGURE 9.8

Select a brand and driver
for your NIC

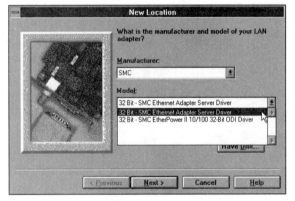

a. The next screen will ask you to select the NIC hardware settings for your driver. Be sure you enter the correct information. You should test and record hardware settings before starting installation.

b. Next, enter the NDS tree or preferred server for the bindery service. The context is the NDS container in which your user object has been created. If you have not created a user object at this time, enter the container name that the Administrator user (default is Admin) was created in. The Administrator account should have been created in the Organization container object, which is the first container below the root of the tree.

11. Configure TCP/IP. The next screen will ask if you would like to add the TCP/IP protocol for your workstation. Windows 3.x clients must use IPX or NetWare/IP to communicate with NetWare 3, 4, or 5 servers, but TCP/IP is required to dial into the Internet.

If you elected to install the TCP/IP protocol stack, select the IP addressing method. For a static IP address assignment, select "No User Specified." To use the other options, you must have configured a DHCP server, configured a BOOTP server, or activated the RARP protocol on a router.

a. If you have selected the option for static IP address assignment, the next screen will prompt you to enter the IP address and subnet mask for your workstation. If you are unfamiliar with IP addressing, see Chapter 4.

b. Next enter the IP address of the router port that is closest to your workstation. This address is often called the gateway address. This address must be on the same subnet as your workstation and becomes the entry point to the internetwork of routers. You only need to enter one address, but if your subnet is attached to more than one router, enter all addresses. The list is prioritized.

c. Next enter the DNS domain name that your workstation belong to, and the address of the DNS server that is designated to handle name resolution requests from your workstation. If you have not established a DNS domain at this point, you can leave this blank and enter the information at a later date.

12. You will be returned to the Create Location screen to create additional location parameters. When finished, you will be prompted to reboot. During the reboot, Windows DLLs and DRV files will be extracted and copied to the Windows directory for each location.

NOTE

Windows 3.x versions often do not directly update configuration files (CONFIG.SYS, AUTOEXEC.BAT, SYSTEM.INI, WIN.INI, and so on). Pay close attention to Windows dialog boxes during setup. You may receive a message indicating that changes were made to a backup file instead of to the proper configuration file. Windows will save changes to STARTUP.00x and NET.00x (where *x* increments from 0 with each install). The name of the file that changes were saved to along with instructions will be shown on your screen.

Login

After your Novell DOS client files have been configured and loaded, they should execute when your computer is booted. When the CLIENT32.NLM module is executed in the STARTNET.BAT file, you should see a message indicating that you have attached to a server. If you cannot verify this step, press F8 during boot to execute startup files one line at a time.

Once you have attached to a server, you can log in. Switch to drive F, or whichever drive letter is your first NetWare drive, and type **login**. You will be prompted to enter your user name and password. You can log in before running Windows, or else you will see the Novell Login screen when Windows executes.

After Login

You can log in before starting Windows or allow the Windows NetWare login service to log you in after loading Windows. In either case, be sure that you receive the message "Attached to *tree_name*" before Windows is started.

Your Winsetup utility will create a Novell Client program group with helpful utilities to manage network connections, dial-up connections, logins/logouts, client configuration options, help, and README files. You should use these utilities instead of using the Windows Network Control Panel applet, the Windows Network Setup applet, or other Windows utilities (such as File Manager). When you attempt to use File Manager to map a network drive, the NetWare User Tools application will be loaded instead of the Microsoft network browser.

If you make changes in the Windows Network Setup applet, you may adversely affect NetWare connectivity. This option is used to configure Microsoft networking options, but the Novell client software is used instead. Configuration options in Network Setup were adjusted to use Novell's ODI drivers with the NDIS helper (ODIHLP.EXE). If you alter this option, you can cause your NetWare connections to be disabled. You cannot use Network Setup to configure NetWare client options; instead, the Client Control Panel applet is used in the Novell Client program group.

TIP

If you have difficulty gaining access to Microsoft servers, consider installing IPX support on those servers. You can use the Novell IPX drivers to enable access to Windows for Workgroups, Windows 95, and Windows NT servers.

The following utilities are provided to manage your Windows 3.*x* NetWare client.

Client Control Panel

The Client Control Panel applet enables you to edit the configuration of the Novell Client for Windows 3.*x*. To edit this applet, follow these steps:

1. In the Network Control Panel, select the Novell NetWare Client → Locations → LAN Location → Properties and choose the Connection tab.

2. Edit Access the Properties button to edit NIC configuration parameters. Edit protocol configuration options by selecting the Protocols button.

3. Use the NetWare tab to configure your NDS tree, preferred server, Windows login, and drive/printer connection settings.

WARNING **Use the Advanced button in the Locations screen to edit your NET.CFG and STARTNET.BAT files. These files configure and execute your NetWare client modules. You should not edit these files manually.**

Novell Login

You can log in before or after starting Windows. To log in within Windows, use the Novell Login applet for NetWare login and logout while Windows is running. Select the tabs to configure NetWare login, connection, and login script options.

NetWare User Tools

The NetWare User Tools applet is used to:

▸ Map and disconnect mapped drives.

▸ Capture and disconnect captured printers.

▸ Manage server and tree connections.

▸ Manage configuration options for NetWare User Tools, connection, startup, and login options.

NetWare User Tools uses the NetWare browser to search for bindery and NDS objects as well as Microsoft resources. Some of the configuration options in this utility overlap with options presented in the Novell Login applet.

Dialer Assistant

The Dialer Assistant applet is used to dial up remote servers. Use this dialer to remotely access your network or the Internet. The Dialer Assistant is designed to be the client for the NetWare Remote Access Server (NetWare Connect).

Novell Client Help

The Help applet accesses context-sensitive help screens. The help facility uses hyperlinks and can be searched for help on any related topic.

Novell Client Release Notes

Check the release notes for known problems and solutions at the time your client software was released. You can find later fixes and patches at Novell's Web site.

If you have installed the IP-IPX Gateway, the following utilities will be installed.

IP Gateway Switcher

Use this utility to configure the IP-IPX gateway and gateway server, and the IP-to-IP gateway server addresses.

IP Gateway WinPing

This utility is used to "ping" other IP hosts. When using the utility, enter the IP address or host name of the IP-IPX gateway server. This utility tests for connectivity between your workstation and other IP hosts through the gateway. Use this utility to test connectivity between your workstation and any IP host.

Troubleshooting an IPX Install

The IPX option installs server drivers before starting Windows 3.x. The following files have been altered and should contain these entries:

```
CONFIG.SYS

FILES=40

BUFFERS=30
```

```
LASTDRIVE=M  (or higher)

DEVICE=<Novell client directory path>\LOCATION.EXE


AUTOEXEC.BAT

PATH = <existing path>;%PATH%

@CALL <Novell client directory path>\STARTNET.BAT


STARTNET.BAT

REM ******************************************

REM this section is not to be modified manually


@ECHO OFF

<Novell client directory path>\ISINPATH <Novell client
directory path>

if errorlevel 1 goto skippath

PATH=<Novell client directory path>;%PATH%

:skippath

SET NWLANGUAGE=ENGLISH  (or other client language)

C:

CD <Novell client directory path>


<Novell client directory path>\NIOS.EXE

LOAD <Novell client directory path>\NBIC32.NLM

LOAD <Novell client directory path>\LSLC32.NLM

LOAD <Novell client directory path>\CMSM.NLM
```

LOAD *<Novell client directory path>*\ETHERTSM.NLM (or other TSM module)

LOAD *<Novell client directory path>**<NIC driver.LAN>* *<hardware configuration options>* FRAME=*<frame type>*

LOAD *<Novell client directory path>*\TRANNTA.NLM

LOAD *<Novell client directory path>*\IPX.NLM

LOAD *<Novell client directory path>*\SPX_SKTS.NLM

LOAD *<Novell client directory path>*\CLIENT32.NLM

REM **

NET.CFG

; Location: LAN Location

Link Driver NCOMX

    INT 3

    PORT 2F8

Link Support

    Buffers 8 1500

    MemPool 8192

    Max Boards 4

    Max Stacks 4

Netware DOS Requester

    First Network Drive = G

    NETWARE PROTOCOL = NDS,BIND

    VLM = AUTO.VLM

```
        Preferred Tree Tree

        Name Context "Org"

        SHORT MACHINE TYPE = IBM


    Protocol TCPIP

        PATH TCP_CFG <Novell client directory path>\TCP

        TCP_SOCKETS 15

        UDP_SOCKETS 15

        TCP_WINDOW 10240


    NIOS

        LINE DRAW CHARS = "_¿þ03Ž"


    Link driver SMC8000

        FRAME <frame_type>

        FRAME Ethernet_II

        PORT=300
```

Troubleshooting an IP Gateway Install

The IP Gateway option installs server drivers before starting Windows 3.*x*. The following files have been altered and should contain these entries. Check them against your files.

The CONFIG.SYS and AUTOEXEC.BAT files are the same for this installation.

STARTNET.BAT

```
REM ****************************************

REM this section is not to be modified manually
```

```
@ECHO OFF
<Novell client directory path>\ISINPATH C:\ <Novell client
directory path>
if errorlevel 1 goto skippath
PATH=<Novell client directory path>;%PATH%
:skippath
SET NWLANGUAGE=ENGLISH (or other client language)
C:
CD <Novell client directory path>
LOAD <Novell client directory path>\NIOS.EXE
LOAD <Novell client directory path>\NBIC32.NLM
LOAD <Novell client directory path>\LSLC32.NLM
LOAD <Novell client directory path>\CMSM.NLM
LOAD <Novell client directory path>\ETHERTSM.NLM (or other TSM
module)
LOAD <Novell client directory path>\<NIC driver.LAN>
<hardware settings> FRAME=<frame type for IPX>
LOAD <Novell client directory path>\<NIC driver.LAN>
<hardware settings> FRAME=Ethernet_II
LOAD <Novell client directory path>\TCPIP.NLM
LOAD <Novell client directory path>\TRANNTA.NLM
LOAD <Novell client directory path>\IPX.NLM
LOAD <Novell client directory path>\SPX_SKTS.NLM
LOAD <Novell client directory path>\CLIENT32.NLM
REM *****************************************
```

Supporting Access to Microsoft Servers in Windows for Workgroups 3.11

When you load the Novell Client for Windows 3.*x*, the Microsoft protocol stack will be disabled. Novell supports access to NetWare by installing 32-bit drivers before starting Windows. The process for adding support back in for Microsoft hosts is the same as using "real mode" drivers — drivers are loaded, and then ODINSUP is used to stack the Microsoft client on top of the Novell drivers.

To support simultaneous access to both NetWare and Microsoft servers from a Windows for Workgroups 3.11 workstation, you must load the following support modules:

- ODINSUP.386

- NIOS.EXE

- NBIC32.NLM

- LSLC32.NLM

- CMSM.NLM

- A TSM file (for example ETHERTSM.NLM is used for Ethernet NICs)

- A NIC driver

These modules provide access to the Microsoft client in Windows using the Novell NIC driver and protocol stack. The following procedure will configure Windows for Workgroups for access to both NetWare and Microsoft hosts.

1. Start Windows for Workgroups and exit all applications.

2. In Program Manager, select the Network program group, Network Setup, and then Drivers. If Microsoft Networking was not previously installed, select Windows Setup and install Networks.

3. If an NDIS driver has been installed, remove it. Select the driver from the Network Drivers list and then select Remove.

4. From the Networks Setup screen, select Add Adapter and then select Unlisted or Updated Network from the list.

5. You will be asked for the location of the driver. You will need access to the files ODINSUP.386 and OEMSETUP.INF, which are located on your Z.E.N.works CD in the \PRODUCTS\DOSWIN32\WINDRV directory. The driver should be shown as an NDIS3 driver — if it is not:

   a. Select Setup.

   b. From the Driver Type list, select Enhanced Mode NDIS Driver.

6. Verify that both the Novell and Microsoft protocol stacks appear under Network Drivers. If they do not:

   a. Select Add Protocol.

   b. Select the appropriate protocol from the list.

7. Save your work by selecting OK when closing each screen until you have exited Network Setup.

8. Manually edit the STARTNET.BAT file to be sure that each of the modules were loaded.

For information about the correct order in which the drivers should be loaded, and to optimize the load order, see "Optimizing Module Load Order" and "32-Bit Load Order Examples" in your Z.E.N.works documentation under the Novell Client for DOS and Windows 3.1*x*, Optimizing heading.

► · ◄

Troubleshooting the Novell DOS/Windows 3.*x* Client Setup

The best strategy for troubleshooting a failed installation is to reinstall the Novell Client software from the Z.E.N.works Starter Pack. Here are some tips:

· · · · · ·

- ▸ Check the startup files, CONFIG.SYS, AUTOEXEC.BAT, STARTUP.BAT, and NET.CFG. Look for missing commands or statements.

- ▸ Reinstall the Novell DOS/Windows 3.x Client from the Z.E.N.works Starter Pack that came with NetWare 5.

- ▸ If you still cannot connect, remove the Novell DOS/Windows 3.x Client and restore the original CONFIG.SYS and AUTOEXEC.BAT files as they were before the upgrade. Reinstall Microsoft Networking and reestablish connections with your existing Novell and Microsoft servers.

- ▸ Once again, reinstall the Novell DOS/Windows 3.x Client from the Z.E.N.works Starter Pack that came with NetWare 5.

CHAPTER 10

Windows 95/98 and NT Clients

This chapter discusses installing the Novell Client for Windows 95/98 and the Novell Client for Windows NT software, which is often called "Client 32" in your Novell documentation. Pay close attention to the Notes, Tips, Warnings, and procedures contained in this chapter. They refer to situations that are commonly known to cause problems. You will also find a troubleshooting section at the end of the chapter that will help you resolve most client installation problems. You should also refer to the Troubleshooting and Maintenance section of this book, specifically Chapter 14, "Client Connectivity," for additional help.

Novell Client for Windows 95, Windows 98, and Windows NT is 32-bit software that provides access to NetWare servers, NDS trees, and all NetWare resources. The Novell client includes several new features, including Remote Access Services, which provides dial-out access to external bulletin boards, NetWare servers, and Internet service providers (ISPs). This product meshes well with the 32-bit Windows environment.

The Novell Client for Windows 95/98 and NT can access a NetWare 5 system with IPX/SPX or with pure TCP/IP — no IPX protocol bindings are required at all. The Microsoft TCP/IP protocol stack in Windows 95/98 and NT is used — a Novell protocol stack does not need to be installed. The Client 32 module binds to the Windows 95, Windows 98, and Windows NT TCP/IP transport.

NOTE

The Novell Client for Windows 95/98 and NT is often called "Client 32" in your Novell documentation. Client 32 is actually the client requester module — the Novell Client for Windows 95/98 and NT consists of Client 32, protocols, several additional services, and online documentation.

Under certain conditions the Novell Client for Windows 95/98 and NT installed with TCP/IP only can access NetWare servers running IPX through the Compatibility Mode. This enables you to install one driver and one protocol stack to support access to NetWare 5, NetWare 3, NetWare 4, and Microsoft servers regardless of whether they are using IP or IPX.

Clients and Protocols for NetWare Access

You have several client and protocol options for accessing NetWare systems. Each solution includes a:

- Client module

- Protocol stack or "transport"

- NIC driver

Client Modules

Windows 95, Windows 98, and Windows NT have client modules that connect to NetWare servers and NDS trees. Table 10.1 lists various products made to access NetWare networks.

TABLE 10.1 _Client Products for Accessing NetWare Networks_	OPEPRATING SYSTEM	MICROSOFT PRODUCT	NOVELL PRODUCT
	Windows 95 Networks	Client for NetWare	Client for Windows 95/98
	Windows 98	Client for NetWare Networks	Client for Windows 95/98
	Windows NT Workstation 4	Client Services for NetWare	Client for Windows NT
	Windows NT Server 4	Gateway (and Client) Services for NetWare	Client for Windows NT

Microsoft's Client for NetWare Networks in Windows 95/98 and NT does not have the capability of accessing NetWare 5 resources. Perhaps by the time you read this book, Microsoft will have added this capability and released updated client software. However, you should find Novell's client software far more robust for supporting NetWare clients. For NetWare 3 and 4 systems, Microsoft's client is less capable than Novell's client software in accessing NDS trees and adjusting NetWare protocols and communications parameters. The Microsoft client software will allow a Windows 95/98 and NT client to access NetWare resources, but protocol adjustments and use of different login names for Microsoft and NetWare user accounts are among features that are not supported. The Novell Client for Windows 95 has many features that are lacking in Windows 95/98 and NT's built-in client software.

The Microsoft Client for NetWare Networks is helpful for occasional access to NetWare environments, or for temporary access in order to upgrade the client's software to the Novell Client for Windows 95/98 and NT.

TIP

Many Windows workstations are shipped from the manufacturer with Networking installed. Often the Microsoft clients for Microsoft and for NetWare networks are both installed. If you have set up client install directories on a server, or a server CD that is shared, you can access the Winsetup application from the Z.E.N.works Starter Pack using the Microsoft client software.

The Microsoft products previously listed support basic login to NetWare servers and NDS trees using Microsoft NDIS drivers and Microsoft protocol stacks. While Microsoft clients and protocols can connect Windows workstations to NetWare networks, you will find that the corresponding Novell products provide more features, options, adjustments, and capabilities.

The original Windows 95's Client for NetWare Networks did not have the ability to support NDS. Later versions of this client module supports NDS and are available in Windows 95 OSR2 and the Windows 95 Service Pack for Administrators.

NOTE

The Novell products just shown use a combination of Microsoft and Novell protocols. The latest client products for Windows 95, 98, and NT all use Microsoft NDIS drivers.

Microsoft TCP/IP and IPX/SPX Protocol Stacks

The Novell Client for Windows 95/98 and NT uses the Microsoft TCP/IP protocol stack to communicate with NetWare networks. The Microsoft TCP/IP stack in a Windows 95, 98, or NT computer will provide adequate connectivity service. It is not necessary to replace the Microsoft protocols. For this reason, the Windows Client is installed on top of the Microsoft TCP/IP protocols.

When you install IP with IPX Compatibility, the Novell IPX 32-bit Protocol for the Novell NetWare Client is installed. Client 32 binds and communicates with the Novell IPX protocol, which in turn communicates with the Microsoft TCP/IP protocol.

If you install IPX when installing the Novell Client for Windows 95/98/NT, the Novell 32-bit IPX protocol will be installed and bound to the NDIS driver even if you have NWLink installed. Microsoft's NWLink protocol is an emulation of Novell's IPX protocol. Novell's IPX stack has many features that are not included in NWLink.

TIP If you have Windows 95 OSR2 or if you have applied the latest Microsoft Service Pack for Windows 95, setup will be much easier for you. If your operating system is updated prior to attempting client setup, chances are much better that your client installation will go smoothly and work without glitches.

NDIS Driver Support

The Novell Client for Windows 95/98 and NT also uses existing NDIS drivers so there is no need to install an ODI NIC driver in addition to your Windows NDIS driver. This makes installation and support much simpler than was the case in previous Novell clients. NIC driver developers no longer have to develop and support a separate ODI driver for NetWare clients.

Viewing or Setting Up Client Online Documentation

The Z.E.N.works Starter Pack makes it easy for you to view the online documentation before you install and afterward. When you install the Novell Client for Windows 95/98/NT, you will have the option of installing the online documentation. You can install the documentation as a separate step or view the documentation from the CD without installing it. These options are available from menu selections when you run Winsetup and select Windows 95/98 and NT Client on your Z.E.N.works CD. Another way to run the online documentation is to execute RUNME.EXE or VIEWDOC.EXE located in the \DOCUMENTS directory of the Z.E.N.works Starter Pack CD.

Online documentation will run with Netscape Navigator 4 or Internet Explorer 4 on Windows 95, 98, or NT. If one of these products in not already installed on your system, you can install Netscape Navigator 4.04 from the Z.E.N.works CD. To install Navigator, execute N32E404.EXE in the \PRODUCTS\NETSCAPE \WIN32\ENGLISH directory of your Z.E.N.works CD.

Client Setup Options

To install a Windows 95, 98, or NT client, run the NetWare 5 client setup utility for your workstation operating system:

▶ Windows 95/98 Client

▶ Windows NT Client

Novell has made using these programs as bullet-proof as possible. The Winsetup utility will install your client software and a system tray applet for accessing server client utilities. Your local Registry will be updated, and you will be able to log into and log out of NetWare without shutting down Windows. Your existing Microsoft networking logins and connections will remain undisturbed.

You can set up your clients:

▶ Directly from the Z.E.N.works CD

▶ From a network directory

▶ From a shared CD volume

Regardless of which method you use, your setup program is the same. The only difference is the path from which you will execute the setup utility.

NOTE To automate client installation and updates, see your Z.E.N.works Starter Pack. It has many options to make centralized system administration much easier. For a complete reference on Z.E.N.works open your online documentation in the Z.E.N.works Starter Pack and then select Contents → Desktop Management Services → Z.E.N.works Overview.

Copying Client Setup Files to the Network

You can set up clients from the network if they are already attached to an existing tree or server from the Z.E.N.works Starter Pack or from files downloaded from Novell's Web site. The following provides instructions for both procedures.

Installing Client Setup Files From the Z.E.N.works Starter Pack

You can install setup files for all your clients on a network server from your Z.E.N.works Starter Pack. The process is automated with the help of the Z.E.N.works Setup Wizard. To load client software for DOS/Windows 3.*x*, Windows 95, 98, and NT clients:

1. Log into a tree or server with sufficient rights to create, install, and access a directory to be created to house the client files, from a workstation running the Novell Client for Windows 95/98, or NT software.

2. Insert your Z.E.N.works CD into your CD-ROM drive.

3. Run the Z.E.N.works Setup application (SETUP.EXE) from the \Products \Zenworks directory.

4. Follow the instructions provided by the Z.E.N.works Setup Wizard shown in Figure 10.1.

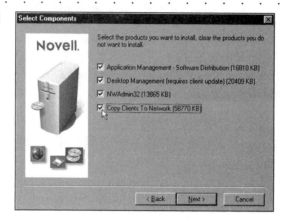

F I G U R E   10.1

The Z.E.N.works Setup Wizard

Manual Network Directory Preparation

To prepare a network directory for installation, follow these steps:

1. From a client workstation, copy the Z.E.N.works Starter Pack CD and all subdirectories to a directory located on a shared volume. For example, if the CD is in drive D: and drive F: is mapped to the root of SYS:, type:

```
XCOPY D:\*.* F:\PUBLIC\CLIENTS /s /e
```

Using the NetWare NCOPY command, type:

```
NCOPY D:\*.* SYS:PUBLIC\CLIENTS /s /e /c
```

2. Map root a drive letter to the directory. To map drive letter I: to the same directory, type:

```
MAP ROOT I:=SYS:PUBLIC\CLIENTS
```

3. Assign Read and File Scan Rights to Files and Directories to the setup network directory. For example, to assign Read and File Scan rights to the Admins group, type the following command:

```
RIGHTS SYS:PUBLIC\CLIENTS RF /GROUP=ADMINS
```

To set up a client:

1. Log in as a member of the Admins group (assuming that group has been created and has sufficient NDS rights to use the network install directory).

2. Execute WINSETUP.EXE from the mapped drive.

Networked CD Preparation

You can update a client that is already connected to a server by installing from the Z.E.N.works CD mounted in a networked CD-ROM drive. Installing from a networked CD also requires mounting the CD as a NetWare volume. This step was done during server installation, but the process may not have been automated.

To mount a CD as a NetWare volume on a NetWare 5 server:

1. Insert the CD into the CD-ROM drive.

2. Switch to the console screen (colon prompt).

3. Type the command **LOAD CDROM**.

4. Add the LOAD CDROM statement to your AUTOEXEC.NCF file to load support full time for CD-ROM drives.

NOTE

On a NetWare 5 server it is not necessary to issue any commands to mount a CD volume once the CDROM.NLM module is loaded. When you remove a CD, the volume will be dismounted. When you insert a CD, the volume will be mounted automatically.

CDROM.NLM supports ISO 9660 format CDs. To load support for Apple HFS format CDs, at your server console type the command **CDHFS.NSS**. To mount a CD as a NetWare volume on a NetWare 3 or 4 server:

1. Insert your Z.E.N.works Starter Pack CD in the server's CD-ROM drive.

2. From the server console (colon prompt), enter **LOAD CDROM**.

3. Enter **CD DEVICE LIST** and notice the No. listed for the CD.

4. Enter **CD MOUNT 1** (or substitute the No. listed for the CD you wish to mount). This command will mount whichever volume is shown in position number 1, which is, normally, any CD in the drive.

You can map to the volume using the CD volume label as the NetWare volume label. For example, if the Z.E.N.works CD is in your server's CD-ROM drive, map drive I: with the following command:

```
MAP I:=NW5_CLNT:
```

You may then execute WINSETUP.EXE from drive I:.

Client Setup

Before you install the Novell Client for Windows 95/98 or NT, you must first install Microsoft networking components into your Windows operating system. At least the network adapter driver and protocol must be installed. Novell's Winsetup utility adds functionality to these components. If you were to attempt to run Winsetup with no network adapter (NIC) or network protocols installed, the installation would fail — a dialog box would inform you that the Microsoft TCP/IP or NWLink protocol must be installed.

Setting up Microsoft Networking

During Windows 95, 98, or NT you have an opportunity to install and configure networking components.

NOTE

If Microsoft networking is not functional, your Novell Client 32 software will not work. Novell adds Client 32 on top of existing Microsoft networking adapter drivers and protocols. Most troubleshooting problems with Windows workstations are related to Microsoft networking configuration problems.

Set up your adapter first and then set up protocols. The following procedure will help you get your Windows 95/98 workstation's networking up and running. Windows 95/98's plug-and-play features detect hardware devices, such as NICs during boot, and run a Setup Wizard the first time the computer is booted after the device has been physically installed. If a device has been improperly installed and/or configured, it cannot be reinstalled until the device driver is removed.

The following procedure will help you if you install or reinstall a NIC in Windows 95 or 98.

1. Physically install the NIC in your computer.

2. Select the Device Manager in the Control Panel System applet.

3. See if a network adapter is currently installed in your system. In the list of devices, search for the network adapter. It may be listed under Network Adapters, or you may find it under Unknown Devices. In most cases, the adapter has been installed improperly and must be removed before the appropriate driver and configuration can be accepted.

4. Remove the device from the list. Highlight the device and then select Remove.

5. Reboot your computer.

6. During boot, a dialog box should appear indicating that new hardware was detected. A Setup Wizard may run to ask for user configuration input. You may need to locate your Windows files (.CAB files found in the \Win95 or \Win98 directory of your Windows CD) to load a new device driver, or you may need to insert a vendor disk with the driver files. Be sure you install the correct driver for the NIC. By default your adapter will be installed with NetBEUI and IPX-Compatible protocols.

7. After the driver is installed, select from the Network applet in Control Panel, click Add, select Protocols from the list, and select Microsoft and then TCP/IP. If you are to use IPX, select Protocols and then IPX/SPX Compatible Protocol.

8. Select TCP/IP protocol and then configure the IP address and mask information. When all configuration is finished, click OK to exit. You should be prompted to reboot. Your configuration will not be effective until you do.

9. You should also set up Microsoft or NetWare networking clients modules and connect to an existing server or tree to verify that the Microsoft networking components and physical devices are installed and working properly.

Windows NT version 4 is not fully plug-and-play compatible, so detection of an existing device during boot is not activated. Windows NT has different Control Panel functionality and plug and play does not normally detect a new device upon boot. The following procedure will help you install an adapter in Windows NT Workstation or Server version 4.

To add the networking components follow these instructions:

1. Physically install the NIC in your system.

2. Open the Adapters tab in the Control Panel Network applet. If no adapter is installed, select Add.

3. Select your NIC from the list of drivers, or select the Have Disk button. When selecting Have Disk, enter the path where the vendor driver files are (typically on a floppy disk) and then select the correct driver from the displayed list.

4. Configure the adapter's properties. The configuration screens are part of the vendor driver and will vary from NIC to NIC. You will be prompted to insert your Windows NT CD or the vendor driver disk. When finished, you should be returned to the Adapters screen.

5. Select Protocols. If the TCP/IP and/or NWLink IPX/SPX Compatible Transport protocols are not shown, select Add and then add the protocol you intend to use (IP or IPX).

6. Select Bindings. This will update the relationships between the adapters and the protocols.

7. In the Protocols screen, select TCP/IP and then Properties (if IP protocol is being installed). In the IP Address screen select Obtain an IP Address from a DHCP Server or select Specify an IP Address and then enter the IP address and mask. Enter the Gateway address (the IP address of the router attached to your local network segment). If configuring NWLink, select this protocol and then configure the Properties, including the frame type, network number, and internal IPX network address.

8. When finished, select OK to save your configuration and exit. You will be prompted to reboot.

Installing the Novell Client for Windows 95/98 and NT

To install the Novell Client for Windows 95/98 or NT, run WINSETUP.EXE in the root of Z.E.N.works Starter Pack. If your system is set up for it, this file will autostart when you insert the CD in your CD-ROM drive. Follow these steps.

1. Select the language to be used. You will see the screen shown in Figure 10.2.

2. Select Windows 95/98 Client or Windows NT Client.

3. Select Install Novell Client.

4. Approve the License agreement.

5. Select Typical or Custom installation. You should select Custom in order to have control over all configuration options. You can view the latest release notes by selecting the Readme button.

6. Select Install. The Setup Wizard will be configured to guide you through your installation.

▶ . . . . ◀

F I G U R E 10.2	
The opening Z.E.N.works Starter Pack screen	

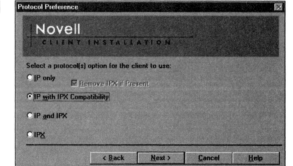

Protocol Preferences

When you continue, you will see the Protocol Preference screen shown in Figure 10.3.

▶ . . . . ◀

F I G U R E 10.3	
The Protocol Preference screen	

When you are installing the Novell Client for Windows NT protocol, preferences are presented after selecting custom options.

NOTE

You have four options for supporting IP and IPX protocols:

▸ *IP Only* — This option installs Client 32 with the IP protocol only in your Windows 95 or Windows 98 computer using the existing Microsoft TCP/IP protocol stack and NDIS driver. The client will be able to effectively communicate with NetWare 5 servers where IP is installed as well as other TCP/IP-based hosts. This option will not allow you to communicate with NetWare 3 and 4 servers.

▸ *IP with IPX Compatibility* — This option allows IPX services and applications to communicate in an IP-only network by converting IPX packets into IP packets at the workstation. This option will install the Novell client IPX Compatibility Mode Driver (CMD) and the Novell IPX/SPX protocols. The client CMD will interface with the Microsoft TCP/IP protocol stack and NDIS driver.

To communicate with IP-only NetWare 5 servers, the server Compatibility Mode Driver (CMD) must also be installed. See Chapter 11, "TCP/IP Services," for instructions on setting up the CMD.

NOTE

This option also allows IP services and applications to work on an IPX network. However, the CMD Migration Agent and the Service Location Protocol (SLP) Directory Agent must be enabled on a NetWare 5 server on your network to support server broadcasting normally handled by Service Advertising Protocol (SAP) in an IPX network.

▸ *IP and IPX* — This option allows the client to use the IP protocol to communicate with IP-only NetWare 5 servers and the IPX protocol to communicate with NetWare 3, 4, and 5 servers running IPX. This option is the default. It should be used for mixed networks consisting of NetWare 3, 4, and 5 servers.

▶ *IPX (IPX Only)* — This option support access to NetWare 3 and 4 servers, and to NetWare 5 servers where the IPX protocol is installed.

NOTE

IPX clients can communicate with IP-only NetWare 5 servers using the CMD. If IPX is not bound to a LAN interface on a NetWare 5 server, the CMD is installed for every IP binding. However, this option is not as optimized as the previous options. It is best to communicate with IP-only NetWare 5 servers using the IP protocol. The IPX-only option should be used when all NetWare servers use the IPX protocol. However, the CMD must be loaded both on the client and on the NetWare 5 server. See Chapter 11, "TCP/IP Services," for details.

The next screen you will see asks you whether the client is to log into an NDS or bindery (NetWare 3) environment.

Custom Options

The next screen you will see presents a list of custom options that you can install on your computer as shown in Figure 10.4. You may check boxes to install these options.

FIGURE 10.4

Custom Options

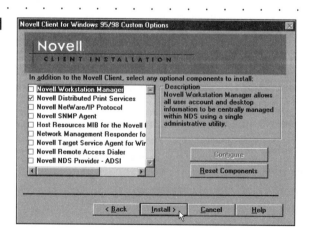

NOTE

The options that appear on your screen may vary from the figures shown in this section if you are installing the Windows NT client. This section combines setup options for both Windows 95/98 and Windows NT client installations, since the differences are minor.

Select the options you want to install by selecting the check box to the left of the option. Each of the following options can be installed.

▸ *Novell Client for Windows NT (Required)* — This listing appears only for Windows NT clients and cannot be unchecked. Though this option does not appear for Windows 95/98 client setup, the Novell Client for Windows 95/98 (Client 32) will be installed.

▸ *Novell Workstation Manager (Windows 95/98 only)* — Enables you to set up user accounts in NetWare Administrator and simultaneously set up a local Windows 95/98 user account and profile. This module allows the user accounts both in NetWare and on the Windows workstation to be managed simultaneously from NetWare Administrator.

▸ *Z.E.N.works Application Launcher NT Service (NT only)* — This service updates the Windows NT local Registry when Application Launcher applications are installed. To use this service, you must install Z.E.N.works on your network.

▸ *Novell Distributed Print Services* — Install this option if you wish to use NDPS resources. NDPS establishes real-time bidirectional printer support along with other features as an alternative to traditional queue-based printing. See Chapter 19, "Printing and NDPS," for details.

▸ *Novell NetWare/IP Protocol* — This option installs the NetWare/IP client support modules. This option is only presented in the Windows 95/98 setup. The same functionality is offered later in the Windows NT setup when protocols are selected.

NOTE

Do not select the Novell NetWare/IP Protocol option unless you need to support NetWare/IP that is already installed on a server. This option is not used to support access to IP-only NetWare 5 servers.

▶ *Novell SNMP Agent* — Makes this workstation an SNMP agent that will report network error conditions to a workstation containing an MIB database.

▶ *Host Resources MIB for the Novell Client* — Enables SNMP management console and polls SNMP clients for inventory information.

▶ *NetWare Management Responder for the Novell Client* — Provides OS, BIOS, and ODI information and services to the network manager. This option is used to support Z.E.N.works capabilities to accumulate client configuration information.

▶ *Novell Target Service Agent* — Allows this workstation to be backed up by an SMS server-based backup device and application.

▶ *Novell NDS Provider - ADSI* — Allows Microsoft Active Directory Service Interfaces to communicate with NDS.

▶ *Novell Remote Access Dialer* — This software provides client dial-up service to Novell Internet Access Servers. See Chapter 12, "Novell Internet Access Server," for details on using this software.

▶ *Novell IP Gateway (NT only)* — This option provides IPX Compatibility Mode access to IP-only NetWare 5 servers. You will not see this option in the Windows 95/98 client setup because it is offered as part of the protocol selection options.

Once you select Next, several activities take place: existing client software is removed, a wizard is configured to handle the rest of the installation, and a file copy installs the required files. You will then be prompted to reboot the workstation.

You may be presented with several screens to enter configuration data for the custom options you have selected. Help is available in each wizard screen.

Managing Client 32

When you install the Novell Client for Windows 95/98/NT, you will notice that a red N has been installed to your system tray. If you have not moved your taskbar from the bottom of your screen, look for the red N in the lower-right corner of your screen. Move your cursor onto the N, and click the right button on your mouse. This will bring up a menu of several NetWare client applications as shown in Figure 10.5.

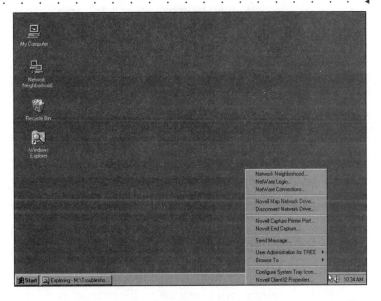

F I G U R E   10.5

The NetWare Services menu available from the red N icon in the system tray

Many of these options simply provide shortcuts to existing components. For example, selecting Network Neighborhood will bring up the same screens as if you clicked the Network Neighborhood shortcut on your default Windows 95 desktop. Novell Client 32 Properties will bring up the same configuration screens accessible from Control Panel's Network applet. However, other selections bring up Novell applications provided to assist you in managing your NetWare options.

Additional Client 32 Services

Some of the NetWare Services menu selections add functionality over and above those provided in Windows 95, 98, or NT. You will find several items that take you to preexisting Windows utilities. These items are not discussed in this section.

- ▸ *NetWare Connections* — This utility shows your Novell network attachments. You can see the NDS and server attachments that are currently serviced, the connection number in use, the Authentication state, and the Transport Type (IP or IPX). This is not a big deal, but it is quite helpful to know this information when troubleshooting. You can also use this utility to terminate a connection or set which is your primary connection.

- ▸ *Novell Map Network Drive* — This utility is an enhanced version of the Map Network Drive option in Windows Explorer's Tools menu. In this utility you can map root, map a search drive, or put the search drive at the beginning or end of the path, in addition to the options provided in the Microsoft Map Network Drive utility.

- ▸ *NetWare Login* — This option allows you to log in again, using the same or a different user name.

- ▸ *Novell Capture Printer Port* — This utility is an abbreviated version of the Microsoft Add Printer Wizard, but it enables you to select Capture options.

- ▸ *Send Message* — This enables you to send a text message to other work-stations, using the same mechanics as the SEND command line utility.

- ▸ *User Administration for tree or server* — You can look up user account information that a user can access in NetWare Administrator. Because this utility is user-oriented, it is not necessary for users to have access to the NetWare Administrator utility. All options that the user typically has rights to access in NetWare Administrator are available from this submenu. The user can view some user properties and edit others. The following options, which are shown in Figure 10.6, are available:

  - • *Personal Information* — Allows the user to view and change some user account-related properties found under the NetWare Administrator's Identification button in Object → Details.

- *Work Information* — Allows the user to view and change other user account-related properties found under the NetWare Administrator's Identification button in Object → Details.

- *Mailing Information* — Allows the user to view and change some user account-related properties found under the NetWare Administrator's Postal Address button in Object → Details.

- *Edit Login Script* — Allows the user to view and change that user's own personal login script.

- *Login Account Information* — Allows the user to view login statistics and time restrictions.

- *Novell Password Administration* — Allows the user to change passwords and to view password restrictions.

- *Group Memberships* — Allows the user to see group memberships and security equivalences.

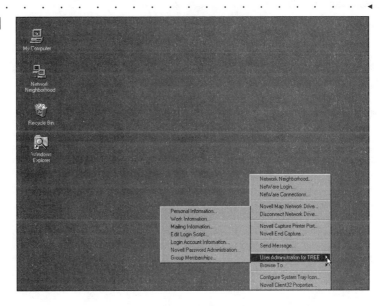

F I G U R E   1 0 . 6

The User Administration menu

▸ *Browse To* — Allows the user to go to My Computer, Network Neighborhood and to edit the browsable paths to eliminate objects from their browser.

▸ *Configure System Tray Icon* — Allows the user to configure mouse clicks and their functions when pointing at the N system tray icon.

▸ *Novell Client 32 Properties* — Enables you to adjust client, login, protocol, capture, and other client-related options. This menu selection brings up the same screens that are accessible from the Network applet in Control Panel if you were to select the Novell NetWare Client.

Novell Client 32 Properties

You can adjust the Client 32 and related properties by accessing the red N system tray icon or by selecting Control Panel's Network applet. You will find the red N in your lower right-hand corner on the taskbar. You will find the Client 32 properties in the Network applet of Control Panel, Novell NetWare Client, Properties. You will see the screens shown in Figure 10.7.

▸ · ◂

FIGURE 10.7

Novell Client 32 Properties

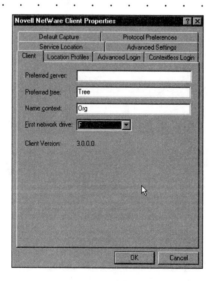

The following options can be adjusted in these screens.

▸ *Preferred Server* — This is the server that should service client attachment in a NetWare 3 or bindery-based environment.

▶ *Preferred Tree* — This is the tree that should service a client attachment in an NDS environment.

▶ *Name Context* — This is the NDS container in which the user account object is located.

▶ *First Network Drive* — This is the drive letter that should be assigned to the initial network attachment. This drive letter must not conflict with a local drive letter.

Location Profiles

Location profiles are used to set different settings for Client 32 depending upon different user login names. Windows 95, 98, and NT can have multiple user profiles on the same computer. Location profiles are used to configure client options differently for different login names. For example, a notebook user may have a location profile called Desktop for logging in at work, and a login profile called Traveling for logging in by modem from a remote location. Each user account would have different desktops in Windows, and each would have different Client 32 options.

When you edit the Properties of a Location Profile, you will see the Novell Client configuration screen shown in Figure 10.8. This feature provides for the use of different login names, passwords, network attachments, login script executions, and dial-up options.

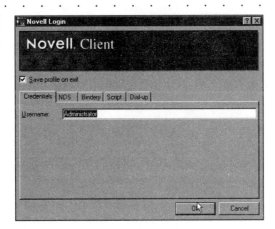

F I G U R E   10.8

Novell Client Location Profile Properties

Advanced Login

This screen enables you to show various options upon login. You can also reference different policies. You can configure your client to show just a login screen, or a login screen with up to four buttons for changing the following login options:

▸ Show Location List on Login

▸ Show Advanced Button on Login

▸ Show Variables Button on Login

▸ Show Clear Connections on Login

Contextless Login

This option enables you to log in without a default context. In order to use this feature, you must have Catalog Services installed on a NetWare 5 server that is available to the client. Catalog Services must be configured to locate and list objects in the user's context.

Service Location

This option enables you to access SLP Directory Agents and scopes. These configuration options are here to configure the client to work with CMD and SLP services running on a NetWare 5 server.

Advanced Settings

This option enables you to adjust NCP protocol settings, such as options that were set in the NET.CFG file of a DOS client. These options are quite advanced and should only be adjusted when problems occur and you know what adjustments to make.

Default Capture

This option enables you to adjust the configuration options for printing to a network printer.

Protocol Preferences

This option enables you to set priorities on which protocol is to be used, and which name resolution method should be used.

► . . . . ◄

After Installation

After installing your client software, you still have modifications to be made, and steps to be taken.

Installing Client Documentation

To install client documentation, access the Z.E.N.works Starter Pack, and execute WINSETUP.EXE in its root, or the autostart feature will execute it.

1. Select the language to be used.

2. Select Novell Client for Windows 95/98/NT.

3. Select Install Documentation as shown in Figure 10.9. A Setup Wizard will be configured to guide you through the process.

4. Select the directory in which to install your documentation files.

5. Select the language that the documentation will use. As you can see in Figure 10.10, your current space statistics are displayed. You can select the Services button to deselect portions of the documentation that you do not wish to install. The Novell Client for Windows 95/98 and NT has two documentation sections: Clients and Desktop Management Services.

The next screen verifies the destination directory and the portions of the documentation that will be installed. When you select Next, documentation files will be copied to the destination directory. A final screen for the Documentation Data File Wizard will be displayed indicating that the files were installed successfully.

▶ · ◀

FIGURE 10.9

Install client documentation

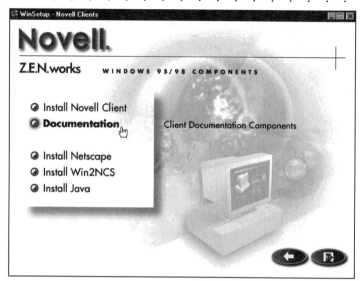

▶ · ◀

FIGURE 10.10

The Select Services screen

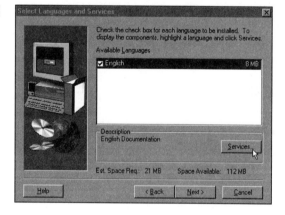

The next step starts another wizard to install the Knowledge Server. This product provides adds search and print capabilities to your documentation that would normally be performed by a Web server. If you already have Netscape Navigator 4 installed, a bookmark will be added. If you do not have Navigator 4, it will be installed.

Another wizard will be assembled to install Adobe Acrobat Reader. Some of the online documentation is in .PDF format. Acrobat enables you to see these files in their graphical form without having the software, which created them. The Acrobat Setup Wizard will simply ask you where you want the Acrobat program files to be installed.

The Knowledge Server and Netscape Navigator Wizard will confirm where the programs will be installed, and where the online documentation data files that it will read are stored.

You will see a dialog box indicating that you will need to reboot your computer before the Knowledge Server will work properly. You will then have to option to view README files for the Z.E.N.works Starter Pack documentation and terminate the wizard.

Adding/Removing Client Components

You can change your mind at any time, and Winsetup will assist you in editing your client installation. When you run Winsetup and change installation options, Winsetup will add components that you have selected and remove components that you have not selected. Each time you make changes, your client and protocols are removed, re-added, and reconfigured without your having to run through the entire setup process again. To change configuration properties, edit the Novell NetWare Client in Control Panel's Network applet.

Removing the Novell Client for Windows 95/98 and NT and Related Components

Winsetup does not provide an option to completely uninstall the Novell Client for Windows 95/98/NT. You can remove all components by removing them in the Network applet of Control Panel. The Registry entries are not eliminated when you use this method. You can delete all Registry entries by executing UNC32.EXE, found on the Z.E.N.works CD in the \PRODUCTS\WIN<version>\IBM_<language> \ADMIN directory.

Rerunning Winsetup

When you restart Winsetup, you will be asked if you would like to start a Default or Custom setup. Select Custom to edit your installation. You will next be asked to select your protocol options. A Setup Wizard will be configured according to your answers and your existing configuration.

Winsetup will enable you to install another protocol, to remove an existing protocol, to install the IP-IPX Gateway, or to remove it. You will find that the IP stack works quite well, and it may not be necessary at all to install IPX. The IP-IPX Gateway is quite effective at providing access to hosts regardless of whether they run IP or IPX.

The very same screens you encountered during setup can be accessed in Control Panel's Network applet. Just select Novell NetWare Client, Properties. Refer to previous Figure 10.4, which shows the Custom Options that can be added and removed by rerunning Winsetup.

Installing Remote System Administration

To install NetWare Administrator, create a shortcut. Look in Public\Win95 or Public\Winnt directory for NWADMIN.EXE. The first time you execute it, the NDS schema will be updated. Select Modify to agree. There are no setup program to be run and no configuration options to be decided. If you want to add NetWare Administrator to your Start menu, use Settings → Taskbar from your Start menu. If you use NetWare Administrator from a workstation often, you can drop a shortcut onto your desktop.

You will also find the Remote Console utility — NWRCON.EXE — in the same directory. You can use this utility to access your server's Remote Console. This is a 16-bit DOS application that is configured to run properly on Windows 95. When you access the Remote Console utility, ignore the dialog box indicating that the application may be unstable when running under Windows.

Troubleshooting Client Setup

When client modules fail to work properly, you have just a few avenues to pursue. The following sections deal with the most common problems that prevent Client 32 from working. These topics are generally presented in the order of the most frequent to the less frequent problems that you might encounter.

Troubleshooting Windows Network Adapter (NIC) Drivers

Network adapter driver failure is the most common reason network connectivity does not work. The adapter driver may fail due to conflicting hardware settings, the use of the wrong driver, or improper driver configuration. Windows 95, 98, and NT have good utilities to check for driver functionality, so it is relatively easy to troubleshoot driver failure.

TIP

To be sure your Microsoft adapter and protocol settings are correct, install the Microsoft Client for Microsoft Networks and/or the Client for NetWare Networks. Once you are able to browse the Network Neighborhood and see Microsoft and/or Novell resources, you are certain that the driver and protocol options are set up properly.

Windows 98 has the same network configuration screens and device management utilities as Windows 95. Windows NT Workstation version 4 and Windows NT Server version 4 share the same configuration screens and utilities but differ from Windows 95/98.

NOTE

Be sure the latest Service Pack has been applied after the network adapter driver has been loaded. Service packs often update drivers that are known to be defective.

Windows 95/98

The following steps will help you locate and resolve most resource conflicts in Windows 95 and 98 workstations.

To troubleshoot NIC driver conflicts and driver configuration problems:

1. Select Network Adapters in the Device Manager tab in the Control Panel System applet. You will see a list similar to the view shown in Figure 10.11.

2. Listed under the Network Adapter heading you will see any network adapters that are installed. Select your network adapter Properties, Resources. You will see a screen similar to Figure 10.12.

Windows 98 Device
Manager

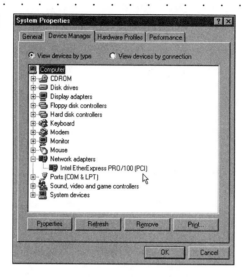

Resource Properties

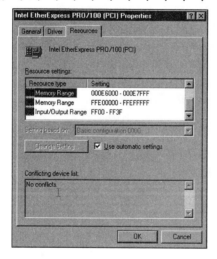

3. If a device is displayed with a yellow exclamation point, the device is not working. If you see two drivers listed for one physical device, one or both of them are not working. Remove both of them and reinstall the device again.

4. If no devices are shown under Network Adapter, look under Unknown Devices. If your NIC is listed here, it was improperly installed at one time and should be removed. When you reboot, Windows should detect new hardware and launch a wizard to help you install it. Be sure you have the latest driver available.

5. Check for resource conflicts. When you edit settings for plug-and-play adapters, the hardware settings will be updated upon reboot.

6. For assistance, select the Start → Help → Troubleshooting entry "If you have trouble using the network" or "If you have a hardware conflict." The troubleshooters will guide you through questions to help you locate and resolve the problem.

Windows NT 4

Windows NT has more conflicting resource problems than Windows 95/98. Be sure Service Pack 3 or higher is installed. If it is possible that the service pack was loaded after the network adapter was loaded, you should reapply the service pack. If a newer driver is available, install it.

TIP

Sound adapters have several hardware resource settings and often cause resource conflicts. Check Adapters → Settings in the Control Panel Multimedia applet to view resource settings. If you suspect the sound card is causing a conflict with the network adapter, remove or disable the sound card and reboot. You may need to remove and reinstall the network adapter driver. If you get the network adapter working, you may add the sound adapter again. Plug and play may then be able to configure new settings that will not conflict.

The following suggestions should help you to troubleshoot Windows NT 4 Resource Conflicts.

To troubleshoot and repair NIC driver conflicts and driver configuration problems:

1. Check NT Diagnostics to see if your driver has loaded. Select Start → Administrative Tools → Windows NT Diagnostics → Resources. If your NIC driver is listed, it is functioning. If your driver is not listed, it was unable to load.

2. Check the System Event Log. Select Start → Administrative Tools → Event Viewer → Log → System. View each entry with red stop signs since the last entry labeled " Event Log." If you find entries indicating that the network adapter driver failed to load, a specific reason may be shown, such as "due to device conflict with. . . ." The Event Log listing may show which resource and setting is conflicting. To fix the problem, resolve hardware conflicts. If the driver still fails to load, remove and reinstall the driver in the Network applet of Control Panel.

3. Remove and reinstall the NIC driver. Select Adapters in the Network applet in Control Panel. Select your NIC driver and then click Remove. Select Bindings, NIC, and protocol relationships will be updated. Select Adapters → Add. Select your NIC from the list, or select Have Disk to load the latest driver from floppy disk or other location. Select Protocols → TCP/IP and then select the down arrow to the right of the network adapter box, select the NIC, and reconfigure the settings. When finished, select OK. You will be prompted to reboot.

You will find that it is more difficult to resolve hardware conflicts with Windows NT 4 than it is with Windows 95/98. Windows NT 4 is not fully plug-and-play compatible — it can read a plug-and-play device configuration, but if you change settings in Control Panel the device hardware settings may not be updated. To resolve hardware conflicts, you should refer to the plug-and-play settings in your BIOS setup. You may be able to manipulate conflicting resource assignments, causing the NIC plug-and-play resource assignments to change. As a last resort, you may need to boot to DOS and then run the DOS plug-and-play configuration utility. This will enable you to update plug-and-play adapters with nonconflicting settings. When you reboot, Windows NT will autodetect the new settings and should load the drivers. In some cases, you may need to remove and reinstall the drivers.

When you remove a network adapter, you may need to reinstall protocols and client modules after adding the new network adapter driver.

NOTE

Troubleshooting TCP/IP Protocol Configuration

Very often failure to connect is due to improper TCP/IP protocol configuration. See Chapter 4, "TCP/IP Protocols, IP Addressing, and Name Resolution," for basics on configuring TCP/IP.

Use the following troubleshooting steps to check your TCP/IP protocol configuration in Control Panel.

To troubleshoot IP addressing issues:

1. Check the IP address assignment for errors.

2. Check the mask for invalid subnet numbers. Refer to Appendix C, "Protocol Reference Guide," for invalid subnet mask tables.

3. Check the Default Gateway setting. The address entered here should be the IP address of the router port connected to your network segment. See your router configuration to determine the correct address.

Troubleshooting IPX/SPX-Compatible Protocol Configurations

When communicating over IPX, your Windows client settings may not be configured properly.

To check your IPX settings in Control Panel:

1. Select your IPX protocol properties in Control Panel's Network applet.

2. Be sure the correct frame type has been entered. If the Autodetect Frame Type radio button is selected, select Manual instead and manually enter the frame type and network address for each frame type.

3. Check the network address for each frame type. This address points to the logical network (typically the network segment) to which this NIC is connected. See Chapter 3, "Novell Protocols and IPX Addressing," if you are uncertain about the value that should be entered here.

NOTE The Internal IPX network address field is only relevant if a Windows shared resource is shared over IPX. When a Windows workstation shares a resource over IPX, this address must not conflict with any other internal or external network address.

Reinstalling Client 32

If your client installation fails to get you connected to a tree or server, check all the configuration options discussed in this section. If the troubleshooting steps fail to get you connected to a tree or server, or if you resolved problems but still cannot connect, reinstall your Novell Client for Windows.

To reinstall Novell Client for Windows 95/98 or NT:

1. Uninstall Client 32. You will find the UNC32.EXE uninstall utility on your Z.E.N.works Starter Pack in the \Products\Win95\ibm_enu\Admin directory.

2. Reinstall, paying close attention to protocol options and settings.

Troubleshooting Compatibility Mode

If you are unable to connect with a pure-IP NetWare 5 server from an IPX workstation, check the following items.

1. Be sure you have configured the Novell Client for Windows 95/98 or NT to be installed with IP and IPX Compatibility (Windows 95/98) or IP Gateway (Windows NT) options enabled.

2. Refer to Chapter 11, "TCP/IP Services," for instructions on setting up the CMD on your NetWare 5 server. The only requirement to support IPX Compatibility Mode clients is that the SCMD.NLM module is loaded on the NetWare 5 server that will service the attachment to the network.

3. Check the CMD network address at the server and the workstation. The default is FFFFFFFD. This address must be the same for the server CMD (found in INETCFG) and in the Client 32 properties. Unless this number was changed in either place, they should be the same.

4. In a complex network, it may be necessary to support IPX tunneling over an IP backbone or IP tunneling over an IPX backbone. To support this feature, Compatibility Mode Migration Agent and SLP Directory Agent servers must be available to the client. See Chapter 11, "TCP/IP Services," for instructions on how to set up and configure these services. If this mode is enabled, check Client 32's Name Resolution property page to see that SLP is checked as one of the name resolution providers. For more on troubleshooting Client 32, refer to Chapter 14, "Client Connectivity."

TCP/IP Services

This chapter discusses several TCP/IP-based services that are included with NetWare 5. Some of these services are native TCP/IP-based services, while others are based on the NetWare Core Protocol (NCP). Both types of service can use the TCP/IP protocol stack for delivery. They key difference is whether a client must be a NetWare client or can access the service with a TCP/IP protocol stack without using the NetWare client software and NCP. Native TCP/IP services are available to all clients using the TCP/IP protocol, including UNIX clients.

The following services are server-based and are installed from your NetWare 5 operating system CD, either during or after server setup:

- Protocol options and configurations

- The Compatibility Mode Driver and related components

- Domain Name Service (DNS)

- Dynamic Host Configuration Protocol (DHCP)

- Monitoring and troubleshooting components

This chapter also discusses configuring and maintaining protocol options. IPX/SPX, TCP/IP, and AppleTalk protocols are based on the NIC drivers and protocol bindings/configurations. Protocol bindings and configurations are activated during the server boot procedure and maintained through configuration files on your server. These files are maintained in your AUTOEXEC.NCF file — Novell has developed applications to make protocol configuration easier. The INETCFG.NLM application is discussed in Chapter 12, "Novell Internet Access Server."

CHECKLIST

The term *service* describes application software running on a NetWare server.

The term *server* refers to the logical object in an NDS tree that represents the service (DNS servers, DHCP servers, and NetWare servers). Remember, in a directory service environment, a logical object points to a service running on a host computer.

The term *host* refers to the physical computer that hosts the service.

If you keep these definitions in mind, you will find this chapter easy to understand.

Protocol Options and Configuration

Before we explore TCP/IP services, let's look at providing services to IP and IPX clients on the network. NetWare 5 offers several protocol options at the client and similar options at the server. Protocol flexibility makes NetWare 5 easy to integrate and provides access for applications based on TCP/IP and traditional IPX protocols.

Client Options

Windows 3.*x*, 95/98, and NT workstations can connect with NetWare 5 servers using TCP/IP or IPX/SPX protocol stacks. Novell's Client 32 module can be installed with the following protocol options:

> ▶ *IP Only* — Uses TCP/IP only for network communications, cannot communicate with NetWare 3, 4, and 5 servers running IPX protocol only or NetWare/IP servers.

> ▶ *IP with IPX Compatibility Mode* — Installs IP as the only protocol to be used for network communications, converts IPX communications into IP using the Compatibility Mode (discussed in "The Compatibility Mode" section later in this chapter), and allows the client to communicate with both IP- and IPX-based servers.

When installing the Novell Client for Windows NT, the "IP Gateway" function refers to IPX Compatibility Mode.

NOTE

▶ *IP + IPX (Default)* — Installs both the TC/IP and IPX/SPX protocol stacks with direct bindings to the LAN drivers. By default, the primary protocol is IP, but this setting can be changed in Client 32's properties. Communication will be established with servers on a case-by-case basis; the client will use whichever protocol a target server responds with.

▶ *IPX Only* — Only the IPX/SPX protocol is installed, restricting communications to NetWare servers using the IPX protocol. Because the NetWare 5 server installs both the IPX/SPX and TCP/IP protocol stacks, it can communicate with any of the preceding client configurations.

NOTE
DOS clients can only be supported with either IPX or NetWare/IP. IPX Compatibility Mode is not an available option for DOS clients, and DOS clients are not able to use native IP services.

Because NetWare 3 and 4 servers require IPX/SPX communications, the client configuration determines which servers a client can communicate with.

DOS and Windows 3.1 clients can communicate with NetWare 5 servers using IPX/SPX or TCP/IP protocols. The IP-IPX Compatibility mode is not available on DOS or Windows 3.1 systems.

Server Protocol Options

Until NetWare 5, all NetWare services required the IPX protocol. However, NetWare 5 can run natively on TCP/IP without any assistance from the IPX protocol. Changing your network protocol strategy involves some consideration to providing support for existing NetWare clients and servers. The following discussion may help you decide whether you need to support IPX/SPX, TCP/IP, or both protocol stacks.

AppleTalk protocols are also supported in all current NetWare versions. If you have installed NetWare for Macintosh, you will find that protocol configuration for AppleTalk is the same as for IPX/SPX and TCP/IP.

NetWare 5 Servers

NetWare 5 servers can be installed with TCP/IP only, IPX/SPX only, or both protocol stacks in addition to AppleTalk protocols. By default, both protocols are installed. Installing both protocol stacks makes communications with all NetWare clients very simple. Some organizations prefer to support only one protocol stack on their networks, in which case the NetWare 5 Compatibility Mode is recommended.

NetWare 5 servers using the Compatibility Mode are able to communicate with both TCP/IP and IPX/SPX clients using the Compatibility Mode Driver (CMD). A NetWare 5 server must be running both the CMD and the Migration Agent (MA) to support IPX clients when only IP is installed on the server. CMD also requires Service Location Protocol (SLP).

NetWare 3 and 4 Servers

All NetWare 3 and 4 servers require IPX protocol, even when NetWare IP is installed. NetWare 3 and 4 servers use a version of NetWare Core Protocol (NCP) that can only work with IPX. NetWare IP tunnels IPX packets inside of IP packets, so reliance on the IPX protocol is still required. NetWare 5's improved NCP binds directly to TCP/IP, eliminating the need for IPX/SPX protocols on the network.

NOTE **When integrating NetWare 5 with previous versions, you should load all current server patches on your NetWare 3 and 4 servers. You will find the patches on your NetWare 5 server operating system CD, or at** www.novell.com.

Compatibility Mode

The Compatibility Mode uses IP for delivery and provides backward compatibility with applications that use IPX/SPX function calls. The Compatibility Mode can perform three functions. It allows:

▶ Clients using IPX to access pure-IP NetWare 5 servers

▶ IPX communications to be forwarded over an IP network

▶ IP communications to be forwarded over an IPX network

Supporting the Compatibility Mode

To enable IPX clients to access a pure-IP NetWare 5 server requires two components: the client Compatibility Mode Driver (CMD) and the server CMD. The client CMD is installed when the "IP with IPX Compatibility Mode" option is selected and installed on the Windows client. This option is only available when setting up the Novell Client for Windows 3.x, Windows 95/98, or Windows NT. The server Compatibility Mode is automatically enabled when the IP protocol is bound on a network interface, and IPX is not bound. When IP-only is installed on a network interface, an IPX virtual network is enabled through the server CMD.

For more information on how Compatibility Mode and SLP work, see your NetWare 5 online documentation. Select Contents → NetWare Server Documentation → Communications → Understanding Network Communications.

NOTE

Some NetWare-ready applications use IPX/SPX calls and may generate software errors when used in a pure IP environment. The Compatibility Mode was designed to provide backward compatibility for IPX/SPX applications when migrating to a pure IP NetWare 5 environment. The Compatibility Mode ensures a smooth transition by enabling various IPX/SPX communications even when the IPX/SPX protocol stack is not used on the network. Figure 11.1 shows a NetWare-based client/server application using the Compatibility Mode to convey IPX/SPX calls between client and server application software.

To support clients where IP with IPX Compatibility was installed, a CMD server that will service the client attachment must also be running the server CMD module (SCMD.NLM). If you set up a server with IP only, CMD will be set up by default. If you set up Windows clients with IP and IPX Compatibility, the default configuration should allow you to use the Compatibility Mode. If the CMD server and the CMD client are not on the same subnet, you may need a Migration Agent to use IPX over the network.

NOTE

▶ • ◀

F I G U R E   II.I

*A client/server application
using IPX calls over an IP
network*

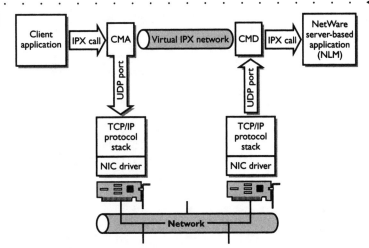

The Server CMD

The server CMD handles IPX/SPX communications from client CMDs that are received from the TCP/IP protocol stack. CMD can also process tunneled requests received from an MA. The MA's role is discussed later in this chapter in the section titled "The Migration Agent."

Migration Agents are not required to support CMD clients on the same IP subnet. Migration Agents are required to support forwarding services from one network segment to another.

NOTE

The Client CMD

The client CMD forwards IPX/SPX calls in UDP packets for delivery over the existing TCP/IP protocol stack. In doing so, the client CMD acts as a logical adapter to a virtual IPX network. At the server end, CMD is required to receive the IPX/SPX requests from the virtual IPX network.

Figure 11.2 shows a Windows NT 4 client's Network properties in Control Panel. Figure 11.2 demonstrates that the client CMD — shown as the Novell IPX Compatibility Adapter — is installed as an NIC.

F I G U R E I I . 2

The Compatibility Mode Driver installed on Windows NT 4

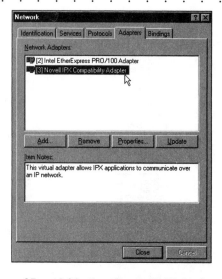

NOTE

In Windows 95 and 98, the client CMD is shown as a network adapter as the Compatibility Mode Driver. In Windows NT 4, the CMD is shown as the IPX Compatibility Mode Adapter. In either case, this module acts as a logical adapter to capture IPX packet information and forward it to UDP for delivery over IP.

Select Protocols and then Microsoft NWLink IPX/SPX Compatible Transport, and notice that the CMD is configured with an IPX network number as shown in Figure 11.3. The CMA's internal network number represents the virtual IPX network. NWLink processes the IPX/SPX function calls and then forwards them to the CMA for transmission over the Microsoft TCP/IP protocol stack.

During Winsetup on a Windows client workstation, one of the setup options — IP with IPX Compatibility Mode — installs the client CMD. When this option is chosen, Client 32 is installed with the existing Microsoft TCP/IP, NWLink, and CMD. IPX/SPX calls are directed to NWLink, which forwards them to the CMA for transport over the TCP/IP stack. CMA is installed as a 32-bit Windows DLL — its impact on local processing is negligible.

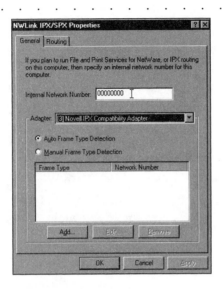

FIGURE 11.3

The CMD and internal IPX network number

The CMD IPX Network Number

The Compatibility Mode private IPX network must be assigned an IPX network number. This network number represents a virtual network when the forwarding feature is used. When the CMD is set up in your server's protocol configuration, the default number is FFFFFFFD (hex). This number can be changed if it conflicts with any NetWare server internal network numbers or network numbers assigned to IPX network segments. However, you should not change this number unless necessary, as it is the default for each client and server CMD. If you change this number, you must also change all other client and server CMD numbers.

NOTE

Do not confuse the CMD network number with the IPX internal network number. When setting up clients with the CMD, the internal network number previously shown in Figure 11.3 is used only for sharing Microsoft resources over IPX. It is not the same network number as the CMD. The internal network number must have a unique IPX network number only when Microsoft file and print sharing is enabled.

Supporting Tunneling

When forwarding is necessary, the Compatibility Mode requires the services of one or more Migration Agents. Forwarding allows larger internetworks to maintain compatibility without reconfiguring existing networks. This feature is intended to make migration from IPX to IP smoother and simpler. For example, forwarding can connect several IPX network segments over an IP backbone network.

Forwarding depends upon the Migration Agent (MA) and Service Location Protocol (SLP) Directory Agent services. These two services must be running on a NetWare 5 server accessible to Compatibility Mode clients and servers. These services are not set up by default and must be enabled manually. The MA is loaded by loading SCMD.NLM with a /g (gateway) switch. The SLP Directory Agent (SLPDA.NLM) must also be loaded.

The Migration Agent

The Migration Agent (MA) provides flexibility in using existing IPX network segments to handle IP traffic and using IP network segments to handle IPX traffic. The MA provides IPX transport over IP networks and IP transport over IPX networks. The MA also allows IPX clients to access IP servers and IP clients to access IPX servers through the CMD. It uses the CMD and the server's internal router to route packets to and from IPX and IP networks.

NetWare 5 servers installed with the MA enabled are capable of communicating directly with other NetWare 3, 4, and 5 servers running any protocol option, and they can communicate directly with clients running any protocol option. They are also capable of routing network traffic between IP and IPX systems.

MA encapsulates (tunnels) IPX/SPX packets into UDP/IP packets for delivery over an IP network. MA also encapsulates IP packets into IPX packets for delivery over an IP network. Figure 11.4 shows two IPX networks joined by an IP network backbone, and two IP networks joined by an IPX network backbone.

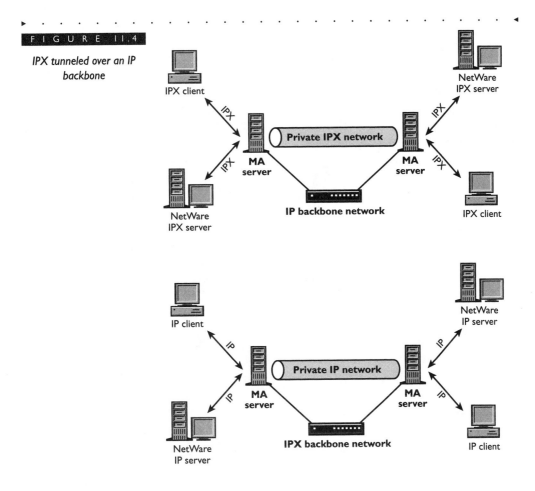

FIGURE 11.4

IPX tunneled over an IP backbone

MAs create a private virtual IPX network between themselves. Packets are wrapped, tunneled through the private virtual network, and forwarded from the local IPX network segment to the IPX destination network, where another MA receives and unwraps or forwards the packets. In the destination network, a NetWare 5 server with the CMD or another MA must be present to receive the tunneled communications. When two separate networks using the same protocol are separated by a network backbone using a different protocol, MAs are required on the origination and destination networks, as demonstrated previously in Figure 11.4. When an IPX client attempts to communicate with a pure-IP server on a different network segment, an MA must be available on the local network segment, and the CMD driver on the IP network interface can receive tunneled communications as shown in Figure 11.5.

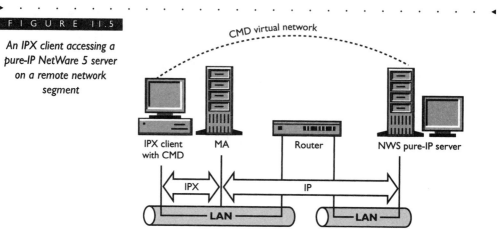

FIGURE 11.5

An IPX client accessing a
pure-IP NetWare 5 server
on a remote network
segment

The CMD and the Migration Agent can be configured during server setup, or manually. In either case, the commands loading SCMD.EXE (for CMD only) or SCMD.EXE /g (CMD with Migration Agent) are added to the AUTOEXEC.BAT.

Installing the MA

The MA is set up one of two ways: during server operating system installation, or manually after installation.

During the graphical portion of your NetWare 5 server installation you must:

1. Bind both the IP and IPX protocols to the same NIC and driver. This is configured in the Protocols screen shown in Figure 11.6. See Chapter 8, "NetWare 5 Setup," Step 7, "Select and Configure Networking Protocols."

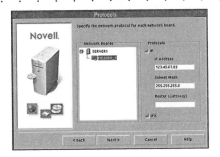

FIGURE 11.6

*Selecting networking
protocols*

2. Select the Migration Agent check box in the Compatibility Mode screen.
This option is configured in the Product Customization screen shown in
Figure 11.7. Select Protocols → Compatibility Mode. See Chapter 8,
"NetWare 5 Setup," Step 12.

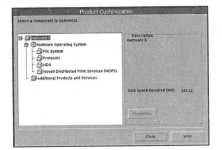

FIGURE 11.7

*Product Customization
screen*

To install the MA manually:

1. Bind both the IP and IPX protocols to a NIC driver. Load INETCFG →
Bindings. View which protocols are bound. Select and configure the
protocol that is not bound. Both IPX and IP protocols must be selected and
configured correctly according to your network configuration.

2. Edit or add the command **load SCMD /g** to your AUTOEXEC.NCF. You
can use INETCFG.NLM, NWCONFIG.NLM, or the EDIT.NLM utility.

3. At the server console type **load SLPDA.NLM**. If this module has not been loaded before, the SLP setup will run, creating and configuring required NDS objects. Add this statement to your AUTOEXEC.NCF.

Service Location Protocol

In a pure IP environment, Service Location Protocol (SLP) replaces Service Advertising Protocol (SAP). SLP is therefore necessary to substitute for SAP in a pure IP environment. Chapter 3, "Novell Protocols and IPX Addressing," goes into detail about SAP's role in NetWare SLP registers services that are available on the network, for example, print servers, print brokers, file servers, and remote access services.

Three types of SLP agents are used in discovering resources.

1. Service agents (server services—NLMs—to be registered) running on a NetWare 5 host.

2. Directory agents register the presence, services, and locations of service agents within the same IP subnet.

3. User agents search for network services (service agents) by contacting the directory agent on the local subnet. User agents are embedded in Client 32.

NDS's Role in SLP   Because SLP Directory agents only acquire information about local SLP Service agents, a few NDS objects are required to propagate SLP service information throughout the entire internetwork.

1. The SLP Directory Agent object represents each SLPDA.NLM service that is running. The SLPDA service receives broadcasts on the local subnet from server-based services (NLMs) as they are loaded. Each SLPDA reports SLP Service agent information to the SLP Directory Agent object.

2. The SLP Scope Container object collects and imports data from SLP Directory Agents. This allows SLP data to be available throughout the entire internetwork. The SLP Scope Container makes server services available to all User agents within the NDS partition. SLP Scope Container objects can be replicated to other partitions or trees to make services available outside of the local NDS partition.

3. An SLP Service object is created for each service registered. When a service is loaded, an SLP Service object is created to represent the service. The User agent gains access and finds the location of the service through access to the Scope Container object.

4. NCP Server objects are created for each NetWare 5 server. Each SLP Service object is located on a NetWare 5 server. The NCP Server object is used to locate the distinguished name of the server on which the registered service is running.

How to Set up the SLP Directory Agent and NDS Objects   When you load the SLPDA.NLM on a server for the first time, the required NDS objects are automatically created. An SLP Directory Agent object is created to represent the SLPDA service that is being loaded. If no SLP Scope Container object exists within the local partition, one will be created.

Setting Up and Configuring the Compatibility Mode for Tunneling

The Compatibility Mode can also support IP forwarding over IPX backbones and IPX forwarding over IP. This functionality requires the addition of the CMD MA with the /bs option, which in turn requires the SLPDA service.

To support the MA forwarding option, load SCMD with the /bs (backbone support) switch. You must have an MA with the /bs option loaded on the source and destination network segments to serve as gateways to the private IPX virtual network.

Table 11.1 shows the components required to make CMD and the MA's work properly.

TABLE 11.1	SERVICE/APPLICATION	DESCRIPTION
Required Components of CMD and MA	SCMD.NLM /g	CMD with the gateway option (the Migration Agent)
	SCMD.NLM /bs	CMD with backbone support (for tunneling)
	SLPDA.NLM	SLP Directory agent

Table 11.2 shows the objects that are created when SLPDA is first loaded on the host server.

TABLE 11.2	NDS OBJECT	NDS LOCATION
NDS Objects Created for SLP	SLP Directory Agent (SLPDA) server object	Same container as replica server (host server)
	SLP container	Same container with the host server object and the SLPDA
	SLP scope	In SLP container

If you study Figure 11.8, you can see the NDS objects that are created for SLP.

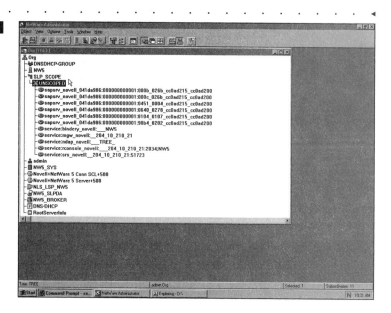

The default SLP Scope objects and properties

To make the MA backbone services available, you must load two modules. Required NDS objects will be created the first time the modules are loaded:

1. Log in as Admin or with Supervisory rights to the container that contains the host server where SLPDA, MA, and CMD are to be loaded. This server must be a replica server.

2. Load SLPDA.NLM from the server console prompt. If SLPDA has not been set up, loading will pause to ask if you would like to create the default configuration.

NOTE

Step 2 is very important. You must create the NDS objects for the SLPDA by loading SLPDA on a replica server. When you load SLPDA.NLM, answer Yes the query about creating the default configuration. Notice in Figure 11.8 that a scope is created with complex properties that it would be very difficult to create manually.

3. Answer Yes to create a default configuration. This step automatically creates the required NDS objects in a default configuration.

4. From a workstation, log in as the tree Administrator (or with supervisory rights to the container that holds the master replica and MA).

5. Run NetWare Administrator.

6. Load SCMD.NLM with the /G (gateway) option. This sets the server into gateway mode. The default IPX network number for the private IPX network is FFFFFFFD and can be changed with the /net=*network_address* option.

7. Add the following commands to the end of your AUTOEXEC.NCF file:

```
load SLPDA
load SCMD /g /bs /net=network_address
```

Enable IPX tunneling through IP. Load INETCFG, and then select Protocols →
IPX → IPX Protocol Configuration. In this screen,

Enable Tunnel IPX through IP

Enable Address Mapping Gateway

Under Address Mapping Gateway Configuration enter the Address Mapping
Network Number as FFFFFFFD (default) or enter the address assigned
to the CMD in step 6.

The CMD, MA, and SLP functions are now available to all network segments
where the private IPX network number has been assigned.

NetWare DNS/DHCP Services

NetWare 5's DNS and DHCP services are installed as one set of server-based
applications. This section discusses implementing the DNS/DHCP Service that is
included with your NetWare 5 distribution CD.

If you have not installed the DNS/DHCP Service during installation, you will
need to install it at this time. To set up and manage this service, Novell has built
a Windows-based remote management application — you will also need to install
the DNS/DHCP Management Console.

You will find that there are a few surprises in NetWare 5's DNS/DHCP. Using a
directory service platform adds new functionality to these age-old services.
Novell's DNS/DHCP handles services that are not available in most other DNS
server products. It also scales up well on very large intranets — it is designed to
handle very large systems with far more flexibility than traditional DNS systems.

Because DNS and DHCP are combined into one service, this section is
organized as follows:

▸ Installing the DNS/DHCP Service

▸ Installing the DNS/DHCP Management Console

Installing the DNS/DHCP Service

DNS/DHCP Services can be installed during the NetWare 5 Additional Products and Services phase of server installation, or they can be installed manually after installation. In either case, a few NDS objects must be created and the appropriate NDS trustee rights must be granted to make these services available throughout the tree. If you elected to add DNS/DHCP Services during installation, the required NDS objects were created.

Installing the DNS/DHCP Service during NetWare 5 Server Setup

During installation, you were asked to select Additional Products and Services. Among them was a check box for Novell DNS/DHCP Services. If you added the DNS/DHCP Service during installation, the service was installed and the DNS/DHCP Locator, Group, and RootServerInfo objects were created. You may proceed to the later section titled "Installing the DNS/DCHP Management Console."

Installing the DNS/DHCP Service after NetWare 5 Server Setup

If you did not install this service during installation, you will need to run the DNIPINST.NLM module on a host server. To add the DNS/DHCP Services after installation:

1. Switch to your NetWare 5 server's console screen (with the colon prompt).

2. Type the command

   ```
   load DNIPINST
   ```

3. Follow the on-screen instructions. You will need to log into NDS with Administrator rights in the container in which the DNS/DHCP Locator, DNS-DHCP Group, and RootServerInfo objects are to be created. You should create these objects in the same context as your master NDS replica server.

In a larger network, you may want to organize the DNS/DHCP objects in a separate container such as a resource container or one designated for DNS/DHCP use only. If you do so, place a master replica in this container — you may even wish to partition it. For instructions on replication and partitioning, see Chapter 18, "NDS Infrastructure and Repair."

TIP

Reinstalling the DNS/DHCP Service after NetWare 5 Server Setup

You may need to reinstall the DNS/DHCP Service if you did not configure this service during server installation, or if the NDS object creation process was aborted when DNIPINST was run. If the required objects already exist, the object creation part of the program will fail and terminate the procedure. To resolve the problem:

1. Delete the following objects in NetWare Administrator or Console One utilities: Locator, DNS-DHCP Group, and RootServerInfo.

2. Load DNIPINST with the -F switch to fix (repair) the setup as follows:

```
load DNIPINST -F
```

If you receive an message indicating a schema extension error, execute DNIPINST.NLM in the regular mode (without the -F switch). This error indicates that the schema may have already been extended.

3. Install and execute the DNS/SHCP Management Console utility on a Windows 95, 98, or NT workstation. Set up and configure the DNS server as discussed in "Setting Up DNS Servers and Resource Records" later in this chapter.

4. Next load the DNS server module. At the server console, enter

```
load NAMED
```

You should always unload NAMED.NLM before making major changes to the DNS server configuration and then reload it when finished. Adding, deleting, and changing resource records is okay, but changes to server configuration must be updated offline.

Installing the DNS/DHCP Management Console

The DNS/DHCP Management Console utility is the client software application used to set up and manage DNS and DHCP server services. You can run this application from any workstation to manage DNS servers throughout your NDS tree.

When you install the DNS/DHCP Management Console, menu selections will be installed to your Windows Start menu, and as a snap-in on the Tools menu of the NetWare Administrator utility. To install this utility, you must install the NetWare Administrator if you have not already done so. You will also need to locate the NetWare Administrator's executable file.

The DNS/DHCP Management Console utility is designed for a Windows 95, 98, or NT workstation with 1024 × 768 resolution. If you use any lower resolution, you will have to scroll to see buttons and portions of the screen. This application will not run on a Windows 3.x system, and there is no DOS or server equivalent.

You can only run this utility under TCP/IP — it will not run under IPX. The management workstation will therefore need to have the TCP/IP protocol set up and working properly, and the user must log into the NDS tree with the appropriate NDS rights as discussed in the text that follows.

You must have the appropriate NDS rights to create and manage the DNS-DHCP Locator object in the NDS tree. The Locator object should be created in the same container as the server that will host the DNS/DHCP services.

The DNS-DHCP Locator, Group, and RootServerInfo zone objects are created when the DNS/DHCP Management Console is run for the first time. These objects should be placed in the same container as the server that is to host the DNS/DHCP service. Installing these objects in the correct context provides the appropriate NDS rights to properly run these services.

Table 11.3 shows the NDS object and property rights required for installing, configuring, and viewing the DNS and DHCP services and related functions.

T A B L E I I . 3		
NDS Rights Required for DNS/DHCP Use		
DNS/DHCP OBJECTS	OBJECT RIGHTS	ALL PROPERTY RIGHTS
FOR ADDING DNS/DHCP-RELATED OBJECTS:		
Locator object	Browse	Supervisor
Group object	Browse	Supervisor
Host server/container	Supervisor	Supervisor
TO MANAGE DHCP SERVICES, SUBNETS, DNS ZONES, AND RESOURCE RECORDS:		
Locator object	Browse	Read
Group object	Browse	Read
Host server/container	Browse, Create, Delete	Supervisor
TO VIEW DNS/DHCP SERVICE CONFIGURATION:		
Locator object	Browse	Read
Group object	Browse	Read
Host server/container	Browse	Read

One utility is used to manage both the DNS and the DHCP services. To install the DNS/DHCP Management Utility:

1. Execute the SETUP.EXE utility in SYS:\public\dnsdhcp\Setup.exe.

2. When the Setup Wizard asks, check the box to Copy the Snap-in Files.

3. When asked, enter the path of the executable file for the NetWare Administrator utility. By default its location is SYS:\public\win32\nwadmin.exe.

You can execute the DNS/DHCP Management Console one of three ways:

► By selecting DNS/DHCP from your Start menu

▶ By selecting DNS/DHCP from the Tools menu in the 32-bit version of NetWare Administrator (NWADMIN32.EXE)

▶ From a shortcut that you copy to your desktop

NetWare 5 DNS

DNS in NetWare 5 conforms to Internet RFC standards. However, NetWare 5's DNS differs from a traditional DNS environment in having added features. DNS is grafted into the NDS schema to integrate this service into a robust directory service environment. Without compromising conformity to standards, NetWare 5's DNS:

▶ *Uses a remote console* — DNS configuration and resources records can be managed from any Windows 95, 98, or NT workstation using a remote Java utility.

▶ *Replicates data through NDS* — no secondary DNS servers are required for this purpose.

▶ *Is secure* — Server console access is controlled by NDS login security and rights.

▶ *Can be organized logically instead of physically* — Physical infrastructure can be based on logical Zones of Authority rather than using a direct correlation to domain structure.

DNS is integrated and replicated within NDS. NDS objects are created to provide the link between DNS and DHCP services, physical servers, and clients. Resource records are stored as properties of the DNS server in the NDS database. The DNS schema can be completely logical with less reliance on the physical infrastructure of your DNS domain tree. This design allows remote access to the DNS server from any workstation, and access is controlled by NDS. DNS integration into NDS also requires creation of a few NDS objects.

This section discusses:

- ▸ DNS basics

- ▸ DNS hierarchy

- ▸ DNS replication

- ▸ Resource records

- ▸ Domains versus zones of authority

- ▸ Zone mechanics

- ▸ Remote DNS management

- ▸ NDS considerations

- ▸ Setting up DNS servers and resource records

For more discussion of DNS structure and basics, refer to Chapter 18, "NDS Infrastructure and Repair."

TIP   **If you are experienced with DNS setup and configuration, you can skip this section on DNS basics. However, configuring a DNS system in an NDS environment has a few twists that all readers should review. If you have not dealt with Zones of Authority, you should refer to the section "Zones of Authority" later in this chapter.**

DNS Basics

Domain Name Service (DNS) provides name-to-address resolution. When for instance a server or a printer must be located, the host name is used. For example, when you open a URL in your Web browser or send an e-mail message, the host name is referenced. DNS provides the translation from the host name to the IP address that is used to deliver your requests. DNS is always used to locate mail destinations.

Name resolution is not a problem in a NetWare environment because NetWare does not need DNS to find servers and resources within NDS — server and other object names and their corresponding addresses are stored in servers' binderies or NDS databases. Outside of handling the NDS rights, nothing needs to be added from your basic installation to allow clients to find servers and resources within your NDS tree. However, when accessing a TCP/IP host computer that is not within NDS, DNS is used to locate the TCP/IP resources.

The DNS Hierarchy

In larger intranets a domain is subdivided into subdomains. For example, the fictitious domain xyz-corp.com can be divided into subdomains:

```
sales.xyz-corp.com

corp.xyz-corp.com

service.xyz-corp.com
```

In very large organizations, subdomains may be divided into more levels beneath the root. For example, sales.xyzcorp.com might be further divided into the subdomains:

```
neast.sales.xyz-corp.com

south.sales.xyz-corp.com

west.sales.xyz-corp.com

mwest.sales.xyz-corp.com
```

Generally, domains are subdivided because the subdomains represent geographically disparate locations, and perhaps each domain is managed by a different support group. Normally one level beneath the top domain level is sufficient. Another, probably more efficient way to subdivide the preceding example would be as follows:

```
corp.xyz-corp.com

service.xyz-corp.com

neastsales.xyz-corp.com

southsales.xyz-corp.com

westsales.xyz-corp.com

mwestsales.xyz-corp.com
```

As you can see, a DNS hierarchy allows subdivision into many domains in both width and depth to suite the unique needs of small, large, and very large organizations.

DNS Replication

In a traditional DNS environment, changes can only be made at the primary DNS server, and periodically secondary DNS servers request updates. The primary servers are masters, and the secondary servers are slaves — the process of replicating to the secondary DNS server, called a *zone transfer,* consists of copying the entire DNS database from the primary to the secondary. The slave-master relationship has several disadvantages, notably that all changes must be made at single physical location — the primary DNS server. Another potential problem is the amount of traffic that is generated for a zone transfer. When primary and secondary DNS servers are separated by a WAN — which is most often the case — the amount of traffic can consume a large percentage of the WAN's bandwidth on a periodic basis. NetWare 5's DNS reduces bandwidth consumption by sending only the changes using the NDS replication process, which is far more efficient than a normal zone transfer.

If the NDS physical infrastructure is properly designed, NDS automatically balances DNS loads and provides fault tolerance among NDS replica servers without the need for secondary DNS servers. DNS structure should closely parallel the NDS structure, relying on replicas to distribute, replicate, and partition the network.

NOTE

DNS will only be as stable as your NDS replication. NDS replication is automatically configured when the first three servers are installed into a tree. If you have removed any servers that contained NDS replicas, your NDS replication may not be configured satisfactorily. Before installing DNS/DHCP Services, you should review your tree and partitioning status in NDS Manager to be sure that NDS replication is configured appropriately.

In a NetWare 5 internetwork that does not contain any WANs, only one primary DNS server is necessary for an entire tree. When a portion of the tree is remote (separated by a WAN), the remote network should have its own NDS partition and also should have its own DNS zone.

Resource Records

A DNS server provides name-to-IP-address lookups. The records that hold this data are called *resource records*. Resource records are added to the DNS server's database along with DNS server and zone configuration data. There are several types of resource records, all of which consist of at least a DNS name and an IP address. These records are referenced by DNS clients for name resolution. There are several types of resource records, including those shown in Table 11.4.

RECORD TYPE	DESCRIPTION
A	Normal host pointer record consisting of the host name, IP v4 address, NDS context, comments
AAAA	Defines an IP v6 address record
AFSDB	Subtype and host name fields
CNAME	Alias name for host
HINFO	CPU and OS
ISDN	ISDN address and subaddress
MB	Mailbox name
MG	Mail group member name
MINFO	Responsible and error message mailboxes
MR	Mail rename mailbox
MX	Reference and exchange information
NS	DNS server domain name
PTR	Domain name
PX	Preference — domain names in Map 822, and x.400 addressing formats
RP	Responsible person's mailbox and TXT RR name
RT	Preference and Intermediate information
SRV	Service, proto, priority, weight, port, and target information
TXT	Comments and text in multiple strings
WKS	Protocol and bit map information
X25	PSDN/VAN address

TABLE 11.4
Resource Record Types

NOTE   You will find this table of NetWare 5 DNS resource record types on
the CD that accompanies this book in the Protocol Reference Guide,
and in Appendix C, "Protocol Reference Guide."

Zones of Authority

In NetWare 5, DNS domain structure is managed by *Zones of Authority*. A Zone
of Authority is a logical grouping of domains and subdomains for which an
organization has administrative authority. NetWare 5's DNS uses these logical
zones instead of domains as the basis of its physical infrastructure. In many DNS
systems, each domain and subdomain has its own primary and a secondary DNS
server as shown in Figure 11.9. Each secondary DNS server has a read-only replica
of the primary's database. If the intranet is large enough, each physical location
will have its own DNS domain and will be administered separately.

▶ · ◀

FIGURE 11.9

Traditional DNS

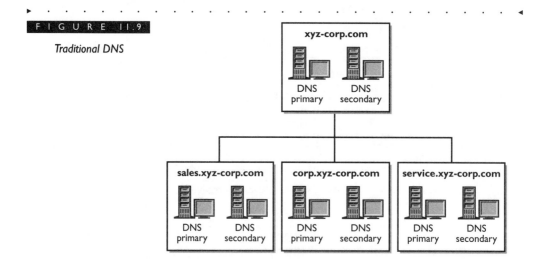

When using Zones of Authority, physical constraints are removed—each
domain does not need to have its own primary DNS server. Zones of Authority are
established in each geographical location and can be administered separately,
while domains within each zone can be organized logically with less consideration
of geographical locale. Figure 11.10 illustrates a NetWare 5 DNS system where
each zone represents a separate geographical location.

FIGURE II.I0

NetWare 5 Zones of
Authority and domains

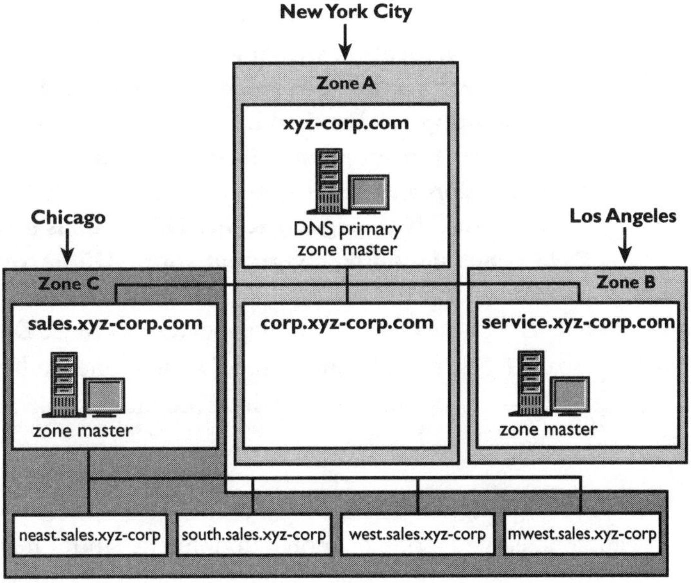

As you can see by comparing Figures 11.9 and 11.10, DNS configuration can be constructed with better logic and efficiency when using Zones of Authority. More important, domain naming can reflect an organization's logical structure, whereas zones are established to handle geographic considerations. Each geographic location — New York City, Chicago, and Los Angeles — can have a separate zone, and each can be administered separately. The NetWare 5 DNS system illustrated in Figure 11.10 requires only three DNS servers, one for each zone. To accomplish equivalent functionality in a traditional DNS environment would require four primary DNS servers — one for each domain — and should have four secondary DNS servers — for a total of eight DNS servers. The NetWare DNS servers logical servers and should be hosted on the NDS replica servers, to reduce the number of required DNS servers. The traditional DNS system would have more complexity than the zoned DNS system. You can see from this illustration that NetWare 5 DNS can reduce the number of required servers, complexity, and associated administrative costs.

NOTE

In an NDS environment, only one DNS server is required for an entire tree. At least one NDS replica server is created for each geographical location within a tree. Because the DNS configuration and resource records are stored in the NDS database, replication and load balancing are handled by NDS. Each zone should have its own DNS server, but more than likely, each zone also has a separate NDS tree partition and replica server which should host the DNS server for that zone. If an organization's NDS tree is properly configured, DNS zones should be congruent with NDS partitions.

NDS data is replicated to NDS replica servers. Because DNS data is stored in the NDS database DNS, replication, load balancing, and fault tolerance are handled through NDS — it is not necessary to have secondary DNS servers to provide these services.

Zone Mechanics

Each zone contains one or more subdomains, and a master zone contains the top-level domain. As discussed previously, zones of authority are used to divide larger DNS databases into more efficient portions, which are easier to manage and maintain than a single, large DNS database.

One or more domains/subdomains are placed into each zone. A single DNS server can manage one or more than one zone, but each zone must be assigned to only one DNS server. DNS zones of authority are typically established geographically on the same basis as NDS partitions — each zone is typically separated from the rest of the intranet by a WAN.

Primary and Secondary DNS Servers and Zone Masters

In a traditional DNS environment, each domain generally has a primary and a secondary DNS server. The primary DNS server holds all the records for a domain, and a secondary is a read-only replicated copy that is provided for fault tolerance and better performance. This configuration ensures that a DNS server is always available and DNS requests are handled expeditiously. Because NDS replicates DNS data, it is normally not necessary to have secondary DNS servers for this purpose.

Secondary DNS servers are used in NetWare 5 to link zones together — not for load balancing or fault tolerant reasons. A secondary DNS server imports foreign or parent DNS records into a domain. A DNS server in a parent domain is configured as a primary, and a DNS server in a child domain is configured as secondary. The secondary DNS server periodically requests updates, and the primary transfers records to the secondary.

In a NetWare 5 DNS zone, a Zone Master is the primary DNS server for the zone. The Zone Master is configured as the primary DNS server for the zone. Because the Zone Master configuration and records are replicated to other NDS replica servers along with other NDS data, no secondary is required for fault tolerance or to improve performance. A child zone can be linked by configuring the Zone Master of the child zone as a secondary DNS server to the Zone Master of the parent zone. In this manner, zones import and export data.

Organizing Zones of Authority

Domains are established on the basis of many considerations. Each domain is accompanied by substantial hardware and administrative costs and therefore usually constitutes a large grouping of hosts. Designing a domain hierarchy constitutes a balancing act between geographic, organizational, and size considerations. Establishing Zones of Authority mitigates these costs substantially. Existing NDS replica servers are used to host DNS servers, no secondary DNS servers are required, and a single administrator can manage an entire zone remotely, regardless of how many domains the zone contains.

Zones provide a mechanism for managing DNS along geographical divisions, while domains can be structured according to the organizational needs. For example, an organization located in LA and NYC may wish to structure its domains according to function, such as sales, marketing, and manufacturing. It can establish domains according to sales, marketing, and manufacturing while establishing and administering DNS in LA and NYC zones.

Each zone can have one or more than one Zone Master. However, only one Zone Master can be configured as the primary DNS server for the zone. The other Zone Masters must be secondaries to that primary. This configuration provides support for zones that are geographically distributed. If you were create a single zone with WAN links between locations, you would want to have a Zone Master in each location, with a parent location configured as the primary DNS server and the remote locations configured as secondaries. Only the primary can do "zone in" transfers from foreign domains.

Authoritative DNS Server

Each zone must have a primary DNS server that is designated as an Authoritative DNS Server. A DNS server is a logical server, which is hosted on a physical server. The DNS service is the DNS software that is running on the NetWare server. An Authoritative DNS Server is the NetWare server that hosts the DNS service for a zone. In NDS, all network resources are logical objects, so the Authoritative DNS Server is actually the NDS server object that represents the NetWare server on which the DNS server service is running. One NetWare server must be assigned as the Authoritative DNS Server for each zone. Other DNS servers in a zone can be assigned as Authoritative DNS Servers but are not necessary. When more than one Zone Master is in a zone, one is configured as a primary DNS server, and the others are configured as secondary DNS servers referenced to the primary Zone Master.

When selecting an Authoritative DNS Server in the DNS/DHCP Management Console utility, you will see a listing of primary DNS servers from which to choose. The first primary DNS server in the NetWare 5–based intranet should reside on the NDS master replica server. Zone Masters should also be placed on a NDS replica servers.

Remote DNS Management

Another difference between traditional DNS and NetWare 5's DNS is management. In a traditional DNS environment, the DNS server must be managed locally—the administrator must log in locally to the host computer that is running the DNS service (daemon) to configure the DNS server. Resource records can only be added at the primary DNS server because the secondary servers are read-only. In NetWare 5, administrators can manage DNS servers from any 32-bit Windows client workstation within the NDS tree. Remote management is made possible by the NDS objects that were added to place the NDS servers into NDS and the NetWare 5 Java interface. Because DNS is managed under NDS, security is controlled through NDS rights and organization regardless of where the administrator physically resides.

Novell's DNS server enables remote management through the Java-based client utility, the DNS/DHCP Management Console. DNS changes and updates can be done from anywhere on the network, even over a modem link, and access is secured through NDS. Weaning DNS management off a main server console provides more flexibility, and better control.

NDS Considerations

As discussed previously, NetWare 5's DNS/DHCP relies on NDS for replication and load balancing. But it also uses NDS to distribute DNS services throughout an NDS tree. This design enables administrators to utilize the same physical infrastructure in place for their NDS tree to manage and replicate DNS and DHCP. Three NDS objects are to be used by the DNS/DHCP services:

▸ DNS/DHCP Locator object

▸ DNS/DHCP Group object

▸ RootServerInfo Zone

In most systems, managing DNS and DHCP servers requires physical access to the DNS and DHCP servers. However, the Novell DNS and DHCP servers are managed remotely — from client workstations — and access is controlled through NDS. These three objects provide a link between the physical network/internetwork and the NDS tree and control remote access to DNS/DHCP services and resources.

Each of these objects must exist in your NDS tree, and the DNS server, the DHCP server, and the DNS/DHCP Management Console must have access to them to effectively manage these services.

The DNS/DHCP Group object provides access to the DNS and DHCP servers. The DNS/DHCP Management Console is a member of the DNS/DHCP Group object and therefore has the ability to manage the DNS and DHCP servers.

These two services rely on the Locator object in the NDS tree to control DNS processing. The context for the Locator object, Group object, and RootSrvrInfo Zone was specified during installation. These objects should have been installed into the same container as the NetWare server object that was being installed. Without the Locator object you will not be able to configure the DNS or DHCP services.

Setting Up DNS Servers and Resource Records

DNS servers and resource records are set up and configured in the DNS/DHCP Management Console utility. You can run this utility and manage the DNS server from anywhere on your network. The following instructions are divided into simple (single zone) and more complex (multiple zone) configurations.

Setting Up a Basic DNS System with a Single Zone

Most intranets only require one zone. As discussed previously, a zone is a logical object which can include one or multiple DNS domains. If your tree is wholly located in a single physical location — no WANS separate portions of your tree — create a single zone. If there are more than 1,000 hosts in the zone, you might consider creating additional zones for performance reasons.

A single-zone system requires a one primary DNS server. The primary DNS server will be the Zone Master for the zone. No secondary DNS servers are required for a single zone.

In the steps that follow, the example names shown in Table 11.5 will be used.

T A B L E 11.5	OBJECT	OBJECT NAME
Example Names	NetWare 5 NDS master replica server	NW5G.org
	DNS primary server name	DNS_NW5G
	NDS container	org (O=org, Tree = tree)
	Private domain name	pvt-dom
	Primary zone name	zone-corp

The steps for creating a single-zone DNS system are as follows:

1. Create the primary DNS server in the organization.

2. Create the primary zone.

3. Create the pointer record for the host server.

4. Create the IN-ADDR.ARPA zone.

5. Start the DNS server.

6. Configure clients to use the DNS server.

7. Enter resource records (pointer records) for host computers.

NOTE

When using the DNS/DHCP Management Console, you will need to scroll down or across to see the entire screen unless your display settings are configured for 1024 × 768 screen resolution.

Step 1: Create the Primary DNS Server in an Organization   To create the Primary DNS Server in an organization:

1. Execute the DNS/DHCP Management Console utility either from your Start menu or from the Tools menu selection in NetWare Administrator.

2. Select the DNS tab.

3. Select the All Zones object in the left pane.

4. Select the Create button (labeled with a cube) from the toolbar at the top of the screen.

5. Select the DNS Server line in the Create New DNS Record dialog box and then OK. The Create DNS Server dialog box will appear.

6. Enter the server configuration data as shown in Figure 11.11.

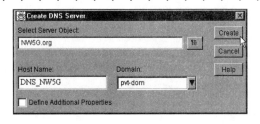

FIGURE 11.11

Create DNS Server dialog box

a. Select the Browse button to the right of the Select Server Object and then locate and select the NetWare 5 NDS master replica server. Example: NW5G.org

b. Enter the host name to be assigned to the DNS server. Use the name DNS_<*host_server_name*>. Example: DNS_NW5G

NOTE

The server name assigned in this step will be the Authoritative DNS Server for the root DNS domain and zone.

c. Enter the domain name. The domain name is the private DNS domain name. Typically this domain name has been assigned by the InterNIC or another international Internet authority. Example: priv-dom

7. Select Create. It is not necessary to define additional properties at this time.

If you have successfully created the primary DNS server, you will see the DNS server object displayed on the lower part of the screen.

Step 2: Create a Primary Zone Object   To create a Primary Zone object:

1. Select the DNS Services tab in the DNS/DHCP Management Console. Select the All Zones object on the left pane.

2. Select the Create button on the toolbar, select Zone in the Select DNS Record dialog box, and then select OK.

3. In the Create Zone dialog box shown in Figure 11.12, configure the following parameters:

▶ · ◀

FIGURE 11.12

Creating a DNS zone

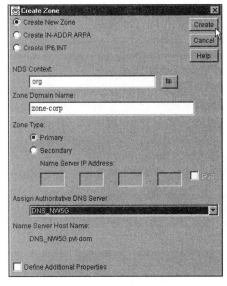

a. Select the radio button for Create New Zone. Example: zone-corp

b. Enter or select the NDS Context in which the zone will be created and managed. The primary zone should be in the same context as the host NetWare 5 server on which the primary DNS server resides. Example: org

c. Select Primary for the Zone Type.

d. Under Assign Authoritative DNS Server, select the down arrow to see a list — select the primary DNS server created in Step 1. Example: DNS_NW5G

e. The Name Server Host Name will be assigned automatically. The name will be the DNS server name and domain name.

f. Select Create. It is not necessary to define additional properties at this time.

A notification box will remind you to create a pointer record (resource record type A) for the host server domain name and a corresponding PTR record in the IN-ADDR.ARPA zone.

Step 3: Create the Pointer Record for the Host Server   To create the pointer for the host server:

1. Select the DNS Service tab in the DNS/DHCP Management Console screen. Select the primary zone created in Step 2. Example: zone-corp

2. Select Resource Record in the Create New DNS Record dialog box and then select OK.

3. In the Create Resource Record dialog box shown in Figure 11.13, enter the Host Name — the name of the NetWare 5 server that hosts the primary DNS server. Example: NW5G

▶ · ◀

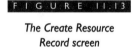
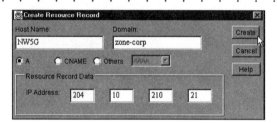

The Create Resource Record screen

4. Select the Record Type A radio button.

5. Enter the IP address of the NetWare 5 server that hosts the primary DNS server. Example: 204.10.210.21

Step 4: Create the IN-ADDR.ARPA Zone   To create the IN-ADDR.ARPA Zone:

1. Select the DNS Services tab in the DNS/DHCP Management Console. Select the All Zones object on the left pane.

2. Select the Create button on the toolbar, select Zone in the Select DNS Record dialog box, and then select OK.

CHAPTER 11

TCP/IP SERVICES

3. In the Create Zone dialog box shown in Figure 11.14, configure the
following parameters:

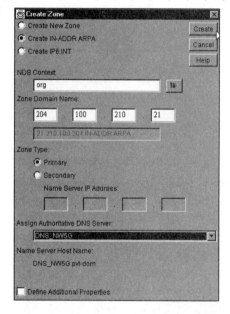

FIGURE 11.14

*Creating the IN-
ADDR.ARPA zone*

a. Select the radio button for Create IN-ADDR.ARPA.

b. Select the NDS context for the NetWare 5 server that hosts the primary
DNS server. Example: org

c. In the Zone Domain Name field enter the IP address of the NetWare 5
server that hosts the primary DNS server. Example: 204.10.210.21

d. Select the Primary radio button for the Zone Type.

e. Click the down arrow to the right of the Assign Authoritative DNS
Server field, and select the primary DNS server. Example: DNS_NW5G

4. Select Create. It is not necessary at this time to define additional properties.

Step 5: Start the DNS Server   To start the DNS server:

1. At the NetWare 5 server that hosts the primary DNS server, access the console and then load NAMED.NLM. To access the console, strike Alt+Esc until you see the screen with the colon prompt. To load NAMED, enter the command

    load NAMED

2. Return to the management workstation where the DNS/DHCP Management Console is running and then select the Refresh button (the page symbol) on the toolbar.

NOTE **Notice the DNS Server applet in the lower-left corner of the DNS Service screen. The red circle with a strike through it should disappear, indicating that the DNS server has started and is ready for service. Be patient — it may take a few minutes for the DNS server to be acknowledged.**

Your DNS server should be functional at this point.

Step 6: Configure Clients to Use DNS   To configure clients to use DNS:
You must configure client workstations to use the DNS server.
For Windows 95 and 98 workstations:

1. Select Control Panel, Network applet, TCP/IP —> <NIC_driver>, Properties.

2. Select the DNS tab, enter the host name (computer name) of this workstation, the domain or NetWare 5 zone, and the IP address of the DNS server as shown in Figure 11.15.

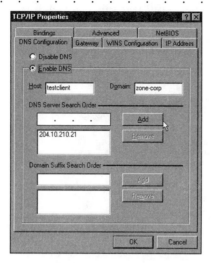

FIGURE 11.15

Editing the Windows 95/98 DNS properties

NOTE

Microsoft computer names and DNS host names may be different because Microsoft networking allows computer names that include spaces and underscores that are not valid in DNS. A host name entered in the DNS properties page will be used for DNS purposes in lieu of the computer name.

For Windows NT workstations:

1. Select Control Panel, Network applet, Protocols, TCP/IP Protocol, and then select the Properties button.

2. Select the DNS tab. You will see a screen similar to the one shown in Figure 11.16. Configure the DNS properties as follows:

   a. Enter the computer name or the DNS host name for this computer.

NOTE

If the same name is used for both the Windows computer name and the DNS host name, DNS name resolution can resolve names for both systems. You should assign a computer name that is valid for both Windows and DNS — never use underscores (_) or spaces in a Windows computer name.

You can reassign the computer name if necessary in the Identification screen of the Network applet. If you rename the computer, all drive mappings pointing to that computer must also be changed.

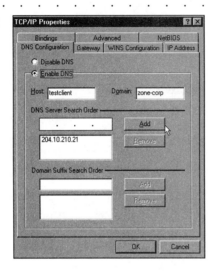

F I G U R E 11.16

Updating Windows NT 4's DNS client configuration

b. In the domain name field, enter the domain or zone name.

NOTE

Logical zones are treated as domain names in NDS.

c. Use the Add button to enter the address of the primary DNS server, which is the same as the address of the NetWare 5 host computer on which the DNS service is running.

d. Select OK.

3. Select OK to exit the Network applet.

Step 7: Enter Resource Records for Host Computers   To enter resource records for host computers:

1. Select the DNS Services tab, select the zone in which to create the resource record in the left pane of your screen and then select the Create button.

2. Select the Resource Record line in the Create New DNS Record dialog box and then select Create.

3. Enter the Host Name and the IP address of the host computer for which you are creating a record.

4. Select the record type. Standard host entries are A records — a CNAME is a canonical name, sometimes called a primary or alias name. For a full list of record types, see Table 11.2, or refer to the CD that accompanies this book for a list of other types of resource records.

Step 8: Load the DNS server module   Once the DNS services are configured, you must load the DNS-DHCP module at the NetWare 5 server with the following console command:

```
load NAMED
```

Your DNS server is not on line and ready for service.

Importing and Exporting DNS Records

DNS records can be imported using the Import DNS Database button on the DNS Service screen's toolbar. The file must be in the DNS BIND Master file format. When importing a file, the zone is created at the same time. DNS records can be exported using the Export DNS Database button on the DNS Service screen's toolbar.

These options can be used to upgrade DNS servers and to revise DNS server configurations. You can export a zone database, edit the header records, and then import the records into a new DNS zone database. For example, if you have configured your system with a single zone and entered all your resource records, and then you decide to break the zone into multiple zones, follow these steps:

1. Export a database.

2. Separate the records into multiple files.

3. Edit the header records.

4. Import the files back into new zones.

Creating Secondary DNS Zones

Secondary DNS zones can cut DNS loads down to manageable levels in larger organizations. Each zone is controlled by a Zone Master, which is the Authoritative DNS Server for the zone. Each Zone Master is a primary DNS server for the zone and is also a secondary DNS server for an Authoritative DNS Server in another zone. Zones are organized hierarchically — a master zone at the top, with one or more zones beneath it.

More than one zone is required only in larger networks/intranets. It is assumed that a larger intranet will consist of many NetWare servers. A secondary Zone Master DNS server must be placed on a different NetWare 5 server from the DNS server for the primary zone.

Each zone master should be placed in a separate NDS partition.

Once a primary zone has been created as discussed previously in this chapter, secondary zones can be added. The procedure consists of creating an additional DNS server and then creating a secondary DNS Zone object.

To create a secondary zone:

1. Select the DNS Services tab and then select the primary (parent) zone in which to create the new zone in the left pane of your screen. Select the Create button.

2. In the Create a New DNS Record dialog box, select the Zone line.

3. Configure the Create Zone screen as follows:

    a. Select the Create New Zone radio button.

b. Select the NDS context using the Browse button. Place the new zone in the same context as the NetWare 5 host computer that will contains the new DNS server.

c. Enter the new zone name in the Zone Domain Name field.

d. Select Secondary as the Zone Type, and enter the IP address in the Name Server IP Address fields.

e. Enter names in the Authoritative DNS Server and Name Server Host Name fields. It is not necessary to enter this information. If you prefer to enter these properties, the Authoritative DNS Server is the primary DNS server that will export its zone database, and the Name Server Host Name is the NetWare 5 server that hosts the DNS zone master.

f. Select Create. A notification box will remind you to create the pointer record for the NetWare 5 computer that hosts the DNS server, and to create the pointer record for the IN-ADDR.ARPA zone.

4. Configure the secondary DNS zone to download zone transfers from the primary zone:

a. Select the secondary DNS zone and then select the SOA Information tab.

b. Enter the primary DNS zone name in the Zone Master field.

c. Enter the e-mail address as root.*<primary_zone>*.

The IN-ADDR.ARPA Zone

The IN-ADDR.ARPA zone provides reverse lookup capabilities. The IN-ADDR.ARPA records provide the capability to resolve a name from a known IP address. This database is made up of a Start of Authority record and Pointer (PTR) records. However, the pointer records in this file are written in reverse order and appended with "in-addr.arpa." The process of creating an IN-ADDR.ARPA zone object is discussed previously in this chapter.

Forwarding List

A Forwarding List is used to redirect unresolved queries to other DNS servers. A DNS server will often receive requests for host names that are not listed in its local DNS database. If the request cannot be resolved by one of the forwarded servers, or if no forwarding list exists, the request is forwarded to the root DNS server.

Linking with Foreign DNS Servers

NetWare 5's DNS is fully compatible with other DNS systems. DNS records from foreign DNS systems are imported into NetWare DNS zones by Zone In servers. Zone transfers are exported to foreign DNS servers using the same procedure as any other DNS system. The following procedures are used to link to higher foreign domains, and to link with lower foreign domains.

The Zone In Server   In a traditional DNS environment, higher-level domain information is imported into the private domain with a primary - secondary relationship. The primary DNS server in the private domain is configured as a secondary to the DNS server above it in the domain structure. This links the two domains together without propagating the private DNS data to the higher domain. The primary DNS server in the private domain is then replicated to the secondary DNS servers and to primary DNS servers in subdomains.

Novell DNS supports the traditional method of importing data from a foreign DNS server, except that only one Novell DNS server is required to propagate data to an entire zone instead of propagating to each secondary DNS server. To import data, a NetWare 5 DNS server must be configured as a secondary DNS server, and as a Zone In DNS server. This configuration imports zone transfers from the foreign primary DNS server into the NDS database. A NetWare 5 primary DNS server can also be configured as a secondary for the foreign system. The Zone In DNS server configuration puts the data into the Zone Master's database for the NetWare 5 zone, thus making it available to all NetWare 5 DNS servers throughout the NDS tree.

NOTE   NetWare DNS servers can be configured as both primary and secondary DNS servers. Create the server object as a primary and then configure the primary DNS server as a secondary to another zone or foreign domain.

Supporting Foreign Secondary DNS Servers Supporting other DNS servers, such as UNIX DNS servers, is accomplished through the classic primary-secondary DNS server relationship. A NetWare 5 primary DNS server will send a zone transfer to all secondary DNS servers, NetWare and non-NetWare alike.

Your only consideration in configuring a primary and foreign secondary relationship is your NetWare DNS zones. In a larger NetWare DNS configuration, each zone has a primary DNS server—in most other systems each domain has a primary DNS server. Match each foreign secondary DNS server with a NetWare primary zone DNS server.

A NetWare primary DNS server is also known as a NetWare DNS Zone Master.

NOTE

The Designated DNS Server for Dynamic DNS Updates A Designated DNS server is required to receive updates from a DHCP server. When an IP address is reassigned or relinquished by the DHCP server, the Designated DNS server is informed, and the appropriate resource records are saved to the Zone Master as shown in Figure 11.17. Because the address update is stored in the NDS database, updates are immediately available to all DNS servers. Because changes are stored in the NDS tree, they are automatically available to foreign secondary DNS servers.

A Designated DNS server must be hosted by an NDS replica server in each primary zone. Novell Designated DNS servers can only import data from Novell DHCP servers.

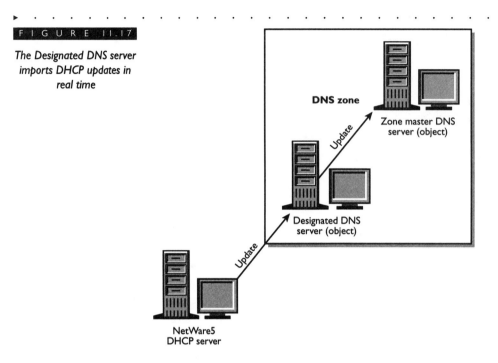

FIGURE 11.17

The Designated DNS server imports DHCP updates in real time

Other DNS Server Configurations

A few more configuration options are available for other DNS options.

Forwarding Client Queries to Root DNS Servers Your DNS configuration was installed with a RootServerInfo object, which handles the job of forwarding client DNS queries to the root name server(s). No further configuration is required to effect this process.

Cache-Only Server Configuration Cache-only servers are used to handle DNS queries for Internet access. A cache-only server can speed up name resolution requests to Internet hosts significantly. The process of setting up a cache-only server is as follows:

1. Create a DNS Name Server object.

2. Do not assign any zones for it to serve.

3. Add the ISP's name server address to the Forwarding List found in the DNS server properties screen. To locate this screen, select the DNS server at the bottom of the DNS Services screen of the DNS/DHCP Management Console and then select the Forwarding List tab.

4. Configure clients to reference the cache-only DNS server. Windows 95, 98, and NT workstations are configured in Control Panel's Network applet under the TCP/IP Protocol Properties.

Supporting Child Zones   Child zones are supported with glue-logic records in the zone DNS database. The parent zone must be configured with:

- A Name Server record — type NS — for the zone server

- A Name Server record — type NS — for the child zone

- An Address Pointer record — type A — for the child zone's DNS server

When a zone is configured in this manner, queries directed to the parent DNS zone are returned with a reply from the child zone.

NetWare 5 DHCP

NetWare 5 supports three methods of allocating IP addresses to clients:

- Dynamic BOOTP

- Manual (static)

- Dynamic DHCP

Bootstrap Protocol (BOOTP) was developed to automatically allocate IP addresses to clients from a server without controlling which host on a subnet will receive which address. A table of address assignments is configured on a DHCP server, and the addresses are permanently assigned as hosts connect to the network. This method reduces administrative time and effort but does not handle conditions where IP addresses must be reallocated. For example, mobile users may log into a different subnet. This method also does not provide additional address and name resolution configuration, so trips to the desktop are sometimes required anyway.

With the manual (static) method, an IP address assignment can be permanently configured to a host in the DNS/DHCP Management Console utility. The assignment is made once to the host as it attaches to the network. This method is roughly similar to the Dynamic BOOTP method.

Dynamic Host Configuration Protocol (DHCP) leases IP addresses to client computers and can provide additional address and name resolution configuration data to clients. Leases are temporary assignments that last a given period of time, which is then usually renewed at the end of the lease period. Leasing IP addresses provides two significant benefits: It makes changing IP address assignments easier, and it extends the number of IP addresses available for occasional users.

In many cases, DHCP is necessary for mobile users—when they log in at different locations, an IP address must be assigned that falls within a subnet that relates a specific router port (the gateway address). Because a change of physical location may require a subnet change, a change of other addressing information such as the gateway address may be furnished by the DHCP server. Just about any addressing or name resolution information can be provided by the DHCP server.

Required NDS rights

Novell's DHCP shares the use of the DNS/DHCP Locator and Group objects with DNS. They are used for the same purpose—they provide controlled administrative and user access to the DHCP servers. You must have the appropriate NDS rights to manage the Locator and Group objects as discussed previously. See the section in this chapter entitled "Installing the DNS/DHCP Management Console" for the NDS rights that are needed to set up and manage the Locator and Group objects.

Terminology

The following terms are used in setting up and managing the DHCP service.

TIP
Studying these definitions will assist in understanding subsequent sections of this chapter. When a term is capitalized, the term refers to a proper name used in configuration screens and in documentation.

DHCP Server

The DHCP server is the logical server object that runs as a service on a NetWare server. The DHCP server is set up using the Create DHCP Server option in the Create New DHCP Record dialog box.

Subnet

A Subnet record identifies the subnet that the DHCP server will service. You must create a subnet record for each subnet that the DHCP server will service. Subnet records are modified with other types of DHCP records. Addresses and ranges of addresses within a subnet can be included and excluded as discussed in the text that follows.

Subnet Pools

A subnet pool defines a grouping of subnets for use in configuring Virtual LANs (VLANs). Some network switches can automatically partition ports — and therefore user workstations — into separate subnets to reduce shared bandwidth on a physical network segment. NetWare 5's Subnet Pools facilitate this feature and prevent routing problems when subnet addresses for various nodes are changed.

Subnet Address Range

A Subnet Address Range is a range of IP addresses. Subnet Address Range records can be created to configure address ranges for use with DHCP and BOOTP services, and to include or exclude address ranges from assignment.

Address Assignment Policies

You can configure assignments with one of the following policies:

▸ *Delete Duplicate* — Assigns new address, deletes previous assignment.

▸ *Allow Duplicate* — Assigns new address, retains former assignment.

▸ *No Duplicate* — Retains same address assignment if valid.

Inheritance Rules

Options assigned at the lowest level override options assigned at a higher level. If, for example, an option is assigned at the global level and a different option is assigned at the subnet level, the subnet level option will take precedence. If a different option is assigned at the IP address level, it would override options set at the global and subnet levels.

Configuring DHCP

The DHCP service is installed along with the DNS service as discussed previously in this chapter. The DHCP service is set up and managed using the DNS/DHCP Management Console utility. You must install and run the DNS/DHCP Management Console utility before you can set up your DHCP server.

Creating a usable DHCP service requires the following steps:

▸ Create a DHCP server

▸ Create a Subnet record

Creating a DHCP Server

The following procedure will create a DHCP server. Once the server is created, it can be configured by entering resource records.

1. Execute the DNS/DHCP Management Console utility either from your Start menu or from the Tools menu selection in NetWare Administrator.

2. Select the DHCP tab.

3. Select the Create button (marked with a cube).

4. Select DHCP Server from the Create New DHCP Record dialog box.

5. Enter the name of or select of the NetWare server on which the DNS service is to run. Enter a unique host name for the DNS server (different from the NetWare server name).

Creating Subnet Records

DHCP uses subnet records, with related records to issue addresses. A DHCP server requires a separate subnet record for ranges of addresses to be issued in each subnet. That subnet record is modified by range and address records as follows:

▸ First, a subnet record is created for each subnet to include addresses to be issued by the DHCP server. Subnet records are modified by the following types of records.

▸ Range records specify a range of addresses within the subnet that are to be included or excluded from DHCP server assignments to clients.

▸ Address records are created to exclude individual addresses from being assigned to clients.

Each of the preceding types of records have several properties to configure them for use by DHCP, BOOTP, and other types of address assignment methods as discussed previously in this chapter. The following instructions demonstrate how to create subnet and subsidiary records.

When you create a subnet record, IP addresses in the subnet are available to be assigned to client computers as they attach to the network. A subnet record is required for all addresses to be assigned that lie within a subnet range.

You can create a subnet record for any valid subnet mask—by default all addresses in the subnet are included in the range of addresses to be assigned except the subnet and the broadcast addresses.

To create a subnet record:

1. Select the DHCP Services tab in the DNS/DHCP Management Console.

2. Select the global Our Network object in the left screen pane and then select the Create button on the toolbar. You will see the screen shown in Figure 11.18.

FIGURE 11.18

Creating a subnet record

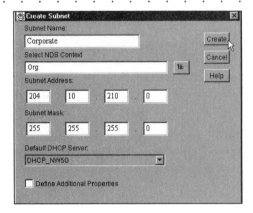

3. Enter the subnet number — the first IP address in the subnet — and the subnet mask.

4. Select Create to save the subnet record.

Figure 11.19 shows a subnet record for the class C subnet 204.10.210.0. The address 204.10.210.0 is excluded because it is the address of the subnet itself, and 204.10.210.255 is excluded because it is the broadcast address for this subnet. These addresses may not be assigned to clients.

FIGURE 11.19

Subnet and broadcast address exclusions are created by default.

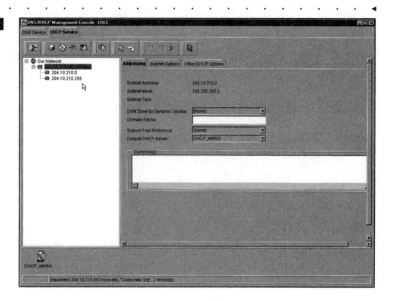

WARNING

Under some circumstances, DHCP will permit issuance of invalid addresses. See Chapter 4 for a discussion of subnetting rules and classful versus classless addressing. Several subnet masks are invalid for classful addressing, while the same masks may be valid when using classless addressing. To use classless addressing, you must assure that the proper conditions must be met. DHCP cannot modify these rules.

Including and Excluding IP Addresses and Ranges

You can exclude IP addresses within a given subnet so that they will not be assigned. Addresses may be excluded for several reasons — IP addresses may have been statically assigned to printers, servers, and such; or addresses may be reserved for a variety of other reasons.

IP addresses can be included and excluded for a given subnet in two ways:

▸ You can create IP Address records to exclude individual IP addresses.

▸ You can create Subnet Address Range records to include or exclude ranges of addresses.

Excluding IP Addresses   Once a Subnet record has been created, you can exclude individual IP addresses from being assigned by creating an IP Address record for each address to be excluded. IP Address records modify existing Subnet records.

To create an IP Address record:

1. Select the DHCP Services tab in the DNS/DHCP Management Console.

2. Select the subnet record to be modified in the left screen pane.

3. Select the Create button in the toolbar.

4. Select the IP Address line in the Create New DHCP Record dialog box and then select OK.

5. Enter the IP address to be excluded, and select Excluded in the Range Type field as shown in Figure 11.20.

F I G U R E   11.20

Excluding an address range

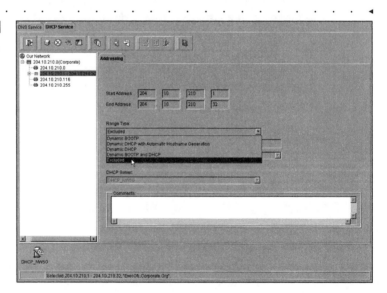

6. Select the Define Additional Properties check box and then select Create.

NOTE

The Manual Assignment Type is used to exclude a specific physical address — and therefore device — from assignment. For example, you may exclude a network-attached printer by specifying the device's MAC address as well as its static IP address. When using this Assignment Type, you will be permitted to edit the MAC Type, Hostname, and NDS object fields in the Addressing properties page for this IP Address record.

7. (Optional) You can enter the Client Identifier (serial number, asset tag, or the like), MAC Address, and comments for this record. You can also edit the Usage Properties page to make the assignment permanent or reserve the address for a given period.

When a Subnet record is created, the entire subnet is made available for assignment by default. You can exclude addresses within a subnet or within a subnet range by creating an address exclusion record for each IP address to be excluded.

Including and Excluding Address Ranges   You can include and exclude address ranges for each subnet. To modify a subnet assignment range:

1. Select the DHCP Services tab in the DNS/DHCP Management Console.

2. Select the subnet record to be modified in the left screen pane.

3. Select the Create button on the toolbar.

4. Select Subnet Address Range from the Create New DHCP Record dialog box and then select OK.

5. In the Create Subnet Address Range dialog box:

    a. Enter a name to be assigned to the Subnet Address Range record.

    b. Enter the starting and ending IP addresses for the range.

    c. Select the Define Additional Properties check box.

    d. Select Create. The record will be created, and you will view the Subnet Address Range record's property screen in your right screen pane.

6. In the Range Type field select the down arrow and then select the record type as shown in Figure 11.21. The first four options include the range for issuance. The Excluded type excludes the range from issuance.

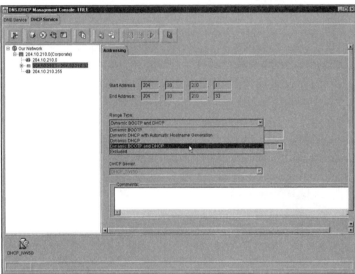

Including a standard DHCP address range

> IP Address records cannot be used to exclude an address from Subnet Address Ranges. To exclude an address from a range, create two ranges — one ending before the address to be excluded, and another after the address to be excluded. Then create the IP Address exclusion record.
>
> NOTE

Subnet Address Range Types   The following types can be specified for a Subnet Address Range record:

▸ *Dynamic BOOTP* — This type of record is used for BOOTP-only requests (not DHCP).

▸ *Dynamic HHCP with Automatic Host Name Generation* — This type of record is used for DHCP-only requests where host names are to be assigned from a pool and then dynamically update DNS. Host names are appended and incremented by an integer when configured in the Auto Host Name Starts With parameter of the record's property page.

▸ *Dynamic DHCP* — This type of record is used for DHCP-only requests (not BOOTP). If this type is specified, the Dynamic Update or Always Update parameter can be specified for use to automatically update NetWare 5 DNS records.

▸ *Dynamic BOOTP and DHCP* — This type of record is used for both DHCP and BOOTP requests.

▸ *Excluded* — This type of record excludes the range from use, whereas all the preceding types include and configure the use of the range.

Importing and Exporting DHCP Records

You can import and export records using DHCP version 2.0 or 3.0 format. Select the Import or Export buttons on the toolbar to execute these functions. This feature is helpful for adding records in bulk — it can also be used to save a backup record of DHCP database records.

You can create an importable file by exporting a file, editing and adding fields, and then importing them.

TIP

Dynamic DNS (DDNS)

NDS resource records are generally entered manually. However, using DNS with DHCP can be problematic because addresses are often reassigned. DDNS is used to update DNS records in real time as DHCP assigns, reuses, and reassigns addresses.

DDNS requires the following configuration:

▸ A DNS Zone object must exist to receive DHCP updates.

▸ The Subnet Address Range objects that will use DDNS must be set to range type Dynamic BOOTP and DHCP or Dynamic DHCP.

Follow these steps to configure DDNS:

1. Select the DHCP Services tab in the DNS/DHCP Management Console.

2. Select the Subnet record for which DDNS is to be activated.

3. Select the DNS zone to receive DHCP updates in the DNS Zone for Dynamic Updates field.

4. In the Subnet Address Range's Addressing property page:

   a. Change the Range Type to Dynamic BOOTP and DHCP or Dynamic DHCP.

   b. Enter the DNS domain name (optional).

   c. Change the DNS Update Option to Always Update.

5. Select another object in the left screen page to save your changes.

Load the DHCP Server Module

The last step in setting up your DHCP server is to load the DHCP service. At the NetWare 5 server console enter the following command:

```
load DHCPSRVR
```

DHCP services are now on line and ready for service.

Monitoring and Troubleshooting

Several applications and tools can be used make protocol configuration easier and to troubleshoot configurations that may not be working properly. This section addresses issues related to monitoring and troubleshooting.

DNS Auditing

Auditing enables management to track changes made to DNS and DHCP. DNS/DHCP Services has robust auditing features that are required in many organizations. DNS Auditing retains a record of DNS record changes.

Auditing is not turned on by default. The administrator must configure the DNS services to log audit activities.

Configuring DNS Auditing

DNS auditing is set up in the DNS/DHCP Management Console. The following procedure will configure your DNS service for auditing:

1. Log in with a user account that has sufficient NDS rights to manage DNS. Select the DNS Services tab in the DNS/DHCP Management Console.

2. Select the DNS server for which auditing is to be configured. Select the Options tab for the Options Properties screen.

3. In the Event Log box, select the Major Events or the All radio button.

4. Check the Enable Audit Trail Log check box.

5. Select the Save button on the toolbar.

Viewing the DNS Event Log

The following procedure will enable you to view the Event Log for a DNS server:

1. Log in with a user account that has sufficient NDS rights to manage DNS. Select the DNS Services tab in the DNS/DHCP Management Console.

2. Select the DNS server to be managed, and select the View Events/Alerts button on the toolbar. Accept or enter the dates to audit The Events Period - Event Log dialog box.

3. Select OK to view the Event Log.

The Event Log lists audit log entries with the following:

► Entry time

► Severity

▸ State

▸ Description

You can select Display Options to select a new date range and to select or view the severity and state of individual events.

Viewing the DNS Audit Trail Log

The following procedure will enable you to view a DNS server's Audit Trail Log:

1. Log in with a user account that has sufficient NDS rights to manage DNS. Select the DNS Services tab in the DNS/DHCP Management Console.

2. Select the DNS server to be managed, and select the View Audit Trail Log button on the toolbar. Accept or enter the dates to audit The Events Period - Event Log dialog box.

3. Select OK to view the Audit Trail Log.

The Audit Trail Log displays the following:

▸ Entry time

▸ Type

▸ IP address

▸ Domain name

▸ DNS transaction

You can select Display Options to select the date range to be viewed or to select various transaction types.

DNS Events/Properties That Are Audited

The following types of transactions are saved to the Audit Trail Log:

▸ *Agent Ready* — Indicates the SNMP agent is active and can send/receive SNMP requests.

▸ *Query Received* — Acknowledges receipt of queries.

▸ *Query Forwarded* — Acknowledges that a query was forwarded to another DNS server or client.

▸ *Response Received* — Acknowledges a response to a query.

DHCP Auditing

Auditing is not turned on by default. The administrator must configure the DHCP services to log audit activities.

Configuring DHCP Auditing

DHCP auditing is set up in the DNS/DHCP Management Console. The following procedure will configure your DHCP service for auditing:

1. Log in with a user account that has sufficient NDS rights to manage DHCP. Select the DHCP Services tab in the DNS/DHCP Management Console.

2. Select the DHCP server for which auditing is to be configured. Select the Options tab for the Options Properties screen.

3. Configure the following options:

   a. In the Set SNMP Traps Option box select Major Events or All.

   b. In the Audit Train and Alerts Option box, select Major Events or All.

   c. Check the Enable Audit Trail Log check box.

   d. In the Mobile User Options box, select one of the following radio buttons: No Mobile User Allowed, Allow Mobile User but Delete Previously Assigned Address, or Allow Mobile User but Do Not Delete Previously Assigned Address.

4. If desired, check the Ping Enabled check box.

5. Select the Save button on the toolbar.

Viewing the DHCP Event Log

The following procedure will enable you to view the Event Log for a DHCP server:

I. Log in with a user account that has sufficient NDS rights to manage DHCP. Select the DHCP Services tab in the DNS/DHCP Management Console.

2. Select the DHCP server to be managed, select the View Events/Alerts button on the toolbar. Accept or enter the dates to audit The Events Period - Event Log dialog box.

3. Select OK to view the Events/Alerts log.

The Audit Trail Log displays the following for each entry:

▸ Entry time

▸ Severity

▸ State

▸ Description of each event

You can select Display Options to edit the date range and/or to select records according to severity and state.

Viewing the DHCP Audit Trail Log

The following procedure will enable you to view a DHCP server's Audit Trail Log:

I. Log in with a user account that has sufficient NDS rights to manage DHCP. Select the DHCP Services tab in the DNS/DHCP Management Console.

2. Select the DHCP server to be managed, select the View Audit Trail Log button on the toolbar. Accept or enter the dates to audit The Events Period — Audit Trail Log dialog box.

3. Select OK to view the Audit Trail Log.

DHCP Events/Properties That Are Audited
The Audit Trail Log displays the following information for each entry:

▸ Entry time

▸ IP address

▸ Type

▸ Status

▸ Hostname

▸ Hardware address

▸ Client ID

▸ Lease type

You can select Display Options to edit the date range of entries to view or to view one or more of the following types of address leases:

▸ Manual

▸ Dynamic

▸ Automatic

▸ Exclusion

▸ Unauthorized

▸ IPCP

Viewing TCP/IP Protocol Statistics

You can view many TCP/IP protocol statistics in the TCP/IP Console utility. Access this utility by loading TCPCON.NLM from a console prompt, or access it through NIAS or INETCFG.

The TCP/IP Console is useful to verify that communications are effectively received or sent, and to view the configuration for each of the TCP/IP protocols in the protocol stack.

Simple Network Management Protocol

Simple Network Management Protocol (SNMP) provides a standard protocol and format for locating and reporting network errors. In NetWare 3 and 4 SNMP support is built into the TCP/IP Console Monitor (TCPCON) and other server-based modules. All SNMP-related management and viewing is incorporated into Novell Internet Access Server (NAIS), which is included with NetWare 5 at no additional cost. NetWare's SNMP services are also available to SNMP-based management software. Novell's ManageWise, Hewlett-Packard's OpenView, Bay Networks' Optivity, and other management software packages use SNMP for extensive network management and monitoring. However, the built-in SNMP tools provided with NetWare 5 are very helpful.

This protocol, like other TCP/IP services, is client/server-based. SNMP server agents are implemented in software and firmware and are installed on computers and other network-related devices. SNMP server agents generate trap messages—SNMP client software collects traps in Management Information Base (MIB) format for viewing and interpretation. SNMP is a universal standards-based protocol that is used in many network-related software and hardware products.

SNMP management and reporting is contained within NIAS, which in turn uses the following server-based modules:

- ▸ *INETCFG.NLM*—Configuring and viewing protocols and information for configuring SNMP management

- ▸ *TCPCON.NLM*—Console management utility used to view TCP/IP statistics

▸ *SNMP.NLM* — The agent that generates trap messages

▸ *SNMPLOG.NLM* — To receive trap messages and log them to the MIB (SYS:ETC\SNMP$LOG.BIN)

NetWare 5 SNMP installation and setup is handled within NIASCFG or INETCFG (which is autoloaded from NIASCFG). In NetWare 3 and 4 versions, SNMP setup and management are handled through INETCFG and the preceding utilities.

Configuring SNMP Parameters

When setting up SNMP, you must configure *community name* options. Communities organize SNMP devices and management software into logical divisions. When an SNMP agent or management station is included in an organization, it shares the same MIB and traps. Smaller networks need only a single community, whereas larger networks may have separate communities, each one managed individually.

Three types of community names are to be configured:

▸ Monitor community

▸ Control community

▸ Trap community

Membership in each of the preceding types of communities is configured individually. Configure community memberships under in INETCFG under Manage Configurations → Configure SNMP Parameters.

Configuring SNMP Information

Configure the following parameters. The only required field is the Node Name; the others are optional.

▸ Node Name for SNMP (server name by default)

▸ Hardware Description (optional)

▸ Physical Location (optional)

▸ Human Contact (optional)

Configuring the SNMP Log

SNMP traps are logged to the SNMP$LOG.BIN file in binary format by the SNMPLOG.NLM utility. Because the log file is in binary format, you must use the a utility to read it, such as TCPCON, IPXCON, PPPCON, or FRCON — all of which are found in NIAS.

The procedure of configuring SNMP in your system consists of two steps:

1. Load SNMPLOG.NLM on the host that is to log traps. SNMPLOG.NLM needs only to be loaded on the TCP/IP host that will intercept and log the traps. If you do not require trap message logging, or if trap messages are directed to another TCP/IP host computer, do not load SNMPLOG.NLM. When SNMPLOG.NLM is loaded, traps are sent to the local host by default.

2. Configure other SNMP agents to send traps to an SNMP manager in NIAS or INETCFG. In NIAS select Configure NIAS → Protocols and Routing — this will bring up INETCFG. Select Protocols, TCP/IP, SNMP Manager Table and then Ins to enter the IP address of the host that is to log the traps. You can edit the SNMP configuration file SYS:ETC\TRAPTARG.CFG manually.

All SNMP agents should be configured to send traps to the same host in your local network or community.

Viewing the Trap Log

You can view the trap log in its raw state by selecting Display Local Traps in the TCP/IP Console utility (TCPCON).

NOTE

Once you have loaded SNMPLOG.NLM, be sure to delete the log file, SNMPLOG.BIN, periodically. Log entries will continue to accumulate, causing the file to grow. If you delete this file, a new file is created automatically the next time a trap is to be logged.

Viewing SNMP Statistics

SNMP traps are viewed as statistics under the TCP/IP Console (TCPCON). Load this module on your server using NIAS or INETCFG, or else go directly to TCPCON. The first menu selection is the SNMP Access Configuration menu selection. It shows the community name and other configuration statistics. It also shows the number of IP and TCP communications received, sent, and forwarded.

Other TCP/IP Services

A few other TCP/IP services are available in NetWare 5.

Remote Console Access for Pure IP

Most NetWare administrators have grown accustomed to accessing their NetWare servers using RCONSOLE, but this utility only works with IPX. NetWare 5 includes the RCONSOLEJ utility, which is used for IP remote console access.

RCONSOLEJ features a Windows interface, shown in Figure 11.22. This utility has a character-based console window. Surrounding this window are Back and Forward control buttons and a selection box to select which console screen to view. As with RCONSOLE, you can access any character-based screens and perform any tasks as if you were physically seated at the server. You will not, however, be able to access the Server Graphical User Interface or ConsoleOne graphical application from this utility.

The RConsoleJ utility

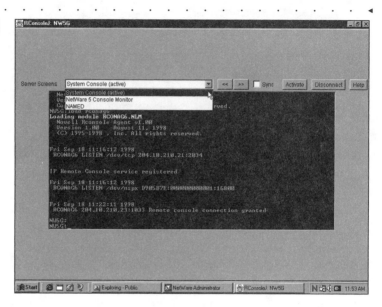

To set up RCONSOLEJ:

I. Load RCONAG6.NLM on your NetWare 5 server, you will be prompted to enter a password and then the TCP port number for the remote console to use. You can strike Enter to accept the default port number.

2. From your Windows 95/98/NT workstation, run NetWare Administrator. You must have Supervisory NDS rights to manage the server.

3. Select Tools → Pure IP Remote Console. You will be prompted to enter the password that was entered in step 1.

The server RCONSOLEJ module can be used to access other NetWare 5 IP servers remotely. You can access RCONSOLEJ from the graphical Console One utility.

1. From your server's graphical console, select Start → Console One. You must have Supervisory NDS rights to manage the server.

2. In the left window pane, select Tools → RconsoleJ.

3. Enter the server IP address and password. You will then be able to view the remote server's Console One utility, just as you would from a 32-bit Windows workstation. This password will be sent over the network encrypted.

NOTE **You can synchronize the server and the RconsoleJ screens from a menu selection on the RconsoleJ main screen. This will prevent the infrequent problem of a local and remote user accessing different screens at the same time.**

Console One Remote Java Console

You can access Console One, the graphical Java console utility used on your NetWare 5 server, from any 32-bit Windows workstation running TCP/IP.
To run Console One:

1. From a Windows 95/98/NT workstation where the NetWare 5 Client 32 is installed, search for the SYS:Public\mgmt directory using the Start menu's Run option or Windows Explorer. You must have Supervisory NDS rights to manage the server.

2. Execute the CONSOLE1.EXE application.

You can create a shortcut to this application if you wish to access it frequently.

Netscape FastTrack Server for NetWare

NetWare 4.2 and 5 include Netscape FastTrack Server for NetWare. One of the top web servers available now runs on NetWare. The same web applications can be run on many different platforms. The Netscape FastTrack Server for NetWare software is not copied to your server during installation. Follow these instructions to install FastTrack server on your NetWare 5 server. You must have at least 100 MB of disk space available on the target server, and your server must have at least 64 MB of RAM.

1. From a workstation with the Novell Client for Windows 95/98 or NT software installed, map root a drive to the SYS volume on your NetWare 5 server.

2. Insert the NetWare 5 Operating System CD into the workstation's CD-ROM device.

3. From the \Products\Webserv directory on the NetWare 5 Operating System CD, execute SETUP.EXE.

4. The FastTrack setup wizard will run. Follow the prompts through the web server setup. When queried for the installation target, enter the drive letter mapped previously in step 1.

Changing a Server's IP Address

Changing an IP address for a server can cause serious problems throughout an entire internetwork. It could take as long as 30 minutes for an IP address change to update all replicas in an NDS tree. You can force an update with the DSTrace server console command. The DSTrace SET parameter adjusts the NDS replication update period. By default, NetWare 5 sets this parameter to once every 79 seconds. You can force an update and then set the parameter back to its default. After changing a server's IP address, enter the following command at the server console:

```
Set DSTrace = 5
```

After five seconds, set the parameter back to its previous value. The following command sets this parameter to its default value.

```
Set DSTrace = 79
```

CHAPTER 12

Novell Internet Access Server

Novell Internet Access Server (NIAS) is a new server-based management utility (NIASCFG.NLM) that represents many protocol and remote access features in NetWare 4.11, 4.2, and 5. NIAS provides the administrative interface for two major functions: It manages network interfaces and protocol complexities, and it manages Routing and Remote Access Services (RRAS). NIAS is far more than a utility, however — it is the interface for several server components included in NetWare 5 that were previously licensed as separate products. RRAS consists of the Novell Communications Services (NCS) dial-up server — formerly known as NetWare Connect — and Novell's Multiprotocol Router (MPR). These two products provide remote network access over all types of LANs, WANs, synchronous, and asynchronous interfaces. NIAS includes several management consoles to make all these interfaces and protocols easier to configure and manage. NIAS also includes menu utilities for managing protocols so that the administrator will not have to deal with complex load and bind commands, syntax, and the need to edit configuration files manually.

NIAS replaces several third-party products and services. To equal the communications features built into NetWare 5, you would have to purchase several server applications and dedicated hardware devices. This product makes NetWare 5 the most universally connectable networking product in the industry.

The Internetwork Configuration portion of NIAS has been available in NetWare 3 and 4 versions for many years, but many of the communications options in NIAS made their debut in BorderManager. The biggest difference in NetWare 5 is that so many of the communications options that were previously available in BorderManager are now included in NIAS at no additional cost. Though BorderManager provides additional services, such as remote Windows-based management, NIAS and all its features are now part of NetWare 5 with no additional cost.

NIAS, especially the Internetworking Configuration portion (INETCFG), is an essential tool in troubleshooting and reconfiguring your system. Experienced NetWare professionals are accustomed to loading INSTALL.NLM to manage NIC drivers and protocol configurations. You used to load SERVMAN or MONITOR to manage routing and service protocols. Now these functions are handled in NIAS. You will find this application to be an invaluable tool for troubleshooting as well as reconfiguring your servers.

NIAS Components

NIAS contains so many components that it is necessary to take a moment to define the components and services that are discussed in this chapter. NIAS includes the following services, components, protocols, and interfaces.

Internet Network Configuration

Internet Network Configuration (INETCFG) is incorporated into NIASCFG. INETCFG is loaded from the NIAS menu when you select Configure NIAS → Protocols and Routing from the NIAS Options menu. You can even load INETCFG separately, without using NIASCFG. Once INETCFG is used, commands related to loading NIC drivers and configuring protocols are migrated into the INETCFG database. From that point on, you are not to manage NIC drivers and related protocol configurations by editing the startup files. Instead you must use INETCFG, which parses and stores the same information in separate files.

INETCFG is a substantial utility by itself. It consists of ten menu selections, some of which have as many as seven selections, and others that have several selections once you have chosen a device or protocol to manage. This utility is one of the most important tools for viewing and modifying server configuration properties. If you add remote access modules, even more devices and protocols are included in its interface.

Multiprotocol Router

Multiprotocol Router (MPR) has been available from Novell as a separate product but is now a basic feature in NetWare 5. It is discussed in the "Routing Part of Routing and Remote Access Services" section of your NetWare 5 online documentation. While NetWare 5 includes the standard internal router for IPX and IP, MPR provides robust routing protocols, including RIP II and OSPF. More important, MPR provides the ability to interface with LAN and WANs that require several data-link protocols. You can build a very sophisticated router right on your server using MPR. MPR supports ATM, Frame Relay, X.25, and PPP at the data-link level. These protocols are required to support many brands and models of digital WAN adapters, including ATM, T-1/E-1, and frame relay devices. All these protocols can interface with IPX/SPX, TCP/IP, and AppleTalk transports.

Novell Communications Services

Novell Communications Services (NCS) is the remote access server that is standard in NIAS. It is the Remote Access Services part of Routing and Remote Access Services mentioned in your NetWare 5 documentation. NCS was previously known as NetWare Connect and was sold separately and included in BorderManager. It now has new capabilities and has been integrated into NIAS and therefore into NetWare 5 with no additional cost. NCS provides dial-in, dial-out, and dedicated access for remote users. It handles synchronous and asynchronous interfaces, including everything from an external modem connected to built-in serial ports to multiport asynchronous serial adapters and T-1/E-1 and other digital communications adapters.

NetWare Asynchronous Services Interface

NCS uses the NetWare Asynchronous Services Interface (NASI) APIs to provide an interface to redirect asynchronous communications over the network. For example, you are when dialing out of a NCS modem with third-party communications software, the communications need to be redirected over the network to the shared AIO ports. Most communications software is designed to communicate with COM1, COM2, and so on. However, communications software that supports the NASI interface can be configured to redirect communications to a network API. NASI also allows remote access to network computers via NCS.

Win2NCS

Z.E.N.works includes the Win2NCS Windows-based application to support NASI mappings at the client end. Win2NCS is included at no additional cost to support Windows 95/98/NT, OS/2, and Macintosh clients. The NCS server and Win2NCS on the client end provides a communications medium that allows clients to use remote control software, such as pcAnywhere and Carbon Copy, to take control of a network workstation from a remote computer. This allows a dial-in user to execute and work with any application just as if he/she were seated at a local desktop workstation.

WAN Data-Link Interfaces

In addition to all previously supported LANs and frame formats, NetWare 5 supports extensive WAN and remote access protocols. WAN protocols are supported with extensive server modules, management, and monitoring including the following:

▸ Asynchronous Transfer Mode (ATM)

▸ Frame Relay

▸ X.25

▸ Point-to-Point Protocol (PPP)

▸ Synchronous and asynchronous dial-up over digital lines, ISDN, and modems

All of the services named use drivers and protocols that require configuration, console management, and the ability to view statistics. The dial-up server software also requires port and modem configuration/management. Because one or more protocol stacks are bound to each access protocol, configuration and management can become quite complex. For example, let's say that your server is to contain analog modems, a Frame Relay interface, and a T-1 adapter with IPX/SPX, TCP/IP, and AppleTalk protocol stacks. You will need to support at least nine protocol bindings in addition to your NIC protocol bindings. This is where you will come to appreciate NIAS — it makes the job of configuring these drivers and bindings manageable.

NetWare 5 includes support for remote access over IPX/SPX, TCP/IP, and AppleTalk protocol stacks using all the previously described LAN, WAN, and dial-up access protocols. NIAS provides local and remote management for all these options in one utility, broken down into several menu selections and configuration screens.

LAN, WAN, and Remote User Consoles

The MPR portion of NIAS includes several management consoles to manage and monitor remote access protocols and traffic. Table 12.1 shows consoles found in NIAS.

	UTILITY	USED FOR
TABLE 12.1	NWCCON	NetWare Connect (NCS) remote console utility
NIAS Consoles	NWCSTAT	NetWare Connect (NCS) remote access usage reporting
	IPXCON	IPX/SPX protocol and router console
	TCPCON	TCP/IP and SNMP console
	ATCON	AppleTalk console
	ATMCON	Asynchronous Transfer Mode console
	FRCON	Frame Relay console
	X25CON	X.25 console
	PPPCON	Point-to-Point Protocol console
	NCSCON	NetWare Asynchronous Services Interface (NASI) console

NIAS has several options for remotely supporting these console utilities, as shown in Table 12.2.

	UTILITY	USED FOR
TABLE 12.2	NWCSTAT	Reporting remote access status in NetWare Connect
NIAS Options	AIOCON	Configuring and viewing communications I/O ports
	AIOPDCON	Configuring X.25 packet assembly-disassembly profiles
	PPPRNCON	Configuring and viewing Point-to-Point Protocol Remote Node Services (PPPRNS)
	ARASCON	Configuring AppleTalk Remote Access Service (ARAS)
	NCSCON	Configuring NetWare Asynchronous Services Interface (NASI) and Novell Communications Services (NCS)

NIAS enables the administrator to manage these functions from any point on a network or from a dial-up connection. The RCONSOLE utility provides the ability to access NIAS from a client workstation. NIAS's remote access service feature also provides console access from dial-up connections.

NIAS is a valuable component that can make these services affordable even to the smallest shops. For example, it may be exorbitantly expensive for an organization to support wide area networking small branch offices to a corporate headquarters with dedicated hardware devices. NIAS incorporates remote networking into each remote branch's server. A single support staff can manage all servers remotely from a central point, reducing administrative and support costs. The cost and complexity of supporting branch offices can be downsized to affordable levels with NetWare 5's NIAS.

Of course, you can purchase separate dedicated routers to accomplish these tasks. But to support all the previously described options, you will spend tens of thousands of dollars and you will need to learn completely different administrative and configuration tasks that are unique to each piece of hardware and its operating system. More than likely you will need to purchase several hardware devices to handle the tasks discussed. NetWare 5 can consolidate all these services into one server.

NOTE

See "Novell Internet Access Server 4.1 Management and Optimization" in your online documentation that comes with NetWare 5. You will find that the section on using NIAS is well done. All NetWare 5 documentation uses HTML with links and figures, making the documentation easy to use. You will also find a search option (the magnifying glass icon in the lower-left part of the browser interface) to activate a Java search applet.

The documentation is presented so well that it is not necessary to duplicate much of the material in this book.

NIAS Setup and Configuration

The NIAS character-based opening menu provides two options: Configure NIAS and View Statistics for NIAS. The Configure NIAS menu selection provides two submenu options, one for Remote Access (NCS) and another for Protocols and Routing (INETCFG). Under each option are utilities for managing and configuring or for viewing statistics relating to many LAN, WAN, internetwork, and asynchronous dial-up communications functions and the protocol stacks that are bound to them. You can access NIAS from the server console by typing the command **LOAD NIASCFG**.

NOTE

NetWare 3 and 4 servers have INETCFG.NLM, which is just one of several applications in NIASCFG. This utility can be used to handle complex NIC and protocol configurations in the same manner as discussed in this chapter. MPR and RRAS are available at additional cost for NetWare 3 and 4 servers. These services are managed with separate utilities.

During server setup, driver and protocol configuration commands were added to the AUTOEXEC.NCF file. When you first run NIAS, you will be asked if you want to transfer protocol-related commands from your AUTOEXEC.NCF into NIAS. As more related options are added, AUTOEXEC.NCF becomes more complex and difficult to manage. Transferring the protocol-related commands into the NIAS Btrieve database makes these options much simpler to configure and manage.

NIAS's menu interface is deceptively simple — it incorporates several server-based utilities. The NIAS menu transfers the user interface to a Btrieve database to be managed by several server-based utilities — INETCFG is just one of many. The NIAS utilities are divided into two categories:

- Routing and protocols (INETCFG)

- Remote access (MPR and NWConnect)

As you can see by the lists of utilities in Tables 12.1 and 12.2, NIAS's options are quite extensive.

Routing and Protocol Management

Before setting up other NIAS functions, it is necessary to initialize the NIAS database. This process is pretty much the same as was required with INETCFG — LOAD and BIND statements in AUTOEXEC.NCF must be migrated into a Btrieve database. NIAS pulls information from the database, saves updates to the database, and then retrieves it during server load time. Syntax, switches, and load order are handled automatically without user configuration — each configuration component can be handled from menu-based screens without regard to mechanics of how they are executed.

Setting Up NIAS

When you first load NIASCFG, some setup activities must be performed. To manage protocols, you must migrate protocol commands from your AUTOEXEC.NCF to NIAS's database. This is done automatically, if you choose, when you first run NIASCFG.

I. To initialize NIAS, go to your server's console and type **load NIASCFG**. When you first load NIASCFG, you will receive a message indicating that continuing will move your protocol-related commands from your AUTOEXEC.NCF to the NIAS Btrieve database.

Once you continue past this screen, you will always be required to use NIAS to manage protocol configurations. When you continue, you will find that protocol-related commands have been remarked from your AUTOEXEC.NCF file. Figure 12.1 shows the AUTOEXEC.NCF after commands have been migrated to NIAS. Semicolons (;), pound signs (#), or the word REM or REMARK precede remark statements and will be ignored. These commands will be supplemented with many more and are migrated to a Btrieve database for future management and viewing.

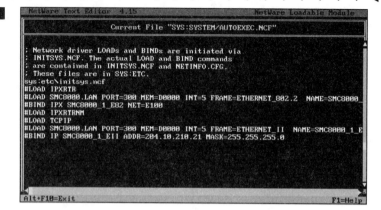

F I G U R E 12.1

AUTOEXEC.NCF after commands have been migrated to the NIAS database

If you prefer to set up NIAS manually, select No, Use the Standard Method and you will see the INETCFG main menu. There is no advantage to using the standard method; you must perform the very same steps if you do. If you elect to use the standard method, follow the same instructions presented in this section.

When using NIAS or INETCFG, you can press F1 at any time to view help screens.

TIP

2. Next you will be asked if you would like to run fast setup. Select Yes, even if you are planning to set up WAN connections, dial-up connections, static routes, or OSPF routing protocol configuration. After running fast setup, you can add more protocols and options at any time.

The fast setup method will install MPR using existing settings and will replace NetWare 5's default internal router. You will see the Configuration Summary screen, listing the NIC drives, frame types, protocols, and addressing options that were configured during server installation as shown in Figure 12.2.

FIGURE 12.2

NIAS board Configuration Summary

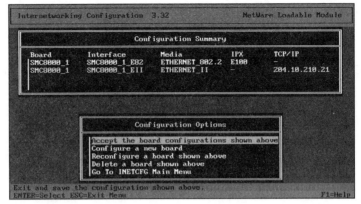

3. Edit or accept the existing configurations and then save your configuration.

Once you finish fast setup, you will see the INETCFG main menu shown in Figure 12.3. Using menu selections, you can add, delete, edit, and save NIC configurations.

FIGURE 12.3

The INETCFG main menu

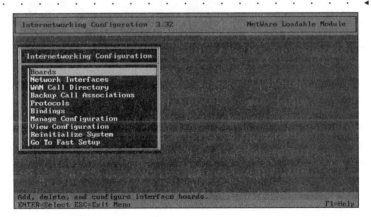

Loading and Configuring Additional NIC Drivers and Protocols

When you use NIAS to set up a network board or protocol, you actually use INETCFG. NIAS transfers — or spawns — the INETCFG.NLM. The process of setting up a NIC in NetWare 3, 4, or 5 is therefore the same. Setting up NIC drivers in NIAS/INETCFG is a little different than using NWCONFIG or the graphical server installation utility. It is more detailed, and each step is selected by the installer individually. You will find that using INETCFG is easier than using NWCONFIG, especially where there is more complexity.

To install a network board using NIAS/INETCFG, follow these steps:

I. Select Boards and you will see a listing of all the NIC drivers installed in your server. You can select a NIC and edit its driver. If your NIC driver is not listed, press Ins at the Select a Driver screen. Enter A:\ or the path name to locate the driver.

2. Once you select a driver, you will see the Board Configuration screen similar to the screen shown in Figure 12.4. Common configuration parameters as well as parameters that are unique to a specific NIC driver will be entered here.

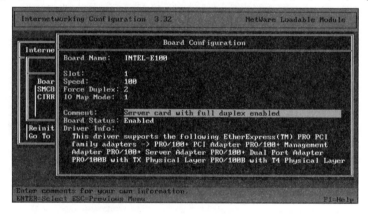

FIGURE 12.4

The Board Configuration screen

3. Select the protocol to be configured in the Protocol Configuration shown in Figure 12.5 from the INETCFG Internetworking Configuration menu. Select each protocol to be used for the selected NIC and enter the protocol configuration options. Protocol configuration options will be unique for each protocol stack.

F I G U R E 12.5

Selecting protocols to be bound to a NIC

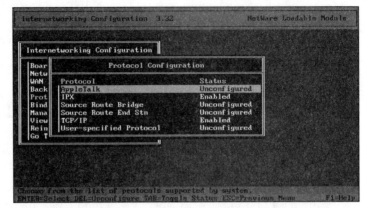

TIP

Notice the green help line at the bottom of the screen showing a brief description of the selected configuration parameter.

4. Select Bindings from the INETCFG Internetworking Configuration screen. Select each board and then review the relationship between the boards, frame types, and protocols. Select Expert Bind Options to enter any parameters unique to that board-protocol combination.

5. Select Manage Configuration from the INETCFG Internetworking Configuration menu. Enter SNMP and Remote Access Console options for this NIC.

8. Select Reinitialize System to load and bind the drivers/protocols you have just configured without rebooting the server.

Loading and Configuring WAN Drivers

Use NAIS/INETCFG as discussed previously to install drivers for synchronous, asynchronous, digital, and other types of communications adapters. Setting up a WAN communications adapter is the same process as setting up a NIC with a few exceptions.

1. Under the Boards menu selection of the INETCFG Internetworking Configuration menu, configuration parameters unique to each type of adapter will be entered in the Board Configuration screen.

2. For ATM, Frame Relay, X.25, and other synchronous or WAN boards, proceed to the Network Interfaces menu selection in the INETCFG Internetworking Configuration menu. Select the board driver you have installed and enter any data-link parameters for that type of board. For example, for a T-1 digital communications board, you will select the board listed in the Network Interfaces screen (or press Ins to load a driver from disk), select the medium (for instance, PPP routing), and then select the interface options. This is where you would enter the type of DCE to be used (such as the brand/model of DSU/CSU).

3. Select WAN Call Directory from the INETCFG Internetworking Configuration menu. Enter the Call Destination.

4. Select Backup Call Destination to enter an alternate call destination in case the primary call destination fails.

5. Select Protocol Configuration from the INETCFG Internetworking Configuration screen shown in Figure 12.5. Select each protocol to be used for the selected adapter just as you would for a NIC, and then enter the protocol configuration options. Protocol configuration options will be unique for each protocol stack.

6. Select Bindings from the INETCFG Internetworking Configuration menu. Select each board, and then review the relationship between the boards, frame types, and protocols. Select Expert Bind Options to enter any parameters unique to that board-protocol combination.

7. Select Manage Configuration from the INETCFG Internetworking Configuration menu. Enter SNMP and Remote Access Console options for this communications device.

8. Select Reinitialize System to activate the new configuration without rebooting the server.

When you select Reinitialize System, all existing remote access and some WAN connections will be interrupted. You should perform this task after hours or at a time when these connections will not interfere with work in progress.

Configuring Protocols

You can edit transport protocol stack configurations in the Protocol menu selection as shown in Figure 12.6.

▶ · ◀

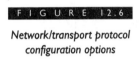

FIGURE 12.6

Network/transport protocol
configuration options

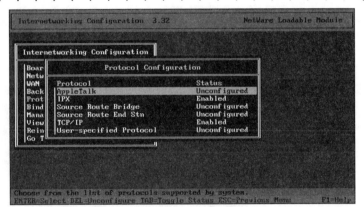

IPX/SPX Protocol Configuration

You can edit IPX-, TCP/IP-, and AppleTalk-related protocols from this menu. Select IPX to see the protocol configuration options that are available, as shown in Figure 12.7.

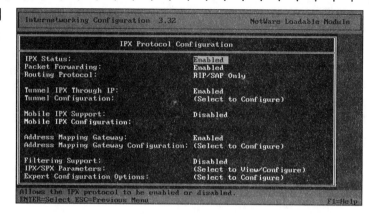

FIGURE 12.7

IPX configuration options in INETCFG

TCP/IP and Related Settings

Select TCP/IP to view and change settings for several configurations as shown in Figure 12.8.

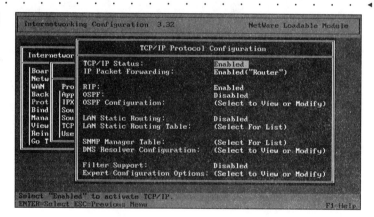

FIGURE 12.8

TCP/IP and related configuration settings

This is how you configure IP routing, SNMP, DNS, and filtering options. For broadcast, BootP, and EGP settings, enable the Filter Support, and select Expert Configuration Options.

You can add static routes by configuring the RIP protocol. Select Protocols → TCP/IP. Set LAN Static Routing to Enable, select LAN Static Routing Table, and press Ins to enter routes. Routes added here will supplement route discovery information obtained from RIP protocol communications. Use this option to configure routes that do not appear automatically. For example, RIP broadcasts may be suppressed over a router, but this option will enable you to establish permanent route information that does not depend upon RIP broadcasts.

Bindings

This menu selection is where you bind the NIC drivers and frame types to the protocols as well as where you assign IPX network addresses, IP addresses, network addresses, subnet masks, and related configurations. The Bindings menu selection is also used to configure routing protocols. NetWare 5 supports RIP, RIPII, and OSPF routing protocols for TCP/IP. To configure these protocols, select a TCP/IP binding to one of your NICs under the Bindings menu.

View Configuration

Use NIAS/INETCFG to view your current protocol configurations. Select View Configuration — you will see the screen shown in Figure 12.9.

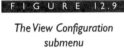

F I G U R E 12.9

The View Configuration submenu

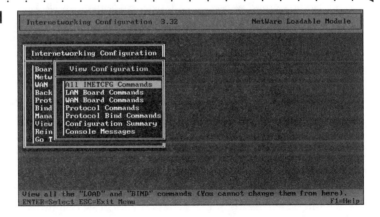

Commands in this screen are presented in the same manner as if these commands were to be executed in the AUTOEXEC.NCF file, but the syntax you see is not stored in this way. NIAS/INETCFG simply provides a more user-friendly way to enter configuration parameters for more complex configurations and then presents it in a way that is familiar to NetWare administrators. When viewing configuration commands in this part of INETCFG, you are viewing LOAD and BIND commands in a read-only mode.

The statements and switches you view in these screens are stored in a relational database so that they can be sorted and viewed in different views. You will see portions of the same commands expressed differently in more than one screen. These commands are not executed exactly as seen, but command execution will have the same effect as if they were executed in the manner in which you view them.

These menu selections provide the following functionality:

▶ *All INETCFG Commands* — This menu selection shows all LOAD commands that have been migrated to INETCFG data files and can be viewed in AUTOEXEC.NCF format.

▶ *LAN Board Commands* — This menu selection shows LOAD driver and BIND protocol commands. These commands contain essential NIC driver switches, frame type switches, IP configuration values including IP addresses and subnet masks, and IPX network numbers.

▶ *WAN Board Commands* — This menu selection shows the equivalent LOAD and BIND commands for WAN boards and their associated protocols, including PPP, ATM, Frame Relay, and X.25.

▶ *Protocol Commands* — The commands viewed in this screen control protocol commands for IPX/SPX, TCP/IP, AppleTalk, and routing protocols.

▶ *Protocol Bind Commands* — These are the BIND commands, which are also viewed under the Boards menu selection.

▶ *Configuration Summary* — This screen summarizes LAN and WAN interfaces, listing frame types and address assignments.

▶ *Console Messages* — When you select this item, you will view the CONLOG file, which lists all console screen messages. CONLOG captures all console screen printing and directs it to the CONSOLE.LOG file for viewing. Use this selection to view screen messages that have scrolled off the screen before you have a chance to read them. For example, you can view error messages that occurred during boot.

Remote Access Services

Remote Access Services (RAS) — also known as Novell Communications Services (NCS) — was previously known as NetWare Connect. This product allows users to dial in and out of synchronous and asynchronous interface devices and ports and to log into a network. Users can then access all remote access services that have been set up and configured and can access all IPX, TCP/IP, and AppleTalk network services through NDS. When remote access consoles in NIAS are set up, remote users can manage the protocol consoles from any network or dial-up connection. RAS supports modems, ISDN, X.25, and many types of digital and analog communications adapters.

Remote Access supports modems and DSU/CSUs as well as the following types of communications devices:

- ▸ Serial ports

- ▸ Serial communications adapters (Digiboards, Equinox boards, and so on)

- ▸ ISDN modems and terminal adapters

- ▸ X.25

- ▸ Multiport communications boards

- ▸ Digital communications adapters (T-1/E-1, digital data service, and so on)

- ▸ Frame Relay interface devices

- ▸ ATM server adapters

Many interface devices are installed and configured as network adapters in the same manner as a NIC. However, other devices, such as ATM and Frame Relay adapters, require special protocol management options. NIAS provides console utilities for managing these devices.

A multiport communications adapter is also installed as a NIC. Once a driver is installed, your system will recognize the onboard communications ports as

COM3, COM4, COM5, and so on. Several brands of multiport communications adapters are available, such as the Digi International's Digiboard products. These products generally come in 4-, 8-, 16-, 32-, and 64-port models with external RS-232 port interfaces and vendor-supplied drivers.

TIP

Look for PCI multiport communication adapters that feature an on-board processor. It is very important to off-load port polling to the board to reduce the impact on your server's processor utilization. You will also find that this type of product generally performs better and is more effective at clearing ports than dumb 16-bit adapters.

Setting Up and Configuring Novell Communications Services

If Novell Communications Services (NCS) has not been used yet, it must be set up. You can use the automatic setup routine, which is executed the first time you access the Remote Access menu selection in NIASCFG. NIAS setup is a prerequisite to setting up NCS. The first time you select the Remote Access menu item within NIAS, the automatic setup utility will run. The automatic setup loads drivers for I/O devices and creates the Connect object in the NDS tree. Once RAS is set up, the NetWare Connect console utility (NWCCON.NLM) will run instead.

Automated setup steps you through three stages of configuration:

▸ Selecting and loading communications adapters

▸ Configuring modem parameters

▸ Selecting which remote access services are to be used.

Before You Begin

Before you execute the automatic setup routine, be sure the following steps have been completed:

1. Physically install and configure all communications devices, eliminating all potential hardware conflicts.

2. Set up NIAS as discussed previously in this chapter.

3. Connect and power-up all external modems and digital communications devices.

4. If you have any synchronous communications adapters, such as X.25, ISDN synchronous adapters, or digital communications boards, first set them up as you would set up a NIC. You should use NIAS's Protocols and Routing menu selection (INETCFG) to select, configure, and load these device drivers before proceeding.

NDS Considerations

Whether you use the automatic setup process or the manual setup process, the Connect object must be created in your NDS tree. The automatic setup places the Connect object in the [Root] of your tree. This placement extends usage to all users in the tree and restricts management to the Admin or other users who have Supervisor NDS rights to the [Root] object. You can use NIAS or NetWare Administrator to move the Connect object after installation if desired.

TIP

You can use any of several techniques to manipulate NDS rights configurations to restrict remote access usage. You can place the Connect object in an organizational unit other than the [Root] container. All users in the tree in and beneath the container in which you place the Connect object will have NDS rights to use remote access services. To assign an administrator for remote access services, assign NDS Supervisor object rights and Supervisor property rights to the remote access administrator. This can be done by making a user (or Role object) a trustee of the Connect object or of the container in which the Connect object is placed.

Another option is to place the Connect object in a separate container, such as an organizational unit dedicated for containing resources. When using this configuration, create a Group object for access to the Connect object and give the Group object Browse object rights and Read object property rights to all properties. When you make users members of the group, they inherit the NDS rights of the Group object. Another alternative is to create an Alias object of the Connect object and place it in the target container.

Remote Access Automatic Setup Procedure

Setting up remote access is simplified with an automatic setup option. Start NIASCFG by typing the command **load NIASCFG** at the server console prompt.

I. Select Configure NIAS → Remote Access. You will be notified that the service is not set up. If you continue, the automatic setup procedure will walk you through a setup process.

2. You will be asked, "Do you have any Synchronous Adapters?" Synchronous adapters includes digital communications boards and X.25 or ISDN adapters. They do not include asynchronous adapters such as Digi or other brands of multiport adapters. If you answer Yes, you will be switched to INETCFG automatic setup. However, these devices cannot be configured in automatic setup. If you have not already set up these devices, you should exit automatic setup without saving changes and load/configure the drivers in NIAS/INETCFG.

NOTE
Asynchronous devices, such as multiport communications adapters or existing serial ports, and ISDN terminal adapters are treated as asynchronous devices, whereas ISDN synchronous devices are treated as synchronous adapters. Many of these devices can also be installed as NICs in INETCFG prior to running automatic setup.

   a. If any synchronous adapters have been installed, answer Yes to this question. Automatic setup will transfer LOAD statements from AUTOEXEC.NCF, if they are located there, and then proceed to configuration steps as required. If the devices have not been set up, automatic setup will then proceed to the MPR fast setup procedure; however, fast setup does not support this option at this time. You should exit and set up the devices manually in NAIS/INETCFG and then restart the automatic setup procedure. If you press Esc, you will be offered an opportunity to abort automatic setup without saving changes.

   b. If you have no synchronous communications adapters, answer No to this query.

3. Now install asynchronous serial port drivers.

  a. If you have physically installed a multiport serial adapter and the drivers for it, you will see a notification box indicating how many AIO devices (ports) are available (see Figure 12.10). If all ports are recognized, skip to step 4.

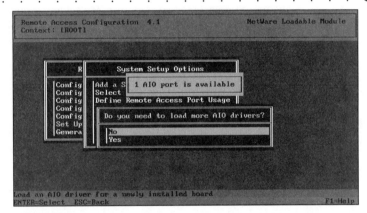

FIGURE 12.10

All AIO devices installed and recognized

  b. If you have physically installed a multiport serial adapter but have not installed the drivers, you will see a notification box indicating that no AIO ports are defined. Press Enter to select a driver that matches your board. You will see a list of AIO device drivers shown in Figure 12.11.

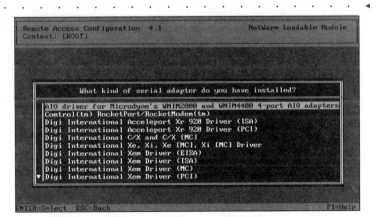

FIGURE 12.11

Serial adapter driver listings

c. If your driver is not found in this list, or if you have a later driver provided by the board manufacturer for NetWare 5, select Other Board Not Listed Above.

d. After selecting the driver, you will be asked to enter the configuration settings for the type of board. If you enter a setting incorrectly, or if a setting conflicts with another device, you will be switched to the console to view the error message. If this is the case, you must physically reconfigure the device so that it is set properly and does not conflict with other devices.

e. After installing your driver, you will see a notification box indicating the number of available AIO ports and a question box asking if you need to load more AIO drivers. If you need to install another multiport serial adapter, answer Yes and repeat the process of installing a driver. If not, and if all ports are available, answer No to continue.

4. In this step, the Remote Access Server will detect modems connected to the AIO ports. Be sure all modems are turned on and functioning and then press Enter to continue. The modem polling process will start in a few seconds; when it is completed, the status screen will indicate how many modems and X.25 and ISDN devices have been located. If all modems were not discovered, select Try Modem Discovery Again. If all modems have been found, select Continue with Automatic Setup.

5. Next, automatic setup will attempt to autodetect the types — brands and models — of modems attached to AIO ports. Automatic setup will then list ports where it has discovered modems.

If automatic setup could not determine the type of modem, you will be notified of this result, and a Modem Names screen will be displayed with a list of modems. If some modems were not discovered, check the modem to see that it is turned on and functioning. If the port was acknowledged, the problem is in the modem cable or the modem itself. Select your modem from the list. If your modem model is not displayed, select Hayes Compatible. You can manually configure the modem in NIAS or enter

setup strings later if needed. When all modems types have been
configured, select Continue with Automated Setup.

8. Select which Remote Access Services are to be used. The following list
describes the available services:

a. *ARAS* — AppleTalk Remote Access Service, to be used for dial-in service
from Macintosh remote clients.

b. *NCS* — NASI (NetWare Asynchronous Services Interface)
Communications Services, to be used to extend dial-out modem
sharing to clients on the network.

c. *PPPRNS* — PPP Remote Node Service, for any type of dial-in client that
uses Point-to-Point Protocol.

d. *RAMA* — Remote Access Management Agent, to provide access to
remote clients using ConnectView (in ManageWise).

**Be sure to select PPRNS for all dial-in ports, and select NCS for all
dial-out ports.**

NOTE

7. Select the transport protocols to be used over each service. When
configuring the IP protocol, you will need to enter a unique IP address and
subnet mask for each port. When configuring IPX, you will need to assign
the server's IPX network number.

8. When you complete this step for each port and protocol, the drivers will be
loaded.

Once you have completed automatic setup, RAS is ready for use. The next time
you access the Remote Access menu selection in NIASCFG, you will not enter
automatic setup.

Editing Configurations

You can edit configurations for AIO ports, modems, and services to be used by
entering NIAS → Configure NIAS → Remote Access → Set Up. Select the menu
item that you would like to configure from the list shown in Figure 12.12.

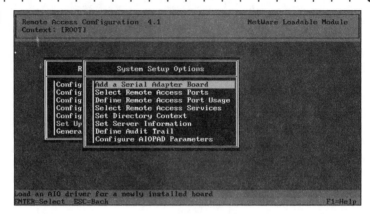

FIGURE 12.12

Reconfiguring Remote Access Server setup options

NCS Dial-Up Clients

Clients have two options for dial-in: remote node and remote control. Remote node service provides a connection to the network, but the connection is limited to the bandwidth provided by the communications medium. For example, if the user dials in with a 28,800 bps modem connection, communications are limited to this rate. Even a T-1 connection only provides 1.55Mbps throughput, which is very limited for many network applications. Client/server applications, including Web-based applications, are designed for this type of connection, but if a user needs to execute an application, such as NetWare Administrator, a remote node connection is not suitable. For this type of service, remote control is mandated.

A remote control connection allows the user to take control of a host workstation where program execution can run at network speeds. The remote user's workstation becomes a terminal to the host computer, executing screen updates and sending keystrokes to the host workstation. This allows the remote user to execute any applications just as if he or she were seated at the host computer. Performance is not as good as when one is seated at the host computer, but it is perfectly acceptable for most purposes when executing Windows applications.

Client workstations with modems can dial in using one of four services:

> ▶ *Point-to-Point Protocol Remote Node Service (PPPRNS)* — Most clients will use PPPRNS. This service binds PPP remote clients to asynchronous ports. It is used for remote node service.

▶ *AppleTalk Remote Access Service (ARAS)* — Macintosh clients use ARAS, which is a protocol in the AppleTalk protocol stack for remote access.

▶ *Remote Access Management Agent (RAMA)* — ManageWise clients use RAMA, which is used to service ConnectView remote console access over TCP/IP.

▶ *NASI Connection Service* (NCS, not to be confused with Novell Communications Services) — NCS is used for remote control; it is to be used with third-party communications software to access network nodes other than the Novell Connection Service server. At the incoming server end, NCS uses NASI to access network nodes. NCS binds the port to the network node, which is one of several functions that NASI handles.

Dial-up clients use a combination of workstation operating system and Novell client components. To support DOS clients, install the DOS 32-bit client and the Novell IPX/SPX protocol stack — the DOS VLMs and NETX are not supported. For Windows 3.1 and Windows for Workgroup 3.11 clients, you must install the Novell IPX/SPX protocol and Client-32 from the Z.E.N.works Starter Pack CD. The Microsoft IPX-Compatible protocol (or NWLink) is not compatible with NASI remote control capabilities. Macintosh clients use AppleTalk components exclusively.

On the Z.E.N.works Starter pack, you will find all that is needed to set up Windows clients. Two components may need to be installed:

▶ Novell Remote Access Dialer

▶ Win2NCS

The Novell Remote Access Dialer is software that is incorporated into the NetWare client login to permit login over a dial-up modem connection. This component is one of the options that is available when installing the Novell Windows client software in the custom mode. It adds a Dial-Up tab to the login screen that has options for connecting and logging into a remote NetWare server over a local modem connection. The Novell Remote Access Dialer uses PPP to access the NCS server.

Win2NCS is a separate utility that polls the network for shared modems and then allows a user to map a local communications port to the shared modems on the NCS server. Win2NCS uses NASI for access to modem resources over the network. Win2NCS enables two features for dial-up users: First, it allows a local port to be redirected to an NCS port and modem. Second, it allows the use of remote control software over NCS to other network nodes. Win2NCS is not required to simply dial in to the NCS server for a direct connection.

The steps to setting up a dial-up connection for Windows clients are as follows:

1. Install Win2NCS if required.

2. Install a modem and configure connection properties.

3. Create a Windows Dial Up Networking Connection (Phonebook entry).

4. Install the Novell Remote Access Dialer.

5. Configure the dial-up properties in the NetWare login application.

These steps will enable you to log in locally, or to log into a remote NetWare server using NCS as your connection to the remote network.

Installing and Configuring Win2NCS

Win2NCS allows users to use remote control software over the network. For example, users needing to access their desktop computers from home can install Win2NCS, pcAnywhere Remote (or another remote control software), and Windows' Dial Up Networking on their home computers, also installing pcAnywhere Host software on their desktop computers. Users can then dial into the NCS server and take control of their office desktop computers.

Figure 12.13 demonstrates the communications process — the remote notebook computer has pcAnywhere remote running with Win2NCS and Windows Dial Up Networking. The remote user is dialed into the NCS server at work, and the host desktop computer is located anywhere on the local network at work. In this illustration, the notebook user is running NetWare Administrator — the program is being executed on the desktop computer, while the notebook is handling keyboard and video traffic only.

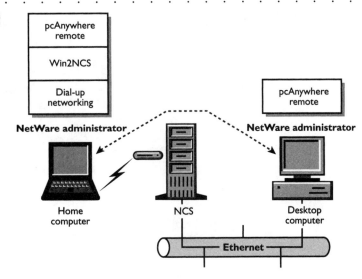

FIGURE 12.13

Remote control over the network via Win2NCS and NASI

You can use pcAnywhere, Carbon Copy, Reachout, Procomm, LapLink, and most any communications software with Win2NCS. Virtually all network-ready communications software supports NASI communications.

To install Win2NCS:

1. Run WINSETUP.EXE from your Z.E.N.works Starter Pack CD. Select Start → Run and enter *drive*:\WINSETUP.EXE.

2. Select the language to use and then select Install Win2NCS from the next screen.

To map a local port to a shared NCS port:

1. Select Win2NCS Com Port Mapping → Win2NCS from your Start menu.

2. From the menu bar select Options → Map Communications Port. Notice that as the next screen comes up, shared ports are polled and then displayed in the Available Services box as shown in Figure 12.14.

FIGURE 12.14

Available services in the
Win2NCS Map
Communications Ports
screen

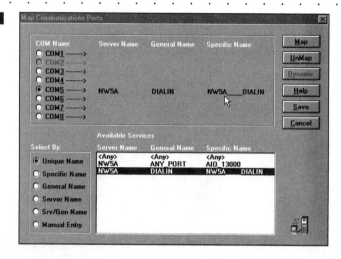

3. Select a shared port from the list in the Available Services box, and then select a radio button next to a communications port from the list in the COM Name box. Use a port that is not physically installed in your computer.

4. Select the Save button to map the port.

Your mapped port will now work like any other local communications port.

Installing Your Modem in Windows

When you run the Install New Modem Wizard in Windows Control Panel, select the check box that says "Don't detect my modem; I will select it from a list." Select the type of modem to be accessed or Standard Modem, Standard 19,200 bps modem. As you continue, the Novell NASI ports will show up along with other ports when the "Select the port to use with the modem" screen appears.

Creating a Windows Dial Up Networking Connection (Phonebook Entry)

The Phonebook entries are configured in Windows' Dial Up Networking applet, accessible from the My Computer applet on your desktop. Select the Make a New Connection Wizard to create a Phonebook entry.

If Dial Up Networking has not been installed:

▸ *For Windows 95 and 98*, Dial Up Networking is installed through Control Panel's Add/Remove Programs applet under Windows Setup. If Dial Up Networking has not been installed, select Control Panel → Add/Remove Programs → Communications → Details. Check the Dial Up Networking box and select OK. When you exit, you will be prompted to insert your Windows 95 or 98 CD, and Dial Up Networking components will be installed.

▸ *For Windows NT*, select the My Computer applet, and then select Dial Up Networking. If Dial Up Networking was not originally installed, it will be installed when this applet is first accessed. The Setup Wizard will also install Remote Access Services (RAS) as a dependency service. When configuring RAS, select the NCS modem port. If you have not set up the NCS modem port, see the instructions earlier in this chapter.

▸ *For Windows 3.1 and Windows for Workgroups 3.11*, you will need to obtain third-party dialer software. Several Windows 3.1*x* dialers are available on the Internet.

To set up a Windows 95 or 98 Dial Up Networking Connection:

1. Select Dial Up Networking in Control Panel, and then select Make New Connection. The Add Connection Wizard will run.

2. Enter a name for the connection. Select the connection for the local modem — or for a NASI port that was configured with Win2NCS.

3. Enter the area code and phone number to be dialed. Select Finish to end the Make New Connection Wizard.

4. Select the Dial Up Networking Connection you just created. In the Dial Up Networking program group, select File → Properties.

5. Select the Server Types tab. For Type of Dial-Up Server select PPP, Windows 95, Windows NT 3.5, Internet if using TCP/IP. If using IPX/SPX Compatible, select NRN: NetWare Connect.

6. Select the protocols to use. If using TCP/IP, select the TCP/IP Settings button.

7. Leave the default Server Assigned IP Address option as is.

8. Select Specify Name Server Addresses, and then enter the DNS server information for the remote network.

You can now use this Dial Up Networking Connection to dial out using NCS. You can create a shortcut for your desktop for quick dialing. Check applications for options for an option to automatically call up the Dial Up Networking Connection when the application is executed.

For a Windows NT Phonebook entry:

1. Create a new Phonebook Entry.

a. If no previous Phonebook Entries have been created, Windows NT will run the New Phonebook Entry Wizard. When running the wizard, enter the phone number for the target server and select the modem — or select the port that was mapped using Win2NCS. Complete the wizard questions, then select the Phonebook entry, and then select the More button to edit the Phonebook Entry properties as discussed in the next few steps.

b. If other phonebook entries have been created, select the New button in your Phonebook Entry selection screen. In the New Phonebook Entry screen, enter the phone number for the target server. In the Dial Using box, select the modem — or select the port that was mapped using Win2NCS.

2. Select the Server tab at the top of the screen. Select or enter the following properties:

- *Dial-up server type:* Select PPP, Windows NT, Windows 95 Plus, Internet.

- *Network Protocols:* Select TCP/IP and/or IPX/SPX compatible.

3. When using TCP/IP, select the TCP/IP Settings button, and then select:

- Server assigned IP address

- Specify name server addresses

Enter the DNS server addresses. You may leave the other check boxes set to their defaults.

Configuring the Dial-Up tab in this manner will enable you to select either a local login or a dial-up login when your NetWare login screen comes up.

Installing the Novell Remote Access Dialer

The Novell Remote Access Dialer is used to log into a NetWare server with a dial-up connection. When this utility is installed, your login screen will include the Dial-Up tab under the Advanced Properties dialog box. The Dial-Up screen can be configured to log in locally or to dial up using Windows' Dial Up Networking.

 Win2NCS is not required for a simple dial-up login and connection to a server.

NOTE

Install the Novell Remote Access Dialer when running WINSETUP.EXE from the NetWare Z.E.N.works Starter Pack CD. During setup, select Custom Installation Options to see the screen shown in Figure 12.15. Select the check box for the Novell Remote Access Dialer to add this to your client setup.

FIGURE 12.15

*Selecting the Novell Remote
Access Dialer in Winsetup*

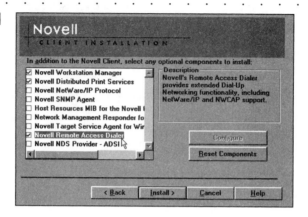

Configuring the Dial-Up Connection in the Login Screens

If you need to log into a NetWare server over a dial-up connection, you must next configure the Dial-Up login tab. This is accomplished by creating a new service in a location profile.

1. Select the Novell icon in the system tray (at the lower-right end of your Windows taskbar), and then select Novell Client Properties.

2. Select the Location Profiles tab. Enter a profile name in the New Location Profile box for the location from which you will be calling, and then select the Add button. You will see the Location Profile Properties screen as shown in Figure 12.16.

3. In the Service box, select the Login Service; in the Service Instance screen, select the Default service; and then select the Properties button.

4. Select the Dial-Up tab to see the login properties screen shown in Figure 12.17.

5. Select the Enable Tab check box, Login Using (Microsoft) Dial-up Networking, and the Phonebook Entry to Dial. Select OK to save your configuration.

FIGURE 12.16

The Location Profile
Properties screen

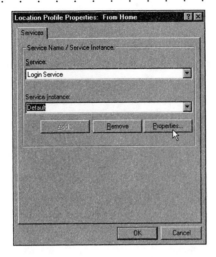

Configuring the Novell
Remote Access Dialer

FIGURE 12.17

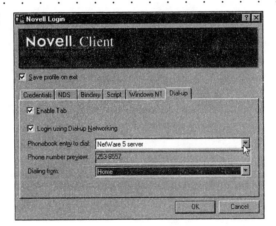

When logging in, you can select or deselect dial-up login by selecting the Advanced button and then the Dial-Up tab of the login screen. Select or deselect the check box for Login using Dial Up Networking.

NOTE

Network Clients Dialing Out

Once your Remote Access Server is set up with modems, network clients can dial out from any network workstation using Windows' Dial Up Networking or any communications package. Win2NCS is used to map a local serial port to a shared NCS port, so that you can dial out on that port as if it were a local port. NASI redirects modem communications over the network transparently.

Win2NCS provides the mechanism to map to shared AIO ports on an NCS server. Using Win2NCS is not much different from mapping to a network volume or capturing a printer—it is used to map a local serial port (COM3, COM4, and so on) to the shared AIO port. The AIO port is given a name in NIAS's Remote Access setup. Win2NCS redirects communications for the mapped local port to the AIO port using NASI.

The user can just dial out with Windows Dial Up Networking or with third-party communications software. The Win2NCS application is shown in Figure 12.18.

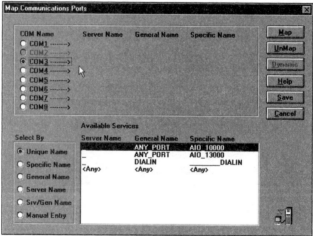

FIGURE 12.18

Win2NCS mapping application

Install Win2NCS from the Z.E.N.works Starter Pack CD as discussed previously in this chapter under " Installing and Configuring Win2NCS." Use Win2NCS to map communications to the general name specified in NCS setup. The default general name DIALOUT is created in NIASCFG Remote Access setup as shown in Figure 12.18. To locate this parameter, at your server load NIASCFG → Configure

NIAS → Remote Access → Configure Services → NCS (which must have been set up under Setup).

▶ · ◀

FIGURE 12.19

NIASCFG Remote Access
AIO port setup

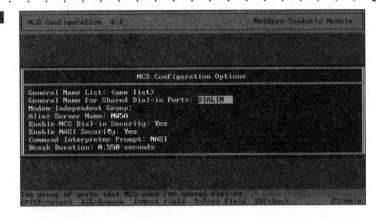

Configuring Remote Console Access

You can manage your NetWare servers remotely using remote console access utilities. The utilities shown in Table 12.3 enable you to access almost all server functions from network and dial-up workstations.

TABLE 12.3

Remote Console Access
Utilities

UTILITY	REMOTE ACCESS OVER
RCONSOLE	IPX/SPX networks
ACONSOLE	Asynchronous modems connected to your server
RCONSOLEJ	TCP/IP networks
Console One	A Java remote console to load the Console One utility over TCP/IP networks
ConnectView	Means to manage server console functions remotely in a Windows-based utility (only in ManageWise) over TCP/IP networks

NOTE

At this time only RCONSOLE will enable you to manage all character-based screens. RCONSOLEJ currently lacks the ability to support NIASCFG over its connections. Watch Novell's Web sites for updates to this utility. You can manage NIAS remotely over TCP/IP with ConnectView, a Windows-based workstation utility included in ManageWise.

Configuring Server Remote Console Access over IPX/SPX or by a Modem Attached to the Server

Configuring remote access over IPX/SPX will enable you to access your server's character-based screens over IPX/SPX networks. The server uses RSPX.NLM and REMOTE.NLM to provide access—the client uses RCONSOLE to access the remote console. For access over a modem directly attached to the server, the server uses RS232.NLM and REMOTE.NLM. A password assigned for this purpose protects access to the console. Setting up remote console access was previously done manually, but now it is handled in NIAS. It still can be done manually, but if the commands are executed in the AUTOEXEC.BAT, your password must be entered manually during server boot. NIAS's Remote Console Access option stores the commands and password in the server's boot database for security and easy configuration.

To configure your server for console access with RCONSOLE:

I. Load NIASCFG and choose Configure NIAS → Protocols and Routing → Manage Configuration Configure Remote Console.

2. Select the Remote Console Access field, press Enter, and then toggle the entry to Enabled.

3. Configure your remote console for access using RCONSOLE and/or ACONSOLE as shown in Figure 12.20. An RCONSOLE connection is made over IPX, and an ACONSOLE connection is made over a modem. Use the Expert Modem Setup to enter any modem setup strings that may be required for your modem.

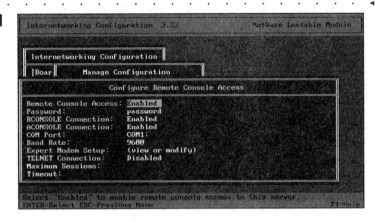

F I G U R E   12.20

Setting up Remote Console
Access

Once you have saved your changes, you will need to reboot your server or enter the commands manually at the console for them to become effective. To manually establish the remote console server environment:

1. At the server console enter the command

```
load RSPX
```

2. Assign a remote console password when prompted for the password.

You can now access the console from a client workstation.

Accessing the Remote Console from an IPX/SPX Client or Modem
To access the remote console from a workstation using IPX/SPX:

1. Log into an IPX- or IPX Compatibility–enabled workstation with NDS rights as supervisor of the server object.

2. Map a search drive the SYS:PUBLIC directory of your NetWare 5 server.

3. Execute RCONSOLE.EXE. Select the server to access from the list. All servers with the remote console properly enabled for IPX/SPX will be listed.

4. Enter the remote console password previously assigned for this server.

You will then see the character-based server screen that is active. Press Alt+F1 for a menu to switch to other character-based server screens.

To access the remote console from a remote workstation using a modem directly connected to the server:

1. Log into a workstation with a modem properly installed with NDS rights as supervisor of the server object.

2. Execute the ACONSOLE.EXE application. Copy this file to a local directory from the SYS:PUBLIC directory of a NetWare 5 server, or execute the application from the NetWare 5 server directory.

3. Select the Asynchronous menu selection. Enter the phone number to be dialed to access the remote server.

4. Select the server from the list, and then enter the remote console password assigned previously.

You will then see the character-based server screen that is active. Press Alt+F1 for a menu to switch to other character-based server screens.

Configuring Server Remote Console Access over TCP/IP

To load remote support for viewing character-based server screens over TCP/IP:

1. At the NetWare 5 server console enter the command

   ACONAG6

2. When asked for the password, enter a password to be used to access this console.

3. When asked for the TCP/UDP port number, press Enter for the default port number 2034, or enter the port number of your choice.

WARNING

If you enter a custom port number, be sure it will not conflict with any TCP/IP application. The same port number will need to be entered from a workstation to access the console.

4. When prompted for the IPX socket (port) number, press Enter to accept the default of 16800.

You can now access this console over TCP/IP from a client workstation.

Accessing the Remote Console from a TCP/IP Client

To load remote console support over TCP/IP, follow these steps:

1. Log into a Windows 95, 98, or NT TCP/IP-based client workstation with NDS rights as supervisor of the server object.

2. Execute RCONSOLEJ.EXE. You will find this application in the SYS:PUBLIC/MGMT directory of your NetWare 5 server.

3. Enter the server IP address, the TCP port number, and the password, and then select the Connect button. You will then be able to view the character-based server screens.

4. Select the forward (>) or backward (<<) buttons to scroll to different screens, or select the Server Screens box's down arrow for a list of available screens. You can synchronize the remote and server console screens.

Configuring Remote Access over an NCS Dial-Up Connection

You can also access a server console remotely over a dial-up connection when you are dialed into an NCS server and Win2NCS is installed at the workstation. Once dialed in, you can access RCONSOLE or RCONSOLEJ as long as all the requirements are met as discussed for network clients.

If you are to access any applications remotely, it is necessary to use remote control communications software. Executing any applications remotely requires far too much traffic over the connection to be practical with a T-1 connection or less. The only utility that will work from a practical standpoint is RCONSOLE.

PART III

Troubleshooting and Maintenance

CHAPTER 13

LAN and Cabling

The LAN to which your servers and clients are attached is a platform—if the platform is unstable, the whole network is unstable. LAN problems cause downtime and cost organizations thousands of dollars in lost revenues, lost productivity, and support costs. If a portion of the costs are captured and invested in preventing problems, these costs can be reduced significantly.

Though this chapter deals with the cold, hard reality of troubleshooting cabling and LAN problems, you should be aware that a well-designed and properly installed cabling system is the foundation of the entire network. You will never have to spend much time wrestling with the problems discussed in this chapter if you have followed the suggestions offered here and in Chapter 5.

In this book, the term *LAN* is used to mean the Ethernet, Token Ring, FDDI, or other type of local area network.

NOTE

A LAN is made up of at least two layers—the physical layer and the data-link layer. The physical layer consists of cabling, LAN devices, NIC circuitry, and such. The data-link layer consists of software-related functions, such as LAN protocols, frame formatting, addressing, and related functions. The physical layer handles bits and electrical signals that represent bits. The data-link layer handles frames, the protocol data units that carry network packets (such as IPX or IP packets) to their destinations. Some LANs (including FDDI and ATM) include a third layer for managing interaction between the other two layers and reporting potential problems.

In this chapter, only two layers are discussed: the physical and the data-link layers. This book is focused on technologies that you will encounter day-in and day-out in most business environments: mainly Ethernet and Fast Ethernet. These platforms are the overwhelming favorites used between client workstations and servers. Management layers are specific to types of LANs that are less common and more expensive, such as FDDI and ATM.

Statistically speaking, cabling problems alone account for over 50 percent of all network problems. Having realized this fact, many organizations have invested heavily in their cabling plants and have reduced this problem to an occasional connector replacement. A sloppy cable plant causes years' worth of headaches— it is far better to take every step possible to ensure that cabling is installed with meticulous care according to specifications.

Cabling specifications in this chapter relate back to TIA/EIA 568A specifications, which are now well established. See Chapter 5, "Preparing the Server and LAN" for more details on LAN cabling.

 Refer to Anixter's Web site for an excellent guide on cabling rules. You will find the Anixter Structured Cabling System Design guide in their technical library at `http://www.anixter.com/techlib/standard/cabling`**.**

NOTE

LAN Devices

LAN components—NICs, hubs, and switches—are built to last virtually forever but do occasionally fail. Wherever these components fail, the network manager must search for an extraordinary cause. Several problems commonly cause these components to fail including:

▸ Heat

▸ Dust

▸ Lightning

▸ Electrical abnormalities (including surges, spikes, R.F. noise, improper grounding)

Newer buildings and cabling plants are installed according to the TIA/EIA 568/569 standards discussed in Chapter 5. These specifications were not formalized until 1996, so few buildings are fully compliant. Even cabling that was installed with the intention of conforming to these specifications may fail the test of working properly. The goals of these specifications are often defeated by sloppy workmanship and cost-cutting, which are encouraged through inadequate supervision and inspections.

Though building codes mandate strict conformity, inspectors are only able to spot-check and are primarily concerned with issues that present hazards. When violations are observed, corrections are mandated, but the inspectors often do not have the time or interest to come back and review corrections. Oversights result from the many changes that are made during the final construction stages. The bottom line is that even in newer buildings cable plants are often fraught with problems. Electricians are often lax in their attention to details because 110 volt and telephone wiring is quite forgiving — sloppy workmanship rarely prevents lights and power outlets from working. LAN cabling is different, however — even the slightest variation from specifications can cause significant problems that are difficult to diagnose.

This chapter addresses cabling and LAN component problems in simple terms. Sophisticated equipment is available to monitor and diagnose cabling and LAN problems. Day-to-day troubleshooting using common tools and visual observation will often reveal the source of most cabling problems. This chapter emphasizes the day-to-day tools you will use to diagnose and correct the majority of your LAN problems.

Cabling Types

First, let's take a look at what kind of cabling is to be discussed. Today, only two types of cabling are commonly used for all types of LANs: unshielded twisted-pair (UTP) and optical fiber (fiber optics). Both are highly sensitive to seemingly minor problems. In this book, we refer to the TIA/EIA 568A rules for workstation cabling and the TIA/EIA 569 rules for building backbones (between wiring closets). TIA/EIA 568A discusses rules for *horizontal* cabling — the cabling that extends from wiring closets and hubs to workstations. Workstation cabling is almost exclusively UTP today, whereas backbones should include both UTP and optical fiber.

Coaxial Cable

Coaxial cabling was the most popular type of LAN cabling at one time, but it is rarely used or even found today. If you have any coaxial Ethernet cabling (thick-net or thin-net), you can test it with a continuity tester and/or ohmmeter. Thin Ethernet cable should be RG-58a/u or RG-58c/u. Thick Ethernet should be rated for use as Ethernet cabling. Both types are rated at 50 ohms. TV coaxial cable (CATV) and other coaxial cable should never be used. CATV is 75 ohm, and IBM

5250 workstation/ARCnet coax is 93 ohm. Each computer connection must have a tee, and the two end connections must have 50-ohm terminators. Test for continuity at any computer connection: the outside is the ground and the inner connector should carry –5 volts. If you are testing with an ohmmeter, each connection should show 25 ohms of resistance, plus or minus 10 percent.

Optical Fiber

Fiber optic cabling is used for longer distances, generally between hubs. Whereas a cable segment of unshielded twisted-pair can extend no more than 100 meters (321 feet) for Ethernet, fiber optic extends the distance to as much as 2 kilometers (1.2 miles). Optical fiber uses light instead of electrical signals and is therefore immune from many types of electrical interference discussed in this chapter.

Optical fiber comes in two varieties: multimode and single mode. Single mode is thinner and provides better characteristics over longer distances, but both types can be used.

It is no longer completely true that optical fiber is more expensive than other types of cable. The cable itself is about the same cost as other LAN cable types, but terminating (putting ends on) is more difficult and expensive. Amp and 3M now make tools for terminating cable that bring the cost down to reasonable levels and enable you to terminate your own fiber optic cabling. You can outfit yourself with everything you need for under $2,000, including a microscope for visually inspecting your cut surfaces.

Optical fiber is the preferred medium for backbones—the connections between wiring closets. Optical fiber can extend to extreme locations without the need for wide area networking, and it makes fixed cable plants more secure. You will find fiber optic hubs and connections to be far more expensive than their electronic counterparts. Cost is easily justified when configuring a backbone that will connect all hubs or LANs into a single topology.

Shielded Twisted-Pair

Shielded twisted-pair (STP) was often used in IBM 16Mbps token ring LANs. Earlier token ring LANs used extensive cabling rules with variations when using different types of LAN devices. Today, most Token Ring NICs are designed to use category 5 UTP with TIA/EIA 568A rules.

STP should test at 150 ohms plus or minus 10 percent, can use any one of the three standardized pinouts discussed later in this chapter, and should have continuity on pins 3, 4, 5, and 6. Refer to IBM's Token Ring Cabling Guide for cabling rules.

Unshielded Twisted-Pair

Because LANs operate at the extreme range of Unshielded Twisted-Pair's (UTP) capabilities, what seems to be a minor problem to you can be a significant problem to your LAN. The following conditions are often to blame for LAN problems.

Wrong Cabling Type

LAN cabling for most applications should be category 5–rated. TIA rates voice and data cabling into categories, often called *levels*, to assist you in selecting the correct cable for your application. Table 13.1 summarizes UTP cabling applications used in telephony and data networking.

T A B L E   13.1

Twisted-Pair Voice and Data
Cable Applications

CATEGORY	DESCRIPTION	LAN APPLICATION
1	Voice and low-voltage power	None
2	Voice and low-speed data	None
3	Voice and data up to 16 MHz	Ethernet (10Base-T/100Base-T4), 4Mbps Token Ring, ARCnet, 100-VG
4	Voice and data up to 20 MHz	Ethernet (10Base-T/100Base-T4), 4/16Mbps Token Ring, ARCnet, 100-VG
5	UTP, ScTP and STP for voice and data up to 100 MHz	Ethernet (10Base-T/100Base-T4/100Base-TX), ATM OC-3 (155Mbps), FDDI on copper (CDDI), 100-VG

As you can see from this table, category 5 covers the greatest range of options and provides forward compatibility with future LAN applications.

The cable type is typically printed on the outer jacket, but older cabling may not be marked. Check all cable segments to verify the type of cable used in your network. If you cannot tell, you may have to rely on a cable tester to determine the type of cable.

NOTE **Shielded twisted-pair and other types of cabling that might be considered "better" should never be used. Use only UTP or STP that is category 3, 4, or 5 rated. In LANs, "better" is not better — it simply does not conform to specifications and requirements. In most Ethernet environments, problems may not appear until the network is busy — then performance will be poor and connections may be interrupted.**

Excessive Length

TIA/EIA 568A rules limit UTP wiring to 100 meters from end to end for each workstation or server cabling segment. This length, however, includes patch cables from the hub to the punch-down block, and workstation cabling from the wall plate to the NIC. Specific rules concerning *horizontal* cabling are discussed in TIA/EIA 568A specifications. Workstation cables (from the wall plate to the NIC) should not exceed 3 meters (less than 10 feet). The total of patch cables from the hub to the punch-down block plus workstation cables should not exceed 10 meters, as shown in Figure 13.1.

Figure 13.1 demonstrates more detail on this statistic.

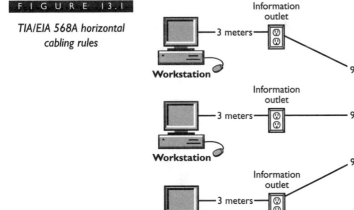

FIGURE 13.1

TIA/EIA 568A horizontal cabling rules

You will find a very good guide for TIA/EIA 568A cabling in Anixter's Technical Library at `http://www.anixter.com/techlib/standard/ cabling.`

Pin-Out and Termination

Nothing is more critical than proper pin-out of your cabling. Modular eight-pin jacks were pinned with three different configurations until just a few years ago. The pin-outs were known as AT&T 268a, TIA, and USOC. AT&T 256A is now TIA/EIA 568B, TIA is now TIA/EIA 568A, and USOC is no longer used. Both 568A and 568B are acceptable for local area networking. USOC was used for PBX and other telephonic applications. USOC does not support Ethernet and most other types of LANs. USOC was preferred for Token Ring in past years, but TIA/EIA 568A is now the preferred pin-out for Token Ring as well as most types of LANs.

All three types pin straight through (that is, 1-1, 2-2, 3-3, and so on). The key difference is in pairing wires and in coloration as demonstrated in Figure 13.2.

FIGURE 13.2

Pin-outs and pairing

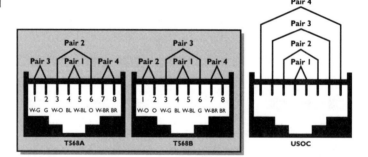

Both 568A and 568B pair lines 1-2, 7-8, 3-6, and 4-5. In these two schemes, pairs are numbered differently and different colors are put in different positions, but electrically, the result is the same. However, USOC pairs 1-8, 2-7, 3-6, and 4-5. Since pins 1, 2, 3, and 6 are used in Ethernet and most other types of LANs, the benefits of pairing the positive and negative lines are defeated in the USOC pin-out. When individual wires are not paired properly, the condition is known as *split pairs.*

Your hub and NIC may show a link light, but if your cable segment has split pairs, data errors will consume much of your bandwidth, resulting in reduced performance. This condition will affect the computer connected to the defective cabling segment, but it will also affect all other computers within the same collision domain. Since bandwidth is shared among all computers connected to a collision domain, problems for one are problems for the many.

UTP is available in both solid-core and stranded varieties. Using the proper type of connector is important also. Modular eight-pin connectors are designed differently for use with solid-core versus stranded-core UTP. For stranded wire, the tines are pointed to pierce the inner core; for solid-core wire, the tines are either shaped more like a blade or are split to make contact at more than one point as shown in Figure 13.3.

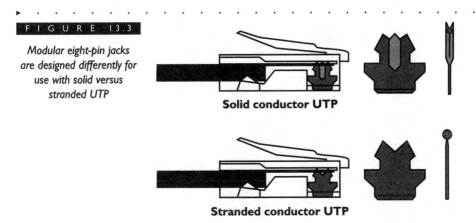

FIGURE 13.3

Modular eight-pin jacks are designed differently for use with solid versus stranded UTP

Solid conductor UTP

Stranded conductor UTP

You will also find that some modular eight-pin connectors are made for flat silver-satin, and others, for rounded UTP. Using the type made for flat wire will cause the crimping tool to jam without depressing the tines completely, resulting in poor connection with the wires.

Never strip more than ½ inch of outer jacket when installing a modular eight-pin connector. The outer jacket of the cable must fit under the crimp, and no more than ½ inch of wire is to be untwisted at any point on your cabling segment.

Multiple Use in the Same Cabling

Never mix telephone and LAN communications on the same cable. Though most LANs only use two pairs in a four-pair cable, the other two pairs should remain unused. Telephone communications within one pair—especially the ringer—can bleed to the LAN pairs, thus causing data errors. This condition is called *crosstalk*. Though early UTP Ethernet rules (IEEE 10Base-T) assumed that a cable should be able to carry both voice and data, engineers later found that doing so is problematic at best.

Kinks, Breaks, and Shorted Wires

Even the best-quality cabling is subject to wear and tear. Something as minor as a sharp kink in a cable can cause reflections, which can be incorrectly interpreted as a collision, thus affecting performance.

Bending a cable too sharply or too often can break solid-core wire very easily. This condition cannot be observed readily by inspecting the outside of the cable. Breaks often cause intermittent loss of continuity, and they always cause strong reflections.

Shorts result when the wiring jacket is not stripped properly, or when the jacket is subject to abrasion. Shorting wires also often cause intermittent loss of continuity, strong reflections, signal loss, and attenuation.

Interference

LAN cabling must not be run in the same conduit or holes with high-voltage wiring. This is stated in the National Electric Code building standards to prevent shorting of high-voltage wiring. However, this is a more important consideration for local area networking. Installing UTP LAN cabling close to high-voltage electrical conductors causes noise and resulting data errors in your LAN.

Visually inspect your LAN cabling for close proximity to electrical sources. Be sure that cable segments remain at least 2–3 feet from 110-volt wiring, and 3–4 feet from fluorescent light fixtures, motors, and other electrical fixtures.

Number of Repeaters in Series

Ethernet LANs are restricted by the number of repeaters (hubs and other types of repeating devices) in series. No more than four hubs should be used from one end of the LAN to the most distant end. Each repeater incurs a minute amount of delay, and a very small amount of delay can be tolerated from one end of the network to the other. Generally, larger LANs are designed with a central concentrator and departmental concentrators as shown in Figure 13.4 to handle longer distances without violating this rule. However, when a hub is added at an extreme end of the network as shown in Figure 13.4, the entire network can be plagued with undetected collisions.

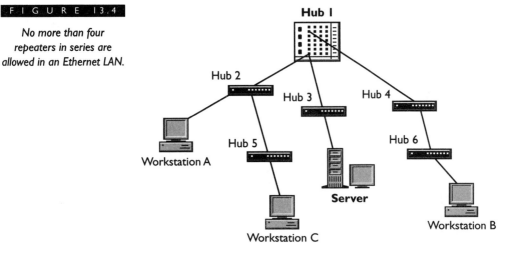

FIGURE 13.4

No more than four repeaters in series are allowed in an Ethernet LAN.

Hub 1

Hub 2

Hub 3

Hub 4

Workstation A

Hub 5

Hub 6

Server

Workstation B

Workstation C

Notice in Figure 13.4 that workstation A has three repeaters between itself and the server, while workstations B and C have four repeaters between them and the server. This configuration is okay but generally not done. Instead hubs 5 and 6 should be connected to hub number 1 (a central concentrator) to keep the number of repeaters in series to a minimum. This will allow a little flexibility throughout the network without causing problems. For example, if the user at workstation B or C wanted to add a small hub to provide an additional port to which a notebook computer would be connected, the four repeaters in series rule would be broken. This can cause performance problems throughout the network.

Fast Ethernet has far more restrictive rules than 10Mbps Ethernet. Fast Ethernet hubs are categorized as class I and class II. Depending upon which type you are using, and whether you are mixing 100Base-TX and 100Base-T4 devices, you are allowed either one or two hubs in series. Switching hubs can be used to eliminate this problem. Refer to your hub vendor's cabling guide for specific rules to be used in your Fast Ethernet LAN.

Electrical Characteristics of Cabling

In order for NICs to work properly, they are designed to send and receive good, clean signals. Various types of LANs use different encoding schemes, but all common types of LANs use digital baseband signaling. Cabling rules and standards are based on how much signal degradation can be allowed between a sender and a receiver. EIA/TIA considered all common types of LANs when developing the 568 rules. Since all the products they considered were digital baseband, the cabling requirements were very similar.

There are four basic problems that affect the ability to read the signals properly:

▸ Propagation delay

▸ Signal loss

▸ Attenuation

▸ Near-end crosstalk

▸ Noise

For each cabling segment, a given amount of each of these electrical characteristics can be tolerated. TIA/EIA 568A rules allow a given level for each of these factors — the amount of each characteristic varies with the cable length. The maximum amount allowable under optimal conditions, combined with the maximum propagation delay that can be tolerated, determines the cabling length. Because the statistics are variable according to length, it is nearly impossible to mechanically calculate allowable levels without some electronic assistance.

Propagation delay limits the length of cabling and the number of repeaters in series. An electron travels down a wire at a given rate of speed, which is known as the *nominal velocity of propagation* (NVP). Of course, the NVP will be less than the speed of light and will depend upon the thickness, quality, and other characteristics of the wire. For example, category 5 UTP should propagate at no less than 66 percent of the speed of light. Only a given amount of propagation delay is allowable in any type of LAN, which in turn limits cabling length. The propagation delay is the maximum time that can be tolerated for a bit to travel to the farthest extremes of the LAN.

Signal loss measures how much the signal's voltage or amperage has degraded over a given length of cable. As the signal travels further on the wire, some of the signal strength will degrade. Figure 13.5 illustrates a strong, square digital signal as would be viewed on an oscilloscope at the sending end, and again at the other end of the cable segment. A given amount of loss is tolerable, but again, the maximum amount is relative to the length of cable.

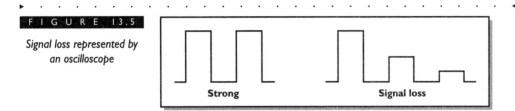

FIGURE 13.5

Signal loss represented by an oscilloscope

Strong   **Signal loss**

Attenuation is a measure of how the signal has lost its characteristic voltage or amperage levels. For example, Ethernet signals at 0 or 5 volts. A good, clean digital signal would shift very quickly from 0 to 5 volts and back to 0 volts with a square pattern represented by an oscilloscope as shown in Figure 13.6. A badly attenuated signal would have a slower transition from one voltage to another — this condition is represented with rounded corners.

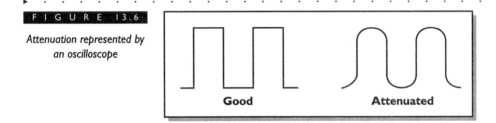

FIGURE 13.6

Attenuation represented by an oscilloscope

Good   **Attenuated**

Near-end crosstalk measures how much signal has bled from one pair of wires to another. Any time an electrical current runs through a wire, a magnetic field is generated around it. The magnetic field induces an electric current in other wires that are in close proximity. The magnetic field causes one signal to be transferred to another wire as represented in Figure 13.7. Near-end crosstalk measures the amount of bleed from one pair to another over a given length of cable.

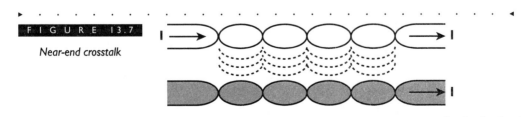

FIGURE 13.7

Near-end crosstalk

Wires in UTP cable are crossed to retain signal over limited distances, and to cancel out the effects of other sources of electrical interference without using shielding. Crossing the positive and negative wires of a single signal causes each to induce a reciprocal signal in the other, which preserves the signal. In category 5 cable, each pair of wires has a different number of twists per foot, reducing the tendency of one pair to bleed signal to another.

Noise is the measure of electrical interference picked up over the length of the cable. Figure 13.8 illustrates noise fluctuations that have been picked up, which interfere with the nice square shape of the data signal.

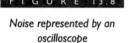

F I G U R E   13.8

Noise represented by an oscilloscope

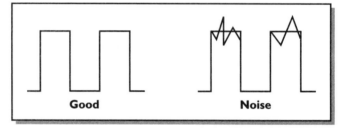

Good   Noise

Crude Cable Testing

You can conduct two types of tests: a crude test to determine if you have continuity and the proper pin-out, and more sophisticated tests to determine the quality of the connection.

Assuming the proper type of UTP and connectors have been used, your first concern is simply one of whether the cable segment has been properly installed. The following suggestions are some crude but highly effective tests that you can use to ensure that the physical link between two computers is good:

1. Check the link light on the hub or on your NIC. Most hubs have one or two lights — normally a green light indicates continuity between the hub and the NIC with pins 1, 2, 3, and 6 pinned straight through. Other lights usually indicate a flow of data. Also check the NIC. Many NICs have link lights. The link lights at both ends will be on, or both will be off. If the link light is off, check your cable; you obviously have an open circuit on one or all four lines in use.

Link lights only test for continuity on lines 1, 2, 3, and 4. Though a link light appears, you can still have a bad cable.

2. Switch cables. If one does not work, try another. It is best to use a cable that you know for sure is good. Verify the cable's fitness for duty by using it on a workstation that can communicate with the server over the network.

3. Bypass the cabling and hubs using a crossover cable directly between a server and a workstation. When you bypass the existing cabling and hub with a crossover cable that is known to be good, you can eliminate the possibility that the cable or hub is bad. You may be able to find a crossover connector (block) that can be used with a normal straight-through LAN cable at a store that carries a large selection of LAN wiring components. The connector is a female-to-female connector that connects two modular eight-pin ends together. You will commonly find them with a straight-through pin-out — crossover connectors are harder to find.

Normally, the hub crosses the transmit pair to the receive pair, and the positive to negative in each pair. A crossover cable emulates the cross in the hub, thereby alleviating the need for a hub to connect two computers. Crossover cables are often used as patch (cross-connect) cables between hubs.

Figure 13.9 shows how to pin-out a crossover cable. Instead of pinning straight through (pinning 1-1, 2-2, 3-3, and so on), pin 1-3, 2-6, 3-1, and 6-2.

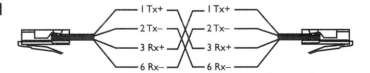

FIGURE 13.9

Crossover cable pin-out

4. Check the hub port for an X, which indicates a crossover. Some hubs have a port with no X, which is provided for a connection to another hub with a straight-through cable instead of a cross-connect. Some hubs have a switch to change the port from crossover to straight-through. Typically, an uncrossed port will be port number 1, or a port that is separated from the other ports.

5. Run your NIC's diagnostic and testing utility. First, check to see if the card is working properly, and then check for communications with another computer. Then run the station-to-station test. Most Ethernet NICs include these utilities. For example, 3Com calls their test the echo server and echo user test. SMC calls their test the responder test.

Advanced Cable Testing

Cable testing is conducted with electronic testing instruments. To adequately measure the proper electrical characteristics of your cabling, you would have to use more than one type of instrument. You would first need to measure the cable length, the NVP, and the level of each of the previously described characteristics, and then to calculate the characteristic in relationship to the length of your cable segment. Your calculations would then need to be compared to tables showing the allowable ranges for each category rating, and for various lengths of cabling. This would be pretty time-consuming and subject to error.

The following instruments can be used to test your cabling:

▶ Continuity tester

▶ Time domain reflectometer (TDR)

▶ Multimeter (or other types of meters)

▶ Cable tester

▶ Cable certification tester

Continuity Testers

Continuity testers simply test for continuity from one end of a cable to another. The link light on your hub is a continuity check on pins 1, 2, 3, and 6. A continuity tester determines if your cable is broken or shorted. It can also tell you if the cable is pinned out properly by testing continuity from one end to another (as from pin 1 on one end to pin 1 on the other end). Very inexpensive continuity testers are available that perform both of these functions when you plug both ends of a cable into the tester. To test a cable that is permanently installed, a signal injector is connected to one end and the tester to the other end. The tester listens for the signal generated by the signal injector.

A continuity tester is the basic instrument you would use to ensure that you have continuity over the length of a cable segment. The link lights on a hub verify continuity from hub to NIC. However, keep in mind that the link lights and continuity tests do not disclose the levels of signal loss, attenuation, crosstalk, and noise, nor do they measure propagation delay or cable length.

Time Domain Reflectometers

Time Domain Reflectometers (TDRs) are used to find breaks and shorts in a cable segment. Most TDRs are able to discern whether a break or short exists, and where the break/short is located. TDRs can also tell us the length of the cable if the type is known, or they can tell us the type of cable if the length is known because every type of cable has a unique NVP. A TDR is therefore a valuable instrument for basic troubleshooting. All cable testers include a TDR feature as part of their design.

A TDR sends a signal on the wire and measures the length of time it takes for a reflected signal to return. A TDR distinguishes a break from a short—a broken wire will return one type of reflection that the TDR can distinguish from a shorted reflection. The distance to the break/short is measured by the time it takes for the reflection to return to the TDR.

TDRs can also be used to measure the length of a cable. You can test for a cable's length if you know the type of cable or the cable's NVP. For example, to inventory the length of cable on a partially used 1,000 foot spool of category 5 UTP, program your TDR for category 5 UTP or 64 percent of the speed of light, attach it to one end of the cable, leaving the other end unterminated, and then run a test. The TDR will tell you that there is a break in the cable and the distance to the break, which translates the length of cable on the spool. You will find that TDRs are quite inaccurate at distances of less than 25 feet but can be accurate within inches when measuring over 100 feet of cable.

Meters

Voltmeters, ammeters, ohmmeters, and multimeters can be used to measure loss, attenuation, and noise but do not measure cable length. A meter can only produce quantitative raw data, which requires interpretation in the context of length. Once the raw measurement is interpreted per length of cable, the resulting statistic must be compared with charts listing allowable ranges. Interpreting raw statistics is time-consuming and introduces the possibility of making mistakes. Meters are rarely used to determine the cable's fitness of purpose.

An ohmmeter can be used to provide a quick check to verify cable type. Short one end of the cable and test from the other end. You should get the following results per 1,000 feet of cable:

▶ Category 3-5 UTP — 100 ohms

▶ STP — 150 ohms

▶ Coaxial Ethernet — 50 ohms

You will need to extrapolate the reading according to the length of your cable. For example, if you are testing a 100 foot cable, your reading should be 10 percent of the proper ohm rating. Readings can vary by 10 percent in either direction. Depending upon the ohmmeter's precision, your readings can be way off for shorter cable lengths. At least you can get a rough indication about whether a coax cable is Ethernet versus CATV or whether twisted-pair is UTP versus STP.

Cable Testers

Cable testers are the most affordable yet comprehensive type of device to use for basic day-to-day cable troubleshooting. Most cable testers are affordable and can be used by almost any technician without training. A cable tester will verify a cable segment's compliance to a given category rating. You can use one to definitively test a cable segment you suspect is defective.

Cable testers combine the functions of several instruments to produce a qualitative pass/fail result. Tables are stored in the cable tester with NVP values for cable types, and with category rating formulas. The cable tester runs tests, interprets, and then compares the results to tables or formulas to produce the pass/fail. Most cable testers require you to run multiple tests, while others have a "one-button test" where all applicable tests are run and interpreted, and the pass/fail result is produced.

A defective cable segment may have been good at the time of installation. Many factors can damage a cable or reduce its performance. For example, a LAN cable segment in a suspended ceiling may have been moved too close to a fluorescent light fixture. A sharp kink in a UTP cable can break a wire. Another common problem is when telephone or alarm systems share the same wiring closet — technicians may fix one system but inadvertently cause problems with other systems in the same closet.

Several companies make testers for LAN cabling. These devices are common and inexpensive enough that you can find them at your local electronics store or computer superstore. Prices range from a couple hundred dollars to several thousand dollars. Simple Ethernet UTP (10Base-T) testers are quite inexpensive, but cable testers that rate category 5 and optical fiber at 100 MHz can cost more than a thousand dollars.

Cable Certification Testers

This type of tester is more sophisticated than a simple cable tester. It can provide qualitative category ratings for a given cable segment — or it can produce quantitative raw data results. Certifying testers are the best type to use for verifying that a new cable segment has been properly installed or for surveying sites to detect potential problems.

The difference between an ordinary cable tester and a certification tester is how the results are produced. You would use a cable tester to test for compliance to a given category — perhaps category 3 — and get a pass or fail. The cable certification tester will test the cable and tell you which highest category the cable segment can support, and it will produce printed, detailed reports to support the test results. It will also tell you why a cable segment does not qualify for a higher rating, and it will point out electrical characteristics that are marginal.

Features built into cable certification testers vary significantly. Many cable certification testers produce elaborate reports giving the category rating and raw statistics on each electrical characteristic, while others provide only pertinent data. Many testers include programmable features to combine your favorite series of tests into a one-button test. Some testers interface with a PC to manage the tester and to download test results. Some devices can even be used to monitor a LAN in real time, paging you when potential problems occur.

Cable testers for optical fiber differ significantly from (and cost much more than) testers for copper cable. Testing light instead of electricity requires entirely different and far more expensive components and technology. Optical fiber components are expensive, and engineering costs for these devices are high. All of these factors add up to an expensive piece of test equipment.

TIP

Before spending thousands of dollars on a cable certification tester, request an evaluation unit or an on-site demonstration. Most dealers will provide a unit for you to try out before you buy, or they will provide a return authorization in case you decide against purchasing the unit.

Diagnosing LAN Problems

You can diagnose many LAN problems with a LAN monitor or protocol analyzer. Many LAN equipment vendors provide software for this purpose. Software packages, like Bay Networks' Optivity and Novell's ManageWise monitor your LANs in an attempt to diagnose problems even before users report problems.

Standards have been developed to enable an interface between LAN components and management software. Embedded firmware agents in LAN hubs, switches, and routers can be used to collect statistical information to be used for this purpose. Software agents can also be installed on servers at strategic points to assist in the job of collecting statistics.

Protocol analyzers are used for more comprehensive LAN analysis. Protocol analyzers monitor protocol statistics and decode LAN protocol data units for analysis. Analysts can evaluate protocol errors and statistics for clues about the source of network problems. Some protocol analyzers like Network Associates' Sniffer are hardware-based, whereas others like Novell's LANalyzer for Windows are software-based. Prices start at a few hundred dollars, but more sophisticated hardware-based analyzers for FDDI and ATM networks can cost as much as

$25,000. Novell's LANalyzer for Windows retails for $1,595 but is included in ManageWise at no additional cost.

Monitoring software and protocol analyzers also report vital LAN statistics that may represent network conditions that are out of the ordinary. Most monitors and analyzers have an interface that can send network messages, activate a pager, or execute an external application to warn the network administrator of impending problems.

Managing Network Communications

Standard protocols and messaging formats have been established in order to monitor network devices and network conditions. These standards were designed so that network hardware can be monitored in keeping with an open-systems approach. Some standards date back to the origination of the TCP/IP protocol stack, but newer standards have been designed to include features that were not anticipated that long ago.

Simple Network Management Protocol

SNMP is a protocol that was developed by the U.S. Department of Defense as part of the TCP/IP protocol stack. This protocol requires TCP/IP and reports typical network conditions that should be monitored. SNMP agents are embedded in many network devices such as intelligent Ethernet hubs. SNMP is not limited to use on a specific type of LAN but is most common in the Ethernet community.

SNMP management strategy consists of three components:

▸ Communications between SNMP agents and management stations

▸ Management Information Base (MIB) message storage

▸ Structure and identification of MIB data, which describes how MIB records are constructed

SNMP standards are handled by the Internet Engineering Task Force (IETF) along with other Internet and TCP/IP standards using Request for Comment (RFC) input. RFCs define MIB and MIB II formats along with protocol codes and standard procedures.

Network management stations accumulate data in one of two ways: through *traps* and through *polling*. Trap messages are sent from managed devices to management stations. Management stations poll managed devices to request current information, such as network usage levels.

SNMP agents provided with NetWare server software are configured through the INETCFG.NLM module. ManageWise provides more SNMP management agents for NetWare servers in addition to Windows-based workstation management software.

Remote Monitoring and Remote Monitoring 2

Remote Monitoring (RMON) is a MIB standard format that provides for collection of real-time data from managed devices. RMON is oriented more toward managing network devices, and it fills in gaps that SNMP does not address. Additional functionality makes this standard more attractive to network equipment vendors for event notification and for propagating alarms. Thresholds are set to define levels where event notification should be established.

Thresholds and Alarms

Alarms and thresholds allow network managers to take a proactive stance in managing a network. With monitoring, software alarms are set off when thresholds are reached. Using managed agents, SNMP, RMON, and other network monitoring techniques, thresholds are set, alarms are set off, and the network manager can be notified of conditions that may require attention. Monitoring software is often configured to notify administrators or operators when alarms are set off.

When using monitoring software, we generally set threshold levels that represent network conditions considered to be out of the normal range. A good example is the 30 percent threshold for network utilization that is commonly used. Network utilization measures how much network bandwidth is currently in use in real time. Though Ethernet can use as much as 90 percent of theoretical bandwidth, 30 percent is the threshold that is normally considered to be heavy traffic. If this threshold is reached too often, we should consider techniques to make more bandwidth available to users—we can use a switching hub, divide LANs into smaller segments, or upgrade to a higher-capacity LAN, such as Fast Ethernet.

Thresholds for the Ethernet statistics shown in Table 13.2 are generally monitored.

TABLE 13.2	EVENT OR STATISTIC	DESCRIPTION
Ethernet Statistics Thresholds	Network utilization	Percentage of network bandwidth in use
	Collisions	Overlapping frames that were retransmitted
	Bad CRCs	Cyclic Redundancy Check (CRC) detects error in frame
	Short frames (runts)	Frames less than 64 bytes with good CRC
	Long frames	Frames more than 1,518 bytes with a good CRC
	Jabber frames	Frames longer than 1,518 bytes with a bad CRC

Various network developers use different terminology to describe these Ethernet conditions.

NOTE

Ethernet does not have much error control or detection. Errors that can be detected are very general in nature and require interpretation to diagnose specific problems. A small number of some of these events are present on the LAN under normal conditions and should not concern us. For example, bad CRCs are part of the normal way that Ethernet works — as traffic becomes heavier, the likelihood increases that two workstations will attempt to send data at exactly the same moment, resulting in a collision. A threshold of six bad CRCs per second is considered to be an abnormal condition. When this level is reached, perhaps a network manager should evaluate network conditions to see if a problem exists.

Token Ring and FDDI have far more features to detect network conditions that are defective. The Active Monitor and the Ring Error Monitor can be observed to see if the ring is working properly. Thresholds for the number of beacons or ring recoveries can be monitored to detect a LAN that has a defective component. LAN monitoring allows us to isolate exactly which device is causing the problem so that we can replace it in short order.

Novell's ManageWise

To stay a step ahead of problems and to troubleshoot your network, use Novell's ManageWise software. Use ManageWise to monitor and troubleshoot everything from physical connectivity to router and server configuration.

ManageWise includes the following functions:

▸ Visual diagramming (mapping) of your internetwork topology

▸ LAN and cable monitoring with alarms and notification features

▸ Management of servers, routers, and workstations from a workstation console

▸ Protocol monitoring, capture, and analysis

▸ Virus detection at the server and the client

▸ Windows client desktop management

▸ Software distribution and control

ManageWise Components

ManageWise installs the following components:

▸ *The NetWare Management Agent* — An SNMP agent that is installed on NetWare servers to detect network problems and to interoperate with ManageWise console using SNMP

▸ *The NetWare LANalyzer Agent* — A server-based NLM to monitor LAN and cabling, and then distribute the data to the ManageWise console

▸ *The NetWare Hub Services* — A server-based module to manage Hub Management Interface–compliant devices from the ManageWise console

NetExplorer maps your network and establishes and early warning system for network problems. When you install ManageWise, the NetExplorer utility maps your internetwork, discovering servers, routers, and other network devices. Using a Windows graphical interface, it displays your network topology and creates a database of all network information. You can then configure it to detect critical thresholds for detecting network problems and activate alarms to notify administrators when thresholds are reached.

The ManageWise console is installed on a workstation to be used as a management station to monitor and manage your internetwork from your desktop. The ManageWise console is the desktop interface for NetExplorer and the ManageWise server-based agents discussed previously.

The ManageWise console also administers virus detection and removal for the network and for the management station. It also is used to manage Windows 95/98 and Windows NT Workstation user desktops to centrally control:

▸ Roaming (roving) user profiles

▸ System policies

▸ NetWare Client 32 updates

▸ NetWare Application Manager/NetWare Application Launcher (NAM/NAL) centrally installed software applications

Managing Windows Software with ManageWise

In addition to managing your physical network infrastructure, ManageWise enables the system administrator to centrally install and manage Windows applications (in a manner that Microsoft has not yet developed) using Novell's NetWare Application Manager (NAM) and NetWare Application Launcher (NAL).

NAM/NAL enables you to install a software application, such as Microsoft Word, in one location and then use that single installation at any workstation where NAL is installed. The process is unique, and it eliminates the need to go to an individual workstation to install or configure applications — all software installation, configuration, and updates can be done at one point for the entire network.

Using NAM, NDS application objects are set up, and software is installed with the NDS application objects as the users for the application. NAL is installed on client workstations' desktops. From the remote desktop NAL remotely accesses NAM's NDS objects to execute the application as if the NAM object is executing the application.

The user can still have unique desktop settings, such as file locations and menu configurations within the application, but the need to install the application locally is eliminated.

Locating LAN Problems

This section provides a summary of recommended troubleshooting procedures gleaned from this chapter to help you locate cabling problems. When cabling and/or LAN problems are suspected, use the information presented here to isolate and correct problems.

Check for Link Lights on Your Hub and NICs

A link light indicates continuity and appropriate pin-outs for a cable segment. If the link light does not activate when the cable is attached to both the hub and the NIC, you do not have continuity on pins 1, 2, 3, and 6.

 A link light does not indicate that the cable segment has the proper electrical characteristics for your type of LAN.

NOTE

Try jiggling the cable while it is hooked up to see if the link light flashes or goes off. Flashing would indicate that the connection is intermittent. The connector must crimp the outer cable jacket tightly so that movement of the internal wires is not possible. The tines in the end of the connector must be fully compressed, and they must properly contact the inner wires. View the connector from the side to verify that the connector is designed for the type of cable you are using. See Figure 13.3 shown earlier in this chapter to determine if the correct type of connector has been used. Replace any connectors that are the wrong type or are not properly installed.

Bypass Installed Cabling and Hubs Using a Crossover Cable

If you suspect that the cabling or hub is defective, bypass the installed cabling using a crossover cable. If the crossover cable works when directly connected, and the installed cabling does not, search for the cause in the installed cabling or hub. Instructions on making a crossover cable were discussed earlier in this chapter. The pin-out is shown in Figure 13.9.

Before relying on your crossover cable, be absolutely certain that it is properly constructed and that it works. Connect it between two network computers and test it by using the NIC's diagnostic utility, logging in, or PINGing between the two hosts.

NOTE

Visually Inspect Your Cable to Verify the Proper Category

Ethernet 10Base-T (10Mbps) and Fast Ethernet 100Base-T4 requires category 3, 4, or 5 UTP cable. Fast Ethernet 100Base-TX requires category 5. Check with your NIC and hub vendors for Fast Ethernet cabling guides for specific rules.

Today, category 5 is used almost exclusively for all local area networking. Category 5 can accommodate almost any type of LAN technology up to 100Mbps. Category 5 is designed to reduce electrical problems that are detrimental to data networking. If you are installing cabling, resist the temptation to save a few pennies on cheaper cabling — it is cheaper in the long run to buy the best.

If you attempt to install Fast Ethernet, FDDI, ATM, or Token Ring LANs on category 3 or 4 UTP, you will experience intermittent problems. Of all major types of LANs, category 3 is only suitable for 10Mbps Ethernet and 4Mbps Token Ring. Category 3 can be used for 100Base-T4 (Fast Ethernet on category 3) and 100VG. However, 100Base-T4 has very limited rules and many restrictions, and special hubs are required. Refer to your LAN equipment vendor's cabling guide for special rules on these technologies.

Check for Different Types of Cabling

Be sure that your entire cable run is the same type of cable (preferably category 5) from end to end. Mixing cable types can cause problems, though the higher grade of cabling may seem to be "better."

Check for "Silver-Satin" (Flat Telephone Wire)

Not even an inch of this type of cable is to be used anywhere on your network. Preconfigured silver-satin is plentiful for use with multiple-line telephones. It is common that someone will use this type of wire between the computer and the wall plate. Using even a small amount of this type of cable can cause serious and intermittent LAN problems.

Check Cable End Pin-Outs

Check for continuity from one end of the cable to the other on pins 1, 2, 3, and 6. Visually inspect the modular eight-pin connector for the same color sequence on both ends. This indicates a straight-through pin-out, which is the standard for a UTP LAN cable. If you have purchased the cable, be sure you have purchased a cable pinned out to TIA/EIA 568A or 568B standards.

Check the Hub Port for an X

An X on a hub port indicates a crossover function within that port. Some hubs have an uncrossed port to be used for hub-to-hub connections (uplink). In some cases a port will have a switch to manually switch the port between crossed and uncrossed states. Be sure all computers are connected to an X port. Crossover cables are often used for uplink connections, but be sure crossover cables are not used with an X port for connecting computers. Be sure an uplink either uses a crossover cable or uses a non-X port. If cables and X's are configured properly, the link light will be on.

What to Do Next

If the problem is not cabling or hub-related, see Chapter 14, "Client Connectivity" for tips on troubleshooting protocol problems.

Client Connectivity

Client connectivity is problematic by nature. Cabling and connectors go bad, and users change their network configuration properties. It seems that a Windows installation is always subject to reconfiguration — Windows software setups often add files and change Registry entries that affect network connectivity. Interaction between Windows, NetWare, and software is tightly integrated — software bugs can be deeply embedded, causing finger-pointing of the most frustrating nature.

Novell's Client for Windows 95, 98, and NT — also called Client 32 — provides a new level of integration with Microsoft operating systems like never before. Client 32 now relies on Microsoft "transports" (protocol stacks). This development simplifies protocol configuration and NOS activity. It reduces competing standards and releases responsibility for driver development — ODI drivers are no longer required for clients. This change accompanies new features and complexity at the client end, making new features more manageable.

This chapter deals with the most common problems you might encounter when administering clients. Use this chapter to find configuration management, troubleshooting, tools to work with, and references to pursue problems that are not covered in this chapter.

Protocol Configuration and Maintenance

The starting point for resolving client connectivity problems is in protocol configuration and maintenance. Microsoft has reduced protocol configuration to managing a few Windows Control Panel screens. Managing servers has become at once more complex and simpler. Administrators must now support pure TCP/IP networking, IPX networking, and the IPX Compatibility Mode.

Protocol complexities at the server end are now managed in Novell Internet Access Server (NIAS), which breaks protocol configuration down to manageable pieces and eliminates the need to use the correct syntax in server load statements. See Chapter 17, "Network Communication and Protocols," for server protocol configuration and maintenance issues.

Protocol complexities at the client end are handled by the Network Control Panel and the Novell Client 32 properties. Novell provides client support for the following workstations in the Z.E.N.works Starter Pack:

▸ Windows 95, 98, and NT (also called 32-bit clients)

▸ Windows 3.1 and Windows for Workgroups 3.11

▸ DOS

Novell support for the following workstations is available by order or by download:

▸ OS/2

▸ Macintosh

Use this section of this chapter to check the most important workstation configuration parameters. This section only discusses the most important factors in configuring client connectivity. More often than not, you will find the problem in this section before moving on to diagnostic procedures.

Novell Client for Windows 95, 98, NT

Novell's Client for Windows 95, 98, and NT supports four options:

▸ TCP/IP only

▸ IPX only

▸ IPX and IP

▸ IP with IPX Compatibility

The first three options are self-explanatory. IPX Compatibility encapsulates IPX/SPX into UDP/IP for transport and requires a Migration Agent somewhere on the internetwork to handle access to NetWare 5 servers. A 32-bit Windows client uses the Compatibility Mode Adapter as a virtual interface between the IPX/SPX and IP protocol stacks.

These options are selected when installing the client software in Winsetup. It is recommended that changing the protocol support should be handled by reinstalling the Novell Client for Windows 95, 98, NT software rather than within Control Panel. See Chapter 10, "Windows 95/98 and NT Clients," for a detailed discussion of configuring 32-bit Windows clients. See the section later in this chapter concerning removing and reinstalling Client 32.

Novell Client for Windows 3.x

The Novell Client for Windows 3.x supports Windows 3.1 and Windows for Workgroups 3.11. This setup has fewer support options — pure IP communications with NetWare 5 servers is not possible. The IP-IPX gateway option provides communications with NetWare 5 servers and IPX networks. NetWare/IP is provided to access NetWare/IP servers. TCP/IP is generally required for Internet dial-up. Configuring the client is a walk-through using a Setup Wizard to guide you.

Novell Client for DOS

The DOS client is far more complex than it used to be, and it limits support even more. The IP-IPX gateway option is not available; only IPX and NetWare/IP support are available.

The Microsoft TCP/IP Protocol

Configuring the Microsoft TCP/IP protocol is handled through Control Panel. It is recommended that you get your Windows workstation communicating properly over TCP/IP before attempting to install the Novell Client for Windows. It is not necessary to install IPX/SPX protocols before installing the Novell Client for Windows — that will be handled according to the protocol options that you select during Winsetup.

Check your TCP/IP Protocol Properties screens shown in Figure 14.1. You should have a static-assigned IP address or a DHCP server available to hand out addresses. The subnet mask must also be properly configured or you will not be able to communicate over the IP subnet.

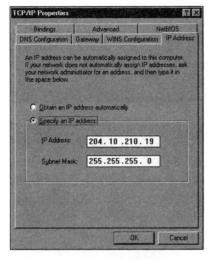

FIGURE 14.1

TCP/IP Protocols Properties screen — IP Addressing

You must also configure the IP Gateway parameter as shown in Figure 14.2. The IP Gateway address maps to the IP address of the router port that is connected to your network segment. Without this address, communications outside of your local network segment are disabled. The IP Gateway address is also known as the Default Route.

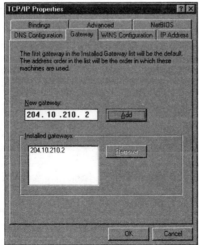

FIGURE 14.2

IP Gateway address

If the Microsoft IPX/SPX-compatible protocol is set up, you will need to check the frame types and internal network addresses in the Advanced screen as shown in Figure 14.3.

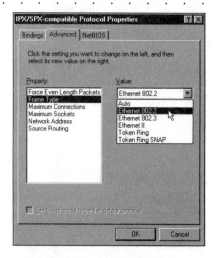

F I G U R E   14.3

The Advanced tab of the IPX/SPX-compatible Protocol Properties

TIP

It is recommended that you manually select the frame type instead of relying on the autodetect. You should also be sure that the correct frame types are selected. Select all frame types in use throughout your network.

Start Here When Troubleshooting

The following troubleshooting suggestions may help to reduce the scope of your investigation. They are divided into the most general categories for the sake of channeling investigation to the proper area.

TIP

Keep in mind that your best bet in locating a problem is to isolate it by being able to replicate the problem at will. If you can replicate the problem, you will eventually find its cause and resolve it. If you cannot replicate the problem at will, your chances of finding the problem are as chaotic as the event is. Persistence is equally important for successful troubleshooting. Some problems are easier to solve than

others, and some technicians are quicker (or luckier) than others, but the most important factor in locating a problem is persistence. If you do not persist, even the simplest problems will not be solved except for luck. No matter how difficult a problem is, you will eventually resolve it given enough persistence.

Is It Plugged In?

The first question any seasoned support technician asks is, "Is it plugged in?" The point is, all troubleshooting should start with the most basic supporting services, verifying what everyone overlooks when embroiled in a problem.

Always check to see that power cords and network cables are all attached firmly. Many network problems have been attributed to connectors that have pulled loose and NICs that have worked loose in their bus sockets. The term, "is it plugged in?" applies to every type of connection that may affect the problem you are viewing.

Failure to Connect to a Server

The most common problem network administrators see is the general failure to connect. The problem can be cabling, LAN drivers, protocols, client software, or server-related.

Consider the following error message:

```
Network Error: Abort, Retry, Ignore
```

This error indicates loss of physical connectivity with a server after having attached to a server. At one time or another most system administrators have seen this error message. The NetWare client software attempts to reconnect several times when connection is broken before sending this message to your workstation console. Generally, this error occurs due to intermittent cable or connector problems.

If this error occurs while loading an application or a data file, or during interaction with a database, file corruption can occur. If the error is noticed when accessing a file after a long period of inactivity, the connection may have been lost during the inactive period. Newer NetWare client modules are more effective at restoring intermittent connections and therefore quite often reconnect without displaying an error. If the problem is persistent, you will eventually receive this error.

A cable fault may occur at times when the workstation is busy and other times when it is not. While a workstation sits idle, no data is being transmitted—therefore no error is reported. The next time you attempt to access the network storage device, the client attempts to reconnect. If it is unsuccessful, an error is reported. Under these conditions network performance is not as good as it could be. If the problem occurs frequently, network performance can be very poor, with the user experiencing delays while loading a program or data file or saving a data file.

When you receive this error and you are able to reconnect without rebooting, look for an intermittently bad connection, normally a cable or connector. If rebooting solves the problem, suspect a NIC that is failing intermittently or a NIC driver that is malfunctioning.

If the problem occurs more frequently when the network is very busy, suspect strong reflections in the cabling. Look for minor kinks, cuts, damage from heavy blows, and places where the cable is or was at one time pinched. If the problem is not related to how busy the network is, suspect a broken or shorted cable. Look for sharp kinks, cuts, and places where cable is bent on a regular basis. If a cable is subject to periodic movement, replace it with a stranded UTP cable with the same category rating. It is often difficult to visually detect damage to internal wires in a cable. A cable tester will uncover the flaw, especially if you are able to jiggle the damaged part of the cable during testing. It is typical of cable flaws to produce intermittent problems. It is typical in an Ethernet environment for damaged cabling to cause overall performance degradation.

Many cabling faults cause intermittent problems. Sometimes you will observe no problems, while at other times connectivity is highly problematic. In some cases, connectivity is not compromised, but performance is reduced. Generally, these problems only appear when LAN bandwidth use approaches higher levels.

The first place to start when searching for a problem is continuity. More advanced and intermittent problems can stem from cabling that has good connectivity but has kinks, split pairs, or bad connections. Detecting this type of cabling fault may require a cabling tester. See Chapter 13, "LAN and Cabling," for details on troubleshooting LANs and cabling.

Isolating the Problem

Here are a few general questions to ask when troubleshooting client connectivity. If the following questions do not resolve your problem, proceed to

"Troubleshooting TCP/IP-Related Problems" or "Known Support Problems and Solutions" found later in this chapter.

Did It Work Before, and If So, What Has Changed?

If you have never connected to the server before, start from the bottom up. Check your NIC settings. Run diagnostic software to test the card and cabling. Then uninstall and reinstall your NetWare client software, making sure that the settings that the client software is configured for match the physical settings on your NIC.

If the system did work before and stopped working, you should first investigate what happened that could have disabled it. As a support technician, you will find that users often try to hide their errors, and the mistake may seem unrelated or insignificant to the user. If you can locate a cause at the outset, you might be able to cut your troubleshooting time down significantly. Try to be diplomatic; if you scare a user, that user may never admit to causing the problem, which simply makes your job harder.

Does the Workstation Have a Good Link?

If a workstation cannot connect during boot or execution of the NetWare requester, first check for a link light (continuity) and then look for a software problem. Assuming you have a good cable installed to specifications, a link light will indicate that the cable is working. If the link light is good, check your drivers and NIC setup.

Does the Problem Affect All Workstations or Just This One?

Check server connections in the server MONITOR. See the troubleshooting procedures using PING (if using TCP/IP) for checking communications from the client end and from the server end. If PING shows no communications, use NIC diagnostics software provided by the NIC vendor to test the physical connectivity. If the server is not working, a NIC is not working, or a protocol is configured improperly, all network nodes connected to that interface or protocol will not connect. If the problem is related to a server interface or protocol, view the server bindings in NIAS (discussed in Chapter 17, "Network Communications and Protocols"). If the problem is a general server failure, such as an abend error, see Chapter 17.

If the problem only affects one workstation, try switching hub connections and then switching cables. As discussed in Chapter 13, "LAN and Cabling," cabling accounts for over half of all network downtime. A cable can show continuity and display a link light but can fail a cable test. In the absence of a cable tester, simply switch to a cable and LAN connection with one that is known to be good. If the problem disappears, you obviously had a bad cable.

Is the Problem Intermittent?

If the problem is intermittent, it points to a bad cable or failing NIC. Look for loose connectors and cabling that is frayed or kinked. A failing NIC is usually tripped when heat rises or when it handles bursts of heavy traffic. Normally, both of these problems will appear and disappear with no apparent cause or correlation.

If the problem is not intermittent, your job is easier. You must attempt to replicate the problem again and again under changing conditions. When you can replicate the problem at will, you can investigate possible contributing factors.

Is the Problem Poor Performance?

Poor performance generally indicates some problem, but like an intermittent problem it may be harder to troubleshoot. Investigate all potentially related components, but don't waste too much time investigating at first. Try removing and then reinstalling the Novell Client for Windows—whatever is wrong may be more simply corrected by removing all components and reinstalling correctly. See sections under "Problem Resolution for Windows 95, 98, and NT" dealing with Client 32 removal, and refer back to Chapter 10, "Windows 95/98 and NT Clients," for reinstallation.

Other General Issues

Several general issues should be checked. The following are issues that show up in many NetWare-based networks on a regular basis.

Checking for Server Attachment

Check to see if you are connected by reviewing the server's connection table. Load the server MONITOR.NLM. Check Connections, and look for a NOT-LOGGED-IN entry for your workstation. As the workstation attaches to the network, a connection should be added at the server. A server attachment indicates that the LAN and protocol stack are installed properly. If you can attach but not log in, look for problems in the Client 32 properties.

Verifying Connections

View the NetWare Connections screen shown in Figure 14.4 to see:

1. That you are connected

2. Which connection number is in use

3. The Authentication State

4. The tree or server to which you are attached

5. Which protocol is in use

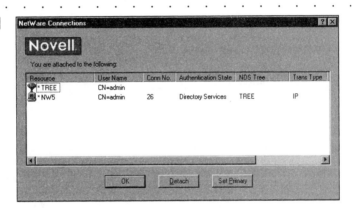

F I G U R E   14.4

Verifying NetWare
connections

If a connection number and protocol are not shown, then look for general LAN, cable, and driver problems. If a connection number and protocol are shown but the Authentication Status does not show "Directory Service," look for Client 32 properties or user account problems that would prevent a login.

Verifying Server Protocols and Bindings

To view the server's protocols and bindings, use NIAS. To review server bindings in NIAS:

1. At your server, load NIASCFG.NLM, and select Configure NIAS →
Protocols and Routing → Bindings.

2. You will see the screen shown in Figure 14.5.

3. Select each protocol and review the details of that binding.

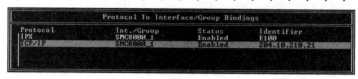

F I G U R E 14.5

Verifying protocol bindings

Verifying Communications over LAN/WAN Interfaces

Verify that communications are flowing over a server's LAN and WAN
interfaces. To verify server connections:

1. Load MONITOR.NLM at your server console.

2. Select LAN/WAN drivers.

3. Select the NIC or network board to monitor.

4. Tab to see statistics.

5. Observe total packets transmitted and received for activity. You should see
a few packets every second, evidencing protocol exchanges between servers
and clients.

6. Observer the ECB block count. A high ECB count indicates a driver or
configuration problem such as insufficient number of packet receive buffers.

The preceding procedure should help you isolate where problems may and may
not be located. Problem elimination will eventually lead you to the cause.

Insufficient NDS Rights

When a user can log in but cannot access some or all resources, check for NDS
rights. By default, all users in a tree can view (Browse) all resources in the tree, but

users may not have NDS object property rights to use the target object. If the user does not have sufficient NDS rights, then resource objects the user attempts to access will not be available.

To check a user's NDS rights to access any object:

1. Log in as Admin or a user with Supervisory NDS rights to the user account to be checked.

2. Execute NetWare Administrator.

3. Select the user to check and then select Object → Rights to other objects. Select a container object that contains the object to be accessed, Effective Rights, and enter or select the object the user has attempted to access.

4. View the effective NDS rights and NDS object property rights as shown in Figure 14.6.

▶ • ◀

Verifying NDS rights in NetWare Administrator

Insufficient Rights to Files and Directories

When a user can log in and access many resources but is limited when attempting to access a file or directory, the problem may be insufficient rights to files and directories. The user may have limited rights to the directory. This situation can be verified in one of several ways.

To verify rights to files and directories with RIGHTS:

1. Log in as the user.

2. Start Windows Explorer and right-click on the folder to evaluate.

• • • • • •

3. Select Properties from the menu.

4. Select NetWare Rights.

5. View the Effective Rights box at the bottom of the screen as shown in Figure 14.7.

F I G U R E   14.7

Effective rights to files and directories

You will see a listing of effective rights in the working directory for this user. This method will also show effective trustee assignments to the directory, detailing direct and indirect (inherited) rights.

Another method of viewing rights to files and directories is to use NetWare Administrator.

To verify rights to files and directories with NetWare Administrator:

1. Log in as Admin or with Supervisory rights to the user's context.

2. Execute NetWare Administrator.

3. Select the volume and directory to be verified, and select Object → Details → Trustees of this Directory. You will view the Access and Inherited rights for this directory as shown in Figure 14.8. To locate the directory

where the trustee assignments are made, move up one directory at a time
and view the Trustees of this Directory button to find where the Rights to
Files and Directories have been assigned.

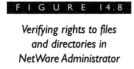

F I G U R E   1 4 . 8

*Verifying rights to files
and directories in
NetWare Administrator*

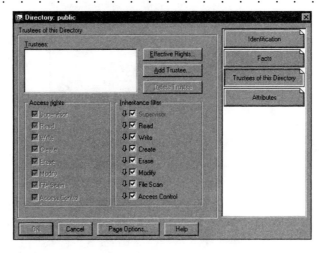

A third method would consist of exiting to a command prompt, changing to the
directory, and then executing the RIGHTS command line utility.

Troubleshooting TCP/IP-Related Problems

Several symptoms may cause you to search the pages of this chapter for a
solution. This section discusses Microsoft Windows TCP/IP services that may need
to be installed or properly configured to resolve network problems.

Checking IP Configuration

Every TCP/IP protocol stack has an IP configuration reporting utility. Windows
95 and 98 have WINIPCFG.EXE, Windows NT has IPCONFIG.EXE. These
utilities show several factors that you should verify before proceeding with other
TCP/IP troubleshooting. Figure 14.9 shows the WINIPCFG More Info screen
showing the TCP/IP protocol configuration parameters currently in use. You will
find this utility in the Windows directory.

▶ . . . . ◀

FIGURE 14.9

The Windows 95/98 IP
configuration utility

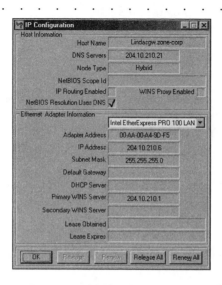

With Windows NT, use IPCONFIG.EXE. You will find this utility in the
<winroot>\system32 directory. Execute the command IPCONFIG /all from a
command prompt. Type IPCONFIG /? to see a list of switches.

**Look for one of several freeware and shareware utilities on the CD
that accompanies this disk. Several Windows-based utilities can
substitute for the Microsoft WINIPCFG and IPCONFIG utilities,
providing more information and helping you troubleshoot TCP/IP.**

NOTE

Troubleshooting with PING

To isolate a problem with IP connectivity, use the PING utility. First PING with
a loopback, and then PING other hosts on the immediate subnet by address and
then by name. These few simple steps help to narrow your search for the
underlying problem.

Ping is executed from any TCP/IP host. The Windows 95, 98, and NT operating
systems have a PING.EXE utility that is executed from a command (or DOS)
prompt.

PING.NLM is also available on NetWare servers that have the IP protocol
installed. Type **PING** or **LOAD PING** at the console (colon) prompt. Enter the
loopback address (127.0.0.1) or destination host address or name.

The following commands are used to test the functionality of the IP protocol and the ability to connect to remote hosts.

Ping Loopback

Pinging the loopback address verifies that the IP protocol is able to communicate with itself through your NIC and LAN cabling. To test loopback with Ping:

1. At a command prompt, type the loopback command:

```
PING 127.0.0.1
```

2. You should see one request and four replies from the same address. If loopback cannot receive a reply from your own workstation, you lack physical connectivity, or your drivers are not working properly — the problem is in the workstation or cabling. Check your cabling, NIC, drivers, and so on to see why you are not connected to the network.

Ping Other Hosts by Address

PINGing destination hosts on your local subnet by address established a communication session and elicits a response from other hosts. To PING other hosts by address:

1. To Ping another host, exit to a command prompt, and type

```
PING <xxx.xxx.xxx.xxx>
```

where *xxx.xxx.xxx.xxx* represents the IP address of an active host on the same subnet.

If the loopback worked but no other hosts on your subnet reply, reinstall the Novell Client for Windows software. This problem indicates that the cable, NIC driver, and TCP/IP protocol stack are working. If you still cannot attach to the network, either your server is not communicating or the client requester portion of your software is not working.

2. Check your server(s) to be sure they are able to service connections. To do so, load MONITOR.NLM and watch for a connection to be established (a server connection will be established when the client software is executed at the workstation — it will be labeled as "NOT-LOGGED_IN" until login) — once you are logged in the user name will appear for the connection.

3. Be sure you are using the latest client software. Look for updates on the Novell Web site.

Ping Your Workstation from a NetWare Server by Address

To verify communications from the server to your workstation, execute the Ping utility from the server and Ping your workstation. To Ping from a NetWare server by address:

1. From the server console, type the command `LOAD PING`.

2. Enter the IP address in the Host name field.

3. Press Esc to initiate the Ping.

4. Press Esc to terminate the Ping.

If you can Ping other computers on your local subnet, you know your NIC driver and IP protocol binding in the server is working. If you can Ping hosts on your local subnet, but not hosts on other subnets, check your router configuration and the IP Gateway address as configured in your server.

Name Resolution

You should suspect that a connectivity problem is based in name resolution when a network object cannot be located. The simplest way to check for this condition is to Ping the host computer you are attempting to reach by address and then by name. If you can effectively communicate with the host by address, but not by name, your problem is Dynamic Name Service (DNS). DNS resolves the name from the DNS server's database, which contains records referencing the host name and its IP address. DNS was not set up by default when you installed your server. See Chapter 11 for details on DNS setup for NetWare 5, or investigate the DNS services on your network.

PING Other Hosts by Name

Pinging hosts by name includes DNS name resolution in the Ping process. If name resolution is problematic, Pinging by name will not be successful. To Ping other hosts by name:

1. Ping another host address by name. Type

    PING <host_name>

where *host_name* is the name of an active host.

2. If Ping times out, try Pinging the domain name.

3. Ping the DNS server address to be sure that the DNS server is online.

If you can successfully Ping by address, but not by name, check name resolution setup in your client properties, and check name service setup on your server(s). If the DNS server is up and you can Ping it by address, but it does not respond to a Ping by host or domain name, check your local workstation name resolution configuration. If your workstation is set up correctly, check the name server for an address record.

NOTE **Name resolution is problematic at time for Windows workstations using WINS resolution. Check Chapter 11, "TCP/IP Services," and Chapter 17, "Network Communications and Protocols," for more on Windows name resolution complexities. It is not unusual to have to delete the WINS database files manually and then reboot the WINS server to get Microsoft name resolution working correctly.**

Troubleshooting Name Resolution

To troubleshoot name resolution:

1. From a network workstation's command prompt or from a NetWare 5 server's console prompt use the following command to check for connectivity:

        PING *ip_address*

If you receive a reply, you can effectively communicate with the host.

2. If the request times out, your workstation is unable to communicate over TCP/IP with hosts on the same subnet. This may indicate 1) lack of connectivity on your workstation's end, or 2) that the LAN may be inoperative.

3. To communicate with the target address over the TCP/IP protocol stack. Try the following:

   a. Ping other addresses on the same subnet. If you receive a reply, your computer's protocol is effectively communicating with the local subnet. If your request timed out, communications are probably not going out from your workstation.

   b. Ping other addresses on remote subnets. If you receive a reply, your computer's protocol is effectively communicating through the local gateway.

   c. If the preceding tests timed out, Ping your local host using the following command:

        PING 127.0.0.1

4. If this test times out, check your local computer — it is not able to establish communications through TCP/IP.

   a. Check cabling.

   b. Check NIC configuration.

c. Check the NIC driver.

d. Check TCP/IP configuration.

5. If the loopback worked, and Pinging by address to the local subnet works, but Pinging to remote subnets does not work, check your gateway address in the Network Control Panel. If this parameter is properly configured but communications cannot go over your router, check the router and its configuration for improper configuration.

IP Addressing and Subnetting

Unless you are quite experienced with IP networking, you will probably experience a few problems with IP addressing and subnetting in your network. Many experienced NetWare administrators will be dealing with the complexity of these issues for the first time. TCP/IP was an elective in the Certified Novell Engineer (CNE) program — the curriculum never required this knowledge.

Chapter 4 discussed the TCP/IP protocol, IP addressing, and subnetting mechanics in detail. This chapter discusses the most common problems you will encounter in effective networking when using these protocols. You may need to refer back to Chapter 4 at times for more detailed discussions on some of the topics presented in this section.

IP Address Conflicts

Given that IP addresses are often assigned manually (static addressing), there is always the possibility that IP address conflicts will occur in your network. When two hosts have been assigned the same IP address, communications for both hosts may be interrupted.

When you boot a Windows computer, a dialog box will inform you if an IP address conflict between this and another host computer exists.

 An IP address conflict often causes the other host with the same IP address to lose connectivity.

NOTE

Subnetting

Subnetting is also a problem for network administrators. Network interfaces and network address assignments for routers and servers must be coordinated for

IP in much the same manner as it is done for IPX; however, IP adds a little more complexity. If you are familiar with the topic of network addressing in an IPX-based internetwork, you will find the same type of configuration required in an IP-based internetwork.

Routers work in concert with network address assignments made when binding the IPX and IP protocols to the server LAN drivers. If you have problems communicating outside of your local IP subnet, check subnet and mask assignments in your router. You should have a map of intranet topology which shows a subnet address number and mask for each subnet. No two network segments should be assigned the same subnet number.

Known Support Problems and Solutions

This section discusses know support issues and solutions. If none of the previous situations solved your problem, check the items in this section for a known issue.

Caching and Lost Data

Novell's Client for Windows 95/98 and NT features network write caching that really improves performance. However, if your workstation crashes or is powered off without exiting all applications, data can be lost. By default, Client 32 holds write requests in local workstation memory until the file in use is closed. This level is beneficial to performance but jeopardizes data integrity if an application or workstation is subject to periodic crashes.

You can adjust caching levels by tweaking just a few parameters. Make adjustments according to workstation memory, performance, applications in use, and stability. To view and adjust Client 32 caching levels, select the red N in the lower-right corner (system tray) of your task bar → Properties → Advanced Settings to see the screen shown in Figure 14.10. The following settings can be adjusted. Please note that a help line in the Description box briefly explains the selected setting.

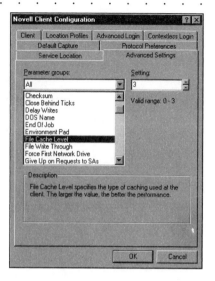

FIGURE 14.10

The Client 32 Advanced Settings screen

File Cache Level

This parameter is set to a value from 0 to 3. A higher number produces better performance, but 0 is the safest level. A high value combined with File write-through can still be safe. The following values are valid:

- 0 — Caching turned off

- 1 — One 4K block per file allocated as read-ahead/write-behind cache

- 2 — Fully cache open files only as long as they are open.

- 3 — Fully cache open and closed files; if, when reopened, the file is detected to be the same, reuse original cache blocks (fastest option).

The default level is 3.

File Write Through

Values are on or off. This parameter controls whether write requests are committed to the network volume at the time of writing. Leaving this on produces stability, since all write requests are sent at the time of writing, but does not interfere with the caching level for read requests.

The default value is on.

Delay Writes

Use this parameter for applications that open and close files repeatedly. Delay Writes On will keep the files open for the amount of time specified in the Close Behind Ticks level. This allows files to stay open, shortening data access times where applications open and close files repeatedly, as is the case in many applications that use overlays.

The default value is off.

Close Behind Ticks

Values are 0 to 65535 measured in ticks. If Delay Writes is turned on, this parameter controls the amount of time a file is held open after an application sends a close file instruction. The delay period is specified in ticks, with about 18 ticks per seconds. A value of 36 is approximately equal to two seconds and is a recommended level.

The default value is 0.

Max Cache Size

Values range from 0 to 49152 in KB. This parameter controls the size of the cache. Larger caches may produce better performance. Memory allocated to cache is not available for use with applications. If a workstation has very little memory (32MB or less), this value should be left low. Over 32MB memory can normally afford a 4KB cache.

The default value is 0.

Auto Reconnect Level

Values range from 0 to 5. When connection with the network is lost, this parameter controls how connections are restored and how the cache is held for reconnection. Setting this level higher ensures data integrity in case the server crashes. If data is written through and held in cache, file updates at the server can be resynchronized at level 4 or 5, or lost at level 3 or below. Adjust this level higher than the default if server stability and data updates are an issue. The following values produce these results:

▸ 0—No automatic reconnect capabilities

▸ 1—Reconnect devices only (connections, drive mappings, printer port connections).

▶ 2 — Reconnect devices, plus read-only files.

▶ 3 — Reconnect devices and read-only files, plus all files and file locks.

▶ 4 — Reconnect devices and read-only files, all files and file locks, plus file writes (data recovery guarantee).

▶ 5 — All the preceding values, plus switch to local disk for storage and resync files later (for NetWare Mobile).

The default value is 3.

Opportunistic Locking

The value of this parameter is not adjustable. Client 32 employs this feature to enable caching for multiuser databases when no one else is sharing a database file and disables caching when the database file has multiple opens pending.

NT Client Login Problems

If you have previously determined that your driver and protocol stack allow you to connect to the network but login fails, you must evaluate user account and NDS configuration. What follows are some common problems that prevent user login.

NDS User Context Not Specified or Not Configured

The following error message indicates that you must configure the user context in a tree and organization in the intraNetWare or NDS:

```
You must enter a valid credential set in order to login
```

The following error message indicates that a connection server is not locatable:

```
Failed to connect to a NetWare service. Please check your
cabling or the event log for a problem.
```

This error indicates a loss of connectivity due to cabling/connectors, NIC malfunction, wrong frame type, driver failure, or any number of protocol configuration problems.

Another reason this error may occur is if NDS servers cannot be found due to an IPX internal network number (also called the server ID in NetWare 5) conflict. Check all IPX addresses for conflicts.

A common problem results when a Windows NT computer shares resources over IPX. The Windows NT internal IPX network address, which is set at 00000000 by default, is only needed when sharing over IPX has been enabled. If the NT server is not sharing resources over IPX, the internal network address is not needed. To be certain that conflicting internal network addresses are not a problem, see that the internal network address for each Windows NT workstation and server is changed to a unique value.

Wrong Frame Type

The following error message generally indicates that the wrong frame type is used for the IPX protocol binding:

```
The tree or server cannot be found.
```

If the situation were the result of lack of connectivity, the "Failed to connect" error would be displayed. In some cases, NT's autodetect frame may not find and load the correct frame type. In the IPX protocol configuration, manually select the frame types to be supported.

Protocol Not Bound to NIC

The following error message indicates that the workstation IPX protocol did not bind properly and is not available:

```
The NetWare redirector cannot find a network transport.
```

In Windows NT, check Event Viewer for critical errors where drivers or protocols failed to load (Windows 95/98 has no such option). In Windows 95 and 98, check your Bindings screen in the Network Control Panel applet. Look for and correct problems such as a conflicting IRQ between the NIC and another device. Reconfigure IPX protocol configuration in Control Panel—you will need to reboot once changes have been made.

Problem Resolution for Windows 95, 98, NT

Support for 32-bit Windows client software setup has been well developed in NetWare 5. The Z.E.N.works Starter Pack includes client setup software that is easy to use and comprehensively handles all the options in a straightforward manner. If you have installed/configured your NIC properly, installation should go quite easily. However, if your client installation fails, this section will provide some tips for correcting a failed installation.

Removing and Reinstalling Novell's Client for Windows 95/98 and NT

As discussed previously in this chapter, sometimes it's just quicker and easier to remove and then reinstall software rather than to try to find and repair a problem. This procedure is the comprehensive solution for just about any problem that is based at the client end. However, a good Client 32 installation depends upon two factors:

▸ The Microsoft network adapter and its driver must be properly installed and working.

▸ You must start with a "fresh" configuration — one that is free from residue from a failed or ineffective installation.

The Windows environment is quite complex — Windows has thousands of files and configuration parameters, and Novell's client software manipulates hundreds of them. In the DOS days, the Novell protocol stack and client shell/requester handled interaction between the workstation operating system and the NetWare server. Today, hundreds of .dll, .drv, and .exe files and Registry entries control interaction between the workstation and the server. Because Novell now uses Microsoft protocol stacks, there are many more complexities over which Novell has no control.

After installation, it does not take much to upset the configuration balance established when Client 32 is first installed. The Registry and Windows folders are updated by service packs, third-party software applications, and the Novell Client software. Setup programs take unexpected actions at times, and the result is often a problem that is seemingly unrelated to the offending setup.

In many cases, you can solve the biggest problems and cut client recovery time to just a few minutes by removing the existing client and then reinstalling the latest client update from scratch. This is why it is recommended that you install an administrative copy of the client setup files on a server and make it accessible to the entire network.

A "fresh" installation is different from a "new" installation. When you reinstall Client 32 and related components, you should first be sure that the workstation has been put back into a state where the operating system and all components are working properly — just like a new installation. A "fresh" installation is one that is free from whatever problems may have contributed to the problems you have experienced.

Here are summarized steps to be taken to perform a fresh installation:

1. Remove the existing Novell client software by executing Unc32.exe. You will find this file on your Z.E.N.works Starter Pack in the \Products\ Win95\ibm_enu\Admin directory. Execute Unc32 from this directory on the CD.

2. For Windows 95 (versions 4.00.950 and 4.00.950A) reapply Service Pack 1. For Windows NT 4, reapply Service Pack 3 or later. Do not apply any service packs to Windows 98 (see the note that follows). Once you have reapplied a service pack, you will need to reboot.

NOTE
Be sure to obtain the latest NetWare 5 Client files, and check release notes for updated instructions. For a later Client 32 release, you may need to install a more recent Microsoft service pack. However, installing a later service pack may upset NetWare connectivity. Current release notes and TIDs available on Novell's support Web site will address these problems.

3. Check your Windows network adapter and protocol settings in the Network Control Panel applet. Verify connectivity over the protocol stack if possible. When using TCP/IP, use the Ping utility to test IP communications loopback and communications with other hosts as discussed in the "Troubleshooting TCP/IP Problems" section earlier in this chapter.

4. Reinstall the Novell Client for Windows from the Z.E.N.works Starter Pack, or from the latest files received from Novell. Select Custom Options and be sure your protocol options are correctly configured. See Chapter 10, "Windows 95/98 and NT Clients," for step-by-step installation instructions.

TIP

Because Client 32 is stacked on top of Microsoft drivers and protocols, you must resolve your Windows networking problems before your Client 32 installation can be successful. If your installation still does not work after the preceding procedure, make sure that the Microsoft adapter driver and protocol stack are able to communicate as discussed in step 3. Most commonly, the problem is hardware conflicts or improper driver configuration.

Updating the Workstation Operating System

If you would like to prevent potential problems, you will check and upgrade Windows clients to the latest version. To view the current version installed on a workstation, select the Control Panel System applet. You will see the version number displayed as shown in Figure 14.11.

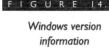

F I G U R E 14.11

Windows version information

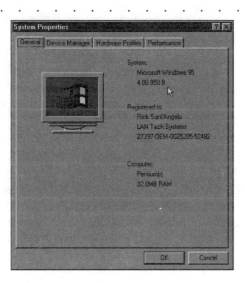

Windows 95/98

Figure 14.9 shows a Windows 95 4.00.950B, which is also called OSR2 (operating system release 2). The following release numbers can be found:

- ▶ 4.00.950 — the original Windows 95 release

- ▶ 4.00.950A — original release with Service Pack 1

- ▶ 4.00.950B — OSR2 (OEM version)

 Look for the SystemInfo utility on the CD that accompanies this book. This freeware Windows utility will tell you what Windows version you are running.

NOTE

All Windows 95 workstations should be updated to 4.00.950A or 4.00.950B. OSR2 is only available from OEMs.

 You can download Windows 95 Service Pack 1 at http://www. microsoft.com/windows/default/asp. **Select Windows Resources, Downloads. Look for Service Pack 1 dated December 31, 1997.**

Windows NT 4

The Windows System applet shows all Windows NT 4 systems as Windows NT version 4.0, build 1381. This version should also have Service Pack 3 or later installed, but the System applet does not indicate whether a service pack is installed or not. To see Windows NT's service pack information, watch during the blue boot screen — at the top of the screen you should see "Microsoft (R) Windows (TM) NT Version 4.0, (Build 1381: Service Pack 3)."

 Windows NT 4 should have Service Pack 3 or later installed before loading Client 32. The System applet does not indicate installed service packs.

NOTE

Order of Installation

You should always install and apply patches in the following order:

1. Install operating system.

2. Install applications.

3. Apply service pack if applicable.

4. Install Novell Client 32.

Reinstalling an operating system will overwrite service pack patches. Anytime you reinstall a Windows operating system, you should reinstall the service pack.

Application software may install new files in one or more of the Windows directories. When you are installing software or applying a service pack, existing files are overwritten with updated files. For this reason, it is sometimes necessary to reapply the service pack after installing software.

A service pack setup also checks for existing Registry entries and may make changes to specific entries if they exist. When you install software after the service pack, appropriate fixes to support files or changes to Registry entries may not be applied.

TIP

It is important to apply the service pack immediately before installing the Novell Client software. When you have installed application software, a support file may have been installed that can cause problems with Client 32.

Replacing Earlier Version Windows Files

Windows updates and third-party software installations both add files and Registry entries — but are the files you end up with the right ones? In some situations, a file that has been updated by a third-party application can conflict with NetWare resource handling. At one time, you may have seen a dialog box asking if you prefer to update an existing file, even when the date is more recent than the update file. Certainly this notification is troubling for many support engineers — how could you know if the older file will remove problems with the newer file, or vice versa?

If you see a dialog box asking if you would like to keep a file with the later date, your best bet is to answer Yes. If you still have the same problem, try the update again, but this time answer No. This will replace the later file with the service pack file and may solve your problem.

Removing the Existing Client

Reinstalling by itself often does not fix a problem. Winsetup, like many applications, checks for existing files and Registry entries and then attempts to work around them. The most perplexing problem seems to relate to existing Registry entries that will not go away. When you remove an application, all related entries should be purged, leaving you with a clean system on which to install your new Client 32. Another situation has to do with replacing older files with newer files, or not replacing older files with newer files. In some cases, you may need to replace newer files with older ones. You can forget all about this if you simply remove and then reinstall Client 32 and related components.

Novell has made an application that will uninstall an existing client, reversing the Control Panel and Registry entries. You will find this utility on the Z.E.N.works Starter Pack CD in the \PRODUCTS\WIN95\ibm_enu\Admin directory.

Run Unc32.exe to completely remove the Novell Client. After running this utility, you may need to adjust your Microsoft Networking properties in Control Panel. Unc32 does the best it can to remove Novell client software without disturbing other configurations. Unc32 is normally effective at this without disturbing other working services and drivers, but this cannot be guaranteed.

NOTE

Use the same utility for removing the Windows 95, 98, and NT client software. Though NT has a separate directory, the Unc32.exe in the Win95 directory is the right utility for all 32-bit Windows versions.

▶ · ◀

Known Windows 3.x Problems and Solutions

You will probably find Windows 3.1 and Windows for Workgroups 3.11 are more difficult to support than 32-bit Windows versions. Having said that, Novell still supports these products and will continue to do so until support is no longer required.

The older method of installing DOS terminate-and-stay-resident (TSR) drivers before starting Windows will not work with NetWare 5. Though DOS TSRs continue to work well for older NetWare versions, new capabilities and stability require 32-bit updated Windows drivers and protocol files. Windows 3.1 and Windows for Workgroups 3.11 can use updated 32-bit drivers with the Windows 32-bit update patch. All Windows 3.x workstations should be upgraded to this level if possible.

IPX Access to NetWare 5 Servers Requires the Compatibility Mode

NetWare 5 supports IPX clients in two ways: with a direct IPX binding or with a Compatibility Mode Driver binding to the IP protocol. The default installation for a server is to install pure IP with IPX Compatibility Mode. However, before your newly installed server can support IPX communications, you must load the CMD (SCMD.NLM) and the SLP Directory Agent (SLPDA.NLM). DNS objects and rights are configured automatically when these modules are first loaded. See Chapter 11, "TCP/IP Services," for instructions on setting up and loading CMD on your server.

Novell Client for Windows 3.x, 95/98, or NT must be installed using IP with IPX compatibility (called IP gateway in NT). When this option is installed, the client should be able to use CMD without modification.

Check the following: NetWare must be the primary login.

Black Screen of Death

Windows 3.x versions are subject to hanging, a condition often referred to as the dreaded "Black Screen of Death" (BSOD). This problem occurs because the operating system has crashed — deadlocked. This condition can occur for a variety of reasons. It is typically impractical to attempt to determine why the condition occurs. There are just a couple situations you should investigate to locate the cause of this problem.

Do not blame the Novell client software for this problem — it can occur with any software at any time when your platform is a 16-bit operating system. The BSOD is more likely to occur when using Novell client software. Networking software relies on drivers and components — when the driver crashes, your system deadlocks. You can get the BSOD at any time should the underlying component fail.

When you get the BSOD, your system is deadlocked with no possibility of recovery — only a cold reboot will solve the problem and may result in the loss of data. Any unsaved work will be lost. To add insult to injury, there is no possibility of obtaining an error message to verify the source of the problem.

Misbehaved drivers are most likely to cause this type of crash. Anytime a 16-bit — "real-mode" — driver fails, it will lock your system. The driver can fail for several reasons: The device or its configuration can be faulty, the driver can have a "bug," or another driver can conflict with the existing driver. For example, if your NIC uses interrupt 3 and your COM2 port also uses interrupt 3, everything can run just fine until a modem is activated on COM2 — then the driver crashes, resulting in the BSOD.

This problem is one of the most significant reasons to update to a 32-bit Windows version with all 32-bit drivers. Newer 32-bit drivers work in the Intel processor "protected mode," which protects 32-bit drivers from crashing your system. Software and drivers running in 32-bit mode are capable of multitasking, which is not possible in a 16-bit environment. Windows' 32-bit environment was designed to handle all types of simultaneous activity — it is safer and faster.

Three conflicts were found between Microsoft and Novell protocol driver files and configurations. The following situations can also cause a BSOD deadlock:

▸ Windows 3.1 requires a Microsoft patch to avoid an interaction problem between the Microsoft VTDA.386 driver and the NetWare requester. The offending file can be updated. This patch is not required for Windows for Workgroups 3.11, since it is incorporated into the official release.

▸ Another conflict was found between Windows' VPICD.386 driver and Novell's VIPX driver. An updated VIPX driver is installed with later Novell client software to eliminate this problem.

▸ A third reason for deadlocks was found to be a configuration adjustment in the SYSTEM.INI file. The TimerCriticalSection= setting in the [386Enh] section must be set to a minimum of 1000, or up to a maximum of 10000.

When installing the latest Novell client software for Windows, these updates are automatically installed to eliminate the possibility of causing a BSOD deadlock. For these reasons, it is not a good idea to manually install NetWare driver files with Windows. If you run a more recent Novell client setup program, the preceding patches and adjustments are automatically applied.

Even though you may have a good device, a working device driver, and all the Novell patches, you can still get BSOD deadlocks due to third-party software. If an application makes calls to IPX/SPX, those calls can cause timeout problems that aggravate interaction between Microsoft, Novell, and the third-party software components. Independent Software Developers (ISVs) must consult the Novell Software Development Kit for specifics about avoiding function calls that may cause BSOD deadlocking.

To resolve the Black Screen of Death in Windows 3.1 or 3.11:

1. Remove the existing Novell client software, and replace it with the latest version. Watch for file copy errors during installation.

2. Check your NIC for hardware port, IRQ, memory, and DMA conflicts with other devices. Normally, NetWare drivers will not load if there is a conflict, but this is not always the case, since not all devices are working at the time the network drivers are loaded.

3. Check for intermittent failure of your NIC. If the NIC fails while in use and you are using 16-bit drivers, you may experience the BSOD. Run your NIC's diagnostic software in repeating cycles to test for intermittent problems. Generally, intermittent problems occur when heat is present from continual device operation combined with heat inside your computer.

4. If all of the preceding components check out okay, the problem may be with a "network-aware" software application. Check with the software vendor's tech support resources for a known IPX/SPX function problem and related patch.

DOS Client Support

NetWare 5 supports DOS clients in a new, very sophisticated way. Instead of relying entirely on outdated 16-bit DOS drivers, Novell has chosen to apply 32-bit server drivers to the DOS client. Server NIC drivers can be used to replace the

TSRs—LSL.COM, IPXODI.COM, VLM.EXE, and .VLM files—that have been used for the past several years.

In the 32-bit driver stack, the NetWare I/O Subsystem (NIOS) handles all other drivers. NIOS.EXE is executed as a TSR. NIOS creates an environment in which NLMs can be loaded. NIC and protocol drivers are then loaded as NLMs.

New 32-Bit Driver Support

Three reasons provided the impetus to develop a new driver/protocol stack for DOS workstations, though DOS workstations are all but obsolete at this point:

▶ First, improvements were required for more sophisticated NetWare 5 features.

▶ Second, Novell wanted to implement 32-bit drivers in the 16-bit DOS environment.

▶ Third, Novell wanted to ensure that driver support for DOS workstations will not disappear. A shift to using server drivers at the workstation reduces NIC vendors' development efforts and provides customers with more options for DOS workstations.

For the preceding reasons, you can select either 16-bit DOS drivers or 32-bit server drivers to install your DOS client.

Failure to Access a NetWare Server

Several potential reasons may prevent your DOS workstation from connecting to a NetWare server.

One or More Drivers Fail to Load

Once you install your DOS client software and reboot, follow this procedure to troubleshoot driver loading:

I. Press F8 during at the beginning of the DOS boot operation to step through your boot instructions one line at a time. Or you can add the /L option to the NIOS.EXE line in the STARTNET.BAT. See the following section for reading the NIOS log file.

2. Observe each line of STARTNET.BAT (called from the AUTOEXEC.BAT). Watch each line to be certain that it executes without errors. Pay special attention to:

   - The driver load statement — check to see that the driver loads. If it does not, check the settings for accuracy or conflicts with other devices.

   - The driver load statement (once again) — check to see that the driver is loaded with the appropriate frame type.

   - The CLIENT32 requester (the last line) — when this module loads, you should see a message indicating "Attached to server *SERVER_NAME.*"

3. At your server console type **TRACK ON** — observe the RIP Tracking Screen. When CLIENT32 is loaded at the workstation, you should see a Specific Route Request coming IN on a line with the network address to which the workstation is connected.

4. At your server console, observe the MONITOR screen's Connection selection. Watch for a connection to be established, with a NOT-LOGGED-IN under the list of Active Connections.

5. At your server console, observe the MONITOR screen's LAN/WAN drivers selection. Select the driver line that shows the frame type the workstation is using, Tab up, watch the Total packets received. You should see a few packets received when CLIENT32 is executed at the workstation.

Analyzing the NIOS.LOG File

When the /L option is added to the NIOS.EXE execution line of the STARTNET.BAT file, a log file will be created when NIOS is executed. The NIOS.LOG file contains a record of messages sent to the screen.

When NIOS.EXE is loaded in the STARTNET.BAT file, you can add a "/L" parameter to enable the logging feature. When logging is enabled, NIOS will write configuration information into the C:\NOVELL\CLIENT32\NIOS.LOG file each time the workstation loads NIOS. If no NIOS.LOG file exists, it will be created. Subsequent loadings of NIOS with the /L parameter append information to the end of the previous log. The log file size can be limited using the Log File Size in Bytes parameter setting in the NET.CFG. The NIOS.LOG should provide some clues if modules are not loading or are producing errors.

DOS Client 32 Does Not Support Pure TCP/IP Access to NetWare Servers

Pure IP access with the DOS client to a NetWare 5 server is not supported. There is an option to install TCP/IP, but this option is only effective when NetWare/IP is installed on your NetWare 5 server.

Tools

In addition to NetWare utilities, many tools are available from third-party developers to help you manage and troubleshoot clients in a NetWare environment. This section presents a few tools that are available from Novell and from independent software developers.

The NetWare Diagnostics Utility for Windows

The NetWare Diagnostics utility, NWD2.EXE, will list all .DLL and .EXE modules currently in memory and their version numbers as shown in Figure 14.12. This utility can help the troubleshooter determine exactly which modules are in use.

This utility is only necessary when a technician must evaluate software and operating system revisions. It is common for an update to replace most but not all modules. At times updates are applied that replace a good module with one that causes problems. Windows makes it very difficult to evaluate the hundreds of files that may be loaded in memory at any given time.

NOTE

This utility is for use with Windows 3.x, 95, and 98. When this utility is used with Windows NT, only 16-bit modules are shown.

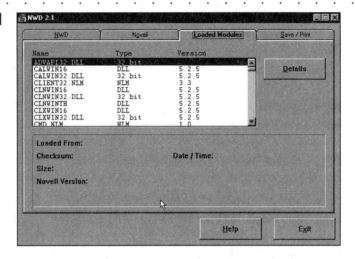

FIGURE 14.12

The NetWare Diagnostics
utility

The NetWare Diagnostics utility tells you:

▸ Module name and path

▸ File date, time, size, checksum

▸ Internal version (Novell files only)

When troubleshooting a software update, use the NetWare Diagnostics utility to see which modules actually are in use instead of assuming all modules have been updated. You can also analyze your Novell Client for Windows software for support module version numbers.

To execute the NetWare Diagnostics application, change directories to the \Products\Adm32\ibm_enu\Diagtool folder and execute NWD2.EXE.

Shareware/Freeware Utilities

Several utilities for troubleshooting TCP/IP are to be found on the CD that accompanies this book. You will find JBRSoftware's selection of NetWare utilities.

You can see a complete listing of JBRSoftware at
http://nz.com/webnz/JRBSoftware.

You will also find a few utilities from Darwin Collins.

 You can access Darwin's Web site at `http://www.fastlane.net/ homepages/dcollins`.

See Appendix E of this book for a complete listing, or see the index of shareware/freeware utilities on the CD.

Dave's Novell Shareware Web Site

David Collins has been collecting NetWare-related shareware and freeware for years, and he has decided to make them available on his Web site. You will find many useful utilities for Windows 3.*x*, 95, 98, and NT and NetWare servers. In this library you will find many utilities that will help you diagnose problems. You will also find many helpful miscellaneous utilities that are helpful for many system administration tasks. Some of the utilities included in David Collins's shareware library are referenced throughout this book.

 Check out Dave's Web site at `http://www.novellshareware.com`.

WinFiles.Com Shareware Collection

This Web site offers a most comprehensive collection of shareware and freeware utilities for Windows 95, 98, and NT. Application are linked to developers' Web/FTP sites, to form a virtual collection. Each application is updated individually, and links are updated twice per week.

WinFiles.Com is like a software superstore, except there is no check-out stand. You are free to download any software on this site and then pay for shareware on the honor system. You will find demo versions of some software packages.

Among other software applications, this Web site has the most extensive collection network/internetwork tools used for monitoring and troubleshooting network-related components.

 You can find WinFiles.Com at `http://winfiles.com/apps/`.

References

You can find references to several resources to help you diagnose and troubleshoot client problems.

Patches and Fixes

Novell provides operating system patches and fixes on a frequent basis. Whenever a problem is found and corrected in NetWare 4 or 5 operating systems, utilities, and drivers, Novell posts patches and fixes for public download. Periodically, patches and fixes are combined into "Service Packs" that can be applied to update all patches and fixes to a stable level where the patches and fixes can coexist peacefully.

To access the most current online patch list with file download links via the Web, check `http://support.novell.com/misc/patlst.htm`.

To search for patches by name, check `http://support.novell.com/search/`.

To search a list of patch and update files contained on Novell's ftp server, see `ftp.novell.com/pub/updates`.

Technical Information Documents (TIDs)

TIDs document current support issues and are kept online as long as they are relevant. TIDs are published in Novell Support's Web site under the Knowledgebase, and are included on the Support Connection CD. On the Web site, you can search according to headings or text, and you can limit the search to most recent documents.

To locate TIDs and relevant patches and files, go to `www.novell.com/support` and select the Knowledgebase link.

Novell AppNotes

AppNotes are published monthly by the Novell Research team and address selected significant technical issues in a "white paper" format. Novell's top support engineers select topics to publish each month — the most current and significant NDS-related topics are discussed in detail in monthly articles. You will find AppNotes dating back several years on the Novell Support Connection CD (available on a subscription basis) and on Novell's Web site at `www.novell.com/support`.

AppNotes are contained in their entirety on the Novell Support Connection CD. However, they are indexed better on Novell's support Web site. You will probably find that searching articles for the past few years is easier using the Web site. For current issues, such as ones discussed in this chapter, look through the most recent AppNotes.

NetNotes

Every later AppNotes issue contains a NetNotes section. NetNotes addresses the most significant current support issues. For the most part, they are derived from TIDs, and they often duplicate TIDs you will find. However, keep in mind that NetNotes are published because they successfully address some of the most common current problems. To find NetNotes, search the AppNotes by issue, select NetNotes from the list of articles, and read through the headings. At least three or four topics are discussed every month.

CHAPTER 15

Storage Devices and File Systems

This chapter provides troubleshooting help for the most common disk- and file system–related problems that are encountered on a day-in, day-out basis. NetWare file systems are different from other file system — indeed, the NetWare file system has advantages in both performance and durability that sets it aside from all other file systems. NetWare administrators need to become acclimated to the uniqueness of this file system in order to be prepared for fast recovery when problems arise.

This chapter discusses:

▶ Using the traditional NetWare file system versus the Novell Storage Services file system

▶ SCSI subsystem setup, configuration, and troubleshooting

▶ File system error handling for the most common problems you may encounter

▶ Unique issues associated with advanced features of the traditional NetWare file system, including file compression, migration, salvaging, and purging

Refer to this chapter when you suspect file corruption or receive I/O (input/output) errors at your server console. Your problems may be due to one of the topics discussed in this chapter.

Traditional versus Novell Storage Services File Systems

NetWare file systems have established a standard for durability, efficiency, and high performance in the networking industry. Each version of NetWare ups the ante on that standard. NetWare 5 is no exception — the addition of the Novell Storage Services (NSS) as an optional file system is a tremendous feature.

NetWare's traditional file system is a self-healing file system — it has fault-tolerant Directory Entry and File Allocation Tables (DET/FAT). Damage to the file listings and FAT does not prevent access to files, and damage is automatically diagnosed and repaired upon boot. NetWare's file caching is legendary and is mostly dedicated to high-speed file access. NetWare's block suballocation provides the most efficient disk storage without sacrificing performance — it provides the performance of a 64KB block size, but retains the efficiency of a 1KB block size. No other company has been able to duplicate this feature. Support for other operating systems' long names and extended attributes are now a default feature, which the system administrator no longer needs to configure. For many reasons, this file system is state of the art.

NSS is also a new feature introduced with NetWare 5 — it allows very large volumes to mount quickly. Larger NetWare volumes take longer to mount due to consistency checking and caching/hashing operations. Very large volumes can require massive amounts of RAM during this process. NSS cuts mounting time and RAM requirements significantly. During volume mount, the NSS volume is not checked for consistency, nor are features added that require building indexes and hash tables. NSS online performance is equal to — or better than — the traditional NetWare file system.

Use NSS for massive storage systems that are fault tolerant and for read-only media. Because NSS does not include features such as compression, migration, suballocation, and mirroring, you should not trust valuable data to this file system. NSS is designed for RAID and CD-ROM drive systems that do not require the features of the traditional NetWare file system. RAID subsystems are fault tolerant and generally quite massive in size — CD-ROMs are read-only and are changed often. For these reasons, the NSS file system is ideally suited to these technologies.

Novell does not recommend using NSS for data on regular disk drives. Use this technology for RAID subsystems — which are fault tolerant — and for CD-ROM drives used for read-only access.
NOTE

You will find very few problems with NSS — it is not designed to handle a lot of problems for read-only and hardware-level fault-tolerant systems. If you experience problems with an NSS volume, you should check the hardware subsystem. Most fault-tolerant disk subsystems are based on SCSI technology. The following section may provide help for both traditional and NSS-based volumes installed on SCSI disk drives and RAID subsystems.

SCSI Subsystem Setup

If your Small Computer System Interface (SCSI) disk subsystem is not installed properly, you will not be able to create NetWare volumes on the drives. This is not a NetWare problem — you need to consult the documentation and setup software for your SCSI adapter. This section provides the basic overview some technicians may find helpful when dealing with SCSI's unique requirements.

Some SCSI adapters have all setup software embedded in firmware on the adapter itself, while others provide a setup disk. If documentation has been misplaced or is not available, see your SCSI adapter vendor's Web site for documentation and helpful FAQs. Another source for hardware setup documentation is Micro House SupportSource technical library. Their hardware document library includes setup manuals for just about every SCSI adapter, hardware configuration settings, instructions, and diagrams.

NOTE **You will find the DELEC SCSI Guide Online on the CD that accompanies this book, provided courtesy of Delec. This guide summarizes SCSI standards, common terminology, specifications, and other information that may help you significantly in understanding, configuring, and implementing SCSI adapters and devices.**

Look for the file SCSIGide.htm.

The following information provides general guidelines for setting up SCSI subsystems. Specific information on how to configure your system is dependent upon the make and model of adapter.

SCSI Technology Overview

SCSI is a bus technology that provides interfacing for SCSI devices with common computer buses. Unlike some disk technologies, the SCSI adapter interfaces your computer bus with a SCSI bus, to which SCSI devices must be connected. The SCSI adapter must be configured with a base I/O address, interrupt request lines, a memory address, and perhaps other configuration settings (such as a DMA channel) to integrate the card into your computer. These settings must not conflict with other adapters installed in your computer, or the card will not work. In addition, you must configure the SCSI adapter, devices, and bus cables according to SCSI requirements.

SCSI subsystems can accommodate either 8 or 16 devices, depending upon the SCSI level. In either case, the adapter counts as one device, leaving the capacity to integrate either 7 or 15 internal drives with one adapter. When using both internal and external drives, you may be able to accommodate the full complement of either 8 or 16 drives. The drives are to be connected to bus cables that run from the adapter to each drive in series, with each bus cable ending at a drive.

SCSI devices include disk drivers, CD-ROM drives, optical drives, and tape and other backup drives, as well as scanners. Scanners are not discussed in this chapter, but all other drives are designed to be configured according to standardized rules discussed in this section.

SCSI Bus Termination

Depending upon SCSI level, a SCSI subsystem uses a 50-pin or 68-pin bus design that requires connections to each device (disk, tape, or CD-ROM drive) and physical termination at both ends. The adapter is normally terminated at one end, and the last drive on the bus is terminated at the other end as shown in Figure 15.1. If you have both internal and external cabling, the terminated devices may be at both ends.

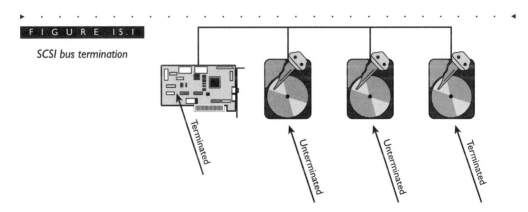

FIGURE 15.1

SCSI bus termination

Most drives and adapters have an automatic electrical termination feature. Terminators are installed on the adapter and on each drive, and an electrical signal from the adapter firmware switches the terminator on or off. Be sure that each drive has terminator(s) installed — if a terminator is missing from the last drive, the switch cannot effectively terminate the bus. Adapters that have automatic electrical termination are generally set to use it by default, but this feature can be turned off — which will require manual installation/removal of terminators. If your SCSI adapter and drives do not support electrical termination, then terminators must be removed from all drives except the last one in the bus.

SCSI Addressing

SCSI devices must be configured with a logical SCSI bus address. Narrow SCSI (8-bit) devices are numbered 0 through 7, and wide SCSI (16-bit) devices are numbered 0 through 15. The adapter is typically software configured with a device number. Most commonly, the adapter is addressed as device 7, while drives are configured as devices 0, 1, 2, and so on. For most SCSI adapters today any number can be assigned to each device as long as the number has not already been assigned to another device. However, the first drive is typically configured as device 0, the second drive as device 1, and so on.

Most SCSI drives are shipped with the device number set at device 0. If no other drives are connected to the same adapter, you should not need to configure any device addresses. When you add a second drive, however, you must change the default SCSI address to another device number, or neither drive can work. The address for each device is set by configuring jumpers or switches that represent binary numbers.

Your drive will typically have three switches or three sets of jumpers, as shown in Figure 15.2.

FIGURE 15.2

SCSI device address jumpers

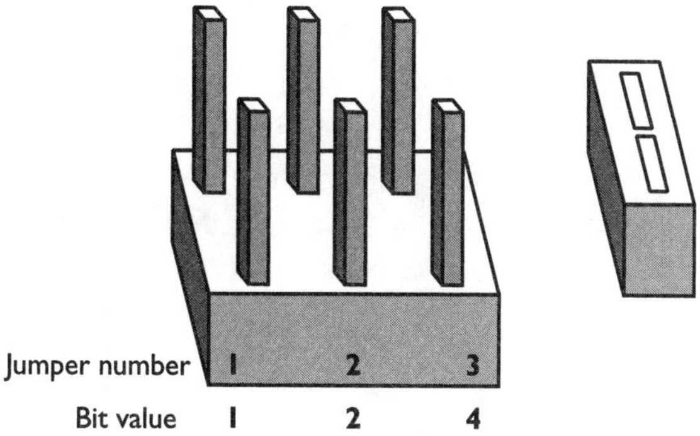

Jumper number   1   2   3

Bit value   1   2   4

Typically, the jumper or switch on the left represents the least significant bit. If all jumpers are off, the device number is 0. If a jumper is placed on the first pair on the left, the device number is set to 1. If a single jumper is installed on the second pair, the device number is set to 2. The third position is 4. Other addresses can be set by combining jumpers. For example, if jumpers are installed on the left and middle pairs, the address is set to 3 (1 + 2). If all jumpers are installed, the device number is seven (1 + 2 + 4). All that is necessary to configure the addresses properly is to set each drive and the adapter to unique addresses.

Logical Unit Number

You may see references to the Logical Unit Number (LUN), which is often confused with the SCSI bus address. Each SCSI drive has its own embedded controller and can accommodate two drives—LUN 0 and LUN 1. This allows each SCSI address to have two drives attached to each bus cable attachment, doubling the potential total number of disk drives that can be supported on a single SCSI adapter. Some SCSI adapters are designed to handle up to 8 LUNs for each SCSI device number (up to 7 for a total of 56 drives on one adapter). This type of configuration should never be used for traditional disk storage, as performance is bound to be poor on each LUN channel. Use this type of configuration for CD-ROM or other types of read-only drives.

One of the tremendous benefits of the SCSI design is that each drive can be configured as a separate intelligent device with associated performance benefits. Using a second drive on a SCSI device defeats this benefit. Though you may see references to LUNs, drives are never installed in this manner. Using secondary drives in this manner hampers performance and is not necessary. If more drives are required, a second adapter should be added, providing greater performance benefits.

BIOS Memory Address

SCSI adapters have BIOS firmware that supplements your computer's BIOS. In order to access the SCSI BIOS, a memory address must be set that is available in your computer setup. NetWare does not require the BIOS — the driver can locate and access the devices. The BIOS is required to enable booting from one of the drives, to configure some or all of the adapter settings, and to run diagnostic routines, which are typically stored in firmware on the adapter.

The BIOS is installed into memory during the computer boot sequence. If the BIOS is disabled, or the memory address setting conflicts with another device, the BIOS will not load. During boot, the SCSI BIOS will display a message when it is successfully installed in memory — some adapters also display a message indicating that the SCSI BIOS is not loaded into memory.

SCSI Setup and Diagnostics

If your adapter has an on-board setup and diagnostics utility, you can run it only if its BIOS is enabled and successfully installed in memory. To execute the setup and diagnostic software, you must press the appropriate key sequence — Ctrl+A is the most common sequence — when the boot message is displayed on your screen. If your adapter's setup and diagnostic software is on disk, you can typically boot from the disk or run the utility from DOS.

Run your SCSI setup and diagnostics program to configure SCSI adapter settings such as bus speed (5 to 20 MHz) and to enable features such as autobooting for CD-ROM drives. Many settings can be adjusted for most adapters. You must be sure that the settings match the capabilities of the connected drives. For example, a SCSI-2 adapter can be set to 5 or 10 MHz, but a SCSI-1 drive can only operate at 5 MHz — therefore the adapter must be set to 5 MHz for a SCSI-1 drive to be recognized. If you get into trouble on these configuration values, you can return all settings to factory defaults. This is typically a good starting point to make your system work. You may then alter settings to improve performance. For example, if everything works at 5 MHz, try changing your bus speed to 10 MHz. If drives do not work, you will know that 5 MHz is the fastest supported speed for your disk drives.

The diagnostics program will poll the SCSI bus, showing you devices that it can recognize. If drives are installed but do not show up, the missing drives are not connected, not addressed, or not terminated properly.

Formatting and Surface Scanning

The setup and diagnostics program that comes with your SCSI adapter also provides user options for formatting and scanning for surface defects. This type of format is a low-level drive initialization that will destroy all existing data including the partitioning tables. Under normal circumstances, formatting is done at the factory — your drive should never need to be low-level formatted again. However, two situations may require you to reinitialize — or low-level format — your drive.

You may need to scan a drive to deallocate drive sectors where media defects are located. If you encounter data errors, your drive may have surface defects that have not been detected. When defects are encountered during a write operation, the controller's verification process will typically find the defect and write the data to another area on the disk. This type of error can show up in file system I/O errors and can be resolved by scanning the drive. Both destructive and nondestructive surface scans can locate and deallocate previously undetected media defects.

You may find that a drive that was previously formatted by one brand of SCSI adapter may need to be reformatted with another brand of adapter to be recognized. This problem was more common in older adapters and is rarely a problem today.

A surface scan will detect media defects and hide them in the bad block table. Surface scans can be destructive or nondestructive. A nondestructive test cannot be as comprehensive as a destructive scan but can often help when you suspect drive problems due to media defects.

Always back up all data before running a surface scan. Before running the surface scan, be sure that you know whether it will be destructive or nondestructive.

WARNING

Setting up and configuring a SCSI disk subsystem is sometimes challenging. This section has provided help and tips to understanding SCSI complexities. Only if your drive hardware is working properly can you move on to the next level of troubleshooting—the logical volume. When you see file and directory errors, always check first to see that your SCSI subsystem is properly configured before moving on to file system error handling as discussed next.

File System Error Handling

You will find many file access error codes that can pinpoint problems by displaying error codes and messages. An error code starts with a hexadecimal code, followed by a brief message. In some cases, the message alone is sufficient to isolate the problem. In other cases, you will need to look up the error code to determine the cause. Sometimes a little detective work is required to follow the error indirectly to its cause.

Look up error codes in the Reference section of your NetWare 5 online documentation. All codes are listed in numeric sequence and are linked to more explicit descriptions. Many error descriptions include diagnostic and troubleshooting suggestions.

NOTE

File system errors can be generated as a result of hardware failure, damaged file or volume tables, or file sharing or software errors. In some cases, it takes some detective work to figure out which is the problem. For example, when you access a file, you may see an error that indicates a file that is open for exclusive use, thereby denying you access to the file. The file sharing error can be generated by a file damage, by hung software, or by a software bug.

File System Mirror Mismatch Errors during Volume Mount

NetWare scans file and directory listings each time a traditional NetWare volume is mounted. If a volume has sustained damage, you will probably see mirror mismatch errors during volume mount. These errors automatically repair themselves in most cases when the volume is remounted a second or subsequent time. If mirror mismatch errors are not automatically eliminated once the volume is mounted three or more times, you must run VREPAIR to fix the damaged DET or FAT.

Mirror mismatch errors are generally caused when a server abends or for any reason when a volume is dismounted without a proper shutdown. Most problems that would normally result in file system corruption will not damage your NetWare volumes, because the Directory Entry Table (DET) and File Allocation Table (FAT) for each NetWare volume are mirrored for fault tolerance.

When mounting a volume where the primary DET/FAT has been damaged, an error indicates that the mirrored copies of the DET and/or FAT do not match. The backup copy of the DET/FAT is automatically used, and the volume mount continues normally. Once the volume is in use, the good DET/FAT is mirrored and the damaged one is abandoned — the repair is automatic.

Transaction Tracking System Backout Messages

If file corruption has been detected on a file protected by the Transaction Tracking System (TTS), an error will be displayed during volume mount. TTS ensures that file corruption will not prevent access to a protected file. TTS provides solid file integrity under the most adverse conditions. TTS protects files that are critical to operating system integrity and makes them fault tolerant. NDS data files and NetWare 3 bindery files are examples of files that need to be protected. Corruption to these files would cause serious authentication and access problems.

When the Transactional attribute is applied to a file, TTS automatically creates a transaction backout file during each file update. Updates are added to the backout file and committed to the actual data file once the updates are completed or on a periodic basis. The actual data file and backout file are combined to work as a single file. This reduces the amount of time the actual data file is opened and exposed to potential corruption. When an update is interrupted, the backout file is left in an open and incomplete state, but the data in the original file is untouched. For example, if a server were to abend while an administrator was in the process of adding or editing an object, the DS database could become corrupted if it were not protected by TTS. TTS will allow incomplete updates to be abandoned, allowing the DS database to be unaltered. The changes to the object will be lost, but the DS database will not sustain damage.

When mounting a volume where incomplete TTS backout files are detected, you are given two options: to add the incomplete transactions, or to abandon the updates. If you are unsure of which action to take, the more conservative approach would be to abandon the updates. In the example given of adding or editing an object, the changes to the object would be lost.

I/O Errors

If you receive an I/O error when accessing a volume, check to see if all storage devices are physically online. If a volume spans more than one drive, failure of any drive will disable access to the volume. Check removable media; if media have been removed, or the device is cycling, access to the volume will become disabled. If any device on a SCSI adapter is not working properly, it can disable all drives connected to the adapter.

Drive deactivation error text generally indicates the reason for the drive deactivation. If an error code is shown, consult the File Service Error Codes in the Reference section of your Novell online documentation. Switch to the console screen to view the error message. If the error has scrolled off the screen, you can locate the error in the console log.

To view the Console Log:

1. Load INETCFG at your server console.

2. Select View Configuration → Console Messages.

3. Scroll toward the end of the log to see the most recent entries.

SYS Volume Fails to Mount

If the SYS volume fails to mount, your system cannot boot. This situation may be due to a malfunctioning disk drive, a defective disk adapter, or a damaged SYS volume. To troubleshoot this problem:

1. Check your disk drives to see that all connectors are fully seated.

2. See that SCSI drives are properly terminated and numbered.

3. Run the SCSI adapter diagnostics to check the adapter and disk drives.

4. Check the DOS boot volume for file corruption.

5. Be sure that the STARTUP.NCF file exists and the disk driver load command is present.

6. Run VREPAIR.

VREPAIR can be run without mounting the SYS volume. You will find VREPAIR.NLM in the DOS server boot directory as well as in the SYS:System directory. Follow this procedure for running VREPAIR from the DOS volume.

WARNING

Always back up a volume before attempting a VREPAIR.

On NetWare 3 and 4.10 or earlier versions where name space support has been installed on a volume, load the long name volume repair support module before running VREPAIR. Failure to do so will remove name support, resulting in irreparable damage to all except DOS files.

This will not be necessary for NetWare 4.11 and NetWare 5 versions. As long as long name space support is loaded, VREPAIR will automatically load long name volume repair support for any name spaces currently loaded. When running VREPAIR on these versions, you will see a message indicating that the long name volume repair support module has been loaded just prior to executing the repair.

To run VREPAIR when the SYS volume will not mount:

1. Boot your server to DOS.

2. Change directories to the server boot directory.

3. Execute **SERVER-NA** (do not execute the AUTOEXEC.NCF file); the SYS volume will fail to mount if that file is damaged.

4. At the colon prompt, load C:VREPAIR.

5. Verify options and then continue.

Server Hangs after Volume Mount

If you server hangs (stops without an error and does not continue loading modules) after the last volume is mounted, the condition may be due to a faulty NIC or driver. A NIC that is loose, is not properly configured, or conflicts with another hardware device can cause this problem. It may seem like a volume or disk problem, but often it is not.

Some Volumes Will Not Mount

If a volume will not mount after a traditional NetWare volume is newly created or expanded, or when long name space support has been added, your server may have insufficient RAM to mount the volume. Changes such as adding long name support to a volume typically precede this type of problem. Other situations can also cause a volume to use more RAM. For example, restoring a large number of files to a volume will cause an increase in the size of the volume tables and will therefore require more memory to mount the volume after the restore.

Each traditional NetWare volume's file system is scanned during mount. This process requires larger amounts of memory for larger file systems. After the volume is mounted, much of the memory required for the volume scan is no longer needed and is returned to the cache buffer memory pool. For this reason, a volume's file system can grow during use, resulting in failure to mount the next time the server is booted.

NetWare 5 has the NSS volume option for this reason. An NSS volume's file system is not scanned during volume mounting. This allows a volume to mount very quickly with far less memory usage. However, your SYS volume cannot be an NSS volume, nor can you upgrade an existing NetWare volume to NSS. To upgrade a volume to NSS, your only option is to back up all data, create a new volume, and then restore the data.

File Compression, Migration, and Suballocation

NetWare 4 and 5 versions include features for file compression, file migration, and block suballocation. File compression and migration can cause file access errors at times, but suballocation is transparent and maintenance-free.

File Compression

File compression is a good feature that has its downside. NetWare's file compression feature does not compress and decompress on the fly. Instead it only compresses files that are not accessed for a given amount of time. By default, files that are not accessed for the configured time period are compressed during off-hours. When a user accesses a compressed file, it is decompressed spontaneously and then accessed. Problems are often related to performance — compression time should be scheduled for off-hours, and decompression can occur at any time. Decompression is most likely to occur when user access is busiest. Spontaneous decompression can cause some significant issues. First, some applications will produce an I/O error when the compressed file is encountered, preventing access to the file. Second, decompression uses up processor power and disk I/O — other active processes must then compete with the compression engine for resources, and performance is adversely affected. Third, additional space is required for both the uncompressed and compressed forms of the file during the process of decompression.

For the first reason stated, you may encounter software that will not work with NetWare file compression. If you encounter I/O errors when accessing a compressed file, try uncompressing the file manually using the NCOPY command.

There is nothing that can be done concerning the adverse affects of running the decompression engine during busy periods. If enough files must be decompressed at one time, which is not unusual for Windows applications, all server processes can grind to a crawl while competing with the decompression process.

Compression can also exacerbate declining volume capacity. Before a file can be accessed, it must first be uncompressed. Compression can temporarily free up disk space, only to exhaust disk space when files must be decompressed.

Because disk space is so inexpensive these days, you might want to reconsider disk compression. Once a volume has been configured for compression, it cannot be turned off. Your best bet is to create a volume that has file compression enabled. Install most of your applications and data on volumes without compression — but store applications and data on the compression volume that are known to work well with NetWare's compression.

Salvaging and Purging Deleted Files

You can recover files that have been deleted in the Salvage tool, available within NetWare Administrator. You will find Salvage under the Tools menu selection. Deleted files are automatically purged on a first-deleted, first-purged basis when disk space is needed. Until files have been purged, you can recover them without loss of data. File listings for deleted files are not available without viewing them in the Salvage tool.

Running Out of Volume Space   When a volume nears capacity, you will receive error messages indicating that the volume is almost full. You should heed these warnings — when a volume is filled, you can suffer file and volume corruption. When a volume reaches capacity, updates to the directory listings and file allocation tables cannot be written. Your volume will normally not become corrupted, because NetWare keeps mirrored directory tables; however, you may lose updates that could not be written to disk.

To quickly check volume space, load MONITOR and check the Volumes menu selection. This will show you an overview of each volume, its total capacity, and its percentage of current use. You can see a more comprehensive evaluation of disk space in NetWare Administrator. In NetWare Administrator, select the volume and then select Object → Details → Statistics. You will see an analysis similar to that shown in Figure 15.3. Another way to check volume space is to exit Windows to a command prompt, change to the drive letter that maps to the volume you wish to check, and then type **NDIR /VOL.**

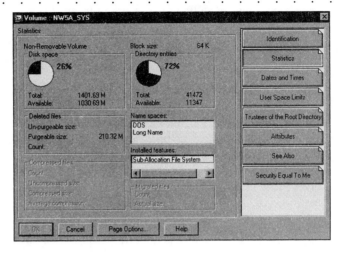

FIGURE 15.3

Volume space statistics

In the Deleted file box, the Purgeable size statistic indicates how much disk space would be available if deleted files on the volume were to be purged. The Unpurgeable size indicates how must space is not reclaimable by purging. Some or all of the unpurgeable space might be reclaimed if the volume were dismounted and mounted again.

You have two options to resolve a volume approaching capacity: delete, archive, or move files; or expand the volume. You can add another disk drive, partition it, and add a volume segment to an existing volume without losing any existing data.

Purging Deleted Files   In case you delete files but additional space does not appear to be available, don't panic. NetWare keeps deleted files so that they can be salvaged. At a command prompt type the command **NDIR /vol.** Look for files that are deleted but not yet purgeable. You can typically reclaim this space by dismounting and remounting the volume.

Volume Corruption

Volumes and directory/file listings can become damaged when software malfunctions, when connectivity is interrupted during an update, or when the volume becomes full. When you suspect volume corruption or file damage, check the volume properties in NetWare 5's NWCONFIG console utility (INSTALL in NetWare 3 and 4). NWCONFIG/INSTALL will provide specific errors when you attempt to access a damaged volume.

To check a volume for damage:

1. At the server console, load NWCONFIG for NetWare 5 or INSTALL for NetWare 3 or 4.

2. Select Standard Disk Options → NetWare Volume Options and then select the volume. If the volume is damaged, you should see a specific error message with text describing what type of damage the volume has sustained.

If VREPAIR cannot fix volume damage, you might try On Track Data Recovery for NetWare from On Track Computing (makers of Disk Manager). This utility provides more options than VREPAIR and provides extensive information concerning the drive geometry, partitioning, volume descriptors, and directory tables on your NetWare volume. On Track Data Recovery for NetWare is an industrial-strength professional tool for analyzing and fixing NetWare drive and file system problems. It also includes extensive surface scanning options.

Mirroring

The only reason mirroring is automatically disabled is because of drive deactivation due to physical failure of one of the disk drives. When one drive fails, an error message is displayed and a beep is sounded, but there is no noticeable interruption of service. The error may scroll off the screen, and you may not even be aware that a drive has failed.

If the error messages that led up to and announced that mirroring has been disabled are not on the console, they may have scrolled off. As discussed previously in this chapter, you may review the console log in INETCFG to find the error messages.

Checking the Mirrored Pair   To see if mirroring is active, check the mirroring options in NWCONFIG/INSTALL's Standard Disk Options.

To check the status of a mirrored pair:

1. Load NWCONFIG (or INSTALL for NetWare 3 and 4 servers). Select the Mirror/Unmirror disk partitions option to see a listing of disk pairs with the mirroring status at the left of the Disk Partition Mirroring Status screen.

2. Select the mirrored pair to see the status of the mirror and each drive.

3. If the status is "not in synch," then the drives are no longer mirrored.

4. Write down the drive information to be sure you do not remove the wrong drive by mistake.

When mirroring is disabled, the administrator should act promptly to replace the defective drive. During the time that mirroring is disabled, your system is vulnerable to failure. In many cases, mirrored drives are in the same lot number — when one drive fails, chances are good that the other drive will also fail soon. For this reason, it is best to use drives from different lot numbers when mirroring.

WARNING

Mirroring will not prevent file system damage caused by software problems, improper shutdowns, abends, or loss of connectivity during an update.

Mirroring does not invalidate the need for data backups. Many other reasons besides drive failure can corrupt or overwrite data. You should never be without good backups.

Replacing a Drive in a Mirrored Pair   When a drive in a mirrored pair is to be replaced, you must first unmirror the drives before removing the failed drive. When the drive has been replaced, the drive configured as the primary is remirrored to the secondary. If you remove the primary and simply replace it, all data on the drive containing data may be wiped out.

WARNING

Always disable mirroring before removing a drive that has failed. Failure to do so can result in loss of all data on the good drive.

To remove and replace a drive in a mirrored pair:

1. Determine which drive has been deactivated by reviewing console logs and the Storage Devices option in the console MONITOR. Select Storage Devices, select the drive, and observe its operating status.

2. Load NWCONFIG (or INSTALL on NetWare 3 and 4 servers). Select Standard Disk Options → Mirror/Unmirror Disk Partitions.

3. Select the drive that is no longer active, and press Del. There will be no interruption of service if you remove the drive that has been deactivated.

Once you have replaced the deactivated drive with a working drive and it is working properly, you may remirror. Remirroring should be scheduled during off-hours. During this process all data on the primary disk partition is copied to the secondary disk partition. User file access will take priority, pausing the remirror process. During busy hours, remirroring can take a very long time to complete.

In order for a drive to be mirrored, the logical partitions must be equal in size. The logical partition is the space available for data once the drive has been physically partitioned and Hot Fix has been allocated. The secondary logical partition must be equal to or larger than the primary drive partition after Hot Fix. When mirroring, NWCONFIG/INSTALL will adjust the existing logical partition size downward if necessary. However, if the logical partition is not large enough, the drives cannot be mirrored.

If a large amount of space remains on the secondary drive, you can create a partition and place a volume segment on it. The additional segment, however, will not be mirrored. For example, if you add a 4GB drive as the secondary drive to a 2GB drive, you will have 2GB of free space remaining. You may partition this space and put a NetWare volume on it. The space can be configured as a separate volume or added to an existing volume.

To reactivate mirroring:

1. Load NWCONFIG (or INSTALL on NetWare 3 and 4 servers). Select Standard Disk Options → Mirror/Unmirror disk partitions.

2. Select Standard Disk Options → Modify Disk Partitions and Hot Fix.

3. Create a NetWare partition on the drive to be added as the secondary drive in the mirrored pair.

4. From the Available Disk Options menu, select Mirror/Unmirror disk partitions. From the list, select an existing drive partition that contains data to be mirrored and press Enter.

5. Press Ins and then select the partition to become the secondary in the mirrored pair. If the partition sizes differ, NWCONFIG will resize the partition to the appropriate size.

6. Press F10 to save the mirror configuration. Remirroring will begin immediately as a background process.

Spanning Volumes

Spanning a volume over multiple disk drives can increase storage capacity in a single volume and improve performance at the same time. The volume size will be the combined size of all the free space used on multiple disk drives.

When data is written to a spanned volume, disk read and write requests can be serviced up to 100 percent faster than data written to a single drive. If the disk drive technology supports simultaneous read/write to multiple devices, data will be written to two or more drives simultaneously.

NOTE

Spanned volumes are frail. Should any drive containing a volume segment fail, the entire volume is lost. When using spanning, also use mirroring to protect from data loss. For example, if you span a volume over two drives, mirror those two drives to two other drives.

SCSI drives are able to take advantage of this feature, because each SCSI device has its own intelligent disk controller, and all SCSI levels allow drives to operate independently of one another.

File Migration

File migration is used for two purposes: to retrieve "near-line" storage as if it were online, and to automatically archive data. File migration leaves file listings on the NetWare volume but marks them with the Migrated attribute and pointers so that NetWare can retrieve the data at any time as if it had been online all the time.

When files are migrated to a secondary storage device, the data is removed and relocated to the near-line device, freeing up space. When migrated files are retrieved, the data is copied back to the NetWare volume and then read. The disk swapping activity will delay access to the file but is a good alternative when massive amounts of data needs to be kept available. The best part of NetWare's file migration is that it is transparent — the application need not be designed specifically for use with NetWare file migration.

File migration poses a couple of manageable risks. First, some software may not work right when files have been migrated. Second, you may run out of disk space when large amounts of data are swapped to the NetWare volume to be accessed. If the application was written to NetWare APIs, file migration should be transparent and should not affect the application. As far as the disk space issue goes, it is necessary to provide sufficient disk space to meet the needs of the users according to your organization's mission and resources.

Reference and Utilities

The following resources are available to locate help on troubleshooting issues, and to locate other resources that will help you track down problems.

AppNotes

AppNotes are published monthly by the Novell Research team and address selected significant technical issues in a "white paper" format. Novell's top support engineers select topics to publish each month — the most current and significant NDS-related topics are discussed in detail in monthly articles. You will find AppNotes dating back several years on the Novell Support Connection CD (available on a subscription basis) and on Novell's Web site at http://developer.novell.com/research/appnotes.htm. You will find that the articles are indexed well and can be found easily on the Web site.

You will find a few good references for maintaining and troubleshooting NetWare file systems in Novell's AppNotes. You can find the following AppNotes on Novell's Developer Web site.

NOTE

This list is ordered by date. More recent AppNotes should be reviewed first, as older AppNotes may address issues that have been resolved or modified in newer versions.

▶ *What's New in NetWare 4.11*, October 1996

▶ *Look into the Future: Distributed Services and Novell's Advanced File System*, December 1995

▶ *Inside Novell's High Capacity Storage System (HCSS)*, February 1995

▶ *Compression and Suballocation in NetWare 4*, June 1994

Micro House SupportSource Technical Library

The Micro House SupportSource hardware library provides documentation for computer components all on one CD. If you handle hardware frequently, one CD can substitute for chasing down documentation for each component in each computer.

Micro House International
2477 55th Street Suite 101
Boulder, Colorado 80301
(303) 443-3388
(800) 926-8299
Home page for Micro House: http//www.microhouse.com
Home page for SupportSource:
http://www.supportsource.com/s2main.htm

DELEC SCSI Guide

DELEC provides online hardware guides at no cost. See http://www.delec.com to review their hardware configuration documents.

Delec has been generous in granting permission to include their SCSI Guide on the CD that accompanies this book. This guide provides a long list of specifications, requirements, and capacities that were too technical to include in this book but may be a significant resource for hardware technicians and system administrators.

See the file SCSIGIDE.HTM on the CD that accompanies this book. You can find the latest information about SCSI specifications and standards at Delec's Web site: `http://www.delec.com`.

> DELEC
> 10 Hughes Ave #103
> Irvine, CA 92618
> USA
> Phone: (949) 859-8592
> Fax: (949) 859-8593
> E-mail: `sales@delec.com`

Darwin Collins

Darwin Collins's Web site is a favorite for NetWare administrators. You will find many file system–related modules and helpful system administration tools to help with evaluating volume data. The following utilities can be found in the Darwin Collins software collection, which is included on the CD that accompanies this book.

You can locate Darwin Collins' Web site at `http://www.fastlane.net/homepages/dcollins/`.

Display Volume Summary Release: September 10, 1997

(Year 2000–Ready)

> File: NVolInfo.zip   Size: 35K

This displays volume information (capacity, available, and free blocks) for all volumes of all servers that you are authenticated to.

Having less than 1,000 blocks of available disk space is a common cause of 100 percent utilization. If you have less than 1,000, then it is time to PURGE /ALL the volume.

NW3/NW4 File Delete/Purge Scheduler Release: September 10, 1997

(NOT Year 2000–Tested)

> File: CleanVol.zip   Size: 5K

This NLM utility will periodically delete and purge obsolete files and directories. You can specify the day name/day number and time that a task will perform. A task can log, delete, or purge files that are older than create, modification, archive, or access date/time stamps.

See the text that follows for other utilities that do automatic volume purges.

JRBSoftware

You will find several file utilities in JRB Software's collection of NetWare utilities. These utilities have been freshly updated to NetWare 5.

John Beard
```
http://JRBSoftware/
```

WinFiles.Com Shareware Collection

WinFiles is a commercial Web site that makes hundreds of utilities available. Their Web site is divided into categories—you will find many software applications in each. Much of the software on WinFiles is for sale, and you can download demo versions. Many software packages are shareware and freeware. The following file system–related utilities are available from WinFiles, or from the software developer.

You can find WinFiles.Com at `http://www.winfiles.com/apps/`.

Volume Segment Calculator Version 1.1, Freeware

Published by Powerahead Computing Ltd., Volume Segment Calculator (16-Nov-97, 668K, Win 95/98/NT) is a freeware utility that enables you to select the block size on your server and then calculate either the size of a segment from the number of blocks or how many blocks are required for a segment of a particular size.

Ontrack Data Recovery for NetWare

Ontrack Data Recovery for NetWare is a tool that provides extensive detail on your physical disk drives, their geometry, volume descriptors, and volume integrity. It has utilities for scanning drive surfaces and repairing volumes. This tool is an important tool for the network administrator who must deal with many servers.

Ontrack is the maker of the Disk Manager product that is included with many new hard drives. Ontrack also operates data recovery labs where data can be retrieved from drives that have gone out of service.

Ontrack Data International, Inc.

Corporate Headquarters

6321 Bury Drive

Eden Prairie, MN 55346

Toll Free: (800) 872-2599

Phone: (612) 937-5161

Fax: (612) 937-5750

http://www.ontrack.com

CHAPTER 16

NetWare Servers

NetWare is unlike any other operating system. It is designed for one purpose only: to be a server network operating system. Server performance requirements differ greatly from those for workstation operating systems. The NetWare operating system is not designed to run user applications — it is not designed for user convenience. NetWare is tuned for multiuser file sharing, DS replication, network interfaces, multiple protocol support, and routing. After 17 generations of server operating systems, NetWare provides the best server platform available today for enterprise networking.

NetWare system engineers know this and are not all that impressed with NetWare 5's graphical user interface and remote graphical utilities, though they are nice to have. NetWare administrators are accustomed to managing NetWare servers remotely when required, and managing security remotely. NetWare is — and has been — just what a network system administrator expects: a darned good network operating system that provides the tools needed to elegantly service small to very large networks.

For the foregoing reasons, you will find some very different aspects of the NetWare server operating system. You need to apply different management and troubleshooting techniques than you would use for a UNIX, Windows NT, or OS/2 server operating system. This chapter discusses management and troubleshooting that is specific to NetWare server operating systems. Just a few tips can help you understand and manage NetWare as easily as any other operating system. The following discussions are presented in this chapter:

- ▸ Remote server management

- ▸ Tuning the NetWare server operating system

- ▸ General server troubleshooting

- ▸ Memory segmentation in NetWare 3 servers

- ▸ 24 × 7 service

- ▸ References to support documentation and troubleshooting tools

▶ · ◀

Remote Server Management

In geographically distributed networks, the system administrator would be quite inconvenienced if he or she would have to physically access each server to be managed. Using just a few tools, NetWare administrators are able to perform almost any tasks that require server console access. NetWare 5 servers can be managed remotely using any one of the following vehicles:

- ▶ *RConsole* — Character utility, IPX-based

- ▶ *RConsoleJ* — 32-bit Windows utility, TCP/IP/Java-based

- ▶ *ConsoleOne* — 32-bit Windows Java utility, TCP/IP-based

- ▶ *ConnectView* — 32-bit Windows utility, TCP/IP-based in BorderManager

NetWare 3 and 4 only have RConsole, but it fulfills the promise of remote administration quite well. It simply does not accommodate access under TCP/IP. See Chapter 12 for a detailed discussion on configuring remote console access to learn to set up these utilities.

HiTecSoft Corporation's Web Console utility provides a Web browser interface to NetWare 3 and 4 servers. This application enables network administrators to securely access and manage NetWare file servers through Novell's Net2000 Network Modular Extension (NMX) standard, which is the most popular Common Gateway Interface (CGI) interface on NetWare and intraNetWare.

Web Console is TCP/IP-based and requires a Web server. It enables the user to access the server console, execute character-based server utilities, and access all other server-based functions from a Web client browser.

 For more information on Web Console, see HiTecSoft's Web site at `http://www.hitecsoft.com/`.

▶ · ◀

Tuning the NetWare Server Operating System

NetWare is self-tuning and generally requires no adjustment to provide peak performance under varying conditions. Since NetWare 3.0, NetWare operating systems have enjoyed floating tuning adjustments with minimum and maximum levels that accommodate the majority of installations.

You may have noticed that NetWare 5 requires far more memory than previous NetWare versions. NetWare 3.12 only requires 4MB of RAM, NetWare 4.11 requires 16MB, and NetWare 5 requires 64MB because of the Java Graphical Server User Interface. If your server has less memory, you can install without the graphical interface. NetWare 5's 64MB requirement may not seem like much to you, but in the past Novell development engineers have always kept system requirements at the lowest levels possible.

In the past, Novell engineers have sought to optimize memory use and server resources, keeping preconfigured operating system parameters to the lowest levels feasible without jeopardizing reliability and performance. This is why you may have needed to manually add a SET command to one of your NCF files to avoid dealing with insufficient resources under various conditions.

NetWare 5 adds many new features and is preconfigured with tuning parameters that handle all known configuration problems — even if it means that memory is not optimized as well as it could be, this policy reduces many common possible problems. For example, because Novell support engineers found that excessive packet receive buffer usage was more common than it should be, the default minimum level is set to 400 in NetWare 5 — the same parameter was set to only 50 in NetWare 3. Because RAM is so cheap today, it just does not make sense to save 350KB or so of memory in exchange for the small number of cases where memory had to be reallocated because this parameter was too low.

Another example is the packet receive buffer size. Ethernet requires only a 1,576-byte buffer, whereas Token Ring and FDDI require 4,224 bytes — the default is 4,224 in NetWare 5, although it was originally 1,576 in NetWare 3.12. Though the vast majority of NetWare servers do not use Token Ring or FDDI, the default is set to accommodate these technologies so that adjustment to this parameter is not necessary. The additional resources required to support the larger packet size use up less than 1MB of memory (when the minimum of 400 packet receive buffers is allocated). Novell support engineers felt that this was a practical investment to reduce support problems for Token Ring and FDDI network administrators.

Many system administrators appreciate that they do not have to adjust SET parameters, and they don't mind overallocating a few KB of memory here and there. NetWare 5 requires 64MB of memory, which is not a lot in comparison to other server operating systems. You will find that NetWare requires far less installed memory when compared with other server operating systems under like conditions. A typical preconfigured server has 128 to 256MB of memory today, which is far more than most NetWare servers require.

However, upon occasion you may need to adjust SET parameters to higher levels under unique conditions. Generally, NLM software developers recommend changes when necessitated by their software demands. Some hardware devices may also recommend adjusting SET parameters to accommodate unique demands for their devices and drivers.

Evaluating Current SET Parameter Levels

Though your server is tuned to provide adequate levels, you may encounter situations that require adjustment under varying conditions. For example, some server NICs require the minimum level of packet receive buffers to be adjusted upward. The higher adjustment accommodates better performance. If a server has several server-based applications, you may need to adjust the maximum level of service processes to a higher level.

Use the server MONITOR to evaluate your server's current levels. Adjusting those levels is also handled in MONITOR for NetWare 5 and NetWare 4.11 — in earlier NetWare 4 releases, adjustments were done in SERVMAN. In NetWare 3, SET adjustments are handled by editing the STARTUP.NCF and AUTOEXEC.NCF files. In NetWare 4 and 5, changed SET parameters are written to these files by the utility instead of manually.

To evaluate SET parameters, view the MONITOR screen. Figure 16.1 shows the MONITOR General Information screen (accessed remotely from the RconsoleJ utility). Notice the current and maximum levels of service processes. Observe your server when it is most active to evaluate whether the maximum level is sufficient to accommodate the current usage level. If the current level reaches the maximum level for an extended period of time (more than a few seconds for this parameter), then you should adjust the maximum level higher.

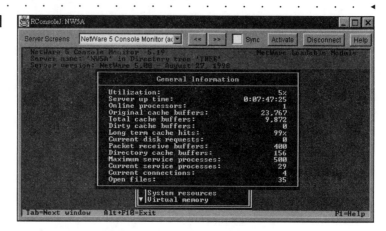

FIGURE 16.1

MONITOR's General Information screen

Other parameters are equally easy to evaluate. You should periodically evaluate the General Information screen and the Disk cache utilization statistics when your server is at its peak levels of utilization. You can see that evaluating these statistics is not all that difficult.

On NetWare 5, you can see the current level of all your operating system SET levels by entering the command **DISPLAY ENVIRONMENT** at the server console prompt. Each level will be displayed with its current setting. In NetWare 4 and 5, you can see better explanations of these levels, their minimum and maximum values, and current settings in the Server parameters menu selection in MONITOR. In NetWare 3 you must type **SET** and then select a category to view. Configuration values and limits will be displayed in a text.

NOTE

Don't expect to squeeze more performance out of your NetWare server by tuning SET parameters. These parameters are adjusted to handle specific conditions where default values are insufficient. In most cases, allocating more resources will not improve performance. NetWare constantly adjusts settings to changing conditions without manual intervention.

In a NetWare environment, getting more out of your server is mainly a matter of upgrading hardware.

Adjusting SET Parameters

Adjusting these parameters does not require a rocket scientist. The job is handled in MONITOR's Server parameters menu selection. Type **Load MONITOR** at your server console prompt. When you select Server parameters, you will see the menu shown in Figure 16.2.

▶ · ◀

F I G U R E 16.2

The Server parameters menu selection

The menu provides 16 categories, each with several SET parameter adjustments in each one. These settings not only adjust server operating system parameters, many of them configure services as well. For example, select the Communications category from the MONITOR menu. Figure 16.3 shows the packet receive buffer settings. Notice that the size and minimum and maximum number of packet receive buffers can be adjusted here.

FIGURE 16.3

Packet receive buffer settings in the Communications category

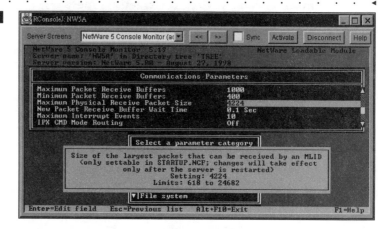

In the Communications category in MONITOR, you can also see the Compatibility Mode has several configuration parameters if the SCMD.NLM (Compatibility Mode Driver NLM) has been loaded. These same parameters can be configured with switches and options in the LOAD SCMD statement. As with the Compatibility Mode settings, many adjustments that are not related to operating system parameters are included in the Server parameters menu selection.

MONITOR's Server parameters menu selection also provides explanations; shows current, maximum, and minimum configuration values; and displays additional help if desired (press F1 to see context-sensitive help). If you change any settings, MONITOR will write the settings to the appropriate configuration file when you exit. You will be asked to confirm your changes at that time.

In NetWare 4.10 and earlier versions, load the SERVMAN application at the server console for the same functionality. In NetWare 3, adjustments are made manually by entering the SET command as shown on the text screens into the AUTOEXEC.NCF or STARTUP.NCF file. For example, to adjust the minimum number packet receive buffers to 200, enter the command

```
SET MINIMUM PACKET RECEIVE BUFFERS = 200
```

This method can also be used for NetWare 4 and 5 versions, but most administrators prefer to use menu utilities.

For additional resources in tuning servers and adjusting SET parameters, see the Reference section of this chapter for references to AppNotes articles. You can access all AppNotes online from an index available at `http://developer.novell.com/research/appnotes.htm.`

▶ · ◀

General Server Troubleshooting

Several problems can cause servers to malfunction. NetWare is especially resilient to traffic-related problems and generally does not crash as a result of excessive traffic or demands. However, you will find that a few problems can cause interruption of a specific service or network interface, or a total halt to server processing. The first place we must start is to define some of the server behavior you may encounter.

As discussed many times in this book, terminology is very important to communicate effectively. When discussing general server problems, it is best to use terms in accordance with Novell technical support. The following discussion will help you to define and communicate your problem.

This section deals with the most common and troublesome problems you might encounter with a NetWare 3, 4, and 5 server. You will find help on the following topics:

▶ Crashing and hanging

▶ Malfunctioning hardware and drivers

▶ Using CONLOG

▶ Abend errors

▶ Using the NetWare Debugger

▶ Before calling for Novell support

Describing System Failures

"Crashes" can occur within a NetWare server operating system. The term *crash* is very vague and is generally not used in Novell documentation or support. Many technicians use the term *crash* to vaguely indicate a system failure at some level. The term *crash* originates in early disk drives where the head of the drive scratched the surface of the disk, causing damage to the disk surface, which in turn resulted in loss of data. The term was also applied to any situation where a computer or component failed. In this chapter, more explicit terms are used. The terms *total system failure, hang,* and *abend* are used and are far more explicit about the nature of the failure.

The hallmark of a total system failure is when the computer fails to boot before loading the NetWare server operating system or stops dead without an error message. A total system failure is a hardware-related problem such as a parity error, power supply failure, or motherboard component failure. Parity errors are the result of a RAM failure — parity errors are normally intermittent and will stop a computer dead in its tracks while the system is running. A parity error may be displayed, or it may not — quite often the problem is instantaneous, and the processor is unable to detect and report the error before processing halts. Similarly, a failed power supply stops a system dead in its tracks. Generally, a failing power supply gives fair warning before a total failure — your computer may fail to boot at times with no beep code and simply stop working at other times. System failure causes are as numerous as the parts in your computer and may exhibit many different behaviors. In most cases, however, motherboard component failures stop your computer dead without an error message. Some failures are so complete that the computer will not boot, and no beep codes or error messages will be displayed.

Beep codes during boot may indicate what type of failure has occurred when a computer is booted; however, some system failures are so complete that no beep or display message is reported at all. Possibilities are many for how and when a total system failure shows up, and they are often intermittent. Most motherboard components fail completely when they malfunction, such that the NetWare operating system cannot be initialized. The worst problem is intermittent failures — your system works sometimes and fails with no perceivable correlation to any event or process.

TIP

Beep codes tell you what type of error is found during the power on self test (POST), which is a function of the BIOS chip. See your BIOS developer's Web site for beep code definitions. AMI, Award, Phoenix, and other BIOS developers use different beep codes but retain the same codes for all brands of computers equipped with their BIOS chips.

Hanging is when the server appears to have stopped processing data but the operating system is paused. If you can enter the NetWare Debugger as discussed later in this chapter, your system has hung, not failed. When a server-based application fails to work properly, the rest of the server operating system may continue to function normally. When a process is paused, the service it is to provide will not be available. This does not necessarily prevent the operating system and other services from working, though some hanging processes do prevent other programs from proceeding. When a process pauses without displaying an abend error, it is said that the service has "hung."

Abends are fatal system errors that are caused by several factors. An abend error brings the operating system to an idle state, and the console displays an error that includes "Abend" in the message. Abend errors are discussed in great detail later in this chapter.

Malfunctioning Hardware or Drivers

Driver problems are usually found during installation. If the driver settings you enter do not correspond with the hardware settings or conflict with another device, the driver normally will not load. However, driver problems can appear later under varying conditions. If a device malfunctions, the driver should remove the device from use gracefully, but this is often not possible. Device failures may cause your system to hang or abend.

Driver problems are a problem for any operating system. It is always best to use drivers that are Novell certified for your version of NetWare. Novell certification provides a high degree of confidence that the driver will perform without problems. However, even certified drivers can have problems that may appear under circumstances that are out of the ordinary.

When a driver fails during installation, you can suspect that the wrong driver has been selected, a configuration is improper, or a driver has a bug. It is usually easy to troubleshoot this type of problem during installation. When you select and configure a driver, NWCONFIG or INSTALL observes the load process and aborts loading the driver if a conflict is present. An explicit error message will be displayed on the console screen (along with a beep), and NWCONFIG or INSTALL will instruct you to switch to the console screen to observe the error statement.

NOTE

Entering the wrong base I/O or memory address will prevent a driver from loading. However, entering the wrong interrupt for a NIC sometimes will not prevent the driver from loading. If the NIC can receive but not send packets, suspect that the wrong interrupt has been entered during setup.

However, drivers can fail after a successful installation. In some cases, drivers can conflict with one another and the conflict may not be detected during installation. For example, two devices may be installed that use Direct Memory Address (DMA) configuration values. Because DMA channels are often only used when I/O traffic is heavy, the conflicting devices may work when the drivers are loaded but may fail when both drivers call on the same DMA channel at the same time. For example, you may have a SCSI adapter that is configured to use the same DMA channel as a multiport communications card. If the disk drive is activated at the same time the multiport card is in use, your server will abend with a processor exception.

This type of problem will typically produce an abend error, halting all processing. However, it is not unusual for a driver to hang, while other processes continue uninterrupted. You need to identify which drivers are involved in the conflict, which is often difficult. To locate the problem, you must observe the system failure several times, making note of exactly what is happening at the time of the failure.

When a Service Hangs

When a driver, application, or service hangs, it is paused, but other processing often proceeds normally. Hanging differs significantly from an abend in a couple ways. First, a hanging process does not jeopardize the stability of other application or caching data. Second, the process may slow or stop, but you can enter the NetWare Debugger and find that the other applications are still active. The other processes may be in a waiting state, but they have not come to a halt. However, a hung process can consume large amounts of processing power, thereby affecting total server operation adversely.

A common example of a hung process is seen when a NIC driver is configured improperly. If the base I/O address or slot number has been entered incorrectly, the NIC driver will hang when loading. As the driver loads, you will hear a beep (generated by the NetWare operating system), a console prompt will indicate that the driver cannot load, and a reason will be stated. A problem of this specific type will remain hung for a short period of time, waiting for user input. The driver will have displayed a message indicating that the NIC could not be found and will request the correct configuration data. If no answer is provided, the driver will eventually abort loading, and the boot process will continue.

Any server-based application or module can hang, but if it is written properly, it will often allow other services to continue. However, this is not always the case. When an application hangs, a more critical problem may occur with memory management, causing an abend error (see "Resolving Abends" in this chapter).

You may experience denial of service problems with Novell or third-party server-based applications and services. Many Novell services are considered part of the server operating system but are loaded as NLMs. Since NetWare 3's introduction in the early 1990s, Novell has increasingly relied on loadable modules in lieu of code integrated with the NetWare operating system core. NetWare 5 has gone even farther in converting basic services into NLMs and other loadable modules, such as driver files. If you observe the boot process on a NetWare 5 server, you may be amazed at how many modules are loaded once the operating system is loaded and the SYS volume is mounted. To view this process, press Alt+Esc when the graphical "splash screen" is displayed. This action will enable you to view the console screen to observe as modules load during the boot process.

Three conditions may occur when a service hangs:

▸ The service may hang, displaying no error message.

▸ The service may hang and display an error message or trap.

▸ The service may hang and result in an abend error.

When a module hangs, review the console messages that occurred at the time the module hangs. If you are not able to see the message, check the CONLOG or ABENDLOG files to scroll through console messages that may have scrolled off the screen. If no message was displayed, look for indications of which service has hung. Abend errors are more serious and are discussed later in this chapter. To unhang the process, switch to the console screen and unload the hung NLM or driver.

When a process hangs, follow this procedure:

1. Observe the entire boot process, watching carefully for console error messages.

2. When a NetWare 5 splash screen is displayed, press Alt+Esc to return to the console screen. You can start SERVER.EXE with the -nl command to suppress the splash screen.

3. As each module loads, typically the module name, a copyright notice, and a confirmation is displayed on the screen before the next module loads.

4. Review messages for error statements, traps, or any type of verbiage that indicates less than perfect conditions.

5. Press Alt+Esc to switch to other screens. See if other modules are running, or if all services have halted. When all services halt, treat the situation as an abend (discussed later). If other services are running, troubleshoot the service that is inactive.

6. Once you determine which module is hung, switch to the console screen (Alt+Esc) and unload the offending NLM or driver. This does not correct the reason for hanging, but if the hung module has dominated the CPU, it allows other processes to resume.

Using CONLOG

Messages scroll by very quickly when a server loads, especially if it is a very fast server. It is often helpful to review all console messages from a file. For this reason, NetWare 5 automatically loads the CONLOG utility at the beginning of the boot procedure. For earlier NetWare versions, you may need to copy CONLOG.NLM to your DOS boot directory and add the command LOAD CONLOG to your AUTOEXEC.NCF file. If you do not have CONLOG.NLM, you can download it from Novell's support Web site at `http://www.support.novell.com/`. Review the console log carefully for messages displayed when a problem, support function, or related module loads.

To review the CONLOG logging file:

1. At your server console load INETCFG.

2. Select View Configuration → Console Messages.

The console logging file is set to a maximum of 100KB. When the file fills up, the earlier entries are purged. If this limit is not sufficient, edit the limit in your AUTOEXEC.NCF file by adding the MAXIMUM=*size* parameter to your LOAD CONLOG statement.

The Mechanics of an Abend

Abend errors occur when a process or application halts, bringing the NetWare server operating system to an idle state. The fault handler interrupts processing so that memory corruption and resulting damage to data will not worsen. For example, if an application has crashed, leaving current data in cache memory, continuing to run the operating system can cause the cache memory to be overwritten, resulting in data corruption for one or all applications currently running.

Abends may halt processing, but they are relatively benign in that data integrity is assured. Because NetWare uses nonpreemptive processing, memory protection is not necessary under normal conditions. Instead, the fault handler generates an abend when memory integrity cannot be ensured. Nonpreemptive processing and memory protection are discussed later in this section.

Abends generate various types of console error messages and always include the word "Abend" in the text:

▸ *Processor exception* — A fault has been detected by the CPU.

▶ *Software exception* — A fault has been detected by the NetWare operating system.

▶ *Nonmaskable interrupt* — A hardware fault detected by the system board logic.

Processor exceptions typically result from hardware failure, malfunction, or driver problems. *Software exceptions* typically result from misbehaved server-based applications (NLMs), for example, when an NLM passes an invalid parameter or function call. *Nonmaskable interrupts* result from an imminent power loss, a bus transfer parity error, or a memory parity error.

In past versions of NetWare, an abend error has meant that the server operating system could not continue to run, and a graceful shutdown could not be executed. You could enter the debugger to troubleshoot the problem if you could analyze assembly code and knew the operating system well enough. For most administrators, the debugger is not a helpful feature. In the hands of an experienced assembly programmer, the debugger can provide essential assistance in finding the cause of an abend.

NetWare 4.11 and NetWare 5 handle abend errors in a new way that is far more eloquent. The improved abend recovery features in these versions can automatically recover from an abend in most cases, and in other cases can allow the administrator enough time to gracefully shut down, thereby preventing data corruption for other activities that are active. A very serious problem can still abend the server, but these cases are rare and usually relate to a bad driver.

Before discussing how to diagnose abends, we must first examine why abends occur and what Novell has done much to reduce abends from occurring in NetWare 4.11, 5 and symmetric multiprocessing versions.

 NOTE **You will find a Novell Research AppNote article on the CD that accompanies this book, which discusses abend recovery in NetWare 4.11. The AppNote applies to NetWare 5 as well. Look for the article "intraNetWare Server Automated Abend Recovery" — it goes into far more detail than this chapter can cover.**

Nonpreemptive Processing

NetWare server operating systems use nonpreemptive processing as a strategy to obtain more power from a processor. The alternative is to use the Intel processor's built-in preemptive processing ring architecture, which causes significantly higher CPU utilization and divides processing time among multiple processes. Nonpreemptive processing is a major factor in delivering performance that is superior to competing server operating systems. Nonpreemptive processing is also the reason that the ubiquitous abend error is necessary at times.

NOTE **Nonpreemptive processing is quite beneficial in terms of performance and has no downside if your system is stable. This feature underscores the need to have solid server hardware, certified drivers, and NLMs.**

Preemptive Processing

The Intel 386 and higher processors have a "ring architecture" feature — processes can be executed in one of four rings, numbered 0 through 3. Ring 0 has the highest priority, and ring 3 has the lowest. Ring 3 has a special mode called the "protected mode" that can be preempted by processes running in a higher ring. Most operating system vendors use ring 3 for executing applications, while the operating system scheduler runs in ring 0. This allows the scheduler to preempt a process — remove it from memory — should it jeopardize system stability.

This processor architecture also includes a related memory protection feature. Memory is partitioned — memory used by one application cannot be overwritten by another. Memory protection prevents a misbehaved application from overwriting memory used by another application.

These features provide protection against software errors and malfunctioning hardware at the expense of large amounts of memory and processing power. Another preemptive processing disadvantage lies in the fact that each process is time-sliced and executed simultaneously with other processes. Processor cycles are divided among active applications, each one only getting only a portion of processor's power.

NetWare server operating systems work differently, however. Each process has full, exclusive access to ring 0 and does not share the processor with other processes. This allows the process to run faster and finish quicker, resulting in better performance. Applications are to be written to relinquish the processor and save memory to disk if long periods are required to finish an operation. Most driver functions are very short in duration and should not need to share processor time. In fact, by not sharing processor time, not only is driver performance enhanced, but other operations are expedited as well because they don't have to be interrupted by driver operations.

If drivers and applications are written properly and are tested well, they should not cause problems, such as consuming excessive processor cycles or crashing. However, when a driver or application does misbehave, the fault handler must take control and generate an abend.

SMP NetWare uses its own preemptive processing mode in which to execute applications while the operating system and core processes run nonpreemptively. For this reason, you can use a multiprocessor server without fear of abends generated by a server-based application. For everyday single-processor servers, a NetWare server operating system can perform as well as a multiprocessor server running a preemptive processing operating system.

Symmetric Multiprocessing and Server-Based Applications

Server-based applications can benefit from a preemptive processing environment. Novell engineers evaluated the conflicting needs of the server operating system and server-based applications. The design goals they pursued demanded that the server operating system and core services such as NDS should not suffer performance degradation because of sharing processor time with server-based applications. Because server-based applications can require massive amounts of processor time, a hybrid of symmetrical and asymmetrical strategies was employed to provide the best of both worlds. Novell engineers developed their own preemptive processing and memory protection strategy to be used in multiprocessor servers.

Many server-based applications do not behave in a way that is conducive to a nonpreemptive environment. For example, a Web server can dominate processor time at the expense of core operating system and I/O operations. Also, server-based applications tend to be less stable than core services built into NetWare. Developers tend to take shortcuts and take advantage of all resources possible, often jeopardizing stability in their wake. Server-based application have more opportunities to "hog" processor time and to cause abends in a nonpreemptive environment.

SMP NetWare uses its own preemptive processing mode in which to execute applications while the operating system and core processes run nonpreemptively. Novell's SMP design is quite unconventional but outperforms other servers in true production environments without jeopardizing server stability. Here's the way it works.

The first processor runs the NetWare server operating system and core services in a nonpreemptive mode. Additional processors are dedicated to a preemptive processing environment for running server-based applications. In a sense, the system is asymmetric in that the first processor is dedicated to one task, while additional processors are dedicated to another task. However, when three or more processors are used, the second, third, and subsequent processors handle server-based applications symmetrically — the processing is spread over each processor equally. Server-based applications can scale up to multiple processor power without affecting the performance and stability of the operating system.

For this reason, you can use a multiprocessor server without fear of abends generated by a server-based application. For everyday single-processor servers, a NetWare server operating system can perform as well as a multiprocessor server running a preemptive processing operating system.

When running server-based applications with NetWare, consider a multiprocessor server. You will realize the benefits afforded by both nonpreemptive and preemptive processing environments.

TIP

In case you wonder why performance testing has not demonstrated the superiority of Novell's approach to SMP, consider this. Performance tests are designed to isolate a specific process — for example, a Web server will be taxed to its limits for the duration of a test bed period. In a real-world production environment, file system access, authentication, and other core services share the server's time with sporadic Web service requests. You can imagine that delayed Web requests are accompanied by delayed core service requests. For example, it may take a very long time to log in or access files while the Web server is busy. When Web and core services are both in use on a NetWare SMP system, core services suffer far less at the expense of server-based application usage. In a real production environment, you can use a single NetWare SMP server for both Web and core network services.

NOTE

If have installed SMP and you experience server problems, first remove SMP using the Multi-CPU options menu selection in NWCONFIG.NLM, resolve your problems, then re-install SMP support.

For detailed information and tips about troubleshooting SMP NetWare, see Technical Information Document #2924364. You can find this document on Novell's support Web site or on the Novell Support Connection CD.

NetWare 4.11 and NetWare 5's Auto Recovery Process

In most cases, a NetWare 4.11 or 5 server operating system will only suspend an offending process, allowing other processes to continue without interruption. The server operating system takes the following actions when an abend occurs:

▸ Information about the source of the abend is displayed on the console.

▸ Information about the abend is written to the ABEND.LOG. The ABEND.LOG is recoverable under all circumstances because it is written to the server's DOS volume and then copied to the SYS:System directory when rebooted.

▸ In most cases, the server recovers from the abend and continues to run normally. A console error message indicates that the server should be shut down and rebooted as soon as possible to clear the abend. In most cases, the server operating system can sustain two or more abends before halting, depending upon the NLM and how it is written. SET parameters can be adjusted to allow self-recovery parameters to be controlled as desired.

▸ A new SET parameter is available to time out a misbehaved application that "hogs" the processor. When an application "hangs" or continues to run longer than the time set in the "CPU Hot Timeout" SET parameter, the application is suspended, allowing other processing to continue normally.

When a server has encountered an abend and continues to run, the server is in a critical state — it should be shut down and rebooted as soon as possible. Care should be taken to have users finish updates in process, after which you should shut the server down and reboot. The administrator should evaluate ABEND.LOG and then diagnose and resolve the problem as soon as possible.

Some drivers can fail in the abend recovery process. When such a driver is found, it should be updated to a later version that supports abend recovery.

NOTE

Resolving Abends

In NetWare 3 and 4 versions prior to 4.11, abend always means the server operating system has come to an idle state — they do not automatically recover from these errors. Though NetWare 5 and 4.11 versions often handle abends without crashing, an abend is a serious problem that requires swift resolution.

When a server abend occurs, an abend error message is displayed with a brief explanation, assembly code is displayed on the screen for the breakpoint, and you are given the option to dump all memory to disk. Though the option is not displayed on screen, you can elect to enter the NetWare debugger.

Dumping memory to disk is not normally required. A memory dump is only useful to Novell support engineers and is only used as a last resort to find a problem that may not have been encountered before. You can do a lot of troubleshooting before you must resort to this resource. The following suggestions provide a proven series of steps to take whenever an abend error occurs.

Be sure you have enough disk space to contain the memory dump. Available disk space in your DOS volume must at least equal the amount of total memory installed in your server. If you do not have enough available space, see the README file in TABND2.EXE on the CD that accompanies this book for tips on saving the memory dump to another server. The only time a memory dump is useful is when an Novell in-house tech support engineer requests it.

NOTE

Nonmaskable Interrupts (NMIs)

NMIs result from hardware failure. NMIs are often intermittent, and their explanations may vary but will always start with "Abend: Nonmaskable interrupt." When you observe this error, pursue hardware-related troubleshooting steps until you resolve the problem. If you only infrequently get NMIs, do not live with the problem — it will not go away, it will only get worse as time goes on. Remember Murphy's Law — the system will fail at the worst possible time, and the failure will cause maximum damage to files and productivity.

NMIs are often the result of poorly conditioned power. Voltage drops, surges, spikes, noise, RF modulation, and other types of power aberrations can generate NMIs. If you do not have an uninterruptable power supply (UPS) that is designed for network server usage, get one and switch it out. Be sure that it contains adequate power conditioning in addition to battery power, or add a power conditioner made for network server usage. Buy a UPS that will provide 15 to 30 minutes of battery power when AC power is lost. You will need adequate time to get to your server and shut it down properly.

Finally, the expenditure for a new server can be far less expensive than the troubleshooting time, lost productivity, and lost data from a malfunctioning one. The problem can be as simple as a failing power supply, a failing chip, or an internal crack in the system board. If you cannot resolve the problem swiftly, replace the server with a new one. Pull the drives and install them in the new server, or restore backups to the new server after installing the operating system on it. Get all-new components if possible. You don't want the problem to follow you from the old to the new server. For the cost of hardware today, it is just not cost-effective to wrestle with a serious problem that an NMI represents.

In the final analysis, your server may be aged beyond its expected lifetime and need to be replaced anyway. You may be able to use the old server as a workstation, or use it in a role that is not as critical. Your first responsibility is to restore the system to a stable state.

TIP

Many companies have a policy of replacing servers every two or three years, retiring the old server for use as a workstation. Take a hint from rental car companies — new cars have fewer maintenance problems than old ones. That's why the rental car companies sell cars as they age. The same goes for computers. It's not like you have to throw them away — using the old server as a workstation retains its value and offsets the cost of a new server.

Preliminary Maintenance Steps

Be aware that any error is a symptom. The error that you observe can mislead you — its cause can be something as simple as a buggy driver, or malfunctioning hardware device. The abend error may provide a clue as to whether the problem is hardware or software related. Before you expend too much energy on troubleshooting the cause of the abend error, you should take the following steps:

1. Be sure your server and its subsystems are in perfect operating condition. Perform preventive maintenance procedures on your server. Intermittent problems are often heat-related. Blow away dust that may have accumulated on chips and from bus slots. Check and clean fans — today's processors can overheat if the heat sink on the CPU is dusty, or if a fan is blocked. Check your power supply and power connectors. Reseat interface cards in their slots; check and tighten all cable connections. Run diagnostics utilities on your hardware.

2. Check SCSI disk subsystems for correct SCSI ID numbers and termination. Check cables carefully, and be sure that SCSI-3, Ultra, and Ultra-2 cables are the proper type. Higher-speed interfaces can incur data errors when older cable types are used.

3. Be sure that high-speed SCSI drives are able to stay cool. Some newer drives run at 7,200 to 10,000 RPM and fail if not adequately ventilated. Many high-availability servers and RAID subsystems provide special cooling fans for drive bays. When a drive overheats, it goes offline and may come back online again once it cools off.

NOTE

Intermittent hardware problems are often heat-related. Be sure that the server environment is cool and ventilated well. Look for heat sources, such as space heaters, electrical equipment, and direct sunlight that can raise the temperature inside your server.

4. Check your uninterruptable power supply and power conditioning equipment. Poorly conditioned power can cause abends that look like hardware problems. If you suspect power problems, you can rent a Dranitz or other type of power tester to record voltage and amperage fluctuations as well as noise and RF modulation.

5. Scan for viruses. NLMs can be affected like any other programs. Use virus scanning software that is designed for NetWare servers, and obtain the latest virus definitions.

6. Update all drivers to the latest revisions. Check NIC and SCSI adapter vendors' Web sites for the latest drivers and release notes on known problems.

7. Apply the latest operating system patches to your version of NetWare. See the minimum patch list at `http://www.support.novell.com/misc/patlst.htm`.

8. Check server-based applications for the latest updates and patches. Visit the each vendor's Web site, looking for updates, release notes, and the latest support issues.

Once your system has been brought to the most updated state, watch it carefully. You may have eliminated the problem, reduced the problem, or changed the problem. Observe circumstances that accompany the abend.

TIP

If applying an update or fixing hardware changes the nature of the problem or the error text, make a note of exactly what the changes were and what the error message is. Though you may not have eliminated the problem, a change is very helpful in isolating the true cause.

Collect As Much Data As Possible

The next step is to accumulate as much information about your system as possible. Don't worry about solving the problem just yet — just find out as much as you can about specifics.

I. Use CONFIG.NLM (filename CONFG7B.EXE or latest version, available from Novell' support Web site at `http://support.novell.com/search/ff_index.htm`). This utility will list all vital statistics, loaded modules, protocol configurations, and load files along with their contents. Review this listing and keep it nearby for information purposes.

2. Be sure you have the correct version of CLIB and BTRIEVE for the applications you are running. Read release notes to see if applications rely on a specific version, or if two applications require different versions.

3. Look for other problems that may seem unrelated. Watch for errors or loss of connectivity on a specific workstation, router error messages, file errors, volumes dismounting, and damage to index files. Though problems may seem unrelated, keep track of all problems until a pattern emerges.

4. Check the CONLOG file. Read all messages as each module was loaded.

Check MONITOR

Check your server MONITOR.NLM for the following statistics. Compare current levels with maximum values as configured. You may need to adjust a SET parameter to handle unusual conditions.

▸ Packet receive buffers should rise and fall or stay at minimum level. If they rise to and remain at maximum level, adjust the minimum and maximum upward. Failure to relinquish packet receive buffers indicates a faulty NIC driver.

▸ If dirty cache buffers should reach 75 percent of total cache buffers and remain there for extended periods (over ten minutes or so), add more RAM. This number is a maximum level, since 25 percent of cache buffers are reserved for read requests.

▸ If current services processes reaches the maximum level, SET the maximum higher.

▸ If CPU utilization hovers at 100 percent for extended periods (more than 10 minutes or so), find the source of the CPU consumption. First look for ISA NICs and SCSI adapters. Replacing ISA cards with PCI bus-mastering cards (normally labeled as server cards) will reduce CPU utilization significantly.

▶ Select each NIC in the LAN/WAN drivers menu selection, and then press
Tab to see statistics. Look for error statistics that may relate to a bad driver
or malfunctioning NIC.

Problem Isolation

If the preceding actions have not revealed the problem, your next step is to
isolate the problem. Here are some suggestions:

1. Attempt to recreate the error. If you can recreate the error at will, you can
   eventually narrow your search to isolate the cause.

2. Remove all unnecessary services. Unload server-based applications and
   hardware devices, reducing services and drivers to a minimum. You can
   either remove them one at a time and then recreate the error — or remove
   all services, add them one at a time, and then recreate the error. Use a pen
   and paper to record exactly what has changed and the exact text of the
   error message. Also make note of circumstances under which the errors
   occurs. Watch for trends and relationships. Execute SERVER with the -NA
   (no AUTOEXEC) switch to load without running AUTOEXEC.NCF. Then
   modules one at a time manually, waiting a short time between each load
   statement to see if the error is related to a specific command or load
   statement. Unload server-based backup software — only load it when you
   are to use it until the problem is solved.

NOTE

**If the abend error changes without any consistency, the problem is
generally hardware-related. If a problem is software-related, you will
typically see a consistent error and a correlation between a software
module and the abend.**

3. Change interrupts on interface cards. Stay away from using IRQs 2, 9, and
   15. Check your hardware setup first to see which interrupts are in use, and
   which are available. For cards that have DMA configuration options,
   change the DMA setting, or disable DMA if it is an option. Run the
   computer setup program, and make sure that plug-and-play options are
   manually configured for ISA cards.

4. Swap out cards that you suspect may be related to the problem. Spare NICs and SCSI adapters should be kept on hand at all times to use for troubleshooting and rapid recovery.

5. Copy a new SERVER.EXE to your server DOS boot volume. Check the volume for file system damage (CHKDSK /F) and viruses.

6. Run INSTALL (or NWCONFIG) and check the partitions, volumes, and mirrored pairs. These utilities warn you if inconsistencies exist in the file system and partitioning, giving very explicit error messages.

7. Run VREPAIR with the options changed to Write Changes Immediately, Purge Deleted Files, and Write All Changes.

WARNING

Before running VREPAIR on NetWare 3 and 4 versions where long name space is supported, load the appropriate name space VREPAIR module, or long filenames and associated data will be lost. Be sure you have a good backup before running VREPAIR.

8. Run a DSREPAIR unattended full repair. Check errors in the error log, and investigate the source of the errors if possible.

9. As a last resort, pull the disk drives and install them in a new computer. In a critical situation, the cost of a new computer is far less than that of allowing the problem to persist, especially if it is intermittent. If this does not solve the problem, you can just about eliminate hardware as the cause.

10. Disconnect network cables from the server NICs. Replace them one at a time, waiting to see if connections generate an abend. This is especially appropriate for Token Ring to reinitialize the NIC and the ring.

11. Perform massive copy operations with XCOPY and NCOPY. XCOPY copies files over the LAN to another location. NCOPY can copy files from one location to another within the same server without going over the LAN. If XCOPY generates an abend, but NCOPY does not, suspect the problem is related to the NIC or the LAN. Try running XCOPY from different workstations to see if the problem is isolated to a specific LAN or cable segment.

12. Check LAN cabling carefully. In an Ethernet environment, faulty cable can cause errors that place an unusual strain on drivers and protocol stacks. Because error recovery is automatic, you may not receive data errors.

Using the NetWare Debugger

The debugger enables you to view breakpoints, register settings at the time of the crash, and all contents of memory. If your skills are good in Intel assembly code, this could help you locate the reason for the crash. If requested, the memory dump can provide Novell support engineers with a picture of all memory at the time of the crash, but it is not useful to anyone else. In order to do a memory dump, you will need to have as much available disk space on your DOS volume as you have memory. For example, if your server has 120MB of RAM, you should have 120MB of disk storage available to capture the dump.

To enter the debugger when an abend error is displayed, press Left Shift+Right Shift+Alt+Esc simultaneously. Type H for help — the debugger key commands will be displayed. Normally you are given an option to dump memory. If this option is not available, you can force a memory dump by entering the debugger and then typing .c from the debugger prompt (#).

You can record the same information for NetWare 3 and 4 servers with the following procedure: Use the worksheet provided on the CD that accompanies this book. The worksheet is provided in .RTF format and is stored in the file ABENDLOG.RTF.

To use the NetWare debugger to research abend causes:

1. When the abend occurs, do not reboot. Instead enter the NetWare debugger by pressing Left Shift, Right Shift, Alt, and Esc simultaneously.

2. At the debugger prompt (#), enter each of the following commands, and then press Enter. Record displayed information for each one.

- *v* enables you to scroll through debugger screens one at a time.

- *r* displays the current register values.

- *?* provides the current instruction's address including the module name, function, and offset.

- *.r* shows the current process that is running.

- *dds* shows the current stack, including module names, function names, and memory addresses.

- *.m* shows the currently loaded modules including name, version, and date.

3. To exit the debugger, type **g** and then press Enter.

Before Calling Novell Support

Before calling for support, be clear about the results of the preceding tests and procedures. Have error messages written down with related conditions. Be sure you have clarity on what may and may not be related to the problem, but keep an open mind.

Check out the TABND2.EXE file on the CD that accompanies this book. Look for Appendix A, "Check/list Summary." Fill out this form and have it ready when calling support. Be sure you have tried all the troubleshooting steps outlined in that document.

Memory Segmentation in NetWare 3 Servers

NetWare 3 may infrequently suffer from memory segmentation problems. Novell has corrected this problem in NetWare 4.0 and later versions. The problem occurs only when servers have run 24 hours a day, 7 days a week and NLMs have been loaded, unloaded, and reloaded repeatedly. The problem is somewhat rare and is easily corrected by rebooting the server.

Server-based applications and processes use memory from the cache buffer memory pool and then give it back when no longer needed. When NetWare 3 was developed, the core operating system was designed with a segmented memory map. Memory used by the operating system is divided into 64KB page segments.

Memory is usable in contiguous segments only — if an NLM requires 72KB of memory, it must use two 64KB blocks of memory. NetWare 3's segmentation often leaves memory fragmented — when memory is returned, some blocks are partially filled, leaving gaps between available memory segments. As a result, some of the memory that is returned to the cache buffer pool is not usable because applications require contiguous memory segments large enough to run the application.

One of the design improvements in NetWare 4 and 5 operating systems is the use of an unsegmented memory map. This eliminates the problem of memory segmentation — when memory is returned, there are no partially filled segments because all memory is returned in a contiguous state.

For this reason, NetWare 3 servers may experience memory fragmentation resulting in running out of available memory from time to time. The problem occurs when NLMs are loaded, unloaded, and loaded again. For example, a server-based backup application may enter and exit memory, so that after several days, memory is so fragmented that the server gets out-of-memory errors when attempting to load.

There is also a problem with the short-term allocatable memory pool. When memory is allocated to this pool, it cannot be reclaimed — it will remain in this pool even if not needed until the server is rebooted. Some NLMs allocate memory to this pool and then when unloaded and reloaded again allocate memory to the short-term allocatable memory pool. As you can imagine, if this happens enough times, not only will large amounts of memory become unavailable, but the short-term allocatable memory pool will become full.

The solution to this problem is very simple — reboot your server. Rebooting reinitializes memory, eliminating segmentation and short-term allocatable memory pool problems. When you reboot, all memory is restored as usable. For this reason, you might consider rebooting NetWare 3 servers once a day or once a week — even if only to reinitialize memory. If this is not acceptable, then you should upgrade to NetWare 4 or 5.

24 × 7 service

If your server must remain up 24 hours a day, seven days a week (24 × 7), you should upgrade to NetWare 4 or 5. NetWare 4 and 5 versions are the operating systems most capable of maintaining 24 × 7 service. Unlike with competing operating systems, you do not have to reboot the server to load and unload drivers, add a disk drive, partition, create volumes, or change an operating system parameter. If it were not for computer hardware, even new interface cards could be added without having to reboot — and even that limitation is resolved in NetWare 5.

NetWare 5 features Hot Plug PCI. With a Hot Plug PCI server, you can even remove and add PCI interface cards without shutting down and restarting your server. Because of this new feature, NetWare 5 is the ultimate server operating system for providing 24 × 7 service and high availability.

References

You may find that this reference list helps you to dig deeper into problems and provides additional background. Over the years, Novell support and research engineers have published many documents on the subjects discussed in this chapter. All of them are at your disposal on the Support Connection CD and the Novell Support Web site.

You will also find many server troubleshooting resources on the CD that accompanies this book. Novell has given permission to include the most recent and important documents and utilities with this book.

Novell's Appnotes

You can view an index of all AppNotes from their inception to the most current issues at `http://developer.novell.com/research/appnotes.htm`. This index is not available on the Support Connection CD, or in the Novell Support Web site. You will find it invaluable for locating articles and NetNotes in any AppNotes issue.

Abend-Related Articles in AppNotes

The following AppNotes articles discuss more detail on abends:

- Brad Dayley, *Troubleshooting Server Problems Using the ABEND.LOG File and Memory Images (Core Dumps)*, October 1997

- Rich Jensen, *IntranetWare Server Automated Abend Recovery,* March 1997

- Todd Peterson and Stan Clark, *What's New in NetWare 4.11*, October 1996

- Dana Henriksen and Ron Lee, *Abend Recovery Techniques for NetWare 3 and 4 Servers*, June 1995

- Rich Jensen, *Resolving Critical Server Issues*, February 1995

NOTE

Updates such as the 3.2 Enhancement Pack address many of the problems discussed in older AppNotes. Always apply the latest patches and drivers to see if a fix has been included for your problem. Release notes with each update discuss problems that have been addressed.

NetNotes Articles in AppNotes

The following NetNotes discuss abends. NetNotes is a section within AppNotes that contains very short articles dealing with a current issue:

- Rich Jensen, *Basic Terminology Surrounding Critical NetWare Server Issues - Why NetWare Servers Abend*, April 1998

- Tom Buckley, *Hints for Handling Server Abends*, March 1998

SMP Troubleshooting NetNotes in AppNotes

The following NetNotes deal with troubleshooting issues discussed in this chapter:

▸ Tom Buckley, *Troubleshooting NetWare 4.11 SMP Issues*, September 1997

Tuning and SET Parameters

The following AppNotes articles discuss more detail on performance and optimization:

▸ Ron Lee, *NetWare 4.x Performance Tuning and Optimization: Part 3*, October 1993

▸ Ron Lee, *NetWare 4.0 Performance Tuning and Optimization: Part 2*, June 1993

▸ Ron Lee, *NetWare 4.0 Performance Tuning and Optimization: Part 1*, May 1993

▸ Ron Lee, *Using Production Workload Characteristics to Validate LAN Performance Evaluation Studies*, March 1993

▸ Ron Lee, *Identifying Test Workloads in LAN Performance Evaluation Studies*, May 1992

Server Troubleshooting Technical Information Documents

You can research the following TIDs online at `http://support.novell.com/servlet/Knowledgebase`. This link will bring you to the Knowledgebase search page. You can enter the TID document number to view and download the document (see Table 16.1).

TABLE 16.1

Technical Information
Documents (TIDs)

DOCUMENT TITLE	TID NUMBER
What Is Drive Deactivation?	500051
Trouble Mounting CDROM's as NetWare Volumes	500052
Register Memory in NetWare 3.x and 4.x	1003164
4.x Backup/Restore	500074
Drive Deactivation Troubleshooting Tips	500089
Support Tips for Adaptec EISA, VL, PCI HBA'S	500362
Intel Pentium Floating Point Flaw on NetWare	500462
SFT III 4.1 Features/Changes Document	21974
Replacing Failed Hard Drive in Mirrored Group	10024983
Compression and High Utilization	10059634
High Utilization and Compression Document	10057362
Suballocation and High Utilization	10054363
NetWare 3.x and 4.x Directory Entries Limit	1202046
PCI Troubleshooting Tips	1202472
SMP General Information and Support Tips	2924364

Server Troubleshooting Tools

The following utilities support troubleshooting activities discussed in this chapter. You will find the latest versions available at no cost from Novell's Web site at `http://support.novell.com/search/ff_index.htm`. Enter the filename and then select the Search button to locate the file. You will be able to download the file immediately.

▶ *TABND2A.EXE: Abend Troubleshooting Guide (updated July 14, 1997)* — This file is the most comprehensive toolkit and documentation for troubleshooting and diagnosing NetWare 3, 4, and 5 server problems. It covers hanging, abends, page faults, general processor protection exceptions, nonmaskable interrupts, and more. This file includes the CONFIG.NLM utility mentioned in this chapter, an abend troubleshooting worksheet, and a comprehensive document that discusses abends, hanging, core dumps, and the NetWare debugger.

▶ *CFGRD6B.EXE: NetWare Windows client Config Reader v2.67 (revised October 14, 1998)* — This file is a Windows workstation utility that analyzes the CONFIG.TXT file generated by CONFIG.NLM.

▶ *CONFG7B.EXE: Server Configuration Information (revised September 1, 1998)* — This utility analyzes the CONFIG.TXT file generated by CONFIG.NLM and is used for all versions of NetWare.

▶ *ETBOX2.EXE: Tools for a NetWare 5 Server v2.01 (revised October 12, 1998)* — This file contains TOOLBOX.NLM which includes several additional server console commands used for troubleshooting and general utility usage. It includes commands that enable you to copy and list DOS files from the NetWare server console.

▶ *TBOX7.EXE: Tools for NetWare 3 & 4 Servers v1.09d (revised October 22, 1998)* — This file contains TOOLBOX.NLM, which includes several additional server console commands used for troubleshooting and general utility usage. It includes commands that enable you to copy and list DOS files from the NetWare server console.

Novell Technical Services Training Videos

Novell's Advanced Technical Training videos offer IT professionals a convenient, cost-effective way to stay up to date with Novell products and technology. These professionally produced tapes feature Advanced Technical Training sessions presented by Novell's most knowledgeable support engineers (see Table 16.2).

T A B L E 16.2	NETWARE OPERATING SYSTEMS	PART NUMBER
Training Videos	*Resolving Critical Server Issues Volume 1: Understanding Abends, Hangs, and Utilization Issues*	476-000204-001
	Resolving Critical Server Issues Volume 2: Knowing and Using the Tools to Resolve Critical Server Issues	476-000205-001
	NetWare v3.x to v4.11 Migration / NDS Disaster Recovery Update	476-000180-001
	NetWare v4.11 Server Updates	476-000182-001

CHAPTER 17

Network Communications and Protocols

Many years ago, Novell found its strength in supporting technical professionals who used and supported their products. As one of the first CNEs, I recall Novell responding to our requests for better error messaging, error message documentation, white papers, and many other tools that enabled us to support their products better. Each version of NetWare showed improvements in each of these areas.

Today, NetWare 5 features a high level of support for viewing, monitoring, and troubleshooting the foundation of the network — the communications protocols. NetWare 4.11 and NetWare 5 includes Novell Internet Access Server (NIAS) 4.1, which provides a central resource for installing, configuring, monitoring, and troubleshooting remote access, routing, and protocols.

NIAS is represented by a utility NIASCFG.NLM. This utility is more than a communication server, however; it provides many tools to assist support technicians in analyzing protocol traffic both locally and on remote servers. NIASCFG is the launching pad for many other utilities that are discussed in this chapter.

Chapter 12, "Novell Internet Access Server," discusses how to install and configure remote access, routing, and protocol configurations. This present chapter discusses using the same utility for troubleshooting those utilities. In addition, this chapter discusses troubleshooting DNS and DHCP. In a TCP/IP network, these services are an essential part of network communications. Because the highly advanced DNS and DHCP services have been built into NetWare 5, and because these services are so newly developed, information on installing, configuring, and troubleshooting has been in short supply. This chapter will help you hunt down typical DNS and DHCP service problems that you might experience.

NOTE   **You will find extensive support for Novell DNS and DHCP services on the CD that accompanies this book. Specifically, you will find two Novell AppNotes that document these services in far more detail than you will find in your NetWare 5 online documentation.**

This chapter discusses troubleshooting:

▶ TCP/IP

▶ IPX

► AppleTalk

► PPP

► DNS

► DHCP

TCP/IP

Novell has made protocol configuration in NetWare 5 as simple as possible. The NIC drivers are autodetected, and default configuration parameters are suggested. If you accept the defaults, your system is going to support both IPX/SPX and TCP/IP clients. For most newer hardware everything you need is installed by default and works without intervention. However, configuration changes after installation can complicate your IP networking configuration.

The NetWare 5 documentation has an excellent troubleshooting section on troubleshooting TCP/IP. Before reading on, check the NetWare 5 online documentation to familiarize yourself with procedures and troubleshooting steps in troubleshooting TCP/IP protocols.

Finding IP Troubleshooting in Your NetWare 5 Online Documentation

To find IP Troubleshooting in your NetWare 5 online documentation:

1. Select the Troubleshooting section of your NetWare 5 online documentation.

2. Select Routing and Remote Access Troubleshooting.

3. Select Troubleshooting Protocol and Routing Connections.

4. Select Troubleshooting IP.

You will find sections for all the following troubleshooting topics. Links in the documentation are quite helpful in moving to various instructions and checkpoints.

The following topics are areas you should investigate when IP connectivity is not working. The topics are presented in a prioritized sequence.

Verifying Effective IP Communications

The following problems can prevent a server or workstation from communicating with the network.

Check for Physical Connectivity to the LAN

Check link LEDs on the hub and local NICs. A link light is generally provided to verify physical connectivity between the hub and the NIC. If the link light is not activated, check for disconnected cabling, a damaged connector, or an inoperative NIC.

 Some NICs do not light up the link light until a driver is installed.

NOTE

Check the Workstation Device to See If It Is Working

To check a NIC driver in Windows 95/98:

1. Select Network Adapters in the Device Manager, found in the Control Panel System applet.

2. See if a NIC is listed. A yellow exclamation point (!) indicates that the driver is not working.

3. Select Properties → Resources for the driver. Check the conflicting device list in the lower part of screen.

If the device is not listed, this indicates that the NIC driver must be reinstalled. When a driver is shown but has a yellow exclamation point, this indicates that the device is not working, generally due to a device conflict.

To check a NIC driver in Windows NT 4:

1. From your Start menu, select Administrative Tools → Windows NT Diagnostics → Resources.

2. Locate the NIC driver, select it and then check its configuration values.

3. Compare the NIC configuration with other devices, looking for potential conflicts.

If the NIC driver is not listed in the Resource listings, it is not loaded, indicating that the device is not working. This condition occurs due to device conflicts or any condition that causes the device to fail.

Loopback Test with Ping

The first test you should try is to Ping another host on the network. Ping is a standard utility provided with most TCP/IP software. The Microsoft Ping utility is included with all Microsoft Windows TCP/IP software and is executed from a command (DOS) prompt within Windows. Other operating systems and TCP/IP driver stacks include this basic utility—the operation and functionality are generally the same.

Use the Ping utility from a Windows command prompt to perform a loopback test. This test checks for the ability to send ICMP packets to the LAN and back testing for a valid IP subnet.

Type the following command at a command prompt:

```
PING 127.0.0.1
```

NetWare 5 servers have a Ping utility executed at a console prompt by typing

```
PING 127.0.0.1
```

The NetWare server version of Ping is menu driven and continues to Ping until interrupted with an Esc.

▶ *Success* — If the test is successful, you should receive replies to the Ping packets, indicating that the IP protocol on your computer can successfully communicate with a valid LAN.

▶ *Failure* — Check local computer cabling connection, the NIC driver, and TCP/IP configuration.

For both servers and clients, check the following potential problems:

1. The NIC is not connected to an operative LAN.

2. The device conflicts with other hardware resources, or the driver is not loaded.

3. The wrong NIC driver has been used.

4. The TCP/IP protocol stack is not installed.

5. A duplicate IP address has been assigned.

6. The IP address assignment does not fall within the local subnet address range.

7. An incorrect IP mask was assigned.

To verify IP configuration values:

▶ *Windows 95/98 workstations* — Execute **WINIPCFG** from a command prompt.

▶ *Windows NT 4 workstations* — Execute **IPCONFIG /a** from a command prompt.

▶ *NetWare servers* — Load **INETCFG**.

See Chapter 14, "Client Connectivity," for a detailed discussion for troubleshooting client problems. Also refer to the Troubleshooting section of your NetWare 5 online documentation.

Ping the Host by Address on a Local Subnet
Ping a remote host on the same subnet to verify that IP communications can be exchanged between two hosts.

Use the Ping utility to ping a host by address. From a command prompt, type

PING *nnn.nnn.nnn.hhh*

where *nnn.nnn.nnn* is the subnet number, and *hhh* is the host number.

- *Success* — If you get replies, communications over IP are working on your local subnet.

- *Failure* — If you get a timeout after a wait period, communications over IP are not working. If this test fails, try Pinging other hosts on the local subnet. If the loopback worked, but this test fails, check your IP address and mask.

Ping the Host by Address on a Remote Subnet

Ping a remote host on a subnet other than your local subnet to verify that IP communications can be exchanged between two hosts over a router.

Use the Ping utility to ping a host by address. From a command prompt, type

PING *nnn.nnn.nnn.hhh*

where *nnn.nnn.nnn.* is subnet number, and *hhh* is host number.

Be sure that the subnet number is different from your local subnet. This will require a router to forward your Pings.

- *Success* — If you get replies, communications over IP are working over the router.

- *Failure* — If you get a timeout after a wait period, communications over IP are not working. If this test fails, try Pinging other hosts on other remote subnets. If the test still fails, check the following:

    1. Gateway address in IP properties

    2. Router connections and configuration

    3. Subnet labeling and router configuration

A router is required to forward IP packets from one subnet to another. Two or more subnets can be attached to a single router port, but routing is required to forward IP packets from one logical subnet to another. Windows NT has an internal router that can forward between logical subnets; check TCP/IP protocol properties in the Routing screen.

> **You will find a helpful TCP/IP Utilities Reference Guide in Appendix D and on the CD that accompanies this book.**

NOTE

Monitor

The NetWare server MONITOR utility is the first place you should look to see if protocols have been properly loaded and to verify that traffic is flowing over the interface.

To monitor network interfaces with MONITOR:

1. LOAD MONITOR at your server console.

2. Select LAN/WAN drivers.

3. Select and view an incident of a driver from the Available LAN Drivers screen.

4. Press Tab to access the Statistics screen. Scroll down to view more statistics.

5. When viewing these statistics, first pay attention to the total packets transmitted and total packets received. This will verify that communications are flowing.

Addressing, Masking, and Subnetting

IP problems in your server can typically be traced to improper BIND and LOAD statements in your system startup configuration. During setup, the INSTALL utility recorded these statements in the AUTOEXEC.NCF file according to your selections of NICs, drivers, frame types, and protocols. From this point on, however, the complexity of supporting multiple NICs, frame types, and protocols mandates that you use INETCFG.NLM. This utility can be executed separately or on NetWare 5 servers from within NIASCFG.NLM.

The first time you enter INETCFG, driver and protocol statements will be migrated from your AUTOEXEC.NCF to a Btrieve database. The complexities and syntax in LOAD statements is simplified greatly by breaking each configuration detail into a separate menu screen within INETCFG, and syntax is handled behind the scenes. You can then view each aspect of protocol configuration; make changes; and add NICs, frame types, and protocols without fear of inadvertently messing up the syntax in any way. Everything about your protocol configuration is easier to understand and makes more sense.

Using INETCFG was discussed in Chapter 12, "Novell Internet Access Server." Refer to that chapter for a more detailed discussion on checking and configuring your TCP/IP protocol configurations. Check the following configurations:

1. IP address assigned to server NICS. Be sure the assigned addresses do not conflict with existing IP addresses, and that the addresses are properly entered. If you are connected to the Internet, be sure that all IP addresses in use are valid addresses assigned by Internet authorities.

2. Mask. Check to see that the mask is properly entered, and that the subnet the mask identifies is a valid network address, configured properly in associated routers.

3. Subnet (network address) portion of the IP address. Check your router configuration to see that subnets have been properly assigned, and that the subnet portion of the IP address space identifies networks in a uniform manner.

4. Gateway address. Be sure that you have properly entered the IP address of the router port to which your network segment is attached.

For more background on TCP/IP protocols, see Chapter 4, "TCP/IP Protocols, IP Addressing, and Name Resolution." For instructions on configuring TCP/IP protocols and services, see Chapter 11, "TCP/IP Services." You will also find TCP/IP utilities and protocol codes in Appendix D and on the CD that accompanies this book.

Monitoring Server TCP/IP Using TCPCON

TCPCON.NLM is a server-based utility that enables you to monitor protocol statistics in NetWare 3, 4, and 5 servers. This module cannot be executed until the TCP/IP protocol stack is installed and all support modules are loaded. For a NetWare 5 system, TCP/IP is installed by default and all support modules are automatically loaded. NetWare 3 and 4 systems require the administrator to load TCPIP.NLM after loading the frame type and binding the IP protocol to NIC at least.

Before TCPCON can be used in a NetWare 5 system, the administrator must load and configure SNMP. The procedure of loading and configuring SNMP is discussed in Chapter 11, "TCP/IP Services."

TCPCON will provide statistics on various components of the NetWare TCP/IP protocol stack. SNMP allows statistics to be gathered from SNMP agents all over the network. Even remote systems can be tested.

You can load this console by typing the command **LOAD TCPCON** at the console prompt, or you can access it from the NIASCFG utility. To load TCPCON from NIASCFG:

1. LOAD NIASCFG at your NetWare 4.11 or NetWare 5 console.

2. Select View Status for NIAS.

3. Select Protocols and Routing.

4. Select TCP/IP Protocol Stack.

TCPCON has options for the following:

▸ Monitoring IP subnets

▸ Viewing protocol configuration for IP nodes where SNMP is installed

▸ Viewing protocol configurations for IP, ICMP, UDP, TCP, OSPF, and EGP

▸ Viewing known IP routes

▸ Viewing trap logs in the local server

The TCPCON utility is documented well in your online documentation. Follow the directions in the previous section "Finding IP Troubleshooting in Your NetWare 5 Online Documentation," to find specific instructions on using TCPCON.

IPX

Most experienced NetWare technicians are familiar with troubleshooting IPX connectivity. IPX is the easiest protocol to troubleshoot: Because addressing and name resolution are automated, there is simply less to configure and less to troubleshoot. The most critical aspect of configuring IPX is to properly assign network numbers (network addresses). See Chapter 3, "Novell Protocols and IPX Addressing," for a detailed discussion on configuring IPX protocol and network addressing.

The NetWare 5 documentation has an excellent troubleshooting section on troubleshooting IPX/SPX. The following directions will take you to the section of your documentation that will assist in troubleshooting IPX and using IPX troubleshooting utilities.

Finding IPX Troubleshooting in Your NetWare 5 Online Documentation

To find IPX Troubleshooting in your NetWare 5 online documentation:

1. Select the Troubleshooting section of your NetWare 5 online documentation.

2. Select Routing and Remote Access Troubleshooting.

3. Select Troubleshooting Protocol and Routing Connections.

4. Select Troubleshooting IPX.

You will find sections for all the following troubleshooting topics. Links in the documentation are quite helpful in moving to various instructions and checkpoints.

Monitor

The NetWare server MONITOR utility is the first place you should look to see if protocols have been properly loaded and to verify that traffic is flowing over the interface. This utility will show all information that is available from other console commands and most other utilities.

To monitor network interfaces with MONITOR:

1. LOAD MONITOR at your server console.

2. Select LAN/WAN drivers.

3. Select and view an incident of a driver from the Available LAN Drivers screen.

4. Press Tab to access the statistics screen. Scroll down to view more statistics.

5. When viewing these statistics, first pay attention to the total packets transmitted and total packets received. This will verify that communications are flowing.

IPXCON

IPXCON.NLM is used to monitor IPX/SPX protocols. In NetWare 5, this console can collect IPX statistics over UDP/IP using SNMP remote systems. You can load this console by typing the command **LOAD IPXCON** at the console prompt, or you can access it from the NIASCFG utility. To load IPXCON from NIASCFG:

1. LOAD NIASCFG at your NetWare 4.11 or NetWare 5 console.

2. Select View Status for NIAS.

3. Select Protocols and Routing.

4. Select IPX Protocol Stack.

IPXCON has options for the following:

- ▸ Viewing known IPX routing paths

- ▸ Viewing the status of known IPX network addresses and routers

- ▸ Viewing virtual connections (operational circuits)

- ▸ Viewing remote routers that have NIAS's remote console features enabled.

The IPXCON utility is documented well in your online documentation. Follow the directions discussed in the earlier section "Finding IP Troubleshooting in Your NetWare 5 Online Documentation."

AppleTalk

ATCON.NLM is used to monitor AppleTalk protocols. You will find this console to be similar to other protocol consoles discussed in this chapter. You can load this console by typing the command **LOAD ATCON** at the console prompt, or you can access it from the NIASCFG utility.

To load TCPCON from NIASCFG:

1. LOAD NIASCFG at your NetWare 4.11 or NetWare 5 console.

2. Select View Status for NIAS.

3. Select Protocols and Routing.

4. Select AppleTalk Protocol Stack.

Your online documentation discusses using this utility. Follow these directions to locate help for ATCON and other aspects of troubleshooting AppleTalk Protocols.

To find AppleTalk Troubleshooting in your NetWare 5 online documentation, look in your online documentation under Troubleshooting → Routing and Remote Access Troubleshooting → Troubleshooting Protocol and Routing Connections → Troubleshooting AppleTalk.

PPP

Point to Point Protocol connections are not set up and configured during server installation — you must load and configure the Routing and Remote Access Service in NIASCFG.NLM. A wizard-type utility will run, walking you through setup and configuration steps.

Once the service is set up, monitoring is accomplished through NIASCFG's View Status → Remote Access screens. This will enable you to view status for ports, services, and alerts.

Use the following utilities to monitor PPP connections.

PPPTRACE

This utility analyzes PPP frames, IPX/SPX, TCP/IP, AppleTalk, and NCP communications flowing over remote access ports and devices. You can monitor communications such as modem initialization strings and login initialization scripts to see if they are accomplishing their intended tasks. PPPTRACE captures and displays decoded PPP packets, which can contain encoded IPX, IP, AppleTalk, SRB, modem control packets, LCP, and NCP packets. It is most helpful to use this utility to view login initialization strings.

If you are not familiar with protocol analyzers and the PPP protocol, this utility may be a bit intimidating. Use it to learn about how these protocols operate, and apply knowledge of protocol mechanics gleaned from Part I of this book, "Networking with NetWare." You can read more about PPPTRACE in the CAPI/ISDN section or under Troubleshooting NetWare Link/PPP in your NetWare 5 online documentation.

To view PPP communications:

1. LOAD PPPTRACE.NLM at the server console prompt.

2. From the menu, select Real-Time Monitor.

3. Press F8 and scroll until you select the port or interface you wish to monitor.

4. Initiate frame capture by pressing F7.

5. View protocol dialogs in the PPP Trace Real-Time Monitor screen. You can review captured traffic using the Play Back or Print options.

To view the captured frames decoded into ASCII, print the capture buffer to a print file instead of a printer. To convert the file to ASCII, use the following command:

```
PPPDISP capture_file_name output_file_name
```

Troubleshooting ISDN Using CAPITRCE

If you cannot locate a problem in monitoring PPP communications over ISDN with PPPTRACE, you must troubleshoot communications between the CAPI Manager (CAPIMGR) and the CAPI adaptation component (WHSMCAPI). The CAPITRACE.NLM utility monitors the ISDN physical interface. This utility accomplishes the same type of functionality as a serial port monitor, but for ISDN devices. This utility captures and decodes negotiations between the CAPI Manager and its drivers, and between the CAPI Manager and its PPP adaptation layer.

To capture and view these communications:

1. LOAD CAPITRACE.NLM at your server console.

2. Select CAPI Manager or one of the ISDN devices listed on the menu.

3. Answer Yes when prompted to create a new trace. You will see the Select Trace Function screen.

4. Accept the default capture filename or edit it, press Enter, and then press Esc.

5. Select Start to begin the trace.

6. Attempt to log in through the ISDN device from a remote node.

7. Stop the trace and select Convert. Configure the output filename using a .TXT extension. Configure the trace to include all CAPI functions by selecting Yes for both the B3 HEX Data and B3 ASCII Data options. Select Yes to include the time stamp.

8. From the Select Trace Function screen, press Esc to exit. Your capture will be converted and saved to the specified filename.

9. To view the trace LOAD EDIT, when prompted enter the pathname **SYS:***file_name***.txt**.

The trace will display the dialog between the two devices. Look for obvious failures and error messages. In some cases, these messages will give you a clue about what is not working.

PPPCON

PPPCON.NLM is used to monitor PPP communications. In NetWare 5, this console can collect PPP statistics locally and remotely using SNMP. You can load this console by typing the command **LOAD PPPCON** at the console prompt, or you can access it from the NIASCFG utility. To load PPPCON from NIASCFG:

1. LOAD NIASCFG at your NetWare 4.11 or NetWare 5 console.

2. Select View Status for NIAS.

3. Select Protocols and Routing.

4. Select PPP.

Use this utility to:

- Display traps.

- View the states of the Link Control Protocol (LCP), Network Control Protocol (NCP), and Link Access Protocol-Balanced (LAPB) layers.

- View PPP interface states.

- Reset modems that are stuck in an error state.

- Verify IPX and IP network addresses.

- View PPP LCP parameters.

- Test PPP links.

To reset a modem when it will not answer or to test the effect of using a setup string:

1. LOAD PPPCON at the console or invoke the PPP menu selection from NIASCFG.

2. Select the PPP Interface menu selection.

3. Select the modem port.

4. Select PPP Reset Modem menu selection and then press Enter.

Wait at least 30 seconds for the script to run. Watch for Success or Failed to in the Status field. If the test fails, check the following:

1. Check the modem type. Obtain an updated driver if available, or try another modem driver if the exact modem model is not shown in the description.

2. Check with the modem manufacturer to locate a modem initialization string that may resolve the problem.

You can obtain the following updated modem initialization string files from Novell's support Web site or on the Novell Support Connection CD.

NOTE

NIASMDM1.MDC — Modem vendors A through L

NIASMDM2.MDC — Modem vendors M through Z

NIASCERT.MDC — Novell certified modems

3. Purchase a new modem that is known to have a modem driver that is listed in the installation/configuration options within NIASCFG.

DNS

Novell's DNS is new and constitutes unfamiliar territory for many NetWare administrators. Even for experienced TCP/IP administrators, Novell's logical zones, implementation of new RFCs, and integration with NDS involves learning new terminology and mechanisms.

DNS setup is discussed in Chapter 11, "TCP/IP Services." Discussion in this chapter will be restricted to troubleshooting—you may need to refer back to Chapter 11 for more explicit instructions on reconfiguring DNS servers, zones, and records.

Prior to NetWare 5's introduction, Novell developers and support engineers investigated the most common problems that administrators encountered. The problems were not with irregularities in the DNS services—on the contrary, the DNS/DHCP services in NetWare 5 were introduced in NetWare 4.11's NetWare/IP product. This section discusses the most frequent problems and suggested solutions.

For more information on Novell's DNS/DHCP, see Chapter 11, "TCP/IP Services." You will also find detailed background and more explicit instructions on using Novell's DNS/DHCP in AppNotes found on the CD that accompanies this book. Look under "Support Technical Documents."

NOTE

You will find help with Novell's DNS in your NetWare 5 online documentation under Troubleshooting → Directory Services → DNS/DHCP Administration.

Resolving DNS Problems

Start your DNS communications troubleshooting by verifying effective TCP/IP communications from the workstation end of the network. Follow the steps discussed previously in this chapter under "Verifying Effective IP Communications." This section is predicated on the assumption that your local computer, server, LAN, internetwork, and router configurations are all working properly and you can Ping throughout the internetwork.

DNS resolution is easily tested. Pinging by name requires a name server to locate the IP address of the destination host from a name. If you can Ping other hosts by address but not by name, you know that name resolution is not working. The following test will determine if DNS is working:

1. Ping the DNS server by IP address to verify that the DNS server is reachable.

2. Ping another host by IP address to verify that the host is reachable.

3. Ping the same host by name. If you can Ping by address, but Pinging by name fails, name resolution is not working.

NOTE

In this test Windows 3.1, 95, 98, and NT workstations should Ping NetWare servers. Windows uses NetBIOS name resolution and may resolve names using an alternate to DNS, rendering your test invalid.

Windows uses name resolution over TCP/IP configuration options as discussed later. Windows primarily uses Microsoft name resolution methods, reverting to DNS only if other methods fail — therefore a successful Ping may not indicate that your DNS server is responding.

Windows Workstation DNS Configuration Issues

Windows workstations can use one or more of several methods for name resolution. Check your workstation's TCP/IP properties to see which of the following methods is used by your workstation. For Windows 95/98 workstations, look in the DNS and WINS screens for configuration options as shown in Figures 17.1 and 17.2. Windows NT's screens are slightly different, but most of the same information can be found.

▶ · ◀

FIGURE 17.1

Windows 95's WINS Configuration screen

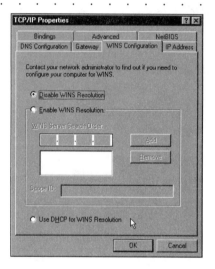

▶ · ◀

FIGURE 17.2

Windows 95's DNS Configuration screen

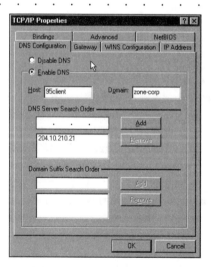

▸ *NetBIOS broadcasts* — If no WINS or DNS configuration boxes are checked, the workstation will broadcast the name resolution request on the local subnet. If a host with the requested name is found on the local subnet, it will respond with a NetBIOS reply, providing its IP address. NetBIOS is not routable — NetBIOS broadcasts are transported by UDP/IP packets, which are, by default, not forwarded to remote subnets by routers.

NOTE

Only computers that use NetBIOS will respond to NetBIOS broadcasts — NetWare servers will not. WINS and other NetBIOS name resolution methods will only register NetBIOS.

▸ *WINS servers* — If a WINS server address is shown in the WINS screen under TCP/IP Properties, the workstation will direct name resolution requests to that WINS server first. WINS servers accumulate NetBIOS name/IP address information from the local subnet and keep it in the WINS database to resolve names. In a routed environment, each local subnet must have a WINS server (or proxy) to accumulate NetBIOS data, and WINS servers must be configured to update one another. A WINS server is a specialized NetBIOS name server. Even when DNS servers are listed in the DNS Configuration page, WINS is checked first.

WINS servers only accumulate NetBIOS names and are not used to resolve other hosts, such as UNIX or NetWare servers.

▸ *DHCP* — If Use DHCP for WINS Resolution is checked, the DHCP server will be checked for name resolution data instead of WINS. DHCP servers contain name resolution data in their lease tables. Even when DNS servers are listed in the DNS Configuration page, DHCP is checked first.

▸ *LMHOSTS file* — When other name resolution methods fail, Windows workstations check the local LMHOSTS file for a listing. LMHOSTS is a text file manually built for this purpose. In many networks where name resolution has been a problem, the LMHOSTS file may have been updated to work around the problems.

▸ *HOSTS file* — A standard BSD HOSTS file can be used, and if present will be checked after the LMHOSTS file.

▶ *DNS* — Only after all the methods described have failed to resolve a name, DNS will be used if DNS is enabled. DNS servers addressed in the DNS Configuration screen will be checked in a prioritized order for name resolution.

If multiple boxes are checked:

1. The workstation NetBIOS cache is checked first. If the name was recently resolved, it will be found here without checking other methods. The cache contains only NetBIOS hosts and will not retain names for non-NetBIOS hosts.

2. WINS is always used first if configured for WINS. DHCP is used instead of WINS if the DHCP radio button is checked.

3. If neither WINS nor DHCP is configured, NetBIOS broadcast is used. When WINS or DHCP fails to resolve, the workstation reverts to NetBIOS broadcast.

4. If all the preceding methods fail, the LMHOSTS file is checked.

5. If all the preceding methods fail, the HOSTS file is checked.

6. If all the preceding methods fail and DNS is configured, the DNS server is checked. If the first attempt fails, additional attempts are made at 5-, 10-, 20-, and 40-second intervals. Subsequent failure results in a timeout.

 Windows NT does not have an option to Use DHCP for WINS Resolution. When both DNS and WINS options are configured, WINS will be checked first, and then DNS.
NOTE

If you intend to use the Novell DNS server, you should be sure that the DNS options are checked and configured, and that no WINS or DHCP options are checked.

TIP

If you reconfigure Windows name resolution options, be sure to reboot before retrying name resolution testing.

Zones

Novell DNS is based on logical zones as opposed to domains. Setting up and configuring zones is discussed in Chapter 11, "TCP/IP Services." See that chapter for more detail on Novell DNS components. The zone introduces an element of logical configuration that can remove restrictions imposed by physical constraints. For example, because Novell DNS is replicated through NDS, it is not necessary to have secondary DNS servers for each domain, and multiple domains can be handled by one DNS zone master server.

CHECKLIST

A zone is a logical DNS container, which can include one or more than one domain.

Some of the issues that may prevent your ability to resolve names may stem from zone configuration issues. Many of the following issues involve zone versus domain issues. Consider that the same type of link records and configurations between parent and child domains must be applied to zones. Once zones are configured, domain names are linked to zones with pointer (PTR) records so that queries directed to the domain are handled by the zone master.

NOTE

You will find a Novell AppNote entitled "Novell DNS/DHCP Services: Design Issues and Troubleshooting" on the CD that accompanies this book. This document eloquently explains zone concepts in addition to many other aspects of Novell DNS services. You will find that this document goes much further than the NetWare 5 online documentation.

Problems and Solutions

When troubleshooting, you may observe the following symptoms. Use these checklists to resolve DNS configuration problems.

Overview of Domain/Zone Name Configuration Issues

Names may be resolved in the local zone, but not in remote zones. This condition may be due to one of a few problems:

1. The DNS server is down.

2. Primary - secondary zone masters/domains may not be effectively linked.

3. Link records between the two zones/domains may not be setup properly.

The first test you should perform is to have the parent DNS server Ping the local NetWare zone master server by address, and to have the local NetWare zone master server Ping the parent DNS server by address. This will ensure that the two hosts are capable of communications.

Once you have verified that the two DNS servers can communicate, run the following tests from a workstation:

1. Ping a host in the local domain/zone by name

2. Ping the remote zone/domain name.

3. Ping a host in a remote zone by name. A zone can contain multiple domains, so be sure to Ping a node in a zone other than your local zone.

Hosts Cannot Access a Specific Host, but Can Access Other Hosts

When you can access a host by name but cannot access another host, you can conclude that the DNS server is working, but a problem exists with some of the records. The following steps can be used to locate the problem:

1. Check for an A record for the destination host.

2. Check to see if the static IP address has changed or if the client is using DHCP. If the address has changed, change the associated A record in DNS zone accordingly.

3. Check to see if the DHCP-assigned address has changed and DDNS does not update the zone. Check that the DDNS configuration is set up properly.

Verify that the subnet object is referenced to a DNS zone. See the subnet object, and check that DNS Zone for Dynamic Update is referenced to the appropriate DNS zone/domain.

Failure to Resolve Names in Remote Domain/Zones

When the Ping is successful in the local zone/domain but fails in the remote zone/domain, you can conclude that "glue" records and configurations between the two zones/domains are at fault.

Check that the following conditions are true:

NOTE

In the following checklist, the parent DNS server can be a NetWare zone master or another type of primary DNS server (UNIX, for example).

1. The parent and child (NetWare zone master) DNS servers are both up.

2. The parent DNS server contains an A record and an NS record for the child (NetWare zone master) DNS server.

3. Each domain name is mapped to a zone. For each domain name in a NetWare zone, a PTR record is required. You will find these records saved under the IN-ADDR-ARPA record located below the zone record.

4. The child (NetWare zone master) DNS server is configured as a secondary to the parent primary.

5. The child (NetWare zone master) DNS server has an A record and an NS record for the parent DNS server.

6. The zone master is configured as a secondary to the parent DNS server.

7. The IN-ADDR-ARPA zone record is be created and configured properly.

8. If the parent DNS server is a non-NetWare server, check the master zone record to see that a NetWare DNS server is configured in the Dynamic DNS Server box. DDNS is required to import foreign records into NDS.

9. If parent DNS server is an Internet DNS server, be sure that the private zone/domain is registered with InterNIC and that valid pointer records exist in the ISP's DNS server.

10. Check RootServInfo zone properties. The Secondary radio button must be checked, and an IP address of the parent DNS server must be entered in the zone master IP Address field.

11. If any name server addresses were changed, seek out all A, NS, and PTR records pointing to that address and change them.

NOTE When Internet root name server IP address change, you must manually update all references to them in your DNS parent zone. For updated root name server information, see `ftp://internic. net/domain/named.root`.

12. The Start of Authority (SOA) serial number must be incremented properly. When changing an SOA record, be sure that the serial number is valid. This is a common problem for UNIX, but generally not for NetWare 5, since the number is automatically assigned and incremented as you create a new zone.

NOTE If a primary DNS server is not NDS-based, you might need to change the SOA serial number manually for a secondary server to recognize that a change has occurred.

Child Zone Cannot Resolve Names

If the remote zone is a child of your local zone, name resolution problems may be slightly different. Check the following items.

1. Check the child zone properties. Make sure that the child zone is configured as Secondary with the IP address and host name for parent zone master, and check to see that the serial number is properly sequenced.

2. Check parent and child zones for PTR records to zone masters.

Recovering the DNS/DHCP Locator Object

Novell DNS relies on NDS for storing its records; however, damage to the Locator object or to the NDS database can disable DNS services. NDS and its replication is very sound—this problem will not occur spontaneously. However, an extraordinary event, such as an administrator deleting or moving the Locator or DNS/DHCP Group objects or removal of a NetWare server from the tree can remove the Locator object, which will disable the DNS service.

To recover from this type of event, use the DNS/DHCP Locator object repair utility. You can obtain this utility from Novell.

1. This utility will locate any existing DNS/DHCP Locator object in the tree and then verify the integrity of the existing object.

2. If the object does not exist, a new one will be created.

3. If an existing Locator object is found, it will be repaired. References to other objects are reconstructed, adding missing objects or references as needed.

NOTE **This tool will create new objects as needed but will not delete existing objects even if they are redundant. You should check the Locator object in NetWare Administrator and manually remove objects that are not needed.**

Cannot Access the DNS/DHCP Locator Object

If you receive an error indicating that the Locator object cannot be found when loading NAMED.NLM or DHCPSRVR.NLM, check to see that the object is located at a point in your tree that is accessible to DNS and DHCP servers. If the object is accessible but cannot be accessed, you may need to repair the Locator object NDS schema extensions.

The Locator object contains DNS- and DHCP-related records. When DNS or DHCP servers load, they check the Locator object for a list of global objects. The first time a DNS or DHCP server loads, a list of global objects is read and stored in the SYS:\ETC\DNS\ROOTSRVR.DAT and SYS:\ETC\DHCP\DHCPLOC.TAB files. From that point on, DNS and DHCP servers can load without access to the Locator object, but updates stored in the Locator object's property pages will not be recognized. When loading the DNS/DHCP Management utility, you may receive the error

```
ENDS26 — Schema has not been extended, or objects may have
been deleted
```

When you receive this error, load DNIPINST.NLM at your server console to recreate the Locator object. If the Locator object already exists, you should remove the Locator object's NDS schema, repair the NDS schema, and reinstall the Locator object with the following procedure.

1. From the server console type **DNIPINST –r**. This will remove the Locator object schema extensions.

2. Load DSREPAIR and select Advanced Options → Repair Local DS Database → Rebuild Operational Schema.

3. From the DSRepair main menu, run a Full Unattended Repair just to ensure that other NDS errors do not prevent a full recovery. When finished, exit DSRepair.

4. From the server console, type **DNIPINST**. This will reinstall the Locator object, update the schema extensions, and assign the appropriate NDS permissions.

DHCP

Dynamic Host Configuration Protocol (DHCP) automatically assigns IP addresses to network workstations as they boot. Novell's DHCP uses NDS to store its records and to make its services available throughout a tree. In an enterprise environment, you will find that Novell's DHCP subnet and subnet pool records can be distributed throughout an NDS tree, reducing the number of DHCP servers required in an organization.

Most problems you will find with this system stem from configuration errors. DHCP setup is discussed in Chapter 11, "Configuring TCP/IP with NetWare." Discussion in this chapter is restricted to troubleshooting — you may need to refer back to Chapter 11 for more explicit instructions on reconfiguring the DHCP server and records.

The following symptoms appear when DHCP and related services fail to assign IP addresses properly.

Name Resolution Problems

In NetWare 5, DHCP is very closely tied to DNS issues that are discussed in DNS section of this chapter. The both DNS and DHCP services are accessed through NDS — the same Locator object, DNSDHCP Group object, and other NDS configuration properties are used for both DNS and DHCP. Therefore, many of the same issues apply to DHCP as DNS.

When you have problems receiving DHCP assignments, check name resolution first and be certain that the DHCP server is locatable. In addition to the issues addressed in the DNS section of this chapter, you must also address DHCP configuration issues addressed in this section.

Windows Unable to Obtain an IP Address or Server Not Found

Should DHCP services fail to assign a valid IP address to a client, the client will not be able to connect to the network. The symptom that will be experienced at the workstation is a message during login that no server or tree could be located. Windows 95/98/NT workstations display the following message when a DHCP server does not respond to BOOTP requests:

```
The DHCP client was unable to obtain an IP network address
from a DHCP server. Do you want to see future DHCP messages?
```

You will then see a Microsoft "Welcome to Windows" local login dialog box. You will not have an opportunity to log into NetWare servers or tree, and you will not be able to log into Windows NT domains. You will see the same desktop as you would otherwise, but IP network resources will not be available. If the user has answered No to the preceding question, the workstation will no longer display this message upon boot.

Lease Expiration and Windows Client Behavior

You may not notice a DHCP failure for a few days. Windows DHCP address assignments are leased for a given amount of time. Until the lease period expires, the assigned address will be used even when a DHCP server is offline. The lease period is specified in the subnet configuration — by default it is set to three days. Here is the process:

1. If the host is online when the lease expires, the same address is automatically reassigned (the lease is renewed), and a new lease period begins.

2. If the client is not online at the time the lease expires, the leased IP address is reserved for 24 hours. If the Windows workstation reboots during that time period, the lease will be renewed, and the same address will be reassigned.

3. After 24 hours, the reservation is dropped and the address is made available for reassignment.

Working around a Disabled DHCP Service

DHCP failure denies network users all access. Until you get DHCP services working, you should use a stopgap measure to IP provide network services until you can resolve the problem.

To work around this problem, assign static IP address assignments. Once you get your DHCP server working, you can reconfigure your clients to use DHCP. If you have many IP clients, the workaround is time-consuming.

To configure Windows clients to use static IP assignments, access the Control Panel Network applet. Under TCP/IP properties, assign the IP address. Don't forget you will also have to manually enter a DNS A record for each client.

Once you get your DHCP server online and working, there is no reconfiguration necessary. If your zone was previously configured for Dynamic DNS, the client A records will be updated automatically.

No DHCP Address Assignment or Duplicate IP Assignments

Explore the reasons why your workstation may not receive an address assignment:

1. Check to see if the DHCP server is started.

2. Check the DHCP server to see if all leases have been assigned.

3. If the DHCP server is separated from a workstation by two or more routers, or delay is caused by a congested WAN, the BOOTP request from the client may time out before the DHCP server can respond. If the client is Windows 98 or NT 4, you can extend the DHCP Relay option to more hops or ticks. If the client is Windows 95, you can obtain a patch from Microsoft. The patch is named DCHCPUPD.EXE, dated 2/12/96, and includes the file VDHCP.386. This patch is included in the system administrators' service pack from Microsoft (on CD or download from the Internet — 14 disks).

4. Check for a duplicate address assignment. You must create an IP record configured as an exclusion for each static IP address in use.

5. Check for an invalid address assignment. Novell's DHCP automatically creates an exclusion for 0 and 255 within classful network addresses, but it does not reserve the subnet number and broadcast number when subnetting a classful address. Another problem is using an invalid subnet address. When subnetting a classful network address, some subnet ranges are invalid. Novell DHCP does not automatically exclude these ranges, because they can be valid when classless subnetting is used. See Chapter 4, "TCP/IP Protocols, IP Addressing, and Name Resolution," for rules about classful versus classless addressing. Tables 4.2 and 4.3 list valid subnets and addresses. These tables are also found in Appendix C, "Protocol Reference Guide." The tables are also to be found on the CD that accompanies this book.

Deleting a Subnet Range, Subnet, or Subnet Pool

When deleting a subnet record, you should unload the server service (DHCPSRVR.NLM) and reload it after changes have been made. A dialog box will warn you that the server should be unloaded. Failure to observe this suggestion can cause problems.

DHCP Not Updating DNS Zone (Dynamic DNS Not Working)

DHCP address assignments can update DNS records through a Dynamic DNS (DDNS) server. The DDNS server is simply a DNS server designated for this duty in the DNS zone record. The following configuration options are required to make DDNS successful:

1. Check the DNS zone record properties. Be sure a server is selected in the Dynamic DNS Server box.

2. Check the DHCP Subnet Address Range — be sure the DNS Update Option is set to Always Update, and be sure a valid DHCP server is shown in the DHCP Server box.

3. Verify that the DHCP subnet record is referenced to a DNS zone. See the DHCP subnet record in DHCP, and check that DNS Zone for Dynamic Update is referenced to the appropriate DNS zone.

4. Check to see that the Range Type is set to Dynamic DHCP or Dynamic BOOTP and DHCP.

5. Be sure the DNS Update option is set to Always Update.

References

The following resources are available at Novell's support Web site found at `http://support.novell.com/`.

AppNotes

Detailed information is available in the following *AppNotes*. You will find an excellent index for looking up topics covered in AppNotes at the Novell developer Web site found at `http://developer.novell.com/research/appnotes.htm`.

- ▸ Bartholomew and Neff, *Easing TCP/IP Network Management with Novell's DNS/DHCP Services*, AppNotes, April 1998

- ▸ Amitabh Sahn, *Novell DNS/DHCP Services: Design Issues and Troubleshooting*, AppNotes, November 1998

 This AppNote is found on the CD that accompanies this book under "Support Technical Documents."

NOTE

Technical Information Documents (TID)

Watch for Technical Information Documents (TIDs) in the Knowledgebase section of the Novell support Web site. TIDs are issued to address support issues as they arise. You will find documents on a couple of issues in the following documents.

- ▸ *Can't Load DHCP Manager; Schema Errors*, October 16, 1998, TID #2943430

- ▸ *DNSDHCP-DHCP Locator Object Issues*, August 20, 1998, TID #2941328

Internet RFC 1912

This Internet document provides information about common operational errors found in both the operation of DNS servers and the data the DNS servers contain. This information is common among all DNS systems.

CHAPTER 18

NDS Infrastructure and Repair

Novell Directory Services (NDS) is a global, replicated database of all user-related and resource-related objects. A directory service has many functions. Its primary job is to control access between user-related and resource-related objects, and to distribute administration of large networks while maintaining authority and control over those distributed elements. A directory service provides a single database from which user and resource objects and properties are stored. Security and other network services are applied to this database, providing a centralized repository with distributed control.

In a large organization, network administration requires a delicate balance of departmental and centralized control — administration must be customized to suit each organization. NDS provides a method of organizing objects into a hierarchical structure that can be tailored to meet the needs of any organization. Because NDS is organized hierarchically, an NDS network is organized into what is called a *tree*. A larger network can have very complex trees and can even have several trees in an internetwork.

CHECKLIST

The NDS database, which contains all objects as well as their properties, is called the *Directory*. The process that maintains the Directory is called *Directory Services (DS)*. A DS server that contains an original or copy of the NDS database is called a *replica server*.

The system administrator configures the NDS physical infrastructure and maintains it. Physical infrastructure includes the mechanisms behind NDS, which consist of replica placement and configuration. This chapter discusses NDS maintenance and troubleshooting, which is based on physical infrastructure.

Replica design and configuration is almost automatic when installing the NDS portion of NetWare server setup. During server installation, the first server in a tree is configured with a master replica. When installing a NetWare 4.11, 4.2, or 5 server into an existing tree, the new server will be configured as a read/write replica server of the tree or in the partition in which it is installed. INSTALL will automatically create no more than three replicas in a partition. In most simple networks this configuration requires no adjustments. The administrator should review the replication configuration in the context of his or her network and determine if altering the replication is warranted. This chapter briefly discusses the changes that should be made to accommodate your internetwork infrastructure and procedures in maintaining and troubleshooting NDS replication.

NDS design and implementation is a subject that can become quite complex. This book is focused on maintenance and troubleshooting. Refer to the "Additional Resources" section of this chapter for references to specific resources on NDS and related topics.

· ◀

NDS Physical Infrastructure Overview

NDS is not a new product — several years of use have produced a rock-solid, mature directory service environment that can operate efficiently with little maintenance and negligible down time. NDS physical infrastructure is the basis of this stability and performance. NetWare 4 and 5 installation defaults will make your system fault tolerant. However, it is up the system administrator to revise the default NDS physical infrastructure for best performance.

NDS is managed through Windows-based utilities. All objects in the Directory are represented with Windows icons and placed into container objects for organizational and administrative reasons. The objects represent record listings in the Directory; each object is associated with properties. Access Control Lists and trustee listings permit access to and control of these objects and their properties through NDS. Objects and their properties are physically contained as records in the Directory, which is in turn hosted on NDS replica servers. A healthy and stable Directory depends upon the physical infrastructure established to host the Directory.

CHECKLIST

The NDS database is physically stored on NetWare 4 and 5 servers, called *replica servers*.

CHECKLIST

The term *Directory* is used to refer to a single or composite instance of all NDS replicas distributed throughout an NDS tree. Because the databases are replicated, the composite Directory functions as a single database even though portions of it may be distributed throughout the tree.

Fault tolerance is especially important in an NDS tree because the Directory controls all user authentication and access to resources. In NetWare 5 networks, even DNS and DHCP services are housed within the NDS database. Many networks, especially in larger organizations, handle mission-critical applications. Therefore, high availability is required. NDS stability, availability, and performance are based on physical considerations such as which servers are to host the NDS database and where they are to be located.

Performance is also a great concern. Larger organizations often build large Directories — as any database grows, performance can become a significant issue. NDS performance is vitally important — the users should not have to wait even a moment for authentication. The tree administrator is responsible for developing a physical infrastructure that services users' and container administrators' needs with stability and performance that renders it transparent.

NDS physical infrastructure is flexible and scalable enough to handle the largest tree. The administrator has NDS design tools to permit large Directories to be fault tolerant and to perform at peak efficiency so that users are not inconvenienced by the complexity of the Directory.

Replication

Replication provides fault tolerance and load balancing.

Replicas are copies of the NDS database. Replicas can be created on any NetWare 4 or 5 server and are distributed over multiple servers to provide fault tolerance and load balancing. If you are familiar with DNS replication, NDS works much the same way except that it is far more sophisticated.

Replication is absolutely necessary in an NDS-based network because NDS is the controlling factor in accessing all network resources. Replication provides fault tolerance — without replication, server downtime disables all logins and all access to resources. This is why replication is an automatic default when installing a server into an existing tree. Unless you revise the default replication, every tree with two or more servers is replicated.

Replication also balances loads for better performance. Any NDS server will respond to authentication requests, but only a master or read/write replica allows a user to log in. Because servers are used for multiple purposes, other processing can interfere with NDS authentication response. Load balancing provides quick authentication with less conflict between multiple tasks running on any one server. When a user is in a remote location, a replicated server can handle the request locally — the user does not need to wait for access to a central server that may be located on the other side of a WAN.

Types of Replicas

Replicas can only be created on NetWare 4 and 5 servers. NDS has four types of replicas:

- Master

- Read/write

- Read-only

- Subordinate reference

The Master Replica

A *master replica* is an NDS database that contains a complete listing of all objects and object properties that reside in a partition. In a tree that has not been partitioned, the master replica contains all records for all objects in the entire tree — only one master replica will exist in any unpartitioned tree. When you install a NetWare 4 or 5 server as the first server in a tree, a master replica is created that will contain the NDS database for the entire tree. In a partitioned tree, each partition has its own master replica. Partitioning is discussed in more detail in the "Partitioning" section later in this chapter.

The Read/Write Replica

A *read/write replica* is also a replicated copy of a master replica. Updates can be made directly to a read/write replica. The changes will then be replicated to the master replica, which in turn updates other read/write and read-only replicas. A read-only replica can be used on the remote end of a WAN to reduce NDS administrative traffic in addition to optimizing authentication.

A read/write replica must reside on a different server from the master replica server. Replication is two-way: all objects are replicated from the master replica to the read/write replica. However, the only traffic coming from the read/write replica to the master replica consists of updates that were written directly to the read/write replica. Either replica is available to service authentication requests and automatically balances loads. Read/write replicas can reduce loads on the master replica server by offloading administrative updates. Read/write replicas are especially helpful to reduce WAN traffic in remote locations where administration is done locally.

The Read-Only Replica

A *read-only replica* contains a replicated copy of the NDS database. A read-only replica cannot be changed directly — instead updates are made to master replica and then replicated to the read-only replica. The read-only replica can provide fault tolerance and load balancing for authentication, but not for login or administration. Updates and logins must be made processed by the master replica; the changes will then be replicated to the read-only replica.

A read-only replica must reside on a different server from the master replica server. Replication is one-way only — from the master replica to the read-only replica. Either replica is available to service authentication requests and automatically balance loads.

The Subordinate Reference

The *subordinate reference replica* facilitates name searches across partition boundaries. Subordinate reference replicas do not contain all object data — they contain only very brief indexed names. Subordinate reference replicas are not effective for fault tolerance or load balancing. They are created to provide NDS with enhanced name resolution whenever a tree has been partitioned.

This type of replica is created automatically when needed and deleted automatically when no longer needed. No maintenance is required for a subordinate reference replica — it is entirely maintained by the system.

Replica Rings

It is recommended that three or more replicas be configured for each partition. A replica ring is formed when a master is replicated to read/write and/or read-only replicas. Read/write and read-only replicas contain an exact duplicate of the master replica for the partition. Figure 18.1 demonstrates a replica ring. NDS authentication requests are handled by any available replica server in the ring.

Administrative updates can be handled by the read/write or master replica. A ring of three replicas in a single location provides outstanding fault tolerance and performance characteristics.

FIGURE 18.1

A replica ring

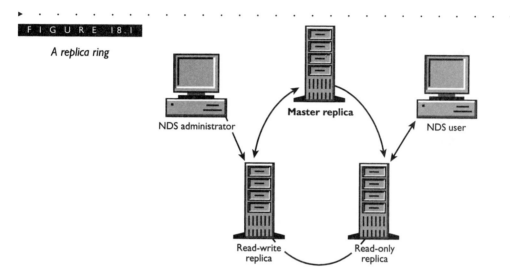

A replica ring works as a unit — users and administrators do not need to consider which server is handling their NDS requests. When a WAN separates portions of the tree, a replica ring in each campus provides local fault tolerance without authentication delays even if the WAN is out of service. When three replicas form a ring, fault tolerance is assured — the chances of all three servers going down at the same time are negligible. Performance is also improved because any one of the three — whichever responds first — handles NDS authentication requests.

When replicating over a WAN, the administrator should carefully consider replication traffic in the context of available bandwidth on the WAN. You will find recommendations for replication over a WAN in the "Partitioning" section later in this chapter.

Replication is configured in the NDS Manager Windows-based utility.

▶ · ◀

Partitioning

In larger NDS environments, the NDS tree can be partitioned to meet one or both of the following goals:

▸ To reduce the size and complexity of the database

▸ To reduce replication traffic

When a tree contains more than 1,000 objects, it is recommended that the tree be partitioned. Partitioning breaks the master replica into smaller units, which are more efficient. Partitioning a large tree optimizes NDS searches, authentication requests, and replication traffic when properly configured under appropriate circumstances.

Partitioning will mean that some replicas contain only portions of the NDS database. Each partition has its own master replica, which contains only the object records for the given partition. Regardless of which partition contains an object, all object records are available as if they were all contained in a single Directory. Like in any other relational database, partition replicas are combined to provide a virtual view of the entire Directory.

Each partition has its own master replica. When partitioning, you can create the new master replica on the same server or on any other NetWare 4 or 5 server. Only master replica servers can contain more than one replica. INSTALL does not have any facilities for creating these partitions — partitioning must be done manually by the system administrator in the NDS Manager Windows-based utility.

NOTE   **Partitioning operations are very sensitive to time synchronization. Be sure to synchronize time in DSRepair before attempting any type of partition change. Be advised that partitioning operations often require excessively long update periods – sometimes many hours even for very powerful servers. Schedule partition changes for long weekends where possible.**

· · · · ·

Partitioning in a Single Location

Partitions are logical divisions that may or may not be congruent with physical locations. You can partition a tree without having to add more servers. To optimize a large Directory, you can create partitions with only one server. When a new partition is created, a new master replica is created for the partition. Figure 18.2 illustrates a new master replica created on the same master replica server. Figure 18.3 illustrates three partitions; each partition has its own master replica, but all three are contained in the same server.

The example shown in Figure 18.2 illustrates how a large Directory is broken down into three smaller databases. In this illustration, the Corporate, Sales, and Manufacturing divisions are separated into partitions. In this illustration, it is not relevant whether each division has its own file/print and application servers. What is more important is that all three divisions are located on the same campus and linked by a high-capacity backbone LAN. This configuration would not be recommended if each division were separated by WANs. This configuration would effectively reduce the size of each master replica.

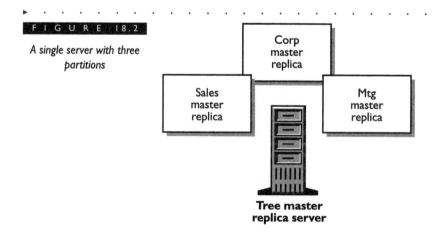

FIGURE 18.2

A single server with three partitions

Corp master replica

Sales master replica

Mtg master replica

Tree master replica server

Partitioning Multiple Locations

Replicating over a WAN will generate replication traffic but provides quick response to authentication requests at the remote site. A normal read-only or read/write replica generates the maximum amount of traffic from the master replica, since all data is replicated. Partitioning reduces the amount of traffic by dividing the data to be replicated into smaller parts. One of the factors an administrator should consider is whether the remote location should be replicated—and if it should, whether it should it be partitioned. Optimization issues are addressed later in this chapter, but the fact remains that a remote facility will most likely benefit from replication should you have sufficient bandwidth to allow it. Normally, partitioning is the best alternative because it will reduce traffic.

If the master replica is created on a separate server from the existing master replica server of the tree, a replicated copy of the partition master replica is retained on the parent server. Figure 18.3 demonstrates a tree with three partitions: Corp, which is located in New York City; Sales, which is located in Los Angeles; and Mfg, which is located in Chicago. The shaded boxes represent partitions, each of which are in separate NDS containers. The dotted lines represent replication. Notice that the LA and Chicago replicas contain only LA or Chicago data, but the NYC replica contains data for NYC, LA, and Chicago.

FIGURE 18.3

A tree with three partitions, one local and two remote

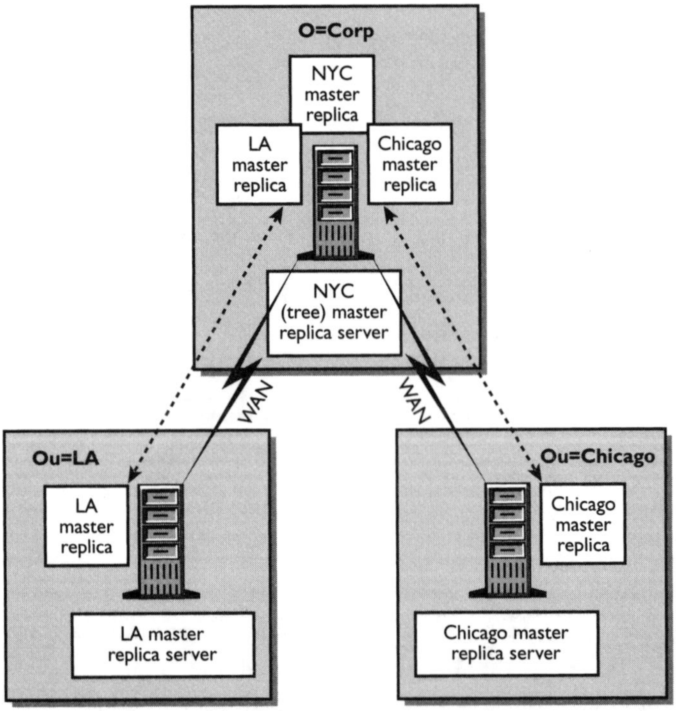

In this illustration, the NYC server contains copies of all three partitions' master replicas and therefore contains all NDS data for the entire tree. However, the Chicago and LA servers only contain data for their respective partitions. In this example, only traffic related to the LA partition is replicated between New York City and LA, and only traffic related to Chicago is replicated between NYC and Chicago. This example illustrates how partitioning over WAN boundaries can reduce the amount of replication traffic between remote locations. This configuration would effectively reduce the replication traffic flowing over the two WANs. If these two remote locations had read-only or read/write replicas, replication for all three locations would be replicated over both WANs.

Figure 18.3 also shows the overlay of the NDS container objects. Notice that each partition is placed into a separate NDS container. In this example, each division has its own NDS container object in addition to having its own partition. Physical location influences both logical NDS tree organization and physical infrastructure.

Subpartitions

Each partition can be subpartitioned. The master replica server for the partition will contain its own master replica plus a replica for each subpartition, as shown in Figure 18.4. In this illustration, the LA partition contains subpartitions for LA-Sales and LA-Mfg. Notice that the NYC server does not contain master replicas of the LA-Sales and LA-Mfg partitions. Each LA subpartition's NDS data is retained in LA and not replicated to the master replica server in NYC — instead subordinate reference (marked as "sub-ref") replicas are created. Subordinate reference replicas contain placeholders to data stored in the subpartitions (LA-Sales and LA-Mfg).

Notice in Figure 18.4 that subordinate reference replicas are created on the NYC master replica server. Subordinate reference replicas are automatically created to optimize searches to subpartitions. This type of replica refers lookups to the appropriate master replica server and contains only name resolution records.

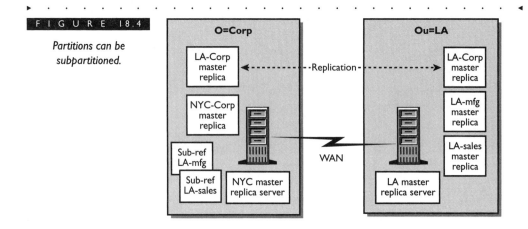

FIGURE 18.4

Partitions can be subpartitioned.

Recommendations for Replication and Partitioning

The following recommendations will help to ensure that your NDS tree is optimized.

Three Replicas at Each Location for Best Fault Tolerance

A replica server provides online backup should the master replica server fail. A master and two read/write replicas should be created in each partition ring to ensure fault tolerance at all times. If there are only two replicas, when one fails, there is no fault tolerance. A third replica provides fault tolerance in the event that one replica server fails. The chance of losing three replica servers at once is minimal if you respond quickly to each system failure as it occurs. If any replica server fails, procrastination is your worst enemy, but we all would like time to solve our problems in a sane and orderly manner. For these reasons, three replicas in a ring are better than two.

Replicating over a WAN

When a remote location is to be included in an NDS tree, the administrator has three options:

- ▸ To rely on the centralized replica server for authentication over the WAN

- ▸ To install a read-only replica to handle authentication locally

- ▸ To install a read/write replica to handle authentication and administrative updates locally

- ▸ To create a partition for the remote location with a replica ring

If the remote location is a small office with little traffic, an on-site replica is not required. A read-only replica provides authentication, but login must be handled by a master or read/write replica. If the branch office has a few logins a day, the read-only replica services authentication every time a resource is accessed. In most small branch offices with just a few users, typical traffic consists of a few logins per day and few if any administrative changes to the objects in that location. In this case, it is advisable to rely on a centralized replica server to service login over the WAN and use a local read-only replica to handle moment-to-moment authentication.

If the location generates a significant level of authentication and infrequent administrative changes are made to objects in that location, the administrator should consider installing a replica server on site. If the location already has a NetWare file or application server on site, it is a good candidate for a read-only replica. A read-only replica handles all authentication requests locally but does not handle logins or updates. It receives changes in replication updates from the master replica server of the tree or from the subordinate reference replica server of the partition.

When the location has local system administration, a read/write replica server is probably more appropriate. When administrative updates are made to objects, changes must be made to a read/write, master, or subordinate reference replica server. For frequent administrative updates, a local read/write replica server is updated, and the update is replicated only to the master replica or subordinate reference replica of the partition. The key to this decision is anticipating the frequency of updates that will occur in the remote office.

Partitioning over a WAN

When a remote location has many users and on-site system administration, a separate partition should be considered for that location. If the location already has two or more servers, a separate partition is more affordable, since the resources for hosting a partition are already in place. In larger departmental groups, a separate partition is highly recommended, as NDS traffic over the WAN can occupy bandwidth and require frequent synchronization.

This consideration should be balanced with the goal of keeping the number of the partitions in the tree to a manageable level. Each partition requires a separate replication process on the master replica server. A discussion of limiting the number of partitions is found within the next few pages.

WAN Bandwidth Considerations

The decision to replicate in a remote office must be considered in the context of available WAN bandwidth. The following considerations should affect the decision to partition, replicate, or rely on the remote replica for authentication.

If the WAN has limited bandwidth (such as 64Kbps) a replica is less attractive. If a T1 is available (1.544Mbps) and the WAN bandwidth is not fully utilized, a replica is a more attractive possibility. If the remote site is linked with frame relay, a Permanent Virtual Circuit (PVC) can be established to dedicate a given amount of bandwidth to replication and authentication traffic. When a given amount of bandwidth is dedicated in this manner, a replica in the remote location is not required, since replication and authentication traffic can be expedited.

TIP

Use WANMAN.NLM to remotely manage NDS updates over a limited-bandwidth WAN or dial-up connection. This new utility is included NetWare 5 and is also available for NetWare 4.x. For help using WANMAN, search for TID 2942079 at `http://support` `.novell.com/servlet/Knowledgebase.`

Another consideration is the service level agreement you have with your data communications provider, in conjunction with your experience with the provider. Even very small amounts of downtime should persuade you to install a local replica in the remote location. If the location has no local replica and the link with the replica goes down, all access to resources is halted.

If the remote location is busy enough to warrant at least two or three servers, perhaps the administrator should consider creating a partition with a subordinate reference replica. If the remote location is administered on site, this makes partitioning more important.

No More Than Seven to Ten Replicas per Partition

More than a few full replicas in any partition may generate excessive replication traffic and in most cases is not necessary. As you can imagine, increasing the number of replicas increases replication traffic exponentially.

This many replicas may be necessary to support existing NetWare 3 bindery contexts. Each bindery context requires a replica and can support up to 16 NetWare 3 servers. If it is not possible to reduce a partition to fewer than ten replicas, consider reorganizing or upgrading your NetWare 3 servers to require fewer NDS bindery replica servers. When more than a few replicas are necessary for any reason, consider creating new partitions. You can tell that replication processing is too high when normal replication causes a server's CPU utilization to approach 100 percent.

Limit the Number of Partitions in a Tree

In each tree, the master replica server contains one replica and associated replication processing for each partition within its tree. The number of replicas on a single server should be limited to a level that the master replica server can handle. When a master replica server contains too many replicas, CPU utilization runs high on a normal basis. Some CPU utilization should be reserved for massive NDS changes, such as revising a partition or moving a container. When CPU utilization reaches 100 percent, replication and authentication processing slow drastically.

A typical NDS master replica server can easily maintain up to 15 partitions in addition to other duties. An NDS master replica server can be used as a file and print server and/or as an application server. However, when it is used in this way, the number of replicas on the server is limited according to the processing demands the other modules place on the server. For example, a busy Web server should probably not be an NDS master replica server at all. A file and print server that rarely rises to 50 percent CPU utilization can host up to 20 or 25 replicas. A good rule of thumb is to establish a dedicated NDS master replica server when more than 15 partitions are required in the tree.

A dedicated NDS master replica server would service only the master NDS database and one replica for each partition — it should not have any other services running outside of normal operating system processes. A dedicated NetWare 4.11/4.2 NDS master replica server can host 100 or more replicas for a typical single processor — perhaps more — depending on several factors in the server's design and replication traffic patterns. A NetWare 5 server can host even more replicas. As more powerful multiprocessor servers evolve, NDS partitioning scalability will climb to higher levels.

When building a dedicated master replica server, be sure to use 100Mbps LAN technology, PCI interfaces, Ultra-Wide SCSI disk drives, and the fastest processor you can afford.

TIP

Guidelines

Just a few guidelines should be observed to maintain synchronization:

1. Always remove resource objects from NDS before physically removing the related devices. If a replica server is to be removed from service for an extended period, remove its NDS server object from the tree before physically disconnecting the server. When removing a server for a short period, be sure that all replicas in its partition are synchronized before disconnecting the server, and postpone massive partition changes until the server is reconnected. Upon reconnection, manually synchronize the partition immediately.

2. Be sure that all replica servers and network segments are up and communicating before making massive NDS changes, such as creating or moving a partition. Though NDS updates are held and propagated when replica servers are back online, best results are obtained when all components are online and operating properly.

When performing a massive update (such as a revision to partitioning), wait for a time when the network is at its lowest traffic levels.

TIP

3. Always check to see that your tree is synchronized before attempting to make massive changes or updates to partition structure. Check synchronization status with DSRepair, and fix any exceptions. Before proceeding, see that communications links are online, and all replicas are responding normally. Check out all exceptions and correct them before proceeding. DSRepair can repair many problems and will force synchronization. However, forcing synchronization will not fix the problem that has caused synchronization to fail in the first place.

4. Once you have synchronized your tree, update your NetWare 4 and 5 servers with the latest versions of Directory Services (DS.NLM) and DSRepair (DSREPAIR.NLM). Be sure to read release notes before applying patches or updating critical services.

WARNING

Your NetWare 5 operating system CD contains updates for your NetWare 4.11 servers. Be sure to apply these updates before adding NetWare 5 servers to your network. Failure to update before adding a NetWare 4.2 or 5 server to your tree can damage NDS and cause downtime. It is not necessary to update 4.2 servers.

5. Run DSRepair and correct all errors before proceeding.

6. Compile all NDS statistics with DSDiagnostics (DSDIAG.NLM). Keep reports on hand so you will have all configuration statistics at hand when needed.

7. Do not experiment on production trees. Use alternative techniques to test your configuration before implementing it.

TIP

See your local Novell office or reseller for a promotional three-user copy of NetWare 5. You can use this for experimenting with replication, partitioning, and repair procedures. *Novell's Guide to NetWare 5 Networks* by Jeffrey F. Hughes and Blair W. Thomas (IDG Books Worldwide) includes a complimentary three-user copy of NetWare 5.

In general, always wait for updates to be propagated throughout the tree before proceeding to the next step. Directory updates can take moments to several hours to be propagated to all affected replicas. Typical updates, such as changing a user password, are propagated in a matter of moments. A complex operation such as a partition move can affect many objects and can take a long time to complete — perhaps even hours. The following factors affect how long it takes a partition update to be completed:

- ▸ The number of objects in the partition

- ▸ The number and complexities of replicas to be updated and synchronized

- ▸ Whether WANs separate replica servers that are affected

- ▸ How busy network segments are that must relay the changes

Diagnostic Procedures

Diagnosing DS problems is handled by observing error messages during the course of normal business, or in operations designated for this purpose in various NetWare 4 and 5 utilities.

Utilities

NetWare 4.11, 4.2, and 5 have four utilities used to view, manage, and troubleshoot DS partitioning and replication services. These utilities are discussed in more detail throughout this chapter:

- ▸ INSTALL and NWCONFIG

- ▸ NDS Manager

- ▸ DSRepair

- ▸ DSDiagnostics

INSTALL/NWCONFIG, DSRepair, and DSDiagnotics are server-based applications that are based on the function to be performed — you select a function and then select the object on which to perform the function. NDS Manager is workstation software that is object-based — you select the object to view properties and perform tasks for the selected object.

NetWare 4's INSTALL.NLM application and NetWare 5's NWCONFIG.NLM are server-based applications that are used to install, remove, reinstall, back up, and restore NDS partitions and replicas. This application is not used for maintenance or troubleshooting. Use these utilities to remove and reinstall NDS. These applications can be accessed remotely using RConsole and RConsoleJ utilities.

NDS Manager is a 32-bit Windows application that is used to manage, maintain, and troubleshoot partitions and replicas once the servers are installed. Use NDS Manager to create new partitions and replicas, as well as to conduct maintaining and troubleshooting operations. For example, you can use NDS Manager to create and synchronize replicas. NDS Manager is the only utility used to create and make changes to partitions and replicas once they have been created.

NDS Manager is not installed on your desktop by default. You must install it by manually creating a shortcut to the executable file, which can be found SYS:Public\win32\NDSMGR32.EXE. This application can be accessed from Windows 95, 98, and NT client workstations anywhere on the internetwork over IPX or IP protocols. No 16-bit or Macintosh version of this utility is currently available.

DSRepair (DSREPAIR.NLM) is used on the server for partition and replica maintenance, troubleshooting, and repair. DSRepair consolidates diagnostic, synchronization, and repair functions into a single utility. It has no facilities for most maintenance operations — for example, you can only create and change partitions and replicas in NDS Manager. Use this utility for troubleshooting, diagnosis, and repair of all NDS operations including time synchronization. This application can be accessed remotely using RConsole and RConsoleJ utilities.

DSDiagnostics (DSDIAG.NLM) is new to NetWare 5 and provides comprehensive reporting on partition and replica status, condition, and errors. Reports can be displayed or saved to files for later printing. Most information that is available in this utility is also available in NDS Manager, but this utility focuses on report generation, while NDS Manager is oriented toward managing NDS partition and replica objects. This application can be accessed remotely using RConsole and RConsoleJ utilities.

NDS Errors

NetWare 5 has extremely explicit NDS error notifications that are displayed when using NDS Manager and NetWare Administrator at your workstation. At your servers DSRepair and DSDiagnostics also provides detailed error reports on screen and in printed form.

NDS error codes can be researched in your NetWare 5 online documentation. To locate NDS error codes and simple-language explanations, follow these instructions:

1. Run the NetWare 5 online documentation by selecting \NOVDOCS\ VIEWDOC.EXE on your NetWare 5 Online Documentation CD.

2. Select the Reference bar in the left-pane menu of your browser.

3. In the right pane select Error Codes → List of All Error Codes → NDS Error Codes → List of NDS Error Codes and then select the error code number in the right pane of your browser.

NOTE

> **Viewing the NetWare 5 online documentation requires that you have previously installed Netscape Navigator 4 or Microsoft Internet Explorer 4 on a Windows 95, 98, or NT computer. You will find Netscape Navigator 4.04 on the Online Documentation CD — it can be executed directly from the CD.**

Checking Replica and Partition Status in NDS Manager

As discussed previously in this chapter, several operations warrant checking NDS status. On a regular basis you should check replica and partition as a maintenance procedure — about once a week works in most organizations. Set aside time during this procedure to fix exceptions you may discover.

When a replica icon has a yellow triangle with an exclamation point (!) as shown in Figure 18.5, an error condition is indicated.

▶ · ◀

FIGURE 18.5

The error flag on a read/write replica icon

When you load NDS Manager or select the Refresh option from the Window menu, all partitions are checked for synchronization status. This process occurs regardless of whether the Tree or Partition and Servers view is displayed. You can detect and view synchronization errors and error text with the following procedure:

1. Log in as Admin or with NDS Supervisory rights to the containers that the replica servers and partitions are in.

2. Run NDS Manager from a 32-bit Windows client.

3. Check replica icons for yellow exclamation point (!) flags. The flag indicates a warning. Selecting the icon enables you to view the error status as discussed previously in this chapter.

4. To check status again, select Window → Refresh.

Checking Partition Continuity

When NDS errors are displayed, check replica rings for synchronization errors. You can use this procedure periodically as a regular maintenance item. This process will work regardless of whether the Tree Partitions or Servers view is currently displayed. To check partition continuity, follow these steps:

1. Log in as Admin or with NDS Supervisory rights to the containers that the replica servers and partitions are in.

2. Run NDS Manager from a 32-bit Windows client.

3. Right-click the partition to be checked.

4. Select Partition Continuity from the menu; the Partition Continuity screen will appear.

5. Replica status will be displayed along with each replica icon as shown in Figure 18.5.

6. If an error condition is noted, right-click the replica and then select Information. Select the question mark (?) to view help on the error message.

7. If a repair is required, select the Repair menu and then select an action to be performed (for instance, Synchronize Immediately). Repair processes that are relevant to the error condition will be activated on the menu as appropriate.

To view synchronization errors, follow these steps:

1. Log in as Admin of the tree, or as container administrator with NDS rights to supervise the replica server.

2. Start NDS Manager from a 32-bit Windows client.

3. Select View → Partitions and Servers. If this selection is grayed out, Partitions and Servers is currently displayed.

4. Check the replica icons. An error condition is indicated by an exclamation point (!) in a yellow triangle. Select the replica icon to view the Replica Information screen shown in Figure 18.6. The error will be shown in the Current Synch Error box at the bottom of the box. Select the question mark (?) icon to the right of the Current Synch Error box for an error description.

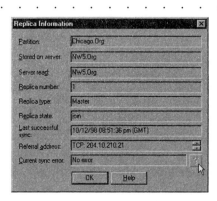

FIGURE 18.6

Help explanations for error notification

Diagnostics Server Utilities

NDS utilities provide status and condition reports on NDS replication, time synchronization, and other related elements. NDS error messages appear on the console screen and within NDS utilities. You can refer to several sources for diagnostic information including the following:

- ▶ Error messages during login, resource access, and other authentication events

- ▶ Error messages when managing objects in NetWare Administrator

- ▶ Status and condition reports in NDS Manager

- ▶ Status and condition reports in DSDiagnostics

- ▶ Status and errors in DSRepair

Novell has refined NDS to produce clear and specific error messages. The utilities described provide the means to check components to see if irregularities are found. Use these tools to find the most common problems. You will find excellent documentation on error messages, indexed and referenced by number and by description, in your NetWare 5 Online Documentation.

DSDiagnostics

DSDiagnostics (DSDIAG.NLM) is a new NDS utility that is provided in NetWare 5. Think of it as a doctor or medical technician for your Directory. The DSDiagnostics Reports Generation menu shown in Figure 18.7 leads to several reports and listings that will assist you in tracking down inconsistencies that can cause DS problems.

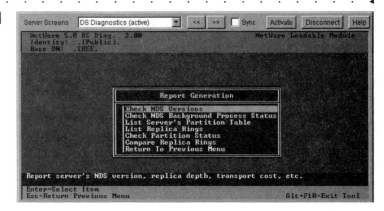

FIGURE 18.7

The DSDiagnostics Reports Generation menu

You will find the following selections in DSDiagnostics' Reports Generation menu.

▶ *Check NDS Versions* — Older versions of the Directory Services module (DS.NLM) are problematic in two ways:

• Older modules may have "bugs" and deficiencies that have been fixed in later versions. Each newer DS.NLM version includes revisions that make Directory Services more efficient in addition to fixing problems.

• Older modules may not interoperate well with newer versions. For example, all NetWare 4.11 servers must be updated to version 5.99 or higher to work properly with NetWare 5. Previous versions did not have support for new features and protocol changes incorporated into NetWare 5.

To update DS.NLM and related files, see a section in this chapter under "Maintenance Procedures." NetWare 4.11 servers' Directory Services can be updated from the NetWare 5 operating system CD, from NDS Manager, from Internet files, or from Novell Support Connection.

▶ *Check NDS Background Process Status* — If a process has been initiated, or you suspect a normal background process has gone into a loop, check its status.

▸ *List Server's Partition Table* — For information purposes only, there will be times when you need to view which partitions are stored on a given server.

▸ *List Replica Rings* — For information purposes only, you should know which servers are members of replica rings, and what type of replica is contained in each server.

▸ *Check Partition Status* — When checking the status of a partition, you will find synchronization problems or missing objects.

▸ *Compare Replica Rings* — Comparing rings enables you to view differences between partitions and objects in those partitions.

DSRepair

DSRepair also provides status and information that will assist in locating inconsistencies. The following options are available to check and report on DS-related status. Figure 18.8 illustrates the reporting options available from the DSRepair Available Options menu.

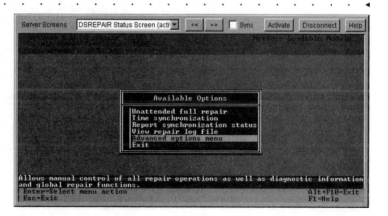

F I G U R E   18.8

The DSRepair Available Options menu

DSRepair's Available Options menu provides logs, statistics, and reports on the following options:

▸ *Time Synchronization* — Checks and reports time synchronization status for each server in the tree. Because replica synchronization is based on time, DS synchronization problems can appear if time issues are not addressed.

▸ *Report Synchronization Status* — Checks and reports replica status throughout the tree.

▸ *View Repair Log File* — Displays logs of all DS repair operations.

DSRepair Advanced Options Submenu

You will find several diagnostic options in DSRepair. Figure 18.9 illustrates the options available from the Advanced Options menu. To access this menu, select Advanced Options → Replica and partition operations and then select a partition/replica to maintain.

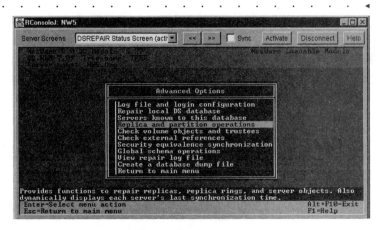

F I G U R E   18.9

The DSRepair Advanced Options menu

The following items found in DSRepair produce reports and check NDS status. You can find these options by selecting Advanced Options from the Available Options menu.

▸ *Check Volume Objects and Trustees* — Trustee lists are properties of directory listings on files, directories, and volumes. When a trustee listing fails, user access may be denied. The error condition is typically the same as if the client did not have the appropriate rights to files and directories.

▶ *Check External References* — This option looks for objects outside of the local partition to see if the objects can be located. Because external objects are typically managed by system administrators outside of the partition, external objects may be removed without removing pointers such as drive mappings.

▶ *View Repair Log File* — When any repair operation is run, the results are recorded in the repair log. View this file to see errors that were discovered and items that were checked with no errors found.

DSRepair Replica and Partition Operations

The following options are found in DSRepair by selecting Available Options → Advanced Options → Replica and Partition Operations. Before viewing the submenu, you must first select a partition/replica ring to view. Figure 18.10 shows the Replica and Partition Operations submenu.

The Replica and Partition Operations menu in DSRepair

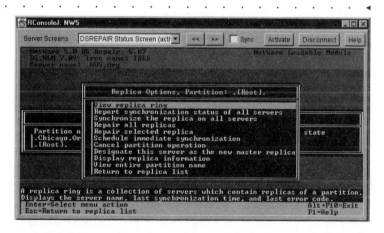

The following selections are available under the Replica and Partition Operations menu in DSRepair.

- *View Replica Ring* — All partitions and replicas that are shown in the local server's Directory database are shown when this selection is activated.

- *Report Synchronization Status on the Selected Server* — This option produces a report showing the current synchronization status of the ring that the server is in.

- *Synchronize the Replica on the Selected Server* — This option synchronizes the replica ring that the selected server is in.

- *Repair All Replicas* — This option is used to repair all replicas in replica ring. If this is the master replica server for the tree, you will have the option to select a replica ring to fix.

- *Repair Selected Replica* — This option enables you to select and repair a specific replica.

- *Schedule Immediate Sync* — This option starts a synchronization operation.

- *Cancel Partition Operation* — This option stops partition operations in process.

NOTE

Partitioning operations are extremely time consuming and should be scheduled for off-hours. Expect any type of partitioning operation to take several hours even on very powerful servers.

- *Designate This Server as the New Master Replica* — Use this option to reconfigure this server as the master, switching roles with the read/write or read-only partition you choose.

- *Display Replica Information* — This option produces a report listing all replicas and the status of each in the working ring.

- *View Entire Partition Name (fully distinguished name)* — This option shows the X.500 fully distinguished name. This is how the partition name must be expressed in DS operations.

When you select the View Replica Ring menu selection from the Advanced Options menu, you must select a replica ring; the submenu will then enable you to perform the following options:

▶ *Report Synchronization Status on the Selected Server* — This option produces a report showing the current synchronization status of the ring that the server is in.

▶ *Synchronize the Replica on the Selected Server* — This option synchronizes the replica ring that the selected server is in.

▶ *Send All Objects to Every Replica in the Ring* — This option sends out updates from the master to all other replicas in the selected ring.

▶ *Receive All Objects from the Master to This Replica* — This option requests updates from the master within the selected ring.

▶ *View Entire Partition Name* — This option displays the X.500 fully distinguished name. Use this name when entering the server name in DSRepair operations.

NOTE

You will find extensive documentation on all DSRepair operations in your NetWare 5 Online Documentation under Troubleshooting → Directory Services → Performing Repair Operations.

Repair Procedures

After diagnosing a problem or determining a problem that is related to a cure, you should find that a few repair procedures should be effective. For example, a resynchronization will fix minor problems that have to do with slow authentication.

Use NDS Manager, DSDiagnostics, and DSRepair to view statistics and test status for your replicas and partitions. Once you find errors and inconsistencies, you will have a good idea of which direction to proceed. The following repair procedures are the most common and should serve to put your system back into efficient and effective use.

If a problem that has caused Directory damage is not fixed, the Directory will continue to experience damage. DSRepair can force fixes but does not automatically fix the contributing factors. Use DSDiagnostics to locate problems and then fix what you can locate before running DSRepair operations.

Resynchronizing

NDS updates are replicated to the replica servers in real time — or *almost* real time. Any network can cause delays in propagating updates, but WANs are especially prone to delays from congestion and are subject to downtime. Because NDS is completely object-oriented, many operations such as moving a container, merging or separating trees, and cutting and pasting can generate massive NDS update traffic. Much of the complexity is based on replication and partitioning in your network. NDS is designed to handle normal delays in stride, but many unavoidable situations — such as intermittent WAN connections — can cause corruption during an update. Because delay is unavoidable, updates are time-stamped and applied in sequential order. Of course you can see that proper synchronization is highly dependent upon time service, but other several other factors can also cause replicated databases to become out of synch.

When a replica server is down, NDS holds updates and forwards them when the replica server is again in service. The time-stamped updates are then applied in sequential order. Because updates are not entire records, even two nonconflicting changes to the same object are applied without one overwriting the other. For example, one administrator can add a trustee to an object while another changes its object properties — both changes will be applied.

Updates consist of very small amounts of data. Under normal circumstances NDS synchronization traffic is minimal. Periodically, you should check for replica consistency and synchronize replicas where necessary. These processes are handled with the DSRepair server-based utility. When administering remote sites, you can use the RCONSOLE or RCONSOLEJ utilities to run DSRepair remotely.

To resynchronize, you may need to send updates or receive updates from a master replica.

NOTE

When performing any DSRepair operations, use the X.500 fully distinguished name. If you do not know what this name is, check for menu selections — wherever the fully distinguished name of an object is required, you will find a menu selection that will display the name for you.

To send an update to all replicas:

1. Log in as Admin of the tree, or as container administrator with NDS rights to supervise the replica server.

2. Start NDS Manager from a 32-bit Windows client.

3. Right-click the master replica.

4. Select Send Update.

5. Confirm to proceed.

6. Confirm that preconditions have been met or answer No if preconditions need to be executed.

7. A confirmation box will indicate that the operation has been submitted to NDS or will indicate why the operation cannot be performed.

To receive updates from a master replica:

1. Log in as Admin of the tree, or as container administrator with NDS rights to supervise the replica server.

2. Start NDS Manager from a 32-bit Windows client.

3. Right-click the read/write or read-only replica.

4. Select Receive Updates as shown in Figure 18.11.

5. Confirm to proceed.

6. Confirm that preconditions have been met or answer No if preconditions need to be executed.

7. A confirmation box will indicate that the operation has been submitted to NDS or will indicate why the operation cannot be performed.

When you right-click a read/write replica, you will see replica status as shown in Figure 18.11.

FIGURE 18.11

A menu obtained from
right-clicking a read/write
replica

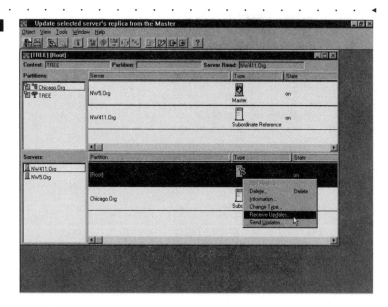

Figure 18.12 illustrates a typical error notification box that may appear.

FIGURE 18.12

A synchronization error
dialog box

To synchronize in DSRepair:

1. Access a replica server console, preferably the master replica server for the tree.

2. Type the command **LOAD DSREPAIR** at the colon prompt.

3. Select Advanced Options → Replica and Partition Operations. Select a partition/master replica to be synchronized from the list of replicas and check Synchronize the Replica on All Servers.

4. Log into the tree as Admin or a user account that has Supervisory DNS rights to the container in which the master replica resides.

To send all updates in DSRepair:

1. Access a replica server console, preferably the master replica server for the tree.

2. Type the command **LOAD DSREPAIR** at the colon prompt.

3. Select Advanced Options → Replica and Partition Operations. Select a partition/master replica to be synchronized from the list of replicas, click View Replica Ring, select the replica to send from, and check Send All Objects to Every Replica in the Ring.

To receive updates in DSRepair:

1. Access a replica server console, preferably the master replica server for the tree.

2. Type the command **LOAD DSREPAIR** at the colon prompt.

3. Select Advanced Options → Replica and Partition Operations. Select a partition/master replica to be synchronized from the list of replicas, click View Replica Ring, select the replica to send from, and check Receive All Objects from the Master to This Replica.

To schedule immediate synchronization:

1. Access a replica server console, preferably the master replica server for the tree.

2. Type the command **LOAD DSREPAIR** at the colon prompt.

3. Select Advanced Options → Replica and Partition Operations. Select the partition/replica master to be synchronized and check Schedule Immediate Synchronization.

In order to clean up all problems and all suspected irregularities at one time, run DSRepair's full repair option. This utility should clear up anything that ails your system or let you know what should be fixed.

To run an unattended full repair in DSRepair:

1. Access the master replica server console (locally, through Rconsole, or RConsoleJ).

2. Load DSREPAIR at the console screen.

3. Select Unattended Full Repair from the Available Options (main) menu.

4. Log in as Admin or with the user account that has Supervisory NDS rights over the master replica server. The full repair will run immediately.

An unattended full repair will run immediately and will display a log when finished.

NOTE

When logging in within DSRepair, always use the fully distinguished name for the master replica server. For example, the default administrator of the tree is CN=Admin.O=*organization_name*. In some cases you will find that a typeless name is not recognized.

If you have already logged in to run a DSRepair process and have not exited the program, you may not need to log in again when running another DSRepair process.

Repair Options in DSRepair

DSRepair provides a single-step solution to diagnosing and fixing all minor inequities in NDS. To perform a comprehensive full repair, select Unattended Full Repair from the Available Options menu. This option performs all DSRepair options and then displays the log report. This option can force some repairs, but it is suggested that you find problems first and then apply a specific fix. In some cases, the unattended full repair cannot force a fix until an error has been resolved.

Repair Operations in the Advanced Options Menu

You will find the following repair options under the Advanced Options menu in DSRepair:

- *Repair a Local DS Database* — Diagnoses and repairs DS database corruption. When corruption is found, you should evaluate how the corruption occurred and how to resolve the problem that caused it.

- *Synchronize Security Equivalences* — This option reestablishes lost pointers to security equivalences. Use this option when group memberships and other security equivalences do not work.

Replica and Partition Operations, View Replica Ring

You will find the following repair options in DSRepair under Available Options → Advanced Options → Replica and Partition Operations. You will need to select a partition to work on before proceeding and then select View Replica Ring.

- *Synchronize All Replicas on This Server* — Performs a full synchronization of all replicas in this partition and other partitions contained in this server. Partitions are hosted by a master replica, and servers that have subpartitions also contain replicated copies of the master replicas for those partitions.

WARNING

This option can cause massive updates to occur that may take several hours and can involve many servers. If your partitioning is complex, execute this process only when partitions are found to be out of synch.

▶ *Repair All Replicas* — This option will attempt a repair on all replicas contained in this server. You should always run a database repair on each replica server — Repair a Local DS Database (on highlighted replica) — before performing this step.

▶ *Repair Selected Replicas* — This option will attempt a repair on the replicas contained in the local server. You should always run a database repair on each replica server — Repair a Local DS Database — before performing this step.

▶ *Schedule Immediate Synchronization* — Schedules a replica synchronization in the working ring.

▶ *Designate This Server as the New Master Replica* — This option is used to exchange roles between a master replica and a read-only or read/write replica in the working ring. Use this option if the existing master replica must be removed from service permanently or for an extensive period. See the section in this chapter entitled "Extended Shutdown and Replica Removal Procedure" for more details.

Global Schema Repair Operations

The global schema is the system or rules and definitions for object properties. The schema establishes the content and format of each object and its relationship with other objects in the DS database. When the global schema is corrupted, DS operations are quite problematic. To update, report, or reset the global schema in all replicas contained on the local server, select Global Schema Operations from the Available Options → Advanced Options menu.

▶ *Update the Server's Schema* — This option updates the global schema of the [root] partition of the entire NDS tree.

▶ *Import Remote Schema* — This option imports a schema from a selected tree so that both trees will have identical schemas.

Maintenance Procedures

Several maintenance procedures are used to keep an existing tree healthy and to make changes to the tree. The following options are maintenance operations that may need to be performed on occasion. As discussed in "Recommendations for Replication and Partitioning," you may need to add remove or merge partitions to accommodate better performance and fault tolerance. NetWare 4.11 servers should be updated before adding NetWare 4.2 and 5 servers. If you need to remove a server from the tree for an extended period, this section provides instructions.

WARNING

Most partition changes, such as a partition merge, are extremely processor-intensive and should be scheduled during off-hours, preferably over a weekend or holiday. Even when no activity is present and the tree is small, some of these operations can take several hours to complete.

Adding a Replica

Adding a replica is done in one of two ways: either the replica is added using the server INSTALL application during server installation, or using NDS Manager after a server has been installed without a replica.

When installing a server into an existing tree or partition, two read/write replicas will be added. When three replicas are found in an existing partition, additional servers are installed without replicas.

To add a replica to an existing ring:

1. Log in as Admin of the tree, or as container administrator with NDS rights to supervise the replica server.

2. Start NDS Manager from a 32-bit Windows client.

3. Select View → Partitions and Servers.

4. Select the master replica server in the top screen pane and then select Object → Add Replica.

5. Select the Read-Only or Read/Write radio button for the type of replica.

6. Select the server in the Server Name box by selecting the NDS Search button. Select OK to create the replica.

Adding a Partition

When you use installation defaults, no partitions are created except the [Root] partition. To segment your NDS tree into partitions, use NDS Manager.

When creating a new partition, be sure that each partition has at least two servers and at least two replicas in its ring. As discussed previously, three replicas in a ring provide more comprehensive fault tolerance.

To partition with NDS Manager:

1. Log in as Admin of the tree, or as container administrator with NDS rights to supervise the replica server.

2. Start NDS Manager from a 32-bit Windows client.

3. Select View → Tree to see the tree view of the network.

4. In the left screen pane, select the Organizational unit in which to create the new partition.

5. Select Object → Create Partition.

Removing a Replica

Removing a replica is an operation that should be planned before execution. Be sure you maintain fault tolerance in every partition with a replica ring of two or three servers.

WARNING

Before removing a replica, be sure you have removed all references to the replica.

To remove a replica in NDS Manager:

1. Log in as Admin of the tree, or as container administrator with NDS rights to supervise the replica server.

2. Start NDS Manager from a 32-bit Windows client.

3. Select View → Tree to view the tree.

4. Right-click the replica to be deleted.

5. Select Delete.

Removing a Partition

Removing a partition is accomplished by removing Directory Services from a server in the INSTALL or NWCONFIG server-based application.

 Removing a partition removes all replicas and DS objects from that partition.

WARNING

To remove a partition in INSTALL or NWCONFIG:

1. Access the master replica server console (locally, through Rconsole, or RConsoleJ).

2. Load NWCONFIG or INSTALL.

3. Select Directory Options → Remove Directory Services from This Server. Observe the warning screen — read it carefully — this step will disable all Directory Services on this server and cannot be reversed. You will be prompted to log in to the tree as Admin or with Supervisory NDS rights to the server.

Merging Partitions

If your intent is to eliminate the partition but retain the NS objects that it contains, you will need to merge the partition with an existing partition in the same tree.

 A partition merge is a very processor-intensive task that can take several hours for even the smallest of trees. Schedule this type of operation on a weekend—a holiday weekend is best.
NOTE

To merge partitions:

1. Log in as Admin of the tree, or as container administrator with NDS rights to supervise the replica server.

2. Start NDS Manager from a 32-bit Windows client.

3. Select View → Partitions and Servers.

4. In the left server pane, right-click the lower-level partition to be merged.

5. Select Merge. You will see a Partition operation status screen. Selecting Close will not abort the operation; however, selecting Abort will. If you close this screen you can abort the partition operation in the DSRepair Replica and Partition Operations menu.

If you need to halt any partition operation, you can do so without causing damage. Updated partitioning is not implemented until the operation is completed.

To cancel an ongoing partition operation in DSRepair:

1. Access the master replica server console (locally, through Rconsole, or RConsoleJ).

2. Load DSREPAIR at the console screen.

3. Select Advanced Options → Replica and Partition Operations → Cancel Partition Operation.

Updating NDS Version on NetWare 4.11 Servers from NetWare 5 CD

When integrating NetWare 5 and NetWare 4.11 servers, all older servers must be upgraded to NetWare 4.11 with Directory Services version 5.99 or later. You will find the DS upgrade on the NetWare 5 operating system CD.

The release notes will tell you that you can install the upgrade manually, but you should install it using the server INSTALL application so that new NDS Manager utilities and help files will be installed automatically.

NOTE **IntranetWare Service Pack 6 is available from Novell at no cost. Included in this update is DS v6.00. You can order Service Pack 6 from Novell or download it. Search for the service pack by name, IWSP6.EXE (or a later version) at** `http://support.novell` `.com/search/ff_index.htm`.

To update a NetWare 4.11 server DS from the NetWare 5 CD:

1. Load INSTALL.NLM at the NetWare 4.11 server console.

2. Select Product Options → Install a Product not Listed.

3. Select F3 and specify the path to NetWare 5 operating system CD in the \Products\411_upg\nds directory. Press Enter to start the upgrade process.

Expect a brief DS shutdown during the procedure. Several files will be upgraded. You will not need to reboot your server.

You can update other servers from a workstation using NDS Manager when a NetWare 5 or updated NetWare 4.11 server is online.

To update all NetWare servers' DS from NDS Manager:

1. Log in as Admin of the tree, or as container administrator with NDS rights to supervise the replica server.

2. Start NDS Manager from a 32-bit Windows client.

3. Select the NetWare Server object to be source for updated DS-related files.

4. Select Object → NDS Version → Update. A list of eligible servers will be displayed. If any servers in or below the target context cannot be upgraded, they will be grayed out.

5. Select the server to updated from the list of servers on the left and then select the right arrow to move the server to the list of servers to be upgraded.

6. Select OK; the update files will be copied to the target servers.

Brief Shutdown Procedure

It is no longer necessary to remove a replica before a brief shutdown. NetWare 4.11, 4.2, and 5 with DS version 5.99 and later can gracefully recover from brief shutdowns without the need for extraordinary precautions.

However, before taking any replica server offline, consider the consequences. In every server's lifetime there will come a time when a brief shutdown is required. To update hardware, replace a failing component, or upgrade server hardware you may have to take a server out of service for anywhere from a few minutes to several days. You may wish to replace a server with a new server, but retain the existing disk subsystem — or you may need to upgrade a NIC, add new ones, or install additional memory. Whatever your reason might be, the procedure will not necessarily require removing then reinstalling NDS on the server if the shutdown period is brief.

In some organizations, a central support staff installs and deploys servers and then ships them to the remote facility. In addition to brief shutdowns, this discussion contains recommendations for remote deployments. If the server can be deployed and resynchronized within a few days, the recommendations for a brief shutdown apply with a few caveats.

A brief shutdown is considered a week or less, but the period is really influenced by the number of administrative changes in your Directory during the shutdown. The stated definitions for brief versus extended periods also depends upon the size of your tree, and the complexity of your replication and partitioning. If a replica server is to be out of service for an extended period, see the section "Extended Shutdown and Replica Removal Procedure" later in this chapter.

During this time, NDS replication traffic will be stored automatically and synchronized when the server is back online. However, you should take a few precautions before the operation, observe some rules during the shutdown period, and follow these recommendations for performing a brief shutdown and resynchronization.

NOTE

Try to keep administrative updates to a minimum during a brief shutdown. Postpone any updates to replication within the partition, and changes to the local partitioning until all replica servers are back online and verified to by synchronized without errors.

Under no circumstances should a new replica be added to the local partition until all replicas are back online.

To perform a brief shutdown:

1. Check replica status, fix all error conditions.

2. Perform all updates possible — clear up backlogged work and try to get ahead if possible.

3. Resynchronize the partition.

4. Make a full backup of the replica server.

5. Pull the plug! But get the server back online as soon as possible.

6. When the server is back online, resynchronize. Select the replica and then use the Receive Updates option in NDS Manager.

Upgrading Server Hardware

When replacing a disk subsystem or an entire server, you can back up DS data stored on a server and replace it on the new system. The option to back up and restore the DS is provided in the NetWare server install program (INSTALL.NLM for NetWare 4.11, 4.2, and NWCONFIG.NLM in NetWare 5).

The following procedure requires two servers — the server to be upgraded and one other that has enough space to accommodate the DS backup.

NOTE

Use the following procedure to back up and then restore when replacing hardware:

1. Do a full backup of all data contained on the server volumes. You do not need to back up the SYS:System or SYS:Public directories.

2. Load NWCONFIG.NLM (or INSTALL.NLM) on the server to be upgraded.

3. Select Directory Options → Remove Directory Services from This Server. Enter the tree Admin user name and password when prompted.

4. When prompted to "Enter the placeholder object distinguished name," enter or select a user object to hold the server references. The default will be the host server name, but only a user object is acceptable — the Admin account is a good choice, but any user object with Supervisory NDS rights to the server that is being removed from service will do. When entering this name, use the fully distinguished name (such as CN=Admin.O-Org).

5. When prompted to "Change from which distinguished name and below" enter the container in which the server object resides or any container that is above the server in the tree. The default is [Root].

6. If the server to be taken out of service is a read-only or read/write replica, you can continue. If the server to be taken out of service is a master replica server, you will be prompted to exchange roles with another replica in the ring. This will make the other replica a master and will make the master a read/write replica. When this process is completed, you will be returned to the Directory Services Options menu.

7. Select Remove Directory Services from This Server. You will see a warning screen. Read the instructions and then press Enter to confirm that you wish to remove Directory Services from the server. You will be prompted to log in with the Admin password to continue. You will not need to reconfigure other objects, since you will restore the replica within a short amount of time.

After completing this procedure, replace the server and/or disk subsystem. Next you will reinstall the operating system on the newly installed system and then restore the Directory Services.

To restore Directory Services:

1. Install the NetWare 4.11, 4.2, or 5 operating system on the server. When prompted to install Directory Services, skip this step. Finish the installation and exit to the console prompt.

2. Restore data backups, but do not restore the operating system or Directory Services — the SYS:System and SYS:Public directories should not be restored.

3. Load NWCONFIG.NLM (or INSTALL.NLM), select Directory options → Directory Backup and Restore Options → Restore References from Another Object to This Server.

4. Enter the fully distinguished name of the placeholder object — the user account that the server references to which the server references were saved in step 3 in the backup procedure. This will restore your replica to its state at the time of backup. This process will reregister the volumes and data without destroying existing data.

5. From a workstation, log in as Admin, start NDS Manager, select the replica that has been restored, and initiate a Receive Updates synchronization. When the synchronization has been completed without errors, the procedure is completed.

6. If the replica on this server was a master replica that was converted to a read/write replica in the backup procedure, you can switch it back to a master replica by following the Change Replica Type procedure discussed in this chapter.

To change replica type:

1. Log in as Admin of the tree, or as container administrator with NDS rights to supervise the replica server.

2. Start NDS Manager from a 32-bit Windows client.

3. Right-click the read-only or read/write replica to be changed, select Change Type from the menu.

4. In the Change Replica Type dialog box that appears, select the Master radio button. This box will list as the server name, the name of the server to become the master replica server.

5. In the Change Replica Type dialog box that appears next, the existing master replica server name will appear. Select Read/Write or Read-Only to configure the existing master replica accordingly. When you select OK, the process will be submitted to NDS for processing, or a dialog box will explain why the process cannot be performed.

Extended Shutdown and Replica Removal Procedure

When taking a replica server offline for an extended period, the DS replica should be removed. However, you must plan and prepare for this type of procedure and follow some recommendations to ensure minimum impact of Directory replication and resource availability.

 Failure to follow the proper procedures for taking a replica offline for an extended period can cause considerable damage to the DS replication process and result in downtime.

WARNING

To remove a server:

1. In NetWare Administrator remove all objects that map to the server to be eliminated. Remove all references to the objects such as drive mappings, printer captures, and replica references in NDS.

2. Remove DS via NWCONFIG or INSTALL.

3. Verify that the server object and volume objects have been removed in NetWare Administrator.

4. When replacing the server, install NDS in NWCONFIG.

Time Service

The time service is necessary to keep NDS information synchronized among servers. NDS relies on a synchronized time service for synchronized NDS information that is almost real time. Without good time synchronization, multiuser administration is not possible, and administrative updates can become confused. There are four types of time servers:

- Single reference

- Reference

- Primary

- Secondary

Even in NDS, a server must service each client attachment to enable login to NDS. During attachment, the client workstation's time is updated. All servers provide time to the workstations that they are servicing. Secondary time servers are updated by Single Reference, Reference, or Primary time servers. This basic mechanism allows the entire internetwork to maintain time in a synchronized manner.

In a small NDS tree where there is only one server, the Single Reference server is your only logical choice. Reference time servers can be substituted for a Single Reference time server. In NDS trees where multiple servers are installed, the Secondary time servers are updated from the Single Reference or Reference time server. When building trees in internetworks where remote locations are connected by WANs, Primary time servers substitute for the Single Reference or

Reference time servers for their locations. For example, if an internetwork had locations in LA and NYC, one location would have a Single Reference or Reference time server, and the other location would have a Primary time server. All other servers would be configured as Secondary time servers and would be updated by the Single Reference, Reference, or Primary time server in the same location. All time servers update client workstation clocks when they attach to a server prior to login.

Single Reference

When installing the first server in a new tree and all servers are connected with LANs, the Single Reference time server provides time to other servers and clients. It takes the time from its hardware clock and updates other servers configured as Secondary time servers. Single Reference time servers do not synchronize with any other time servers; other time servers synchronize with them. There should only be one Single Reference time server in a tree.

Reference

A Reference time server is used when the time is to be obtained from an external source. The Reference time server is simply substituted for the Single Reference time server. If there is more than one Reference time server in a tree, all the Reference time servers should be synchronized by referring to the same source. To effectively use a Reference time server, you must have a time source. You can install a highly accurate internal clock, such as an atomic clock, or use a server-based application to get time from one of several sources on a periodic basis.

Primary

When time servers are separated by WANs, time synchronization must be handled differently between servers in the same geographic location and time servers in remote locations. Each geographic location should be served by a Primary, which will coordinate time with Primary time servers at other sites. Primary time servers poll one another and select a single time value.

Secondary

All servers in a tree that are not Single Reference, Reference, or Primary time servers should be configured as Secondary time servers. Secondary time servers get their time from the other types of time servers and provide the time to clients.

Maintaining Time Service

The following actions must be taken to synchronize time servers that have wandered, and to reconfigure time servers.

Synchronizing Time Service

Before processing any major DS synchronization process, time services should be synchronized. If time service console messages indicate that a server is out of synch with other time servers, synchronize them before starting other operations.

To synchronize time services:

1. Access the master replica server console (locally, through Rconsole, or RConsoleJ).

2. Load DSREPAIR at the console screen.

3. Select Time Synchronization from the Available Options menu.

This process will run immediately. A log will be displayed when completed.

Changing Time Server Type

Time server types just discussed are configured by changing a SET command in your AUTOEXEC.NCF file. You can adjust this parameter manually, or you can use the MONITOR.NLM on your server. You will find that MONITOR is better, since it checks syntax before saving.

To change the time server type:

1. Access the server console for the time server to be adjusted (locally, through Rconsole, or RConsoleJ).

2. Load MONITOR.NLM.

3. From the Available Options menu, select Server Parameters → Time.

4. Scroll down to the TIMESYNCH Type field.

5. Manually enter the type of time server — Single, Primary, Reference, or Secondary — according to the discussion earlier in this section. Press Esc to exit and save.

6. Reboot the server.

7. Load DSREPAIR, and select Time synchronization.

This process will update the time server type and resynchronize time.

Additional Resources

The following resources are available to provide greater depth in NDS design and implementation. You will find that many of these resources are available at no cost.

▸ See your NetWare 5 online documentation. Each topic is organized according to Contents, Procedures, Troubleshooting, Reference, and Novell Links in HTML format that is cross-referenced and easy to use. Look for Directory Services under Network Services at the second or third level in any of these sections.

▸ Novell Education offers an advanced course, *NDS Design and Implementation* (course #575). You can take this course at a Novell Authorized Training Center (NAEC) near you. You will find a detailed outline, current information on this and other Novell courses, certification requirements, and a listing of NAECs in the Novell Education Web site at `http://education.novell.com/`.

▶ Novell Press has several books on NDS. See the Novell Press Web site at `http://www.novell.com/books/`. You will find the following two books helpful to extend material presented in this chapter.

- *Novell's Four Principles of NDS Design* by Jeffrey F. Hughes and Blair W. Thomas (IDG Books Worldwide)

- *NDS for NT* by Jeffrey F. Hughes and Blair W. Thomas (IDG Books Worldwide)

▶ Technical Information Documents (TIDs) address selected significant support issues. Look for current support issues by searching key words in the Knowledgebase index. You will find TIDs on the Novell Support Connection CD (available on a subscription basis) and on Novell's Web site at `http://www.support/novell.com/`.

▶ AppNotes are published monthly by the Novell Research team and address selected significant technical issues in a "white paper" format. Novell's top support engineers select topics to publish each month — the most current and significant NDS-related topics are discussed in detail in monthly articles. You will find AppNotes dating back several years on the Novell Support Connection CD (available on a subscription basis) and on Novell's Web site. The best location to view AppNotes is the Novell DeveloperNet site at `http://developer.novell.com/research/appnotes.htm`. You will find that DeveloperNet indexes the articles and makes searching by topic easier.

You will find several excellent references for maintaining and troubleshooting NDS in Novell's AppNotes.

NOTE

This list is ordered by date. More recent AppNotes should be reviewed first, as older AppNotes may address issues that have been resolved or modified in newer versions and in updates.

▶ Amitabh Sinha, *Novell DNS/DHCP Services: Design Issues and Troubleshooting*, November 1998

- Dave Doering, *Troubleshooting Synchronization using NDS Manager,* August 1998

- Dave Doering, *Troubleshooting Synchronization with NDS Manager,* August 1998

- John Mehl, *Using DSREPAIR to Maintain the Novell Directory Services Database,* May 1998

- Williamson and Anaraki, *Maintaining a Healthy NDS Tree pt 1 and 2,* August and October 1997

- Hendry-Caver and Kneff, *Using the Directory Services Trace (DSTRACE) Screen,* February 1997

- Ron Lee, *Ten Proven Techniques to Increase NDS Performance and Reliability,* April 1996

- Ron Lee, *Universal Guidelines for NDS Tree Design.* April 1996

- Novell, Inc., *Troubleshooting Tips for NetWare Directory Services,* August 1995

You will also find the following Technical Information Documents (TID) discussing NDS. You can locate these documents at the Knowledgebase in Novell Support's Web site at `http://support.novell.com/servlet/Knowledgebase/`.

- *Troubleshooting Tips for NetWare Directory Services,* TID 30065

- *DS Quick Tips,* TID 21875

- *Replica and Partition Operation in DSRepair,* TID 2909077

- *Partition Manipulation,* TID 21559

CHAPTER 19

Printing and NDPS

NetWare's traditional queue-based printing architecture has serviced uncountable print jobs for almost a decade. Queue-based printing is solid — you can depend on your print job being handled with the greatest reliability. NDS and queue-based printing have added the complexity of matching components of the queue-based printing process with NDS rights. This is not a serious complication, but Novell engineers have been concerned about making this aspect easier for novices to use. Administrators have also lobbied for printer exposure with no security restrictions. Your queue can be exposed to all network users without restrictions, but it takes a little more knowledge of NDS "tricks of the trade." Later model printers use bidirectional feedback — an area where the queue represents and obstacle to real-time communications between the printer and NOS. For these reasons, traditional queue-based printing was due for an overhaul.

NetWare 5's Novell Distributed Print Services (NDPS) represents the most advanced network printing environment. NDPS in NetWare 5 is not a 1.0 version — it has been refined since its inception and introduction of NDPS 1.0 with NetWare 4.11. NetWare 5's NDPS version 2.0 in conjunction with vendor-supplied Printer Agents and printer gateways is as solid and dependable as printing can be. NetWare printing reflects many years of experience and combined development efforts with printer manufacturers. The cooperative efforts that produced NDPS version 2.0 make administrators' lives easier and add productivity to the job of producing picture-perfect output and providing new printer features to the end user.

Traditional queue-based printing will not disappear anytime soon, but as administrators use NDPS, they will find it is a more robust, more efficient, and simpler printing architecture. As vendor support increases, the incentives to use NDPS will become more obvious. The additional printer communications features are viewed as indispensable once the administrator gets used to them.

NetWare shops will find it difficult at best to switch to NDPS overnight — and it is not necessary to. This chapter discusses both traditional queue-based, and NDPS, and combined printing services. The best approach for troubleshooting printing is to first make sure you have set up your system properly. This chapter discusses mechanics and setup as well as troubleshooting. In many cases, referring to proper setup is all that is required to deliver print jobs without problems.

Traditional Queue-Based Printing

NetWare's traditional queue-based printing service has serviced networks for many years. Queue-based printing is more complex than the latest alternative, Novell Distributed Print Services (NDPS). NDPS is simpler to set up and manage, and is certainly more advanced, than queue-based printing. However, most Novell networks have established queue-based printing in their networks, and there is no compelling reason to immediately change to NDPS. You can retain your queue-based printing and set up NDPS for new printers. As you acclimate to NDPS, you will probably like it better, and you can take your time converting. Queue-based printing is so prevalent that it certainly cannot be ignored even when the focus is on NetWare 5.

Queue-based printing is all that you can use in a NetWare 3 environment— NetWare 4.11 uses NDPS 1.0 or queue-based printing, and NetWare 5 gives you a choice between NDPS and queue-based printing. In both NetWare 4.11 and 5, you are able to support both NDPS and queue-based printing.

Print Processing

The traditional NetWare queue-based printing environment is made up of the following components:

- Queue object
- Printer object
- PSERVER.NLM and print server object
- Local server port driver support module (NPRINTER.NLM)
- Remote printer port driver support module (NPTWIN95.EXE or NPRINTER.EXE)

The print process has two distinctly separate steps. First, the job is spooled to a queue. Once the print job has finished spooling and the spool file has closed, the print server directs the print job to print to a printer device.

Step 1: Print Redirection and Spooling to a Queue

Every print job must be redirected to a NetWare *queue*. A queue is a file that buffers the print job before it is dispatched to its next step, as shown in Figure 19.1.

▶ · ◀

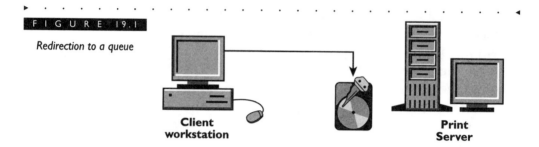

F I G U R E   19.1

Redirection to a queue

Client workstation

Print Server

For Windows workstations, the print job is redirected to the queue through Windows printer setup. A network printer is set up, which is in turn redirected to the NetWare queue. The NetWare queue substitutes for the printer in the Microsoft network print model. As far as the application software that has sent the print job is concerned, delivering the job to the queue has completed the print job. The print redirection components are installed when you install Novell Client 32 or Microsoft Client for Novell Networks services.

For DOS workstations, redirection is accomplished through the NetWare CAPTURE command line utility. CAPTURE redirects print output that was sent to a parallel port to a queue. Alternatively, an application can redirect print output by using NetWare APIs, which accomplish the same result as a CAPTURE command. Few vendors use NetWare APIs for printing. Whichever method is used, the workstation print module in the NetWare DOS client software monitors memory, intercepting and redirecting the print output to the NIC, across the LAN where a file server spools the printing to a binary file. The CAPTURE command is usually automated in a login script, or it can be issued in a menu or batch file at the time the application is executed.

Step 2: Spooling Output to a Network Printer

After the print job is finished spooling to a queue, the NetWare Print Server utility takes over to direct the print job to a printer device. The entire print job must finish spooling to the queue before it can be handled by the print server. The

Print Server is configured to service the queue, and to use the printer object. Every 15 seconds the Print Server polls the queue — when a closed spool file is found, the file is opened and directed to the printer device.

If the printer is server-attached, the job is sent to a local server port. Figure 19.2 traces print jobs redirected to a local server port. Notice that the physical path the print job takes is to be spooled from Client 32 to the disk and then redirected to a port on the print server. The logical path is simply from the application software to the server's printer.

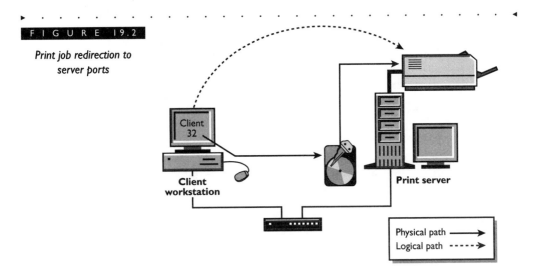

▶ • ◀

F I G U R E 19.2

Print job redirection to server ports

Client 32

Client workstation

Print server

Physical path ——→
Logical path ----→

Remote printers can be used by loading the Windows port driver software (NPTWIN95.EXE), or the DOS port driver (NPRINTER.EXE for NetWare 4 and 5, or RPRINTER.EXE for NetWare 3). Figure 19.3 traces print jobs redirected to a remote workstation port. Notice that the physical path the print job takes is to be spooled to from Client 32 to the disk and then redirected by the print server to a remote printer port serviced by NPTWIN95.EXE. The logical path is simply from the application software to the remote printer.

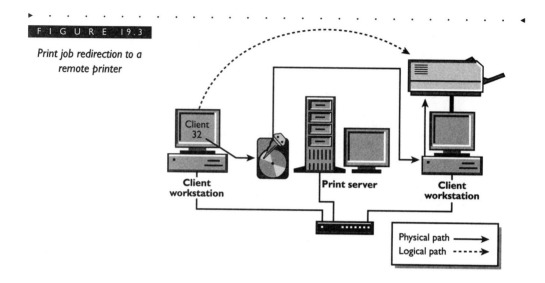

▶ · ◀

F I G U R E   19.3

Print job redirection to a
remote printer

Setting Up Queue-Based Printing

The queue, print server, and printer objects are created and configured in NetWare Administrator or with the PCONSOLE or NETADMIN menu utilities. NDS rights are prominent in configuring the printer objects—the user objects must have access to the queue objects, and the print server object must have access to the queues and the printer objects. User objects do not need to have access to the print server or printer objects.

NDS Rights to Use Queue-Based Printing

A common scenario for creating and configuring print objects is to create a resource container to host all the print objects and print user groups. Making users members of the print user group provides all rights necessary to use the print queue through security equivalences. Another option is to create an alias for the queue object, placing it in the user object's container. Another way to accomplish this goal is to place the queue in the user object's container and then to make the print server a trustee of the queue. There are several ways to extend the appropriate NDS rights as needed. Just remember that without rights, the objects are not accessible.

NOTE To print, the user must have **NDS Browse and Write rights to the queue. For the print server to service the queue, it must have NDS Browse, Read, and Modify rights to the queue and to the printer.**

The Quick Setup Method

During installation, no printer or print server configuration is automatically created for you, and no printing services exist until you create them. The easiest way to set up queue-based printing is to use the Print Services Quick Setup (Non-NDPS) menu selection in NetWare Administrator's Tools menu shown in Figure 19.4.

FIGURE 19.4

The Print Services Quick Setup (Non-NDPS) menu selection

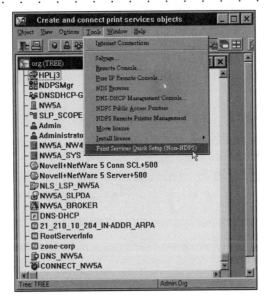

This utility will create a print server object, printer object, and queue object in the NDS container of your choice as shown in Figure 19.5.

► . . . . ◄

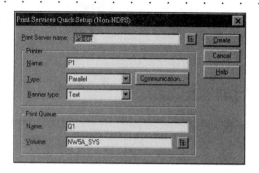

FIGURE 19.5

Creating the print server, printer, and queue objects in Quick Setup

As you can see, Quick Setup makes creating the first printer and queue objects simple. After saving your configuration, you can activate your queue-based print setup by loading PSERVER.NLM at the NetWare server console where the queue volume is located. To provide access to users, create a print queue users group object in the same container with the queue and then make users members of the group. As discussed previously, you can use any one of several methods to provide users with NDS rights to use print queues.

NOTE

In order to perform this process, the administrator must have Browse, Read, Create, Modify, and Write rights (or Supervisor rights) to the container in which the print setup will be created. It is also necessary to have Supervisor file system rights to the volume in which the queue will be created.

When installing a network-attached printer, like a Hewlett-Packard LaserJet with a Jet Direct printer network card or an "Si" (network-prepared) model network model, it is not necessary to load PSERVER or to configure a PSERVER to service the printer. Using Hewlett-Packard's setup software (JetAdmin), you can configure the device itself as a print server.

Once this process has proved successful, you can create more queues and printers. To add more queues and printers, see the steps that follow.

NetWare 3 and 4 also have a quick setup for printing. You will find the quick setup option in the PCONSOLE menu utility in NetWare 3.

Setting Up Queue-Based Print Services Manually

To set up a queue-based print service requires that you manually create three objects and configure assignments among them. You will create:

▸ A printer object (one is required for each printer)

▸ A print server object (only one is required for up to 255 printers)

▸ A print queue object (typically one queue is configured to print to one printer)

NOTE **In order to perform this process, the administrator must have Browse, Read, Create, Modify, and Write rights (or Supervisor) rights to the container in which the print setup will be created. It is also necessary to have Supervisor file system rights to the volume in which the queue will be created.**

Start by setting up the print objects and their configurations:

1. Log in as Admin or with supervisory rights to the container in which you will create the print objects. You must also have browse and create NDS rights to the volume to create the queue.

2. Run NetWare Administrator. Select a container in which your print objects will reside.

3. Create the print queue object. Select Object → Create and then select the Print Queue object. Select the Directory Service Queues radio button, assign a name to the print queue, select the volume on which the queue will be created, and then select OK. Repeat this procedure for each queue to be created.

4. Create a print server object. Select Object → Create and then select the Print Server (Non-NDPS) object. Enter a name for the print server and then select OK. One print server should be created for each collision domain or bridge domain.

5. Create a printer object. Select Object → Create and then select the Printer (Non-NDPS), assign a name to the printer, check the Define Additional Properties button, and then select OK. Select the Configuration button and configure the port configuration properties of the port to which the printer will be connected and then select OK. Repeat this procedure for each printer to be created.

6. Assign the print queue to the printer. Select the printer object and then select Object → Details → Assignments → Add. Locate and select the print queue that is to be redirected to this printer and then select OK. Repeat this procedure for each printer-queue pairing.

7. Assign the printer to the print server. Select the print server object and then select Object → Details → Assignments → Add. Locate and select the printer(s) that is (are) to be managed by the print server.

Next you must set up, and then load, the NetWare Print Server and the port drivers.

1. At the server console, load PSERVER with the server name. For example, if the print server name is PS-LA, and it is in the LA.Org container, type the following command:

```
load PSERVER PS-LA.LA.Org
```

2. Load the port driver module:

a. For a local port on the print server, load NPRINTER.NLM with the print server name and printer number. The printer number is found as one of the printer object's properties in NetWare Administrator. For example, if the printer will be attached to LPT1, which was configured as P1 (printer 0) in the LA.Org container, type the command:

load NPRINTER PS-LA.LA.Org 0

b. For a remote printer port on a Windows 95 or 98 workstation, execute the NPTWIN95.EXE program. You will find this program in the SYS:Public\Win95 directory of your NetWare 5 server. In the Add

Network Printer screen, select the NDS Printer radio button, locate and select the printer object, and then select OK. The Set Properties screen will appear. Select the LPT or COM port to which the printer will be attached and configure the port. Select the interrupt for the port or select Polled. If Activate Printer When Nprinter Manager Loads is checked, the remote printer port driver will remain loaded when you exit this utility.

Loading Remote Printer Support upon Boot

To configure the printer to be available at all times, copy the following list of required modules to the local drive and add NPTWIN95.EXE to the workstation's startup folder. Follow these instructions to set up automatic local loading:

1. Create a directory (folder) on the workstation local hard drive.

2. Copy the following files from the SYS:Public\Win95 directory to the directory created on the workstation local hard drive:

NPTWIN95.EXE

NPTR94.NLM

NPTDRV95.NLM

BIDS45F.DLL

CW3215.DLL

OWL252F.DLL

SH30W32.DLL

NRDDll95.DLL

Support Pack 6 for NetWare 4.11 includes updated drivers.

3. Copy the following files from the SYS:Public\nls*language* directory to the directory created on the workstation local hard drive:

NPTWIN95.DLL

NPTWIN95.HLP

NPTDRV95.MSG

4. Add NPTWIN95.EXE to your Startup folder. Edit the shortcut's properties, and add the /EXIT switch to the Target string. This will execute and then close Nprinter Manager during Windows logon.

All of the preceding files must be saved together in the same directory to ensure proper operation.

NOTE

Novell Distributed Print Services (NDPS)

NDPS is the first major change to Novell print services in many years. This new technology incorporates improved and simplified setup, control, and communications with printers. In addition to other benefits, it enables bidirectional printer communications and simplified NDS setup and rights requirements. In short, any feature a vendor incorporates into its printers can be accessed through NDPS.

NDPS printers can be set up as public printers, or subject to NDS rights and control. Because many printers are to be accessible to all employees, the public printer option is a welcome addition—no NDS rights assignments need be considered. Printers that are to be restricted can still take full advantage of NDS security.

NDPS provides the following benefits:

▶ *Centralized, simplified single-point administration*—NDPS enables the administrator to set up and manage printers in NetWare Administrator, and it never requires trips to the server or use of any other software.

► *Bidirectional printer feedback and control* — NDPS enables real-time bidirectional communication between printers and clients. Bidirectional feedback is as robust as the printer's capabilities. Clients and their software can now communicate with printers to become aware of print job and printer status. The user can see specific printer messages — such as printer warnings, error messages, form changes, and notification when the print job has been completed.

► *Configurable event notification* — NDPS offers improved and more detailed notification options. Users can receive messages from a Windows pop-up and messages can be forwarded to e-mail boxes (using GroupWise), and to log files. APIs are available to permit third-party software developers to direct printer and print job messages to their own software.

► *Tight integration with NDS* — NDPS is designed to take full advantage of NDS features, and to reduce management of each printer to one object only — the printer object. Once an NDPS print system is installed, no other objects need to be created or managed.

► *Automatic printer driver download and end user convenience* — NDPS printing is easier to administer and easier to use. Printer drivers are installed into an NDPS database once and then autodownloaded to clients as needed. The Novell Printer Manager utility enables users to install printers, search for printers with specific features, and gain access to them. It is not necessary to visit each desktop to install a new printer driver.

► *New printer and job configuration options* — As printer manufacturers add features, they are immediately available to NDPS users. Because the printer interface is controlled by the printer manufacturer, full support for new features is available without adding new NetWare components.

► *New job scheduling options* — New configuration options enable users to schedule print jobs according to time of day, job size, or media availability.

▶ *Protocol independence* — NDPS is not dependant upon IPX/SPX or TCP/IP, so NDSP works with either protocol stack, or both at the same time. Printer gateways developed by third parties do not rely on network protocols for their functionality and therefore are also universal. Service Advertising Protocol (SAP) is no longer required to make traditional printers available over NetWare networks. Instead, the print broker registers available services and makes them available without the need for SAP broadcasts. NDPS uses Service Locator Protocol (SLP), which is an IETF standard and will eventually be embedded into printer firmware to provide discovery functionality over TCP/IP networks.

▶ *Compatibility with multiple clients, applications, and operating systems* — All clients and all applications can print to NDPS printers even if they are not NDPS-aware. Novell currently provides NDPS-enhanced client software for Windows 3.*x*, 95, and NT. Only NDPS-enhanced clients can take full advantage of NDPS features. Full NDPS-enhanced functionality will be incorporated into other NetWare clients in the near future.

▶ *Support for existing printers* — Full backward compatibility is ensured in two ways: through existing queues that can be directed to NDPS printers, and through printer gateways. Novell provides printer gateways that are generalized and provide various degrees of NDPS features for existing printers. New printers are currently developed with embedded support for NDPS to provide a full range of printer features to NDPS-enhanced clients.

▶ *Support for Plug and Print* — You can centrally manage printing with NetWare Administration using the IETF standards-based Printer MIB associated with new NDS printer objects.

NDPS Overview

NDPS is structured with several new components shown in Figure 19.6, including:

▶ Printer Agents (server-based or embedded)

▸ Printer gateways

▸ NDS Broker (BROKER.NLM)

▸ NDPS Manager (NDPSM.NLM)

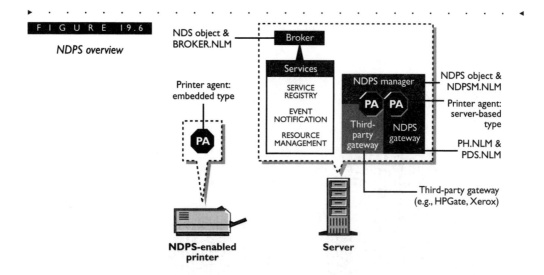

FIGURE 19.6

NDPS overview

▸ *Printer Agents* — The Printer Agent is software either embedded in the printer firmware or server-based that manages print processing between the NOS and the printer. The Printer Agent contains equivalent functionality of the traditional queue-based printer, print queue, print server, and spooler.

▸ *Printer gateways* — When a printer does not have an embedded NDPS Printer Agent, a printer gateway is an NLM that is used to interface the printer to NDPS. A few generalized printer gateways are provided in NetWare 5 — see your printer vendor for customized printer gateways for NetWare.

▸ *NDS Broker* — The NDS Broker is a transparent server-based module that provides three services:

- *Service Registry Service* provides device-specific information. It enables clients to retrieve lists of registered printers that are connected to the network.

- *Event Notification Service* forwards device-specific printer events and print-job status information to users and print operators.

- *Resource Management Service* is a centralized database that hosts printer drivers and printer definition (PDF) files, banners, and fonts for central use.

  ▸ *NDPS Manager* — The NDPS Manager is a server-based module that manages Printer Agents.

NOTE

NetWare 5's NDPS (version 2.0) is not backward compatible with version 1, which was shipped in NetWare 4.11. NDPS version 2 updates are included on your NetWare 5 operating system CD to upgrade your NetWare 4.11 servers. If not upgraded, version 1 and version 2 systems work independently of one another.

Setup

NDPS setup is simplified. The NDS Broker and NDPS Manager are set up automatically when NDPS is selected as an option during NetWare server setup. Once the server components have been installed, all that is ever needed is to create printer objects. When the installer elects to set up a Broker during INSTALL, the remaining print setup — including creation of NDS objects — is automatic with the exception of creating printer objects. NetWare evaluates the need for Brokers and Managers and installs them only when required. The installer may wish to optimize where server components are installed, but default placements will result in a working print system.

Once the server components are installed, the administrator must set up printer objects. This is handled with the help of a Setup Wizard in NetWare Administrator. When printers have embedded Printer Agents, no setup is required — just selecting the printer from a list will suffice. It is no longer necessary to establish each object and then configure a relationship between queues and printers. Printer gateways and printer agents are installed by the administrator when required. Printer gateways are installed to integrate printers that do not have embedded Printer Agents.

If NDPS was not set up during server setup, NDPS printing setup requires three stages: setting up a server Broker, setting up an NDPS Manager, and setting up printers.

Setting Up a Server Broker

The NDPS Broker must be installed on a server that is available to printers and clients. The Broker and its related resources and NDS object can be created during the server operating system INSTALL program, or afterward with BROKER.NLM at the server or NetWare Administrator from a workstation. The following discussions show how to set up a Broker and related components using NetWare Administrator.

Setting Up NDPS During Server INSTALL   If you elect to include NDPS during server setup, INSTALL will check the network for existing NDPS configurations and existing Brokers. If no suitable NDPS setup is found, you are given an option to install a new Broker and set up NDPS version 2.0 services.

If an existing NDPS version 2.0 configuration is found, you are given three options:

▸ Do not install a Broker on this server.

▸ Install a new Broker as a separate service.

▸ Install a new Broker sharing an existing NDPS resource database.

When the first Broker is installed in a tree, the following changes will automatically occur:

1. The NDS schema will be extended.

2. The NDS Broker object will be created in the same NDS container as the server.

3. The command LOAD BROKER will be added to the AUTOEXEC.NCF.

Installing the First Broker in a Tree after Server INSTALL   If NDPS was not installed during server installation, use NetWare Administrator to install a Broker by creating a new Broker object. A Broker must reside in the same NDS container with the server that will load the Broker.

NOTE

In order to set up the first NDS Broker object in a tree, the administrator must have Supervisor rights to the root of the tree, since the NDS schema must be extended. The user must also have Supervisor rights to files and directories to the volume that will host the Resource Management Service.

When the Broker object is created, your tree will be checked for an existing Service Registry Service (SRS), which if found is checked for a list of Brokers. If no Broker is found, the Broker will be installed on the server.

When the first Broker is installed in a tree, the following changes will automatically occur:

I. The NDS schema will be extended.

2. The NDS Broker object will be created.

3. The command LOAD BROKER will be added to the AUTOEXEC.NCF.

Once this process is completed, your server will be ready to service NDPS configurations.

Installing Additional Brokers   BROKER.NLM looks for an existing Service Registry Service (SRS), which if found is checked for a list of Brokers. If a Broker is found, existing Brokers will be checked for suitability. The following checks will occur:

I. The Broker must be NDPS version 2.0 — NDPS version 2.0 and version 1.0 are not interoperable.

2. The Broker must be within three hops from the attached network segment.

3. The server AUTOEXEC.NCF file is checked to see if the Broker module is loaded automatically during boot.

If the preceding requirements are met, you will be informed accordingly — you need not install a Broker. You will have a choice to install an additional Broker if you wish.

Once the first Broker has been installed in a tree, installing an additional Broker requires Read, Write, Modify, and Create NDS rights.

NOTE

If a suitable Broker is found and you elect to install an additional Broker, you will have an option to do so. This option enables multiple Brokers to share the same Resource Manager Service database. If you select the Copy Resource Files checkbox, a duplicate resource database will be created that uses about 60MB of disk space. You can leave this box unchecked to share the existing Resource Manager Service database on an existing Broker server.

Setting Up an NDPS Manager

One NDPS Manager is required to control Printer Agent objects in each tree. There is no limit to how many Printer Agents can be controlled by an NDPS Manager; however, a server that has locally attached printers must have a resident NDPS Manager installed.

You can create an NDPS Manager in NetWare Administrator or by loading NDPSM.NLM at the server, but it is not necessary. When you create a Printer Agent, an NDPS Manager will be created automatically. If you elect to create an NDPS Manager in NetWare Administrator, it must be created in the same NDS container as the server that will host it. During object creation, NDPSM.NLM will be loaded, and the load statement will be added to the server AUTOEXEC.NCF. Once the NDPS Manager is installed, you can manage its properties from NetWare Administrator or from the NDPS Manager server console.

In order to create an NDPS Manager object, the administrator must have Read, Write, Modify, and Create NDS object rights for the container in which the object will be created.

NOTE

Setting Up Printers

You can create two categories of printers: controlled access and public access.

Controlled access printers are through the NDS printer object. Because the printer object is within NDS, access is only available to NDS clients and is subject to NDS rights. Using a controlled access printer requires an NDS login and NDS Browse and Read rights, plus some NDS property rights.

Public access printers are available to all users physically connected to the network. When you create the Printer Agent without having created an NDS printer object, the Printer Agent is exposed to all network users through the NDPS Manager's Service Registry Service without NDS control. All network users have access to the printer, even when using the bindery mode. If the printer is network-attached and set up appropriately, TCP/IP or IPX/SPX software will provide access to the printer — no NetWare login is required. This extends printer availability to UNIX, OS/2, Macintosh, and other network workstations and devices.

The difference in setup is simply the manner in which you set up the Printer Agent. To create a controlled access printer, you start by creating a printer object. To create a public access printer, you simply add the Printer Agent to the Access Control List in the NDPS Manager object.

Creating a Controlled Access Printer   Controlled access printers are set up by creating a printer object in an NDS container. When you create the printer object, you will also create a Printer Agent and install drivers. You can create Printer Agents in the NDPS Manager server console utility or in NetWare Administrator.

The administrator must have NDS Read, Write, Modify, and Create rights for the container in which the printer object will be created, and must be designated as a Manager in the NDPS Manager object's Access Control property page.

NOTE

To create a controlled access printer in NetWare Administrator:

1. Select the container in which you will create the printer object, and select Object → Create. Select the NDPS Printer object and then OK.

2. Enter the name to be assigned to the printer object, select the Create a Printer Agent radio button, and then select Create.

3. Select the NDPS Manager to control this Printer Agent and select the Gateway Type. If you select the Novell Printer Gateway, you will see the Printer Type list shown in Figure 19.7.

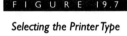
F I G U R E   1 9 . 7

Selecting the Printer Type

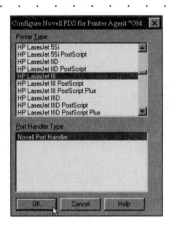

For information about which Gateway Type to select, select each Gateway Type — printer gateway — and then select OK to view a list of supported printers. The Novell Printer Gateway is used to support most legacy printers that are port-attached, whereas the HP Printer Gateway is used for all network-attached printers (HP and others). If you use this printer gateway, you will be required to either select the Printer/Jet Direct device or enter the IP or IPX address and MAC address at this time.

4. When you select the printer and then OK, the Add Printer Wizard will start.

NOTE

Steps 5 and 6 will vary according to what type of printer and port is selected. Complete whichever configuration tasks are requested, and proceed to step 7.

5. Select the Connection Type and Port Type as shown in Figure 19.8. Select Next to continue.

▶ . . . . ◀

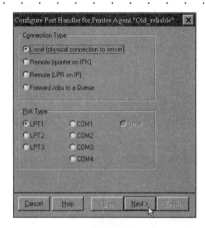

FIGURE 19.8

Setting up an NDPS Printer — Configure Port Handler

6. You will see the Configure Port Handler screen shown in Figure 19.9. Select the Controller Type and Interrupt Request. If you prefer to use no interrupt, select None (polled mode). Select Finish.

▶ . . . . ◀

FIGURE 19.9

Setting up an NDPS Printer — Configure Port Interrupt and Controller Type

7. Select the Printer Drivers for Windows 3.1, Windows 95/98, and Windows NT. The Add Printer Wizard will select the closest match automatically. Verify the driver information screen, and then select OK to save the printer configuration. If you selected Define Additional properties when creating the printer object, you will see the print gateway.

Creating a Public Access Printer   Public access printers are not represented by NDS objects and are available to all network users physically connected to the network without security restrictions. Public access printers can only send print event notifications and are not able to take advantage of detailed bidirectional printer messages. Public access printers are managed through the Tools menu of the NetWare Administrator utility.

The administrator must have Modify rights for the NDPS Manager object, and must be designated as a Manager or security equivalent in the NDPS Manager object's Access Control property page.

NOTE

To create a controlled access printer in NetWare Administrator:

1. Select the NDPS Manager object and then select Object → Details → Printer Agent List → New.

2. Enter the name to be assigned to the Printer Agent and select the Gateway Type.

For information about which Gateway Type to select, select each Gateway Type — printer gateway — and then select OK to view a list of supported printers. The HP Printer Gateway is used for all network-attached HP printers. If using this printer gateway, you will be required to either select the Printer/Jet Direct device or enter the IP or IPX address and MAC address at this time.

4. When you select the printer and then OK, the Add Printer Wizard will start.

Steps 5 and 6 will vary according to what type of printer and port is selected. Complete whichever configuration tasks are requested, and proceed to step 7.

NOTE

5. Select the Connection Type and Port Type. Select Next to continue.

6. You will see the Configure Port Handler screen shown in Figure 19.8. Select the Controller Type and Interrupt Request. If you prefer to use no interrupt, select None (polled mode). Select Finish.

7. Select the Printer Drivers for Windows 3.1, Windows 95/98, and Windows NT. The Add Printer Wizard will select the closest match automatically. Verify the driver information screen, and then select OK to save the printer configuration.

Converting a Controlled Access Printer to a Public Access Printer   To create a public access printer in NetWare Administrator:

1. Create and configure a controlled access printer as discussed previously.

2. Select the NDS container that the printer object to be converted is in, and then select Object → Create. Select NDPS Printer.

3. Enter the name to be assigned for the NDPS Printer Name, select the radio button for Public Access Printer and then select Create. You will see a message indicating that all users of this printer will need to be reconfigured. Select OK to confirm that you realize you will need to reconfigure clients that were previously accessing this printer.

4. You will see the Select Printer Agent screen shown in Figure 19.10. Select the printer to be converted from the list. If the printer is not listed here, check the context in which you initiated the Create Object. If you have selected the wrong context, you will need to cancel and start again.

F I G U R E   19.10

*Selecting a printer agent for
public access*

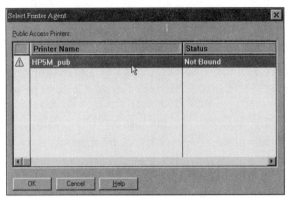

Automated Solutions for Public Access Printers Automated solutions are built
into printer firmware or provided as a server-based NLM. Printer manufacturers
can provide an embedded Printer Agent or a customized printer gateway to
automatically make the printer available as a public access printer. When a public
access embedded Printer Agent or server-based printer gateway is installed on the
network, printer-specific information is registered with a Broker's Service Registry
Service. No NDS object need be used to create a public access printer.

The printer can be made available by accessing the NDPS Public Access Printers
selection in the Tools menu of the NetWare Administrator utility. When this menu
item is selected, a list of printers registered with the Service Registry Service is
displayed. Once the printer is selected, it is available to all network users.

Combining NDPS and Queue-Based Printing

Print jobs submitted to traditional NetWare queues can be redirected to NDPS
printers. This enables clients using traditional queue-based printing to continue
printing without noticeable changes. This also allows NDPS to support
workstations (including OS/2 and Macintosh) where NDPS client enhancements
are not available.

The following procedure configures the NDPS Printer Agent to poll queues, redirecting them to NDPS printers.

NOTE

The administrator must have Modify rights for the NDPS Manager object, and must be designated as a Manager or security equivalent in the NDPS Manager object's Access Control property page.

The following process will configure a Printer Agent to redirect print jobs in a queue to a NDPS printer in NetWare Administrator:

1. Select the NDPS printer, and select Object → Details. The Printer Control screen will be displayed.

2. Select the Jobs button and Spooling Configuration. The screen shown in Figure 19.11 will appear.

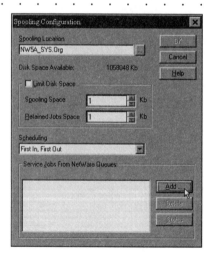

F I G U R E   19.11

The Spooling Configuration screen

3. Select the Add button, then locate and select the queue to be serviced, and then select OK to save changes.

Troubleshooting

In your NetWare 5 online documentation, select Troubleshooting → Print Services → Queue-Based Printing. You will find four categories for troubleshooting:

- Print Server Problems

- General Printing Problems

- Printers

- Printer Stations (remote printers)

You should also check out the troubleshooting section on Novell Distributed Print Services. This section deals with NDPS and queue-based printing in a point-by-point mode. This section discusses:

- Initial Troubleshooting Steps

- Narrowing Your Focus

- Determining Your Platform When Problem Affects Only One Workstation

- Isolating Printing Problems Affecting Only One Windows Workstation

- Tracking Jobs from a Workstation

- Checking Printer Output and Using Test Files

- Printing Problems Affecting All Users

- Printing Problems When Integrating NDPS with Queue-Based Components

Each category includes troubleshooting flow charts and links to related troubleshooting tips, and technical documents dealing with known printer problems that have proven to be most common.

Novell's troubleshooting flow charts are excellent tools for chasing down printer problems. The combination of flow charts and HTML-based documentation with links makes this section hard to improve upon.

Additional Resources

The following resources are available to provide greater depth in NDPS design and implementation. You will find that many of these resources are available at no cost.

White Paper

A Novell white paper has an extensive discussion of NDPS printing. Look for the document entitled "Planning Your Transition to NDPS" at the location `http://www.novell.com/intranetware/products/ndps/`.

AppNotes

The following AppNotes articles have covered printing issues. You can view an index of all AppNotes from their inception to the most current issues at `http://developer.novel.com/research/appnotes.htm`. This index is not available on the Support Connection CD, or at the Novell Support Web site. You will find it invaluable for locating articles and NetNotes in any AppNotes issue.

This list is ordered by date. More recent AppNotes should be reviewed first, as older AppNotes may address issues that have been resolved or modified in newer versions.

- Mark McKell, *Printing in NetWare 5 with NDPS 2.0,* September 1998

- McKell and Whittle, *An Introduction to Novell Distributed Print Services (NDPS),* April 1998

- Wilson and Hegerhorst, *Setting Up Network Printing with IntranetWare Client for Windows NT Workstation,* May 1997

▶ Wilson and Hegerhorst, *Setting Up Network Printing with Client 32 for Windows 95*, November 1996

▶ Liebing, Hemsley, and Hendrick, *Using Novell's NetWare User Tools (NWUSER.EXE) for Client 32 Workstations*, May 1996

▶ Telford and Liebing, *Inside Look at SPX Communications between RPRINTER/NPRINTER and the NetWare Print Server*, December 1995

▶ Roger Montalvo, *Understanding NetWare HostPrint 1.1x*, April 1995

▶ Oler, Bethers, and Davis, *Using Network-Direct Print Devices in NetWare 4*, June 1994

▶ Cottam and Davis, *Optimizing Printing with NetWare 4.x and 3.1x*, September 1993

NetNotes

NetNotes is a section within AppNotes that deals in short with prominent support issues. The following recent NetNote discusses NDPS and printing problems.

▶ *Troubleshooting Print Corruption*, February 1996

Utilities

You can find the following utility and more at `http://www.fastlane.net/homepages/dcollins/`. It is also included on the CD that accompanies this book.

▶ DOS & Windows–based NDS-aware Print Capture Release, Freeware, File: NCAP12.ZIP (Size: 546K)

This utility displays a pick list of all accessible NDS network print queues and print jobs (not used for Bindery Emulation). It enables the user to redirect LPT port print output to the selected queue. Both the DOS and Windows versions can use the same configuration file.

What's on the CD-ROM

This appendix describes shareware, freeware, and other utilities included on the CD-ROM that accompanies this book.

Adobe Acrobat Reader

Adobe Acrobat Reader is a useful program that enables you to read and print Portable Document Format (PDF) files, such as the appendixes included on this CD-ROM.

To install the latest version Adobe Acrobat Reader and view the PDF appendixes:

1. Start Windows Explorer and open the Acrobat folder on the CD-ROM.

2. Double-click rs32e301.exe and follow the instructions presented onscreen for installing Acrobat Reader.

3. To view the PDF appendixes after you have installed Acrobat Reader, open the Appendix folder on the CD-ROM, and double-click on the appendix file you wish to view. All documents in the folder end with the .pdf extension.

For more information on this program from Adobe Systems Incorporated, visit www.adobe.com/prodindex/acrobat/readstep.html.

Novell's LANalyzer for Windows Demo

The accompanying CD-ROM contains a demonstration version of Novell's LANalyzer for Windows protocol analyzer, discussed throughout this book.

To install the LANalyzer for Windows demo:

1. Start Windows Explorer and open the Lzfw folder on the CD-ROM.

2. Double-click Setup.exe and follow the instructions given onscreen to complete the installation.

TIP
For Windows 95/98/NT, adding the directory that holds **LANalyzer** for Windows to your path and executing the Izenet.bat that comes with the program from within your AUTOEXEC.BAT file should load the necessary TSRs to enable the demo programs to work.

For more information on LANalyzer for Windows and its use, please view the included documentation.

JRButils

You will also find the JRButils shareware/freeware from JRBsoftware. These utilities have far greater functionality and flexibility than the tools shipped with NetWare. They are particularly suited for managing large numbers of users, allowing operations to be performed on objects selected via wildcard, container, membership of a group, or a list in a file. When displaying information, filters may be applied.

For example, JRButils can list all users in an NDS tree who have not logged in since a given date, list all objects in a container whose account balance is less than $10, list all compressed files on a volume, or list all files owned by the Macintosh name space. JRButils are suited to batch mode operations, such as mass usercode creation, customization, and deletion.

To install the JRButils:

1. Start Windows Explorer and open the JRButils ⇨ Jrb500a folder on the CD-ROM.

2. View the README.1ST file for installation instructions for and information about the included utilities.

After installing the software, you can view a listing of the JRButils in the accompanying documentation, or you can visit the JRBsoftware web site at www.JRBSoftware.com/.

Darwin Collins: NDS Utilities and Links

I have included several shareware/freeware NetWare utilities from the Darwin Collins: NDS Utilities and Links Web site. You will find many of these utilities helpful for managing NetWare 3, 4, and 5 systems. Darwin Collins is a long-time Novell developer and supporter. You will find his Web site has many helpful links to other NetWare-related resources.

To install the NDS Utilities:

1. Start Windows Explorer and open the NDS folder on the CD-ROM.

2. View the README.TXT file for installation instructions for and information about the included utilities.

 To run the NDS Utilities, you will need to turn off the Windows Read-Only attribute after copying the files to your hard drive.

NOTE

For more information visit the Darwin Collins: NDS Utilities and Links Web site at http://www.novellfans.com/n4util.htm.

Delec SCSI Guide

Delec has been generous in granting permission to include its SCSI Guide on the CD that accompanies this book. This guide provides a long list of specifications, requirements, and capacities that are too technical to include in this book, but may be a significant resource for hardware technicians and system administrators.

To view the Delec SCSI Guide:

1. Start Windows Explorer and open the Delec folder on the CD-ROM.

2. Double-click on the index.html file; your default browser will open the Delec SCSI Guide.

Delec provides online hardware guides at no cost. To review its hardware configuration documents, visit their Web site at www.delec.com.

Appendixes

The CD-ROM includes the following six appendixes to *Novell's Guide to Troubleshooting NetWare 5* in PDF format (located in the Appendix folder):

Appendix A: What's on the CD-ROM
Appendix B: Support Resources
Appendix C: NetWare Requirements and Capacities
Appendix D: Protocol Reference Guide
Appendix E: TCP/IP Utilities
Appendix F: Internet RFC References

To view these appendixes, refer to the installation instructions in the Adobe Acrobat Reader section of this appendix.

Index

Software License Agreement

The LANalyzer 2.2. for Windows Eval software program(s) and documentation ("Software" and "Documentation") you have acquired are protected by copyright laws and international treaties and your use of them is subject to the terms of this License. This License is granted by Novell Ireland Software Ltd. for products purchased in Europe, the Middle East and Africa, and by Novell, Inc. for products purchased elsewhere. Each is referred to in this License as "Novell".

1. **License**. Subject to the terms and conditions of this License, Novell grants to you a non-exclusive, non-transferrable right to one copy of the Software and Documentation for your own internal evaluation. The Software is provided to you solely for evaluation purposes for a period not to exceed 90 days. You may not use the Software in a commercial/production environment. Novell reserves all rights not expressly granted to you.

2. **General**

   a. **Restrictions**. You may not rent, lease, decompile, disassemble, reverse engineer, or create derivative works of the Software. Irrespective of the number of sets of media included with the Software, you may use the Software only as provided in this License. Certain qualifications may apply to the purchase of this License. When present, they are printed on the Software package and form part of this License. If you breach any of the terms of this License, it automatically terminates and you must destroy all copies of the Software and Documentation.

   b. **US Government Restricted Rights**. The Software and any accompanying materials are provided with Restricted Rights. Use, duplication, or disclosure by the Government is subject to restrictions as set forth in subparagraph (c) (1) (ii) of The Rights in Technical Data and Computer Software clause at DFARS 52.227-7013 or subparagraphs (c) (1) and (2) of the Commercial Computer Software — Restricted Rights at 48 CFR 52.227-19, as applicable. Contractor/manufacturer is Novell, Inc. at the address below.

   If you have any questions about this License or special programs for education or charitable organizations, please contact Novell Sales Center, 1555 N. Technology Way, Orem, UT 84057-2399.

3. **Limited Warranty**. This Software is licensed AS IS. Novell® warrants the physical media of the Software against physical defects for a period of 90 days from installation or purchase, whichever is later. Your sole remedy for defective media is replacement. THE SOFTWARE IS ONLY COMPATIBLE WITH CERTAIN COMPUTERS AND OPERATING SYSTEMS. THE SOFTWARE IS NOT WARRANTED FOR NON-COMPATIBLE SYSTEMS. Call Novell Customer Support or your Dealer for information about compatibility.

4. **Disclaimer**. EXCEPT AS OTHERWISE RESTRICTED BY LAW, NOVELL MAKES NO WARRANTY, REPRESENTATION OR PROMISE NOT EXPRESSLY SET FORTH IN THIS LIMITED WARRANTY. NOVELL DISCLAIMS AND EXCLUDES ANY AND ALL IMPLIED WARRANTIES OF MERCHANTABILITY, TITLE OR FITNESS FOR A PARTICULAR PURPOSE. NOVELL DOES NOT WARRANT THAT THE SOFTWARE OR ASSOCIATED DOCUMENTATION WILL SATISFY YOUR REQUIREMENTS OR THAT THE SOFTWARE AND DOCUMENTATION ARE WITHOUT DEFECT OR ERROR OR THAT THE OPERATION OF THE SOFTWARE WILL BE UNINTERRUPTED. Some states do not allow limitations on how long an implied warranty lasts, so the above limitation may not apply to you. This warranty gives you specific legal rights which vary from state to state.

5. **Limitation of Liability**. EXCEPT AS OTHERWISE RESTRICTED BY LAW, NOVELL'S AGGREGATE LIABILITY ARISING FROM OR RELATING TO YOUR USE OF THE SOFTWARE, ASSOCIATED DOCUMENTATION OR ANY SERVICES PROVIDED BY NOVELL AND/OR ITS AGENTS IS LIMITED TO THE TOTAL OF ALL PAYMENTS MADE BY OR FOR YOU FOR THE SOFTWARE AND DOCUMENTATION . NEITHER NOVELL NOR ANY OF ITS LICENSORS, EMPLOYEES, OR AGENTS SHALL IN ANY CASE BE LIABLE FOR ANY SPECIAL, INCIDENTAL, CONSEQUENTIAL, INDIRECT OR PUNITIVE DAMAGES EVEN IF ADVISED OF THE POSSIBILITY OF THOSE DAMAGES. NEITHER NOVELL NOR ANY OF ITS LICENSORS, EMPLOYEES, OR AGENTS IS RESPONSIBLE FOR LOST PROFITS OR REVENUE, LOSS OF USE OF SOFTWARE, LOSS OF DATA, COSTS OF RE-CREATING LOST DATA, THE COST OF ANY SUBSTITUTE EQUIPMENT OR PROGRAM. Some states do not allow the exclusion or limitation of incidental or consequential damages, so the above limitation or exclusion may not apply to you.

my2cents.idgbooks.com

Register This Book — And Win!

Visit **http://my2cents.idgbooks.com** to register this book and we'll automatically enter you in our fantastic monthly prize giveaway. It's also your opportunity to give us feedback: let us know what you thought of this book and how you would like to see other topics covered.

Discover IDG Books Online!

The IDG Books Online Web site is your online resource for tackling technology — at home and at the office. Frequently updated, the IDG Books Online Web site features exclusive software, insider information, online books, and live events!

10 Productive & Career-Enhancing Things You Can Do at www.idgbooks.com

- Nab source code for your own programming projects.

- Download software.

- Read Web exclusives: special articles and book excerpts by IDG Books Worldwide authors.

- Take advantage of resources to help you advance your career as a Novell or Microsoft professional.

- Buy IDG Books Worldwide titles or find a convenient bookstore that carries them.

- Register your book and win a prize.

- Chat live online with authors.

- Sign up for regular e-mail updates about our latest books.

- Suggest a book you'd like to read or write.

- Give us your 2¢ about our books and about our Web site.

You say you're not on the Web yet? It's easy to get started with IDG Books' *Discover the Internet,* available at local retailers everywhere.

WE WROTE THE BOOK
ON NETWORKING

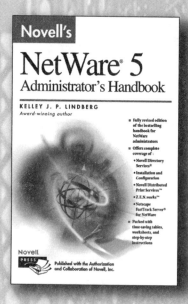
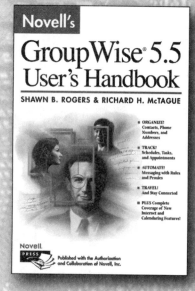
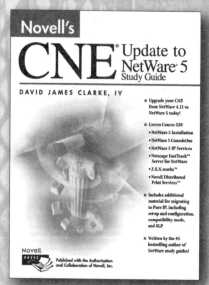

MORE BOOKS FROM NOVELL PRESS™

CD-ROM Installation Instructions

For complete contents and descriptions of the software included on the CD-ROM that accompanies *Novell's Guide to Troubleshooting NetWare 5*, please see Appendix A, "What's on the CD-ROM." Detailed installation instructions are provided for all included programs.

To install the software on the CD-ROM included with this book with Windows 95, 98, or NT 4.0, follow these steps:

1. Place the desired CD-ROM disc in your CD-ROM drive.

2. Click the Start button and select Run.

3. Type the letter of your CD-ROM drive with a colon and backslash (for instance, **D:**) and the directory name that contains the program you wish to run, followed by the name of the appropriate executable installation file. For example, to install the Adobe Acrobat Reader, you would type the following:

   ```
   D:\Acrobat\ar302.exe
   ```

4. Click OK and follow the onscreen installation instructions.